ANCIENT CIVILIZATIONS
OF THE ANDES

Splendid Polychrome Feather-Work Tunic, Showing Blending of Early Nazca and Tiahuanaco II Styles.
Color-plate by courtesy of H. A. Elsberg, Esq., owner of the original.

ANCIENT CIVILIZATIONS
OF THE ANDES

BY

PHILIP AINSWORTH MEANS

NEW YORK

GORDIAN PRESS, INC.

1964

TO MY BROTHER

DR. JAMES HOWARD MEANS

IN GRATITUDE

FOR HIS ENCOURAGEMENT TO ME IN THE

WRITING OF THIS VOLUME

PREFACE

So far as preparation for the writing of this book is concerned, the last nineteen years divide themselves into three unequal periods, the two earlier of a general character, the latest of a more particular nature. These would best be set forth here, but as briefly as possible.

At Harvard, between the Autumn of 1911 and the Spring of 1914, many scholastic privileges were mine which powerfully influenced my work in life. Among them I may mention the splendid courses in Spanish given by Professor J. D. M. Ford and his aides, Doctor Whittem and Doctor Rivera; the courses in anthropology under Doctors R. B. Dixon, A. M. Tozzer, and E. A. Hooton—which courses were taken under the advice of the late Professor F. W. Putnam; and the courses in Spanish and Spanish-American history under Doctor R. B. Merriman. To all eight of these respected teachers I owe an enormous debt, which I gratefully acknowledge.

In the Spring of 1914, through the generosity of my parents, it became possible for me to go to Peru for the first time, going thither as an assistant on the Yale University-National Geographic Society Expedition of which Doctor (now Senator) Hiram Bingham was the director. During my five months in the highlands of southern Peru on that occasion I had the inestimable advantage of being under the orders of Mr. E. C. Erdis, who is a practical field archæologist of the highest ability. He spared no effort in teaching me field archæology and in showing me all the chief sites of archæological importance round about Cuzco, including the famous citadel of Machu Picchu. My gratitude to him is profound.

The second of the three periods referred to began on my return to Boston, in November, 1914, by which time I was fully determined to devote myself to the study of Andean history. This determination was fostered by my friend, Doctor George F. Eaton, of New Haven, a former member of the Yale Expedition, who encouraged me to begin publishing on Peruvian subjects, and by that unsurpassed scholar, the late Sir Clements Markham. With him, in December, 1914, I entered into an active correspondence which ceased only with his lamented death in 1916. He urged upon me the desirability of writing a book such as this, explaining how he, guided by Prescott into the path which he followed faithfully for over sixty years, had formerly intended to do so but had been prevented by the pressure of other duties. In all my other journeys to Peru, occupying most of the time between 1916 and 1921, I bore his advice in mind, particularly so during the years 1920–1921, when I served as Director of the National Museum of Archæology, in Lima.

The third and last period, stretching from October, 1921, to the present year, was important in that it supplied me with a kind of knowledge in which I had been deplorably deficient. This consisted of an intimate acquaintance with the literary source-materials bearing, in a score of ways, upon the subject to which I had given myself. In the years following 1921, and in many libraries and museums of Europe, North America, and Mexico, I strove to make good the deficiency. The result is the present book, in which the reader will find that information is drawn, in equal proportions, from archæology and from literary source-materials.

The friends who have aided me in my task in countless ways are very many. Chief among them I must mention here, with sincere thanks, Miss Gertrude Townsend, of the Museum of Fine Arts, Boston; Mr. H. A. Elsberg, of New York; and Mr. W. V. Alford, of Garrettsville, Ohio, all of whom have provided me with unpublished illustrations for this volume, as well as with innumerable opportunities for study among their books and specimens. To all others who have supplied me with illustrative materials acknowledgment is gladly made in their several places.

PHILIP AINSWORTH MEANS.

POMFRET, CONNECTICUT,
December 1st, 1930.

CONTENTS

ILLUSTRATIONS

ANCIENT CIVILIZATIONS OF THE ANDES

CHAPTER I

THE GEOGRAPHY OF THE ANDEAN AREA AS A BACK-GROUND FOR HISTORY

1. Introductory Considerations

THE Andean area may, for the purposes of this volume, be defined as including the republics of Ecuador, Peru, and Bolivia, together with adjacent portions of Colombia, Argentina, and Chile. One who looks at a good modern map of this area will be impressed by the extremely varied character of the country within it, and also by the vagueness of all save its western borders; for, in truth, no sharply marked natural features separate the Andean area from the rest of South America.

Candor compels the admission that, on purely geographical grounds, there is no justification whatever for the term "Andean area" as it is here used. There is, however, need for such a term, and there is real justification for it on historical grounds; for, as it will be my business to show, this area was formerly the theatre of a great and significant human drama. Indeed, in this region, human beings, by their achievements in many departments of human endeavor, have succeeded most thoroughly in sharply defining an area that, from a geographical standpoint, is arbitrary and artificial. It is as though the greatness of bygone societies had imbrued the very atmosphere with a strong but subtle aroma which forever sets the Andean area apart—at any rate for the historian and his public—from the surrounding wildernesses in which nothing of any special importance ever took place.

At the same time it may be said that in no other region of the world have the forces of Nature played a more formative part in human history than they have always done in the tremendous territory thus designated. In the Andean area

3

man has always been if not the slave at any rate the pupil of that exigeant mistress, Mother Nature, and his history has largely consisted of varyingly successful struggles against many of her enactments, and, in particular, against that one which bade him to live in small groups each one of which had a narrowly circumscribed habitat. As a result of sturdy resistance on the part of man—or rather, on the part of man's leaders—to this commandment of Nature, there came into being in ancient times a political and a resultant cultural cohesion which is not preserved by the boundaries of modern states, a cohesion which represents a human victory over the natural diversity of the country within the area. True, there have always existed—and there still exist—numerous regionalistic tendencies which have led the greater part of human society to form itself into narrow units each one of which displays its peculiar accomplishments and failures. Nevertheless, because of a definite and powerful unifying force to which the entire area was at one period rigidly subjected, namely, the Incaic governmental system, there is an overlying continuity which opposes and abates the regionalistic tendency. In spite of the contrasting divisions within it, the whole Andean area was colored indelibly with the Incaic dye; and to this day, in every part of the territory once ruled by the Incas of Cuzco, one is hourly conscious of the ghost of the Incas' supremacy, manifesting itself in scores of ways, through speech, custom, and material culture.

Nor were the Incas the sole representatives of the unifying force in question. Before their time another empire no less remarkable than theirs had existed, an empire which modern research, both of an archæological and of a literary kind, is slowly bringing within our range of vision, dispelling the mists and shadows which have so long enveloped it. Even now, although our knowledge is far from complete, we know that in western South America no less than in Mexico and Central America the native race of this so-called New World built up and ably administered wide-spreading kingdoms and empires whose history was long, intricate, and admirable.

To examine the theatre wherein this historical drama was acted must, therefore, be our initial task. From early in the Spanish period of South America to our own time it has been axiomatic that the Andean area—as here defined—is divided into three natural geographic and environmental zones which, lying roughly parallel with one another in an approximately north-south direction, each contain many natural sub-divisions. Named from west to east these three zones are: 1, the Coast, or, as the early Spanish writers put it, *los Llanos* (the Plains); 2, the Highlands, or *Sierra*, including the main ranges of the Andes and the lofty tablelands between them; 3, the Forests, or *Montaña*, lying on the eastern slopes of the Andes and stretching indefinitely toward the rising sun.

Such is the usual classification of the natural parts of the Andean area. It has always been—and no doubt still is—quite satisfactory for geographers; but for the historian and for the student of history it does not serve so well because, in addition to being too imprecise, it unduly stresses mountains and other barriers which have been inimical to the growth to greatness on the part of native societies. For the historian, then, and for his public, it is the valleys between the barriers, rather than the barriers themselves, that demand attention.

A study of the suggestive map which precedes the most recent book of Peru's foremost archæologist, Dr. Julio C. Tello,[1] brings home to one who is history-conscious rather than geography-conscious the basic fact that water-courses and their tributary drainage basins are the determining factors in human life and in the history of human culture. It matters little to the historian whether a given valley or basin be at sea-level or high above it; whether a valley be enclosed by mountain-ranges or shut in by vast expanses of solitude; whether the waters which flow through it pour themselves into the Pacific Ocean or into the Atlantic. The great truth in all these cases, for the historian, is: Here lies a naturally formed habitat for a group of human beings, a habitat supplied with water, without which no sort of life is possible, supplied also, either in fact or potentially, with a varied series of raw-materials from which man, if he be sufficiently clever, can construct culture of one type or another.

These fundamental concepts being understood and being held in reserve for further consideration, one may revert to the classic listing of the zones—coast, highlands, and forests—without fear of overworking it. After all, each of those zones had its peculiar human history, the sum, as it were, of the local histories of its component valleys. Even so, the historian is keenly conscious that the characteristics of the zones are far from being constant throughout their length and that, therefore, they demand closer examination.

2. The Valleys of the Coast

Shifting now from the general to the particular, I will describe the valleys of the coast, giving special attention to the historical and cultural value of each series of valleys. In this way a foundation will be laid for a more detailed study in subsequent chapters.

In the extreme north, along the Ecuadorian coast, conditions prevail which accord with the usual conception of the tropical environment; for, in that part of the Andean area, there exist tangled forests crowded with unkempt trees draped in trailing mosses, forests wherein man must combat warm, humid, and enervating air and a too-luxuriant vegetation, not to mention vast stretches of marsh or of spongy, unwholesome soil. In certain districts of the coast, however, as in the vicinity of Cape San Lorenzo and in the country west of the Guayas River, arid conditions assert themselves with the result that the country has a gray and bleak appearance in the dry season, albeit at other times it is pleasant enough. The Island of Puná, at the mouth of the Guayas River, presents a delightful park-like aspect embellished by sightly trees that raise graceful heads above the general expanse of grass and low shrubs. But even this comparatively charming part of the coast is replete with swamps, formerly the abode of yellow-fever mosquitoes, but now happily rendered innocuous. Finally, to the south and east of Puná, along that portion of the mainland shore which forms the eastern and southern bank of the Guayas estuary, forested conditions are found again, extending nearly to the Tumbez Valley in northernmost Peru.

The region thus defined—coastland Ecuador—varies therefore within itself to a marked degree, some of it being, seemingly, almost incapable of supporting human society, the rest of it being, apparently, not unpropitious to mankind. Yet in no part of it, so far as we now know, was any well-balanced culture produced and set upon a rational career. True, manifestations of advanced material culture—stone-carving, pottery-making, etc.—have been discovered there by archæologists; but, as shall be made clear later on, they are almost certainly the product, in every case, of cultural influences from outside the region. Thus, as a whole, the Ecuadorian coast is one of those habitats wherein man was unable to progress without help from outside—or at any rate did not—but wherein, once advanced culture was introduced, it could be carried on.

From Tumbez there extends in an easterly direction a sharp line, partly marked by chains of hills, which divides the hot and humid country to the north of it from the hot and arid country to the south. This contrast is due in large part to the fact that the cool Humboldt current—sweeping northward along the western shore of South America—is here turned in a westerly direction by the conformation of the land-mass south of the line mentioned, and is due in part to the effect of the hills along the line which tend to pocket the winds and to make stagnant, moist heat possible north of them. This very definite line of demarcation was noted by Father Bernabé Cobo, a most intelligent observer, as early as the first part of the seventeenth century.[2] South of that line, and in the Tumbez Valley itself, conditions are found which prelude the coastland desert of Peru and northern Chile.

It is this long and narrow zone which is the most important part of the Andean shore-country, whether we judge it from the geographical or from the historical angle. Lengthwise of the seaboard, where long, unhurrying rollers ceaselessly roar amid a haze of their own making, stretch fifteen hundred miles of barren desert interspersed with westward-dipping streaks of green nestling in valley-bottoms. Even the arid wastes have charm, however, for their sands are of a silvery brilliance, while here and there are jutting hills, close to the shore, with deep purple shadows in their hollows. Inland, shimmering in the pellucid summer sunlight or, at other seasons, half hidden by drifting veils of mist, the desert stretches eastward, a symphony of subtle color—silver, rusty-red, and tints without a name, all blending into one another.

The traveller voyaging along this weirdly exquisite shore gazes long upon the somewhat awful grandeur of these plains, half unconsciously begins to seek, and with satisfaction finds evidences of man's presence and of his industry, crowded for the most part into richly verdant valleys wherein winding rivers flow tranquilly through fields of cotton, maize, and other crops, and through groves of fruit-trees, all of which combine to make a little world hemmed in by high bright bluffs, margins of the deserts beyond. Here and there a small village gleams whitely from among the trees at the border of a valley, and so gives to the landscape that human touch which it needed in order permanently to win the traveller's sympathetic curiosity. At that moment when he discovers the intimate connection of the land with its people does the spell of the Andean coast-country establish itself imperishably in the mind of the responsive voyager.

In winter—from June to November—the aspect of that same coast is grim. A dense pall of metallic-seeming fog hangs fifteen hundred feet above the restless tinsel sea, creating a harsh gray light under which the shore looks forlorn and repellent. Then the only softer hue in the picture is given by the carpet of low-growing flowers which, nourished by nocturnal mists, cling in broad patches to the chaotic hills that rise behind the beaches.

Paradoxically enough, the waters beside this barren shore abound in richly varied life. Birds in multitudes—gulls, gannets, pelicans, cormorants and many others—fill the air with movement, disporting themselves in myriads as they have done from time immemorial.[3] Less easily seen, but fully as important for man, are the sea-creatures, including skates or rays, angel-fish, silversides, flounders, eels, bonitos, sea-bass, sword-fish, and others which have formed an important part of the diet of the coastal folk from earliest times. Equally picturesque, albeit less valuable to the native nations, are several sorts of sharks, porpoises, dolphins, and, on the beaches and off-shore islands, great herds of seals. It is not surprising, in view of the immense diversity of marine life, that fishing should have been for centuries one of the principal occupations of the people along the Peruvian coast.[3]

In order really to grasp the essential character of that wondrous seaboard one must view it from the air. Seen from aloft its conformation, so bewildering to earth-bound wanderers, becomes exquisitely simple; the puzzling jumble of hills, bluffs and hillocks smooth themselves out into sand-clad undulations of merely local importance and combine to form a westward-tilted desert plain crossed frequently from east to west by river-nurtured strips of green—the justly celebrated coastal valleys of Peru.

Naturally enough, settled human life is almost wholly confined to these well-watered portions of the maritime zone. Surprising though it may seem at first there is much fertile land in the valleys separated from one another by wastes of desert. Inland, and behind the whole length of the shore-country, rise the Andes, birthplace of many streams which flow with fructifying effect into the Plains and onwards to the ocean, each stream the life-bringing artery of a small and compact world. The valleys—there are some sixty of them between northern Ecuador and central Chile—are of two sorts, determined by the character of their streams; for some of these are seasonal, flowing only during the highland rainy-season (October to May), while others are perennial, albeit losing a great proportion of their volume in the dry season, as much, according to Father Cobo—an early but sagacious observer—as nine-tenths of their volume.

Of the longer streams, for the most part perennial, it may be said that each passes through several natural phases. Taking their rise in lakes or in melting snow and ice, or perchance in some spring, the waters rush precipitately downwards through narrow gorges in which there are but few human habitations. This initial phase lies within a transitional strip linking the coastland and the highland, a strip sometimes called *ceja de la costa,* "eyebrow of the coast," wherein the traveller from the sea finds that grasses and thickets begin to appear, cold to be felt and, in general, a foretaste of highland conditions to be experienced. The lower or western limit of the *ceja de la costa* is the sharply defined line below which rains do not descend save in abnormal years. The second phase of a characteristic river is one in which its waters roll rapidly and strongly through a V-shaped valley in whose bottom there is enough good soil to permit of agriculture on a small scale, the chief crops being foodstuffs. In the third phase, which is the coastal plain proper, the river, now much increased in volume by its confluents, flows placidly between fertile fields made abundantly productive by its moisture. It is within this third phase that civilizations of long ago took root and grew; it is there that the commercially important part of the seaboard is found to-day. In early times the people therein cultivated not only a wide range of food crops, but also many economically valuable plants such as cotton, maguey, *toquilla* (a riparian reed from which our so-called Panama hats are made, and which was anciently used for basket-work and for matting), numerous kinds of fruit-trees and of nut-bearing trees, and a great variety of herbs valuable as medicines and as delicious savories. In addition to these cultivated plants— or at any rate systematically utilized plants—there are two trees which grow here that demand a word of comment: the *algarroba* and the *balsa*-wood tree. The former is a fantastically gnarled, knotted, and twisted thing rarely reaching to more than thirty feet in height, and having many shoots in all directions. Its roots grip the soil but shallowly, with the result that, when the tree has attained to some size, the winds incline the trunk almost horizontally, causing the future spread of the trunk to assume all manner of fantastic shapes. Naturally enough, such a tree furnishes only a small amount of usable lumber, and that is full of knot-holes and irregular graining; yet the wood of the algarroba tree was the most common source in ancient times upon the coast for timbers in the construction of houses. The pleasantest feature of the algarroba, however, is the fact that it gathers great numbers of delightful song-birds which eat the insects in its flowers and build their nests in its tortuous branches. The balsa-wood tree, on the other hand, is tall and straight. Its wood has the quality of being exceedingly buoyant with the consequence that, from very early times, it has been used for the construction of *balsas* or rafts by the folk along the shore. As it is not a wood capable of sustaining stresses and strains, it has never been used much in buildings.[4]

In this favored territory of the third river-phase the soil is very rich because of the silt laid down upon it annually by the river when at flood and, moreover, the arable land was for centuries considerably extended by skilfully planned works of irrigation, many of which fell into disuse after the Spaniards came, in 1530. Thus, at an early date, the coast valleys became the seat of an intensive and abundantly productive husbandry which cultivated potatoes, maize, squash, beans, sweet-potatoes, peppers, all of which, supplemented by many fruits, nuts, and spices, gave the happy people of the coast one of the best vegetable diets the world has ever seen, and to comestibles of that kind they could add a vast variety of sea-food, and likewise game-birds, venison, and other meats from the higher parts of their valleys. Yet, even in this terrestrial paradise, there was a natural foe: rain. True, it came only rarely; but, when it did come, it was all too apt to be a terribly destructive visitant.[5]

Such are the chief characteristics of those coastal valleys whose streams are of the perennial type. Of the forty-four valleys on the Peruvian coast alone thirty-one have sources high enough on the western slopes of the Andes to ensure a flow, albeit a greatly fluctuating flow, throughout the year. Certain other streams, now seasonal in character, may formerly have been perennial. The Piura River is a case in point. That stream rises sufficiently well within the *ceja de la costa*, where annual rains descend, to ensure a perennial flow of water to its upper reaches; yet, at the present time, and since before 1740, it is a seasonal stream in its lower course. The explanation of this situation, according to the modern people of the Piura Valley, is that formerly the western slope of the Andes was heavily forested but that, during the early part of the colonial period, it was gradually denuded of trees, with the result that the soil in the upper part of the drainage could no longer retain enough water to ensure a continuous flow. If this explanation be correct for the Piura River we may reasonably assume that it holds good also for other seasonal streams with high-lying sources.[6]

In sharpest contrast to the valleys, wherein the most intensive agriculture has been practiced for centuries, the remainder of the coast is now altogether uncultivated and all but uninhabited. Along the very margin of the sea are sporadic hamlets of fisher-folk, with here and there an oil-port or a shipping-centre; but for the most part the interfluvial deserts are picturesque and rather appalling wastes of wind-blown sand dotted by crescent-shaped dunes that wander with deliberate pace from sea to foot-hills, forever impelled by the prevailing south-westerly breezes. But the desert is not uniform throughout its length; for, in the northern half of the Peruvian coast, it is low, some three or four hundred feet, at most, above the valley floors, and it slopes perceptibly towards the sea. Here and there rise from the general surface chains of dark and jagged hills, some of them close to the ocean. In the southern part of the coast, on the other hand, the desert plain lies at an altitude of two or three thousand feet above the sea, and the river itself, at a distance of only twenty miles from its mouth, is, as in the case of the Majes River, at an altitude of a thousand feet or more, and is hemmed in inexorably by the adjacent, but even higher, desert plains.[7] It is little to be won-dered at, therefore, that in valleys of this type, let us say from that of Lomas southwards into northern Chile, no great cultural advances were ever made save as the result of outside influences.

To sum up the cultural and historical significance of the coastal valleys it may be said—and the point will be dwelt upon at greater length in Chapter III—that the business of progressing from simple forms of culture to more complex forms was carried out in the relatively long and open valleys of the northern part of the coast rather than in the shorter and more shut-in valleys of the south. An exception to all general rules is the valley of the Huaraz or Santa River which consists of a freakish pocket in the western face of the Maritime Cordillera. That majestic range splits into two parts of which the more westerly is known as the Cordillera Negra, or Black Cordillera. It is between 14,000 and 16,000 feet in height and has a grim, dark gray appearance and a very even sky-line. To the east of it rises the Cordillera Blanca, or White Cordillera, which is even higher and has lofty peaks, notably Huascarán, 22,000 feet, along its ridge. Between the two chains lies an amazing valley, the so-called Corridor of Huaylas, averaging over 25 miles in width, and having a length of about 125 miles and an average altitude of 8,100 feet above sea-level. Through it, in a northwardly direction, flows the Huaraz River with the towns of Recuay (9,900 feet above sea-level), Huaraz (9,800 feet), Yungay (7,500 feet), Caraz (6,600 feet), and Huaylas (7,000 feet) distributed down its length on or not far back from the river. North of the last-named town the stream takes a sharp turn to the left and, breaking its way through a deep chasm in the Black Cordillera, crosses the coastal desert and enters the Pacific Ocean. The Huaraz or Santa River—only the lower part of it being called by the latter name—is the longest and most varied stream on the Peruvian coast.

3. *The Highlands and Their Valleys*

Behind, and far above, the long series of coastal valleys which we have been considering there lies yet another series of valleys which, from the historical standpoint, is equally important. In general it may be said that the highland zone or *sierra* consists, basically, of the immense elevated mass which is traversed in a north-south direction by the Maritime Cordillera on the west and, with interruptions, by the Central Cordillera and the Eastern Cordillera. These three major ranges are the loftiest portions of a lofty land; inferior only to them are sundry minor ranges which, in any less exalted region, would themselves be lauded as majestic mountains. As a rule both major and minor *cordilleras* lie in approximately a north-south direction; but between and among them are transverse ridges of various elevations which break up the montane mass into divers drainage-basins or valleys, to which Spanish writers apply the convenient term, *hoya*.

In the highland part of what is now the Republic of Ecuador the drainage basins which lie along the intermontane plateau are relatively small and, for the Andes, comparatively low. The western limit of the Ecuadorian *sierra* may be said to be an arbitrary north-south line upon the western slope of the Maritime Cordillera at an altitude of from 2,000 to 4,000 feet above the sea; and the eastern limit is a similar arbitrary north-south line at an altitude of between 3,000 and 4,000 feet on the eastern face of the mountains overlooking the immeasurable wildernesses of Amazonia. Within these limits the longitudinal montane mass rears its vast bulk of which a justly renowned feature is the "avenue of volcanoes." This consists of a double row of snow-clad volcanic peaks—some of them still smoking—which have between them a longitudinal tableland broken into small natural districts by transverse ridges lying roughly east and west. Of the volcanoes the two lowest are Mojanda, over 14,000 feet, and Imbabura, over 15,000, and the two highest are Cotopaxi, about 19,600 feet, and Chimborazo, about 20,500 feet.

The valleys, which alone are historically important, lie between these stupendous but uninhabitable heights and vary in size and in elevation. To be brief it may be said that the average width of the Ecuadorian highlands is about 100 miles and its length about 350, giving an area of some 35,000 square miles from which something—perhaps 10,000 square miles—should be deducted to allow for lands too lofty and too bleak for sedentary occupation by mankind. In other words, an area of some 25,000 square miles, roughly equivalent to New Hampshire, Massachusetts, Connecticut, and Rhode Island added together, was available to societies of the pastoral and agricultural type, the elevation of the area in question varying between about 14,000 feet and about 7,000 feet.

In Peru—to use modern nomenclature—the *hoyas* or drainage areas are much larger and much more easily defined than they are in Ecuador. The northern half of the Peruvian highlands is divided about evenly between the great *hoya* of the Marañón on the west and that of the Huallaga on the east. The southern margin of both is the transverse range known in geographical literature as the *Nudo* or Knot of Pasco; their lateral margins are, respectively, the Maritime Cordillera and the Central Cordillera, enclosing the Marañón Valley between them, and the Central Cordillera and the Eastern Cordillera which enclose the Huallaga Valley. Of the two the *hoya* of the Marañón is, historically, the more important. It is a sizable territory, some 500 miles long from north to south and from 75 to 175 miles wide, which descends towards the north. Although this great area is low enough to be sub-tropical to tropical in character, its environmental conditions are not such as to have prevented the southern highlanders from extending their sway over a good part of it, particularly on the western or left bank of the wide Marañón River. Into the Huallaga Valley, on the other hand, they never succeeded in penetrating with any degree of permanence save in the highest and most southerly part, at Huánuco and in its vicinity. In short, the Marañón basin is one of those regions wherein no cultural progress was likely to be originated for the reason that it was at once too enervating—being rather hot and humid—and too luxuriant in vegetation to stimulate such arts as agriculture, weaving, and pottery-making towards development beyond the initial stages. Nevertheless, it was also a region in which, once the higher types of culture were introduced, they could, under proper governmental supervision, be maintained.

South of the Knot of Pasco the western bulwark of the *sierra*, that is, the Maritime Cordillera, continues to be as definite as ever and, on an average, somewhat higher, with many very lofty peaks along its ridge and with a goodly number of practicable passes, some of which are higher above the sea than is the summit of Pike's Peak or that of Mont Blanc, likewise existing here and there. On the eastern side of this stupendous range there are three great drainage basins: those of the Mantaro, the Apurimac, and the Urubamba (anciently Urupampa) Rivers. All three of them are tributaries to the majestic Ucayali River which flows through the forest country east of the highland zone. A fourth basin should, from a geographical standpoint, also be mentioned, that of the Perené River, likewise a tributary of the Ucayali; but, as in the case of the Huallaga basin, it is of almost no historical importance and so demands no further notice here.

The three basins mentioned here combine to form the highland plateau, about 9,500 to 13,000 feet above the sea, which has, in addition to the still loftier ridges which separate the drainage areas from one another, ramparts on the eastern side which mark it off from the low, hot, sylvan country beyond, ramparts, however, through which many streams make their way, roaring down through sonorous canyons called, graphically enough, *pongos*, from *puncu* the Quechua word for gateway or portal. The area included in these three drainage basins and the high-lying wastes between them measures about 400 miles from north to south and about 150 miles from east to west; all of the territory in question drains into the Amazon river-system.

Travellers who have not previously thought much about the matter are always astonished when they are told that their train—whether on the Central Railway of Peru or on the Southern Railway—is crossing the Continental Divide. It is little surprises like this that make travel in the Andean area so interesting. Such unexpected bits of knowledge likewise prepare one for statements like this: Cuzco, the ancient capital of Ttahua-ntin-suyu, The Land of the Four Sections, otherwise the Inca Empire, lies in the drainage of the Amazon riversystem. Yet this is true, for the small, torrential streams that flow through Cuzco pour themselves into the Urubamba, which is a tributary of the Ucayali, which in turn empties into the Marañón, just as that does into the Amazon.

From the historical standpoint the Urubamba Valley and its tributaries form one of the two most important *hoyas* of the Andean highland zone, the other being the Titicaca basin, of which more will be said presently.

What is there in the environmental complex of this *hoya* of the Urubamba that made it inevitable that it should become the birthplace, the cradle, the home, and the tomb of one of the most remarkable civilizations that mankind has ever constructed? Lying on an average of about 11,000 feet above sea-level, that portion of it which is known as the Cuzco Valley, wherein took place the epochal developments referred to, is a temperate region capable of sustaining intensive agriculture, and, moreover, is productive of the raw-materials for pottery, for textiles, for metal-working, and for architecture in stone. The mere physical presence of these advantageous circumstances is not enough, however, to explain the flowering of advanced culture in that region. In order to be made use of these elements must be able to draw upon a definite amount of human energy, ingenuity, and application. In such a climate as that of the Cuzco Valley man can supply these factors, thereby engendering culture by combining them with those other factors which were so bountifully supplied by Nature. In a clime more enervating man's energies would have been sapped by lassitude; in a colder, they would have been exhausted by the unremitting struggle to keep his body above the freezing-point and by anxiously hunting about for edible

matter. Here there was a felicitous balance of factors and, as
a result, a great civilization was born.

South of the headwaters of the Urubamba River rises
another very important transverse ridge, called the *Nudo* or
Knot of Vilcañota. A relatively easy pass, sometimes called
the Pass of la Raya, sometimes the Pass of Vilcañota, leads
southwards at an altitude of 15,000 feet above sea-level, serving as a natural link between the nuclear region of the Inca
Empire and that of its predecessor, the putative Tiahuanaco
Empire.

Crossing that Pass one enters the basin of Lake Titicaca,
bounded by the Knot of Vilcañota on the north, the Maritime
Cordillera on the west and the Eastern Cordillera—in these
parts known as the Cordillera Real or Royal Cordillera—on
the east. It is a territory which is some 120 miles wide and
some 500 miles long, having towards its northern end the
famous Lake of Titicaca (sometimes called Lake of Chucuito)
which is about 40 miles wide and about 120 miles long, lying
at an altitude of slightly over 12,500 feet above sea-level.
Towards the south this immense area, roughly equal to Maine,
New Hampshire, Vermont, and Massachusetts added together,
is less definitely outlined than in the north for, instead of
being enclosed by ranges, it falls away gradually beyond Lake
Poopó to the great *salares* or salt-beds of Coipasa and Uyuni,
which are, presumably, the vestiges of ancient lakes.

A peculiarity of the Titicaca basin is its hydrography; for,
although the Lake of that name has many inlets, it has but
one outlet, namely, the Desaguadero River, and that merely
flows southeastwardly into Lake Poopó, which has no known
outlet beyond a westward seepage into the salt-beds and an
excessive amount of evaporation. The area in question, therefore, has wide and deep Lake Titicaca at its northern end,
Lake Poopó, at about 12,100 feet above sea-level, and the salt-
beds of Coipasa and Uyuni, a little lower, at its southern end.

It is the country immediately adjacent to Lake Titicaca that
particularly demands the attention of the historian. Here, as
when contemplating the Cuzco Valley, he must ask himself

just how and why this region produced a great civilization. Although it is more than 1,000 feet higher than the Cuzco Valley, the country around Lake Titicaca is, for some distance back from the shore, well below 14,000 feet, which is the upward limit of potato-cultivation. Agriculture was, therefore, possible—but under more difficult circumstances—and the other raw-materials for culture were also present, as were likewise human energy, enterprise, and perseverance. Therefore, this is another region in which we need not be surprised to find that important cultural progress was inaugurated and carried forward to noteworthy culminations.

Still further to the south and southwest we find a tangle of mountains which occupy southern Bolivia, northwestern Argentina, and the northern part of Chile; it is this wide and greatly varying region that modern geographers mean when they speak of the Desert and Puna of Atacama. Within this territory of some 390,000 square miles there were, as we shall see, some interesting cultural and historical developments; but they were mainly brought into the territory from outside, rather than originated in it. This is due not so much to any lack inherent in the environment of those parts as it is to the circumstance that, being rather far south, the inland portions of these regions did not receive their first settlers until after considerable progress in culture had been made by the immigrants who first moved into the territory in question. Only along the coast of Chile—which is merely a continuation of the Peruvian coastal desert—are there traces of relatively backward folk who, in all likelihood, had drifted southward down the shore, supporting themselves chiefly by fishing and by rudimentary agriculture.[8]

Throughout the length of the Andean highlands two major geographical controls play their part in determining the manner of man's existence there. These are: 1, altitude; 2, the courses of rivers. The distinction between the two is far from sharp; indeed, they overlap considerably. Altitude has to do primarily with such matters as heat and cold, as density and rarity of the air, and as the ability or non-ability of plants to thrive at given levels. It is axiomatic that man lives most commodiously in the valley-bottoms, in close proximity to waters that flow perennially between flat alluvial plains and their adjacent fans which, taken together, provide soil capable of sustaining the most intensive sort of husbandry. Above the level of such lands, and contiguous with them, is a belt of mountain-sides which, if painstakingly terraced and irrigated, is also capable of producing good crops. Above that again is another natural belt, one in which steppe conditions prevail, with grass and low shrubs growing abundantly and affording excellent pasturage for flocks at all seasons of the year. Finally, the highest of all, is the belt of the mountain-peaks where there is little vegetation and in the loftiest parts of which there are perennial expanses of ice and snow. In those great heights men live only with effort and never for any long stretch of time; their most elevated parts act now, as they have always done, as barriers that tend to keep the people of one valley from having constant contact with those in the valleys around them. Only by dint of special exertion, usually the product of some long-maturing social polity, can these barriers be over-ridden, and then only by special classes in the body politic.[9] The avenues whereby the governmental forces, whether ancient or modern, have spread themselves far and wide are the elevated passes already mentioned above, nearly all of them being over 13,000 feet above sea-level.

As one might expect, the vegetable products of the highlands are less numerous in kind than those of the coast. Maize will not grow to advantage above 11,000 feet; but other food-crops, including the potato, the *oca*, the *quínua* (a cereal) and certain minor tubers, will grow up to 14,000 feet and, in sheltered spots, a trifle higher. Economically useful plants capable of existing at these altitudes are numerous: *ichu* or *ychu* grass which, growing in tufts, is browsed upon by llamas and vicuñas as well as being used for thatch, matting, etc.; *totora* reed, plentiful on the margins of lakes and useful for basketry and for fashioning into boats or *balsas* of the kind so frequently seen on Lake Titicaca; the *tola*-bush, which attains to a height of a yard or more and is utilized as a fuel, its resinous wood and gluey leaves giving forth a sharp but not unpleasant odor; the *llareta* or *yareta*, a strange plant whose branches, growing compactly, carry a small, dense foliage at their extremities, a foliage so crowded together that it presents to the world a smooth, rounded surface like that of a moss-covered boulder and, when chopped into chunks ready for use as fuel, looks like so many greenish stones; and, finally among the vegetable fuels, there is the *quínua* or *queñua* tree—not to be confounded with the cereal called *quínua*—which is about the size of an olive-tree and is most valuable for firewood. This robust tree fears not the most rigorous conditions of the uplands, boldly and sturdily growing as it does almost up to the snow-line. In this respect it is rivalled by the tree called *quishuar*. This charming tree likewise superficially resembles the olive, but when it is in blossom it is a mass of lovely orange-colored flowers which give forth a delicious scent not unlike that of saffron. The blooms were ground up into a sort of powder or paste which gives a delightful flavor or color to foods much as saffron does. In addition to all this, the *quishuar* tree furnishes the highland Indians with tough wood suitable for the making of *tacllas* or ploughs, and for that purpose they have used it during many centuries.[10]

Of the animals useful to man in one way or another there are, in the *sierra*, a goodly number, prominent among them being, in addition to the wool-bearing llama and vicuña, the *viscacha*, a large edible rodent; deer of several kinds; the *cui*, an edible guinea-pig that abounds in the houses of the Indians; the *yutu*, a sort of partridge; and several sorts of lake fish some of which are excellent for eating.[11]

The *sierra* likewise supplied its inhabitants with an abundance of those mineral substances which were known and used in ancient times in the Andean area. *Cori* or *curi*, Quechua for gold, occurs widely throughout the highlands, as also in most parts of anciently civilized America, and it was extensively used from the earliest times; the same holds true for *collque* or silver. It is probable that copper, called *anta* in

Quechua, came into use somewhat later; and that tin, *chay-anta*, was probably still later, as was also lead, *titi*. Nor was there lacking a considerable variety of building-stone to which in Quechua the general term *checorumi*, literally work-stone, was applied, the work being performed by means of certain small but very hard and heavy stones generally known as *vini*.[12]

In a word, the highland zone, varying as between its deep and fertile valleys and its snow-clad solitudes far above, offered to mankind an amazing range of environmental conditions and of raw materials.

4. The Forests or Montaña

Along the sunrise-greeting slopes of the Eastern Cordillera lies the long, narrow, roughly longitudinal strip which constitutes the third of the natural zones of the Andean area. In geographical parlance it is known as the *ceja de la montaña*, "eyebrow of the woodlands." On the western side it dovetails with the plateau of the *sierra*, from which it slants away sharply towards the east. The topography of the *ceja* is best described as being an alternation of the lofty, jutting spurs of the Andes with deep valleys and canyons through which the *hoyas* of the highlands are drained of their superfluous waters; in other words, the *ceja* links the mountains with the vast, damp, hot, river-veined sylvan wildernesses of Amazonia and of the River Plate drainage.

The valleys of this zone are so many natural avenues leading from the *sierra* into the tropical *montaña* below. Here it is that the Trade-Winds, after sweeping across the lowlands, are forced upward by the rise of the land, with the result that the clouds which they carry are relieved of a great part of their moisture. It is, therefore, a zone of tropical conditions wherein Nature takes on terrifying proportions—terrifying luxuriance of vegetation, terrifying onrush of rivers, terrifying animal life. Never, at any rate so far as we now know, have either the lower portions of the *ceja de la montaña* or the *montaña* itself been the seat of any stable and advanced community; on the contrary, they are properly the habitat of arboreal man in an archaic stage of culture beyond which progress is not possible save under very definite suasion from the outside world. Nevertheless, to certain highland folk—notably the Incas—the *montaña* was always at once alluring and inimical. Guided by the water-courses pouring into it from their homelands, they sought repeatedly to penetrate its mysteries and to establish some kind of dominion over it. But invariably a force, invisible but irresistible, threw their acquisitive plans awry, preventing prolonged residence amid the humid tangle of the woodland world.[13]

5. Geographical Factors in the Shaping of Cultures

During the course of the foregoing description of the Andean area I have commented now and then on the disabilities or abilities of sundry regions from the standpoint of cultural progress. In the next chapter I shall show how, because of the general conditions and phases of development surrounding the settlement of America as a whole, the Andean area was first peopled by folk all of whom had entered—if only to a slight extent—the archaic stage of cultural evolution; that is, even the humblest of them were possessed, at the time of their advent in the Andean area, of at least incipient forms of agriculture, pottery-making, and weaving. This being so, all that was necessary for them to attain to the forms of civilization to which, eventually, some of them did attain was to acquire a cultural impetus strong enough to carry them through the various grades of archaic culture and on into the stage of civilization.

As we shall see in subsequent chapters, this profoundly significant transition took place only in a certain few of the regions into which the Andean area is divided. Does this mean that there is some special combination of geographical factors which engenders in man an ability to achieve the transition? The best way to gain a satisfactory reply to this query is to re-examine the divers regions where progress from archaic to post-archaic culture was made.

First of all let us look again at the coast of Peru, bearing this special problem in mind the while. There we find a very warm, perhaps even a hot, climate, a rich soil (concentrated, to be sure, in valleys contiguous to rivers), and a great variety of plant, animal, and mineral raw materials potentially capable of being employed for the building of advanced culture. Upon examining each of these points in turn we discover that, although the climate was very warm, it was not uninvigorating, this fact being due to the dryness of the atmosphere, and to the circumstance that, owing to the off-shore presence of the cool Humboldt current, the nights are cool and bracing; the up-shot of all this is that man is enabled to maintain a fairly high level of energy. The rich soil made tillage easy and profitable; the presence of plentiful water made irrigation feasible and beneficial; the existence of wild plants susceptible to cultivation vigorously encouraged farming; the populousness of the sea and of the rivers impelled the people early to develop an admirable technique as fishermen, and in like fashion the profusion of game among the foothills led them to become adroit hunters, using both by land and by sea, when in quest of animal food, tools and methods far superior to those which primitive men employ for like purposes; the dense growth along the river margins of reeds suitable for basketry and for mat-making; the sufficient occurrence of clays and pigments acceptable to potters favored improvement in the making of jars, bowls, dishes and other vessels capable of becoming media for the artistic genius of the people; and, finally, the material for adobe being readily obtainable, and algarroba wood (not entirely satisfactory, but still serviceable) being ubiquitously present, the necessary ingredients for architecture were at hand.

Turning now to the Titicaca basin, what do we find? The climate is cold and damp but, for a large-lunged folk, tolerably stimulating; husbandry is favored by the existence of many food-plants and economically useful plants of kinds already mentioned above; weaving draws upon the wool of llamas and vicuñas; copper and other metals wherewith tools can be fashioned abound; excellent stuff wherewith to fashion pots is plentiful; and, finally, various sorts of stone of unsurpassed merit for architectural and sculptural purposes occur copiously.

In the Cuzco Valley practically the same situation prevails with the single difference that the climate is somewhat less austere and less taxing to the human organism.

All three of these regions, then, display the presence of a wide range of raw materials for culture conjoined with climatic conditions which energize man sufficiently to utilize them to the fullest extent. These regions, therefore, stand in sharp contrast to, let us say, the Marañón basin where, although raw materials for culture are not wanting, men, depressed and enervated by the climate, cannot progress to their fullest capabilities; or, again, they stand in contrast to the narrow, deep, and relatively stony gorges along the southernmost shore of Peru and in northernmost coastal Chile, gorges wherein raw materials for culture may exist but where man, psychologically restrained by the frowning bluffs about him, does not expand his imagination and expend himself in constructive labor as he does in the kindlier and more open valleys farther north.

In short, I gather from all this that, in order that the transition from archaic to post-archaic culture may be effected, a perfect balance must be achieved between the sum of Nature's offerings and man's ability and readiness to utilize them. Put energetic men in a stimulating clime which, however, chances to lack materials wherewith they can work culturally and they will either stand still or else retrogress—unless, as usually happens, they save their souls by moving to more propitious surroundings; put other men in a Paradise replete with every conceivable substance for the construction of the most exalted forms of civilization and then nearly suffocate them with hot, damp, breathless air, and they will, at best, remain in the stage of culture which they had on arriving under those conditions or, more likely, they will drop back from mere lassitude, into a state of primitiveness.

Environment, therefore, is not the total causation in culture-shaping; but it is, beyond doubt, the most conspicuous single factor. It works in two ways: in presenting raw materials and in helping to prepare human mentality to utilize them. It likewise functions importantly in furnishing men with trade-routes such as coast-lines, rivers, passes, whereby alien materials and fecundating new ideas may come into a given region. But there is still an indefinable factor which may best be designated quite frankly as x, the unknown quantity, apparently psychological in kind. If x be in harmony with the environmental factors—and it is so comparatively rarely—culture will progress and civilization will be constructed, to continue, we may suppose, until x ceases to be in harmony with the environmental factors. From this it follows that, if x be not the most conspicuous factor in the matter, it certainly is the most important, the most fate-laden. When, through a tardily completed understanding of the significance of life, we achieve mastery over x, then, and not until then, shall we cease to be a race of biped ants and, consummating our age-old desire, join the immortal gods.

NOTES TO CHAPTER I

[1] Tello, 1929.

[2] Cobo, 1890–1893. (As this is the only edition of Father Cobo's great *Historia del Nuevo Mundo*, written between 1642 and 1653, it is cited simply as Cobo after this.)

[3] Murphy, 1923; 1923b; 1925, Chs. ii–vii, inclusive, and Chs. xi and xii.

[4] Markham, 1910, p. 204.

[5] Murphy, 1926.

[6] Alcedo, 1812–1815, IV, pp. 155–156. Raimondi, 1874–1913, I, pp. 356–359.

[7] Bowman, 1916, Chs. viii and ix.

[8] Beuchat, 1912, p. 575. Boman, 1908, I, pp. 67–73. Bowman, 1924, p. 59.

[9] On this point see: Baudin, 1928, pp. 28–33. Means, 1925, pp. 432–444.

[10] Early and still useful descriptions of the various plants here mentioned will be found at the following places: Potatoes—Cobo, Bk. IV, Ch. xiii; Acosta, Bk. IV, Ch. xviii. Oca—Cobo, Bk. IV, Ch. xiv. Quínua (cereal)— Cobo, Bk. IV, Ch. v; Acosta, Bk. IV, Ch. vi. Ichu or ychu—Cobo, Bk. IV, Ch. cvi. Totora—Acosta, Bk. VI, Ch. xiv. Tola—Cobo, Bk. V, Ch. xliii. Llareta or Yareta—Cobo, Bk. V, Ch. lxxii. Quínua or Queñua (tree)—Cobo, Bk. VI, Ch. cxxviii. Quishuar—Cobo, Bk. VI, Ch. xlix.

[11] Viscacha—Cobo, Bk. IX, Ch. xlviii. Cui—Cobo, Bk. IX, Ch. xlvi. Deer —Cobo, Bk. IX, Ch. lvi. For a general discussion of the subject see Eaton, 1925.

[12] Gold—Cobo, Bk. III, Ch. xxxvi. Silver—Cobo, Bk. III, Ch. xxxvii. Copper—Cobo, Bk. III, Ch. xlii. Tin—Cobo, Bk. III, Ch. xliv. Lead—Cobo, Bk. III, Ch. xlv. Building-stone, and quarrying—Cobo, Bk. III, Chs. xiii–xviii, inclusive.

[13] In addition to works already cited, I have used, in writing this chapter, the following authorities: Barrett, 1925, I, pp. 1–30. Bingham, Millicent Todd, 1929. Cisneros, n. d. Denis, 1927. Dyott, 1922 and 1926. Keane, 1909–1911. Levillier, R., 1927, Ch. i. López, F., 1907. McBride, 1921. Ogilvie, 1922. Orton, 1870. Paz Soldán, M. F., 1865 and 1877. Paz Soldán, Mateo and M. F., 1862–1863. Raimondi, 1867, 1873, 1874–1913, 1903. Reiss and Stübel, 1873. Saville, 1907–1910, I, pp. 5–8. Sinclair, 1929. Veatch, 1917. Verneau and Rivet, 1912–1922, I, pp. 1–7. Villavicencio, 1858. Wolf, 1879 and 1892. Whiffen, 1915. Whymper, 1892.

CHAPTER II

THE EARLIEST CULTURES IN THE ANDEAN AREA

THE origins of the native race of America and of its varying degrees and kinds of culture have long stirred the imaginations and the intellects of many people. During three centuries and more men have been making widely divergent conjectures concerning the problem of how America was peopled and how its various societies and polities came into being. Picturesque, alluring theories have been formulated with conviction and eloquence only to be refuted by arguments set forth with equal sincerity, arguments productive chiefly, it must be confessed, of more or less hysterical re-affirmation of the original thesis. So it has gone on, this ancient quest for truth, from century to century, always amid a hail of words by no means always wise and courteous. Regarding the matter in the broad, as it were, one may truly say that the prolonged discussion has been largely a battle between imagination and reasoning, the former fostering all manner of quaint and attractive propositions to the effect that this or that American civilization came from here or from there in far distant portions of our globe, the latter patiently displaying the difference between man-as-an-animal and man-as-a-creator-and-bearer-of-culture.

This is not the proper occasion, however, for dealing with the matter in detail. The scope of this book permits me to give only a brief outline of the subject as it has been seen in the past and to present the currently accepted opinions of reliable scientists.

First of all I will touch briefly upon the theory that the native race of America was originated in the Western Hemisphere and derived no part of its blood from elsewhere. This theory assumes the presence of mankind in America in geologically ancient times, that is, in the glacial and interglacial periods. Various claims have been made in widely scattered localities of America that traces of immensely antique man have been found; but in every case of the kind the implacable light of scientific examination has shown that the pretended age or the pretended nature of the relics was either erroneous or else extremely doubtful.[1] Of particular interest for us is the claim at one time sustained by Dr. Hiram Bingham that remains of geologically ancient man had been found near Cuzco, in southern Peru; for, subsequently, it was shown that those remains were neither entirely human nor ancient, in which finding of science Dr. Bingham himself handsomely concurred when the evidence was complete.[2] The present opinion of competent authorities is, then, that mankind regarded merely as animals did not originate in this Western Hemisphere.

Logically it follows that, if man was not autochthonous in America, he must have come thither from some other part of the earth. Dr. Hrdlička, in the course of many years of the most intensive sort of field work has proved that man, regarded merely as an animal, is not of American origin and that, on the contrary, as the result of a series of unpremeditated, accidental, and long-continued migrations, a portion of the human race reached America from Siberia by way of the Aleutian Islands—formerly a part of the mainland—and Alaska. The migrants were members of the yellow-brown race of Asia and Polynesia. Their drift into America, the beginning of which may be dated approximately as from 25,000 to 10,000 years ago, was chiefly the result of pressure arising from the natural increase in population and the resultant shortage of food in their homeland. It is obvious that the antiquity of even the earliest movements of this kind was as nothing in comparison with that of the populations of Asia represented by the Java Man (450,000 years) and the various interglacial populations of Europe.[3]

The primitive migrations into America from Asia were the result of no fixed plan, nor were they confined to any one period. They were wholly fortuitous and they continued wave upon wave for thousands of years, the latest wave being, perhaps, that represented by the Eskimos in northernmost America. Having arrived in this hemisphere, mankind continued to drift at random, to trickle, to percolate in exploratory groups that fearfully made their way through primordial wildernesses where no man had ever passed before. Thus, to an accompaniment of anxieties and hesitations, man pressed constantly onwards until every region of America had received its first representatives of the human race. It was an unsystematic and protracted process exactly similar to that whereby the birds and the beasts were distributed over the continents.

So much for the advent of man, zoölogically considered, in America. It is now necessary to differentiate, and sharply, between man as an animal and man as an originator and bearer of culture. It is likely that the earliest migrants were extremely primitive in their mode of living and that as time went on the successive waves of newcomers displayed some measure, if only a slight one, of progress. There is no evidence, however, that any of them had passed beyond the hunter-and-fisher stage of being, nor that anything like a sedentary and regulated social system had been developed by them. On the contrary, it is now generally believed by those best qualified to have an opinion that all the advancement towards high material and intellectual culture which was subsequently made by some of the descendants of the initial settlers was made in America with slight, if any, help from outside.

Since no American populations are old in a geological sense, and since all American civilizations took their rise some thousands of years after the advent of man in this hemisphere, it naturally follows that no American civilization can be extremely old. The admirable archæological work of Professor Byron Cummings at Cuicuilco, near Coyoacán, Mexico, makes it clear that the greatest age which can safely be ascribed to any fairly advanced culture is 5,000 years.[4] Most of the high civilizations of America were beyond doubt much less old than this.

Fortunately we possess a chronological guide—albeit one that is far from being wholly satisfactory—useful as an aid in

gauging the antiquity of the various Andean cultural phases
and periods. It is afforded us by the calendrical inscriptions
of the Mayas of Yucatan and of northern Guatemala, supplemented by written matter left to us by the Mayas and by the
advanced native folk of Mexico. In short a situation exists in
America that is faintly analogous to that in the Mediterranean
world of pre-classical times wherein the inscriptions and other
remains abounding in Egypt afford a dating-gauge for the
early periods of civilization in Crete.

Before proceeding to note the chief notches in the dating-
gauge mentioned it is necessary to digress briefly in order to
look at certain aspects of American culture as a whole. Our
present knowledge indicates, as I have said above, that the
initial settlers and the successive waves of immigrants were in
a primitive hunter-and-fisher stage of culture. But, indubitably, there were variations between one group and another:
some were better hunters than their neighbors and so lived
better; some had this or that local advantage—such as good
supplies of flints for tools—which enabled them to construct
more satisfactory shelters wherein to live; some were gifted
with peculiar cleverness in adapting to their needs the growing things around them, thereby taking the first steps towards
a future science of agriculture; some were blessed by the
presence of reeds and grasses capable of being made into
basket-work, which was, perhaps, the common ancestor of the
seemingly divergent arts of the weaver and the potter.

Notwithstanding the minor irregularities of these sorts in
the general cultural level, it remained true that, so long as the
people remained nomadic or semi-nomadic, their lives
remained a struggle in which nearly all of their strength was
absorbed in the grim task of winning a bare subsistence. As
the centuries rolled by, however, even the most backward
made some degree of progress, while at the same time the
most advanced took longer forward steps, until, by slow
degrees, each one of the countless family and kinship groups
made its way into a locality that suited it sufficiently to permit
of its taking root with something very like permanence.

It was on taking possession of their habitats, and on becoming settled therein, that the formerly nomadic groups were able to enter in upon a cultural phase which, for want of a better term, we must call the archaic culture. It is hardly necessary to say that this important change did not take place all at once. Some groups arrived at that point early; others followed at different dates; still others never passed beyond the hunter-and-fisher stage. The best criterion is the presence of pottery, no matter how crude, of agriculture, no matter how rudimentary, or of weaving, no matter how primitive; if any or all of these cultural elements are found associated with a given people it may be safely said that their culture was archaic, that is, post-nomadic or post-primitive. It does not follow, of course, that a people who attained to the archaic stage of culture, as that term is here used, dropped their ancient means of livelihood; on the contrary, they hunted and they fished with increased efficiency because of the better implements therefor with which their enlarged technological repertory provided them.

Like the primitive or purely hunter-and-fisher stage of culture, the succeeding archaic stage was merely a phase in the general series of cultural evolution; at one time or another most American regions have had populations that were, at least temporarily, in the archaic stage of material and intellectual development. Indeed, at the present day, certain archaic cultures still exist: in Amazonia and the Guianas, in the Gran Chaco disputed by Bolivia and Paraguay, in Tierra del Fuego, to name but a few examples. It is apparent, therefore, that it is as great a mistake to regard the archaic culture as representative of any one locality as it is to regard it as representative of any one point in time. On the contrary, it is a phase of culture which may or may not be ancient, but which always underlies any higher brands of civilization that a given region may have possessed or may possess at present. Properly regarded, cultural evolution is like a flight of steps, the lowest landing of which is the primitive, the second landing of which is the archaic, the third is barbaric civilization, and so on, the steps between the several landings being the abovementioned variations in point of excellence that characterize all the phases. Incidentally, one wonders at times whither this stairway will lead us; perchance towards some frightful drop into —what?

The archaic landing, then, is that stage in the evolution of human industries in which germinated, and in a measure grew, various material techniques with their associated intellectual ideas. In a word, it contained the rudiments of and the preparations for barbaric civilization. The variations within the limits of the archaic phase were considerable, just as the variations within the primitive phase which underlay it had been so. In both cases the divergences were the product of varying response to the environment or of varying degrees of advantageousness in the environment of the groups concerned.

Just as these factors determined the contrasting qualities between one representative of the archaic phase and another, so did they determine the degree to which a given group was able, in due course, to pass beyond it. The archaic cultural phase was that wherein not only the arts of prime importance —pottery, weaving, and agriculture—but also such auxiliary arts as wood-carving, stone-working, bone-graving, animal-taming (as a first step in domestication), and social organization, had their inception. The process of passing beyond and upwards from the archaic landing, therefore, was marked by the attainment of mastery over the fundamental technique of each of these. The technological significance of that passing upward lies in the fact that man was thereby released from the necessity of finding out how to employ his materials and was set free to progress in his treatment of them with an ever-increasing sureness of workmanship which brought in its wake all manner of advancement in a multitude of directions.

Some peoples of America never managed to achieve the passage upward to which I refer, and as a result they have, as it were, remained upon the archaic landing. In most cases this has been their misfortune—if it be one—rather than their fault. Other peoples have climbed up the steps which represent progressive elaboration of the archaic culture but have stopped short before reaching the landing which symbolizes the simplest form of barbaric civilization; others, again, have boldly trodden that landing and have gone steadily upwards from it until they stood upon the landing which we may term the feudalistic and agricultural type of civilization. This last, like all the stages of development which preceded it, had its variations, and wide ones at that.

No native peoples of America climbed higher than did the Mayas and the folk of Mexico in the north and the ancient Andeans—or rather, some among them—in the south. Had they gone much further upwards than they did, they would have reached the landing best designated as the international type of civilization, that in which most of Europe found itself from the fall of the Roman Empire to the Industrial Revolution. We, at present, and somewhat to our bewilderment, are on a landing which may be called that of mechanized civilization, one in which the members of the human body, hitherto the principal tools wherewith man has performed his tasks, have been largely and increasingly replaced by machines. What lies beyond this stage none of us can know; at times we suspect that it is not wholly pleasant.

In the scheme of cultural evolution each landing represents an accumulation of wisdom and experience inherited from the stages already passed through. In this sense the various grades of the barbaric and of the feudalistic-agricultural civilizations of America are derivatives from the archaic culture. At the same time, the race of America is a derivative from the primitive immigrants from Asia, but only in a zoölogical sense; for we must bear in mind the fact that, as the primitive migrations took place before men anywhere had reached the archaic stage of culture, before they had ceased to be primitive and nomadic, all subsequent cultural advancement in this hemisphere took place here, and was achieved long after the initial peopling of America.

No part of the subsequent advancement is more spectacular and more impressive than that compassed by the Mayas in

Central America. Moreover, as I have said above, their history is dated, not only in the earliest perceptible periods of their civilization, but also in every part of its career. To begin with, we have, as Dr. Sylvanus Griswold Morley has pointed out, every reason to believe that the Mayas originated in the region now occupied by the Huasteca, on the Atlantic coast of the Mexican state of Vera Cruz and in the country behind it, a region wherein the language is Maya but wherein no trace of the Maya hieroglyphic and calendrical systems has ever been found. Dr. Morley then goes on to show that the earliest dated object representing the Maya culture, the Tuxtla Statuette, 98 B. C., was found at San Andrés de Tuxtla which is roughly mid-way between the Huasteca country and the region occupied by the Old Empire of the Mayas. Finally, he shows that two objects come from well within the Old Empire territory; for we have the Leyden Plate, dated 60 A. D. and Stela 9 at Uaxactun, dated 68 A. D. Furthermore, Dr. Morley makes it very clear that the Mayas passed from the primitive or hunter-and-fisher stage to the archaic stage of culture before they left the Huasteca country.

We may now turn to evidence, presented by Dr. Herbert J. Spinden, relative to the date at which the hieroglyphic and calendrical systems of the Mayas came into being. He demonstrates the probability that the Maya calendar was invented and put into working order between 613 and 580 B. C.[5]

To continue, as briefly as possible, with Maya history, a synopsis of its chief historical periods will be presented.

The so-called Old Empire of the Mayas, which rose, flourished and waned between 50 and 700 A. D., occupied a territory measuring approximately 225 miles on a side in country that is now divided between the Mexican state of Yucatan, the republic of Guatemala, and British Honduras. The area described is to-day a tangled wilderness of forests, lakes, streams and mountains; but in those first seven centuries of our Era more than twenty-five majestic cities flourished there, each one distinguished by the presence of inscribed monuments, altars, and pyramided temples all wrought of stone and imperishably dignified,[6] each one the seat of a beauty-loving people whose artisans fashioned all manner of exquisite objects in pottery, stone, wood and other materials.[7] In short, the Old Empire civilization of the Mayas was worthy to be compared—in spite of certain material lacks which will be noted later—with any that existed in Europe prior to the Industrial Revolution, worthy also to be compared with any of the civilizations of antiquity in Asia or in Africa. And this amazing civilization, be it remembered, was the work of American "Indians" without help from any alien civilized people.

The greatest intensity and vigor of the Old Empire fell in the latter part of its history, roughly between 450 and 700 A. D. It was in that period that the most sightly cities were flourishing and the most memorable art was being produced, in short, that the Mayas were winning for themselves a merited immortality. But it was likewise a period rich in the materials whereof disaster is made; for various factors were working with cumulative effect towards dissolution. Chief among them may be mentioned a general enervation of the physical forces and of the morale of the people, coupled with a general decadence of their morale through super-sophistication operating in large measure through the channels of a priestcraft which had gone rancid. As Dr. Spinden has pointed out,[8] the flamboyant and extravagant art of the latter part of the Old Empire period, although it is weirdly beautiful to our eyes, in truth is expressive of an unwholesome psychological and physical state on the part of its producers. In addition to subtle, intangible moral factors such as those here indicated, there were, as Dr. Morley and Dr. Ellsworth Huntington have shown,[9] from about the beginning of the seventh century A. D., climatic changes in Maya-land which were in the highest degree hostile to a continuation of high material culture there. Conditions of extreme wetness prevailed which made agriculture almost impossible and raised to the nth power the always wasteful methods of husbandry pursued by the Mayas. In order to combat the implacable luxuriance of the forest growth which sprang up overwhelmingly in the humid warmth of the earth and of the atmosphere, the Mayas resorted to a systematic burning-off of the trees and shrubs upon their plantations. Although the charred remnants of the woody growths entered the soil and benefited it, the very burning which produced them consumed the humus in the soil itself with the result that, after each successive burning, a longer and longer period became necessary in order to permit the trees and shrubs to grow anew in the fields. There was, consequently, a perennial conflict between the benefit derived from the charred ashes of the burnt trees and the harm arising from the destruction of humus by the fire.[10]

The up-shot of all these factors in combination was that the region occupied by the Old Empire became intolerable to a highly civilized agricultural people during the course of the seventh century A. D. It need not surprise us, therefore, that, beginning about 450 and continuing onwards until nearly 700, there should have been an increasingly strong centrifugal movement from the Old Empire. At first, no doubt, this movement was in the nature of a colonial enterprise, the product of a strong and proud people's wish to win new territories for themselves; but, as time wore on, and as the conditions already described became more and more overpowering, the colonial off-shoots ceased to be, as it were, imperialistic gestures and became the despair-engendered move of a doomed people away from a habitat that had become obnoxious. Properly regarded this process is a sophisticated version of that whereby the primordial migrants were impelled to enter America from Asia and to distribute themselves over the face of the continent. In the present case, however, the degree of sophistication was great. Although fear was its main motive it was not a movement without order and plan; rather, it was true colonization, determined by social and economic considerations and carried out by an excellently organized governmental machine. In this respect, at least in its inception, the colonizing period of the Old Empire Mayas was more nearly akin to the colonial enterprizes of the ancient Greeks than to the fortuitous wanderings of the first settlers of America.

At first, during the period of Maya colonization—chiefly in a northerly direction, towards the upper part of Yucatan—material and intellectual culture bade fair to maintain themselves at a high level. But, for causes at which we can only guess—climatic conditions, wars, pestilence, who knows what? —there followed, in the new habitat, between 690 and 990, three centuries of decided cultural decline. It was a period analogous in quality to the so-called Dark Ages in Europe.

From 990 to 1200, however, there was, in northern Yucatan, a notable recrudescence of cultural strength, and during more than two centuries new cities, fully as splendid as the now abandoned capitals of the south had been, were founded, grew, and flourished, forming the New Empire of the Mayas. It was a time of peace, prosperity and artistic productiveness. But at the end of the period internecine strife between the various cities and between their ruling dynasties sprang up, greatly weakening the Maya people as a whole, a fact of which the powerful Toltecs of Mexico made use in order to establish their hegemony over Yucatan. Lasting from 1201 to 1458, the Toltec period was filled with brilliant achievement, but it contained the materials for eventual explosion, and after 1458 the Maya-Toltec culture of Yucatan burst into many hostile parts, inaugurating a second decline in civilization which lasted until the Spaniards entered the country.[11]

The significance for us of the facts presented in this all too long digression may be summed up under various heads, as follows:

1. The archaic cultural phase, succeeding to the primitive, hunter-and-fisher phase of culture brought into America by the original migrants from Asia, was very widely distributed throughout the Western Hemisphere, and in various regions it lasted into modern times, albeit in others it was superseded by more advanced types of culture. Because of its catholic character we are constantly finding representatives of its industries in widely separated regions. An artifact of archaic type from one region will often closely resemble one of analogous kind from far away; but a resemblance of that sort does

not denote contact between the folk of the two regions; on the contrary, it merely shows that, at one time or another, the folk of both regions passed through the archaic phase. Moreover, they may have done so at about the same period, or, with equal likelihood, they may have done so at widely separated periods. To cite here but one out of possible hundreds of specific examples I will call attention to the crude stone carvings reported on by Dr. S. K. Lothrop as occurring at Finca Arévalo, in Guatemala, and certain equally crude stone carvings from near Oruro, in Bolivia, described by myself.[12] In both may be seen the same mode of fashioning the eyes and mouths, and the same lack of noses—these last being too intricate for the inchoate artistry of the archaic carvers.

2. The chronology of the Mayas, nowadays resting upon an almost complete understanding of their calendrical inscriptions, is important for us in two respects:

A. The Tuxtla Statuette, bearing a Maya date equal to 98 B. C., is in style fairly well advanced archaic, and is comparable in an æsthetic way to a class of anthropomorphic figures, without inscriptions, which were found under stelæ of Old Empire date at Copán and at a site near Guatemala City. There is an interesting contrast here between the archaic Tuxtla Statuette, which bears the earliest Maya date of which we know, and the archaic figures from Copán and Guatemala City, none of which is dated. It has long been a question in my mind whether the inscription on the Tuxtla Statuette was not engraved long after the figure itself was wrought. But that is beside the point for the present; for, in any case, it is quite clear that the Mayas passed through their archaic phase before their hieroglyphic and calendrical systems were perfected, certain pronounced archaic characteristics persisting into the period when hieroglyphs had become common. This last fact comes out very strongly in the chirography—if that term be permissible—of the Leyden Plate (60 A. D.) and of various early inscriptions at Uaxactun and Tikal, mentioned by Dr. Morley[13] as displaying the influence of archaic technique. It follows from all this that the migrants from Central

America who, accidentally and unsystematically, filtered, generation after generation, along the Isthmus and onwards into South America, bearing with them culture of the archaic sort, must have set out upon their prolonged Odyssey before even the beginnings of writing were made in Central America. Spurious claims to the contrary notwithstanding, science has never discovered in South America a single trace of writing among the native populations. Had even a start been made towards the development of the Maya hieroglyphic system at the time that the members of the Maya stock who began the long flitting through the unknown solitudes beyond the homeland, it would have been inevitable that they should carry with them the germs of the science of writing. But they did not, and we may say, therefore, that the archaic phase of culture was borne into South America prior to 613 B. C.—how much prior, who can tell? It was borne thither, moreover, not by direct descendants of the historic, calendar-using Mayas, but by near kinsmen of theirs who, for motives at which we can only guess, pushed southwards from and far beyond the territory wherein the Old Empire was later to come into being.

B. Having penetrated South America, having distributed themselves along the seacoasts, and having invaded the vast hinterland of the southern continent, the archaic peoples proceeded little by little to find permanent habitats, as indicated on page 32, wherein they took root and grew, each group according to its response to and employment of the environment. Regarding these statements, it will be observed that the migrants were all on the archaic plane of culture, rather than on the primitive, hunter-and-fisher plane. So far as I can see, there were never people in South America whose culture was so low that it could not be considered at least a low archaic culture. Furthermore, it seems to me probable that hunger was the chief motive for the infiltration into South America, and it is not likely that that impelling force could have been operative in pre-archaic times in Central America, for there was a plentiful area suitable for the nascent agriculture of a sparse population. It is well, nevertheless, to admit that there *may* have been a still earlier infiltration of primitive folk in a pre-archaic stage of development, whose traces may lie buried in the shell-mounds along the shores of Brazil. Even so, it is safe to say that the earliest discernible forms of culture in South America in general and in the Andean area in particular were archaic rather than primitive.

It is now necessary briefly to mention a series of theories as to the origins of culture in America which have been presented during the past three hundred years to the attention of the public. It has been claimed, on a basis of superficial resemblances between monuments and artifacts of America and those of various parts of the Eastern Hemisphere, that the civilizations of the so-called New World took their rise from here and there in Asia, Africa, Europe or Oceania. Nearly all claims of this kind fail to make the very important distinction between man-as-an-animal and man-as-a-bearer-of-culture. The conformation of the land-masses of the world is such that it is most unlikely that any considerable numbers of mankind should have reached America save by way of the route from Siberia to Alaska. True, sporadic groups of current-borne and wind-blown mariners might have arrived on one part or another of the American coast, bearing with them a mariners' version of this or that Old World culture; but such groups, if indeed they did so arrive, could not have given rise to the American race, nor could they even have moulded to any considerable extent the evolution of cultures already existent in America. It is the French school of anthropological thought who have most energetically propagated the concept that America was populated from Oceania—from Polynesia and Melanesia for choice—their chief arguments being of the lin: guistic variety. This line of reasoning loses its cogency, however, when one reflects that the Oceanic peoples, no less than the American, were offshoots from the antique population of Asia and that, consequently, it is wholly to be expected that their languages should now and then resemble one another.

In view of all these considerations, it may be asserted that the archaic phase of culture was not only very widely distributed in America but also that it was present in every part of the world wherein the people have progressed beyond the hunter-and-fisher stage of development. From this it follows that when, in due course, growth took place beyond the archaic phase, the arts and industries of America were bound to resemble those of other countries where similar advancement was going on. Such similarities are not, however, evidences of direct contact between distant civilizations; on the contrary they merely prove that, given the same or nearly the same starting-points, and given similar environments, human minds will tend to develop in a more or less uniform manner. After all, pots cannot have more than a certain number of shapes, be it in Peru or in Egypt; doorways cannot take more than a certain number of forms, be it in Mexico or in China; headdresses cannot display more than a certain number of variations, be it in Yucatan or in Africa. The bournes within which the human mind and the human hand can function are in truth rather limited everywhere, and the intellects of men in this or that plane of development the world over are therefore bound to create objects for the use and delight of their makers which vary only between certain not very distant extremes.[14]

Certain aspects of the archaic culture in the Andean area remain to be discussed. If we look upon the question from the geographical angle, we find that there were three main routes by which wandering families and clans could—and no doubt did—enter that part of South America which specially concerns us.

The first of these possible routes is the shoreline of the Pacific Ocean, from Central America to Panama and thence onwards indefinitely along the western shore of South America. This route is of importance in two respects: First, it is probable that those groups which followed it commenced their journey on the Pacific side of Central America, that is, in a region where no traces of Old Empire civilization have been found, but in which certain languages were spoken that had distinct affinity with the Maya tongue, a combination of facts which seems to indicate that, like the Huasteca, the migrants were archaic, pre-calendar-and-hieroglyph-using Mayas, *i. e.*, near kinsmen, as I have said above on page 40, of the historical Mayas; second, the marshy and jungly character of much of the country along this route made it inevitable that a goodly proportion of the wandering be done by sea, rude rafts and crude canoes being used to get about in. Why people whom force of circumstances obliged to become partly aquatic in habit never developed—so far, at any rate, as we now know—anything equal to the admirable boats used by the ancestors of the Maoris and by most of the other folk of Oceania is one of South America's multitude of unanswered questions. As will be pointed out in Chapter VIII, there is no trace of a well-advanced sea-faring technique in South America, and this fact does much to refute the claim that the peoples of Oceania, proficient navigators as they were, gave rise to the population of the Andean area.

The second possible route is that marked out by the northwardly flowing Cauca and Magdalena Rivers. By passing upwards and southwards along their valleys, with long pauses in which the archaic culture was fostered and even, to some extent, made to advance, a migrant folk would eventually find itself in the highlands of Colombia, whence it would be a relatively simple matter to penetrate still farther southwards along the inter-Andean plateaux of Ecuador, Peru, and Bolivia, the process necessitating, of course, many hundreds of years.

The third, which concerns us rather less than do the others, is also a shoreline, that of the Atlantic Ocean, from Central America to Panama and thence along the northern edge of South America and onwards to the coasts of the Guianas and of Brazil. Along this route mighty rivers are frequent, each one hinting at vast hinterlands and powerfully suggesting exploration inlandwards.

By these routes—and more especially by the two mentioned first—the archaic culture was brought into the Andean area.

Like the archaic culture so widespread elsewhere in America, that of the great territory which concerns us was characterized by the rudimentary arts and sciences and industries of peoples in the process of becoming sedentary. To Dr. Spinden we owe an illuminating demonstration that the early forms of agriculture and of animal-taming, of ceramics, of weaving, and of architecture in wood, adobe, and stone are closely bound together to constitute that cultural complex which is here styled archaic.[15] As to the intangible elements in the archaic culture—language and religion foremost among them—we can at present only guess. It seems natural to suppose that they, no less than the tangible elements, were in a nascent stage, but one almost ripe for local developments in this direction or in that which would in time engender the varieties of speech and of religion that we find flourishing subsequently.

Modern investigations, both in the form of archæological field-work and in the form of researches in libraries among the early Spanish accounts of what the native peoples, at the time of the Conquest, had to say about their own history, are daily making it clearer that the archaic culture was a direct ancestor of the higher civilizations which later flourished on the coast of the Andean area and in the highlands. Two points must here be insisted upon, however, the first of which is that the archaic migrants moved much more slowly than did their forefathers of the primitive culture, the second of which is that the passage from the archaic to the post-archaic stage of culture was far from constant either in time or in degree.

These two points demand enlargement. In the first place, it will be clear enough that a given number of people in the hunter-and-fisher stage of culture require a larger territory to support them than does an equal number of people in the archaic stage. As a result of this, they more quickly outgrow a given habitat than does an equal number of archaic folk. This contrast arises from the relatively wide dispersion of the food-supply upon which a primitive people depends and upon the time-wasting and inefficient modes of obtaining food which they of necessity employ, while, on the other hand, an agricultural people can readily and with comparative speed obtain all that they need from a small district wherein husbandry can be carried on. In other words, a hunter-and-fisher group will, by natural increase of numbers, reach the saturation-point of its habitat much more quickly than an agricultural group of equal size will do. Consequently, we may safely picture to ourselves the migratory movements of primitive folk as a fairly steady onward push, and those of archaic folk as an intermittent process, each group sending away its surplus population into new districts as soon as its previous habitat becomes over-populated. Many generations may, there-fore, pass by without the resources of a district being over-strained by an archaic society, and, when it does become nec-essary to send out off-shoots of the parent group, the process is often carried out in a colonizing manner, bonds of sympathy and common interest being maintained between the parent group and its colonies. In the second place, because of diverse local environmental conditions and of varying degrees of re-sponse thereto, one group would stand still, or almost still, while another, perhaps a close neighbor, would march ahead in general culture.

Turning at last to the subject of chronology in western South America, we find, on the basis of what has been said, that, between about 1000 B. C. and the beginning of the Christian Era, people of the archaic culture were filtering into the Andean area by routes already outlined. With the archaic culture, thus introduced into the area, as a foundation prog-ress in many directions was subsequently made by the folk of various parts of the Andean area, thereby giving rise to a series of phases and periods of civilization which, taken to-gether, constitute pre-Spanish Andean history.

It is my present task to offer to the reader an approximate and avowedly tentative chronology of the phases and periods mentioned. The materials for compiling such a chronology are of two chief kinds: The results obtained by field archæolo-gists during the past two hundred years and, more especially, since about 1870; the accounts of ancient matters given to the earlier Spanish invaders by the native peoples of America and, more especially, of the Andean area. As this book proceeds, the reader will find, if he chooses to consult the notes at the ends of the chapters, that various modern writers on archæological and kindred subjects are frequently cited. It is through their field work and through their reports on it that we gain our knowledge of the arts and industries of pre-Spanish times; it is because of their labors that we modern folk in many countries of America and Europe possess numerous richly informative collections of ancient Andean artistic and practical objects which mutely tell us much of what we know concerning their makers' modes of life. Different in quality and yet nicely complementary to the data provided by archæology are the materials for knowledge provided by the historical and descriptive narratives left to us by the early Spanish writers. Taking them as a whole those writers—whom in an earlier writing[16] I have styled collectively "the Chroniclers"— were a remarkable company of men. Among their number were churchmen, lawyers, soldiers, administrators, and three men whose blood was a mixture of the best that the ancient race of America could offer with Spanish. For the most part they were singularly free from that harshness and that intolerance which popular prejudice commonly ascribes to the Spaniards in America. On the contrary, most of the Chroniclers were men of high intelligence and of broad sympathies who frankly admired much that they found in the character of the native folk and in their institutions. It is as a result of their intellectual relations with the upper-class people of Peru during the period between 1530 and 1700, and more especially during the first half of that period, that we possess as much as we do of the pre-Spanish history of the Andean peoples according to their own understanding of it.

More detailed notice of the writers, ancient and modern, who have contributed to our knowledge of the Andean past will be given in the Bibliography at the end of this book. It is enough to say that both archæology and a study of the native Andean folk-history have contributed the data upon which the following Tables of Chronology are based.

TABLE I
CENTRAL AMERICAN AND ANDEAN CULTURAL HISTORY COMPARED

(On a basis of native data recovered by modern research)

B. C.		100	0	100	200	300	400	500	600	700	800	900	1000	1100	1200	1300	1400 1500 A. D.
Central America	Archaic and Introductory	"Old Empire" of the Mayas and period of northwardly expansion into Yucatan								First period of decline			"New Empire"		Toltec period		Second decline
Andean Area	Archaic and Migratory	In the highlands, Advanced Archaic or Tiahuanaco I period								Tiahuanaco II "empire" both on highland and coast		Decline		Early Incas			Inca empire
		Early Chimu and Nazca cultures arising from archaic on the coast										Decline		Late Chimu and Nazca on coast			

It will be remarked that there is a fairly close parallel between the rise and fall of culture-levels in the two regions of America here referred to. The earliest high culture of the Andean area was that of Early Chimu and Early Nazca, roughly coeval with the "Old Empire" of the Mayas. The first period of decline in the Maya area, however, began earlier and lasted longer than did the period of decline in the Andean area. But in both regions culture recrudesced and remained high until 1400 or so, after which, in Yucatan, it suddenly declined again. In Peru, on the other hand, the great empire of the Incas flourished between 1400 and 1530, but it is extremely probable that, at the time of the Spaniards' arrival, the Inca empire was on the verge of disruption such as that which had come upon Yucatan a century earlier. It may be said, therefore, that both regions show the same general historical trend, but that the historical rhythm of the Andean area tends markedly to lag behind that of the Maya area. I venture to call this fact to the attention of Dr. Ellsworth Huntington in the hope that he will give some study to its elucidation.

TABLE II

CULTURAL PERIODS IN THE ANDEAN AREA AS SHOWN
BY MODERN RESEARCH INTO FOLK-MEMORY
AND BY ARCHÆOLOGY

COAST CULTURES	APPROX. DATES	MOUNTAIN CULTURES
Archaic cultured folk gradually arrive in small groups from the north in possession of rudiments of various arts and industries. Gradually Early Chimu culture in the northern part of the coast and Early Nazca in southern part emerge from the archaic stage and attain to brilliant individuality. Intensive agriculture, architecture in adobe, fine ceramics, and superb textile art all characteristic of this period.	? B. C. to A. D. 500	Archaic cultured people arrive from north through inter-Andean plateaux and Amazonia. They gradually build up the advanced archaic culture known as Tiahuanaco I, notable for its sculpture and its architecture.
Contact and conflict with the mountain folk.	500–600	Contact and conflict with the coast-country folk.
Conventionalization in art and other characteristics derived from Tiahuanaco II civilization predominate on the coast throughout its length.	600 to 900	Inaugurated by influences from the coast, the Tiahuanaco II culture, with distinctive characteristics, flourishes far and wide through the highlands.
A period of comparative poverty in cultural matters due to break-down of Tiahuanaco II influences. Earliest phase of Late Chimu and Late Nazca.	900 to 1100	Tiahuanaco II civilization disrupted, a period of neo-archaic conditions follows, with many small, hostile societies.
A recrudescence of the old, distinctive civilization of the coast gives rise to a continuance of the Late Chimu and Late Nazca civilizations which flourish greatly.	1100 to 1400	One tribe, that of the Incas, begins a spectacular climb to imperial power, gradually imposing its sway over all rival societies and laying the foundations of a true empire.

The Incas conquer the coast and establish their imperial power and much of their culture there, receiving, however, much local color from Late Chimu and Late Nazca culture.

1400 to 1530

The Inca empire reaches its greatest power and its greatest glory. A vast imperial society ably governed and well maintained. But, towards the very end of the period, signs of imminent disruption appear.

N. B.—It is my wish and intention that this chronological scheme be considered to supersede and replace all previous schemes of the kind drawn up by me, except the longer version of this same scheme prepared for the Metropolitan Museum of Art, in March, 1930.

NOTES TO CHAPTER II

1 Hrdlička, 1907; 1911; 1912; 1912b; 1912c; 1912d; 1914; 1916; 1916c; 1917; 1917b.

2 The belief that human remains of some 40,000 years ago had been found in a gravel-deposit near Cuzco was set forth in: Bingham, 1912b; Bowman, 1912b and 1912c. The incorrectness of the belief was set forth in: Eaton, 1912; 1913; and 1914; Gregory, 1914 and 1916; and Hrdlička, 1912. In Bingham, 1922, pp. 149–156, there is a handsome acknowledgement of the incorrectness of the first belief.

3 Osborn, 1915, pp. 76–84, 95–115, and 511. MacCurdy, 1924, I, pp. 313–319. Means, 1918e, Ch. iii.

4 Cummings, 1923 and 1923b.

5 Holmes, 1907 and 1916. Morley, 1920, pp. 402–415. Spinden, 1924, pp. 95–98 and 157–159.

6 Totten, 1926.

7 Spinden, 1913.

8 Spinden, 1913, p. 198.

9 Morley, 1920, pp. 447–452. Huntington, 1914; 1914b; 1915; and 1917. Penck, 1914. Arctowski, 1910–1913. Brooks, 1916.

10 Cook, 1909, pp. 11–13. Morley, 1920, pp. 452–456.

11 In addition to the works already cited, the reader will do well to consult the following for the history of the Mayas: Brasseur de Bourbourg, 1857–1859. Brinton, 1882; and 1885. Carrillo y Ancona, 1883. Genet, 1927. Genet and Chelbatz, 1927. López de Cogolludo, 1688. Means, 1917b, Ch. i. Nuttall, 1886; 1901; and 1906.

12 Lothrop, 1926. Means, 1918k.

13 Morley, 1920, pp. 76–77.

14 For a very able treatment of the general principles touched upon in this chapter, see: Dixon, 1928, Chs. ii, iii, and iv.

15 Spinden, 1917; 1917c.

16 Means, 1928.

CHAPTER III

THE HISTORY OF THE ANDEAN AREA UNTIL ABOUT 600 A. D.

1. Native Versions of Historical Events as Reported by the Chroniclers of Peru

THE sixty-odd westward sloping valleys along the Andean coast between southern Colombia and central Chile received their archaic-cultured first settlers during the period already indicated, some immigrants arriving by way of the inter-Cordilleran plateaux and the westward flowing streams on whose sources they chanced to come, others arriving by sea at the mouths of the rivers and later exploring upwards and inlandwards. In either case a determining factor of their movements was the enticing and suggestive influence of flowing water.

Folk-memory of the early shifts of population persisted for many centuries and traces of it drew the attention of Father Miguel Cabello de Balboa, a learned and intelligent Jesuit who, between 1576 and 1586, heedfully studied the Indians' reports concerning their own past. He carefully preserved in writing all that his informants could tell him, both of this early time and of later periods, and from his memorial upon it we gather that, over a long stretch of years, little knots of people were drifting down into the coast-country from the highlands and were establishing themselves in the warm and fertile valleys all along the littoral.

If only we could know the whole truth, we would most likely find that each of the valleys had a dynastic history in which was—or rather would be—summed up the cultural development of its people. As matters now stand, however, only certain valleys in the northern part of the coast of Peru are dynastically recorded in any known writings. One such record, preserved by Father Cabello, tells us of the manner in which one of the valley dynasties established its power, and of what befell it. The story, as told by the good Jesuit, runs thus:

The people of Lambayeque say—and with them agree all the folk living in the vicinity of this valley—that in times so very ancient that they do not know how to express them, there came from the northerly part of this Piru, with a great fleet of Balsas, a father of Families, a man of much valor and quality named Naymlap; and with him he brought many concubines, but the chief wife is said to have been named Ceterni. He brought in his company many people who followed him as their Captain and leader. But those among them who were of the greatest bravery were their officials, who were forty in number, including such men as Pita Zofi, who was the trumpeter or player upon certain great shells that are much esteemed among the Indians. Another was Ninacola, who was in charge of the litter and Throne; another was Ninagintue, in whose care was the drink of that Lord, after the fashion of a Butler; another was called Fonga Sigde, whose duty it was to scatter the dust of sea-shells upon the ground where his Lord was to Tread; another, Occhocalo, was his cook; another had charge of the ointments and color with which the Lord was wont to adorn his countenance, this official being Xam Muchec. Ollopcopoc supervised the bathing of the Lord. Another very important official, much esteemed by his Prince, was called Llapchillulli, and he wrought shirts and clothing of feathers. With this retinue, and with an infinite number of other officials and men of importance, he [Naymlap] brought his person and house, already adorned and established.

With all his possessions this Lord, Naymlap, made port and landed at the mouth of a River which is today called Faquisllanga, and having there abandoned their *balsas*, they went inland, desirous of making a settlement, and having advanced half a league, they built certain Palaces after their fashion to which they gave the name of Chot. And in this house and palace they invoked with barbarous devotion an Idol which they had brought with them made in the likeness of their chief himself and wrought from a green stone. They called it Yampallec, which is to say, "image and statue of Naymlap."

This people having lived for many years in peace and quiet, their Lord and Chief, having had many children, [knew that] the time of his death had arrived. In order that his vassals should not learn that death had jurisdiction over him, his [immediate] attendants buried him secretly and in the same room where he had lived, and they published it throughout the land that he, of his own virtue, had taken wings and had flown away. So great was the grief caused by his absence among those who had followed him at the time of his coming, that, although they now had a great number of descendants and were much attached to their new and fertile land, they abandoned everything and, dispersing without clue or guide, set forth to search for him in every direction. Therefore, there did not remain in the land more people than those who had been born there, which was no small number, for all the rest scattered themselves without rule or order in search of him who, so they believed, had disappeared.

The Empire and power of the dead Naymlap was left to his oldest son, Cium, who married a maiden named Zolzdoñi. By her and by other concubines he had twelve sons, each of whom was father of a large family; and having lived and ruled many years, this Cium placed himself in a subterranean vault and there he allowed himself die, all to the end that posterity might regard him as immortal and divine. After the end and death of this man Escuñain governed; and from him Mascuy inherited the kingdom; and to him succeeded Cuntipallec; and after him governed Allascunti; and to him succeeded Nofan Nech; and to him succeeded Mulumuslan; and after him the power was held by Llamecoll; to whom succeeded Lanipatcum; and after him Acunta ruled.

His successor in the Lordship was Fempellec who was the last and most unfortunate member of this dynasty, for he took it into his mind to move to another place the Idol which we have said had been placed by Naymlap in the palace called Chot. And he made several attempts to carry out his purpose, but without success. At this juncture the Devil appeared to him in the form of a beautiful woman, and so great was the deceitfulness of the Devil and so small was the continence of Fempellec that he slept with her, so they relate, and no sooner had a union so nefarious been consummated than rain began to fall, a thing which had never before been seen upon these plains, and this flood lasted for thirty days; after which followed a year of much sterility and famine. For, inasmuch as it was notorious among the Priests of their Idols and other important men that their Lord had committed this grave crime, they understood that it was the punishment for his fault that his People was suffering, with hunger, rain, and want. And in order to take vengeance upon him, forgetful of the fidelity which is owed by vassals, they took him prisoner and, tying his feet and hands, threw him into the deep sea. With his death was ended the lineage of the native Lords of the Valley of Lambayeque, thus called because of that Idol which Naymlap had brought with him and which was called Yampallec.

During the life of Cium, son and heir of Naymlap and second Lord of these Valleys, his sons set forth, as has been said, to be the beginnings of other families and peoples, and they took with them many followers. One of them, who was called Nor, went to the Valley of Cinto; and Cala went to Tucume; and another to Collique; and others went to other parts. A certain Llapchillulli, a very important man, of whom, as we have said, the Lord Naymlap had made much on account of his valor and because of his skill in making apparel of feather-work, set forth with a great following of those who wished to go with him, and, finding a place to his liking in the valley called Jayanca, settled there. In that locality his progeny and descendants have remained.

We have already seen how, by the merited death which his followers gave to Fempellec, the Lordship of Lambayeque and the country surrounding it remained without patron or native Lord. In that condition remained that populous republic during many days, until a certain powerful Tyrant called Chimo Capac came with an invincible army and possessed himself of these valleys, placing garrisons in them. And in that of Lambayeque he placed a Lord and Chief of his own choice who was called Pongmassa, a native of Chimo. He died a peace-loving Lord, and left as his successor his son named Pallesmassa. To him succeeded his son, Oxa, and it was in his time that the Yngas were passing in their power through the Provinces of Caxamarca, and thus it was that this Oxa was the first one of his lineage to have news of the Ynga Lords; and from this time forward the coast people began to live in constant dread of being despoiled of their Lordships by the arms of the people from Cuzco.

This Oxa was followed in the Chieftainship by a son of his named Llempisan; and when he was dead the Lordship went to Chullumpisan; and to him succeeded a brother of his named Cipromarca; and after him a younger brother was Lord whose name was Fallenpisan. After him the command was held by Efquempisan; and on his death he was succeeded by Pecfunpisan, in whose time our Spaniards entered into this Piru.[1]

The story of the Naymlap dynasty as related above is clearly not the story of an archaic people. The court of King Naymlap and Queen Ceterni was highly organized, and there is much in the tale to indicate that theirs was an advanced culture, even at the very moment of their arrival in the country. Whence they came, and for what reasons, we cannot tell. Cabello's phrasing in this connection is ambiguous, for he says that Naymlap *"vino de la parte suprema de este Piru"* which I have translated above as coming from the north; but, to be frank, it might equally well mean coming from the highlands were it not that there is specific mention of *balsas* or rafts. This is one of those maddening tangles that students of ancient Peru are forever encountering.

We may suppose, then, that the migration of Naymlap was in the nature of a civilized colonizing enterprise and that the subsequent off-shoots from it were so, likewise. The territory involved in this story is roughly conterminous with the modern Department of Lambayeque and it is a region of singular fertility, equable climate and every natural advantage, as some of the first Spaniards in Peru clearly state in their narratives.[2] It is not certain just what river is indicated by the name Faquisllanga in the legend, but it is probable that it designates the Lambayeque River, another name for which is, I seem to remember, Facalá.[3]

The very interesting chronological aspect of Father Cabello's narrative of dynastic history in Lambayeque now demands attention. It is true that he ventures upon no dates himself, but he does provide us with certain rather meagre data for so doing. To begin with he tells us that the dynasty of Naymlap consisted of twelve rulers the length of whose reigns is not specified, but we may safely assume that it averaged twenty-five years just as it does in other dynasties. Then followed an interregnum of indeterminate length which may well represent the period when the mountain folk, whose centre was at Tiahuanaco, were dominant on the coast, as will be told in Chapter IV. Following the interregnum came a period when the Chimu king was overlord of Lambayeque. Finally, the Inca period, lasting four generations, was ended by the Spanish conquest. This material may be tabulated thus:

Naymlap dynasty.

1. Naymlap and Ceterni
2. Cium and Zolzdoñi
3. Escuñain
4. Mascuy
5. Cuntipallec
6. Allascunti
7. Nofan Nech
8. Mulumuslan
9. Llamecoll
10. Lanipatcum
11. Acunta
12. Fempellec

$= 12 \text{ reigns} \times 25 \text{ years} = 300 \text{ years}$

Interregnum of indeterminate length which may represent the Tiahuanaco period on the coast followed by a period of confusion after the downfall of Tiahuanaco.

Dynasty founded by the Chimu.

1. Pongmassa
2. Pallesmassa
3. Oxa
   Inca overlordship begins.................about 1430
4. Llempisan
5. Chullumpisan
6. Cipromarca } (brothers)
7. Fallenpisan
8. Efquempisan
9. Pecfunpisan

Spanish Conquest..1530

The chief lack in the story of Lambayeque as related by Father Cabello de Balboa is that we are given no light upon the subject of how long the interregnum lasted. It is clear, indeed, that this dynastic history is only partly preserved. Therefore, in the absence of evidence to the contrary, and in the presence of archæological proof—to be adduced later in this chapter—that the civilization of the Naymlap dynasty was of the same general type as that which is known as Early Chimu, we may reasonably assume that the Naymlap dynasty flourished some time during the first six centuries or so of our Era or, in other words, during the Early Chimu period.

Of equal importance in the present connection is the material gathered from native informants by the Augustinian historian, Father Antonio de la Calancha, who presents it to us in chapters I and II of book III of his *Coronica Moralizada* (1638). Owing to the fact that the good monk's literary style was prolix and obscure to an amazing degree, I present his material here in abstract rather than in direct quotation.

Book III, chapter I, is entitled "Concerning the celebrated and miraculous Sanctuary of the Most Holy Virgin of Guadalupe in the Valley of Pacasmayo." There are described the topography, situation and particulars of its location, and the names of its first lords, from whom the name of their valleys originated. The gist of the chapter is as follows:

God created, between the slopes of the cold mountains and the shores of an ever-angry sea, a valley which is always delicious to its inhabitants because of the contrast which it affords to the arid wastes around it. The early lords of this valley and of others near it were called Chimo, a term of the same sort as Pharaoh in Egypt. The Chimo had his palace and seat in what is now the city of Trujillo, so named by the Conqueror, Pizarro, in honor of his birthplace, albeit the Indians still call the locality "valleys of the Chimo."[4] The wife of the first Chimo was named Chacma, a name which is found preserved, although somewhat altered, in that of the adjacent Valley of Chicama.

The Valley of Pacasmayo, which the Spaniards called Guadalupe, lay farther north than the original domain of Chimo and Chacma.[5] The Chimo determined to conquer it. Accordingly, he sent a very brave captain of his, chosen for his skill from among his most warlike men, into that valley. After much difficult fighting the victory rested with the captain, and twelve leagues of territory were thereby added to the realm of his master, the Chimo. The name of the Captain was Pacatnamu which, in the language of those people, means Common Father or Father of All. After his victory, the Chimo made him governor of the territory which he had conquered and, because he dealt gently with the conquered without injuring the conquerors, the valley was named Pacatnamu in his honor, being to-day called corruptly Pacasmayo. The hill upon which the captain built his house, the remains of which are still to be seen, is called Pacatnamu to this day, for even those uncultured people know how to preserve the names of those rulers who favor their subjects and protect strangers.

This valley is six leagues wide from the village of Lloco (which to-day is called San Pedro) to the sandy wastes of Saña, and in length it is twelve leagues from the sea up to Chungala, a point which is a league higher up than the village of San Gregorio, the first rung in the ascent up into the mountains, that is, the inland edge of the coastal plains of the Yunca Indians.[6]

Beside the seldom pacific sea there are beaches where some Indian fisher-folk dwell who live upon sea-creatures. Behind the beaches are vast wastes of shifting sand with which the winds sport continually. The Chimos, and afterward the Ingas, used to post watchmen in the deserts in order to guide passers-by and to afford aid to those who had lost their way. In this we see an instance of moral virtue flourishing in gentile hearts, nor would modern travellers suffer there so greatly were the zeal in the hearts of modern rulers as great as that in those of long ago. These sandy expanses are entirely unproductive, except very near to the rivers which flow to the sea. The valley is crossed by a mighty river, which is a dwarf when it is born in the mountains but a giant when it dies in the ocean. It has no other name than Nec, which is the term generally applied to rivers by those Indians. Its two principal parent streams, not to mention minor tributaries, come, the one from the district of la Asunción and the Valley of Condebamba, the other from above the village of San Miguel on the road from Cajamarca.[7] This river (whose waters are clear, clean, and wholesome) is a breeding-place for many kinds of fish, noble and plebeian, great and small.[8]

Near this river, and close beside the sea, rise some mountains three leagues long, quite treeless and, indeed, entirely sterile, even in the season of rains and mists when other mountains of the region produce grass and bring forth flowers. The

mountain nearest to the river is that called Pacatnamu, and
to-day it displays a large number of buildings and ruins, some
of which were the palace of the Chimo's Governor and his
household, others of which were *huacas,* wherein, as though in
temples, they adored their Idols and observed the rites of
their cult.[9]

Among the pebbly and sandy stretches of these hills, and
near to the first settlement of Guadalupe, there are some small
salt-pits which supply the people with a sufficiency of good,
edible salt. A league farther along this hill, in the direction
of the highlands, Providence created upon the summit of the
ridge a hollow in the rock, shaped like a massive canoe, and
filled with water which produces herbs along the margin of
the pool, making it very sightly. This spot is all the more
conspicuous because, for leagues round about, the whole country is of living rock, or, more strictly speaking, of dry stones
altogether dead. It was a kindly act of Nature to create,
among these stony and arid wastes, a bark of water, useful
both for the alleviation of the thirsty wanderer who has lost
his road and for the birds of the region.

Below, amid these dry hills, God placed a valley where the
trees reach the sky and greenness covers the earth. There
every sort of crop may be grown, both of the kinds native to
the country and of the kinds which have been brought into it
from Castile. . . .

The breezes and the temperature are not very cold in
winter, although in summer they are somewhat hot. They
are never so warm as the summer weather in Spain, but more
so than the sultriest weather in Lima, and every wind that
blows is fresh. All shade is pleasant, and there are fewer mists
in winter than on other parts of the coast. The sky has at
times beautiful red clouds. Rains are not at all necessary to
the husbandman because irrigation is possible at all times of
the year, and so the people grow their crops whenever they
wish.

The chapter is brought to a conclusion by the good friar with
an impressive medley of monkish learning, in the course of

which he locates the Valley of Pacasmayo with surprising accuracy, and then avers, again with surprising accuracy, that the antipodal point thereto is Comari, in the state of Goa, southern India.

Book III, chapter II, is entitled "The first Lords who conquered those valleys are told of, and also the Inga, who made them tributaries to himself; their Gods, Idols, and ceremonies before the entry into the country of the most holy Virgin of Guadalupe." The gist of the chapter is as follows:

In the most ancient times those valleys were all in disorder in the matter of government. The oldest member of each family was the lord of his group; villages were few in number and their inhabitants were without culture.[10]

A chief of what is now Trujillo, called the Chimo, being of high-spirited temperament and gifted with an ambitious mind, built up a large empire, as the Incas did later, which at last extended from Parmunga[11] up to Payta and Tumbez. As time went on the Chimos grew in majesty and might, and everywhere that their rule penetrated they introduced their language, which is called Quingnam. This tongue became general in the valleys from Pacasmayo down to Lima, and farther to the north a tongue called Muchic was spoken which is still preserved in the district of Motupe. Besides these two languages there were others, one called Sec, one that was spoken by the people of Olmos, and a third dialect, very guttural and primitive, which our author calls la Pescadora because it was spoken by the fisher-folk (*pescadores*) along the shore.[12]

The Chimo imposed upon all his vassals the duty of paying tribute, and among other things he employed six thousand Indians to bring to him from the highlands gold, silver, copper, and other products. There was, in general, a good deal of commerce, which was carried on with the help of the two principal tongues, Quingnam and Muchic, a good deal of inconvenience being suffered at the same time because of the great number of local dialects.

The Chimos went on, generation after generation, increasing in wealth and power. The last of their line was he whom the highland Indians called Chimo Capac, or the Great Chimo. He raised up a very large army against Topa Inga Yupangui, tenth Inga, greatest of all that dynasty, who conquered the country between Lunaguana and Quito and between Arica and Chile, inclusive. This king also built a road one thousand leagues long which no other human monarch would ever have dared to undertake. The Chimo had enormous wealth in his *guacas* or temples. From the one which is a quarter of a league from Trujillo the Spaniards took gold and silver worth more than eight hundred thousand *pesos,* giving as royal fifth to our King one hundred and four thousand ducats. And from another *guaca,* called Tasca, which is smaller and is on the road to Guanchaco, Escobar Corchuelo and a friend of his took more than six hundred thousand *pesos'* worth.[13]

It cost the Inca Topa Yupangui a great many troops to conquer the coastal plains, for the dwellers by the shore were stronger and more used to hard labor than were the highlanders. But at last, by sheer force of numbers, the Inca vanquished the Chimo, and afterwards he carried him off to Cuzco where he treated him as an equal and loaded him with honors, sending him back at last to his own land in order to rule there as a prince who was a vassal to the Inca. The Chimo always honorably observed the terms imposed upon him. . . .[14]

The Indians of Pacasmayo worshipped the Moon as their greatest deity. They did so because she predominates over the elements, causes crops to grow, brings about disturbances of the sea, and makes thunder and lightning. Her temple was in a *guaca* called Sian, which, in the Iunga language,[15] means House of the Moon. They held her to be more powerful than the Sun because he did not appear by night, whereas she allowed herself to be seen both by night and by day. Another reason for their opinion was the fact that the Moon often eclipsed the Sun but that he never did eclipse her. They were wont to celebrate the eclipses of the Sun with great rejoicings in honor of the Moon's victory over him, but the eclipses of the Moon (by the earth's shadow) were marked by mourning and dances expressive of sadness that lasted as long as did the shadow upon the Moon.

The Indians of the coastal plains believed that when the Moon did not appear she was in the other world castigating thieves who had died. Thievery is the vice which is most abhorred by those people. Children of five years old were sacrificed to the Moon upon piles of colored cotton, together with much *chicha* (maize beer) and many fruits of the earth.

The Indians of Pacasmayo also worshipped the sea, which they called Ni, offering to it white maize-meal, red ochre and other trifling things in order to induce it to refrain from drowning them and to give them many fish. The only marine creature adored by these people was the whale; for its size seemed to them to be expressive of sanctity. They did not adore any fish, looking upon fish merely as food.

The Indians of Pacasmayo and the Yungas in general adored a certain stone which to-day they call Alecpong, or God in Stone. These stones were, apparently, numerous, and they were so much venerated that the people never went within sight of them without making very submissive gestures and paying tribute with a small stone or a stick, of which there are great mounds near those deities. They were regarded as the progenitors of the people among whom they stood, for it was thought that the stones were sons of the Sun who, in a rage because of the death of the woman by whom he had had them, had turned them into stone, commanding later on when his anger was past, that the descendants of each stone adore it.[16]

They also adored and deified three stars which they called Patá, which are those that the Spaniards call *las tres Marías*. The Indians held that the three stars were a thief and his captors to whom he was bound, for that is the meaning of the word Patá. They, the Indians, believed that the Moon, wishing to punish the thief, had sent the two stars to take him prisoner and to lead him away to be devoured by vultures. These last are represented by the four stars just below the group of three. A further custom of these Indians was this:

in times of famine they were wont to fast themselves and to make even their domestic animals do likewise, and also they abstained from intercourse with their wives.

The Indians of the coast believed that humankind descended from four stars, two of which gave rise to the Kings, Chiefs, and Nobles, and the other two to the poor and lowly working classes. The Archbishop of Lima, Don Bartolomé Lobo Guerrero, tried in vain to eradicate this belief.

The Indians of Pacasmayo and the Yungas in general did not calculate the year by Moons, nor yet by the course of the Sun, but by certain stars which the Spaniards call *las Cabrillas*[17] and which they call Fur. These stars were held to be productive of all manner of good for the people, and so, out of gratitude, they honored them in this way.

The mode of marriage among these people was as follows: A new pot filled with maize-flour and the tallow of young llamas was placed before the man and woman who were marrying. It was set on fire and the celebrants kept poking and stirring it until it was entirely consumed. Then the sponsor of the marriage said to them, "Now you are married, but bear it in mind that you must always be equally industrious and equally ardent in love, for you must always be equals in the state into which you are entering."

Against thieves they proceeded very rigorously. The guilty man, even though the thing stolen were of small value, was hanged alive until half dead. When the thief's identity was not known, they set up a pole in the centre of the highway, and from it they suspended ears of maize and green branches. This meant that thieves were about, and it inspired everyone in the neighborhood, whether his own possessions had been taken or not, to help in the search for the perpetrator of the crime. Sacrifices were made to the Moon and to Patá in order that their aid might be gained in the hunt for the guilty. He who sheltered a thief was held to be as much a criminal as the robber, and was punished accordingly. Because of the strictness of the law against thievery, the people never felt the need of doors and locks.

Burials took place five days after death, the interval being spent in wailing and mourning. The body was washed and the knees were brought up under the chin. Adulterers were thrown down alive from cliffs. . . .

The Indians of Pacasmayo had doctors called Oquetlupuc, comparable to those in the highlands called Anpicamayos.[18] They were very skilful in making cures with herbs and simples. Although they were held in great respect and were well rewarded for their efforts, they were killed by flogging if their patients died under treatment. A medical-man whose patient died was tied to the dead body, which was duly buried, while the body of the doctor lay above ground until the birds of prey devoured it. People who were guilty of sacrilege or of lack of respect to the King or to a Chief were buried alive among the bones of other such people and among the remains of unclean animals. The crime of sodomy was sternly punished by burning the guilty and destroying their goods. Finally, it is said by Father Calancha that Demons were present at the dances and feasts of the people of Pacasmayo and of other parts of the coast and that they made replies to questions addressed to them through the mediation of the idols and *guacas*.

Such is the gist of Calancha's narrative of early times in the northern part of coastal Peru. It will be observed that his account of the matter is even more vague, from the chronological standpoint, than is that of Father Cabello. Nevertheless, it is clear enough that the time represented by this record is a long stretch of years, for we have unmistakable references to people of archaic culture with whom the Chimus had to fight when it came to conquering the Pacasmayo Valley; and, at the more recent end of the chronological series, we have references to the conquest of the Chimu by the Incas. My own judgment with regard to this narrative is that the culture of the northerly part of the coast varied very little save for trivial details during some fourteen hundred years. True, there was the Tiahuanaco period—of which the present narrative gives no hint whatever—but that did not, as we shall see, really alter the fundamental characteristics of coastal civilization. I conclude, therefore, that the narrative represents the earliest as well as the later periods of high culture on the coast, this opinion being supported not only by archæological evidence—to be presented later in the chapter—but also by Father Calancha's mention of famines, which could not have happened save in the earlier parts of the civilized period before the irrigational system of the coast was brought to its eventual state of perfection.

The narratives of Father Cabello and of Father Calancha, although written quite independently of one another and separated in point of time by more than fifty years, corroborate and supplement one another nicely. The reason is of course that both are based on the collective folk-memory of the coastal peoples. Nor do they stand altogether alone in this respect; for, here and there among the pages of the early Spanish writers, we find stray bits of auxiliary information which is worth mentioning with some particularity in the present connection.

We have, for example, a document written between 1541 and 1544 as a report to the Governor of Peru, Don Cristóbal Vaca de Castro, concerning what a number of *quipu-camayoc-cuna* (keepers of the quipus or knotted-string records) had to say on the subject of Incaic and pre-Incaic history, one in which such officials would be likely to be specially well versed.[19]

The record-keepers told their interlocutors that long before the Incas were ever heard of a great chief called Chimo Capac ruled all the coast from Nazca in the south to beyond Piura in the north, and perhaps as far as Puerto Viejo (in what is now Ecuador). He received rich tribute from his wide realms in the form of emeralds, *chaquira* (gold and silver beads and bangles), and other prized things, but he had little commerce with the highland folk. Within his own possessions he ruled pacifically and well during an infinite number of years. He was the pinnacle of an elaborate feudal structure made up of chiefs great and small, some of the minor rulers being women variously called *tallaponas* or *capullanas*.[20]

This material, likewise, is indecisive from a chronological

point of view. Nevertheless it has value if only because it indicates that the power of the Chimus at one time extended much farther south along the coast than is generally recognized.

Two further narratives have been left to us by sixteenth-century churchmen, Bishop Bartolomé de las Casas—the celebrated "Apostle to the Indies"—and Friar Jerónimo de Román y Zamora. Although neither one of these historians ever went to Peru, their writings are important for the reason that both were in the habit of obtaining the fullest and most reliable information procurable from travellers—both lay and clerical—in the various regions of America. The data thus assembled were woven into consecutive histories replete with valuable facts.[21]

Casas makes it clear that folk-memory in Peru preserved a remembrance of two distinct periods of culture. The earlier lasted some five or six hundred years. At first the whole country was divided into a great number of chieftaincies, some larger than others but none of any great extent. The moral tone of the chiefs was one of genial paternalism, each state having its peculiar institutions and its own economic life. Between the peoples of adjacent communities there was a primitive kind of commerce whereby products of one kind were bartered for those of another. There was, therefore, some slight trade between neighboring states, but none at all between widely separated localities. This idyllic condition of affairs lasted for some time, but later on wars and discords gradually came into being, chiefly provoked by questions relative to land- and water-rights.[22]

The people of the coast, during this early period, used darts or javelins in their wars, whereas the contemporary highlanders used slings as their chief weapons of offense. The lords of the shore-country were wont to build their palaces upon the summits of hills or, if no suitable hill were available, they would cause their people to pile up vast amounts of earth so as to make an artificial eminence.[23]

The chieftaincies did not pass by any rule of primogeniture; rather, the chiefs of the early coastland kingdoms chose their heirs from among their sons or from among their brothers, according as to where among their near kinsmen the most able man was to be found. The chosen successor was always made known to the people beforehand so that they might accept him as their future ruler, and thereafter he was carefully trained to fill worthily the high place to which he was destined. In the Piura-Tumbez region, where the people went by the name of Tallanas, there were chieftainesses who ruled in their own right and were called *capullanas* by the Spaniards.[24]

In short, we have evidence in the writings of the Chroniclers thus far cited to show us the general trend of the history and the general character of the culture of the Early Chimu kingdom and its people. The account of Bishop las Casas, like that of the Quipucamayocs, covers a very long stretch of time, but it surely refers in part to the period under consideration. Friar Jerónimo de Román y Zamora very largely corroborates the account of Bishop las Casas, for he tells us that there were two distinct cultural periods in pre-Hispanic Peru, the earlier of which lasted for many centuries and terminated about six hundred years before his time or, in other words, about the end or middle of the tenth century A. D. This is, therefore, one of the most precise narratives that we have, from the chronological standpoint at any rate. Friar Jerónimo goes on to say that at first there was no general overlord, but that there were many petty rulers each of whom was merely the chief man in his village. They made it their business to punish evil-doers, but in the beginning their power was far from great. Gradually, however, wars became frequent and the custom grew up among the highlanders of building villages in elevated and easily defended positions. The weapons in use among the mountain folk at this early period were slings for offense and shields for defense. The sundry petty kingdoms traded with their immediate neighbors, but not with distant populations, for there was a great diversity of tongues at this time. The folk in the mountains wore little or no clothing in those days.

Regarding the coastal population at this period, Father Román speaks in almost exactly the same terms as does Bishop las Casas, depicting a generally higher and more polished state of culture, with artificial mounds supporting palaces and temples, with spears hurled by spear-throwers, and all the rest of it.[25]

Father Román, aside from confirming what other Chroniclers say about the earliest period of high culture on the coast, does us a great service in speaking, albeit rather vaguely, of culture in the highlands at that time.

Much more specific is the somewhat gossipy, but at times very informative, Dominican Friar Reginaldo de Lizárraga, who was travelling and studying in Peru between 1555 and 1599. In his "Description of the Indies" he writes as follows:

There are found in these realms [Peru], and particularly in the Plains [the coast], certain burial-places commonly called *Guacas*, which are like hills, being made of piled-up earth, in which the lords of these Plains were interred and with them, as both rumour and actual discoveries testify, they placed a great deal of gold and silver, but chiefly silver, in the form of large jars and other vessels and drinking-cups of the kind that we call *cocos*. The most celebrated *guaca* was one situated a little more than a league from the city of Trujillo, on the opposite side of the river, built partly of banked-up earth and partly of large bricks, or rather small *adobes*.

This edifice was very high, its circumference . . . being slightly less than half a league. There is no remembrance of the builder, nor did the Indians hear of him from their ancestors. It must have occupied a vast number of men during a long stretch of years to erect it, for its greatness cannot be believed save by seeing it. It has always been understood to have been the sepulchre of many lords of that Valley of Trujillo, who are said to have lived long before the Incas and to have been extremely powerful, as well on account of their wealth as on account of their intention to bring a great part of this kingdom [Peru] under their rule. Indeed, because four leagues from the city of Guamanga [Ayacucho] another edifice has been found which, though different, is adorned with figures of Indians like those of Trujillo, it is inferred that the domains of these lords did reach anciently as far as that place, and even beyond it, into the Collao; for, in a village of the Collao, called Tiaguanaco, another building is to be seen, of masonry and of very large and well-worked stones similar to those near Guamanga. . . . The first time that I went thither [to Tiahuanaco] was twenty-nine years ago, in company with two other friars, and we saw the work and marvelled greatly at it because, since these Indians had no picks, nor hammers, nor carpenters' squares wherewith to work those stones, it is wonderful to see them shaped as though skilled quarrymen had done the cutting.

A little farther on the good friar reiterates his belief that Tiahuanaco, the structures near Huamanga (now Ayacucho), and that which he mentions as being near Trujillo were all built by the Chimu kings.[26] This is decidedly interesting, not because of the friar's theory that Chimu power was spread so far into the highlands as Tiahuanaco, but rather because in his jumbled statement of the evidence we have strong documentary support for the historicity of the spread of Tiahuanaco power to the coast, a spread which was probably faintly recorded by the folk-memory and reported to us topsy-turvy by the friar.

The best light that we have on the early history of the highlands and of the coast and on the relations between their inhabitants at this early period is provided by Father Fernando Montesinos, about whom, even at the cost of interrupting the thread of my narrative, I must say a few words. He was that *rara avis*, an ignorant and gullible Jesuit. Nevertheless, his *Memorias antiguas historiales del Perú* is a book of importance for us because it embodies, albeit in garbled form, the historical data gathered by an earlier and infinitely more intelligent Jesuit, Father Blas Valera, who, between 1571 and 1590, had travelled widely in Peru and in the country around Lake Titicaca. Father Valera, being of mixed blood—son of a Castilian gentleman-adventurer and of an upper-class Indian woman from the northern part of the Peruvian highlands— was able to mingle on friendly terms with the native aristocracy. From its members he learned all that he could concerning the ancient history of the Andean folk. Thus informed, Father Valera drew up a long list of chiefs and kings who had ruled in the Peruvian highlands since remotest discernible times, the last ten or so on his list being the Incas. Into this

list Father Valera inserted such historical events as were
reported to him by the native sages and knot-record keepers
whom he consulted. As it originally stood, the Valera list was
probably a fairly accurate and detailed history of the highland folk in pre-Incaic and Incaic times. This, then, was the
material which Father Montesinos, writing between 1629 and
1644, used as a basis for his *Memorias*, but in so doing added
thereto much apocryphal matter and certain distortions of
Valera's work. Therefore, in order to get the greatest possible
good out of the *Memorias*, one must strip away from the narrative therein all the patently unauthoritative matter inserted
by Father Montesinos.[27]

When this is done, we gleam from the *Memorias*, the following outline of ancient history in the highlands of the Andes
and in the coastal zone:

During the first three to six centuries of our Era, highland
states in an archaic stage of culture were gradually growing in
strength and working towards civilization. This was the period
in which that culture flourished which, for want of a more
accurate name, we call Tiahuanaco I. It was a prelude to the
subsequent period of civilization which is now generally
designated Tiahuanaco II. As the nascent states of the highlands grew more and more populous and also more and more
strong, they naturally came into martial collision with the
already well-developed states upon the coast. In order to
defend themselves against incursions from the lowlands, the
mountain folk built various fortresses at strategic points along
the western slopes of the Maritime Cordillera. It must be
remembered that Father Valera wrote primarily from the
standpoint of the mountain folk and that, consequently, it is
not surprising to find that his adapter, Montesinos, portrays
the Chimus as terrible giants of unbridled ferocity and sin-
fulness.[28]

In the presence of a constant menace of invasion by a people more advanced than themselves, the highlanders were
spurred on to a marked cultural progress, the earlier phase of
culture containing—in its architecture, in its art, and in its

material aspects as a whole—the germs of the later one. It is well to note in passing that Father Montesinos always speaks of the earlier kings on the list as ruling from Cuzco, implying that from there they gave instructions for the building of the fortresses of Huáitara, Quínoa and others.[29] It is not until he comes to the reign of the earliest historical Inca that he mentions Tiahuanaco by name;[30] but he does so then in an interesting fashion, mentioning the "kings of Vilcas, Guáitara (Huáitara), and Tiaguanaco." From this we may safely infer that these localities—and very many others likewise—had their local dynasties, probably of great antiquity.

With these accounts of the past agrees, in the main, that given to us by the very great Chronicler and Jesuit, Father Bernabé Cobo who, like Father Lizárraga, brackets the ruins at Tiahuanaco with those near Huamanca (now Ayacucho).[31]

Such, then, is the chief evidence given by the natives of the Andes to the various Chroniclers of Peru and by them set down in writings on the subject of Andean antiquities and ancient history. With great care the more intelligent Spanish settlers in Peru sought to preserve the native lore, doing so not merely from idle curiosity but rather in order to gain a good understanding of the native population and of its political and spiritual needs. The writings of the Chroniclers, therefore, represent the folk-memories of ancient and powerful states along the coast and of contemporary but, at this time, less advanced, societies in the highlands. This is all excellent, so far as it goes; nevertheless, it would be but shadowy stuff were it not amply corroborated by the results of archæological work in modern times.

2. Archæological Evidence Concerning the Early Chimu Period and Its Culture

I will now indicate how much support is given to these native records of the past by the findings of archæology. It must be borne in mind, however, that Andean archæology is still in its infancy, and that many localities and even whole regions have never been touched by the spade of a trained

archæologist. Of the many thousands of ancient Andean artifacts now existing in the museums of the world only a small
number have been collected under strictly scientific principles.
Nevertheless, because of the labors in the field of a few
trained archæologists—of whom Dr. Uhle is the acknowledged
Dean—we do possess a few very precious stratigraphical data
which serve to guide us in the chronological placing of innumerable specimens that were not scientifically collected. Thus
it comes about that we have a series of well-defined styles of
art, borne on sundry kinds of industrial products, to each of
which styles we are able to assign approximate dates. These,
then, are the archæological materials with which I shall now
deal.

On earlier pages I said that at least a part of the coastal
population of Peru migrated southwards from Central America, following the Pacific shore line and importing with them
culture still in the archaic stage. Let me now amplify this
assertion by pointing out the probability that there were also
post-archaic movements in the same direction not, however,
in the form of accidental drifting but rather in that of systematic and purposeful colonizing, conquering, and spreading of
the kind already referred to on previous pages. The story of
Naymlap and his followers unmistakably indicates something
of the sort; and for that story, as will presently be made clear,
there is broad archæological support.

As an example of the manner in which archæologically derived
evidence aids in historical interpretations, let me cite a concrete instance. Dr. Aleš Hrdlička found in a very old *huaca* or
mound in the Chicama Valley two vessels which were accompanied by brachycephalic skulls of Central American physical
type.[32] Not only that, but also the two dishes themselves, one
a pedestal-foot dish, the other a tripod, are of distinctly Central American type, both as regards their forms and as regards
the kind of painted decoration upon them, being representatives of types of pottery produced during long periods in the
territory now occupied by Costa Rica, Nicaragua, and
Panama.[33] Furthermore, Dr. S. K. Lothrop, in speaking of his

study of the museum collections in Lima, says: "Almost every detected likeness to Central America in all parts of Peru occurred in types [of artifacts] to which Dr. Tello assigns an early date—as is also the case with the stratified remains from Ecuador."[34]

With the foregoing as a point of departure, and with a frank recognition of the underlying kinship between archaic and immediately post-archaic Central American culture on the one hand and the earliest phases of Peruvian coastal culture on the other, let me now turn to the advanced civilization which, for lack of a better term, I have been wont to designate as Early Chimu.[35] It was a direct outgrowth of the archaic phase of culture, and its people were in contact with other people—ethnically their kinsmen—who lingered in the archaic phase, contact which was largely of a bellicose nature.

This knowledge, and many other precious bits of information, are conveyed to us by the Early Chimu pottery which, being adorned with highly realistic paintings and modelled figures, possesses a great documentary value. It is from this angle that we shall first study the pottery of this period, leaving the æsthetic aspect of the subject for later consideration. Nevertheless, it is convenient to classify the pottery designs according to criteria that are in part æsthetic, as follows:

Group 1. Landscapes and scenes from daily or from ceremonial life. (This group includes painted decorations and modelled.)

Group 2. Portraits, either of single figures or of groups. (This category is made up chiefly of modelled decorations.)

Group 3. Decorative designs, whether naturalistic, formalized, or conventionalized. (Predominantly painted decoration.)

Group 4. Miscellaneous decorations. (Both painted and modelled.)

Landscapes—and indeed all classes of designs—vary greatly in point of elaboration, some being simple, yet quite realistic, as is the adjoining Figure 1, where we see a field of growing plants, possibly maize, thriving under cultivation. Others, like

Figure 2 are very intricate. In the latter we are shown the design painted around the flaring rim of a large, deep vessel. An Early Chimu cloth-factory is here displayed. The personage in charge of the work appears on the right, seated under a rustic canopy and elaborately clad. With him are three minor officials who appear to be receiving his instruc-

FIG. 1. Early Chimu vase-painting.
After Lehmann and Doering.

tions, together with a supply of food or water in a bowl. Proceeding clockwise, we next come to five humble-looking persons each of whom is working at a loom. They, too, are sheltered by a rustic roof. Each of them is provided with a bit of cloth from which to copy, and with a jug, probably containing liquid refreshments of some kind. Then comes another official who seems to be in charge of the kitchen of the establishment, with a minor personage to help. Venison is cooking on the hearth, and in dishes in the background we catch glimpses of fish and vegetable food. Evidently the workers in this particular weave-shop fared well. Lastly there come three more weavers similar to the first five.[36]

This scene is replete, then, with documentary evidence of the high stage of material culture to which the people who produced it had attained. Because of it we are justified in saying that the textile arts had reached a high development in Early Chimu times.

Almost as informative is the portrait-pot—or perhaps one

would better say effigy-pot in this instance—shown in Figure 3, where we see a representation of a person of rank who, comfortably squatting upon a small raft, is towed over the water by three swimming servitors, clad in abbreviated trunks and in turbans. Again, the handsome stirrup-spout bottle shown in Figure 4 tells us exactly how the Early Chimu warrior dressed and how he was armed. The fighter there displayed wears a cone-shaped helmet surmounted by an axe-head, perhaps of totemic or heraldic significance, and from the helmet over his back streams a curtain-like flap with an attractive design upon it. In his right hand he carries a business-like spear-thrower and two sharply pointed javelins. In his left hand he bears a large club with a deadly-looking end, and also a small square buckler, apparently of wood. His body is covered with a knee-length tunic having short sleeves, and from his waist hangs a large axe-head which, one would think, must have jabbed him cruelly now and then as he walked. His face is heavily painted with dark pigment save around the eyes, in which we find an interesting corroboration of what Father Cabello de Balboa has to say concerning Xam Muchec, guardian of the royal face-paints. His legs likewise appear to be painted. Further evidence of the prevalence of face-painting will be found in specimens to be described presently, as will also evidence regarding the use of ear-studs such as that shown in the vase-painting under discussion.

Hunting- and fishing-scenes are of common occurrence in Early Chimu vase-paintings and in modelled decorations upon pots. In Figure 7 we see three men doing to death a couple of deer which have been driven into a netted-in enclosure. The weapons used are the club and the javelin-with-thrower, the manner in which the latter is here manipulated being specially interesting on account of its deft daintiness. The slaughtering of game under conditions such as those here shown has the same *abattoir*-like quality the pre-war German stag-drives had, but no doubt it was an effective way of obtaining a supply of fresh meat. Again, in Figure 5, we have a stirrup-spout vessel carrying both a modelled and a painted hunting-scene. In the

FIGURE 2. Design from the rim of an Early Chimu vase of the flaring-mouth type. From near Chan-Chan (Trujillo).

Photograph by courtesy of the British Museum.

FIGURE 3. An Early Chimu pot with a modelled group representing a Chief riding upon a raft which is being towed by swimming servitors. From Chan-Chan (Trujillo).

FIGURE 4. An Early Chimu pot with painted decoration showing warriors fully armed for war. From Chan-Chan (Trujillo).

Originals in the National Museum of Archæology, Lima.

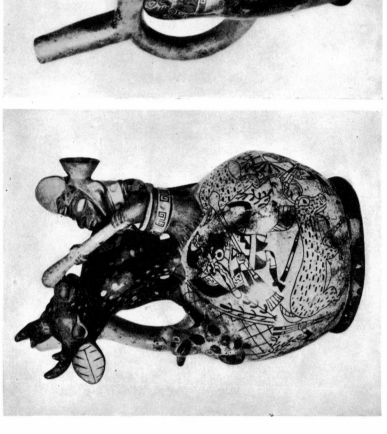

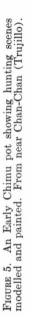

FIGURE 5. An Early Chimu Chimu pot showing hunting scenes modelled and painted. From near Chan-Chan (Trujillo).

FIGURE 6. An Early Chimu pot with a modelled group representing some ceremonial. Below it is a landscape, beautifully engraved. From near Chan-Chan (Trujillo).

Photographs by courtesy of the Peabody Museum, Harvard University.

former a man accompanied by a small dog faintly resembling a wire-haired fox-terrier is giving a blow to a deer with a mighty club. It is not clear just why the deer stands there so meekly to receive it, but the likelihood is that the poor thing

FIG. 7. An Early Chimu vase-painting showing a hunting scene.
After Baessler.

—very obese—has been rendered breathless by a prolonged chase! In the painted scene upon this same vase the javelin-and-net technique is being employed.

Knowledge of the kinds of sea-going craft used by the Early Chimu folk, and of their methods of fishing, is gained from designs like those appearing in Figures 8 to 11, inclusive. The

FIG. 8. A design in bas-relief from an Early Chimu pot, showing a fishing scene, with masked figures, a dog, and a boat.
After Baessler.

boat shown in the first picture of this series looks as though it were made of planks, but it is more likely that it was constructed either of logs or else of bundles of dried grass such as those now employed in boat-building on Lake Titicaca. There is a canopied cock-pit amidships at one end of which stands a jar, presumably for drinking-water or some other beverage. Both the bow and the stern of the boat—and to be perfectly frank a yachtsman would be at a loss to say which is which—are adorned with carved animal-heads, possibly of totemic or heraldic meaning. The lines, hooks, and sinkers used by fishermen are clearly shown, as are also the skate that has been

FIG. 9.   Fishing scene from an Early Chimu vase.
After Baessler.

caught by the bird-like personage in the centre, and the small terrier-like dog. Patently these particular fishermen are no ordinary folk; two of them have the aspect and mien of chiefs, and the remaining three are masked and clad as birds and a fox. No doubt there were ceremonies intended to placate the sea-gods and to ensure a good catch for the fishing community in general. In Figures 9, 10, and 11 we find other fishing-scenes which well repay study if one would form an accurate and detailed notion of maritime life in Early Chimu times.

Of ceremonials we have many representations, almost all of them showing either men disguised as animals and birds or else animals and birds wholly or partially anthropomorphized; it is often difficult to say which is the case. In this we see, no doubt, the results of an animistic cult to which the folk of

that time adhered. In Figure 6, for example, we see a modelled
effigy of a deity, or perchance merely of a dignitary of some
kind, who sits with a semi-circle of partly humanized animal
figures before him, the group evidently being in some sort of
conclave together. Incidentally, the body of this vessel bears
a charming naturalistic landscape, showing trees—*zapote*

Fig. 10.   Marine scene from an Early Chimu pot.
After Baessler.

trees, most likely—cactus bushes, and sandy hillocks such
as one sees in many parts of the northern coast-country, the
whole scene executed in an unusual technique of lines shallowly engraved in the burnished surface of the pot and afterwards filled in with some white substance. Were this same
scene applied to a bit of modern glass-ware from Bohemia or
from Italy, it would command a high price and much admiration from the purchasing public. As things go to-day—in
contrast to the way in which they went some thirty years ago
—this very specimen, if put up for sale at any respectable
European or North American auction-rooms, would command
ten times as much as would a similar modern work of art.

A painted scene of the ceremonial kind is shown in Figure
12, where we behold an elaborate ritualistic dance by men
masked and winged as birds. The verve and sweep of the six

vital and swiftly moving figures compel the admiration of any modern artist who chances to behold them. Moreover, the problematical nature of the object held in the left hand of each dancer arouses one's curiosity. These winged men masked as birds recall the traditional end of King Naymlap, as related by Father Cabello; and, besides, they probably represent some

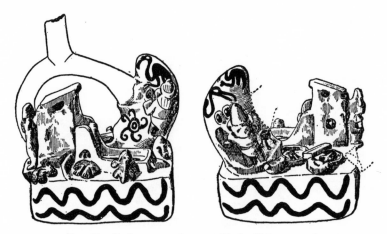

FIG. 11.   Seal nursery, from an Early Chimu vessel.
After Baessler.

ancient folk-tale of the Andeans, for bird-men will be prominently mentioned again in connection with the art of the Tiahuanaco II period.

Pottery-paintings and other types of pottery-designs in general representing battle scenes are likewise frequent in the ceramics of the Early Chimu culture. In Figure 21 we see a justly celebrated vase from Chimbote, now in the Ethnological Museum in Berlin. It is surmounted by an impressive modelled portrait of a chief in a ceremonial attitude, and around the body of the vessel are painted representations of fully accoutred and gorgeously panoplied warriors who seem to be going to and fro in a sandy country replete with cactusbushes. This is one of the masterpieces of Early Chimu art in clay. Hardly less important, both as documents and as beau-

tiful objects, are vase-paintings such as Figure 13, which
shows a battle going on between well-armored and well-
equipped warriors and others who are not so well prepared for
war; such as the flaring-mouthed vase adorned with warriors

FIG. 12.   An Early Chimu vase-painting showing a ceremonial dance.
After Baessler.

with centipede attributes, as shown in Figure 14; such as Figure 16, in which we see a fanged warrior standing against
an aureole-like conventional background; such as the fanged
vegetation-bearing and snake-accompanied personage shown
in Figure 15. Then, too, there are a large number of vase-

FIG. 13.   Elaborate representation of a battle, from an Early Chimu vase.
After Baessler.

embellishments representing the ghastly jollifications of the
dead.

Pottery-designs representing litters, although relatively rare
in Early Chimu art, do occur—as shown in Figure 24—fre-

quently enough to assure us that carrying-chairs or litters, more or less elaborately decorated, were used by the great as a mode of transportation, exactly as Father Cabello's story of Naymlap implies that they were.

Representations of houses are met with more often. In Figure 17 we see an elaborate structure consisting of a three-

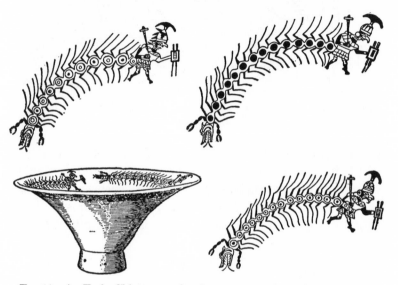

FIG. 14.   An Early Chimu vase showing representations of warriors with centipede attributes.

After Baessler.

terraced mound surmounted by a large house with a gable roof in the ends of which are circular windows. Along the eaves and the ridgepole are some curious objects which seem to be clubs of the sort which we have seen in several previously mentioned designs. Naturally, one can but guess as to the meaning of these things, but a credible explanation is that the building here shown is a meeting-place for warriors—a club-house, in fact, as a female member of a mid-West audience of mine once complacently suggested.

Another type of house appears to have consisted of rustic posts which supported a roof under which were ranged benches of adobe upon which the owners were wont to take their ease while the evening breezes played around them and the pageantry of the coastland sunset delighted them. Pleasure pavilions of this kind appear in Figures 18 and 19.

A feature of many houses of the more solid sort was a massive roof-comb, step-shaped and seemingly useless save

FIG. 15. An Early Chimu vessel with relief ornamentation representing a fanged god with serpents and plants.

FIG. 16. An Early Chimu vessel showing a fanged god in relief against a background of rays.

After Baessler.

for purposes of adornment. Readers who have given some share of their attention to Maya art and architecture will remember that the roof-comb—developed far beyond the proportions common in Peru—was characteristic of Maya architecture both in the Old Empire and in the New.[37]

A final type of house is an improved version of the pavilion type already mentioned. An example of it appears in Figure 20, where we see a throne-like structure upon a high dais. The roof over it is elaborately decorated with carved animal heads that recall those on the boat mentioned on page 75. In the present instance, however, calamitous events are tak-

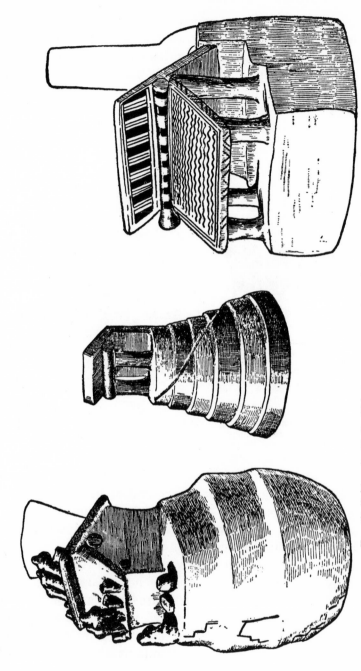

FIG. 17 (left).   An Early Chimu vase representing a house.
FIG. 18 (centre).   An Early Chimu vase showing a pavilion atop a circular pyramid.
FIG. 19 (right).   Another and more elaborate pavilion.

After Baessler.

ing place, for the unfortunate personage within the house is being furiously beset by angry demons of several shapes, but especially by a centipede-like creature having at each end of his long body a head with protruding tongue and a pair of crab-like claws. The scene is highly complicated but well repays careful examination, for it is not more confused than its esoteric quality would inevitably make it for us at this

FIG. 20.   Scene from a vessel near Trujillo.
Original in the Ethnological Museum, Berlin.   Drawing made by W. v. d. Steineu.
After Lehmann and Doering.

distant day. The designer obviously had some symbolical story to tell, and no doubt the picture was perfectly comprehensible to the audience for which it was intended. The same thing may be said regarding designs containing centipede-like creatures with protruding tongues which, as shall be demonstrated presently, occur frequently in Early Nazca art.

Portraiture in clay reached an even higher level of realism and of charming beauty than did the best landscapes and scene-paintings of the Early Chimu pots. As in every other class of pottery of this and of other periods, the degree of excellence varies from specimen to specimen. Comparatively humble as portraits are pots such as those reproduced in Figures 22, 23, 25, and 26; but as "documents" they are valuable for the reason that they give us precise information regarding the dress and the mode of resting prevalent among the Early Chimu people. The supreme glory of Early Chimu art, however, is that relatively small class of vessels which comprises portrait-vases of such excellence as those shown in Figures 27 and 28, before which even blasé and sophisticated modern sculptors pour out a reluctant libation of half-envious admiration. Of these two that in Figure 28 is the better. For delicacy of modelling and fineness of finish this portrait cannot be surpassed anywhere, in ancient times or modern. The matchless, tranquil dignity of the countenance here shown, and the somewhat austere richness of the head-dress, are eloquent of the royal repose and stateliness which must have been characteristic of the Early Chimu ruling caste in its best moments.

Enough material is now in the possession of the reader to permit him to see how thoroughly the realistic pottery of the Early Chimu people corroborates Father Cabello's and Father Calancha's accounts of the culture prevailing in very early times on the northern half of the Peruvian coast. In only one important particular is there a discrepancy between the two kinds of evidence: It is indicated in the two Chronicles cited that women had a high position in the society of that day, some of them even being rulers in their own right. Yet portrait-vases showing women are very rare indeed, and when they do appear, either in portrait- or in effigy-vases or in genre paintings—as, perhaps, in the case of the weavers in Figure 2—they are almost always shown in the performance of hard work, in the exercise of witchcraft, or else in the acts of physiological kind peculiar to their sex.[38] As to the causes of their non-appearance in the more stately sort of portraits one can, at this late date, but guess; it may have been the result of social customs and religious taboos of which we now know nothing.

It has now been amply demonstrated that the fundamental spirit and intention of Early Chimu art were realistic and representational. Nevertheless, designs do occur in considerable numbers which, like Figures 29 and 30, are of slight, if any, realistic import. Rather, they fall within that class of embellishment which modern art-jargon calls "pure design,"

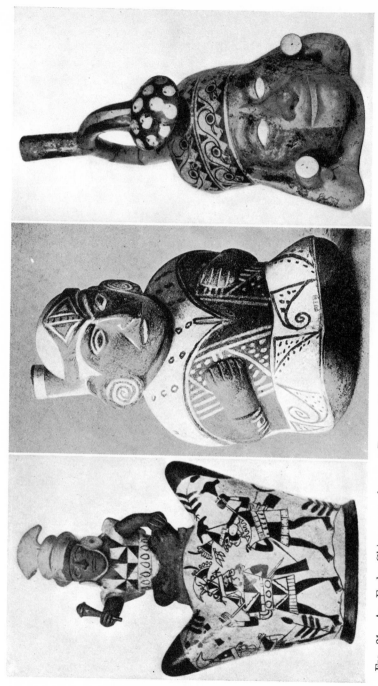

FIG. 21. An Early Chimu pot from Chimbote. The original is now in the Ethnological Museum, Berlin. *After Baessler.*

FIG. 22. Early Chimu portrait-vase showing a richly clad man. From the Chicama Valley. Original in the Drouillon Collection, Musée du Trocadéro, Paris. *After Réal.*

FIG. 23. An Early Chimu portrait vase. *Courtesy of the Peabody Museum, Harvard University.*

Fig. 24. Decorative panel from an Early Chimu vase showing the type
of carrying chair or litter then in use.

*The original is in the Ethnological Museum, Berlin. Drawing by W.
von Stemen. After Baessler.*

Fig. 25. Two Early Chimu portrait vases, probably from the region
of Trujillo.

The originals are in the National Museum of Archæology, Lima.

and constitute linear decoration for the mere sake of prettiness, with little or no attempt to convey any kind of message. Yet no one will deny that they are pleasing to the eye and that they do beautify the vessels which carry them.

The media in which Early Chimu art is found include, first and foremost, pottery, then wood, stone, and miscellaneous substances such as shell and mosaic. This brings us to an important query anent Early Chimu civilization: Did the people of that day have a knowledge of metal-working, and, if so, what metals were used by them? Baron Erland Nordenskiöld, García y Merino, and Dr. J. A. Mason, by using archæological evidence of various kinds, have shown conclusively that metal *was* extensively used for weapons, implements, and ornaments. It is obvious that axes, knives, spear-thrower hooks, and personal adornments such as those seen in very many of the figures mentioned must have been made of metal. To Baron Nordenskiöld we owe valuable evidence that "an age of copper" preceded, in Peru, an "age of bronze," and we are thereby justified in believing that it was pure copper that the Early Chimu folk used as material for metal-work of the more ordinary sort.[39]

Copper is not a particularly difficult metal to work, and for that reason its occurrence in certain high archaic cultures such as that of Chiriquí, need not surprise us. True, silver and gold were used fully as much as copper, being regarded not as "precious" metals, but merely as metals easily wrought, this being the attitude in the matter both of the high archaic folk in various parts of America and of divers post-archaic folk who derived their culture from the archaic plane.[40] The fine Early Chimu knife shown in Figure 31, for example, is made of copper, with a separately cast bird finely wrought in gold of great purity.

Æsthetically considered, Early Chimu art is youthful but not infantile. The difficulties involved in the manipulation of the various materials and tools had all been overcome during the archaic phase. The artists of the Early Chimu period were masters of their instruments and of their media. They were, therefore, released from purely mechanical considerations and were in readiness to progress along æsthetic and psychological lines, in short, to develop their art in accordance with the dictates of a subtle blending of the two. On account of all these factors it came about, with the passage of time, that a considerable diversity came into being in the character of Early Chimu designs. Regarding some of them in an objective way we can declare them to be merely straightforward—but masterly—representations of commonplace situations and occurrences. Figures 1–5; 7–13; 17–19; 21–28, for example, show us compositions whose creators' minds were free from morbid introspection, free, also, from servitude to priestcraft and its accompaniments of symbolism and superstition. Such psychological forces as those dominate an aging, not a maturing culture. But the range of Early Chimu art is rather wide, and manifestations of attainment to maturity are not wanting. With the passage of time the artists of that period tended to abandon the superficial aspects of their world, to cease portraying the personal appearance of their rulers, to give up the habit of representing their fishing, their hunting, and other activities, doing all this in favor of an effort to interpret, in terms of art, the great mysteries of Nature as they understood them. To this deep-reaching tendency we owe such effigies as that of the king beset by demons, shown in Figure 20, such, finally, as the warriors with centipede-like tails displayed in Figure 14. In even the most esoteric of Early Chimu designs, however, realism is present, usually to a marked extent. It was, in truth, one of the strongest fibres of Early Chimu art.

In point of color Early Chimu ceramics are rarely noteworthy; emphasis fell upon line and form, not upon color. The great majority of vessels belonging to this period are of reddish clay covered at least in part with a fine white or cream-colored slip whereon are painted the designs in black, brown, or reddish-brown. Sometimes a realistic effect was obtained by leaving certain areas—such as faces, hands, and feet of human figures—uncovered by the slip, allowing the natural tint of the clay to give them a lifelike aspect which, in

Fig. 26. An Early Chimu portrait vase.
From Chan-Chan (Trujillo).

*The original is in the National Museum
of Archæology, Lima.*

Fig. 27. Early Chimu portrait head from
Chimbote. *After Schmidt, 1929.*

*Original is in the Baessler Collection,
Ethnological Museum, Berlin.*

Fig. 28. An especially fine Early Chimu portrait vase. *After Harcourt, by courtesy
of M. Albert Morancé.*

The original is in Museo Alexander, Lima.

Fig. 29. An Early Chimu vase of flaring-mouth type. From the Valley of Chicama, and now in the Gaffron Collection, Schlachtensee, near Berlin. *After Lehmann and Doering.*

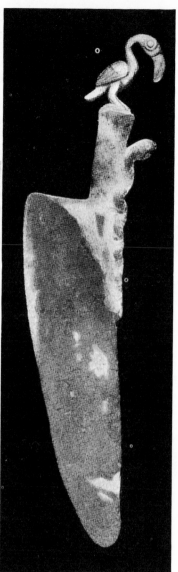

Fig. 31. Copper knife with bird-ornament in gold. Length about 5½ inches.

Courtesy of the Museum of the University of Pennsylvania.

Fig. 30. An Early Chimu pot of unusual shape, with a fine white slip upon which are painted conventionalized sea-creatures and a band of decorative motifs. *After Réal.*

The original is in the Trocadéro Museum, Paris.

such superfine specimens as those in Figures 27 and 28, was heightened by careful burnishing with a smooth hard pebble or with a shell. Sometimes, albeit rarely, hues other than these very simple ones were used, crimson, yellow, orange, and blue being occasionally found on Early Chimu pottery.

Heretofore we have been considering the art of the Early Chimu culture as a whole, without reference to specific localities. But the realm of the Early Chimu culture, whether or not it was at this time a closely knit kingdom, was large; artifacts representing it come from all the coastal valleys from the Gulf of Guayaquil down to the Pativilca Valley in which stands the Chimus' frontier fortress of Parmunca. An admirable air-photograph of that imposing structure appears in Figure 32. On the east this cultural region which, at any rate in later times, was a well-organized monarchical and feudal state as well, was bordered by the Maritime Cordillera; on the west by the Pacific Ocean. In other words, it was a territory some 450 miles in length and some 50 miles in width on an average—approximately 22,500 square miles of desert, valley, and foothill country, roughly equal in size to Connecticut, Massachusetts, and New Hampshire combined.

This interpretation of the geography of the Early Chimu culture cannot, however, be accepted at present without a certain allowance for possible error. Valuable data pertinent to the subject are provided by Dr. Kroeber, the most recent North American field-worker in Peru.[41] He opines that the "Chimoid style"—by which bizarre term he designates, supposedly, all phases of Chimu art, whether Early or Late—occurs along the Peruvian coast from latitude 5° south to latitude 10° south, or, from Piura down to the Casma Valley. This region he sub-divides arbitrarily into five areas which, contrary to the usual procedure, he lists from south to north, as follows: I. Casma; II. Chimbote to Chicama, inclusive; III. Pacasmayo and Chepén; IV. Lambayeque; V. Piura. Dr. Kroeber, after studying the specimens gathered by Dr. Uhle for the University of California's Museum of Anthropology, concludes that the Proto-Chimu style—our Early

Chimu—is characteristic only of area II, viz., from the Chicama Valley down to Chimbote. He says: "With all its æsthetic superiority, therefore, Proto-Chimu remained a local style. It evidently fell in a period of limited communications, probably of restricted political units."[42]

If this be correct, my contention, expressed above, that the Early Chimu cultural area—and perhaps and Early Chimu kingdom on feudal lines—extended from the Gulf of Guayaquil down to Pativilca is incorrect. Perchance the discrepancy is to be explained by the fact that at present we have only the beginnings of an archæologically derived knowledge concerning this period of culture—as, indeed, concerning all periods of ancient culture in the Andean area. Nevertheless, we already possess enough specimens of Early Chimu art from beyond the narrow limits set by Dr. Kroeber to justify us in accepting the wider distribution which I have suggested. The chief support, thus far, to this contention of mine that the Early Chimu culture extended from the Gulf of Guayaquil to Pativilca is the circumstance that Father Calancha, cited on page 59 above, ascribes those limits to the Chimu state; this is, I confess, rickety support, as he may be speaking here of the Late Chimu kingdom—although there is naught in his narrative that indicates this specifically—nor is the evidence strengthened by the fact that both Dr. Uhle and I failed to find incontrovertible testimony that Proto-Chimu— or Early Chimu—culture had flourished to any great extent in the Department of Piura.[43] It is to be hoped that in the future systematic archæological field-work will clear up this rather important point in a definitive manner.

Meanwhile, we know that Chan-Chan, lying between the sea and the Spanish walled city of Trujillo, on the right side of the Moche River but some five miles from its margin, was the capital of the Early Chimu kings. Both archæological and literary evidence points this out as true. The ruined city occupies the southern end of the Plain of Chan-Chan which is bordered on east and north by mountains, on the south by the Moche or Chimu Valley, and on the west by the Pacific Ocean.

Fig. 32. An aerial photograph of the fortress of Parmunca (Paramonga, the modern La Barranca), which defended the southern frontier of the Chimu kingdom.

Fig. 33. Vestiges of a patio-garden in one of the palaces at Chan-Chan (Trujillo). The white serpentine lines mark the site of the ornamental *acequias*, or irrigation ditches, and they are made by the saline deposits laid down by the water formerly in the ditches.

Photographs by courtesy of Major Otto Holstein.

FIG. 34. Vestiges of Early Chimu wall-frescoes at Chan-Chan (Trujillo).
Photograph by courtesy of Major Otto Holstein.

FIG. 35. Masonry of the Tiahuanaco I period: the western wall of the
Acapana at Tiahuanaco. *After Posnansky.*

This plain, thickly studded as it is with vestiges of settlements, pyramid-mounds, or *huacas*, streets, open squares,
reservoirs, aqueducts, enclosures where tastefully laid out

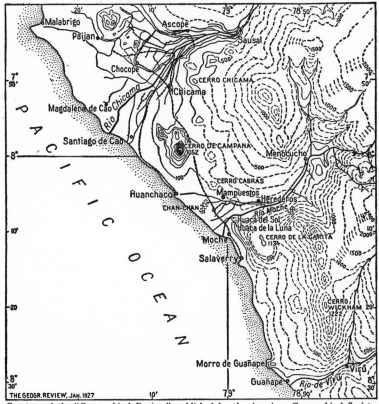

Courtesy of the "Geographical Review," published by the American Geographical Society
of New York.

Fig. 36.   Map of the vicinity of Trujillo showing the site of Chan-Chan.
Drawn from the compilation prepared for the Trujillo and Piura sheets of
the American Geographical Society's Millionth Map of Hispanic America.
Scale 1:1,000,000.

water courses supplied moisture to verdant pleasances, the
ghost of one of which is shown in Figure 33, and countless
other mementos of civilized occupation, was long ago, and
over a protracted period, a metropolitan area of great impressiveness.   Major Holstein's admirable map of the district
appears in Figure 36.

The standard description of the wonders of Chan-Chan was, until recently, that of Squier. It has been improved upon, and largely superseded, by the work done in the Trujillo district —and from the air over it—by Major Otto Holstein.[44] From his very important article I draw the following facts.

The Moche River, a perennial stream, provided water which, from the earliest civilized times, was conducted through an intricate series of reservoirs and ditches that made the whole plain a truck-garden yielding several crops a year. The city of Chan-Chan itself covers some eleven square miles of ground and was enclosed in a high wall, various wards of the city being delimited by subsidiary walls. There was a marked tendency towards rectangularity in the general plan of the city, but an irksome monotony that might have resulted therefrom was obviated by the irregularity of the placing of the pyramidal huacas whose vast bulk and great height relieved the eye and stirred the imagination here and there through the city and in the surrounding plain. When in its hey-day the capital, as already hinted, was embellished by greenery and gaily colored flowers in public gardens and in palace patios, and the now drab-colored mud walls were then coated with white plaster upon which were painted animated scenes depicted in the same æsthetic style that we see in the vase-paintings. Remains of such wall-frescoes appear in Figure 34, and Major Holstein shows two more which are at the Huaca of the Moon.[45] This structure and its larger neighbor, the Huaca of the Sun, stand south of Chan-Chan itself and on the opposite side of the Moche River. Both were built of adobe and both suffered terrible damage during the rains of March, 1925, as did all the other structures, ancient and modern alike, on the northern part of the Peruvian coast.[46]

To sum up the matter of the ancient aspect of Chan-Chan I will quote the late Sir Clements Markham, who wrote thus: "The great mounds presented a very different appearance in the time of the Chimu. Originally they were in terraces, on which buildings were erected with pitched roofs, and tastefully painted walls. Verandahs, supported by the twisted stems of

Fig. 37.

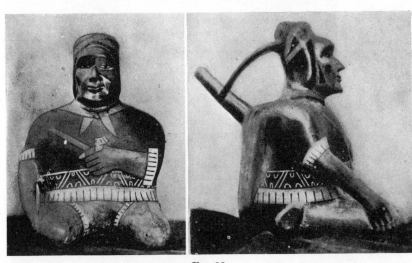

Fig. 38.

Photographs by courtesy of the Boston Museum of Fine Arts.

Fig. 39.

Fig. 37. Front view and side view of an Early Nazca portrait vase. The original is owned by Señora Doña Hortensia Cáceres de Porras, of Lima, by whose courtesy these photographs are allowed to appear here.

Fig 38. Front view and side view of an Early Nazca portrait vase.

Fig. 39. An Early Nazca vase showing a man running with a plumed staff. On the right, an Early Nazca double vase with men bearing plumed staffs.

Originals are in the Gaffron Collection, Schlachtensee, near Berlin. After Lehmann and Doering.

FIG. 40.

Original in the Trocadéro Museum, Paris.
After Réal.

FIG. 41.

Original in the Trocadéro Museum, Paris.
After Berthon.

FIG. 43.

Original in the Trocadéro Museum, Paris.
After Réal.

FIG. 42.

Courtesy of the Peabody Museum,
Harvard University.

FIGS. 40, 41, 43. Three Early Nazca pots representing the portrait tradition derived from Early Chimu art, but with progressive loss of realism.

FIG. 42. An Early Nazca pot showing a considerable degree of realism, but with a strong formalistic trend also.

algaroba trees, afforded shade, and there were communications
with the interior passages and chambers. From the seashore
these structures, with gardens at their bases, must have presented a magnificent effect."[47]

The "documentary" pottery fully justifies us in giving
credence to this description. In all the northern coast valleys
of Peru there are unnumbered pyramidal structures, great and
small, the largest being hundreds of feet on a side and as much
as two hundred feet in height. Naturally enough, edifices so
huge were not built all at once, nor even during a short period;
but we may safely assume that many of them had at any rate
their beginnings in the Early Chimu period.

*3. Archæological Evidence Concerning the Early Nazca Period
and Its Culture*

As I said above, on page 50, every coastal valley in Peru
doubtless had a dynastic history of considerable length which,
if we could but know it in full, would summarize the cultural
development of each valley concerned. Nevertheless, as matters stand now, our knowledge is sadly fragmentary in this
respect, so much so that we can only study the data yielded
by modern archæology in the southern part of the coast, just
as we have done for the northern part.

Proceeding southwards we find what seems to be a curious
scarcity of definite indications that there were, at this period,
any of the higher types of culture in the region between the
Pativilca Valley and the Chincha Valley. True, in all the
region designated there are huge pyramidal structures of
adobe, and also many other signs of intensive occupation of
the valleys, which may well date, at least in part, from this
period. True, also, in some of the valleys, notably in that of
Chancay and in that of the Rimac (Lima), there are types of
pottery which may or may not date wholly or in part from
the first six centuries A. D. Amidst all this uncertainty, however, one thing is quite certain: The earliest style of art represented by any considerable number of vestiges at Pachacamac, a few miles south of the Rimac Valley, is that of Tia-

huanaco. Only a few trifling wall-paintings of sea-creatures at the base of the great pyramid at Pachacamac even faintly resemble Early Chimu art, and they are so fragmentary that it would be rash to identify them as being Early Chimu.[48]

Only when we reach the Chincha Valley do we find the beginning of a new cultural area that does indubitably date, at least in part, from the first 600 years A. D. That area includes the Chincha, Pisco, Ica, and Nazca (or Rio Grande) Valleys. South of that, again, comes a stretch of coast which is but slightly known to archæology, and that is followed, in its turn, by the Tacna and Arica region which, as Dr. Uhle has shown, was in an archaic state of culture during the period now under consideration.[49] Indeed, it is possible to assert that archæological evidence—mostly given to us by Dr. Uhle— shows that only the Pisco, Ica and Nazca (or Rio Grande) Valleys were the seat of Early Nazca culture.[50]

As briefly as possible I shall now describe—from an objective point of view—the Early Nazca art found in the narrow region of the three valleys mentioned. In so doing I shall speak chiefly of Early Nazca art as a whole, only occasionally referring to specific sites, for no other course seems to me feasible under the circumstances.

As Early Chimu art was, in general, distinguished by the marked realism of its designs, by the subordination of color to line, and by the slow but sure interpenetration of formalism and even of conventionalization in such of the designs as may be said to be symbolical rather than representational, so also did Early Nazca art have its peculiarities and its characteristic tendencies. For one thing, realism, although seen to be strongly surviving in many Early Nazca specimens, is not there the dominant characteristic save in rare examples such as Figures 37–39; rather, it may safely be said to be a waning element in Early Nazca art as a whole. On the other hand, color will inevitably be regarded as the peculiar splendor of Early Nazca art. The vases and the textile stuffs of this culture glow with splashes of crimson, scarlet, pink, yellow, orange, green, various shades of blue, brown, and gray, and,

A   In the Gaffron Collection, Ethnological Museum, Munich.

B

C   In the Gaffron Private Collection, Schlachtensee-bei-Berlin.

FIG. 44.   Spotted cat designs from Early Nazca pots.
After Seler.

finally, black and white. Finally, stylistic dogmas which, in Early Chimu art, were struggling for control of the artists' imaginations, are here seen to be reigning in triumph, with the result that, in most of the specimens which display the symbolical creatures who make up as it were the *dramatis personæ* of Early Nazca art, there is but little left of the old freedom of concept and representation. That this loss of realism was not accompanied by any corresponding loss of beauty will become apparent when a number of examples of Early Nazca art shall have been studied.

The assertion made above, on page 48, that Early Chimu and Early Nazca art were closely connected and were to a large extent contemporary must now be tested. An important proof of its correctness appears in Figures 37 and 38, which show two Early Nazca portrait-pots fully as realistic in conception and in execution as any Early Chimu portrait-pots could be. Even their spouts are significant in the present connection, being almost midway between the stirrup handle-spout so characteristic of Early Chimu pottery and the double-spout-with-bridge which, as will appear from the illustrations to be described, was equally characteristic of Early Nazca pottery. The clothing, weapons, posture, and general aspect of the two figures resemble strongly the corresponding points in Early Chimu portraits; indeed, the one conspicuous difference lies in the matter of coloring, as study of the pictures here offered will reveal. These two specimens alone would serve to establish the close connection and the contemporaneity of the two cultures, but it is well to strengthen the argument by further examples. We have, for instance, portrait-pots like those in Figures 40, 41, 42 and 43, which display a progressive loss of realism coupled with a corresponding gain in formalism and in symbolism. Here, as in cases already cited, the chief contrast with the Early Chimu prototypes of these designs is in the matter of coloring, as one can tell even from non-colored reproductions.

It has already been said that even Early Chimu art, highly realistic though it was in general, did possess elements which

FIG. 45.   Cat-demon designs from Early Nazca pots.

A and *B* in Gaffron Private Collection. *After Seler.*
C, D, E—From "La Crónica," Lima, Peru, 10 January, 1916.

must be considered formalistic, if not conventional. Such will be found even in the most realistic portrait-vases where they are to be seen in the sitter's apparel or in the devices upon his shield.[51] Early Nazca art, in contrast with Early Chimu, is chiefly esoteric, symbolical, in short, an art built up around many fabulous personages whose identity, functions, and significance are now lost to us. True, realism, as already stated, does survive in the Early Nazca art; but it is there an intrusive note, not a dominant one. Yet, even in the conventionalized and symbolical elements of Early Nazca art there is a connection with the analogous portions of Early Chimu art.

An examination of the characteristics of certain leading personages of Early Nazca art will serve to bring this last statement into proper perspective. To the late Dr. Eduard Seler we owe the most complete general treatise on Early Nazca art.[52] Using his masterly study as a basis, I shall now present the most conspicuous of the Early Nazca personages.

The Spotted Cat, Bringer of the Means of Life, is shown in Figure 44, which makes it clear that there was at least an occasional faint trace of realism in this strange creature's portrayal, particularly in the tail and back. In calling it *Bringer of the Means of Life,* Dr. Seler was, of course, indulging in scholarly conjecture; but it certainly is true that very often *The Spotted Cat* is bringing in his paws things that look like seeds, leaves, or pods. Sometimes these things are shown attached to other parts of his person; sometimes they are altogether lacking in the design.[53]

The Cat-Demon appears in Figures 45 and 46, where he appears as a terrible being who is very likely to be brandishing a club or otherwise to present a bellicose aspect. Almost always he bears in his hands, or has somewhere about his person, one or more decapitated human heads, usually grasped by the hair of their heads. Sometimes, as in Figure 45, E, he is shown grasping a luckless human being who, in his turn, grasps by the hair a head that is obviously mummified. Indeed, a large proportion of the decapitated heads, with thorns passed through their lips, seem to be mummified.[54] In short, *The*

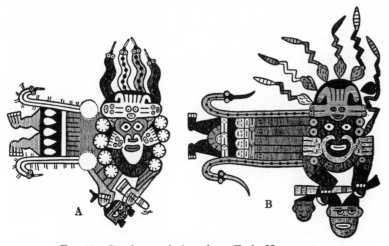

FIG. 46.   Cat-demon designs from Early Nazca pots.
A. In Gaffron Private Collection.
B. In Gaffron Collection, Ethnological Museum, Munich.
After Seler.

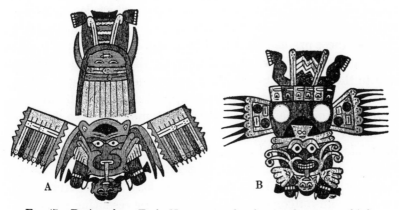

FIG. 47.   Designs from Early Nazca pots, showing cat-demon as a bird.
Originals in Gaffron Collection, Ethnological Museum, Munich.
After Seler.

Cat-Demon appears to have been, among other things, a war-god and a formidable deity in general.[55] Nor did the fact that he seems to have assumed various shapes make him any less redoubtable. In Figure 47 we see him either as a bird or as a man-masked-as-a-bird, but always with his characteristic aura of cruelty and rapine.[56]

The Bird-Demon is a creature whose personality is not always sharply differentiated from that of *The Cat-Demon-as-a-bird* but who, at any rate in his clearer portrayals, is obviously a bird, and not a man masquerading as one. *The Bird-Demon* is variously depicted in Figure 48.[57] In all of them it is evident that he is no less malevolent and rapacious than are others of the Early Nazca pantheon.

The Multiple-Headed God is, to us, even more incomprehensible and consequently more frightful than the demons or gods whom we have already considered. He is so, at least in part, because he is even further removed from any natural life form than are any of the others. As a rule, he is a spindly-legged fellow with mis-shapen hands and feet and with puny, weazened arms. In lieu of a proper head he has a cluster of faces, all of them highly conventionalized, which leer unpleasantly at one with lozenge-shaped eyes. These inscrutable countenances are usually edged by a number of curling, featherlike projections or rays, and they are linked to one another and to the central torso by their own projecting tongues or by their chins, headdresses or other appurtenances. All this becomes as comprehensible as it can be hoped to make it if one examines Figure 49 wherein two versions of the grotesque *Multiple-Headed God* are displayed.[58] It seems to me quite possible that this personage is a late development in Early Nazca art, perhaps of the late fifth or early sixth century, and that he is an outcome of the custom of representing sacrificed heads, these last being shown in *The Multiple-Headed God* figures, as hyperconventionalized secondary heads of the type already described.

The Centipede God is the last of the gods or demons whom we will mention here. Dr. Seler does not individually mention

A

B

C

FIG. 48. Bird-demon designs from Early Nazca pots.

A. In Sartorius Collection, Linden Museum, Stuttgart.
B. In Gaffron Collection, Ethnological Museum, Munich.
C. In Buck-Seler Collection, Ethnological Museum, Berlin.

After Seler.

him, including him, instead, with *The Cat-Demon* figures. But long ago I pointed out the characteristics of *The Centipede God,* and I have never seen the necessity of abandoning him to oblivion.[59] Good portrayals of him are shown in Figure 50.

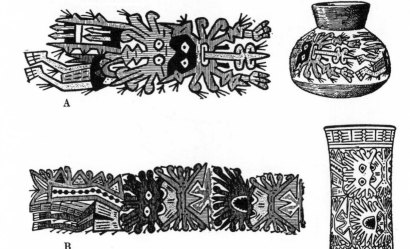

FIG. 49.   Multiple-headed god. Designs from Early Nazca pots.
A. In Zembsch Collection, Ethnological Museum, Berlin.
B. In Macedo Collection, Ethnological Museum, Berlin.
After Seler.

In seeking the ancestry and derivation of *The Centipede God,* we recall the centipede figures which occur on Early Chimu pots, as shown in Figures 14 and 20. They have the same general aspect, the same partially human form, and the same air of hostility to mankind as do the Early Nazca representations of *The Centipede God.* In all this we see one more testimonial to the close connection between Early Chimu and Early Nazca art and culture.[60]

Such are the chief personages of the Early Nazca pantheon, if we may call it so. In studying them as he goes along the reader will notice that all the creatures, as portrayed on ceramics and textiles, have certain highly distinctive attributes in common, attributes which are the most salient peculiarities

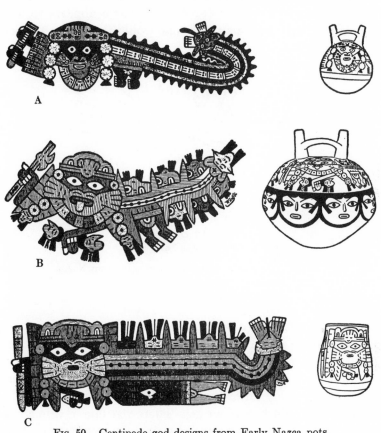

Fig. 50.   Centipede god designs from Early Nazca pots.
A. In Seler Collection.
B. In Macedo Collection, Ethnological Museum, Berlin.
C. In Buck-Seler Collection, Ethnological Museum, Berlin.

of Early Nazca art. It is well to speak of each of them briefly here.

The mouth-mask, a curious adornment which is to be seen in nearly all Early Nazca designs, consists, in its simplest form, of a number of whisker-like protuberances which stand out stiffly under the nose and on each side of it, after the fashion of a cat's bristles, and of a broad, flat band which hangs under the mouth and over the chin of the wearer. Sometimes, apparently, this queer and barbaric ornament was in one piece; sometimes in two or even three. The whole appears to have been supported—very painfully one would think—by the sep-

Fig. 51. Tri-partite mouth-mask of gold, from Nazca.
Original in Gaffron Collection, Schlachtensee.
After Lehmann and Doering.

tum of the nose, into which was thrust a pair of pin-like points. In the illustrations are seen a few of the numberless variations of the mouth-mask. We would, perhaps, be at a loss to understand this trinket and to jump at the conclusion that it was merely an artistic dogma, were it not that actual specimens of mouth-masks exist. There was one of thin sheet-copper with repoussé faces and designs in the collection of the late Dr. Prado, of Lima; there is one of thin sheet-gold, similarly embellished, in the collection of Señora Doña Hortensia Cáceres de Porras, also of Lima; and, finally, there is a very handsome mouth-mask of gold repoussé in three pieces in the private collection of Herr Gaffron at Schlachtensee-bei-Berlin. This last is shown in Figure 51. A point that has not, so far as I know, been made hitherto is this: The mouth-mask seems to have been the peculiar property of the dead and of the gods or demons. The specimens just cited all occurred with mummy-packs. Moreover, although mouth-ornaments similar to the semi-lunar lower part of the typical mouth-mask, sometimes occur in Early Chimu portrait-vases, nothing in the

FIG. 52.   Early Chimu vessel, showing conventionalized figure, perhaps a puma, with fangs, protruding tongue and spotted body.

Original in Gaffron Collection, Schlachtensee.

After Lehmann and Doering.

nature of a mouth-ornament or of a typical Early Nazca mouth-mask is to be seen, as a rule, in Early Nazca designs which represent realistically human beings, birds and so on. This bears out my assertion that the mouth-mask belonged to the dead and to the gods.

The protruding tongue or the protruding tongue-like ornament is a second characteristic feature of the non-realistic paintings and textile designs of this culture. Practically all the formal or conventionalized human or pseudo-human heads in Early Nazca art have either protruding tongues or else some object that comes forth from between the lips in such a way as to suggest a tongue. Sometimes the "tongue" does not issue from the lips but instead, starts just below them. What the symbolical meaning of this feature may have been we do not know; somewhere or other, I believe, the late Dr. Seler suggested that it was derived from the female puma's habit of lapping her young, but this seems a trifle far-fetched because, among other reasons, there are no young in the Early Nazca designs, and because there is no special indication that the figures with protruding tongues are females, still less female pumas. An Early Chimu design showing a puma with protruding tongue appears in Figure 52.

The headdress, always presenting the same general appearance in spite of innumerable variations in detail, occurs on nearly all the more formalized Early Nazca personages. Always the headdress is ornamented with secondary faces, human, feline, or nondescript.

Hands and feet with too-few digits are found in a large proportion of Early Nazca patterns; in the cases where hands and feet have the natural number of digits it will usually be found that realism in other respects is also present. Sometimes, but rarely we find a corollary to this abnormality in a too-great number of digits.

Ceremonial staffs or weapons are borne with great frequency by the various sorts of creatures shown in Early Nazca art. Not only the more realistic designs but also some of the most highly conventionalized possess, in this respect, a documentary value almost equal to that of some of the Early Chimu vase-paintings. The weapons shown in Early Nazca art are clubs of divers types, spears and spear-throwers much like those already mentioned as being characteristic of Early Chimu culture, and slings like those found by Dr. Hrdlička in various sites on the southerly borders of the Early Nazca cultural region.[61]

In the face, then, of such facts as the holding-over of realism—and particularly of the habit of portraiture—such facts also as the presence of the centipede element in both Early Nazca and Early Chimu art, how can anyone deny a close relationship between the two? The urgent question now is: Which came first?

Readers versed in the general laws that govern the evolution of art the world over will be surprised that this question need be put. Yet, because numerous writers have claimed that Early Nazca art represents an older cultural phase than Early Chimu, it needs must. To me it is obvious that Early Chimu art is fresh and youthful and that Early Nazca art, growing out of it, is more cynical and more mature, especially in its more formalized phases. *The Cat-Demon, The Centipede God* and, most of all, *The Multiple-Headed God,* are, progressively, more and more nearly devoid of natural characteristics suggestive of contact with the real world; they can only be the product of priestcraft, of a religion whose mainspring was terror, of grossly cruel superstition; and from all such things, at any rate in their initial phases, the Early Chimu folk were largely free.

The creeping in of the new forces here hinted at, forces that tended to draw men's minds away from naturalism and to lead them into the perchance sinister realm of dogma and conventionalism, did not, as I have said before, entail a loss of beauty or of vigor in the artistic productions of the day. Indeed, we have to thank the Early Nazca culture for what are, perhaps, the two most noteworthy textiles in the whole range of ancient American art.

One is the superb featherwork-shirt shown in the Frontispiece. It bears a version of *The Cat-Demon* that is different from the usual portrayals of that personage, not only because of the exigencies of the medium but also because of the lighter than usual tonality of the design. The ground is of rich yellow having at the bottom margin a geometrical arrangement of alternating yellow and pink. The central horizontal band of four panels is enclosed between parallel lines of black, and in the four panels we find light blue, dark blue, yellow, buff, light green, pale pink, and black, a truly amazing symphony of colors. Indeed, we see in this gorgeous mosaic of feathers an admirable example of the completeness with which the Early Nazca designers had learned two laws of composition, *e. g.,* that normally discordant tints cease to be inharmonious if they are separated by a black line; and that hues which are not inimical do not need thus to be separated. This masterpiece of polychromatic harmony in featherwork vividly illustrates these two principles of design.*

The other super-specimen to which I refer above is the now celebrated fabric known as the Paracas Textile. It is a piece of cotton cloth, loosely woven, having a painted conventional design, and bordered by an astonishing series of about ninety human and animal figures wrought in closely knitted vicuña wool of the finest quality and each one designed in accordance with the dictates of Early Nazca artistic tradition. In spite of the difficulties arising from the technique of the border there is a great degree of realism in many parts of the border, as shown in Figures 53 and 54 and, side by side with it, an equal degree of conventionalization.[62]†

A word or two must be said about the provenance and the age of the Paracas Textile. The burial in which it was found was that of a small old man, mummified and in the drawn-up or fœtal position common in ancient Peruvian interments. The mummy-pack was encased in a basket of woven straw and was wrapped in a white cerement cloth measuring some thirty-seven feet in length by over a yard in width. Inside of that came a dark-blue blanket—to use Mme. Levillier's term —beautifully embroidered in many colors, then came a number of other fabrics which had all rotted away, and, finally, next to the corpse, there was the exquisite Paracas Textile itself.[63] The body was evidently that of a person of very high degree, but whether a priest or a king who can say? His skull had been profusely adorned with embroidered fillets and with golden ornaments which, however, at some time previous to the final disinterment of the mummy, had been torn off and carried away, the head being dislocated in the process, the skull and the corpse being afterwards hastily re-buried.[63] With

*The owner of this splendid featherwork-shirt is Herman A. Elsberg, Esq., of New York City, to whose generous kindness I am deeply indebted, because he has given me the color-plate which serves as the Frontispiece of this volume.
†The owner of the Paracas Textile is Don Rafael Larco-Herrera, of the Hacienda Chiclín, Chicama Valley, Trujillo, Peru.

Figs. 53-54. Portions of the Paracas Textile, taken from the water-color drawings made by Srta. Elena Izcue and first published by Mme. Levillier, 1928.

Fig. 55.   Examples of Tiahuanaco I sculpture. *After Posnansky.*

Fig. 56.   Three pieces of crude pottery probably representing the Tiahuanaco I period and style. The originals belong to Colonel Don Federigo Diez de Medina, of La Paz, by whose courtesy these photographs have been allowed to appear here.

the mummy were the bodies of three very young children and of two older ones, and also many ears of maize and bags of coca-leaves. The depth at which the body was found was between six and seven metres. The fashion of the man's head-dress was similar to that so frequently seen in Early Nazca polychrome vase-paintings.[64] Indeed, the whole aspect of the Paracas Textile itself and of the circumstances of the burial is eloquent of identity with the Early Nazca culture. Yet Dr. Tello and Mme. Levillier ascribe a pre-Nazca age to the Paracas cemetery and its contents.[65] The chronological discrepancy is not so great, however, as one might think, for Dr. Tello uses the term "Nazca" to designate the period just prior to the Incaic, namely, our Late Nazca period.[66] It follows from this that Dr. Uhle's Proto-Nazca and our Early Nazca period came much earlier, indeed, at about the date that Dr. Tello ascribes to them.

If one regards the Paracas Textile merely as a document, he may justly say that it is a synthetic description of the daily and ceremonial life that went on in Early Nazca times. The intricate border shows us the elaborate costumes then worn, the weapons used, the llama haltered and laden with ears of maize, the cultivated plants, the puma, *The Centipede God* and very many other figures whose significance can only be guessed at to-day.

The presence, already noted, of both realism and formalism, the presence, too, of both coastal and highland elements, not only in the design (cotton-plants and the llama, respectively, for instance), but also in the materials of the specimen (cotton in the centre and wool on the border), lead me to date it —at any rate tentatively—as being close to 500 A. D., a time when coastal and highland cultures were beginning to come into stimulating contact with one another.

In short, we have ample evidence, archæologically acquired in recent years, and largely through the instrumentality of Drs. Max Uhle and Julio Tello, that the southern part of the coast, no less than the northern, was the seat of a remarkable and well-advanced culture which flourished during the first six centuries A. D. Future field-work will, it is to be hoped, supplement the knowledge that we have already gained with new details, but even now the broad outlines of the matter are clear.

4. Highland Culture During the First Six Centuries A. D. as Revealed by Archæology: The Tiahuanaco I Culture

Earlier in this chapter we noted that certain Chroniclers of Peru—including Fathers Montesinos, Lizárraga, and las Casas—speak very distinctly concerning early contact between the coast folk and the highlanders, contact—according to them—that was chiefly of a warlike nature. In so doing, they mention certain specific localities as being places where defensive works were erected. In support of this, archæology shows us a series of ancient edifices and other remains that may well be studied in this connection.

Father Montesinos, for example, speaks of Huáitara—which is in the highest part of the Pisco Valley and therefore adjacent to if not truly included in the region of Early Nazca culture—as being a point of martial contact between the coast-landers and the highlanders at an early period.[67] It is well known that there are many ruins, not only in the village of Huáitara itself but also throughout the district of that name and, in general, in all parts of the Province of Castrovirreina wherein Huáitara lies. So far as I know none of these ruins has ever been studied by trained archæologists. It is usually assumed that they are Incaic, and so they may be, in part; but it is entirely possible that other parts of the structures in question are far older than the Incas.[68] In like manner, Father Montesinos mentions Quínoa, some fifteen miles north of Huamanga (now Ayacucho), as possessing some remains of very ancient buildings, and in this case, too, it is well known that important vestiges of the past are awaiting the advent of scientific archæologists.[69] Again, there are the ruins at Viñaque, also near Huamanga, which Cieza de León visited and, very unsatisfactorily, described.[70]

In fact, until archæological investigations have been made

at a whole series of sites which are strung out along the Cordilleras, which series includes, as Don Marcos Jiménez de la Espada pointed out thirty-eight years ago, Cuélap (in Chachapoyas), Huamachuco, Huánuco el Viejo, Chavín de Huántar, Vilcashuamán, and the whole northern half of the Titicaca Basin to at least as far south as La Paz,[71] we shall know but little concerning the cultural history of the mountain folk and their contact with the coastlanders of the Early Chimu and Early Nazca period. True, we already have faint glimpses of the archæological significance of some of these sites: In 1893 Dr. Bandelier made a hasty and not very conclusive reconnaissance of the Chachapoyas region wherein stands the great fortress of Cuélap;[72] Huamachuco is briefly mentioned by Cieza, but chiefly in connection with the Inca's conquest of that province; ruins, notably at Marca Huamachuco, two leagues northwest of the Spanish town of Huamachuco, and at Viracocha-Pampa a short league north of the town, there are extensive ruins which may be in part very ancient;[73] Huánuco el Viejo has been superficially described by Squier and, more recently, by Mr. C. R. Enock.[74] Of Chavín de Huántar and of the good archæological work done there in recent years by Dr. J. C. Tello, I shall speak later. Regarding Vilcashuamán I will speak very briefly here.

Vilcashuamán, sometimes called Vilcas, is mentioned at some length by Captain Pedro de Cieza de León who visited it within twenty years of the Spanish conquest.[75] He, however, ascribes almost all of the edifices there to the Incas. This is in direct opposition to what Father Lizárraga has to say on the subject; for he, as was indicated on page 67, specifically links the structures at Vilcashuamán with the Early Chimu kings. The only modern description of Vilcashuamán known to me is that of the French traveller, Charles Wiener,[76] who gives plans and drawings of the ancient buildings there, some of which are reproduced in Figures 57 and 58. From the material provided by him it is possible to see that a large proportion of the structures is indeed in the Incaic style of architecture, but one edifice, a rectangular pyramid with three terraces

and a steep stone stairway up one side, is certainly pre-Incaic.
Save that it is built of stone and not of adobe it closely resembles the pyramids so common on the coast. It is, in short,

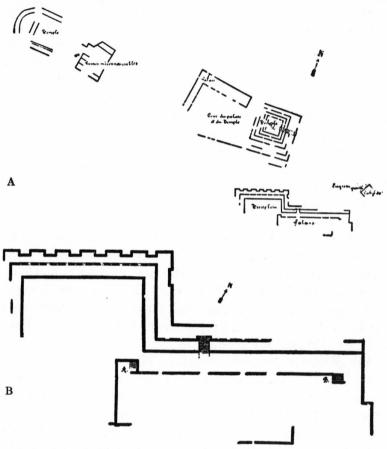

Fig. 57. *A*. General plan of the ruins at Vilcashuamán. *B*. Detailed plan of
the Pyramid Temple.

After Wiener.

as different as could well be from the neighboring Incaic constructions, and from Incaic architecture in general.

As things now stand the most important task awaiting the
field archæologist in the Andean area is a careful survey of
the various sites mentioned above, and of countless others

scattered all up and down the highland zone. True, good work has already been done in Ecuador and in Argentina, as will be shown in the next chapter; but, save for Chavín de Huántar,

Fig. 58. The Pyramid Temple at Vilcashuamán.
After Wiener.

also to be discussed later, practically nothing of the necessary sort has been done, in the highlands of Peru. At Machu Picchu, the site which has received the most sustained, intelligent, and intensive attention from archæological science in recent times, almost nothing ante-dating the Incas was found, a point to which I shall revert further on.

On the other hand, at the justly renowned ruins of Tiahuanaco, near the southern end of Lake Titicaca and on Bolivian soil, archæological work has been carried on in a fitful way by sundry investigators, among them Herr Arthur Posnansky to whom, in spite of the fantastic quality of some of his ideas, we owe a great debt because of his having shown quite clearly that there were *two* successive and easily distinguishable cultural periods at that site. For the sake of convenience I call them, respectively, Tiahuanaco I and Tiahuanaco II. The masonry of the earlier period, as Herr Posnansky has pointed out, is cruder and more roughly finished than that of the later, and its material is soft, reddish-brown sandstone readily obtainable in the neighborhood, whereas, on the contrary, the hard volcanic andesitic stone used for the later constructions had to be brought from considerable distances.[77] The building which most thoroughly represents the Tiahuanaco I period at the name-site itself is a rectangular enclosure measuring approximately 98 feet by 98. It is marked 9 on Herr Posnansky's admirable plan of the ruins, reproduced on page 125. Also, the huge artificial mound known as Acapana, which is about 680 feet long and almost as wide, is in part of this same style and period. Distinguishing points about Tiahuanaco I masonry include, besides the matter of its material, the following: Large stones, rather roughly finished and measuring six feet or more in height, were set up at short intervals, and between them smaller stones were laid in mud, some of which were nicely finished and others hardly worked at all,[77] as shown in Figure 35.

In short, it was a type of architecture such as one might expect to find among a people who, living in a region where easily worked stone was at hand, were gradually passing through the archaic culture's successive stages and preparing unconsciously to pass beyond it. The sculptures of this period, shown in Figure 55, are likewise patently archaic in style, the work of artists who had by no means won mastery over their tools and over their materials, although even within the scope of the Tiahuanaco I culture, a study of the various stone carvings shows a perceptible progress. In pottery, likewise, of which a few examples appear in Figure 56, there is a contrast between extremely coarse incised vessels and almost equally coarse, but painted, vessels.[78]

To sum up I may say that our present very incomplete knowledge of highland Andean archæology seems to indicate that, during the first six centuries of our Era, at a time when high cultures were flourishing along the coast, the mountain folk were slowly and laboriously working up through the stages of the archaic culture and were approaching the point where, as a result of stimulus from outside, they would be able to produce a really finished art, expressive of a well-developed culture.

NOTES TO CHAPTER III

1 The material presented thus far in this chapter is derived from the *Miscelánea Antártica* of Father Miguel Cabello de Balboa, Part III, Ch. xvii, pp. 507–516 of the unpublished Manuscript, preserved in the New York Public Library. As the two existent printed editions of this great Chronicle are very unsatisfactory and incomplete, all citations of the work of Father Cabello will be to the N. Y. P. L. MS. The long quotation given here comes from pages 510–516. Truncated versions of the Lambayeque tale will be found in Markham, 1910, pp. 222–223; and Joyce, 1912, pp. 50–52. (This author seems to think that Lambayeque is in Ecuador, for he inserts the story of Naymlap in his chapter on that country.) Beuchat, 1912, pp. 584–585, also refers to it.

2 Cieza, Pt. I, Ch. xlvii. Xerez, 1872, pp. 32–33. Anonymous, Conquest of Peru, 1929, pp. 27–29. These narratives were all written soon after the Spanish conquest.

3 Middendorf, 1894–1895, II, p. 282, identifies the Faquisllanga with the Facalá; but I am not perfectly certain whether the Lambayeque is or is not the same as the Facalá.

4 There is a slight error of fact here. The city of Trujillo is an entirely Spanish foundation, dating from the establishment of the place by Marquis Pizarro in 1534. It was a walled town, oval in outline, and it stood amid fertile lands dotted with innumerable vestiges of early civilization. See: Feyjoo de Sosa, 1763; Holstein, 1927, for admirable data on this region.

5 The nucleus of the Chimu kingdom occupied the lower reaches of four neighboring valleys, viz., Chicama, Moche or Valley of the Chimu (in which the ancient city of Chan Chan stood), Viru, and Chao.

6 The dimensions given by Father Calancha in his definition of the valley of Pacasmayo (otherwise called San Pedro, Guadalupe, Jequetepeque) are approximately correct. The town which he calls Lloco is San Pedro de Lloc. Chungala (or Changala) and San Gregorio lie some twelve or thirteen leagues inland and within the border of the Department of Cajamarca. For all practical purposes a league—the distance-measure employed by all the Chroniclers—may be reckoned as three miles.

7 Correct in the main.

8 With regard to sea-life, see Chapter I.

9 It is quite true that there *are* such hills as those mentioned, but I do not

know what their archæological content may be. On the map of the Department of la Libertad in Paz-Soldán, 1865, there is a point marked Talambo which is near the right bank of the river and at the southern end of a range of hills. At the northern end of the range, or rather a league west from the northern end, is a point marked "Ruinas." Either of these may be the site of Pacatnamu's palace.

[10] In other words, there was a state of affairs similar to that described above in connection with the archaic phase of culture. In fact, it was the archaic phase that these people were passing through at this early time.

[11] Otherwise Parmunca or Paramunca. Descriptions of it appear in Cieza, Pt. I, Ch. lxx; Proctor, 1825, p. 175; Squier, 1877, pp. 101–102; Larrabure y Unánue, 1893, pp. 279–280; and Beuchat, 1912, pp. 643–644. A magnificent picture of it, taken from the air, by Major Otto Holstein appears in Fig. 32.

[12] This passage relative to the languages of the northerly part of coastal Peru is extremely important. Some day a qualified student will, let us hope, make an intensive study of the matter. The chief works now existing that bear upon it are: Carrera, 1644 and 1880; and Middendorf, 1890–1892. The first edition of Carrera's grammar is of supreme rarity, and the re-issue of it, edited by the late Dr. González de la Rosa, is rare also. The Sec language was studied in 1863 by the late Richard Spruce, who collected a vocabulary of 37 words, none of which resemble equivalent words in other idioms. I found Sec faintly surviving in the vicinity of Sechura, Department of Piura, in 1918. Olmos, near the northern side of the Department of Lambayeque, still has a dialect of its own, albeit most of the people habitually speak Spanish. Muchic, however, the language studied by Bishop Carrera and by Middendorf, is generally held to be the most important of the tongues spoken in that part of Peru.

[13] Peru still reeks with tales of lost treasure and of treasure unearthed by fortunate searchers. In the stories there is, as a rule, a large basis of fact, and because of the yarns of successful treasure-hunting, some of the most important archæological sites have been unsystematically dug into and thereby ruined by eager persons intent on sudden wealth.

[14] Mention of the wars between the Chimu's subjects and the Inca will be found in Chapter VII. Father Calancha speaks of it interestingly and at some length, but as this material is not pertinent to the present chapter, I omit it here.

[15] It is not clear whether Father Calancha, in speaking of the Iunga, or Yunga, language means Mochica or whether he means Quingnam.

[16] Jijón y Caamaño, 1919, pp. 402–403, says that this word is Muchic or Mochica and that it comes from *Aiplen,* meaning Creator, and *Pong,* meaning stone.

[17] The Pleiades. Concerning this group of stars one may read, on p. 73, Vol. XVIII of the Encyclopædia Britannica, 14th edition, as follows: "The spring rising and early winter setting of the Pleiades . . . are important dates for the farmer. . . . This group is physically connected, being distinguished from the background stars by community of proper motion." It is, therefore, quite conceivable that time should be counted on a basis of the movement of the Pleiades or *Fur.*

[18] The general term for medical-man in Quechua is *hampi-camayoc,* which

means remedy-keeper. See González Holguín, 1607, p. 138. See also Chapter VIII.

[19] Quipucamayocs, 1892 and 1920.

[20] Quipucamayocs, 1920, pp. 15 and 16.

[21] Casas, 1892. Román y Zamora, 1595. Accounts of these two writers and their works will be found in Means, 1928, pp. 334–342 and 442–452.

[22] Casas, 1892, pp. 106–107.

[23] Casas, 1892, pp. 107–108.

[24] Casas, 1892, pp. 108–111. I do not find this term, however, in the dictionary of the Royal Spanish Academy, and I am not sure what it means.

[25] Román y Zamora, 1595, Vol. III, folios 162, verso, to 163, verso.

[26] Lizárraga, 1909, pp. 495–496.

[27] These points are fully discussed in Markham, 1910, pp. 12–14 and 303–305, and also in the introductions to Montesinos, 1920, by Sir Clements Markham and P. A. Means. See also, for data on the relations between the writings of Valera and those of Montesinos, Means, 1928, pp. 402–411 and 497–507.

[28] Montesinos, 1920, Ch. ix.

[29] Montesinos, 1920, Ch. ix, p. 41. The walls of the ancient fortress of Huáitara are now incorporated with those of the parish church. (Almanaque of la Crónica, Lima, 1918, art. Huáitara.)

[30] Montesinos, 1920, Ch. xvii, p. 75.

[31] Cobo, Bk. XII, Ch. i.

[32] Hrdlička, 1911, pp. 10–11.

[33] A good grasp on the meaning of this resemblance can best be got by studying the types of Central American pottery shown by Holmes, 1888; MacCurdy, 1911; Lothrop, 1926b; Linné, 1929; and then comparing the two dishes found in the Chicama Valley by Hrdlička.

[34] Lothrop, 1926b, Vol. II, p. 406. We thus have the foremost of Peruvian archæologists in agreement with a leading authority on Central American archæology. Dr. Tello has already been mentioned, in Chapter I.

[35] Dr. Uhle, on whose labors are based all acceptable chronologies of ancient Peruvian cultures, uses the terms Proto-Chimu and Proto-Nazca. But, since 1918, I have found the terms Early Chimu and Early Nazca to be more satisfactory because they are early phases of one civilization rather than separate civilizations in themselves. But compare: Uhle, 1910; 1912; 1913; and Means, 1918j.

[36] This specimen, now in the British Museum, will be found described in Joyce, 1922.

[37] Totten, 1926.

[38] Carrión Cachot, 1923. Schmidt, 1929, p. 149, shows a very touching modelled nativity scene in which the mother, the mid-wife, and the mid-wife's assistant are all shown with graphic fidelity, as is also the face of the Little Stranger itself.

[39] García y Merino, 1894. Uhle, 1907b. Nordenskiöld, 1921, pp. 71–108. Mason, 1928, studies examples of spear-throwers from several parts of America, i. e., the Eskimo region, our own southwest, Florida, and Mexico, as well as from Peru.

[40] Holmes, 1887; 1888. Baessler, 1906. MacCurdy, 1911. Beuchat, 1912, pp. 683–688.

[41] Kroeber, 1925, pp. 224–228. Dr. R. L. Olson, of the American Museum of Natural History, has also been doing archæological work in Peru, but none of his results have been published to date (October, 1930).

[42] Kroeber, 1925, pp. 228–229.

[43] Means, 1919b. Uhle, 1920.

[44] Squier, 1877, Chs. vii, viii, and ix. Holstein, 1927.

[45] Holstein, 1927, Figs. 31 and 32.

[46] Murphy, 1923b.

[47] Markham, 1910, p. 211.

[48] Uhle, 1903, pp. 19–21.

[49] Uhle, 1917b; 1919; 1919b.

[50] Kroeber and Strong, 1924 and 1924b.

[51] Means, 1917c, pp. 339–369.

[52] Seler, 1923b.

[53] Seler, 1923b, pp. 174–183.

[54] Tello, 1918.

[55] Seler, 1923b, pp. 183–210.

[56] Seler, 1923b, pp. 211–225.

[57] Seler, 1923b, pp. 225–238.

[58] Seler, 1923b, pp. 267–284.

[59] Means, 1917c, pp. 344–345.

[60] Uhle, 1906d, pp. 583–585, illustrations. Cobo, Bk. IX, Ch. xiv, speaks in a general way of the deadliness of centipedes.

[61] Means, 1919d.

[62] Mme. Levillier, 1928.

[63] Mme. Levillier, 1928, p. 18.

[64] Mme. Levillier, 1928, p. 19.

[65] Mme. Levillier, 1928, pp. 11 and 16. Tello, 1928; 1929, pp. 117–149.

[66] Tello, 1929, p. 25.

[67] Montesinos, 1920, Chs. iii, vi, and ix.

[68] Raimondi, 1874–1913, II, p. 92. Almanaque de la Crónica, 1918, pp. 108–109 and 192–193.

[69] Montesinos, 1920, Ch. ix. Almanaque de la Crónica, 1918, pp. 390–391.

[70] Cieza de León, Pt. I, Ch. lxxxvii.

[71] On this point see the interesting note by Don Marcos Jiménez de la Espada in Vol. III, pp. 111–112 of his edition of Cobo.

[72] Bandelier, 1907.

[73] Cieza de León, Pt. I, Ch. lxxxi. Raimondi, 1874–1913, II, pp. 30 and 53. Almanaque de la Crónica, 1918, pp. 194–195.

[74] Squier, 1877, pp. 216–217. Enock, 1907, Ch. xxii.

[75] Cieza de León, Pt. I, Ch. lxxxix, and Pt. II, Ch. xlviii. Also see brief report made in 1586 by Don Pedro de Carabajal and printed in *Relaciones geográficas de Indias*, I, pp. 146–147.

[76] Wiener, 1880, pp. 264–270.

[77] Posnansky, 1914, Ch. vii.

[78] Stuebel and Uhle, 1892. Créqui-Montfort, 1906. González de la Rosa, 1910. Nestler, 1910 and 1913.

CHAPTER IV

THE TIAHUANACO II CULTURE, ITS CHARACTER AND ITS INFLUENCE

FATHER MONTESINOS leads us to believe that, between the sixth and the tenth centuries of our Era there flourished in the highlands of Peru a noteworthy civilization, based upon agriculture, possessed of a rather high type of religion, and filled with martial vigor. It is true that the "kings" whom he mentions in connection with that civilization and period ruled from Cuzco, as indeed may have been the truth—in part—of the matter. Nevertheless, Cuzco cannot have been the metropolis of the mountains at this time, for, with the exception of such vestiges as the northern walls of the fortress of Sacsahuamán and as certain structures still to be seen at Ollantaytambo, archæology can show almost nothing, at any rate so far, that can be safely ascribed to the period in question, or to an earlier period. There is little doubt in my mind that the northern walls of Sacsahuamán, shown in Figures 59 and 60 and the wall to which I refer at Ollantaytambo, shown in Figure 61, represent the Tiahuanaco I culture which was spoken of in Chapter III.

Tiahuanaco, perhaps the most important archæological site in South America, is clearly the metropolis of the mountains so far as the period here under consideration is concerned. It lies in a wide, flat-bottomed valley that drains into the southernmost part of Lake Titicaca. The site had been occupied by a people sufficiently advanced culturally to know how to hew stone and to lay out huge buildings of a crude sort, a people who lived and wrought in that locality during the Tiahuanaco I period mentioned in the previous chapter. They were a people who, on their own initiative, had been able to make decided progress and who were in need only of directional stimulus from outside that would push their progress

117

still further, enabling it to attain to civilization of no mean worth in some respects.

The present indications are that it was the Early Nazca culture which met with and reacted upon the Tiahuanaco I culture, thereby engendering the Tiahuanaco II culture. It is true that the great stretch of country between the seat of the Early Nazca culture and that of the Tiahuanaco I and II cultures is anything but propitious to intercourse between their respective inhabitants, but still, given motives sufficiently strong, barriers of space and time such as those present in this case are wont to be overcome by peoples advancing culturally along parallel lines. It is probable that trade, not to mention its accompaniment, war, was a channel of contact between the peoples in the two regions. The coast lacked certain commodities, wool, good building-stone, timber, copper, silver, gold, and coca, commodities which could only be obtained as a result of contact with the highland folk who either possessed themselves these valued articles or else were adjacent to the forest-folk who did possess them. The highlanders, on their part, lacked certain things which could be obtained on the coast, cotton, many sorts of vegetable-foods, sea-foods and fruits, and, perhaps most important of all, æsthetic ideas. An interchange of coastland cotton for highland wool would alone produce an important degree of contact between the two regions, and the fact that both materials are found in both regions from a very early period shows that trade of the barter type did indeed exist.[1]

At this time, roughly between 500 and 600 A. D., the art of the Early Nazca culture was in a highly conventionalized stage, with much tradition and dogma imbedded in its æsthetic concepts, and having certain tenets as to color and representation of living models that could not fail to be preserved if it were to influence a less developed art and to impress upon it a new individuality. Tiahuanaco II art, as we shall see, is exactly what one would expect an art to be which was derived from Tiahuanaco I developed by stimulating contact with Early Nazca and, to a less extent perhaps, with Early Chimu.[1a]

FIG. 59. A detail of the northern walls of Sacsahuamán, close to Cuzco.
Photograph by Max Vargas, Arequipa.

FIG. 60. A detail of the lowermost of the three northern walls of the Fortress of Sacsahuamán. The large stone on the right weighs about 150 tons.
Photograph by courtesy of W. V. Alford, Esq.

FIG. 61. Remains of three terraces in the older part of the Fortress of Ollantaytambo.
Photograph by L. D. Gismondi, La Paz.

FIG. 62. Incaic terraces at Ollantaytambo. In extreme upper right-hand corner is seen one end of the older terrace of large blocks shown in FIG. 61.
Photograph by courtesy of W. V. Alford, Esq.

Before going on to an examination of Tiahuanaco II art, however, it is necessary to speak briefly concerning Tiahuanaco as a site, as a centre of civilization. It is a locality which has long occupied the attention of travellers, and a few of the early accounts of the place, left to us by the Chroniclers of Peru, are worth noticing.

That Tiahuanaco, more anciently known as Taypicala,[2] is of pre-Incaic date, and that it is associated with the worship of a Creator-God whose name is best spelled Viracocha— although it appears in literature under many forms—is a two-fold fact to which several Chroniclers testify, with varying degrees of precision. Father Acosta, for example, says: ". . . and they (the Indians) report that out of the great Lake Titicaca came one Viracocha, which staied in Tiahuanaco, where at this day there is to bee seene the ruines of ancient and very strange buildings, and from thence came to Cuzco. . . ."[3] Others, notably Betánzos, Calancha, Cieza, Cobo, and Sarmiento, link pre-Incaic Tiahuanaco with Viracocha-worship in a quite definite manner.[4]

Of the early accounts of the ruins at Tiahuanaco three stand out with special prominence and so merit quotation. Captain Pedro de Cieza de León, who was there during some part of the decade from 1540 to 1550,[5] speaks thus of the vestiges of the past to be seen at this place: "Tiahuanaco is not a very large village, but it is celebrated for the great edifices near it, which are certainly things worth seeing. Near the buildings there is a hill made by the hands of men, on great foundations of stone. . . ." This is the mound now known as Acapana or Akapana, which, as we have said, is partly of the Tiahuanaco I period. Cieza continues: "Beyond this hill there are two stone idols, of the human shape and figure, the features very skilfully carved, so that they appear to have been done by the hand of some great master. They are so large that they seem like small giants, and it is clear that they have on a sort of clothing different from that now worn by the natives of these parts. They seem to have some ornament on their heads. Near these stone statues there is another building. Their antiquity and the want of letters are the causes why it is not known who built such vast foundations, and how much time has since elapsed; for at present there is only a wall very well built, and which must have been standing for many ages. Some of the stones are much worn. At this part there are stones of such enormous size that it causes wonder to think of them, and to reflect how human force can have sufficed to move them to the place where we now see them, being so large. Many of these stones are carved in different ways, some of them having the shape of the human body, which must have been their idols. Near the wall there are many holes and hollow places in the ground. In another place, more to the westward, there are other ancient remains, among them many doorways with their jambs, lintels, and thresholds, all of one stone. But what I noted most particularly, when I wandered about over these ruins writing down what I saw, was that from these great doorways there came out other still larger stones upon which the doorways were formed, some of them thirty feet broad, fifteen or more long, and six inches in thickness. The whole of this, with the doorway and its jambs and lintel, was all one single stone. The work is one of grandeur and magnificence when well considered. For myself I fail to understand with what instruments or tools it can have been done; for it is very certain that before these great stones could be brought to perfection and left as we see them, the tools must have been much better than those now used by the Indians."[6]

In concluding his account of the ruins, Cieza de León tells us that the edifices at Tiahuanaco were never completed; that even in his day they were held to be more ancient than the Incas, who imitated their masonry in building the city of Cuzco and even thought of making Tiahuanaco their capital. He was told that a race different from the Incas built Tiahuanaco long, long ago, and also the edifice at Viñaque (Huiñac) which is mentioned in the previous chapter.[7]

The Inca Garcilaso de la Vega, although he tends very strongly to ascribe all native culture in Peru to the Incas, his kinsmen, does us a good service in this connection by quoting in full an account of Tiahuanaco given him by his old friend and foster-brother, Father Diego de Alcobasa, which runs thus:

In Tiahuanaco, in the province of Collao, amongst other things, there are some ancient ruins worthy of immortal memory. They are near the lake called by the Spaniards Chucuito, the proper name of which is Chuquivitu.[8] Here there are some very grand edifices, and amongst them there is a square court, fifteen *brazas*[9] each way, with walls two stories high. On one side of this court there is a hall forty-five feet long by twenty-two broad, apparently once covered, in the same way as those buildings you have seen in the house of the sun at Cuzco, with a roof of straw. The walls, roofs, floor, and doorways are all of one single piece, carved out of a rock, and the walls of the court and of the hall are three-quarters of a yard in breadth. The roof of the hall, though it appears to be thatch, is really of stone. For as the Indians cover their houses with thatch, in order that this might appear like the rest, they have combed and carved the stone so that it resembles a roof of thatch. The waters of the lake wash the walls of the court. The natives say that this and the other buildings were dedicated to the Creator of the universe. There are also many other stones carved into the shape of men and women so naturally that they appear to be alive, some drinking with cups in their hands, others sitting, others standing, and others walking in the stream which flows by the walls. There are also statues of women with their infants in their laps, others with them on their backs, and in a thousand other postures. . . .[10]

This account is given here in full for a particular reason, viz., because it is not wholly consonant with the truth as shown to us by archæology, yet is sufficiently so to give some specious support to the erroneous contention that Tiahuanaco was at one period a port. First of all, in considering what Father Alcobasa has to say, we must take with a good deal of skepticism his remarks about the large monolithic chamber with a stone roof sculptured to resemble thatch. Much though one would like to give credence to this priestly yarn, he really cannot do so, for the thing is inherently unbelievable. In the second place, Father Alcobasa is mistaken—if not deliberately mendacious—in asserting that there are statues of women with children at Tiahuanaco, for all the sculptures now visible there are of men, or, perchance, of gods. Finally, the statement that the Lake once flowed to the city of Tiahuanaco is unconsciously contradicted by the good Father himself when he speaks of statues of people walking in *the stream which flows by the walls*. That Lake Titicaca ever laved the walls is, on many accounts, including topographical and archæological grounds, incredible; but one can readily believe that the small stream which flows northwardly through the Tiahuanaco Valley was once brought, in artificial channels, to the city. It is far more likely, however, that the inhabitants of Tiahuanaco were in need of leading water away from their city rather than to it, for the locality is very damp, and the channels that remain in that vicinity were in all likelihood drainage canals.[11] Moreover, the level of Lake Titicaca above the sea is 3,854 metres, and that of old Tiahuanaco is 3,897 metres, this according to the best map of which I know, the map made by J. B. Pentland, utilised, with additions, by Stuebel and Uhle.[12] Inasmuch as the Lake's *sole* outlet, the Desaguadero (literally, Drain) River, leaves the Lake through a wide gap in the Quimsachata range and flows very slowly at a scarcely perceptible gradient for miles through a wide valley, it is evident that no material increase in the volume of lake water could possibly have existed within the period during which man has existed, for the configuration of the drainage is such as to prevent any great rise in the lake-water's level.[13]

With the account of Tiaguanaco (as he calls it) given by Father Cobo we enter upon rather firmer ground. But even here we tend to be tangled in terminology because he misapplies certain names, confounding Puma-Puncu—the Gate of the Puma—with Acapana. It is well to pause here long enough to clear up this question of names at Tiahuanaco once and for all.

As the late Don Manuel González de la Rosa has pointed out,[14] there is probably far more of Tiahuanaco below the soil than there is above it. The whole significance of the site will not be shown until an exhaustive and systematic excavation of the whole area in which the ruins occur shall have been undertaken and fully carried out. Meanwhile, we can only say, as does Mr. Ogilvie,[15] that an area of several square miles is crowded with vestiges of the ancient city, vestiges that are patiently awaiting exploration and excavation of the sort which I have mentioned. It is already apparent that the area in question contains distinct parts and sub-parts, as follows:

1. Tiahuanaco proper, carefully surveyed by Herr Posnansky in 1904 and again in 1912, his map being partially reproduced in Figure 63. This area is an oblong bounded by a ditch, and it measures approximately 1,000 metres from east to west by 450 metres from north to south, or, in English measurements, about 3,280 feet by 1,470 feet. This considerable extent of ground is crossed on the north by the highway from Guaqui to La Paz and on the south by the railway between those points. Remains, ranging from single worked stones to whole buildings of great size, but now much ruined, are scattered over the area, the two most important being:

A. The natural mound called Ak-kapana, Akapana, or Acapana (which spelling, for simplicity's sake, I use here), which lies near the middle of the southern edge of the area. It measures about 210 metres (690 feet) by about 210 metres, but is not rectangular, having sixteen sides which form as many bastions. Although the mound is of natural origin, it has been shaped by man in the fashion indicated, and faced with cut stones,[16] some of the work being of the Tiahuanaco I style. In the centre of the mound is a deep depression which reaches down to the level of the plain and contains stagnant water. The height of Acapana is about 15 metres (49 feet). What the mound, so painstakingly improved by the ancients, who even took the trouble to drain the central cavity with a stone-lined sewer running out at the southern side, was intended to be we do not know. Squier calls it a fortress,[17] but that term does not seem to fit very well.

B. The nearly rectangular enclosure called Kalasasaya, Kalisasaya, or Calasasaya (which spelling is the simplest) lies northwest of the Acapana. M. Georges Courty, who did some excavating there in 1903, mis-names it, in his plan, calling it Ak-Kapana,[18] but in so doing he follows the precedent given by Stuebel and Uhle,[19] who call it Ak-kapana and distinguish the mound by calling that the Mound of Ak-kapana. Bandelier and Posnansky designate the enclosure Kalasasaya,[20] and it is their example that I shall follow here, although I might equally well follow that of Squier and of Mr. Joyce, both of whom use terms such as "temple" and "megalithic enclosure" when speaking of this building.[21]

The Calasasaya, then, measures about 135 metres (440 feet) from east to west, according to Posnansky, and somewhat less from north to south. Its outer margin is marked by walls in the Tiahuanaco II style with lava pillars of varying size at short intervals and smaller stones, also of lava, laid in courses between them. One notable feature of the masonry is the high degree of finish still observable, in spite of weathering, in the lava blocks, great and small; and another is the use of cast copper clamps, some of them T-shaped, others I-shaped, which were sunk into sockets prepared for them in the stones and so aided powerfully in holding the wall together.[22]

At the eastern end of Calasasaya is the so-called Monolithic Stairway, of six steps hewn from massive blocks of lava and having a huge upright monolith of the same material at either end of the stairway. See Figure 64. This admirable construction gave access to a rectangular enclosure with three concentric lines of pillars around it. The outer dimensions of this *sanctissimum*, as Posnansky calls it[23] are about 60 metres north and south by about 64 metres east and west, or about 195 feet by about 208 feet. In the northwest corner of the Calasasaya stands the famous Monolithic Gateway, of which I shall speak presently in detail. The western wall of the Calasasaya does not form a straight line as do the other three walls, for it has a bastion some 55 metres in length that projects northwards 6 metres, which is shown in Figure 65.

C. To the east of the Monolithic Stairway, at a distance of about 150 feet, is a Tiahuanaco I structure measuring about

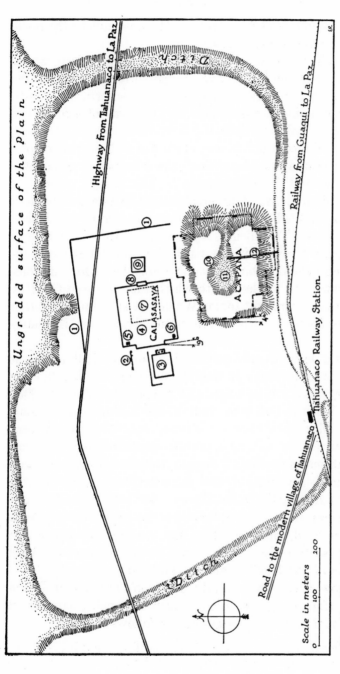

Fig. 63. Plan of the ruins of Tiahuanaco, based on surveys made in 1904 and 1912 by Arthur Posnansky, Engineer, and greatly simplified for the present volume.

1. Remains of a Tiahuanaco II Wall.
2. Vestiges of Walls or Terraces.
3. Remains of a Tiahuanaco II edifice with a stairway in colors on its eastern side. Called "Palace of the Sarophagi,"
4. Calasasaya or Kalasasaya, of the Tiahuanaco II style of masonry.
5. The Monolithic Gateway on the Eastern Face of which is the Frieze of Viracocha and his attendant Personages.
6. The Monolithic Statue called "The Friar" or "The Bishop."
7. The Inner Enclosure or Sanctissimum within Calassasaya.
8. The Monolithic Stairway.
9. Remains of an edifice of the Tiahuanaco I style of masonry.
10. Remains of the Acapana or Akapana, with its Natural Mound and outside Walls of the Tiahuanaco I style of masonry.
11. A natural depression in the middle of Acapana.
12. Masonry-lined Drain, probably of the Tiahuanaco II period.

30 metres square (98 feet square). It was sufficiently mentioned in the preceding chapter.

D. Another rectangle, commonly called the Palace, which lies just west of the Calasasaya. It measures about 60 metres (196 feet) east and west, and somewhat less north and south. At its eastern side it has an entrance stairway of a few steps with traces of coloring upon it.

2. Puma-Puncu, the Gateway of the Puma, lies quite remote, some quarter of a mile, from Tiahuanaco proper, to the southwest and beyond the area covered by Posnansky's survey. It is a natural eminence of no great height. Upon its northern side lies a jumbled mass of carved lava blocks in the Tiahuanaco II style. The niches, sockets, and other indentations painstakingly wrought in the hard stone compel the admiration of the beholder, but they inevitably leave him in complete darkness as to the use to which they were destined by the cutters who wrought them. We do not even know whether the edifice for which they were intended was ever in reality set up.

Such is a description of the chief features of Tiahuanaco as that site is at present. It was my privilege to visit the site for a very brief while, under the guidance of the late Don Manuel Vicente Ballivián and of his son in law, Colonel Federico Diez de Medina, in November, 1917, but my time and resources did not then permit me to conduct any real investigations at the site. I depend, therefore, on the writings of men more fortunate in this respect than myself, drawing from their frequently contradictory assertions, measurements, and interpretations what order and sense I can. The reader is frankly warned, however, that my account of the site is doubtless as full of errors in detail as are those of all other describers of the locality, ancient and modern.

It is now worth while to take up Cobo's account of Tiahuanaco.[24] His description is long, much of it being superfluous for us, but important passages run as follows:

Two facts do I find in these buildings worthy of not being passed over in silence and without reflection: the first is the remarkable size of the stones throughout the structures; and the second, their great antiquity. Who, indeed, will fail to marvel at the strange hugeness of the stones which I have described, and who will not wonder how, they being so large, they could have been carried by human strength from the quarries where they were cut to the places where we now see them? And the matter becomes all the more puzzling when it is remembered that no such stones as these exist for leagues round about, and that it is well known that all the folk of this New World were lacking in inventions such as machines, wheels, and windlasses, not to mention draft animals. I confess that I cannot comprehend with what force they could drag the stones, nor with what implements and tools they could work them. Moreover, we must admit that, before they were worked and perfected, the stones were even larger than they now are, as we see them, perfectly finished. All of these stones are of two or three kinds, some being sandy, red, and easily worked, others brown or ash-coloured, and very hard. The cutting upon them is varied, but all very different from our work. The nicety of the workmanship appears most clearly in their smooth, flat finish, than which nothing could be better.

Inasmuch as the Indians lacked letters, we cannot find out many things about them, and as a result we must proceed by guesswork. This we must do in the present case when wishful to investigate the origin of this ancient place and to ascertain what men built it and how long ago these edifices were made. It is only certain that, among the Indians now there, no remembrance lingers as to this, for they all confess that the work is so ancient that they know nothing of it. But they all agree that, many centuries before the Incas began to rule, these buildings were already erected. Indeed, it is currently reported among these same Indians that the Incas made their great structures at Cuzco and elsewhere throughout their kingdom after the models found here.

Here the good Father wanders a bit in order to recount various fantastic tales to which, as he himself says, the size of the ruins gave rise. He then goes on to say that the degree to which the stones above ground are weather-worn is one argument in favor of their great age.

The second argument [he continues] which I find in favour of their great antiquity, an argument which carries even more weight than the first, is the multitude of wrought stones that lies beneath the soil. Sooth to say, numerous though those are which are seen upon the surface, whether fallen from the buildings or scattered about, those beneath the earth are even more wonderful because of their numbers. The ground of this locality being flat, even, and grass covered, free from gullies and crags, it is possible to dig anywhere within half a league of the ruins and to find, at a depth of one or two estados,* a quantity of well wrought stones, some of them being very large and beautifully finished slabs, so that it is apparent that a whole great city is here buried. After I passed by these buildings for the first time, in the year 1610, they dug up a big stone which I myself measured on my returning thither, and I found it to measure twenty feet long by fifteen feet wide, highly finished and polished like the rest.

Father Cobo then goes on to tell how his friend, the priest of Tiahuanaco, wishing to make an ornamental tank in the court of his house so that it might be beautiful enough to receive the Bishop of La Paz who was to pass that way, caused an excavation to be made, as a result of which some finely finished stones were found. Moreover, the priest, who had charge of the building of the church in the village, ordered his mason to carve two statues, of Saint Peter and Saint Paul, and when the artificer complained that he had no stone with which to do it, the priest told him that suitable material could be found wherever he might dig, and in order to prove it, he caused the man to dig in the very spot where they were. Stones large enough for the purpose were found, and the two statues are to be seen to this day at the entrance of the church. They appear in Figure 66, being, of course, statues of the Tiahuanaco I period which the lazy mason foisted upon the priest who renewed their usefulness to humanity by renaming them Saint Peter and Saint Paul.

Finally, Father Cobo tells us of the first archæological work ever carried out at Tiahuanaco. The excavator was Don Juan de Vargas, who was the first encomendero (holder of vassals) of Tiahuanaco. It seems that, in the 1540s, he was in Spain, trying to advance his interests at Court and not succeeding. One day, when he was feeling very depressed, a stranger came to him and asked him why he was so sad, he who was owner

*An estado is equal to somewhat more than a yard and three-fourths.

Fig. 64. The Monolithic Stairway (so-called) at Tiahuanaco, in the centre of the eastern side of Calasasaya.

Fig. 65. A detail of Tiahuanaco: part of the Palace of the Sarcophagi looking northwards along the western wall of Calasasaya.

Photographs by Max Vargas, Arequipa.

Fig. 66. Façade of the Spanish church in the village of Tiahuanaco. To right and left of the gateway are seen stone images in the Tiahuanaco I style. Practically all of the masonry in the church is made of stones carried away from old Tiahuanaco.

Photograph by L. D. Gismondi, La Paz, Bolivia.

FIG. 67. A view of the margin of Lake Titicaca.
Photograph by courtesy of W. V. Alford, Esq.

FIG. 68. One of the lesser monolithic gateways at Tiahuanaco. *After Lehmann and Doering.*
FIG. 69. One of the monolithic statues in the Tiahuanaco II style at Tiahuanaco. It is
popularly known as "The Friar" or "The Bishop."

Photograph by courtesy of the late Dr. Joseph Clark Hoppin.

of the richest village in the world, Tiahuanaco. The stranger gave to Vargas a memorandum of how to find among the ancient buildings great wealth. Having returned there, after the conclusion of his business at Court, Vargas dug in accordance with the instructions which he had so mysteriously received, and he found many jars containing fine cloth, and also stools and flagons of silver, a quantity of beads or bangles, a large human skeleton, and finally a huge human head of gold whose face was like that of the statues round about. The night after this last find was made, Vargas suddenly died, and archæological curiosity was thereby greatly discouraged.[25]

The theory of Father Cobo that far more remains below ground at Tiahuanaco than is to be seen above it is in accord with that of Dr. González, already cited.[14] Decidedly archæological work of the most efficient description must be done, perhaps even with the help of aeroplanes, a paradoxical but very useful aid to the digger, as the work of Mr. O. G. S. Crawford and others in England has amply proved.

So much for Tiahuanaco itself. Although most of the emphasis in both ancient and modern writings falls upon the ruins at that site, we must not lose to view the presence of like remains at other places in the Titicaca basin. Localities around the Lake of Titicaca, such as Chililaya and Pucarani, some thirty miles north of Tiahuanaco, such, too, as Calaqui, or Kalaki, and other places on the Peninsula of Huata, are already vaguely known archæologically; various points on the Islands of Titicaca and Coati have yielded vestiges of Tiahuanaco art of both cultural phases;[26] Hatuncolla and Sillustani near the northwestern corner of the Lake have carved monolithic pillars which recall Tiahuanaco II art;[27] and Llojepaya, described by Dr. Uhle,[28] on the borders of the Lake, as well as other sites on its margin, belongs to the Tiahuanaco II period, at least in part.

In short, we already have sufficient reason for believing that Tiahuanaco was the metropolis of a strong state, perhaps of a theocratic character, whose "home counties," as it were, occupied the whole of the Titicaca basin. The locality is not, at any rate to-day, one that seems propitious to the development of high civilization. A flattish valley, gray to red in hue, sodden with stagnant water in many places, hemmed in by rounded hills, grim in their sterile grayness, a zinc-colored sky that seems to weigh upon one's very head, and a prevailing sombreness and faintness of daylight, these go to make up the scene in the vicinity of Tiahuanaco as I saw it. Perhaps at seasons of the year other than November, when the rainy-season is on, the landscape is less forlorn and repellent. Even in November, however, Lake Titicaca is beautiful, particularly at the hour of sunset, with the tall reeds along its margins swaying in the evening wind, and with the all too rapidly passing glory of the sky mirrored in the water. Here and there a reed balsa with a sail of matting floats with an air of immeasurable antiquity, and quaintly clad modern Indians go silently and patiently about their mysterious affairs. Far off to the west and south snow-clad peaks of the Eastern Cordillera—Sorata, Huayna Potosí, and Illampu—bite into the sky with glistening white teeth. The traveller looks upon it all and sees that the keynote of that land is majesty, distinctly cold and grim, but majesty all the same, and very seldom tempered by any softer or more genial note. A characteristic scene on the shore of Titicaca appears in Figure 67.

The art of the region corresponds well with the quality of the country which saw its rise. Its media include stone, pottery, metal, and textiles, and in whichever one of them it appears the Tiahuanaco II art invariably displays a style so highly individual that it is a relatively easy matter to trace, by its means, the spread of great Tiahuanaco's intellectual and æsthetic influence, if not of its political paramountcy.

Conveniently enough, a general conspectus of Tiahuanaco II art appears on one monument, the celebrated Monolithic Gateway which stands in the northwestern corner of Calasasaya. The intricate carvings upon its eastern face are shown in Figures 70 and 71. Study of them puts one in possession of the chief characteristics of Tiahuanaco art as it was at the height of its development. On the frieze above the doorway we behold a splendidly conceived and executed bas-relief which shows a central figure with a large square face and an elaborate headdress decorated with projecting embellishments that stand away from the face like a fringe and have at their ends either conventionalized puma profiles or else circular patterns of unknown significance. From the large round eye-sockets of this personage tears course down the cheeks, giving rise to the modern fashion of calling him the Weeping God of Tiahuanaco,[29] albeit there is little doubt but that he is the Creator-God, Viracocha, principal deity of the highland folk in Tiahuanaco times, of whose place in Andean religious thought I shall speak in Chapter IX. In his two hands, which have only four digits, the figure holds ceremonial objects, different in detail but alike in general appearance, that in his right hand seeming to be a highly conventionalized spear-thrower, and that in his left hand a highly conventionalized quiver containing two spears. Viracocha, if I may thus specifically name him, is dressed in an elaborately adorned tunic, bound by a girdle embellished with puma heads, from which depends a fringe made up of conventionalized faces suggestive of the puma. In like manner, every part of the design upon the frieze is laden with a wealth of ornamental detail involving conventionalized representations of men, animals, birds, and fish, as well as a variety of precisely carved symbolical motifs the significance of which we cannot surely know.

On both sides of Viracocha are twenty-four attendant personages who face towards him. The upper and the lowermost rows of these minor figures are made up of winged men bearing staffs or spears and wearing headdresses; the middle row consists of partly personified birds, similarly arranged. All of these personages are shown running rapidly towards Viracocha as he stands upon a terraced pyramid or throne. Below the parts of the design referred to, and immediately above the doorway, is a narrow horizontal band of decoration in which appear æsthetic elements similar to those already mentioned.

Regarded either as a whole or in detail, this composition is an amazing sculpture. In spite of the high conventionalization

which is its chief æsthetic quality, it possesses a degree of
vitality that is in no wise diminished by the rigid symmetry
and balance of the design. In the rendering of the hands, legs,
and wings of the various figures we see a vigor which expresses
great strength and liveliness of imagination on the part of the
artists who conceived and executed the frieze, in short, a spirit
still virile in spite of the weight of artistic dogma, perchance
engendered by priestcraft, under which it labored.

Whoever has thoroughly acquainted himself with the frieze
of the Monolithic Gateway will have seized the essence of Tiahuanaco II art. In order to point out the consistency of
quality which is one of its most important aspects, I shall now
briefly comment on a few other typical instances of the art in
various media.

Art in stone includes, besides numerous minor monolithic
gateways such as that shown in Figure 68, a great variety of
statues. One, popularly known as "the Friar" or "the Bishop,"
appears in Figure 69. It is considerably more lifelike, especially about its left hand, than is the figure of Viracocha, but
it has the same general aspect and the same square-edged cutting as the figures on the frieze. Because of the wear and tear
of weather, not to mention bullet-wounds inflicted by persons
who have used it as a target in modern times, some of the
detail is lost, but enough remains to show us that this personage is wearing a girdle adorned with spider- or crab-like
creatures conventionally rendered, and that the cup held in
the left hand is embellished by bird-heads closely resembling
those to be found among the ornamentation of the Monolithic
Gateway. Quite different, however, are such carvings as that
shown in Figure 72 which, although it comes from Tiahuanaco
and represents the second phase of culture there, does not
resemble the carving of the frieze at all save for the fact that
they have the same square-edged cutting. It seems to me, on
æsthetic grounds, that it represents a later period, one in
which, because of excessive conventionalizing tendencies,
designs had lost much of their coherence. This specimen
closely resembles the three bas-reliefs shown in Figures 73,

FIG. 70. The eastern face of the monolithic gateway at Tiahuanaco.
After Posnansky.

FIG. 71. Detail of the frieze on the monolithic gateway at Tiahuanaco.
After Posnansky.

FIG. 72. FIG. 73.

FIG. 74. FIG. 75.

FIG. 72. Stone carving from Tiahuanaco.

The original is in the collection of Sr. F. Buck, La Paz, by whose courtesy this photograph is used.

FIGS. 73–75. Three low-relief carvings in stone, probably representing the latter part of the Tiahuanaco II period. They are said to come from Peru.

The originals are in the Musée Ethnographique du Trocadéro, in Paris. After Réal.

74, and 75, which are said to come from Peru (locality not specified by M. Réal), and which are now in the Musée Ethnographique du Trocadéro, Paris.

The pottery of the Tiahuanaco II period, not only at Tiahuanaco itself but also wherever it occurs, is strictly consistent with the canons of art that we see observed on the Monolithic Gateway. Bowls, jars, bottles, vases, cups, etc., occur upon which one sees painted, in rich but sombre colors, pumas and other creatures very like those carved on the Monolithic Gateway. Typical examples of the pottery appear in Figures 76 and 77.

Of artistically interesting objects in metal from Tiahuanaco and its vicinity, and representing this period, we have almost nothing, although bronzes and articles of gold and silver from other regions do show a pronounced connection with the art of the Tiahuanaco II period. True, animal-figures in the style of this time have been found, one by Bandelier on the Island of Coati,[30] others at Asángaro, a considerable distance north of the Lake;[31] true also, that gold was found by Don Juan de Vargas when he was delving into the earth at Tiahuanaco in the middle of the sixteenth century, as Father Cobo tells us. But in general it remains true that the great majority of metal artifacts representing this period come from elsewhere than Tiahuanaco.

Exactly the same statement may be made regarding textiles. We know, of course, from the statues and from the other carvings at Tiahuanaco, that the ancient inhabitants of the region wore elaborate clothes, embellished by ornaments of various kinds. But the damp climate of the highlands is not propitious to the conservation of fabrics, and as a result the very few that have been preserved to us represent the Inca period rather than that which we are now considering. As in the case of metal objects, however, we are possessed of numerous specimens of Tiahuanaco II art in textiles, albeit the examples of them all come from other regions than that of Tiahuanaco.

The question of the ethnic identity of the people who built the Tiahuanaco II culture has never been settled. It is known that the Colla folk—incorrectly but very generally called Aymará—were the chief occupants of the Titicaca basin in immediately pre-Incaic times, and their language is widely spoken throughout central Bolivia to-day. The misuse of the term Aymará came about in this way: Long before the Spanish Conquest the Incas had settled a colony of Aymará on the shores of Lake Titicaca, near Julí. These people, like the Incas themselves, were members of the great linguistic stock whose homeland was in the valleys of the Urubamba and the Apurimac Rivers; their tongue was the Runa-Simi, more commonly called Quechua or Quichua. The folk among whom the transplanted Aymará were settled were members of another ethnic stock, the Colla, itself divided into a number of tribes, such as the Pacajes and the Lupacas. In the latter half of the sixteenth century, the missionary priests who entered that region failed to differentiate between the two language-groups and so came to apply the name of the Quechua-speaking Aymará to the older Colla-speaking folk round about. The misuse of the name appeared in print for the first time in 1583, and it has persisted in general usage to this day.[32] In these pages, however, I shall use the term Colla to designate the natives of the Titicaca basin and of the country around Chuqui-apu or La Paz.

The only other considerable ethnic group in this region and in the valley of the Desaguadero River is the Uru or Uro folk, who constitute one of the most interesting problems in the native history of the Andean area. One of the earliest and best accounts of them is to be found in a report on the Province of the Pacajes written, about 1586, for the Spanish government by Don Pedro Mercado de Peñalosa.[33] He speaks with some particularity of the Urus who dwelt in the upper part of the Desaguadero Valley, just south of the Lake, stating that they were mingled with the Aymará (Colla) population and spoke their language, but that formerly they had inhabited the shores of the Lake and had lived by fishing and by eating the roots of certain plants that grew wild there. He goes on to say that they were held in slight esteem because they were poor laborers and unskilful agriculturists, and that the Incas, on conquering the region, had thought so little of them that they did not trouble to teach them Sun-worship, merely commanding that they pay tribute in fish and by making baskets. For their fishing they used *balsas* (rafts) of totora-reed—see Figure 67—and nets made of ichu-grass.[34]

Ever since Mercado's time the Urus have lived in small groups scattered over the southern part of the Titicaca basin and along the Desaguadero River. They are by natural tendency fishers and hunters, and only when bulldozed by the Incas or by the Spaniards have they tried their hand at husbandry, with conspicuously bad results. Their language is the Puquina or Pukina tongue which, at the time of the Spanish Conquest, extended all over the region under discussion and even down to the Pacific shore in northern Chile,[35] existing side by side with the Colla language. It was one of the great native languages of Peru in the late sixteenth century, for Bishop Oré deemed it worth while to give his Compendium of Christian Doctrine not only in Spanish but also in Quechua, Colla, Puquina, Mochica, Yunca and other native languages then widely spoken.[36]

The Urus, nevertheless, have always been looked down upon by their neighbors and have been generally treated like pariahs and outcasts. The reason for this is not, I think, merely that they are of capacities inferior to those of their neighbors, but is due rather to their being aliens among the mountain population in whose country they long ago settled. This opinion is supported by a statement by Mercado to the effect that it took two Urus to do the work of one *serrano* (mountaineer),[37] which implies that the Urus were *not* mountaineers. Furthermore, in modern times it has been demonstrated pretty conclusively that the Puquina tongue belongs to the great Arawak linguistic stock of eastern South America, and it has been shown that, very probably, the Urus migrated long, long ago across the Amazonian wilderness and up into the highlands around Lake Titicaca.[38]

Clearly enough, the Urus, whether regarded from the standpoint of material culture or from that of their psychological characteristics, do not bear the stamp of a race of empire- and culture-builders. We may safely conclude, therefore, that they did not create the civilization of Tiahuanaco II. It is conceivable, of course, but not very likely, that they were the Tiahuanaco I folk, who were afterwards submerged by the builders of the second and higher cultural phase. They are, at any rate, an excellent example of an archaic-cultured folk surviving into modern times. But it seems to me far more probable that they were the destroyers of the Tiahuanaco II civilization than that they were the creators of any high culture whatsoever. To this point I shall revert presently.[38a]

We are left in doubt, therefore, whether it was the Collas who created the Tiahuanaco I and II cultures or whether it was the Quechua-speaking folk. At the present time there are two leading opinions on this subject. The one holds that the Collas are and have been for many centuries the chief people of the Titicaca basin and that they were the creators and propagators of Tiahuanaco culture; the other considers that the Quechuas were the folk of Tiahuanaco in its great days and that they carried its influence far and wide throughout the Andean area. There are good arguments on both sides, as Don José de la Riva-Agüero has shown in his masterly summing-up of the problem,[39] but nothing really conclusive has yet been produced. The matter turns largely upon the study of languages and of mythology, a study which, in spite of much excellent preliminary work, is still in its infancy. To my mind, the crux of the problem is this: How closely, if at all, are the Colla and the Quechua languages related? If it should be demonstrated conclusively that they are very nearly akin, we would be justified in assuming that the Tiahuanaco folk spoke a language which was mother of them both, they being but variations of one system of speech which developed differently in different regions; if, on the other hand, they are found to be profoundly dissimilar, it will be necessary to trace out their respective histories.

This brings us to the question of the spread of Tiahuanaco

influences, cultural if not political, throughout the Andean area. Undoubtedly the nucleus of both Tiahuanaco I and Tiahuanaco II culture had its seat at the southern end of Lake Titicaca. As I said, on page 117, it is conceivable that the northern walls of the fortress of Sacsahuamán, above Cuzco, and of parts of the fortress of Ollantaytambo represent the Tiahuanaco I period, although they both differ somewhat from the masonry of that age at Tiahuanaco itself. But the admirable work carried out by Mr. E. C. Erdis at Machu Picchu, under the direction of Dr. Hiram Bingham, head of the Yale University-National Geographic Society Expeditions to Peru, failed to reveal the presence, below Ollantaytambo, of walls even remotely resembling those of the Tiahuanaco I style. Nor is the Tiahuanaco II period represented, so far as I know, by any wall now standing in Cuzco itself.

In fact, almost the sole evidence that I can think of which would establish at Cuzco the sometime presence of Tiahuanaco II influence is a certain vase, now in the Ethnological Museum in Berlin, which is shown in Figure 78. It is said to have come from Cuzco, but from what part of the city and under what circumstances we do not know.[40] Nevertheless, it is worth while to study this pot briefly.

Ugly though the decoration upon this vessel is, it has a considerable interest for us because it clearly displays the presence of elements derived from three sources: The ornamentation of the nose and forehead of the face and of the rim of the pot is purest Tiahuanaco II in style; the fanged mouth distinctly recalls the fanged personages so frequent in Early Chimu art; and the painting of the hands with too-few digits which grasp decapitated heads by their hair is strongly reminiscent of Early Nazca art. It seems to me, therefore, that we have here conclusive proof that these three arts met and mingled in order to produce this far from beautiful pot. As to the date at which it was made we can only conjecture, but my personal guess is that it represents the early part of the Tiahuanaco II period and the latest part of the Early Chimu and Early Nazca periods or, in other words, about 600 A. D.

Evidences of Tiahuanaco influence all along the Peruvian coast are far more conclusive than this, particularly at Nazca and Pachacamac. From the former of these localities we have superb fabrics in the style of Tiahuanaco II, as well as much pottery in the same style.[41] And at Pachacamac, where the art of Tiahuanaco II style is very heavily represented, it appears to have been the first high civilization of the locality.[42] Again, in the region ascribed to the Early Chimu culture, we have not only plentiful archæological evidence of the reality of a Tiahuanaco period,[43] but also a hint in the folklore of the region. It will be remembered that Father Cabello, in recounting the early history of Lambayeque, mentioned a period which he called "a republic," not specifying its duration, nor saying anything about it. It is at least conceivable that this interruption was nothing more nor less than the period in which Tiahuanaco influence was paramount on the coast. Not always, of course, did the invading art of the mountain folk succeed in obliterating the æsthetic traditions of the peoples among whom it was introduced. The Early Chimus and some of the folk farther south, at Nazca, for example, had an artistic tradition far too strong to be thus overcome.

The length of time during which the Tiahuanaco II civilization flourished was probably not much more than three hundred years. Representative not only of its northward spread through the highlands but also of its later phases are certain sculptures found at Chavín de Huántar in the valley of the Puccha River, which is a tributary of the Marañón River. Chavín lies, therefore, on the eastern slope of the White Cordillera, which separates it from the Corridor of Huaylas. The archæological content of the Chavín district is already somewhat known, thanks to the work of Raimondi, Mr. Enock, and, especially, that of Dr. Julio C. Tello.[44]

The most celebrated of the carvings found at Chavín is the so-called Raimondi monolith, a slab of greenish granite or, more accurately, diorite, measuring nearly seven feet in length. It is now preserved in the National Museum, in Lima, and the design which occupies one side of it is shown in Figure 80. Let me now briefly describe the design.

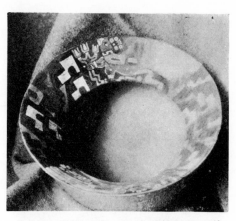

Fig. 77. A bowl decorated with step-motif and with partly humanized mythical creatures, quadrupeds with birds' heads, grasping a plant which may be a conventionalized rendering of the cotton-bush.

Fig. 76. A *quero* or cup found at Tiahuanaco and representing the highest stage of ceramic art in that locality.
The originals are the collection of Sr. F. Buck, La Paz, by whose courtesy they appear here.

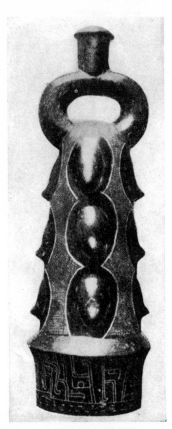

Fig. 78. A jar in Tiahuanaco II style, said to come from Cuzco. *After Schmidt, 1929.*

Fig. 79. A black-ware vessel, probably in the Chavín style, from near Morropón, Department of Piura, Peru.

The original is in the collection of Don Luís Elías y Elías, Morropón.

Fig. 80.   Fig. 81.   Fig. 82

Fig. 80. The bas relief on the Raimondi monolith from Chavín de Huántar. The original stone, about 7 feet high, greenish granite, is in the National Museum of Archæology, Lima. *After Lehmann and Doering.*

Fig. 81. A carved granite monolith from Chavín de Huántar. *After Tello.*

Fig. 82. A carving about 8 feet high found by Dr. Julio Tello in the temple of Chavín de Huántar in 1919. *After Tello.*

Fig. 83. Stone seat from Manabí. *After Saville.*

Fig. 83.

Clearly it falls into two halves, a lower and an upper, but there is a certain cohesion between the two for the reason that the upper half may be interpreted as being the headdress of the personage in the lower half. That personage is unquestionably derived from the same fundamental concept that inspired the Viracocha figure of the Monolithic Gateway at Tiahuanaco. But with what a difference! A difference made all the greater by the underlying similarities which exist between the two. On the Raimondi monolith the face of the chief figure is square and is edged with serpent-heads faintly reminiscent of the ornaments upon the headdress of Viracocha. The features of the Chavín personage are, however, quite different from those of the Weeping God of Tiahuanaco; *his* were distinctly human features, albeit conventionalized, but those of the Chavín creature cannot be readily referred to any natural model, and, moreover, when examined closely, they contain some surprises for the beholder. Examine the rectangular area between the creature's shoulders and the crosswise line just below the headdress. You will see a curiously bovine face with small eyes under elaborately conventionalized eyebrows, with nostrils between strange decorations, with a fanged mouth whose lips recall on shape those of a Tragedy mask, and, finally, with an odd neck-ornament. Now turn the design upside down and see what you have. The mouth and chin of the creature have become a pattern which can be taken in two ways: either it is a much conventionalized feline (puma?) face seen from in front, or else it is two snarling feline faces, nose to nose, seen from the side. In other words, we have here something extremely rare in Andean art, namely a trick for the eye, a trick, however, which can readily be duplicated in Maya art, in Alaskan art, and doubtless elsewhere in ancient American art. Now, keeping the design wrong side up, we find just below the puma face, or faces, a strange fanged countenance below which, again, comes a series of four vaguely feline faces with fangs, the lowermost two of which closely resemble one another, the other two being different, but all four having protruding tongues that

recall Early Nazca art. Indeed, this half of the design, whichever way one looks at it, is strongly reminiscent of the Multiple-Headed God motif so frequent in the Early Nazca designs. Now returning the decoration to its upright position
you will note another similarity to the Viracocha figure. This
Chavín creature grasps highly conventionalized weapons or
staffs in its hands, which have too-few digits, and its apparel
is somewhat similar to that of Viracocha. But here, again, the
æsthetic differences are great, for, although the weapons held
by Viracocha balance one another perfectly, they are not
alike; but the staffs of the Chavín figure are identical and are
so highly ornamented that it is impossible to say what they
are meant to represent. Furthermore, although the hands of
Viracocha lack each one a finger, they are unmistakably
human hands; these, on the contrary, not only lack two fingers each, but also possess hardly any human attribute. The
same may be said of the feet of the Chavín personage. An
additional æsthetic point is this: In Tiahuanaco art there is
a pronounced tendency toward bilateral symmetry of design,
a tendency observable also, but to a less extent, in Early Nazca
art. In the Chavín design this tendency is carried to such
extremes that, if one draws a line down the middle of the
monolith, the pattern on one side will be found to be an exact
duplicate of that on the other. In this we see a culmination
of long-continued æsthetic evolution along the line of conventionalization which is so general among decorative arts the
world over.

Mystifying and weird though the design on the Raimondi
monolith undeniably is, it nevertheless has beauty. The immense intricacy of details, the featherlike and snake-headed
side ornaments, the fang-motif, the feather-motif, and the
puma-face motif being all arranged with a masterly precision
and balance that inevitably makes for an imposing richness of
embellishment.[45] It is of historical interest as well, for, in
addition to the fundamental concept, which is clearly connected with Tiahuanaco II art, there are elements suggestive
of influence from the Early Chimu art and from that of Early

Nazca. The fangs and the feather-like ornaments recall the more formal or esoteric parts of Early Chimu designs, and both are lacking in the designs of Tiahuanaco itself; the multiple-headed headdress recalls one of the chief personages of Early Nazca art, and it, also, is not found in Tiahuanaco art proper. The cutting of the relief is, however, of the same square-edged sort that is so characteristic of Tiahuanaco II carvings and, highly conventionalized though the pattern is as a whole, even here there is a feeble survival of the realistic spirit. One finds it in the portrayal of the arms and legs of the creature, remarkable for their pudgy roundness.

As to the age of this bas-relief one can only guess. Its style is decidedly more mature—one might almost say more nearly senile—than that of the Monolithic Gateway. Some twenty years ago Sir Clements Markham summed up the connection between the two thus: "The two compositions are, I think, the work of the same people, with the same cult, the same art, and the same traditions, but with an interval of a century or two between them." He goes on to speak of the need of seeking "the transition from the earlier and simpler style of Tiahuanaco to the more elaborate and corrupt work on the stone of Chavín."[46] In this opinion of the connection between the two compositions and of their relative chronological positions González de la Rosa likewise concurred,[47] as will anyone at all versed in the laws of æsthetic evolution. Assuming, therefore, that the date of the Raimondi monolith is about 800 A. D., how does one explain the presence in its design of elements clearly derived from Early Chimu and Early Nazca art, which were in their hey-day some centuries before that?

Naturally various explanations can easily be concocted—all of them guess-work—but my own conjecture, for which I am far from claiming correctness, merely offering it tentatively, is this: Tiahuanaco influence, on spreading to the coast, there found well-developed art whose modes and manners cheered and charmed the highland designers. Moreover, it is quite possible that the spread of artistic influence from the mountains was the result of a political spread, similar in nature to the Incaic expansion of later times. If this were so, it would naturally follow that the priest-ridden ruling class of the supposed Tiahuanaco empire would adopt those elements in the coastland art that pleased them, and would mould and turn them into conformity with their own rigid æsthetic and pietistic notions. The result of such a process would be an art exactly like that seen on the Raimondi monolith, a result achieved, perhaps, only after two or three centuries of contact between the relatively naturalistic coastal art and the highly dogmatized mountain art of the Tiahuanaco II period.

The process mentioned was one which could not, logically, stop short at the point represented by the Raimondi monolith. Nor does it. There are other carvings from Chavín de Huántar which have been made known to us in recent years by Dr. Julio C. Tello, of Lima, whose labors in the Chavín district have produced important results, among them a magnificent collection of artifacts from that part of Peru, which collection is now admirably displayed in the Archæological Museum of the University of San Marcos, in Lima. Figure 81 shows a monolith seen and studied by Dr. Tello in one of the pitch-dark inner chambers of the pre-Incaic structure at Chavín. Its shape is that of a three-sided prism 2.20 metres (a bit more than 7 feet) in height and of irregular thickness.[48] A study of the design shows that the creature here represented is a fanged monster somewhat like that on the Raimondi monolith and, like him, lavishly adorned with snake-heads, puma-heads, and various ornamental motifs. Regarded as an artistic composition, this carving is on a far lower plane than that on the Raimondi monolith, being not only hideously grotesque but also incoherent. If, as seems probable, Dr. Tello is right in regarding this creature as the Supreme Divinity of its creators, one can only say that their minds had fallen into a lamentable state of confusion and terror, a state no doubt induced by the increasing dominance of those ever-growing powers of priestcraft at which, from time to time, I have hinted in these pages.

A still further stage of artistic and psychological disintegration is made evident by the carvings on the so-called Chavín obelisk which was discovered in the palace at Chavín by Dr. Tello, in 1919, and which is now in the Museum of the University of San Marcos. One of these carvings appears in Figure 82. The height of the obelisk is 2.52 metres, somewhat over 8 feet. Looked at as it stands upright this design is almost incomprehensible, but if we turn it so that the right-hand side is downwards we find that it represents a dragon-like monster, richly decorated and having a formidable head armed with fangs. According to Dr. Tello the creature is shown in the act of devouring serpents, condors, and fish,[49] all of them highly conventionalized. Various secondary attributes—puma-heads, fangs, plants, snake-heads and so on—appear in divers parts of the carving. The genital organ of the creature is in the form of a fanged puma-head from which issues a plant-like object perhaps emblematic of fertility. In this element we have a faint suggestion of that wistful phallicism which so often accompanies the degeneration of art among people desirous of fertility who dimly realize that their vitality is at low ebb. Incidentally, it is worth while to note that the creature or divinity on the opposite side of the obelisk, although much like the other, has a clearly feminine genital organ. In later times, at any rate, as we shall see in Chapter IX, the Creator-God, Viracocha, was considered to be of both sexes, and this monolith may well be a monument to that belief.[50]

My historical interpretation of these three Chavín carvings —the Raimondi monolith, the prism, and the obelisk—is this: They are all related to the art of the Tiahuanaco II period, if not integral parts of it in the widest sense. The various decorative motifs, the personality of the central figure, and the rendering of eyes, noses, tails, mouths and other parts of the various personages in the designs all refer back to Tiahuanaco II art; but they are very far removed from the relatively simple and realistic presentation of the persons and creatures on the Monolithic Gateway. It seems to me, therefore, that Tiahuanaco II art, having spread as far north as Chavín, and having adopted some of the artistic traditions of the coast

folk—which it proceeded to convert to its own purposes—
entered in upon a period of rapid intellectual and material
decline. Civilization was still high; but it was enervated,
whether because of the now too-great power of priestcraft or
because of loss of control over the soil, who can say? Montesinos, let us note in passing, leads us to believe that, in the
period between 700 and 900 the civilized mountain folk were
constantly menaced by fierce barbarians east and southeast of
them.[51] This would be still another cause of decline on the
part of the Tiahuanaco empire and its subject peoples, particularly if it were powerfully aided by adverse climatic conditions, as may have been the case.

Thus far I have been tracing the spread of the influence of
Tiahuanaco II culture into the central highlands of Peru and
along the Peruvian coast. It is now my duty to speak of its
still more remote irradiations.

In northernmost Peru, in the mountainous section of the
Department of Piura, are found some faint traces of the Tiahuanaco culture. Here, as so often elsewhere, these traces
would no doubt be more numerous and more definite had more
archæological work ever been done in that part of the country. With the exception of one zoölogical expedition from
Harvard University, participated in by Drs. Tello and G. K.
Noble, and of rapid archæological journeys to that region by
Dr. Uhle and by me, almost no scientific attention has been
given to that very interesting corner of Peru. Nevertheless,
two important, but not scientifically assembled, collections of
ancient artifacts have been formed in the Department of
Piura, namely, those of Don Luis Elías y Elías, at Morropón,
and of the late Senator Dr. Don Victor Eguiguren y Escudero,
in the city of Piura.[52] In the Eguiguren collection there are
no specimens from the Piura region which can be safely attrib-
uted to either the Tiahuanaco culture proper or to its derivative, the Chavín culture. In the Elías collection, however,
there is a very remarkable vessel made of highly polished fine
black clay. It is shown in Figure 79. The vessel is about one
foot high and is chiefly remarkable for the band of incised

ornamentation around its base. Meaningless at first glance, the design presently resolves itself into an arrangement of highly conventionalized birds' heads, the eyes and the beaks being the only parts shown, and these being in the ultimate stage of æsthetic disintegration. Although far more crude as to workmanship than the stone carvings noted as representing the last gasp of Chavín art, this vessel is clearly the product of either the Chavín culture itself or else of some as yet unidentified culture in a similar condition of evolution.[53]

This specimen remains, I think, the earliest artifact now known to us as coming from the Piura-Tumbez region. Because it shows us Chavín art in its latest stages it may be reasonably dated as between 800 and 1000 A. D. This would seem to imply, in the absence of evidence to the contrary, that no part of the Piura-Tumbez region was intensively occupied by folk of high culture before that time.

Happily, however, evidence to the contrary *is* forthcoming, and of two sorts, archæological and folklorical. Dr. G. K. Noble illustrates a small carving strongly suggestive of Tiahuanaco influence, a cat-figure rather crudely wrought in relief on stone, which he found not far from Huancabamba;[54] and Dr. Tello found, in more or less the same vicinity, a number of painted cloths which display the influence of Tiahuanaco art. These are now in the Peabody Museum at Harvard University. Finally, the folk-memory mentioned in the preceding chapter makes it clear enough that the early coastal kingdoms did intensively occupy the region under discussion. The Piura-Tumbez region, however, is still a part of Peru practically unknown to archæological science.

Turning now to the possible penetration of Tiahuanaco influence in territory now occupied by the republic of Ecuador we find a peculiar state of chaos prevailing at the present time because of doubt that has been cast upon an authority formerly held to be absolutely reliable and because of modern archæological work whose entire significance has not yet been revealed. In other words, there is an apparently irreconcilable difference between the ancient history of the Kingdom of

Quitu, *i. e.*, Ecuador, as told by Father Juan de Velasco, S. J., and the opinions held by many modern investigators of unquestionable erudition.

First of all I shall give my readers a succinct version of the story set forth by Father Velasco.[55] Then I shall summarize the attack made upon the veracity, intelligence, and honesty of this Jesuit historian. Finally, as briefly as may be, I shall display and comment upon the results of archæological work in Ecuador.

According to Velasco the first historical period of the Quito region extended from "a few centuries after the general Deluge" until about 1000 A. D. when the Kingdom of Quitu was conquered by the Caran Scyri. The second period lasted from about 1000 until 1487, during which time the Caran Scyri and his descendants ruled the land. The third period extended from 1487, when the Incas conquered Quito, to the advent of the Spaniards in 1531. Of these three periods only the first two concern us here.

The Kingdom of Quitu was a territory about 50 leagues square lying in the inter-Andean plateau and having Quitu or Quito more or less in its centre. It is unknown, says Abbé Velasco, whether the people of the Kingdom were all of one stock or whether they had originally belonged to divers tribes and nations which eventually united themselves to form the Kingdom of Quitu. At any rate, there were 40 provinces, the names of 34 of which are remembered. Nor is it known who and how many were the chieftains so long dominant in the land save that the last of the line was called Quitu. In like manner, nothing is known of the laws and customs of the people in that early period, albeit it is supposed that they were rather barbarous.

The original Kingdom of Quitu, with its 40 provinces, accounted for only a part of the territory afterwards included in the Kingdom of Quitu; for there were more than 50 independent states, some of them as large and strong as Quitu itself, others smaller. It is clear that a number of them were made up of formerly independent tribes which were subsequently welded together to form the states in question. Among the most important of these states were the following: North of Quitu: Cayambi, Otovalo, Ymbayá or Caranqui; south of Quitu: Latacunga, Puruhá, Cañar, Zarza; on the coast: Paita, Tumbez, Lapuná, Manta, Cara, and Tacámes or Atacámes.*

Regarding the matter dispassionately one finds nothing very startling in the political and tribal conditions of very ancient Ecuador as described by Abbé Velasco. He merely tells us that there were numerous confederacies each made up of sundry once independent tribes, and that of these the chieftaincy or kingdom of Quitu was the most important. Of the material culture and general attainments of these early people Abbé Velasco tells us almost nothing.

He does, however, vouchsafe the information that the state of Cara, on the coast, became, about 700 or 800 A. D., the seat of a powerful nomadic tribe who arrived on rafts under the leadership of a chief named Caran who had for his title the epithet *Scyri,* meaning overlord. He founded upon the shore of a bay a city to which he gave the name of Cara, and the bay itself is still known by the name he gave it: Caráques. The subjects of Caran, however, did not at once abandon their nomadic way of living; for they were not satisfied with their new habitat. Forsaking their ancient custom of travel by sea, they at length moved inland, eventually arriving in the neighborhood of Quitu about 1000 A. D. In this connection it is well to note that Caran and his people are not the only roving folk whose odyssey is recorded by the worthy Abbé. He also tells us of an earlier maritime invasion by giants who arrived in the province of Manta in the first centuries of the Christian Era, causing much dismay and slaughter among the earlier peoples there.

Abbé Velasco makes his second period begin about 1000 A. D. with the arrival at Quitu of the people led by the Caran Scyri of that day. He says quite definitely that the enervating environmental conditions of the coast, coupled with the dis-

*The spelling of proper names here used is that given by Father Velasco.

covery of an easy way up into the mountains by way of the
Esmeraldas River, induced them to seek a more salubrious
home such as that which they finally found at Quitu. Eight
or ten successive Scyris ruled them during the period of the
drift from the coast to Quitu. About 980 A. D. the Caras
found themselves far up the Blanco River, a tributary of the
Esmeraldas on the western slopes of Mount Pichincha. On
the eastern slopes of that same mountain were some of the
provinces subject to the King of Quitu, and against these the
Caras delivered their initial attack. After a struggle the
invaders vanquished the native king, Quitu, and made his
realm their own.

Under the Caras, from about 1000 A. D. onwards, a higher
kind of polity was formed in the Quito region than had prevailed there under the earlier and ruder dynasty. Worship of
the Sun and of the Moon was formally established, and on the
west side of the city a Sun-Temple was built which had its
main entrance on the east, overlooking the city, and it was
flanked by two tall columns which were used for calculating
the solstices. Round the temple were twelve other gnomons
destined to like purposes. The Moon-Temple stood on the
east side of the city and faced towards the west.

The government was a monarchy with a very powerful
nobility. Only sons could inherit offices and property. If a
chief or a noble died without sons, his eldest nephew, son of
one of his sisters, was his heir. In the case of inheritance of
the Scyri-ship the great nobles had to pass on and accept the
heir or else to elect in his place one of their own number.

In burying the dead the Caras departed from the custom of
their predecessors, the Quitus. The latter had been wont to
make deep, well-like sepultures in the ground with human
remains and artifacts at the bottom; the Caras, in contrast to
this, placed cadavers on the surface surrounded by the most
cherished possessions of the deceased. A low wall of rough
stones was built around the body after the funeral observances,
and stones were used to form a rude vault over it somewhat in
the shape of an oven. Above this earth was heaped until a

mound was formed, called a *tola*, which was large or small according to the station of the person buried.

The Caras had no writing, nor even so imperfect a substitute for it as the *quipu* of the Incas. Instead, they had "certain archives or deposits made of wood, stone, or pottery, with sundry compartments in which they placed little stones of divers sizes, colors, and shapes, for they were notable lapidaries. With the various combinations of these they perpetuated the memory of their deeds and formed their accounts of every sort."[56]

In architecture they were backward for the most part, albeit they did know the use of arches and vaults. But they excelled as lapidaries, even knowing how to cut emeralds and other hard stones.

They were remarkable weavers of cotton and wool, and were even more skilful in the tanning of leather. Their garments were made of cloth and of leather and were very simple. The Scyri wore a double diadem of feathers with a large emerald over the middle of the forehead. The nobles wore double diadems without the emerald. All other men capable of bearing arms wore a single fillet of feathers.

Ordinary men had but one wife and no concubines, albeit the wife could be divorced for frivolous reasons. The nobles had one legitimate wife and a few concubines. The Scyri had a wife and an unlimited number of concubines.

The dominant passion of the Scyris was war for conquest. Although they were ever striving to enlarge their realms at the expense of their neighbors, they never displayed that genius for consolidating their conquests which was so prominent a trait of the dynasties ruling farther south.

The earliest conquests made by the Caras after their arrival in the highlands all lay to the north of Quitu, and included Cayambi (or Cayambe), Otovalo, Tusa (the modern San Gabriel near to the present northern frontier of Ecuador), and other localities. Abbé Velasco says "In all the newly conquered provinces they built their strongholds, which were rectangular terrepleins of one or two terraces provided with ramps having drawbridges. . . . Near each of these fortresses there was always established a village wherein dwelt the officials and captains who were stationed there on the pretext of teaching the inhabitants the art of war and the use of arms. The ruins and traces of those citadels may be seen to this day, and at the first glance they may be distinguished from the fortresses which, at a later date, were erected by the Incas."[57]

The good Abbé then goes on to relate the deeds of various Scyris of the Caran line. The seventh Scyri it was who began the custom of making conquests to the south of Quitu. With but slight difficulty he vanquished the populous but pacific province of Latacunga, after which he came hard up against the still larger and very bellicose province of Puruhá. This last-named state had long been waging bitter war against some of the coast peoples as well as against the redoubtable chieftaincy of Cañar, farther south in the mountains. During generations of strife the Puruhá folk had developed extraordinary proficiency in the use of certain long-range weapons, as well as in the use of the usual lances and clubs. Their special weapons were the sling, which they used in the chase as well as in war, and with which they could bring to earth any designated fruit hanging aloft in the trees, and a small club for throwing, called *huicopa,* which was as deadly in their hands as a musket. Altogether it is not strange that the Scyri of Quitu decided that Puruhá and its allied states of Chimbo and Tiquizambi was too tough a nut to crack. So a friendly alliance was made between the Scyris and the chiefs of Puruhá which seems to have lasted for several generations. With the eleventh Scyri the masculine line of the Caran dynasty became extinct; nor did any sister of the eleventh Scyri have a son. His sole child was the Princess Toa who, under the existing laws, could not inherit the chieftainship. But the Scyri called together his sages and his nobles and formally asked their aid in repealing the old law so that Toa could succeed and reign conjointly with whatever man she should freely choose as her consort. This eleventh Scyri seems, indeed, to have been a canny politician—if, that is to say, Abbé Velasco speaks truly concerning him—for his proposal was accepted with enthusiasm by the assembly. Using his daughter as a powerful weapon he then proceeded to vanquish the kingdom of Puruhá by means of an alliance between her and Duchicela, the eldest son of the aged Condorazo, chief of Puruhá. This arrangement being successfully carried through, a new dynasty of Scyris came to the dual chieftainship of Quitu and Puruhá. This change took place about 1300. Like some of the Peruvian "kings" mentioned by such writers as Montesinos, Huamán Poma de Ayala, and Sarmiento, Duchicela was appallingly long-lived. His eldest son, Autachi Duchicela, thirteenth Scyri, succeeded him in 1370 and reigned for sixty years. The Scyris of the house of Duchicela were far less pugnacious than the Caran Scyris had been, and in general theirs was a time of peaceful political expansion in the Kingdom of Quitu during which alliances were made with the chiefs of Cañar and of other powerful southern states as far as Paita. One motive for this policy was a desire for union against the Incas of Cuzco whose steadily growing power was being anxiously watched by all of these chieftains. About 1430 Hualcopo Duchicela, fourteenth Scyri of Quitu, began his reign. He was a younger son of Autachi Duchicela—the eldest son, and normal heir, Hualca, generally abhorred for his evil courses, having been deposed by the council of nobles.

The Scyri period came to an end about 1450 when the Inca Tupac Yupanqui began his campaigns against the southern allies of Hualcopo Duchicela. The conquest of what is now Ecuador by that Inca and his successor was rapid and decisive, as will be told in Chapter VII, hereafter.

Such, briefly outlined, is the pre-Incaic history of the Kingdom of Quitu as related by Father Juan de Velasco, S. J. Strictly speaking only the period down to about 1000 A. D. concerns us in the present chapter, but I have deemed it best to tell the whole story here for the sake of continuity. Presently I shall speak in greater detail of the culture of Ecuador prior to that date and I shall endeavor to show to what extent the narrative of Abbé Velasco and modern archæology corroborate one another.

It is now my duty to outline the attacks that have been

made upon the historical narrative of Velasco. Into our own day his story has been accepted by students of the first importance. As Señor Jijón y Caamaño has pointed out, the history related by Velasco has "struck deep roots into the national soul" of Ecuador, largely because of the "popular" re-statements of it issued by such writers as Don Pedro Fermín Cevallos and as M. Louis Faliès.[58] Nevertheless, a group of very important modern critical scholars now invite us to discard it, notwithstanding the fact that other and equally important investigators still adhere to it.

Prescott was the first writer, so far as I know, to cast doubt upon assertions made by Velasco. The innuendo which he indulges in at the Abbé's expense[59] is not, however, directed against his history of Quitu, but against his rose-tinted portrayal of the Incas' methods of conquest.

The shrewd and conscientious German traveller, Theodore Wolf, though he never hesitated to contradict Velasco, especially in those parts of his book which refer to volcanic and other natural phenomena, nevertheless accepted literally the story told by the Abbé, incidentally deploring his carelessness in not clearly indicating his sources of information.[60]

It was that extraordinarily prolific Spanish historian after whom the noisiest street of noisy modern Madrid is named, Don Francisco Pi y Margall, who, in 1888, first called in question the good-faith and general acceptability of Abbé Velasco's narrative. A few years later the most celebrated Americanist ever produced by Spain, Don Marcos Jiménez de la Espada, set forth adverse views on the History of the Kingdom of Quito in a well-formulated and carefully considered pronouncement. Then, most portentous of all, came the rejection of Velasco by the most eminent Ecuadorian writer on history, the late Archbishop of Quito, Don Federico González-Suárez, who, in earlier writings, had accepted Velasco without reserve.[61] Thus it came about that, between 1888 and 1904, the foundations were laid for an imposing body of anti-Velasco opinion shared in by Señores Jijón y Caamaño and Viteri Lafronte and other students.[62]

On examining the life-story of Abbé Velasco and his aptitude for writing of the pre-Incaic history of Quito, we find the
matter to stand as follows:

Juan de Velasco was born at Riobamba, of noble family, in
January, 1727. In July, 1747, he began his novitiate among
the Jesuits. By 1761 he had become a fully ordained priest
and a member of the Society of Jesus, and in that year he was
working hard at scholarly labors in the city of Ibarra, considerably to the north of Quito. On April 10, 1763, he received his
doctorate from the University of San Gregorio Magno at
Ibarra. When, in 1767, the orders of Charles III expelling the
Jesuits from all of his dominions were carried out, Father
Velasco was living and teaching at Popayán, in what is now
southern Colombia. As did nearly all the Jesuits, Father
Velasco had a difficult and painful time of it after the expulsion, but at length, in 1769, he arrived in Italy and settled at
Faenza where, often in poor health during long stretches of
time, he remained until his death, which took place in 1819.
From the point of view of his writing, his years may be
grouped as follows:

1756–1762   Voyages and observations in what is now Ecuador.
1762–1763   A year of probation for his doctorate.
1763–1765   Researches in the libraries and archives of Quito.
1765–1767   Years spent at Popayán.
1767–1769   Years filled with painful wanderings after expulsion.
1769–1778   Years of poor health and resultant literary inactivity.
1778–1788   Ten years of neglect of his History.
1788–1789   A final burst of renewed activity resulting in the com-
            pletion of the History.

This arrangement, be it remembered, is an adaptation of
that drawn up by Dr. Jijón[63] in his impressive attack upon
Velasco. I will now present not all, but the most important,
points brought against the Abbé by his detractors. They are
as follows:

1. When, in 1767, the Jesuits were expelled from Spanish
America, Velasco was at Popayán, and thence he made his
way northwards to Cartagena and so to Italy. The Jesuits

were not permitted to carry with them any books save a breviary or a book of devotions and, if he did bear with him notes on his previous researches, they must have been meagre enough to be concealed about his person.

2. A long and damning list can be made of the important early writers who never heard of Velasco's Scyris, the chief of the authors in question being: Cieza de León, Santillán, Cabello de Balboa, and Montesinos.[64] Nor did Garcilaso and Cobo ever say a word about the Scyris.

3. Velasco does cite, however, three authorities on whom he bases his History. They are: Friar Marcos de Niza, whose opportunities for studying the subject in hand were, at best, of the most cursory description and whose alleged writings on ancient Ecuador are unknown to anyone except Velasco; Dr. Melchor Bravo de Saravia, said by Velasco to have been the author of a book on the Antiquities of Peru which, however, was never seen by anyone save Velasco himself; and Cacique Jacinto Collahuaso, a chief in the vicinity of Ibarra, whose manuscripts and books were burned by official persecutors not long after Velasco had studied them. It is upon these decidedly dubious and feeble bibliographical supports that Father Velasco's narrative largely rests.[65]

4. According to Dr. Jijón, the History was written, in Italy, after a lapse of twenty-four years' absence from Quito had weakened the author's memory regarding both his personal observations and his literary researches in Quito. It is further charged that, because of his illness and other misfortunes, Abbé Velasco could not keep abreast with historical studies during his years at Faenza and that, as a result, he wrote according to the dictates of his unreliable memory and of his lively imagination.[66]

Regarding the first three of these points I have nothing to say in rebuttal at present. Concerning the fourth I will say this: At the time when Father Velasco was living at Faenza there was, in Italy, a larger group of scholars interested in American antiquities than is generally remembered nowadays. Among them may be mentioned, first and foremost, Count

Gianrinaldo Carli, and likewise such men as Count Algarotti, Father Gilii, and Abbé Clavigero. If it should ever be proved —and I think it not at all improbable—that Abbé Velasco, during his years at Faenza, was in touch with such men, some of the distrust of his work would melt away. It would then become clear that he never really lost contact with his Americanist studies, that he always continued to regard himself as a student of and as a writer on American history. One argument that we already have in his favor is the fact that he was a subscriber to the first edition of Clavigero's *Storia antica del Messico,* issued at Cesena in 1780–1781, in four volumes. His name, and that of Don Joaquín Larrea, also a Quiteño, are printed in Italianate form in the list of subscribers, they being set down as residents of Faenza. Because he, although poor, ill, and an exile, subscribed to a work which must have been costly and which did not directly concern his native land, it is evident that he was still an enthusiastic student of ancient American history. The other Quiteño subscriber, Don Joaquín Larrea, was, no doubt, a member of the distinguished family to whom the subsequent publication of the History was chiefly due, which constitutes another point in its favor; for, it is an indication that, at a time when, according to Dr. Jijón, Abbé Velasco was neglecting his History, he was in reality making a careful investigation of ancient American history in general. Of this fact his fellow expatriate, Larrea, cannot have failed to know, particularly as they were both dwelling in the same small Italian city.

Let me now, after this long but unavoidable digression, return to the subject of culture in Ecuador at the time when the Tiahuanaco II culture was flourishing in the regions to the south. Dr. Marshall Saville, in his archæological work along the coast of Ecuador, found traces of an advanced civilization which neither he nor Dr. Manuel González de la Rosa hesitated to associate with the Caras mentioned by Abbé Velasco. Furthermore, Drs. Verneau and Rivet accept Velasco's History as a basis for their own very important work.[67]

In addition to the work, already mentioned, of Drs. Saville,

Rivet, and Verneau, we have also various other archæological contributions which concern either the whole or parts of what is now Ecuador. Among them may be mentioned, as particularly important, those of Archbishop González Suárez, Dr. George A. Dorsey, and Dr. Jijón y Caamaño.[68] It is the last-named and most recent of these investigators who has given

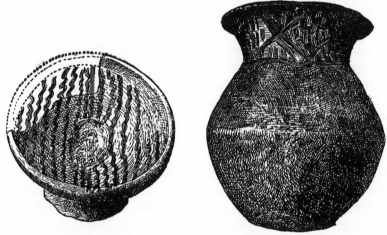

FIGS. 84–85.   Proto-Panzaleo I pottery, dated by Jijón as prior to 200 B. C.
After Jijón y Caamaño.

us the most complete seriation of cultural styles and periods, with approximate dating. His chronology, strictly speaking, refers only to the Puruhá region, in the Province of Chimborazo, which, as Abbé Velasco makes clear, was a powerful state in olden times; but, in preparing it, Dr. Jijón has borne in mind the work done by Dr. Uhle in Peru and also his own labors at Maranga, near Lima. His cultural periods, with approximate dating, are, then, as follows:

Proto-Panzaleo I .... ? – 200 B. C.
Proto-Panzaleo II .... 200 B. C. – 0
Tuncahuán .... 0 – 750 A. D.
Guano, or San Sebastián .... 755–850 A. D.
Elén-pata .... 850–1300 A. D.
Huavalac .... 1300–1450 A. D.
Incaic-Puruhá .... 1450–1532 A. D.[69]

After careful study of the ample illustrations given by Dr. Jijón I find that this chronology does not seem to me to be

86   87

88   89

FIGS. 86–89. Painted Proto-Panzaleo II pottery, dated by Jijón as of 200 B. C. – 0 A. D.

After Jijón y Caamaño.

acceptable. Only by commenting on his graphic material can I show why the chronology fails to win my confidence.

The Proto-Panzaleo I specimens, shown by Dr. Jijón in his Plates V–X, inclusive, and represented by Figures 84 and 85 herewith, are clearly enough low-archaic pottery with incised decoration. The Proto-Panzaleo II specimens, Jijón's Plates XI–XIX, inclusive, and represented by Figures 86, 87, 88, and

89, herewith, are merely somewhat higher archaic pottery in which incised decoration partly yields to painted decoration, simple at first, but improving to a marked degree. With the Tuncahuán pottery, Jijón's Plates XIX–XXV, inclusive, and our Figures 90–95, we come to a period in which both the painted decoration of the pottery and the forms of the vessels themselves show marked progress, albeit both remain well within the bournes of the archaic stage of culture. Modelled human figures were made, but were exceedingly crude; the same may be said of human effigies wrought in stone, one of which is shown by Dr. Jijón in his Plate XXVII, the effigy there displayed being inferior to the best of the Tiahuanaco I sculptures from around Lake Titicaca. The pottery of the Guano, or San Sebastián, type and period appears in Dr. Jijón's Plates XXXIV–LII, inclusive, and examples of it in our Figures 96 to 100. It ranges from very low archaic pottery, some of it with incised embellishments, up to vessels with crudely modelled human faces. A few of the vessels are tall and rather narrow jars upon which very crude modelling is found in conjunction with quite excellent conventionalized painting in black on a white ground, painting which contains motives reminiscent both of Central American and of different styles of Peruvian art. An equal and closely similar range of types is found in the Elén-pata pottery, shown in Jijón's Plates LIII–CIX, inclusive, and in our Figures 101–103. Finally, the Huavalac pottery, shown in Jijón's Plates CXIII–CXXIII, inclusive, may be mentioned in almost the same terms as the classes which Dr. Jijón designates as Guano, or San Sebastián, and as Elén-pata.

To my mind one of the objections to Dr. Jijón's dated chronology is the fact that, in his classification of pottery types, he fails to show the existence of any vivid and deep-reaching contrast between his various types of pottery, such a contrast, for example, as that between Early Chimu and Early Nazca. It is quite possible to lump all of his types together and to say of them merely that they represent a culture which, beginning as a low archaic culture, an integral part

90   91

92   93

94   95

FIGS. 90–95. Tuncahuán pottery, dated by Jijón 0–750 A. D.

After Jijón y Caamaño.

of that so wide-spread in Central and South America, gradually worked its way up through the various grades of the
archaic stage until it attained to a stage which, though preserv-

96   97

98   99   100

FIGS. 96–100.   The more elaborate types of Guano or San Sebastián pottery,
dated by Jijón 755–850.

After Jijón y Caamaño.

ing traces of archaicism (in the modelled human faces particularly), was nevertheless on a par with Tiahuanaco II art
in its later years and, like it, was possessed of a metallurgic
art.[70] Throughout all this long and gradual upward climb
influences were received far more constantly from the north,
i. e., from Colombia and Central America, than they were

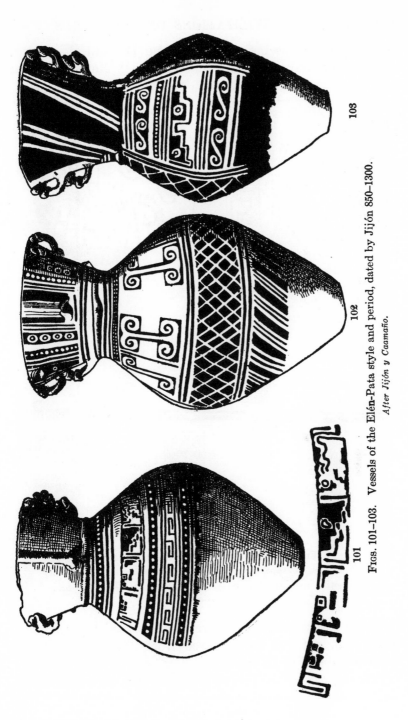

FIGS. 101–103. Vessels of the Elén-Pata style and period, dated by Jijón 850–1300.

After Jijón y Caamaño.

from the south, as both Dr. Jijón and Dr. Uhle have very emphatically indicated from time to time.[71] Nevertheless, as

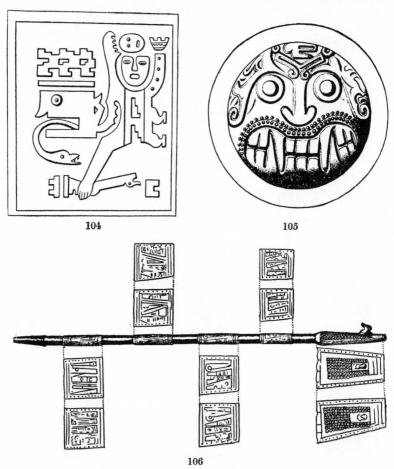

104   105

106

FIGS. 104–106. Gold objects from Ecuador.
FIG. 104. An engraved gold plaque from Patecte, near Chordeleg.
FIG. 105. A gold plaque from Chordeleg.
FIG. 106. A ceremonial spear-thrower adorned with gold, from Chordeleg.
After Saville.

Dr. Jijón also points out,[72] there are clear evidences of influence of an æsthetic sort derived from Tiahuanaco II art towards the end of its career.

This suggests a new line of inquiry which we would better

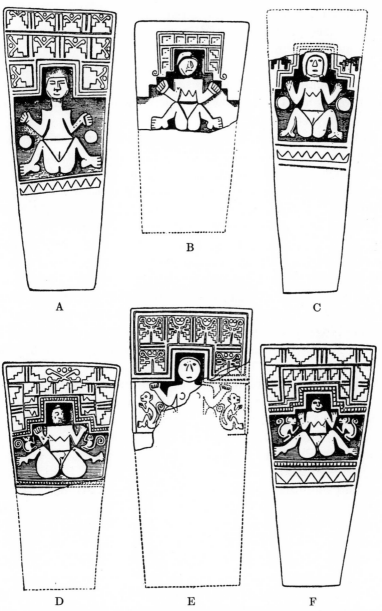

A   C

D   E   F

Fig. 107, *A–F*. Carved slabs from Manabí, coast of Ecuador.

After Saville.

follow for a time. To what extent can direct influence from Tiahuanaco II art be found in Ecuador, and what does its presence there mean?

The archæological work done on the coast of Ecuador by Dr. Marshall Saville[73] revealed the presence of an interesting culture which I shall now briefly describe according to my own interpretation of it.

Most individualistic of all the artifacts representing that culture are great numbers of stone seats which, although they vary considerably in detail, may, in general, be said to consist of a U-shaped seat, without a back, supported by a crouching human- or animal-figure whose spine usually lies in the same direction as does the trough of the U-shaped seat above.[74] The æsthetic qualities of these seats vary widely from marked crudity to fairly respectable high-archaic workmanship such as that seen upon the specimens shown in Saville's Plate XXI and our Figure 83. In these seats, unlike anything found elsewhere in America but, as Dr. Saville shows, probably related to seats and to legged grinding stones in other regions,[75] there is only an occasional and very faint hint of influence from Tiahuanaco II art as, for instance, in the relief embellishment at the edge of the stone seat shown in Figure 83.

Equally characteristic of the culture in question are certain stone slabs adorned with relief carving, some of it deeply cut, some of it shallow.[76] Drawings of these slabs, given by Dr. Saville in Plates IV to VII, inclusive, of his second volume, are represented herewith in Figures 107 and 108. Here, at last, we find definite resemblance to Tiahuanaco II art, both as it is found at Chavín de Huántar and as it is found at Hatuncolla, near the northwestern margin of Lake Titicaca. Compare the Manabí bas-reliefs shown in Figure 108 with the Chavín monoliths shown in Figures 80, 81 and 82 and with the Hatuncolla monoliths shown in Figure 109.[77] It at once becomes apparent that there is kinship of some kind, and rather close kinship at that, between them all.

Again, the beautiful stone puma-urn shown by Dr. Saville and found by him near Caráques[78] has a very strong family

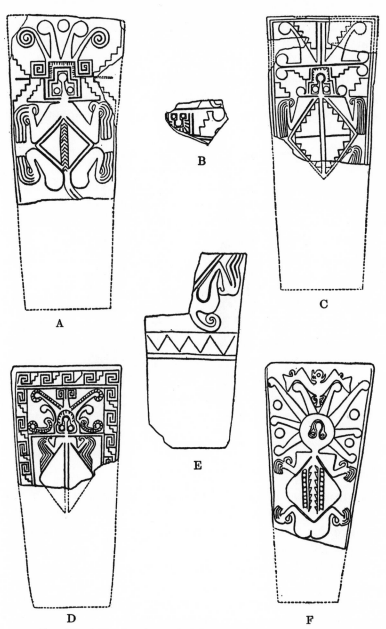

B

A

C

E

D   F

FIG. 108, *A–F*.   Another series of carved slabs from Manabí.

After Saville.

resemblance to equally well-wrought stone vessels of pre-Incaic style found in the Cuzco region and illustrated by Schmidt.[79]

On the whole, the Ecuadorian artifacts which display the closest affinities with Tiahuanaco II and other styles of Peruvian pre-Incaic art are various objects of gold and other

Fig. 109.   Carved stone columns at Hatuncolla, west side of Lake Titicaca.
After Squier.

metal from sites in the Province of Azuay, which lies in the highlands east of the inland end of the Gulf of Guayaquil. We have, for example, a golden plaque from Patecte, measuring some 28 inches in length and bearing a design reproduced in Figure 104, herewith.[80]   The pattern—which, truth to tell, is curious rather than beautiful—is engraved upon the gold with a precision of line that precludes one's describing it as archaic.   Indeed, there is nothing crude about it; on the contrary, it is æsthetically mature, and in it one finds motives and elements that seem to be derived from Early Chimu (the hand holding a spear-thrower and the legs), Early Nazca (the protruding tongue), and Tiahuanaco II art, this last being represented by the step-motive and the general appearance of the pattern. Again, we have the series of splendid gold objects described by Dr. Saville as coming from Sigsig.[81] Not only do the golden crowns, the personal adornments, the gold-banded spear-throwers and sundry minor objects in the series recall pre-Incaic Peruvian art in a general way, but also certain other pieces recall it in a more particular way. The golden breastplate from Chordeleg shown by Saville[82] and reproduced here in Figure 105 is very similar to the central face of the Tiahuanaco II style golden breastplate from Cuzco, likewise shown by Saville, but in another work,[83] and discussed later in the present volume. Finally, the ceremonial golden weapon from near Chordeleg reproduced in our Figure 106 is strongly suggestive of direct contact with Tiahuanaco II art.

In a work of the sort to which the present volume belongs it is impossible to adduce every shred of possible evidence in support of every point. I trust, however, that I have now brought forward enough data to make it clear that the following beliefs held by me are not unreasonable:

1. Along the coast of Ecuador there anciently existed a culture—or a series of cultures—which progressed from a low archaic stage to a stage resembling, if not directly influenced by, the civilization, art, and characteristics which we designate Tiahuanaco II. Competent critics have not hesitated to identify this Ecuadorian coast-culture with that of the Caras, mentioned by Abbé Velasco, in the days prior to their migration into the highlands.[84] Personally, I am far from greeting this interpretation of the matter with the derisive comment that has been turned against it by Dr. Jijón.

2. In the highlands of Ecuador, also, there are many traces of ancient culture which range from low archaic to a stage very like that represented by Tiahuanaco II culture. There are various specimens, particularly from the more southerly regions of Ecuador, which almost certainly indicate direct con-

tact with the Tiahuanaco II culture or with the early coastal cultures of Peru.

3. In both the coastal regions of Ecuador and the highland regions, as Dr. Uhle has shown,[85] there are many indications that influence was received from the north—even from so far away as Central America—as well as from the south. In view of the fact that no traces of Maya hieroglyphs have ever been found in Ecuadorian artifacts which display affinities with Central American art, and in view of the further fact that such evidences as we have that refer to Peruvian art all concern those cultures which existed during the first nine centuries of our era, we are safe in saying that the influences from the north are older than those from the south, for they all represent Central American art at a time when it was either squarely in the archaic stage or very slightly removed from it.

There is in all this, so far as I can see, no general disproof by modern archæology of the gist of the story told to us by Abbé Velasco. According to him, the Caras came in from the north long ago; about 700–1000 they were moving up into the highlands where they found a crude people upon whom they imposed themselves, introducing mound-burials (*tolas*) instead of well-like graves, and various other modifications in culture. In short save for certain minor matters mentioned by Velasco, such as arches, vaults, and drawbridges, which necessarily leave us doubtful as to the facts, there is no real conflict between the broad lines of the story told by the Abbé and the broad lines of the story told—thus far—by archæology. On the other hand, there is, in some cases, very real correspondence between the two, as, for instance, in the matter of counting-devices. (See page 327 of Chapter VIII, in this volume.) No doubt Abbé Velasco did make mistakes, sometimes bad mistakes, in his History. Who, writing in the circumstances that surrounded him, would not do so? But the main thread of his story is, I am convinced, sound and reliable. As Don Isaac Barrera, one of Velasco's few defenders among the contemporary intellectuals of Ecuador, has pointed out, the narrative left to us by the Abbé requires scientific scrutiny and correction, but it does not deserve, for itself and for its author, the scorn and derision which have become fashionable in its regard.[86]

Turning now from Ecuador to the other extreme of the Andean region, *i. e.*, to territory that is now the northwestern part of Argentina, we discover an almost embarrassing mass of archæological data which have not, thus far, been satisfactorily coordinated and interpreted. This being so, all that I can attempt to do here is to point out a few of the major indications of contact between various pre-Incaic cultures of Peru and various pre-Incaic cultures of northwestern Argentina.

The foundations of Argentine archæology were laid by such field workers as Ambrosetti, Debenedetti, Lafone Quevedo, and Boman—to name the most prominent among them—whose chief works are cited in the Bibliography of this volume. All of them tended to link, or at any rate to compare, the various types of culture which they unearthed in Argentina with analogous types in other parts of America both near and far.

Subsequently, possible connections between this or that type of culture in the Diaguite region—as the archæologically important part of Argentina is usually called—and this or that culture in Peru were discussed by Boman, Uhle, Posnansky, Levillier, von Rosen, and others.[87]

These writers, with the exception of the late M. Eric Boman, have felt that there was a definite connection between the several phases of culture in Peru and the various types of artifacts which have been found in the Diaguite region. It seems to me too early, however, to lay down any fixed laws in this connection. Beyond pointing out that the archaic culture was certainly one of the phases which existed in northwestern Argentina at some time or other,[88] I find it impossible to be sure just what was the culture-sequence in the Diaguite region and what was its correspondence with the Peruvian culture-sequence. The work done by Ambrosetti, Debenedetti, Lafone Quevedo, and others, as well as the later writers already cited, has been immense;[89] but, it seems to me to be merely a preparation for an analytical and synthetical study of interpretation.

In our present knowledge of the archæology of Chile, at least for the pre-Incaic period, there is a similar confusion and a general incompleteness of data. The principal writers on Chilean pre-Hispanic history, particularly of the pre-Incaic period, are Messrs. Capdeville, Latcham, and Magallanes.[90] Of these the first comes closest to giving us a good basis for a culture-sequence and a chronology, but even his scheme is as yet too immature and too liable to be upset to justify detailed study here. It is better to be cautious and to echo the opinion of Sr. Magallanes who makes it clear that, prior to the Incaic period in Chile, culture was archaic and society fluid and greatly broken up.

Having now indicated the main facts concerning the character, influence, and distribution of the Tiahuanaco II culture, so far, that is to say, as our far from complete present knowledge of that period permits, I will conclude this chapter by pointing out that the causes of the final disintegration of the Tiahuanaco II civilization—probably about 900 A. D.—are more or less clear. Folklore, as preserved by Father Montesinos and other Chroniclers, contains numerous hints of many kinds of calamities, such as invasions by hostile strangers, changes of climate, divine displeasure, epidemics, and earthquakes. The vivid Fourteenth Chapter of the *Memorias antiguas* of Montesinos—one of the most authentic-seeming parts of that work —preserves a definite folk-remembrance of a time full of tumult and terror during which superstition overwhelmed orderly religious thinking, a time, also, of wide-spread disruption on the part of central government supplemented by a setting-up of innumerable small tribal communities throughout the highland zone. We are told that at length a remnant of the formerly ruling caste of Cuzco—*not* of Tiahuanaco— sought refuge in a place called Tampu Tocco, Window Tavern, and that there they remained during a number of generations, a weak tribe of herders, in no wise different from hundreds of others up and down the tablelands. "Thus," says Montesinos, "was the government of the Peruvian monarchy lost and destroyed. . . . In each province they elected their own king. . . ."[91]

NOTES TO CHAPTER IV

[1] Latcham, 1910.

[1a] One piece of pottery, reported on by Dr. Uhle (1913b, p. 363), almost constitutes in itself a proof of the blending of Early Nazca art into Tiahuanaco II art. The vessel in question is a shallow bowl from Tiahuanaco upon the broad rim of which is painted, but in the style of Early Nazca, a serpent whose head, however, closely resembles the puma-heads so often seen in Tiahuanaco II art. The fact that the vessel comes from Tiahuanaco proves that Early Nazca art penetrated thither, and its association on the same vessel with Tiahuanaco II art proves their close kinship.

[2] Modern usage employs the name Tiahuanaco, but it is to be noted that an earlier name for the place appears to have been Taypicala. According to Cobo, Bk. XIII, Ch. xix, and Bandelier, 1911, pp. 222 and 243, this name has the meaning of "Stone in the Centre," i. e., of the world. Apparently it is derived from the Colla terms, taipiri, centre, and ccala, worked stone, so defined in the Vocabulario políglota incaico, Lima, 1905.

[3] Acosta, Bk. I, Ch. xxv.

[4] Betánzos, Chs. i and ii. Calancha, Bk. I, Ch. xiv. Cieza, Pt. I, Ch. xxxviii; Pt. II, Chs. iv and v. Cobo, Bk. XII, Ch. i. Sarmiento de Gamboa, Ch. vi.

[5] Means, 1928, p. 343.

[6] Cieza de León, Pt. I, Ch. cv, Markham's translation, pp. 374–376.

[7] Cieza, Pt. I, Ch. cv, Markham's translation, pp. 376–379.

[8] The name Titicaca is properly that of an island in the Lake, but usage has applied the name to the whole Lake and the name Chucuito is now seldom employed.

[9] A braza is about 6 feet.

[10] Garcilaso, Pt. I, Bk. III, Ch. i. Quotation taken from Markham's translation, Vol. I, pp. 211–212.

[11] Stuebel and Uhle, 1892, show in their pictures the proximity of the Tiahuanaco River to the ruins and to the modern village. Bandelier, 1911, pp. 224–226, speaks of the watery condition of the valley and of the need of drainage.

[12] Stuebel and Uhle, 1892.

[13] Ogilvie, 1922, pp. 98–100, and illustrations at pp. 23 and 24. Neveu-Lemaire, 1909.

[14] González de la Rosa, 1910, pp. 406–407.

[15] Ogilvie, 1922, p. 138.

[16] Bandelier, 1911, p. 222.

[17] Squier, 1877, pp. 279–281.

[18] Créqui-Montfort, 1906, p. 535.

[19] Stuebel and Uhle, 1892.

172   ANCIENT CIVILIZATIONS OF THE ANDES

[20] Bandelier, 1911, p. 223. Posnansky, 1914.

[21] Squier, 1877, pp. 278–279. Joyce, 1912, p. 169.

[22] Squier, 1877, p. 281. Bandelier, 1911, p. 228. Nordenskiöld, 1921, p. 89.

[23] Posnansky, 1914, Plate XXXXIII.

[24] Cobo, Bk. XIII, Ch. xix.

[25] Cobo, Vol. IV, pp. 65–74. Cieza, Pt. I, Ch. cv.

[26] Bandelier, 1910, passim.

[27] Squier, 1877, pp. 385–386.

[28] Dr. Uhle, in a very adverse review of Posnansky, 1914, describes the ruins called Llojepaya on the southern shore of the peninsula of Copacabana. The vestiges now visible consist of a terrace made of massive stones and measuring one hundred and sixty paces by one hundred and forty-five by three and one-half metres thick. This terrace, when seen by Dr. Uhle in 1894, was practically at lake-level and only twenty-five paces from the water's edge. Furthermore, Dr. Uhle mentions other ruins equally of Tiahuanaco type, and all lower than Tiahuanaco itself. These ruins are: Taaq'ani, on the western end of Cumaná Island, about twenty-five metres above the Lake; and Luquimata on the peninsula of Taraca, fifteen to twenty metres above the Lake. (See: *Revista Chilena de Historia y Geografía*, II, pp. 467–479, and especially, pp. 475–476.) Santiago, 1912.

[29] Joyce, 1913c, uses this term for the first time.

[30] Bandelier, 1910, Plate LXXVIII.

[31] At Arequipa, in November, 1917, I was shown a magnificent collection of gold objects belonging to a gentleman named Sr. Neri. Nearly all, if not all, of the specimens were in the Tiahuanaco II style. They included personal ornaments, face masks (perhaps intended for the dead), and other objects of a decorative or ceremonial character, all of them beautifully wrought. The collection had been found, so I was told at the time, at Asángaro, in the Peruvian Department of Puno, at the northern end of the Lake.

[32] Markham, 1910, p. 315.

[33] Mercado de Peñalosa's *Relación de la Provincia de los Pacajes* appears in *Relaciones Geográficas de Indias*, II, pp. 51–64, Madrid, 1885.

[34] Mercado, 1885, pp. 54–55.

[35] Polo, 1901.

[36] Oré, 1607. Means, 1928, pp. 425–427.

[37] Mercado, 1885, p. 55.

[38] Ogilvie, 1922, pp. 136–137. Grasserie, 1894. Créqui-Montfort and Rivet, 1914, 1914b, and 1925–1927. Rivet, 1913.

[38a] Yet González de la Rosa, 1910, pp. 411–413, would have us believe that the Urus are the descendants of the builders of the high civilization of Tiahuanaco.

[39] Riva-Agüero y Osma, 1910, pp. 61–113; 1921, pp. 18–30.

[40] Seler, 1893, Pl. VII, Fig. 8, published this pot for the first time, and with it various other Tiahuanaco II and Early Nazca specimens which are said to have come from Cuzco. In the series are two Tiahuanaco II vessels shaped for all the world like the heads of golf-clubs of the "putter" sort. Fuhrmann, 1922, I, Plate XX.

[41] Kroeber, 1927. Means, 1917; 1917c.

⁴² Uhle, 1903. Baessler, Vol. IV.

⁴³ Uhle, 1910, 1913.

⁴⁴ Raimondi, 1873, pp. 214–215; 1874–1913, I, pp. 153–154. Enock, 1910, Ch. vii. Polo, 1899.

⁴⁵ Tello, 1923, pp. 298–304.

⁴⁶ Markham, 1910b, p. 393.

⁴⁷ González de la Rosa, 1910, p. 409.

⁴⁸ Polo, 1899. Raimondi, 1873, pp. 214–215. Middendorf, 1894–95, III, pp. 99–100. Wiener, 1880, p. 575. Tello, 1923, 305–309.

⁴⁹ Tello, 1923, pp. 274–283.

⁵⁰ Tello, 1923, Plate I.

⁵¹ Montesinos, Chs. xi, xii, and xiii.

⁵² I saw the Eguiguren and the Elías collections in 1918 and 1919. Since that time Dr. Eguiguren has died. He was a charming, urbane, and hospitable gentleman of the old school, a Spanish hidalgo, and a representative of the best in blood and tradition of South American good breeding, kindliness, and wisdom. He was deeply interested in Peruvian history and was a friend to all who shared his interest. Don Luis Elías, although extremely busy at the times when I visited him, showed me the most generous hospitality in his house, and aided my studies in every possible way. To these two gentlemen, and to numerous members of the Checa family of Hacienda Sojo, in the Chira Valley, as well as to Dr. Don Luis Carranza, of Piura City, and to Señora Carranza, I owe the various opportunities that I had to study, albeit briefly, the ancient history of Piura. To them all, likewise, I owe innumerable pleasant memories for countless kindnesses which they showed me. Whenever I hear the word "hospitality," I think of Piura, and of the many kind and charming people whom I knew there.

⁵³ Means, 1919b. In this short paper I declared that this specimen was in the Tiahuanaco style. In so doing I was mistaken; I give my final opinion above. Dr. Tello ascribes the specimen to the Chavín culture; Dr. Jijón y Caamaño links it to the art of the coast of Ecuador. See: Jijón, 1927, p. 210. Tello, 1923, p. 269. Uhle, 1920, p. 166, links this specimen with the early cultural period of the Peruvian coast, and for this there is justification in the shape of the handle-spout, which closely resembles the stirrup handle-spout of Early Chimu vases. But it equally resembles the handle-spout of Chavín vases, of which Dr. Tello shows us numerous examples. See: Tello, 1929.

⁵⁴ Noble, 1921 and 1921b.

⁵⁵ Velasco, 1789, 1789b, 1837–1839, 1840, 1841–1844.

⁵⁶ Velasco, 1841–1844, II, p. 7.

⁵⁷ Velasco, 1841–1844, II, p. 8.

⁵⁸ Jijón, 1918, p. 35. Cevallos, 1870; 1886–1889. Faliés, n. d., II, pp. 260–268, 399–417.

⁵⁹ Prescott, Bk. I, Ch. ii.

⁶⁰ Wolf, 1892, pp. 496–511.

⁶¹ Pi y Margall, 1888, I, p. 308. Jiménez de la Espada, in Appendix IV of Vol. III of the *Relaciones geográficas de Indias*, Madrid, 1897. González-Suárez, 1904, 1908, and 1915.

⁶² Jijón y Caamaño, 1918. Viteri Lafronte, 1917.

[63] Jijón, 1918, p. 39.

[64] Jijón, 1918, pp. 39–43.

[65] Jijón, 1918, pp. 43–49. Means, 1928, pp. 415–416, 455–462.

[66] Jijón, 1918, pp. 39 and 49.

[67] Saville, 1907–1910, II, p. 242. González de la Rosa, 1908c. Verneau and Rivet, 1912–1922, I, pp. 11–65.

[68] González Suárez, 1878, 1890–1903, 1892, 1904, 1908, 1915, 1922. Dorsey, 1901. Jijón y Caamaño, 1912, 1914, 1918, 1918b, 1919, 1919b, 1920, 1920b, 1927, 1929.

[69] Jijón, 1927, p. 182.

[70] Jijón, 1927, Pls. XXVI, CX, CXI.

[71] Jijón, 1927, pp. 115–143. Uhle, 1920b, 1920c, 1922, 1922c, 1923, 1923b, 1926.

[72] Jijón, 1927, pp. 110–111.

[73] Saville, 1907–1910.

[74] Saville, 1907–1910, I, Pls. IV–XXVII, inclusive.

[75] Saville, 1907–1910, II, pp. 88–123.

[76] Saville, 1907–1910, I, Pls. XXXV–XXXIX, inclusive.

[77] Squier, 1877, pp. 385–386.

[78] Saville, 1907–1910, II, Pl. XCIX.

[79] Schmidt, 1929, p. 459.

[80] Patecte is near Chordeleg, in the Cantón of Gualaceo of the Province of Azuay. In ancient times this region was a part of the Cañar state, mentioned by Abbé Velasco. See: González Suárez, 1890–1903, Atlas, Pl. II, and Verneau and Rivet, 1912–1922, I, pp. 325–326.

[81] Saville, 1924.

[82] Saville, 1924, Pl. V, Fig. 2.

[83] Saville, 1921.

[84] González de la Rosa, 1908c. Buchwald, 1908, 1908b, 1909b, 1909c, 1909–1910, 1918b, 1918c, 1920.

[85] Uhle, 1920b, 1920c, 1922, 1922c, 1923, and 1923b.

[86] Barrera, 1918, p. 144.

[87] Boman, 1903, 1904, 1905; 1908, pp. 187–212; 1923 and 1923b. Uhle, 1910b and 1923c. Posnansky, 1913. Rosen, 1924. Levillier, R., 1927, pp. 3–75.

[88] Boman, 1908, Pl. I.

[89] Ambrosetti, 1897, 1897c, 1899, 1901, 1902, 1902b, 1902c, 1904, 1904b, 1904c, 1905, 1906, 1907, 1908, 1910. Debenedetti, 1908, 1910, 1911, 1912, 1912b, 1928. Lafone Quevedo, 1892, 1904, 1905, 1908.

[90] Capdeville, 1921, 1921b, 1921c, 1922. Latcham, 1903, 1909, 1910, 1914, 1915, 1924. Magallanes, 1912. Medina, 1882.

[91] Montesinos, 1920, p. 62.

CHAPTER V

THE PERIOD OF DECLINE, BETWEEN THE FALL OF THE TIAHUANACO II CULTURE AND THE RISE OF THE INCAIC CULTURE, ABOUT 900 TO ABOUT 1400

The Tiahuanaco II culture having been intellectually, if not politically, dominant in the mountains and on the coast of Peru during a period of some three hundred years, suddenly lost vitality at its very core, through causes which we can see only in broad outline, and so ushered in a period of decline which made itself felt throughout Peru, and, perhaps, even far beyond the territory now occupied by that nation. The degree of the decline, as may perhaps seem natural, was greater in the highlands—where the factors causing it were probably particularly active—than on the coast; likewise, it lasted longer in the highlands than on the coast.

Moreover, the ancient, pre-Tiahuanaco culture of the shore folk was sufficiently strong to have resisted, in large measure, change through the influence of Tiahuanaco when that culture was at its height. True, the coast-cultures were colored by the dye of Tiahuanaco, but when that dye wore thin, they stood forth much as they had been before, with the same social structure, the same fundamental architectural and artistic ideas, and the same characteristics in general that they had had in pre-Tiahuanaco times.

Another point is this: In the previous chapter we saw that Tiahuanaco II art was partly engendered by Early Nazca art and that, in certain of its phases—notably at Chavín—it was deeply imbued with elements derived from Early Nazca and Early Chimu art at a period long after their finest florescence on the coast. This constitutes a sort of carry-over by one ethnic group—in this case the Tiahuanaco folk or their mountaineer subjects—of the artistic and intellectual tradition of

175

another—here the coastal population in general. It is not too great a stretch of the imagination to guess that workers in pottery, stone, and other art media were imported into the highlands, early in the Tiahuanaco II period, from the coast, and were there set to work, under the influence of the rulers of Tiahuanaco, to create works of art into which, inevitably, much of their own artistic dogma crept, albeit changed and exaggerated by contact with their new masters' notions. Perhaps hereditary trades or craft-guilds were established here and there in the highlands—at Chavín for example—which, after the fall of the Tiahuanaco II empire, naturally sought the homelands of their forebears—on the coast.

We thus have two possible channels whereby the artistic, intellectual, and material culture of the Early Chimu-Early Nazca period might be transmitted, half hidden, through the Tiahuanaco II period to the Late Chimu-Late Nazca period which followed it. The one channel—on the whole more easily demonstrable than the other—is on the coast itself and consists simply of the power of the coastal people to preserve their own individuality even under the cloak, temporarily worn, of Tiahuanaco art. The other is in the highlands, where Early Nazca and Early Chimu art seems to have been strongly influential even in the great days of Tiahuanaco II art.

Cloak though it was, Tiahuanaco II art on the coast was not a cloak that could be discarded all at once. The art of the great mountain culture was imposing, significant, and worthy of respect from any observer of it. Why, therefore, should it vanish like a flash the instant that the nucleus of the civilization which it represented was overwhelmed by calamities? Because of its inherent excellence in many respects, Tiahuanaco II influence long continued on the coast.

In order to take care of this influence chronologically and stylistically, Dr. Max Uhle concocted the term "Epigone Style" derived from a Greek word which means "one born afterwards." He defines his term thus: "For lack of a more fitting term, we designated as the Epigone style that cultural type which, although closely related to the style of Tiahuanaco, is inferior to its famous prototype in almost every respect."[1] Elsewhere, Dr. Uhle has declared that he found the Epigone style at various points on the Peruvian coast, including Ica, Pachacamac, Ancón, Chancay, Huacho, the Casma Valley, and at Moche near Trujillo. Not only that, but also he found it at such inland sites as Huamachuco and Chavín de Huántar.[2]

It has been shown by Dr. Uhle that Tiahuanaco style objects and others in the so-called Epigone style have occurred in the same graves at Pachacamac.[3] A careful study of the Epigone style artifacts found by him at that site and very clearly presented in his great monograph[4] has led me to think that the best of his Epigone style specimens are perhaps integral parts of Tiahuanaco II art on the coast and that the less excellent examples are either representatives of the fading-away of Tiahuanaco influence on the shore-country or else that they are merely unskilful attempts by coastland artists to copy the characteristics of Tiahuanaco II art. Arguing *a priori* one would say that there must have been a considerable period—a century at the least—during which the tenets of Tiahuanaco art were gradually losing their grip on the collective artistic imagination of the coastland folk. This loss would be but the natural outcome of the cessation of the Tiahuanaco II civilization in its homeland, the Titicaca basin and the highlands in general. A certain sediment was left, as we shall see, chiefly in the form of minor motifs of decoration, in the artistic repertory of the shore-country artists of the post-Tiahuanaco period, much as our own decorative art of to-day is laden with the sediment derived from all the previous periods of which we are the inheritors.

To what extent, if any, the paramountcy of Tiahuanaco II influence upon material culture on the coast represents a political paramountcy we cannot surely know. It seems quite possible that there was a real political empire dominated by Tiahuanaco as well as a widespread intellectual influence; but of its reality we have as yet no proof. All that we do know is that, along the Peruvian seaboard, there were a number of powerful states which, at the time of the Inca conquest of the coast, were organized in a fashion almost feudal.

It is to these states, the natural inheritors of the Early Chimu and Early Nazca culture, as also of the intrusive Tiahuanaco II culture, that we must turn our attention if we are to gain some understanding of this period intervening between the fall of Tiahuanaco and the rise of the Incas of Cuzco.

The northernmost of the great coast states was that of the Chimu, with its centre at Chan-Chan and with a territory which came to include all the shore from the Gulf of Guayaquil down to Parmunca (Paramonga or Pativilca). This was the realm of the Late Chimu kings and of their culture. As recorded in Chapter III, there was, at Lambayeque, an intermediate period between the old line of local kings of Lambayeque and the new line established under the suzerainty of the Great Chimu of Chan-Chan. This period is called by Father Cabello de Balboa "a republic."[5] It seems to me quite likely that the "republic"—a term vaguely synonymous, to a man of Cabello's training, with any interruption of constituted authority—was merely the predominance of Tiahuanaco control over the coast states. When that state of affairs terminated the coast states were left free to resume their autonomy, and they proceeded to fall into the inevitable condition of rivalry with one another, rivalry which resulted in the stronger imposing their rule upon the weaker states. Ultimately the chiefs of Chan-Chan came out on top, for, beginning in their home valleys, they conquered other valleys, to north and south, one by one, adding them to a growing kingdom constructed on feudal lines. Father Calancha speaks of these conquests in some detail, mentioning the fact that, as they grew in greatness and majesty, the Chimu kings "were wont to collect tribute in the form of apparel and food, and likewise they obliged six thousand Indians to bring to them from the mountains gold, silver, *chaquiras* (small beads or bangles of metal), and copper."[6] The practical motive for the Chimus' conquests is thus clearly revealed.

The character of the control exercised by the Late Chimu

kings over the various valley states was almost beyond question feudal rather than direct, except, of course, in their own home valleys wherein they were hereditary lords of the soil and of the people. Some of their vassals did not offer them very good materials for empire-building. The folk of Tumbez, for example, are always described in disparaging terms by the Chroniclers, for, apparently, neither the Late Chimu kings nor the Incas were successful in making them decent in their personal habits. They had chiefs at whose courts buffoons, singers, and dancers whiled away the time for their masters; they were given to unnatural vices; they worshipped wild animals; and they practiced human sacrifice for their deities. Besides these traits, they were possessed of agricultural skill and also of skill in weaving and in making fine raiment. Finally, they were very warlike, their traditional enemies being the people of the Island of Puná, in the Gulf of Guayaquil, whose ruling family was that of Tumpala or Tumala.[7]

In short, the people of Tumbez were by way of being a buffer state between the warlike but depraved and rather low-cultured peoples of the Ecuadorian coast north of them, and the equally warlike but more civilized subjects of the Chimu south of them. It seems to me that, although the lord of Chan-Chan may have been theoretically the liege of the chief of Tumbez, his real power began, on the north, in the Chira Valley. From there southwards the archæology—so far as we know it up to the present—of the country reveals consistent evidences of intensive occupation of the land by people closely akin to, if not identical with, the folk of Chan-Chan as they were during the Late Chimu period. In the matter of architecture, for example, we have many pyramidal structures of adobe in the Chira Valley and in the Piura Valley, and from there onwards down the coast. In December, 1917, through the courtesy of Don Miguel Checa and of his son, Don Alfredo Checa y Eguiguren, I was able to do some digging at the interesting huaca (pyramidal structure) of Sojo, hard by the mansion-house of the Hacienda de Sojo, owned by the Messrs. Checa. The huaca, anciently named Chira, was the seat of one of the thirteen chiefs who divided between them the lordship of the rich and populous Chira Valley. The structure was found to measure 280 feet east and west, 360 north and south. At its northern side, overlooking the broad and fertile Chira Valley with the Hills of Amotape or La Brea in the distance, was a platform or terrace 280 feet by 220 feet and some 10 feet high; behind it came a second terrace, 280 feet by 80 feet and about 30 feet above the ground-level; finally, at the southern end of the structure, there was a third terrace measuring 280 feet by 60 feet and between 50 and 60 feet high. The material of which the huaca is built is adobe mixed with earth. Within the mass of the third terrace some traces of walls were found, very strange in shape, being ten feet or more broad at the base and tapering to a point. In height they were not more than fifteen feet. Although they had originally been neatly finished with plaster or fine clay upon which a few vestiges of bluish paint appeared, they had later been submerged by new masses of rough adobes so that, ultimately, the third terrace, like the rest of the huaca, was solid adobe-and-earth. My finds of artifacts in the huaca were few, but interesting, consisting of several sherds of pottery of Late Chimu type and of a small fragment of yellow woollen cloth with Late Chimu figures worked in it. I believe that, later on, the Messrs. Checa did some further digging in the huaca and recovered other fragments of pottery all of the same general character.

There has been practically no archæological work done in the Chira and Piura Valleys so far as I know. Dr. Uhle and I, at about the same time, but quite independently of one another, made hasty archæological surveys of the region, reporting on them very briefly.[8] Each of us, as I say, quite without consultation or co-action of any kind, found that what little could be learned of the pre-Spanish history of the Piura and Chira Valleys was to be derived from existing archæological collections, chief among which were those of Senator Don Victor Eguiguren y Escudero, of Piura, and Don Luis Elías y Elías, of Morropón. Although neither of the collections was formed under scientific conditions, it may be said that the

FIG. 110.

FIG. 111.

FIG. 112.   FIG. 113.   FIG. 114.

FIGS. 110–114. Five specimens in the Eguiguren Collection at Piura, possibly representing
the Early Chimu culture but more probably the Late Chimu, which was really a continuation of it.

Photographs by Montero, Piura, through the courtesy of Don Víctor Eguiguren.

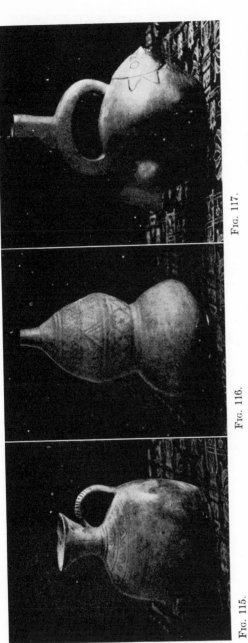

FIG. 115.

FIG. 116.

FIG. 117.

FIG. 118.

A   B

FIG. 119.   A   B   C

FIGS. 115–119. Eight specimens of Late Chimu pottery in the Eguiguren Collection, at Piura, Peru.
Photographs by Montero, Piura, through the courtesy of Don Victor Eguiguren.

Eguiguren collection represents the lower reaches of the Piura and Chira River Valleys and that the Elías collection represents the district in the Piura Valley which lies adjacent to the foothills of the Maritime Cordillera.

In the Eguiguren collection I found five pottery vessels which might conceivably be Early Chimu. They appear in Figures 110 to 114, inclusive. In the absence of scientific data concerning their provenance and the circumstances of their discovery, it is not, however, safe to state that they prove an Early Chimu penetration of that region. Nearly all the rest of the collection is either clearly Late Chimu or else Incaic. In Figures 115 and 116, we see two vessels made of red clay covered with a white slip upon which are painted in brownish black designs of the kind called by Dr. Kroeber, "cursive."[9] The other specimens shown in Figures 117–119 are all typical Late Chimu one-color ware, in this case dark red, highly burnished. Æsthetically Figure 119a is the most pleasing; for the modelling of the vicuña and the panels of low relief is excellent. Figure 119b is amusing because it shows a person who is devouring corn-on-the-cob with evident gusto. Both specimens in Figure 118 have documentary value, for they show the mode in which persons of consequence were borne along in hammock-like litters.

In the Elías collection there are other specimens of interest. A score of representative examples appear in Figures 120 and 121. All of them are typical of the Late Chimu period. One-color ware of both the dark red and the black varieties is here found in Figures 120a, b and c and e–g and in Figure 121. The two specimens not mentioned, namely, Figures 120d and 120h, show, respectively, a strange animal with its tail in its mouth and a painted design reminiscent of the step-motive in Tiahuanaco II art, and a double jar with a charming group of three birds surmounting a rectangular vessel decorated in the "cursive" style.[10]

Enough material has now been presented, I trust, to justify the assertion that the Chira and Piura Valleys were intensively occupied by people of Late Chimu culture. In order to give greater point to this claim I will now study Late Chimu art as it is found farther south.

The pottery of the Late Chimu period is so distinctive that it always stands out prominently in any collection of Andean antiquities. The greater part of it consists of blackware vessels adorned with designs in relief and with figures in the round. The material used is a black or very dark gray clay capable of taking a high burnish, sometimes because of the presence in the clay of graphite or some similar substance. Closely analogous to the blackware pottery is the redware, which is like it except that the clay is of dark red or of reddish brown color. In both the same or closely similar designs appear, and also the shapes of the pots are very much alike. One may sometimes call the two one-color ware.

Blackware was known to the Early Chimu people,[9] and it was also used to some extent during the Tiahuanaco period of the coast. It constitutes, according to Dr. Kroeber, only 3% of the Early Chimu pottery; but 75% of the Late Chimu is blackware. In this we see a definite carry-over from Early Chimu to Late Chimu. Another is the stirrup handle-spout, characteristic of both periods; another is the double-bodied jar. But features found only in Late Chimu ceramics are numerous, also, including: the double-spout linked by a bridge, a form derived from Early Nazca pottery via Tiahuanaco coast pottery; flattened or oval, rather than globular bodies of pots; a complete absence of the spirited and beautiful realistic paintings of persons and of genre-scenes or landscapes which were so characteristic of Early Chimu art; a strong tendency to use a whistling-device in the double-bodied jars.[10] True, there are cases of Early Chimu whistling jars, but they are very rare; it is only in Late Chimu times that the use of this curious trick became common. It consists of an arrangement of narrow passages in the bird- or animal-figure which surmounts one of the spouts such that, when the water is poured out of the other spout, a whistle is made by the air rushing in at the other.

To my mind, the fundamentally important fact regarding

F   G   H

FIG. 120. Eight specimens of Late Chimu pottery in Elías Collection at Morropón.
Photographs through courtesy of Don Luís Elías.

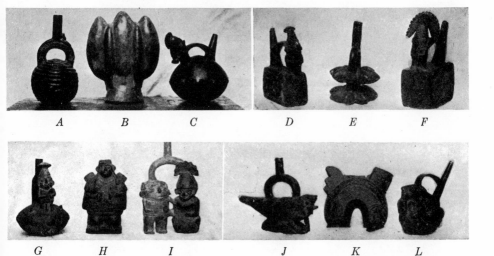

FIG. 121. Twelve examples of one-color ware, some of it black, some dark red, in the
Elías Collection at Morropón. All these specimens are of the Late Chimu style.
Photographs by courtesy of Don Luís Elías.

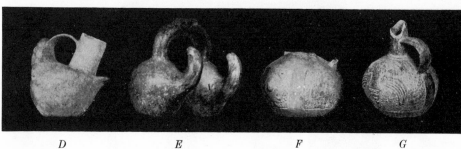

A   B   C

D   E   F   G

FIG. 122. Seven specimens of Late Chimu one-color ware found in a huaca west of Lima by The Foundation Company.

By courtesy of The Foundation Company.

A   B   C

FIG. 123. Three Late Chimu black-ware pots from the coast of Peru.

By courtesy of the Peabody Museum, Harvard University.

Late Chimu ceramics is this: The designs, on both the black-ware and the redware, were often of realistic intent, particularly in the modelled part of the ornamentation, but they never achieve the lifelikeness or the vigor of the best Early Chimu decorations whether painted or modelled. The explanation of this loss of skill, for such it seems to have been, lies perhaps in the cloying and conventionalizing influence of Tiahuanaco II art, so long paramount on the coast. For the most part, as a study of Figures 122 and 123 will show, the designs were more or less formalized, and so fell short of complete realism; others were frankly geometric in character and, in their panels of rigidly conventionalized relief wrought in the material of the vessel, they clearly show the inherited influence of Tiahuanaco II art. Only very rarely do we find realistic designs equal to the bird in Figure 122a. In short, the contrast between the art of the Early Chimu period and that of the Late Chimu period can best be summed up by saying that, whereas the former was capable of producing masterly portraits in clay of dignified personages, the best that the latter could do was to fabricate likenesses of animals or of vegetables such as those in Figures 122a, d, e and g.

Fictile decoration is not limited to pottery in the Late Chimu period. Very characteristic ornamentation, obviously related to some of the more conventionalized ceramic designs, is to be seen on adobe walls at Chan-Chan and elsewhere. Figures 124 and 125 show good examples of it. Stucco-like reliefs of this kind may have been suggested in the first place by the reliefs in stone so important in Tiahuanaco II art, but they were completely absorbed by the Late Chimu architects who used them exactly in the same way that Early Chimu architects had used wall-paintings. (See Figure 34.)

The fabrics of the Late Chimu period will be studied in some detail in Chapter XI. It suffices to say here that they were rich and harmonious in color and design, and that the weaving in them was excellent. The civilized dwellers in the shore-country seem always to have had a weakness for rich raiment for their persons and for sumptuous hangings for their houses. Even the doorways had large curtains worked by cords in a quite sophisticated manner, as is made evident by rare pottery pieces that I have seen in private collections in Peru.

Such are the chief features of the art of the Late Chimu state. We may safely think of it as a well-organized kingdom which, towards the end of its period of greatness and independence, stretched from the Chira Valley to the Pativilca Valley and from the Pacific to the summit of the Maritime Cordillera, a kingdom, in other words, of some 22,500 square miles, roughly equal in area to New Hampshire, Massachusetts and Connecticut added together. That it was a territory carefully welded together in spite of its deep-seated tendency to break up into small regions each having a river as a nucleus, is made evident by the fact that the Chimu kings, and after them the Incas, maintained a service of guides in the inter-fluvial deserts so that travellers and governmental emissaries might be led safely across the wastes. Calancha aptly styles this service, which is at once merciful and practical, the result of "moral virtue in the hearts of gentiles," and he bewails the failure of the Spaniards to continue the good work.[11]

To the south of the kingdom of the Great Chimu came another great feudal state, that ruled by a house whose head, at the time of the Inca conquest, bore the name or title of Cuismancu. His domains included the country from the Huamán Valley (the modern La Barranca), just south of the Pativilca Valley, down to and including the Pachacamac Valley (the modern Lurín Valley). The chief claim to fame of the Cuismancu dynasty was that its members had built the mighty temple of Pachacamac[12] and also the countless huacas and other buildings which dot the valleys of the Rimac and adjacent streams. Some of these are of small dimensions, but others are of incredible size, as we shall see in Chapter XII wherein architecture will be dealt with briefly.

The great huaca or pyramidal temple at Pachacamac was a place of pilgrimage for people from all parts of the Andean area. The god there worshipped was the Creator-God Pachacamac who, as will be shown in Chapter IX, was the coastal counterpart of the highland Creator-God Viracocha, worshipped at Tiahuanaco and elsewhere in the sierra. Only great lords and the priests of the fane were allowed within the temple precincts, however, and they were wont to make offerings of animals and other things or of imitations of them wrought in gold and silver, and, on the grandest occasions, they were wont even to make human sacrifices. The town adjacent to the great temple was divided into two parts, the one intended for the subjects of Cuismancu, the other for the thousands of visitors that flocked thither from far and wide. Here and there through the great city were lesser huacas which were the special chapels, as it were, of villages, provinces and kingdoms. Calancha leads us to think that certain families (perhaps those of other coastland rulers) were in the habit of maintaining shrines at Pachacamac in connection with the Creator-God's cult.[13]

On Dr. Uhle's showing,[14] Pachacamac was founded in the Tiahuanaco II period. It seems quite probable that the Viracocha-worshippers of the highlands deliberately colonized Pachacamac and there set up a great centre of their cherished religion. They may even have used the city thus established as a coast-country capital and as a distributing centre for their intellectual and political influence up and down the coast. The artifacts discovered there by Dr. Uhle and others[15] include pottery, textiles, gold, and wooden objects; they show a gradual and logical progression from the purest Tiahuanaco II style through the "Epigone" style, the red-white-black style to the Inca style. Curiously enough, blackware is not a feature of Pachacamac archæology. But Baessler shows us[16] a full-length portrait vase of a man carrying a carcass on his back and holding a knife in his hand. It is reproduced in Figure 131. Were it not that there is no distinct trace of an Early Chimu period at Pachacamac, and were it not that the truncated cone headdress of the man is quite different from the headgear of the Early Chimu portraits, not to mention its being decorated with "cursive" designs, one would be inclined to regard this as an Early Chimu specimen, so excellent is it. As matters stand, however, it is safer to call it Late Chimu in period, and to hail it as the best Late Chimu portrait pot on record.

The Rimac (Lima) Valley, some twelve miles north of Pachacamac, was also a great religious centre. At Rimac-Tampu (now called Limatambo), there was an idol reputed to speak and utter oracular statements. It was kept in a rich temple which, however, was less grand than that of Pacha-camac, and the rulers of the various regions of Peru were wont to send emissaries to consult it on questions that concerned their policies.[17]

Among the various classes of pottery found in Peru, none is more distinctive than two ceramic groups whose places of origin are, respectively, Chancay and Nievería (in the Rimac Valley above Lima), both of which fall within the central part of Cuismancu's kingdom as it was at the time of the Inca conquest.

Dr. Uhle's field work, as presented to us by Dr. Kroeber,[18] reveals five styles of pottery at Chancay which the last-named writer lists as follows, beginning with the latest: Black-on-white, three-color geometric ware, Epigonal (3 and 4 color) ware, White-on-red ware, and Interlocking ware. Although it is of the Black-on-white ware, the latest, that I wish to speak particularly here, I will say in passing that the Uhle-Kroeber Interlocking style[19] seems to me to be a pre-Tiahuanaco pottery of poor execution and decidedly provincial aspect but interesting because it shows the influence of both the Early Chimu and the Early Nazca arts; and that the Uhle-Kroeber White-on-red, Three-color, and Epigonal wares, equally provincial in aspect[20] seem to me to represent the period of Tiahuanaco II influence on this part of the coast, mixed with various influences derived from the Early Chimu and Early Nazca arts.

There is no doubt at all but that the fifth style, the distinctive Chancay Black-on-white, of which examples are shown in Figures 126, 127 and 128, is post-Tiahuanaco and pre-Incaic, probably dating from the latter half of the intermediate

FIG. 124. Wall arabesques at Chan-Chan (Trujillo), in the Late Chimu style.
Photograph by courtesy of Major Otto Holstein.

FIG. 125. Late Chimu arabesques on walls at Chan-Chan (destroyed by the rains of 1925). *After Lehmann and Doering.*

FIG. 126.   FIG. 127.   FIG. 128.

FIGS. 126–128.   Five specimens of Chancay black-on-white ware found in a huaca west of Lima by The Foundation Company.

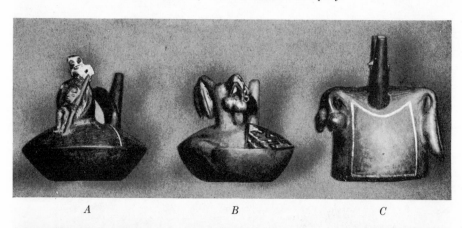

A   B   C

D   E   F

FIG. 129.   Six specimens of Nievería pottery, called 'Proto-Lima' by Drs. Uhle and Gayton.

The originals are in the National Museum of Archæology, Lima.

period which we are considering in this chapter. Dr. Kroeber, in describing Dr. Uhle's results at Chancay, found it to be late, and Dr. Strong, in his paper on Dr. Uhle's results at Ancón, found it to be so late as to impinge upon the Inca style.[21]

Having thus approximately dated the Chancay Black-on-white ware, I shall describe the specimens shown in Figures 126, 127 and 128. It will be seen at once that, although the ware is crude both as to modelling and as to painting, it is very striking. There is here a curious contrast between the would-be realism of the modelled ornamentation and the pronounced geometric character of the painted decoration. We may assume that two distinct tendencies here met and, if not blended, at any rate combined with one another. From the Early Chimu realistic tradition was derived the modelled element in this ware, and from the Tiahuanaco II conventionalized tradition was derived the painted embellishment. At least, that is my diagnosis of the situation, which I offer for the reader's consideration. The strange crudeness of the ware, made at a period when the other coast folk were producing highly finished pottery, is a point that I cannot explain. Mere local differentiation or provinciality does not suffice to interpret it, for this ware was manufactured in the heart of a powerful and civilized kingdom.[22] It is conceivable that the crudeness is in reality an artistic mannerism deliberately utilized for the sake of achieving an aspect of bold originality. If so, it certainly accomplished its purpose.

Chancay Black-on-white ware has been found not only at the home-site of the ware, but also at Ancón and in the Rimac Valley. Much light was thrown on the archæology of the country near Lima some years ago by The Foundation Company, of New York. That important concern was engaged in building a road for the Peruvian government, and during the course of the work it was found necessary to slice off a part of one of the enormous huacas between Lima and the Pacific. (See Figures 214 and 215.) In so doing pottery specimens of various types were brought to light, including the five Chancay Black-on-white specimens already discussed, and those shown in Figure 122. Quite clearly these last, although apparently contemporary, more or less, with the black-on-white pots, are not productions of the Rimac Valley folk; they are intrusive artifacts of northern provenance, in all probability. But this is a wholly natural situation when we remember that the shrine of the oracle-god at Rimac-Tampu was visited, as we have noticed above, by people from all parts of Peru. It would not be at all surprising if, as a result of exhaustive archæological study of the lower Rimac Valley, pottery from every region of the Andean area were discovered there.

The pottery found at Nievería, higher up the Rimac Valley, stands in a class by itself, seemingly restricted to the two sites called Nievería and Cajamarquilla, which lie close together about midway between Lima and Chosica. So far as I know, the only serious archæological work done at Cajamarquilla and at Nievería to date has been performed by Dr. Uhle—whose results are presented by Dr. Anna Gayton—and by M. Raoul d'Harcourt.[23] The best collections of specimens from this district are those in the National Museum, Lima, in the Museum of the University of California, and a few in the Museum of the University of Pennsylvania. The six specimens shown in Figure 129 are all in the first-mentioned collection, and they were placed there, I think, by Dr. Uhle while he was director of the Museum.

Dr. Uhle, and after him Dr. Gayton, calls certain pots not dissimilar in the main to the Nievería vessels shown in Figure 129 "Proto-Lima." The last-mentioned author makes an hypertechnical study of the ceramics in question, from which study, after much toil, one deduces that the Nievería style is post-Tiahuanaco and contains elements derived from the earlier cultural phases of the coast. Certainly the influence of the realistic tradition of Early Chimu art seems to be present in Figure 129, but present only in the modelled part of their embellishments for, so far as the painted ornamentation is concerned, particularly in the case of the second specimen in that Figure, the affinity seems to be with the Late Nazca ceramic paintings which we shall study presently in this chapter. The same may be said of the sixth specimen, which combines would-be realistic ornamentation in the round with painted decoration similar to that found in the south at this period. Only the fourth specimen seems to be wholly of northern inspiration, recalling as it does, at least superficially, some of the more conventionalized monster-designs of Late Chimu and Early Chimu art. The fifth specimen, essentially realistic, also recalls Early Chimu art, in part.

Whether it is because our information is as yet fragmentary or whether the indications that have been presented tell the truth, I cannot say; but at all events the impression remains that the kingdom of Cuismancu was far more highly developed in the Rimac and Pachacamac Valleys than it was in the northern part of its territory. It may be that future work will reveal material capable of altering the impression. Even as it is, the work performed long ago by Reiss and Stuebel at Ancón shows the presence in the cemeteries there of thousands of artifacts eloquent of high culture, but Ancón is a locality devoid of architectural remains, and one cannot, therefore, declare it to have been a great urban centre such as Pachacamac or such as Chan-Chan. The archæological richness of Ancón does not, therefore, serve to counteract the mentioned impression that the northern half of Cuismancu's kingdom was relatively backward.

South of the realm of Cuismancu was another multi-valleyed state, that of Chuquimancu (as the ruler was named at the time of the Inca conquest), lord of Runahuanac, Huarcu, Mala, and Chilca. All of these valleys, so Garcilaso tells us, "were under one chief called Chuquimancu, who was treated as a king, and exacted homage from all the neighbouring tribes, though they were not his vassals."[24] This kingdom was smaller than that of Chuquimancu, but it was fully as civilized. Its people were special adepts in agriculture, having worked out a system of cultivation that commands respect even in modern breasts. Cieza describes it thus: "From this temple of Pachacamac . . . the road leads to Chilca, and at that place there is a thing that is well worthy of note, for it is very strange. It is

this,—that neither rain falls from heaven, nor does any river
or spring flow through the land,[25] and yet the greater part of
the valley is full of crops of Indian corn, of roots, and of fruit
trees. It is a marvellous thing to hear what the Indians do in
this valley. In order to secure the necessary moisture, they
make broad and very deep holes where they sow their crops,
and God is served by their growing with the aid of dew alone;
but by no means could they make the maize grow if they did
not put two heads of sardines to each grain, these sardines
being small fish which they catch with nets in the sea. At the
time of sowing, these fishes' heads are put with the maize in
the same hole that is made for the grain, and in this manner
the grain grows and yields abundantly. It is certainly a notable thing that in a land where it does not rain, and where
nothing but a very fine dew falls, people should be able to
live at their ease."[26] The Mala Valley was and is watered by a
river supplemented by irrigation ditches; the same is true of
the Huarcu Valley (the modern Cañete Valley) in the upper
part of which is the district of Runahuanac (Lunahuaná). In
short, the small but close-knit realm of Chuquimancu was, in
pre-Incaic and Incaic days, a delicious region blessed with
abundant crops, with fruit trees, and with shady thickets in
which nested pigeons and other birds.

As we shall see when we come to the history of the conquest
of the coast by the Incas, the chief Chuquimancu and his
people were far more virile and warlike than others of the
coast-dwellers. It need not surprise us, therefore, to find that
one of the two greatest military constructions on the coast of
Peru was in the Huarcu Valley. True, both Cieza de León and
Garcilaso de la Vega lead us to suppose that the fortress which
dominates the Cañete Valley from a bluff on its southern side
was built by the Incas;[27] but here, as so often, the Chroniclers
tend to give to the dynasty of the Sun all the credit for works
which were begun long before their day and which they only
added to or completed. I do not doubt but that the altar which
surmounts the fortress and faces towards the rising sun was
built by the Incas, but the bulk of the edifice is probably

purely coastal in construction. The admirable plan of the
fortress by Don Emilio Harth-Terré is shown in Figure 130.

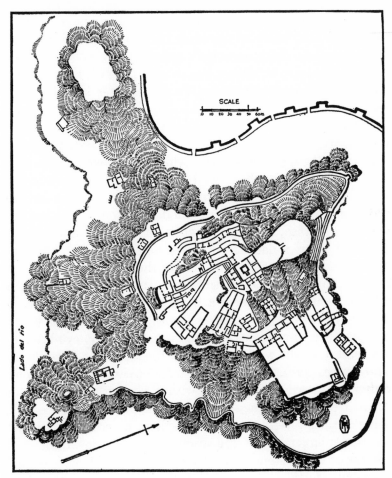

FIG. 130. Plan of the fortress of Chuquimancu, in the Huarcu (Cañete)
Valley.
After E. Harth-Terré, 1923.

The fortress may date in large part from the time when Chuquimancu was fighting to maintain his independence against
the Incas; and other parts of it may well be much more
ancient, for there must have been constant warfare between

the various ethnic groups along the coast in the period when
the various coast states—that of Chuquimancu among them—
were being formed. Moreover, in the country behind and
above Runahuanac, there lived the warlike but somewhat
backward Yauyu folk whose land, being rugged and difficult,
did not satisfy them, on which account they no doubt cast
envious glances downstream toward the fat, rich realm of the
house of Chuquimancu. Cieza, in the chapter already cited,
specifically mentions folk-memory of ancient wars between
the Sierra people, i. e., the Yauyus, and the coast-dwellers.
Both Garcilaso and Sarmiento de Gamboa testify to the
bravery of the Yauyus in terms which make one suspect that
they sometimes gave the coastal people a good deal of trouble,
for they were subsequently highly prized as soldiers by the
Incas who had some trouble in subduing them.[28] It does not
seem unduly rash, therefore, to guess that at least a portion of
the great fortress dates from the time of the early wars between the highland folk and those of the coast.

The Yauyus and their neighbors to the north and west, the
folk of Huarochirí, deserve a word in passing for the reason
that they are typical of the long series of ethnic groups which
occupied the so-called ceja de la costa (literally, eye-brow of
the coast, i. e., the western slopes of the Maritime Cordillera).
They were, perhaps in large part for environmental reasons,
rather backward as compared with the coastlanders west of
them. Nevertheless, they practiced agriculture with some skill,
using artificial terraces and well-planned irrigation ditches
for the enlargement of the arable acreage; they built rude
edifices of uncut stone in a style of masonry called pirca; and
they built fortifications, made burials in caves in the cliffs,
and manufactured rude sorts of pottery.[29] In a word, they
were in a high archaic stage of culture which contrasted greatly
with the advanced civilization of the more favored neighbors
downstream and to the west of them. Of the strange religious
cults prevailing along the ceja de la costa, and also in many
parts of the highlands proper, Fathers Arriaga, Avendaño and
Avila speak in great detail, having been shocked into profound

study of the infidel religions which they were bent upon stamping out.[30] To this subject I shall revert in Chapter IX. For the present it suffices to call attention to the Yauyu and Huarochirí folk simply as representatives of the hinterland and *ceja de la costa* peoples whose culture, with minor local variations, was very widely distributed throughout the mountain regions at this period.

Returning now to the kingdom of Chuquimancu,[31] I will mention the lamentable fact that almost, indeed quite, nothing is known concerning the pottery and other artifacts made by the subjects of Chuquimancu and his forebears. The region in question is, potentially, one of the richest archæological fields in all Peru. Let us hope that some of the younger fieldworkers of that nation will turn their attention to it.

South of the realm of Chuquimancu comes a series of valleys which were linked together culturally, if not politically, in this period. These are the valleys of Chincha, Pisco, Ica, and Nazca (or Río Grande). The Chinchas, according to legends preserved by Cieza and Garcilaso, were invaders of the coast where they early vanquished and obliterated the low-cultured folk already resident there, introducing a higher order of polity and their cult of the sea. Having made good their hold upon this portion of the coast, the Chinchas continued to foster an aggressive policy towards their inland neighbors, with the result that there was much give-and-take of cultural elements between the coast and the highlands accompanied by warfare that may have led to the conquest of the coast by the Tiahuanaco people, as Mr. Joyce has suggested.[32] At any rate it is clear that, at the period which we are considering in this chapter, the Chincha folk and their associates in the other valleys mentioned constituted an ancient, proud, and warlike confederation of civilized valley-dwellers.[33] Light is thrown on the immediately pre-Incaic history of Chincha by Father Cristóbal de Castro, a well-known churchman and missionary, and Don Diego de Ortega Morejón, *corregidor* (magistrate) of Chincha, who, in 1558, wrote as follows:

All the old *curacas* (chiefs) of these valleys are agreed that, before they were made subjects of the Incas, the ruler and lord of this valley (*i. e.*, Chincha) was Guabiarucana, whose house is still extant, and whose kinsfolk and hereditary properties are known. And in the Valley of Ica, at this same time, the lord was Aranbilca, whose houses, farms, and kinsfolk are known to this day. And in the Valley of Limaguana (correctly Runahuanac) the lord who ruled at this time was called Caciarucana. Each one of these governed apart by himself in his own valley, reasonably and with justice. There were also chiefs for the divers tribes, each division having farms for its use, and each Indian having land for his maintenance. These people were ever at war with the Indians who were their nearest neighbors, without ever passing beyond their vicinity into other districts, without even knowing of such districts, unless it were by hearsay, without being acquainted with other peoples. This was because the people were constantly killing one another, unless it chanced to be in time of peace or of truce. The most common way to attain tranquility between neighbors was to exchange women with them. The folk of these valleys did not adore the sun, but they did have the same rites, sacrifices and fasts as at the present time.[34]

We have here, as I see it, a vivid documentary portrayal of the formation of one of the great coastal kingdoms. Not only do we find that there was definite connection with the Runahuanac folk, neighbors of the Chinchas on the north, but also, as is made evident by the personal name of the lord of Chincha, with the Rucana people who dwelt in that part of the *ceja de la costa* which is behind and above the valleys in question. Moreover, we have a very definite hint that each valley had its chief lord and a number of lesser chiefs under him—in other words, an incipient feudal system. Again, war and peace evidently alternated with one another, being but parts of the process of kingdom- or of confederation-building. The localized interests of the valley-dwellers is explained, no doubt, by the fact of their having formerly been ruled with a strong hand from Tiahuanaco, the result of which was to turn their gaze only at their neighbors without thinking of more distant conquests. Finally, in the interchange of women, we see, I think, a practice which inevitably tended to amalgamate the blood of these valley-dwellers and to distribute their type of culture more or less evenly throughout their region—the four valleys mentioned, those of Chincha, Pisco, Ica, and Nazca.

The work done by Dr. Uhle and by his continuators, Drs. Kroeber and Strong, throws interesting light upon the matter of the archæology of this region.[35] They have shown us that the semi-circular Valley of Chincha, watered by irrigation ditches which tap the Chincha River and dry it up before it reaches the sea, contains many remains of huge edifices that represent both pre-Incaic and the Incaic periods. One vast congeries of buildings is known as La Centinela and it measures some 1,800 feet east and west by about 1,000 feet north and south, with a height ranging from about 30 to 50 feet above the soil. The construction is of adobe. This huge mass of material contains rooms and halls of considerable dimensions. As Dr. Uhle clearly shows, the western end of La Centinela is mainly Incaic, but the eastern end is largely earlier than that and therefore belongs to the period which here concerns us. This building was evidently a fortress and a palace combined. Another great structure is the Huaca de Tambo de Mora—as it is now called—evidently a palace built in pyramid formation around a court. Dr. Uhle suggests that this cluster of terraced structures, provided with stairways to the platforms on their summits, was the residence of a prominent chief.[36] This huaca, as a whole, measures some 500 feet by about 400 feet. A third imposing structure, known as La Cumbe, a terraced pyramid some 50 feet high, was probably the sanctuary of the chief local deity, called Chincha Camac by the Incas, whose shrine was established in this valley in imitation of the great temple to Pachacamac, up the coast.[37]

In a word, the Chincha Valley was, in pre-Incaic times, an urban centre comparable to Chan-Chan, Rimactampu, and Pachacamac. Together with the Ica and the Río Grande (Nazca) Valleys to the south, it constituted during some five hundred years, from about 900 to about 1400,[38] the seat of the culture which I have called Late Nazca.

Drs. Kroeber and Strong[39] in taking over the materials

acquired in the field by Dr. Uhle and publishing them have injected a meaningless tangle of subdivisions into the discussion which will require years to unravel. In like manner, the culture sequence of the Ica Valley has been studied by them[40] with an elaborate attempt at classification which only obscures the main trend of cultural history. In spite of their elucidations, however, it is quite clear that, in the Ica region, there was a long series of cultural phases including Early Nazca, Tiahuanaco, and the later pre-Incaic styles.

It is these last, represented by Figures 132–136 of the present volume, which are particularly characteristic of the period in question. Some of them are very strongly influenced by Tiahuanaco II art; others again display the heritage from Early Nazca art, both as regards their rich and sombre coloring and as regards their manner of depicting human- and animal-forms.

The most distinctive of the pots belonging to the Late Nazca period are those which have geometric patterns obviously inspired by textile art. These designs constitute a new form of painted embellishment on pottery and they are peculiar to this southerly region of the Peruvian coast during the Late Nazca period.

We have now made a rapid, and necessarily incomplete, survey of the civilization of the states which were strung out along the Peruvian coast in the period between the fading away of Tiahuanaco influences and the advent of Inca influences. It is well to sum up our impressions by pointing out that, local variations in pottery, architecture, customs, etc., notwithstanding, the coastal civilization of this period was, in the main, a whole, and that its fundamental elements, modes, and manners were constant throughout the area covered by this survey. This fact was tacitly recognized by many of the best Chroniclers who, very often, speak of the shore-folk as a whole, under the name of Yunca. A typical passage, illustrative of the material elaboration of the coast cultures in general, occurs in the writings of Cieza de León, who says: "These Yuncas were very refined, and the lords were luxurious and

FIG. 131. Late Chimu portrait vase.
After Baessler.

FIG. 132. Late Nazca pottery from Ica.
After Schmidt.

FIG. 133. Late Nazca pottery from Ica. *After Schmidt.*
The originals are in the Ethnological Museum, Berlin.

FIG. 134.

FIG. 135.

FIG. 136.

FIGS. 134–136. Late Nazca pottery from the region of Ica. *After Lehmann and Doering, and Schmidt.*

The originals are in the Ethnological Museum, Berlin.

fond of festivities. They travelled on the shoulders of vassals, had many women, were rich in gold and silver, cloth, precious stones, and flocks. In those times they were served with much pomp. Heralds and buffoons went before them, porters attended on them, and they observed religious ceremonies."[41] Passages of like importance can be duplicated in the works of several other Chroniclers.

The coastal districts beyond Ica and Nazca must now be passed in rapid review. Archæologically the Provinces of Camaná and Islay, which together compose the seaward side of the Department of Arequipa, are practicaly speaking *terra incognita*. It is known in a general way, that they were well peopled at the time of the Inca conquest. This is made evident by Dr. Hrdlička, whose photographs of various sites in the northwesterly part of the region show us vestiges of rather humble adobe buildings like the less pretentious edifices elsewhere on the coast.[42] There were also at least two fortified hills with crude stone structures now much ruined. Dr. Hrdlička also collected a number of slings which I studied and found not to be different from similar weapons elsewhere on the coast.[43] This is all that the available data permits me to say concerning the archæology of the coastal region designated. Let us hope that before long some of the Peruvian field workers, or else archæologists from other countries, will make an intensive study of this part of Peru.

Almost equally vague is our knowledge of the pre-Incaic culture of Moquegua, anciently Moquechua. Dr. Montenegro y Ubaldi, in his brief remarks about the early history of that region,[44] leads us to suppose that the people there were only fairly well advanced, but enough so to construct pyramidal tombs of stones and earth, measuring some three feet in height. They had cloth garments, pottery of a sort unspecified, and various implements; but they lacked the use and even the knowledge of metals. Their food was provided in part by agriculture. As Dr. Montenegro has pointed out, the chief importance of Moquegua historically arises from the fact that it was the first coast province to be conquered by the Incas.[45]

They did so, however, not without difficulty, for the natives of Moquegua made a stand against the invaders at a poor little fortress which they had in a place called Cochuna, among the foothills of the Maritime Cordillera.[46] We thus see a pathetic combination of relatively modest cultural attainments with intense devotion to their independence, a combination which reminds one very strongly of the Araucanos of Chile, of whom we shall speak in a later chapter.

There now remains to be considered only the archæology of the Tacna and Arica region. As usual—one may say—Dr. Max Uhle is our chief informant concerning the archæological content of this region.[47] He found there a series of artifacts representing a number of cultural periods. Up to Tiahuanaco times and the related Epigonal period, which he dates together about 600 to 900 A. D., culture was of the archaic type and was characterized by wooden objects, basket-work, crude textiles, nets, lines, spears and spear-throwers, stone implements (but apparently no metal ones), and other things which one would expect to find among an archaic-cultured fishing and hunting people who, somehow, had failed to become agriculturists. Strangely enough these people mummified, or at any rate preserved, the dead at full length, not in the bent position usual in the Andean area.[48]

The Tiahuanaco-Epigonal period of Tacna and Arica was not different from the corresponding period elsewhere in the coastal region. The *queros* or cups and bowls which represent it might come from almost any part of the Peruvian shore-country. Following it came the period which Dr. Uhle calls Atacameño, for the reason that it bears affinities with the regions south and southeast of this. He dates it 900–1100 A. D. The pottery is coarse and heavy, being decorated with ill-arranged designs that have a certain boldness and vigor but no beauty. The shapes of the pots, however, are interesting in that they have clearly some relationship—of a nature to be discussed later—with Incaic pot-shapes. These same shapes persist into and are emphasized in the succeeding Chincha-Atacameño period, 1100–1350 A. D., according to Dr. Uhle.

But the designs in this period are far better and richer than in the earlier time, doubtless because of the influence of Chincha or Late Nazca art which, as we have seen, was producing excellent textile-like designs. Historically, the pottery of the Chincha-Atacameño type is valuable in connection with the study of Inca pottery.

In the highlands the general cultural level was so low, after the disintegration of the Tiahuanaco II culture, that, in some localities, it might fairly be called a neo-archaic culture. Arts, crafts, and aspirations towards earthly magnificence were all lost—swept away by a great wave of disaster. Only the rudimentary forms of them remained. Of this situation Montesinos, in passages already cited and quoted, gives us a vivid picture, and the Inca Garcilaso de la Vega corroborates him by almost always describing the mountain-folk, whom the Incas later conquered, as being mere barbarians. In a word, the small tribal or clan groups which came into being after the central authority of Tiahuanaco—whatever the nature of that authority may have been—died away at its source, were not greatly different from that series of peoples to whom, earlier in the present chapter, I have referred as dwelling along the *ceja de la costa*. More specific descriptive comment upon these small and humble societies will be made in the course of my narrative of the growth of the Incaic empire, in Chapters VI and VII.

Nevertheless, there were still societies which managed to remain above the general level of mediocrity. As one might expect, one group of these, representing an intermediate culture which I have been wont to designate as the Colla-Chulpa culture, or as the Tampu-Toco cultural period,[49] had its seat in the Titicaca basin, precisely where its predecessor, the Tiahuanaco II civilization, had had its centre and its greatest strength.

Certain of the Chroniclers would have us believe that a general condition of warfare between small states organized on patriarchal lines was prevalent throughout the Andean highlands at this time;[50] but others lead us to suppose that there were confederacies, or even nascent kingdoms, of considerable strength. Cieza de León, for example, speaks of two great rival lords or tyrants in the Collao (Titicaca basin) whose names were Sapana and Cari, and Garcilaso, correcting him, calls them Chipana and Cari.[51] He describes them as being the last of two long dynasties of pre-Incaic chiefs whose respective houses had long been at deadly feud. Likewise, he differs from Cieza in placing them in the neighborhood of Lake Paria or Aullagas, which receives the waters of the Desaguadero River. Father Morúa is even more informative, for he tells us that, in pre-Incaic times, there was a great state which extended from the Pass of Vilcañota—where there was a frontier wall—down into Chile. Three chiefs of this extensive realm are mentioned, Tocai Cápac, Pinan Cápac, and Javilla. They all ruled before the Incas and had as a captain in their service a certain Choque Chuman.[52] It is possible that Morúa is here mentioning pre-Incaic chiefs of the line whose history is described so unsatisfactorily by Father Montesinos, for on the list of kings given by the latter we find the 41st king named Toca Corca Apu Capac, which faintly resembles the name Tocai Cápac, but no names in the least like Pinan Cápac or Javilla appear, so that the possibility is not very great after all.

We may safely say, however, that in the Titicaca basin, usually designated by the Chroniclers under the name of Collao —the land of the Collas—there were chiefs whose power was greater than that of most of their contemporary highland rulers.

From the archæological standpoint the most interesting remains of this period are the strange edifices called *chulpas*. Strictly speaking these are towers of stone or of adobe, sometimes rectangular, sometimes circular in plan. Various uses have been suggested as having been theirs at the time when they were built. On the whole it seems probable that most of them were tombs of chiefs.[53] The chulpas vary considerably in architecture, in dimensions, and, no doubt, in age. The simplest of this class of buildings are round towers made of uncut stones laid in clay or mud, which style of masonry is usually called *pirca*. Some of them are broader at the base than above; but all have carefully made, if somewhat rustic-looking, cornices and conical roofs. On the inside of the structure is a small chamber with a cone-shaped vault formed by causing each layer of stones to overlap slightly the layer below it until the apex of the vault is reached. The same principle was used by the Maya architects in their most grandiose constructions.

Although it is impossible for me to enter into a detailed discussion of the various types of chulpa, I can summarize the matter by saying that the most primitive type of chulpa is found at Quellenata, near the northern end of the Lake, and at Ullulloma, some fifty miles northwest therefrom. Other examples occur at Sillustani, a peninsula in the Lake of Umayo west of the northern end of Lake Titicaca; at Calaqui (or Kalaki), on the eastern shore; and at Coni and Curahuara, far to the southeast of the Lake.[54] In a word, the pre-Incaic chulpa, whatever the degree of excellence its construction may display, may be said to abound in most parts of the Titicaca basin, the southernmost group of which I know being at Pucará, in Bolivia, some 85 miles south of La Paz, where some chulpas made of adobe and measuring two metres square by four high were found by M. Sever.[55]

Chulpas, or at any rate chulpa-like buildings, are not, however, confined to the Titicaca basin. The late Dr. Farabee found some rectangular adobe chulpas at Colocolo, "on the high plateau between Oroyo and La Paz,"[56] and he also found some very interesting stone *pirca*-style chulpas set close together like houses in a city block.[57] My friend, Mr. W. V. Alford, also found chulpa-like buildings in the vicinity of Oroya, at a place called Pachacayo, some of which stood alone, others being in blocks, but all having flat tops, two storeys, and being in the *pirca* style of masonry. See Figures 137 and 138. These buildings, it will be observed, have well-made doors and windows. Dr. Hrdlička also reports on and pictures chulpa-like burial towers of *pirca* masonry, those which he describes being in the district of Huarochirí.[58] Finally, Sr. Villar Córdova, in his archæological work in the Province of Canta, which lies in the upper part of the Chillón and Chancay (or Pasamayo) River-Valleys, northeast of Lima, found some very interesting and well-made chulpas at Canta Marca. One of them has an exceptionally good vaulting, held up by a circular central column with niches in it, the burial being in the floor at the base of the column.[59] It is not entirely certain, however, whether these structures are pre-Incaic or Incaic. The tribe which built these structures was that called Atauillo or Atavillo, and it was of Colla origin, probably having been settled in the Canta region by the Incas.[60] We cannot, therefore, take the rather good masonry described by Sr. Villar as being typical of the stone work done by the *ceja de la costa* folk whose pre-Incaic culture was probably lower than this.

Not wishing to pile Ossa upon Pelion in the way of evidence about a point that is not, after all, wildly exciting, I will refrain from further citations concerning chulpas. In concluding this chapter, however, I feel called upon to justify its title by reminding the reader that, following the breakdown of the Tiahuanaco II civilization, there was a distinct decline in culture throughout Peru and Bolivia, a decline far greater and longer lasting in the highlands than on the coast. In the latter zone, as we have seen, particularly in the central and northern parts of it, culture quickly rallied from the shock of the cessation of Tiahuanaco II influence, and new states, with new architectural and artistic abilities, soon entered in upon a new period of growth some of whose chief manifestations we have passed in rapid review. In the mountains, on the other hand, there was little or no recovery of this sort, until the enlightened Incas made good their control over the highland populations.

NOTES TO CHAPTER V

[1] Uhle, 1903, p. 26.
[2] Uhle, 1906c, p. 575.
[3] Uhle, 1903, p. 22, and Plates IV and V. Kroeber, 1927, p. 262.
[4] Uhle, 1903, Ch. xi, pp. 26–34.
[5] Cabello de Balboa, N. Y. Public Library MS., pp. 515–517.
[6] Calancha, Bk. III, Ch. ii.
[7] Accounts of Tumbez include: Garcilaso, Pt. I, Bk. IX, Ch. ii; Cieza,

Pt. I, Chs. liv, lv, and lix; P. Pizarro, 1921, I, pp. 152–155. The fact that the same family retained the chieftaincy of Puná until after 1570 is attested by the Licentiate Salazar de Villasante, who wrote his *Relación General de las Poblaciones españolas del Perú* in 1573–1574. He mentions the chief of Puná, Don Diego Tomalá, and his son, Don Francisco, as being good Christians. (*Relaciones geográficas de Indias,* I, pp. 9–12.)

[8] Uhle, 1920. Means, 1919b.

[9] Kroeber, 1925, p. 216.

[10] Kroeber, 1925, pp. 216–218.

[11] Calancha, Bk. III, Ch. i.

[12] Garcilaso, Pt. I, Bk. VI, Ch. xxx. Cieza, Pt. I, Ch. lxxii; Pt. II, Ch. lviii. Cobo, Bk. XIII, Ch. xvii. Córdoba y Salinas, 1650, Ch. xiiij.

[13] Calancha, Bk. II, Ch. xix.

[14] Uhle, 1903, Ch. xv.

[15] Uhle, 1903; Baessler, Vol. IV.

[16] Baessler, Vol. IV, Pl. 155.

[17] Garcilaso, Pt. I, Bk. VI, Ch. xxx.

[18] Kroeber, 1926b, pp. 290–291.

[19] Kroeber, 1926b, Plates 88, 89, and 90.

[20] Kroeber, 1926b, Plates 83–87, inclusive.

[21] Kroeber, 1926b, p. 269. Strong, 1925, pp. 188 and 189, where he analyzes Reiss and Stuebel's Plates 91 and 92.

[22] Kroeber, 1926b, p. 270, seems to support the provincial theory. An argument in support thereof is the fact that all the earlier styles at Chancay look "provincial," also. R. and M. d'Harcourt, 1924, pp. 23–24, briefly mention Chancay ware.

[23] Harcourt, R., 1922; 1924, pp. 24–30. Gayton, 1927.

[24] Garcilaso, Pt. I, Bk. VI, Ch. xxix.

[25] This is correct. See Atlases of Paz Soldán and Cisneros, and also Markham's notes to the passage quoted.

[26] Cieza, Pt. I, Ch. lxxiii, p. 255 of Markham's translation, 1864.

[27] Garcilaso, Pt. I, Bk. VI, Ch. xxix. Cieza, Pt. I, Ch. lxxiii.

[28] Garcilaso, Pt. I, Bk. VI, Ch. xvi. Sarmiento, Ch. lxiii.

[29] Hrdlička, 1914, pp. 7–8. Joyce, 1912, p. 152. Markham, 1910, pp. 180–181.

[30] Arriaga, 1621; Avendaño, 1648; Avila, 1608, 1611. See Means, 1928, pp. 299–303 and 306–310, for data on these writers.

[31] Interesting material will be found in: Cheesman Salinas, 1909, and Larrabure y Unánue, 1874 and 1893.

[32] Joyce, 1912, p. 187.

[33] Cieza, Pt. I, Chs. lxxiv and lxxv, Pt. II, Ch. lix. Garcilaso, Pt. I, Bk. VI, Chs. xvii and xviii, tacitly accepts the Chinchas' accounts of themselves. But in Ch. xix he denies that the Yuncas, *i. e.,* the Chinchas, ever invaded the highlands, averring that, had they done so, they would have died from terror because of the thunder and lightning in the mountains, unlike anything in their own region. This argument, however, is vitiated if, as may have been the case, the Chinchas were themselves of mountaineer stock; and it is rendered negligible in any case by its obvious psychological falsity.

[34] Friar Cristóbal de Castro and Don Diego de Ortega Morejón wrote

204 ANCIENT CIVILIZATIONS OF THE ANDES

Relación y declaración del modo que este valle de Chincha y sus comarcanos se gobernaban antes que hobiese ingas y después que los hobo hasta que los cristianos entraron en esta tierra. It is dated at Chincha February 22, 1558, and is published in Vol. L of the Colección de documentos inéditos para la historia de España, pp. 206–220, Madrid, 1867, edited by the Marquis of Miraflores and Don Miguel Salvá. (My quotation from pp. 206–207.)

35 Uhle, 1924. Kroeber and Strong, 1924, 1924b.

36 Uhle, 1924, p. 65.

37 Cieza, Pt. I, Ch. lxxiv. Garcilaso, Pt. I, Bk. VI, Ch. xvii. Alexander, 1920, p. 224. Uhle, 1924, pp. 67–69.

38 Uhle, 1920b, p. 458; 1924, p. 69.

39 Kroeber and Strong, 1924.

40 Uhle, 1924b, 1924c, 1924d. Kroeber and Strong, 1924b.

41 Cieza, Pt. I, Ch. lviii.

42 Hrdlička, 1914.

43 Means, 1919d.

44 Montenegro y Ubaldi, 1906.

45 Montenegro y Ubaldi, 1906, pp. 70–71.

46 Montenegro y Ubaldi, 1906, pp. 72–73. Cochuna is now known as San Agustín de Torata. It is a well-known health resort for persons suffering from pulmonary diseases. Garcilaso mentions Cuchuna as being the place where the coast peoples' fort was. (Pt. I, Bk. III, Ch. v.)

47 Uhle, 1917b, 1919, 1919b.

48 Uhle, 1919b, pp. 4–21.

49 Means, 1917; 1917c, pp. 330–333.

50 Calancha, *Discurso*. Casas, 1892, Ch. i. Cobo, Bk. XII, Ch. i. Garcilaso, Pt. I, Bk. I, Chs. ix–xiv, inclusive. Lizárraga, Pt. I, Ch. lxv. Oliva, Bk. I, Ch. ii. Polo de Ondegardo, 1873, p. 154. Román y Zamora, Pt. III, Bk. II, Ch. x. Sarmiento de Gamboa, Chs. viii and ix.

51 Cieza, Pt. I, Chs. c and cii. Garcilaso, Pt. I, Bk. III, Ch. xiv.

52 Morúa, Bk. III, Ch. xxi. Means, 1928, p. 414. Garcilaso, Pt. I, Bk. I, Ch. xviii.

53 Squier, 1877, p. 388. Nordenskiöld, 1906b, p. 29. Markham, 1910, p. 187. Joyce, 1912, pp. 135–136. Beuchat, 1912, pp. 577–578.

54 Tschudi, 1868, Vol. V, pp. 202–210. Markham, 1871, p. 308. Squier, 1877, Chs. xviii, xix, and xx. Nordenskiöld, 1906, 1906b. Bandelier, 1905; 1910, pp. 165–240. In the latter place Dr. Bandelier shows that the modern Indians differentiate between the Chulpa (or Chullpa) period and artifacts, and the Incaic. Posnansky, 1911b, p. 17.

55 Sever, 1922.

56 At least so Farabee, 1922, p. 180, phrases it, but this passage ought, perhaps, to read: "at Corocoro, on the high plateau between Oruro and La Paz." See Farabee's Plate 23.

57 Farabee, 1922, p. 180, and Plate 24a.

58 Hrdlička, 1914, Plates 3 and 4, and pp. 9–10.

59 Villar Córdoba, 1923.

60 Villar Córdoba, 1923, p. 4.

CHAPTER VI

THE ORIGINS OF THE INCA DYNASTY AND THE HISTORY OF THE EARLIEST REIGNS

THE origin of the great dynasty, which shaped for the ancient peoples of the Andean area the amazing final phase of civilization found there by Francisco Pizarro and his followers in 1530, is still, to a certain extent, shrouded in mystery. But here, as in other parts of this general field of study, research into the folklore and into the material vestiges of early culture is little by little bringing to light facts upon which firmly founded knowledge will eventually be based. An examination of the folk-memory concerning the origins of the dynasty, as reported by the leading Chroniclers of Peru, will throw the best possible light upon the major points of the matter.

As I have pointed out in detail in an earlier writing[1] the Chroniclers of Peru fall, for the most part, into two groups or "schools," the one being that which I have called the Toledan School, the other the Garcilasan School. The former might equally well be dubbed the Discouragistic or Denigratory School, for, under the guidance of the Viceroy Don Francisco de Toledo, in the 1570s, it became the official version of Incaic history, its chief purpose being to display the Inca dynasty before the world as a line of usurpers, tyrants, and murderers. The underlying objective of this school was to justify the establishment of Castilian power in the Andean area and elsewhere in America, this end to be served by showing the Incas to have been bastards and usurpers whom Charles I and Philip II of Castile, descendants of those questionable sovereigns, Sancho IV and Henry II of Castile, had every right to supersede, not only because they were so much superior in their hereditary right to rule, but also because America was only a fitting reward for the services rendered to God during the

eight centuries of the Reconquest in Spain, and also because
Alexander VI—that holy pontiff—had given them the right.[2]

The chief exponent of the Toledan School was Captain Don
Pedro Sarmiento de Gamboa, Cosmographer of Peru, obedient
henchman of Toledo. In his *History of the Incas,* written in
1572 at the Viceroy's behest,[3] he tells us that four brothers,
whose names were Manco Capac, Ayar Auca, Ayar Cachi, and
Ayar Uchu, together with their sisters, Mama Ocllo, Mama
Huaco, Mama Cura (or Ipacura), and Mama Raua, dwelt
some six leagues or eighteen miles from Cuzco at a place called
Paccari-Tampu, which means *Tavern of the Dawn.*[4] A hill in
that locality bore the name of Tampu-Tocco, meaning *Tavern
of the Windows,* which had in it three windows called Maras
Tocco, Sutic Tocco, and Capac Tocco. It is said that from
these windows issued various clans, the brothers and sisters
coming forth from the central window, Capac Tocco, Rich or
Splendid Window. Under their leadership, ten *ayllus*—clans
or tribes—marched from Tampu-Tocco to the Cuzco Valley
where they waged war upon the people already living there
and finally imposed their authority upon them. It is interesting to note in passing that the Cuzco Valley, according to Sarmiento, was early occupied by three ayllus called Sauasera,
Antasaya, and Hualla, and that, prior to the arrival of the
Incas, three other ayllus peacefully entered the Valley and
settled there, led by chiefs whose names were Alcaviquiza, Copalimayta, and Culumchima.[5]

The crux of this tale is that, not only did the four brothers
and the four sisters constitute a ruling class at the time when
they left Paccari-Tampu—for they were leaders of ten ayllus
whom Sarmiento names—but also, on arriving in the immediate vicinity of Cuzco, Manco Capac and his spouse proceeded
to make the six tribes already living in the valley their subjects also, thus laying the foundation for an imperial career.
This came as a sequence to various deeds of violence performed in the course of their slow march on Cuzco, during
which they managed to rid themselves of most of their brothers and sisters. On the journey, also, while dwelling at a place

called Tampu-Quirao, Inn of the Cradle, Manco Capac begot
a son on his sister Mama Ocllo, the lad being given the name
of Sinchi, or Cinchi, Roca.[6]

This tale is also told, albeit with differences in detail, by
Cieza de León, who was in Peru more than twenty years before
the time when Sarmiento wrote. This honest and intelligent
adventurer was, moreover, a lover of historical truth, and he
certainly bore no special grudge against the Inca family. It is
interesting, therefore, to note that he corroborates Sarmiento,
the arch-enemy of the Incas.[7]

The Inca Garcilaso de la Vega, undoubtedly the greatest
and most authoritative of the Chroniclers, avers that the Sun
created a man and a woman, his children, and placed them on
an island in Lake Titicaca. He gave them a staff of gold, and
bade them to go whithersoever they wished and to settle down
permanently in whatever place it might be that the staff, at
one blow upon the earth, should sink into the ground and dis-
appear. The pair journeyed northwards, testing the earth with
their staff wherever they halted. For a time they rested at
Paccari-Tampu, seven or eight leagues south of Cuzco. Thence
they at length went onwards to the Valley of Cuzco, and there,
on the hill of Huanacauti hard by the site of the city, the
golden staff vanished into the earth. At that time the Valley
was densely forested, and the people living there were plunged
in a dismal state of vice, misery, and confusion. The prince
and the princess went about through the country, he to the
north and she to the south of Huanacauti, calling the people
together in the name of their Father, the Sun. With the multitude which they thus assembled they founded the city of
Cuzco, dividing it into two parts, Hanan Cuzco or Upper
Cuzco where those people whom the prince collected were settled, and Hurin Cuzco or Lower Cuzco where the princess's
followers were established. Thus did the Inca Manco Capac
and the Coya (Queen) Mama Ocllo found their city and state.
Thereafter, the Inca "taught the Indians those occupations
which appertain to a man, such as breaking up and cultivating
the ground, and sowing corn and other seeds, which he pointed

out as fit for food and useful." The Coya did likewise for the women, instructing them in weaving, sewing and other household duties. This was the version of the myths relating to the origins of the Incas that the youthful Garcilaso had from an Inca who was his maternal uncle.[8] He tells it with considerable, and entirely creditable, feeling, adding to it the version of the matter which was current in the regions south and west of Cuzco. It ran as follows: After a great flood—perhaps the universal deluge—a man appeared at Tiahuanaco who was so powerful that he divided the world into four parts over each of which he placed a king. The first of these kings was called Manco Capac, the second Colla, the third Tocay, and the fourth Pinahua, and they were made lords of the North, South, East, and West quarters of the world, respectively. (It will be remembered that, towards the end of the previous chapter, reference was made to these chiefs.) Each of these kings was ordered by the creator to go into his own land and to govern it. Accordingly, Manco Capac went northwards to Cuzco, and there, using the surrounding people for material, he founded a kingdom.[9]

This tale is corroborated in part by Father Calancha, who says, "The Indian Mancocapac, first King of Peru, was a native of Tiaguanaco or of some small village nearby."[10] Father Cobo relates several myths without, however, subscribing to any one of them for the reason that he considered them all to be ridiculous fables. The migration from Paccari-Tampu to Cuzco and that from Titicaca to Paccari-Tampu and thence to Cuzco are both set forth by him. He gives the names of the brothers and sisters much as Sarmiento does, speaks of the hill of Huanacauri (as he calls it), and mentions the divisions of Upper and Lower Cuzco as Garcilaso does. Like him, also, he goes on to show how Manco Capac, having founded the city, assumed the rôle of culture-hero, assuming the heavy task of lifting the people out of the forlorn state in which they had been blindly struggling for some generations past.[11]

The myths referred to thus far possess many features in common and constitute a definite cycle of tales. In certain of the Chronicles, however, we find another type of legend which can best be designated as the Shining Mantle Story.[12] Its chief points are as follows: Mama Siuyacu, whose name means *the gradually widening ring* and may have been prophetic of the Incas' future greatness, perceived and lamented the misery, bestiality and ignorance in which the people were living throughout the highlands. Being an audacious woman and richly endowed with initiative force, she determined to improve matters for the benefit of every one, particularly her own kindred. Accordingly, she took her beautiful son, Roca or Rocca, and, after arraying him in a specially prepared costume of fine cloth shining with closely sewn bangles of gold (a kind of cloth called *chaquira* in Quechua), she placed him in a certain cave in the hillside overlooking Cuzco. The lad was carefully instructed to appear at the mouth of the cave at a certain moment and to announce himself to the people as Son of the Sun and as one sent by his Father to rule over the land. All went as the astute dame Siuyacu had calculated: the youth duly appeared at the mouth of his cave; the rays of the sun fell upon his bangled garment and caused it to flash and glitter blindingly; the credulous people, seeing this marvel, believed all that was told them concerning the divine origin of the boy. Thus, by a bit of well-planned chicanery, was the dynasty of the Incas founded, if we are to accept this fable as historical—as to which point, more anon.

A point that all the fables examined thus far have in common is this: They fail to give to Manco Capac and his sister-spouse a specific earthly ancestry. One story, however, recorded by the Jesuit, Father Oliva, supplies this deficiency in a distinctly unexpected manner. His version of the origins of the Incas runs thus:

Father Oliva opens his recital by telling us that he had been unable to obtain any information concerning the antecedents of Manco Capac until, in some papers given to him by Dr. Bartolomé Cervantes, a canon of the cathedral of Charcas or La Plata (anciently Chuquisaca, but now called Sucre), he found some notes based on the narrations of one Catari whom

Canon Cervantes declared to have been a former keeper of the *quipus* or knot-records under the Incas. Although Catari was still living towards the end of the sixteenth century, his information was far older, for he had inherited his office and the knowledge of native lore that went with it from a certain Ylla or Illa who had been keeper of the *quipus* under Mayta Capac, one of the early Inca rulers.

According to Catari, then, as reported upon by Oliva who transcribes from the Cervantes papers, the remote forebears of the Indians were driven to America from the Old World after the Deluge, and eventually some of them reached Caracas, which may possibly be identified with Caráques, on the Ecuadorian coast, rather than with the inland capital of modern Venezuela. Others landed at Sampu, called by the Spaniards Santa Elena, and also on the Ecuadorian coast. This last group was led by a chief named Tumbe or Tumba. After a time he sent forth many of his followers under one of his most trusted captains, ordering them to seek for more spacious and fertile lands and to return within a year to Sampu in order to make their report. The explorers departed, but they never returned to Sampu, for they wandered far away and eventually peopled the lands of Brazil and of Chile. Tumbe assumed that they must all have perished, and yet he gave orders for a relief expedition, but his own death overcame him not long afterwards.

Quitumbe and Otoya, the two sons of Tumbe, quarrelled bitterly after their sire's death, and Quitumbe presently led his followers southwards from Sampu, reaching in due course a pleasant plain where he founded a city which he named Tumbez in honor of his father. Quitumbe was married to a beautiful woman named Llira whom he left behind him at Sampu, in a state of pregnancy, the understanding being that he would return thither and rejoin her. Llira bore a son whom she named Guayanay and who was destined to be the forebear of the Incas.

Otoya, meanwhile, the younger son of Tumbe, remained at Sampu, giving himself up to evil courses. So great was his wickedness that presently a race of giants, even more nefarious than he, invaded his dominions and, first imprisoning him, overwhelmed his people with their inordinate lechery.

During this same time, Quitumbe was sending out expeditions from Tumbez in all directions, as well to learn about the surrounding country as to find, if possible, traces of those whom his father had sent forth. As time went by, he ungratefully forgot his wife, Llira, and, learning of the fate which had overtaken his enemy and brother, and wishing to avoid its like, he caused canoes to be built for himself and his people. At first they planned to settle on the island of Puná, but, finding it too arid to suit them, they passed over to the mainland and up into the highlands of Quitu or Quito, to which region Quitumbe gave his name. From there, later on, some of Quitumbe's people went southwards through the mountains, and eventually they settled in the provinces of Cuzco and Charcas (now south-central Bolivia). Later on, always according to Catari as reported upon by Oliva, Quitumbe went and dwelt in the region of Rimac, where he built a great temple in honor of the god Pachacamac. There he died, at an advanced age, leaving as his heir his rapacious son, Thome, who succeeded him and subjugated many neighboring nations.

Llira, meanwhile, seeing herself thus cavalierly abandoned, was filled with implacable hatred for her husband and, with Guayanay, her son by him, she went up into the highlands of Jancar—possibly Huántar or Jauja—where she addressed fervent prayers to Pachacamac, beseeching him to aid her. A fearful thunderstorm and a great earthquake thereupon convulsed heaven and earth, and Llira took them to be a sign that the god had heard her supplications with favor. By way of thanks she planned to sacrifice Guayanay. She made him bathe in a fountain as a preparation to being consumed upon a pyre which she now prepared. But a royal eagle—that is, a condor—swooped down from the sky and carried off the lad to the isle of Guayán, lost amid the waves of the sea. There the boy lived until he became a beautiful youth of twenty-two. At that age he built himself a raft upon which he journeyed to the mainland where he was promptly captured by savages dressed in pelts who haled him along to their chief. This personage imprisoned poor Guayanay under a strong guard, and doubtless it would have gone ill with the youth had not the chief's daughter, the lovely Ciguar, seen him and fallen in love with his beauty. She managed to give her adored one an axe with which he slew four of his six guards and, while the remaining two were running to tell their chief, Guayanay and Ciguar escaped, making their way to Guayán where, in a plain besprinkled with flowers, and under a tree whose succulent leaves gave them an abundance of sweet water, they made their idyllic home. For many years thereafter the descendants of Guayanay and Ciguar continued to dwell on that mystical isle lost amid the waves of the sea. All went well with them until invaders came, led by a son of Guayanay's cruel half-brother, Thome, who was then ruling the coast-country and the kingdom of Quito. This severe king had passed a law condemning all adulterers to be cut up into small pieces, and his own son and heir, being found guilty of the proscribed crime, was forced to flee with some of his companions. Their intention was to journey along the shore until Thome's wrath should be appeased, but a tempest swept them from their course and for twenty-two days they were the plaything of the waves. At this time Atau, son of Guayanay and Ciguar, was ruling twenty-four people who had been dwelling in peaceful plenty upon the isle of Guayán. When at length the fugitives from the mainland disembarked upon the isle, Atau perceived that the slender resources of his home would soon be overstrained and that, as a consequence, his people would better seek more ample homes on the mainland, the great extent of which he now learned for the first time, from the wanderers whom he had welcomed to his island home. But Atau was very old, and knowing himself near death, he called to him his son, Manco, and bade him to make the move as soon as possible after he, Atau, should die. Manco was a brave, clever, and affable lad, well beloved by his vassals. It was clear to all that some great destiny awaited him for, when he was but six or seven years old, a condor had descended close to him and never left him more, sheltering the child's head with her wings from the heat of the sun, making her nest in his house, and there raising her little ones. All of which was interpreted as an omen of future felicity.

Atau died at length, and Manco, now aged thirty years, obedient to his father's command, went with his followers to the mainland. They touched first near Rimac but, displeased by an earthquake, went on to Ica. There Manco was again disgusted, this time by the boisterousness of the sea, and he determined to go inland, and, like other great adventurers before and since, he burned his boats behind him and marched eastwards and upwards into the bleak and unfrequented country later known as the Collao. Presently Manco and his people arrived at the Lake of Chucuitu or Titicaca which was so large that they thought that it must be some mysterious inland sea. Manco decided to explore the strand of the Lake unaccompanied. To his people he gave orders that, if he did not return to them within a certain time, they should disperse in all directions and that, to all persons whom they encountered during their search for him, they should announce that they were looking for the Son of the Sun who had been sent to earth by his father to rule the land.

Manco then turned to the left—that is, to the north—and after wandering for some days, not without considerable deprivations, arrived at a place called Mamaota, a league and a half from Cuzco. There he found a number of caverns in one of which he hid himself. Later it received the name of Capac-Toco or Royal Window. When the period which he had fixed for his followers had expired, they set themselves to seek him in every direction, and some of them determined to cross the Lake which, so they judged, could not be very wide, for pigeons and other birds were constantly traversing it. Having constructed two or three canoes, they arrived at a great island where they were astonished to find a vast cavern shaped by the hand of man. Its walls were all covered with ornaments of gold and silver, but it was entered only by a very narrow door. They destroyed their canoes and took up their abode in the cavern, agreeing among themselves that they would tell all comers that they had issued from that mysterious cave in order to seek the Son of the Sun, and, in order to recognize one another, in case they should chance to be separated, they pierced their ear-lobes and inserted in them great rings of a reed called totora, which much enlarged the holes. Some days later, at the time of the full moon, they saw the arrival of several canoes filled with Indians who were astonished to find there a cavern and to learn that those who had issued from it were seeking for the Son of the Sun. Thenceforward it was the custom of the Indians to make sacrifices in that place.

Very soon the rumor was spread throughout the country that the Son of the Sun had come forth from the cavern of Capac-Toco and that he had appeared at Pacaritambo in a costume ornamented with plates of gold. It was also said that, on coming forth, he had hurled with his sling a stone which had shattered a rock more than a league away. An immense multitude of Indians quickly assembled around him, and all the chiefs of the countryside sent messengers to find out the truth of the reports. Manco caused them to gather before Capac-Toco, and at sunrise he came forth covered with plates of gold that shone so brightly in the rays of that heavenly body that he seemed to rival it in radiance. His own majestic mien indicated a monarch made to govern the whole earth, and the people did not hesitate to prostrate themselves before him and to recognize him as their king. Thus the monarchy was founded, without the shedding of a single drop of blood, and during the three months of festivals that followed Manco took for the first time the name of Inca, derived from the word *Inti*, which means the Sun.

During these festivals Manco showed himself to the public only five or six times. He retained the most important chiefs near him, ordering the others to retire to their homes and to announce his advent to their people. They were all to return at the end of a year, bringing with them all who were disposed to follow them. The reunion took place at the moment fixed

upon, and at the same time Manco saw the arrival of those
companions of his whom he had left at the Lake of Titicaca,
all of whom were of the same blood as himself. He swore them
to secrecy concerning their origin, and they preserved it always. Then he commanded that all who had brought him
tribute should be ranged on one side and that those who had
not done so should be drawn up on the other in order that
they, as well as their women and children, might be massacred.
Among the latter were the descendants of Thome. Nevertheless, some of them escaped the slaughter, and thus, through
them, was preserved the tradition of the origin of Manco-
Capac, for his own people always kept it an inviolable secret.[13]

Such is Father Oliva's report of Catari's account of the origin of the Incas. Nor is Oliva the only Chronicler who ascribes
a mortal pedigree to the founder of Inca greatness. Another
who does so is the Augustinian, Friar Alonso Ramos Gavilán,
who lived at about the same time as Oliva and, like him, labored as a missionary in the region of Lake Titicaca.[14] Ramos
tells us the following tale:

A chief who ruled near Cuzco had two sons, the elder being
in appearance like the other Indians, the younger—whose
mother died in bearing him—being blond and fair-skinned.
Astonished by his younger son's looks, the father consulted a
great wizard who was a friend of his, and the two came to an
understanding about the lad. When the old chief died, the
ordinary elder son succeeded him; the younger, meanwhile,
was being brought up in great secrecy which was shared only
by the Indian woman who was the child's nurse. Growing to
manhood, the lad became so beautiful that the wizard won-
dered if he were not the Son of the Sun, whom those people
adored as their chief god. The Devil aided him to come to the
conclusion that this was so, and when the boy was still very
young the wizard slew the nurse for the sake of greater secrecy.
Thereafter he instructed the boy in what he was to do, and
taught him to believe that he was indeed the Son of the Sun.
At the same time, he wedded him to his own sole daughter.
When the young man was twenty years old, the wizard ar-

rayed him in specially prepared garments thickly sewn with
gold leaf, placing a splendid headdress of gold and brilliant
feathers on his brow, and at the proper moment he displayed
him upon the slope of a hill above Tambo where his apparel,
shining in the rays of the newly risen sun, drew the glances of
the multitude of Indians below who were enjoying an orgy of
drinking. Well drilled in his part, the young man advanced
before the wonderstruck people, and made a speech in a loud
voice, saying that it was the Sun himself who spoke, having
come down to earth in compassionate mood in order to announce to them that, eight days later, he would send his son,
in appearance like himself, to rule over the people as sole lord.
The hearers, credulous always, but especially so at that moment from drunkenness, believed what they heard. The shining figure suddenly vanished from their sight, by the simple
expedient of darting into a cave in the hillside. Then the
wizard went about among the people, fostering their wonder
and their acceptance of the story, and, at the appointed time,
a vast concourse of people having in the meanwhile assembled,
the lustrous lad again appeared, and he was generally ac-
claimed as Son of the Sun, and as king.[15]

A version of the Shining Mantle fable is also related by
Bishop Oré, who tells us that the first Incas came from Lake
Titicaca to Pacaritampu, three or four leagues from Cuzco.
There Manco Capac showed himself in resplendent raiment
and, proclaiming himself as Son of the Sun, he was accepted
by the people as their lord.[16]

It is Father Cabello de Balboa, however, who throws the
most penetrating light upon the fog of misty legends surrounding the origins of the Incas. He makes a clear distinction between the myths current among the ordinary folk and those
current among the members of the Inca caste. The people, so
he tells us, held to the fable of Paccari-Tampu or Tampu-
Tocco, and believed that Manco Capac and his three brothers
and four sisters—whose names he gives in the usual way—
came from there to Cuzco by very slow stages and that, during
their long-lasting migration, a son, Sinchi Roca, was born to

Mama Ocllo and Manco Capac, an event that considerably shocked the rest of the group until, after reflection, most of them became resigned to the situation. One brother, Ayar Auca, was irreconcilable, however, and said such cutting things to the incestuous pair that he was finally shut up by all the others in a cave. Subsequently, during the farther part of the leisurely advance, another brother, Ayar Cache, insulted a powerful wizard and was punished by being turned into a stone. The remaining members of the little band thereafter dwelt for years at Matahua, and there the young prince, Sinchi Roca, came of age, his ears being pierced at a suitable ceremony now held for the first time. During their stay at Matahua, "these deceitful brothers and sisters" were in the habit of "giving the people to understand a million fabulous and vain stories, thereby preparing the way for themselves, who already intended to seize the overlordship of that entire district, a plan which they later carried out."[17]

This, so Father Cabello avers, is the story as told among "the uninstructed vulgar." The Incas themselves related it in a very different manner, deriving their historical knowledge from the royal quipus or knot-records. According to their version, the history of the dynasty began in the year 945 A. D. At that time a certain barbarous family living in the highlands of Peru began to have great ambitions and to look disdainfully upon the humble folk around them. The family consisted of four brothers and four sisters, as told in the popular legend, and they resolved to make themselves great, if not by right or by force, then by guile. Accordingly, the four sisters busied themselves during many days in the manufacture of a new style of clothing which all of them were to wear. The new raiment was made in great secrecy, and the makers gave it every beautiful color of which they had knowledge. To make it still more splendid, they covered the surface of the garments with many spangles of burnished gold.

When these preparations were completed, the group slipped away from their old home and, by hidden roads that were seldom used, they journeyed, always by night and without being seen by anyone, as far as certain buildings which they found at a spot some five leagues from Cuzco. Although the buildings themselves were unused, there was a small square nearby where the folk of the vicinity were wont to congregate from time to time in order to hold a market. On the day after their arrival the members of the barbarous family rose at dawn and arrayed themselves in their new and resplendent apparel. Then they all filed through one of the windows of the house where they were directly into the square where the unsus·pecting natives were holding their market. They told the astounded onlookers that they had come from Heaven, that they were the children of the Sun, and that they had been sent to earth by him. Marvelling at the magnificent attire and dignified bearing of the lordly strangers who had thus appeared, as if by a miracle, among them, the simple rustics made no difficulty about acknowledging their divine origin, and all the folk for a league or two around hailed them as their rulers.

Shortly after this, Mama Ocllo became pregnant by her brother, Manco Capac. This sort of thing was condemned by the people of that day, and their brother Ayar Auca especially resented it, threatening to reveal the truth to the tribes which were now flocking thither from all sides. Manco Capac, fearing lest his new subjects come to despise him and so withdraw their obedience, resolved to slay Ayar Auca. This was done by means of a trick. Later, when Mama Ocllo was on the point of giving birth to her child, it was announced that she had been made pregnant by the Sun. In due course, apparently at Matahua, Sinchi Roca was born, eldest son and heir of Manco Capac, who was now lord over a considerable realm.

The remainder of the group continued at Matahua for twenty years, spreading about all sorts of fables concerning themselves. The group dwindled, however, as time went by, for Ayar Cache was poisoned by a wizard, and Ayar Uchu and Mama Rahua died without children. The survivors, Manco Capac, Mama Ocllo, and Mama Huaco, announced that the departed had been taken up into the sky again. Mama Huaco, who was very warlike and mannish, yet wise in counsel and of great prudence, threw two golden rods in such a way that one fell at a place two cross-bow shots from Matahua while the other landed in the Huaca Pata (Holy Terrace or Square) in the city of Cuzco. The first of these rods entered but a little way into the earth, but the second buried itself deeply in the soil, from which it was argued that the destination of the group was Cuzco.

The rest of the story is tedious—and likewise unpleasantly gory—for it relates how the Incas, finally arriving at Cuzco, caused the inhabitants of that place greatly to suffer, chiefly through the bloodthirsty activity of Mama Huaco. Thanks largely to this vigorous but unscrupulous lady, the Incas finally overcame Copalimayta, rightful king of Cuzco, and made themselves at last lords of that city. Poor Copalimayta, on resigning his power into their hands, went away to a place where none could see him. His parting message to the victors was that, whenever on some lofty pass in the mountains they should see the snow lying, they were to think of him, for there his exiled spirit would be lingering.

Manco Capac and his family now settled at Coricancha where a temple was laid out in honor of the Sun. He also planned the city of Cuzco in a new way for his kinsfolk and his now numerous following. Four wards were designated, wherein this tale is different from some others, which speak of two wards, only, as we have seen.[18]

Such, very briefly presented, are the principal legends relative to the origins of the Inca dynasty. It now remains to comment upon them from the standpoint of common sense.

It will have been observed that the legends fall into two major groups: those which are simple migration myths, and those which, in addition to being migration myths, contain memories of astuteness and chicanery of the Shining Mantle type whereby the Inca rule was established over the drink-sodden and gullible folk of the countryside around Cuzco.[19]

Of the latter group of tales that derived from Catari and recorded by Father Oliva demands special attention. Its significance appears to me to be this: It seems probable that in

Catari's day (early or middle sixteenth century) some vague folk-memories were still extant of a time when the pre-Incaic highlanders had had more or less constant intercourse with the peoples of the coast. Catari, *apud* Oliva, is the only authority who makes the Incas descendants of dwellers on the coast; but this may reasonably be taken in a figurative sense merely as typifying a former cultural relationship, perhaps even a political one. It should be noted in passing that Oliva makes it out that Tiahuanaco was pre-Incaic, for he avers that it was anciently called Chucava and that popular belief held it to have been constructed by "the mighty Huyustus, lord of the entire world," some of whose administrative arrangements Sinchi Roca adopted.[20] In a remark like this we discern a vague but interesting remembrance of the Tiahuanaco empire. The fact that the myth displays the forebears of the Incas as coming up from the coast into the highlands at a time subsequent to the disintegration of that empire simply means, I conjecture, that the Inca tribe, doubtless following the example of many others at that time, was shifting its habitat and that, in so doing, they preserved shadowy traditions of a former time when they had had to do with the folk upon the coast.

Another bit of evidence, in the Catari-Oliva version of pre-Incaic history, of folk memory of the Tiahuanaco cultural period is the fact that Quito, Tumbes, Rimac, and Pachacamac are all specifically mentioned as having been ruled anciently by ancestors or by kinsmen of Manco. This seems to indicate that the Inca dynasty was indissolubly connected in the popular mind with an empire earlier than that inaugurated by Manco.

It is clear enough, as Professor Louis Baudin has lately pointed out,[21] that there were two sets of native historical narratives, the one designed for the people, the other strictly reserved to the imperial family. Cabello makes it quite plain that the dark side of the historical picture was pretty well suppressed in the story as told to the populace, but that, among themselves, the Incas dared to remember the devious methods

whereby they came to power. This, from a politician's standpoint, is entirely right and desirable. Both sets of histories,
however, were probably based in part upon quipus and were
recited and taught by the *amautas* or professional sages of the
Incas' court.

It is best now to consider some of the most important modern theories concerning the origin of the Incas. Some of them
turn upon a study of the native languages.

Garcilaso states that the Incas had a language peculiar to
themselves.[22] Cobo thinks that this language was merely a
dialect of the Quechua tongue and that it was spoken by the
tribes in the Valley of Tampu.[23] This, and much cognate evidence, is carefully studied by Drs. Patrón and Romero in an
important article of some seven years ago in which, with reason, they conclude that "the special language of the Incas—
if, indeed, it ever really existed—was nothing more than a
dialect of the Quechua tongue."[24]

To Dr. Max Uhle is due the credit for marshalling a particularly impressive array of linguistic and archæological evidence concerning the origin of the Incas. He has shown us that
the Quechua language was used only in a small area round
about Cuzco until the Incas gave to it the great distribution
which it had at the time of the Spanish conquest. On the
other hand, Aymará, or rather Colla, was spoken not only in
the Titicaca basin but also along the coast as far north as the
Rimac Valley and in the highland region behind that part of
the coast. He takes care to point out, however, that most of
pre-Spanish Peru was bilingual in that people spoke their own
local dialects as well as the more widely distributed official
language. Therefore, if Colla was indeed the language of the
Tiahuanaco empire—and this constitutes a very great unanswered problem—the wide pre-Quechua distribution claimed
for that tongue is highly significant. Dr. Uhle supplements his
remarks concerning the area of the Colla idiom by a study of
pottery from Arequipa, Urubamba, Yucay and other places in
southern Peru which have yielded up not only what seem to
be the crude beginnings of ceramic forms that were later per-

fected by the Incas, but also incipient versions of sundry decorative motifs that were later characteristic of the highest art of the Incaic period.[25]

On a basis of folklore combined with archæological evidence, it is possible to arrive at a general idea of the probable facts of the matter. It seems quite likely that the Incas were originally but a small tribe of llama-tending, potato-growing mountaineers apparently not a whit different from hundreds of others existing throughout the highlands after the collapse of the Tiahuanaco II culture. Whether their habitat was south of Cuzco or whether Tampu—mentioned by several Chroniclers—was the place now called Ollantaytambo, in the Urubamba Valley, is a point that has not yet been settled conclusively. Humble though they were, the Incas were providentially gifted with a genius for rulership and with a robust, pugnacious temperament not hampered by undue scrupulosity so that they were impelled irresistibly to go forth from their cramped home in order first to establish their authority over the peoples whose territory they invaded, second to consolidate a nucleus for a strong expansive polity, and finally, through gradual growth, to build up one of the most amazing empires the world has ever seen. The fact that other highland tribes were taking much the same course as themselves by establishing dynasties and shaping nascent polities was a circumstance which had much influence upon the Incas' upward career, for the rivalries resulting therefrom engendered recurrent struggles for mastery, and the struggles bred strength and ever more strength in the victors.

* * *

As briefly as possible I shall now trace the history of the Inca empire reign by reign, chiefly following the light thrown by the great Inca historian, Garcilaso de la Vega, and by others of his School, a group including as its chief members Cabello, Calancha, Cieza, Cobo, Montesinos, and Morúa. Of Manco Capac little further need be said here. It has been conclusively shown in recent times that he was a legendary character, of the same shadowy stuff as the fabled chiefs, heroes and kings who open the history of many another country.[26] So far as he was real at all, he was a culture-hero, an innovator, a reformer fired by great ambitions. More than this one cannot say without entering the realm of mere conjecture.

We may picture the condition of things in the Andean highlands in the eleventh century as having been this: Innumerable small societies in a neo-archaic cultural status were ruled by petty chiefs whose authority varied from one *ayllu* or tribe to another. In the less advanced of these ayllus the *sinchis* or chiefs—literally "strong men"—were wartime leaders only, chosen by the heads of the households in their ayllus to direct military operations against unfriendly neighbors and, with the restoration of peace, they were shorn of their power, becoming again mere heads of households like the electors. As happens everywhere under like circumstances, the sinchis perceived that a continuance of warfare meant that their own power became permanent. They accordingly set themselves to make armed aggression a permanent thing.

The first Inca chief of whom it can be said that he was an historical figure was Sinchi Roca. The appearance in his name of the title "sinchi" is significant, for it shows quite clearly that he was merely a war-chieftain of the type referred to above. True, there is evidence, in the Chronicles, that he early succeeded in rendering his authority permanent, doing so either by some stratagem of the Shining Mantle type or else by a studied policy of martial activity or by a combination of the two, and that he thus prepared the ground for the founding of a definite dynasty. He thus became the permanent ruler of a compact little hegemony of tribes in the Cuzco Valley, some of his subjects being members of his own ayllu, and others the original inhabitants of that Valley and its vicinity.

Sinchi Roca, whose dates were about 1105–1140,[27] first consolidated his authority in the immediate vicinity of Cuzco, and then turned his attention southward. There were a number of tribes in that direction whose general culture was similar to that of his own subjects. He seems to have decided to add them to his realm by peaceful means, if possible, but by force or by other methods if necessary. With astuteness character-istic of his family, he hit upon an efficacious way of attracting outsiders to him of their own accord. This consisted of en-riching the life at his court with ceremonies and jollifications of kinds never seen before. These novel and delightful pas-times awakened the curiosity and the envious admiration of other tribes round about, increasing the prestige of Sinchi Roca not a little, while at the same time making him seem less terrifying.[28]

With a technique that deftly combined tact, diplomacy, timely allure, and martial aggression, Sinchi Roca extended his realm southward from Cuzco through the uppermost por-tions of the Urubamba Valley and so to the Vilcañota Pass. The country in that direction, particularly at Piquillacta—Flea Town—and in its neighborhood, is filled with vestiges of this period in the shape of buildings constructed in the *pirca* style of masonry to which I referred in Chapter V.[29]

At the Pass of Vilcañota, Sinchi Roca came to the southern brim of the Incas' original habitat. It stands at the head of the Urubamba (or Vilca-mayu) Valley, of which the Huata-nay River, on whose banks Cuzco stands, is a tributary; and beyond it lies the Collao, land of the Collas, in the Titicaca basin. At the Pass of Vilcañota—sometimes called La Raya, the Line or Frontier—there are still visible the remains of a defensive wall of pirca masonry and of a number of houses perhaps intended to shelter a garrison. This wall, however, is in all likelihood far older than the Incas, for it is quite prob-able that it was a traditional boundary between the Quechua-speaking and the Colla-speaking peoples.[30] Sinchi Roca seems to have paused for a time, at any rate, on his side of the wall, peering over the top of it, as it were, in order to regard with calculating eye those chiefs beyond the wall who were doing exactly as he was doing himself, namely, shaping young states of steadily increasing power.

Such a cessation of the process of expansion was natural enough for, as shall be made clear, it was ever the policy of the Incas to consolidate and inwardly organize their conquests as they went along the triumphant path which Fate had ordained for them. To this aspect of the Incaic polity, recently emphasized by M. Louis Baudin, of Dijon University,[31] I shall return later on.

Connected with the formation of a strong state was the question of Sinchi Roca's marriage, his chief marriage, rather. If we are to believe Garcilaso, Cieza, and Montesinos, Sinchi Roca took as his *Coya* or Queen his own sister, Mama Cura. Sarmiento says that the Coya of Sinchi Roca was Mama Cuca of the town of Saño, and Cabello states that she was Mama Coca, daughter of Suti Guamán, chief of Saño.[32] If those who aver that this Inca's marriage was of the incestuous kind are correct, it follows that dynastic pride must have developed very early among the Incas. On the grounds of common sense and inherent probability, however, it seems to me much more likely that the head of a newly established ruling family would most naturally seek to strengthen his position by taking as his queen the daughter of a neighboring chief. But, as will appear in later pages, the whole question of the Incas' marriages—particularly those of the early rulers—cries aloud for careful analytical study.

It is certain, at any rate, that Sinchi Roca laid the foundations of Incarial pomp and ceremonial. This, again, is a subject of extreme intricacy, for the Chroniclers give us a wealth of ill-assorted data concerning the ordinary and the festive apparel and accessories of the Incas and their subjects, data which have never been reduced to orderly sequence by modern analytical study. It is fairly clear, nevertheless, that the essential facts of the matter were somewhat as follows: Three distinguishing marks were characteristic of the Incaic caste, *viz.*, the *llautu*, a thick fillet bound several times around the head and being of several colors, for the Inca himself, but black for the others; the shaven head upon which only a thin lock was left; and the bored ears distended to a great degree by the use of stoppers, the ears being more or less distended according to the rank of their owner. The *llautu* is also called *huincha* by some of the early writers. With it was associated, on special occasions, a gay-colored feather headdress variously called *suntur paucar* or *masca paycha,* which seems to have been a gorgeous affair bright with plumage and adorned by tassels. This, apparently, was a badge of the imperial office. Upon his person the Inca wore a tunic reaching to the knees and called *uncu* or *capac uncu,* over which could be donned a square mantle richly wrought called *yacolla.* At ceremonies the Inca bore in his hands a mace or war-club which seems to have served him as a sceptre or wand of office. Finally, his feet were protected from bruises by sandals called *usuta.*[33] Doubtless all of these personal embellishments began modestly enough, but there is every reason to believe that as time went on and the grandeur of the Incas' worldly position increased from reign to reign, they also increased in splendor and intricacy.

To return now to the subject of Sinchi Roca's additions to his realm, I will say that it is not certain whether he ever made a serious attempt to extend his sway beyond Vilcañota. Garcilaso hints that there is authority for believing that he did extend his power to the northern end of Lake Titicaca, but he does not himself affirm this, stating that Chuncara, near the modern village of Santa Rosa, was as far as he went in his conquering career.[34] It may be that Sinchi Roca only conducted preliminary explorations and skirmishes beyond that point, leaving the task of conquest and consolidation to his successor.

Lloque Yupanqui, *circa* 1140-1195, though far from being the only child of his father, was his legitimate heir and so followed him as wearer of the *suntur paucar.* His name was one of happy augury, for it signifies "Left-handed one who will be renowned for pious actions."[35] His first official act was to inaugurate an excellent custom which was ever afterwards observed by the Incas on coming to power. After the period of state mourning for his father was passed, he made a thoroughgoing tour of inspection in all parts of his realm. This had the twofold result of informing the new ruler as to the circumstances of his kingdom and of putting the ruled into direct contact with their sovereign. Furthermore, it brought Lloque Yupanqui into touch with various *curacas* (chiefs who had become permanent rulers instead of being mere *sinchis*) who were his neighbors and who, in many cases, now became his vassals voluntarily. Among those who did so were Huamán Samo (Samo the Falcon) curaca of Huaro (the modern Huarocondo) and a certain wise old man named Pachachalla Viracocha. A wife was found for this Inca—who seems to have been a trifle hard to please—by Pachachalla Viracocha and the Inca's brother, Manco Sacapa, in the person of Mama Cava, daughter of the curaca of Oma, near Cuzco.[36] The Inca married her amid the bibulous rejoicings habitual at the court of Cuzco.

During the reign of Lloque Yupanqui there were three periods of aggressive warfare for the purpose of increasing the realm. The intervals between were devoted to internal organization. This alternation of war with intensive consolidation was one of the secrets of the Incas' strength.

The conquests of Lloque Yupanqui were all in the northerly portion of the Titicaca basin and along the western shore of the Lake. In those districts lay the lands controlled by the strong confederacy of the Collas, whose principal centres were Hatun-Colla and Paucar-Colla, both of them near the northwestern margin of Titicaca. As already mentioned, the Collas were at this time building up a state similar in character and aspirations to the Inca's own, and it was therefore inevitable that the two growing powers should come into collision and should struggle for mastery. For the Incas this was the first of a series of formidable conflicts by which, in a remarkable crescendo, their strength was tested ever more and more severely and, after each successive victory, enlarged and justified.

By means of several campaigns in which martial vigor was aided by diplomacy and by skilful propaganda, Lloque Yupanqui extended his dominion all down the western shore of the Lake. At strategic points he established his garrisons and introduced his governmental institutions. The Inca's army at this period, according to Garcilaso,[37] numbered 10,000 warriors. This figure may at first seem excessive, but if we allow ten non-combatants to every fighting-man we find that the population of the realm was only about 100,000 at the end of the reign, which certainly is a modest estimate for a territory three hundred miles long by fifty, on an average, wide. This area is roughly equivalent to that of Massachusetts, Connecticut, Rhode Island and Long Island taken together.

Mayta Capac, the third Inca, *circa* 1195–1230, followed the example of his father by making a preliminary inspection of his empire. During his father's lifetime he had received a valuable training in the arts of war and of government, for another secret of the Incas' great strength as a dynasty was the invariable custom of preparing the heir to the *llautu* for the heavy tasks and responsibilities which would eventually descend upon him.

The territory brought within the empire by Mayta Capac was both extensive and varied. In his earlier wars the principal foe encountered by him was the still unsubjugated portion of the Colla stock. Beginning, after due preparations and inspections, at the southwestern corner of Lake Titicaca, the Inca led his forces to the Desaguadero River. Crossing it on a fleet of balsas, he went onwards around the end of the Lake and so reached the valley where Tiahuanaco lies. For the first time the Incas now beheld the imposing remains of the great city which had been the centre of the ancient empire of their predecessors. Intelligent as they were, they could not fail to be deeply impressed by the many evidences that met their eyes of superior skill in masonry and in the handicrafts. Moreover, the mystery which surrounded the ruins awakened their curiosity, but all their efforts to learn the history of the place from the debased folk whom they found living meanly in huts among the ruins were quite in vain.

Both Garcilaso and Cobo make it plain that the most important result of the acquiring of Tiahuanaco was the increase which it gave to the Incas of technological skill in several directions, particularly in wall-building.[38] This is wholly natural considering the fact that, up to the time of their arrival at Tiahuanaco, the Incas' masonry had all been of the *pirca* kind, neat—if executed painstakingly—but never impressive. At the site of which they were now become the owners they found stone-work that stimulated them to improve their own masonry.

Beyond the Tiahuanaco Valley, in an easterly direction, lay two great provinces called Hatun Pacasa and Cacyaviri, both of which were occupied by well-organized folk of the Colla stock. The territory included in these provinces took in all the country between Lake Titicaca and Chuquiapu (La Paz). It was an easy matter to bring it under the Inca's sway.

In later campaigns of this reign the Inca power was carried all around the Lake and also for a considerable distance eastward and northward from its shores. Furthermore, the Inca's armies entered the coastal zone for the first time, entering the province of Moquehua or Moquechua (Moquegua) from the eastern or inland side. The incursions into that region appear to have been tentative forays led, not by the Inca personally, but by trusted captains of his. At about the same time, as a result of a campaign lasting three years, Mayta Capac in person added to the realm a great stretch of country southeast of the Titicaca basin. In doing this he was greatly aided by the prestige won for him by a hanging bridge of *chahuar* (aloe) fibre which he had caused to be built across a canyon, much to the wonderment of the simple folk round about.[39] This structure was, perhaps, the first of its kind to be built by the Incas, but later on many like it were constructed in all parts of the empire.

After a period of peaceful internal organization came the final campaign of Mayta Capac. His armies had already crossed the Maritime Cordillera in descending upon Moquehua, but now the Inca himself, assisted by his ablest generals, added to the empire all the country lying west and southwest of Cuzco as far as the Maritime Cordillera. In that region of tangled mountain ranges and narrow tortuous valleys dwelt the folk known as Quechuas and Aymarás, who were closely akin to the Inca tribe itself and spoke the same tongue, Runa Simi, better known as Quechua, which, under the Incas, became the official language of the whole empire.

Having done so much, Mayta Capac and his generals proceeded to do still more. Marching by way of Villilli, Allca, and Taurisma, the Inca led an army of 20,000 men over the Maritime Cordillera and down into the country beyond it. On the western slopes he found a number of large, sparsely settled provinces, including Cotahuasi, Pumatampu (Inn of the Puma), and Parihuana-cocha (Lake of the Flamingo).[40] An idea of the town of Pumatampu is clearly given by Figures 139–142. These places occupy the upper part of the western slope of the Maritime Cordillera and, being rather difficult country, were added to the empire only after considerable trouble. Soon afterwards the districts of Aruni, Coropuna, Collahua, and Arequipa were, in like manner, brought under the rule of the Inca.[41] Thus, though the Inca's armies had not yet penetrated the lower part of any coastal valley, they had mastered a very extensive area which included the upper portions of all the river-systems from the Moquehua River up to the Acarí River.

Regarding the Coya of this Inca there is even more confusion than usual, among the Chroniclers. Garcilaso avers that she was Mama Cuca, sister to the Inca. Cieza calls her Mama Cahua Pata and makes her daughter of the lord of Oma, in all of which he mixes up this Inca with his predecessor. Sarmiento says that she was Mama Tacucaray, native of the town of Tacucaray. And Cabello names her Mama Coca Taucaraz, of the village of Taucaraz. From contradictions such as these one despairs of extracting an orderly interpretation until, upon reflection, he sees that, even yet, the incestuous type of marriage was not logical for the Inca and that, on the contrary, alliance with some friendly chieftain's daughter, or some strong vassal's, would be. But in vain does one seek upon the map for Taucaraz or Tacucaray. On the whole, therefore, Father Cobo's statement is the most convincing, for he tells us

FIG. 137. Pachacayo, a ruined pre-Incaic (?) town on the hills beyond Oroya.

FIG. 138. Detail showing *pirca* construction.
Photographs by courtesy of W. V. Alford, Esq.

FIG. 139. A general view of Pumatampu. Near the upper right-hand corner is the isolated ruin of the Sun-Temple, erected by the Inca.

FIG. 140. A detail of the architecture of Pumatampu.

Photographs by courtesy of W. V. Alford, Esq.

that the Coya of this Inca was Mama Tancaray-Yacchi, daughter of the chief of the Collahuas who dwelt between Aruni and Arequipa in the country conquered by Inca Mayta Capac in his last campaign. Such a marriage as that is altogether credible.[42]

According to Father Cabello an internal development of some importance psychologically took place at this time. It was the formal recognition, by the Inca Mayta Capac, of a great variety of wizards, soothsayers, herbalists and such folk who, for a long time, had carried on clandestinely their more or less sinister professions. The Inca who, sapiently enough, thought that they would do less mischief if they were brought out into the open, gave to the formerly illicit practitioners a recognized place in the body of society, and from that time onwards, until more than a century after the Spanish conquest, they continued to be a conspicuous element in Andean sociology.[43] Indeed, only a self-blinded optimist could say that they have now ceased to exist in Peru. In this benevolently astute policy of the Inca towards the spell-casters we have an example of the profound commonsense which was one of the strongest characteristics of the dynasty.

Capac Yupanqui, fourth Inca, *circa* 1230–1250, after the usual preliminaries of state mourning and inspection of the realm, assembled an army of 20,000 men and prepared it for active warfare. In due course he led his forces southwestwardly from Cuzco and, first crossing a wonderful aloe-fibre suspension bridge which he had had built across the Apurimac River, he and his troops entered the region beyond, which had been added to the empire in his father's latest campaigns. There he further strengthened the imperial authority and regulated the governmental institutions, at the same time intensifying the cultural education of the people by the use of the customary Inca methods.

This ruler was the first of his dynasty to weave any part of the shore-country solidly into the fabric of his realm. It is interesting to note here that Capac Yupanqui did not always lead his armies in person, in which fact we see the result of the now greatly augmented scope of the imperial office.[44] In the earlier reigns, when the realm was still relatively compact, the Inca could attend to the affairs of government and, at intervals, also conduct in person the military operations intended to enlarge the empire. From the time of Capac Yupanqui onwards, however, there was an increasing tendency to delegate military matters to the heir apparent and to other close kinsmen of the Inca, leaving the sovereign himself free to direct the government from Cuzco or from whatever place he might be in temporarily. Many of the Inca generals, all members of the imperial caste—the *"orejones"* (big ears) of the Spanish writers—were men of high ability. In the reign of Inca Capac Yupanqui the captain-general of the armies of aggression was the monarch's brother, Auqui Titu, and he had as his chief colleagues four other Incas.[45]

These able leaders put the finishing touches to the conquest of certain mountain provinces which had been imperfectly dominated by the previous Inca and then, acting on behalf of Capac Yupanqui, they conducted a campaign on the coast, adding to the empire the Quilca and Acarí Valleys and all the country on the coast between them. It is significant that they chose for their first operations in the *llanos* a territory not dominated by any of the more powerful coastland chiefs. They were doubtless aware that they had an intangible foe to face in the environment of the lowlands, so different from that of their highland home, and so they did wisely in selecting a region wherein the human enemies against whom they would have to contend were weakest. Thus they gained invaluable experience in the best methods of handling highland troops under coast-country conditions, experience which was to prove a decisive factor in the more difficult campaigns of later times.

After an interval of peaceful construction within the empire, the Inca himself took the field, marching southwards from Cuzco through the Titicaca basin, and down the Desaguadero River, which he crossed by means of a remarkable bridge laid upon pontoons of *ychu* grass. The vast regions around Lake Aullagas or Poopó, on the west, and the rich, warm Cochapampa Valley on the east, were added to the empire, partly by warfare, but largely also by diplomacy of the divide-and-rule variety.

Capac Yupanqui married, as his Coya, Mama Curi Ilpay. As usual there is confusion about her, Garcilaso stating that she was the Inca's sister, Cieza maintaining discreet silence, Sarmiento declaring that she was a daughter of the wealthy Sinchi of Ayamarca, Cobo and Cabello making her a lady of Cuzco.[46] This tangle is but one more evidence of the obscurity of the whole problem of the Incas' marriages.

It is known, at any rate, that the heir of Capac Yupanqui was his son by the Coya, known by the name of Inca Roca or Rocca. During the last years of his father's reign this prince was placed at the head of the army, and in that post he conducted a campaign in the highlands west of Cuzco and on the coast, in the Nazca Valley, adding extensive territories to the empire in those regions.

At this time was begun one of the most ingenious practices of the Incaic political system—that of transferring whole communities of conquered people from their homes to districts already thoroughly Inca-ized. Such colonies were called *mitmaccuna* or, in Spanish form, *mitimaes,* the term meaning transferred persons, *i. e.,* colonists.[47] There was a corollary to this practice, also, namely, that of setting down a large number of well-disciplined folk in a newly won district in order that they might educate their new neighbors in the Incaic idea. Often, no doubt, colonies of this type partook of the nature of garrisons. The first mitmaccuna of the former sort were taken from the Nazca Valley and settled in a warm part of the Apurimac Valley. So great was the geographic wisdom of the Incas that they always chose for the colonists environments in accordance with their natural inclinations, never putting hot-country folk in a cold climate, or vice-versa.

The Inca empire at the death of the Inca Capac Yupanqui contained about 120,000 square miles and was, therefore, approximately equal to New England, New York and New Jersey added together or, in other words, perceptibly larger than

Italy. It was a territory of great diversity, including parts of each one of the three natural zones of the Andean area as described in Chapter I. In all of these zones the disunifying tendencies inherent in the topography of the land had been nullified to a large extent by means of highroads, causeways, bridges and even balsas. In every corner of the realm the Incas set up governmental machinery that welded every district firmly to the central authority: The Inca at Cuzco, or wherever he might be. By planting garrisons in suitable places, and by establishing focal points for the spread of Incaic culture—points such as Pumatampu must have been, with its temple, official buildings, storehouses, and so on—the Incas took the most efficacious measures possible for converting their variegated possessions into a unified empire, countless inimical natural barriers notwithstanding.

From this time forward the Incas were masters of their environment, and could devote all their intelligence and valor to overcoming the increasingly powerful human enemies whom they were henceforward to encounter.

Naturally enough we know but little of the art of the Incas at the end of this initial period of their history. To Dr. Max Uhle we owe a debt of gratitude for having indicated, at any rate in a general way, the salient traits of the Incas' ceramic art as it was in its earliest stages.

NOTES TO CHAPTER VI

[1] Means, 1928, pp. 518–525.

[2] Sancho IV, second son of Alfonso X, the Learned, seized the throne of Castile in 1284, in direct violation of the last testament of his father. Enrique II, bastard son of Alfonso XI by Leonora de Guzmán, first slew his legitimate half-brother, Pedro I, and then usurped the kingly office, in 1369. As for Alexander VI, one need only remark that he was né Borgia.

[3] Means, 1928, pp. 462–478.

[4] In giving Quechua names for persons, places, and things, I shall not attempt pedantically purist perfection. Neither shall I cumber my pages with the extraordinary Germanic neo-Quechua phonetical spelling. My reason for holding to this somewhat dogmatic attitude is twofold: time has blurred the facts concerning classical pronunciation of the language used by the Incas so that no amount of well-intentioned jugglery of letters will ever really reproduce it; Spanish orthography, when properly understood and employed, is far

more truly phonetic than any artificial system can be, and is far less repellent to the eye of the average reader.

[5] Sarmiento de Gamboa, Ch. ix.

[6] Sarmiento, Chs. ix–xiii, inclusive.

[7] Cieza de León, Pt. II, Chs. vi, vii, and viii.

[8] Garcilaso, Pt. I, Bk. I, Chs. xv, xvi, and xvii.

[9] Garcilaso, Pt. I, Bk. I, Ch. xviii.

[10] Calancha, Bk. I, Ch. xiv.

[11] Cobo, Bk. XII, Chs. iii and iv.

[12] Morúa, Bk. I, Ch. iii. Montesinos, Chs. xvi and xvii.

[13] Oliva, Chs. iii and iv, 1857, pp. 25–39.

[14] Material relative to the lives of Oliva and Ramos will be found in Means, 1928, pp. 416–420 and 434–435.

[15] Ramos Gavilán, 1621, pp. 5–9.

[16] Oré, 1598, Ch. ix.

[17] Cabello de Balboa, Pt. III, Ch. ix, pp. 372–389 of New York Public Library Manuscript.

[18] Cabello, Pt. III, Ch. x, pp. 390–402.

[19] Attention is called to the admirable summary of Inca legends in Alexander, 1920, pp. 210–220.

[20] Oliva, Ch. v, 1857, pp. 41–50.

[21] Baudin, 1927; 1928, p. 2.

[22] Garcilaso, Pt. I, Bk. I, Ch. xviii.

[23] Cobo, Bk. XII, Ch. iii.

[24] Patrón and Romero, 1923.

[25] Uhle, 1912b.

[26] Castaing, 1888. González de la Rosa, 1912.

[27] The dating here used is that which is drawn up in Means, 1921. It is, of course, only tentative and approximate, a guide to the reader's imagination.

[28] Cabello, N. Y. P. L. MS., pp. 409–411.

[29] Good descriptions of the archæology of this region will be found in Squier, 1877, pp. 419–425, and Bingham, 1922, Ch. vii.

[30] Lizárraga, Pt. I, Ch. lxv. Bingham, 1922, pp. 117–119. Means, 1925, p. 448.

[31] Baudin, 1929.

[32] Garcilaso, Pt. I, Bk. I, Ch. xxv; Bk. II, Ch. xvi. Cieza, Pt. II, Chs. viii and xxxi. Montesinos, Ch. xviii. Sarmiento, Ch. xv. Cabello, Pt. III, Chs. x and xi.

[33] Garcilaso, Pt. I, Bk. I, Ch. xxii; Bk. IV, Ch. ii. Montesinos, Ch. xvii. Cabello, Pt. III, Ch. xi. Sarmiento, Chs. xiv and xxxi. Cieza, Pt. II, Chs. vii and x. Cobo, Bk. XII, Ch. v. Calancha, Bk. I, Ch. xv. Oré, 1598, Ch. ix. Uhle, 1907. Montell, 1929, pp. 222–225.

[34] Garcilaso, Bk. II, Ch. xvi. Bingham, 1922, pp. 110–116.

[35] Garcilaso, Pt. I, Bk. II, Ch. xvii.

[36] Cabello, Pt. III, Ch. xii. Sarmiento, Ch. xvi. Garcilaso, Pt. I, Bk. II, Ch. xx. Cobo, Bk. XII, Ch. vi. But Cieza de León, Pt. II, Ch. xxxiii, makes her the wife of the next Inca, saying nothing specific about this one's wife.

[37] Garcilaso, Pt. I, Bk. II, Ch. xx.

[38] Garcilaso, Pt. I, Bk. III, Ch. i. Cobo, Bk. XIII, Ch. xix.

[39] Garcilaso, Pt. I, Bk. III, Chs. vii and viii.

[40] Garcilaso, Pt. I, Bk. III, Ch. ix. Cieza, Pt. II, Ch. xlvii. Bingham, 1922, Chs. iii and iv.

[41] Garcilaso, Pt. I, Bk. III, Ch. ix. Bingham, 1922, Ch. ii.

[42] Garcilaso, Pt. I, Bk. III, Ch. ix. Cieza, Pt. II, Ch. xxxiii. Sarmiento, Ch. xviii. Cabello, Pt. III, Ch. xii, p. 434, N. Y. P. L. MS. Cobo, Bk. XII, Ch. vii.

[43] Cabello, Pt. III, Ch. xii. Montesinos, Ch. xiv.

[44] Garcilaso, Pt. I, Bk. III, Ch. x. Cieza, Pt. II, Ch. xxxiv. Cobo, Bk. XII, Ch. viii.

[45] Garcilaso, Pt. I, Bk. III, Ch. xii.

[46] Garcilaso, Pt. I, Bk. III, Ch. xix. Sarmiento, Ch. xviii. Cobo, Bk. XII, Ch. viii. Cabello, Pt. III, Ch. xiii.

[47] Garcilaso, Pt. I, Bk. III, Ch. xix; Bk. VII, Ch. i. Sarmiento, Ch. xxxix. Cieza, Pt. II, Ch. xxii. Cobo, Bk. XII, Chs. xxiii and xxiv.

CHAPTER VII

THE LATER REIGNS OF THE INCA DYNASTY

INCA ROCA, fifth Inca, *circa* 1250–1315, was a far more important personage, from the mundane point of view, than his namesake had been, the war-chief of two centuries earlier. In accordance with the now well-established dynastic custom, he had been thoroughly grounded during his youth in the military arts of his people, and, on donning the imperial *llautu*, he had every reason to believe that it would be his duty and his privilege to expand the empire, exactly as his forebears had all been wont to do. But he was destined to another fate; for, in his reign, and in the two after it, the Incas passed through the gravest and the most decisive crisis of their history.

About one hundred miles west of Cuzco lies the Valley of Andahuaylas, drained by a tributary of the Pampas River which, in turn, is a confluent of the great Apurimac River. There, in the time of Inca Roca, dwelt a strong and warlike folk who formed the so-called Chanca Confederacy. It consisted of a number of tribes, each having its own curaca and a hierarchy of minor chiefs. The leading Chroniclers agree in saying that there were various tribes in the confederacy and that it occupied a considerable territory which, however, it had not possessed for more than three or four generations.[1] Dr. Lafone Quevedo has shown, by linguistic evidence, that the origins of the Chanca tribes probably lay in the forest country and that they were not mountain folk at all but, rather, were closely akin to the fierce and low-cultured people of Amazonia and of the Gran Chaco region, to the east and southeast, respectively, of the Incas' realm.[2]

At all events it is clear that it was a numerous and a bellicose people, strongly organized for defence and for aggression, who, in a most formidable way, blocked the northward ex-

237

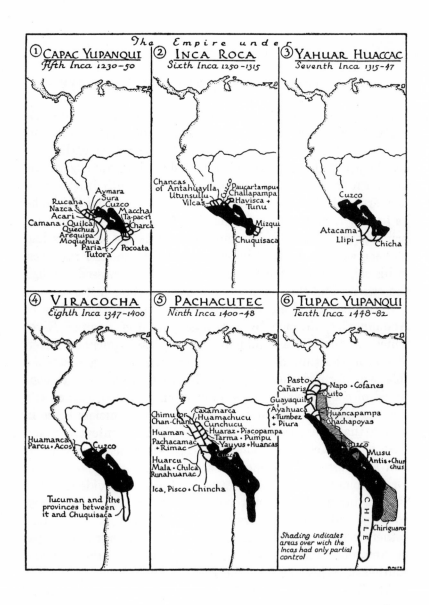

The Empire under

① CAPAC YUPANQUI
Fifth Inca 1230-50

Aymara
Sura
Cuzco
Rucana
Nazca
Acari
Camana · Quilca
Quechua
Arequipa
Moquehua
Paria
Tutora
Maccha
Ta-pac-ri
Charca
Pocoata

② INCA ROCA
Sixth Inca 1250-1315

Chancas
of Antahuaylla
Utunsullu
Vilcas
Paucartampu
Challapampa
Havisca +
Tunu
Mizqu
Chuquisaca

③ YAHUAR HUACCAC
Seventh Inca 1315-47

Cuzco
Atacama
Llipi
Chicha

④ VIRACOCHA
Eighth Inca 1347-1400

Huamarca
Parcu · Acos
Cuzco

Tucuman and the
provinces between
it and Chuquisaca

⑤ PACHACUTEC
Ninth Inca 1400-48

Chimu or
Chan · Chan
Huaman
Pachacamac
+ Rimac
Huarcu
Mala · Chulca
Runahuanac

Ica, Pisco · Chincha

Caxamarca
Huamachucu
Cunchucu
Huaraz · Piscopampa
Tarma · Pumpu
Yauyus + Huancas
Cuzco

⑥ TUPAC YUPANQUI
Tenth Inca 1448-82

Pasto
Cañaris
Guayaquil
Ayahuaca
+ Tumbez
· Piura
Napo · Cofanes
Quito
Huancapampa
Chachapoyas
Cuzco
Musu
Antis + Chun
chus

CHILE

Chiriguana

Shading indicates
areas over wich the
Incas had only partial
control

pansion of the Inca empire. The foe was a redoubtable one, even for the Incas, and it is no exaggeration to say that the long struggle, beginning in the time of Inca Roca and continuing throughout the reign of his son and successor, Cusi Hualpa, better known as Yahuar Huaccac, was a crucial contest for the dynasty of Cuzco.

There is no need to trace out here all the events of the Chanca War, for presently, in connection with the Inca Viracocha, we shall take notice of the final outcome of it. Let it be remembered, in the meanwhile, that the hovering menace of the Chanca was a constant and terrifying peril during the middle reigns of the Inca dynasty.

Three groups of conquests were made in the reign of Inca Roca, either by the sovereign in person or by his generals. The districts of Vilcas or Vilcashuamán, Utunsullu, and Antahuayla, all in the modern Departments of Apurimac and Ayacucho, were within the territory dominated by the Chancas, and the Inca's grasp upon them, after his invasion of them, was correspondingly precarious. Indeed, his campaigns to win and to hold them were an integral part of the Chanca War in general. Another series of conquests, towards the east, carried the Inca's power well into the fringe of the sylvan wilderness, into the so-called *ceja de la montaña,* wherein lie the desirable districts of Paucartampu, Challapampa, Havisca, and Tunu, all of which were added to the empire at this period.[3] From this favored region was drawn a considerable part of the *coca-*crop so important in both ancient and modern times for its narcotic properties. Finally, a conquest in the far south, that of the region around Chuquisaca (the La Plata of colonial times and now called Sucre), rounded out the empire in that direction.[4]

The internal reforms of Inca Roca were, if anything, more important and far-reaching than his military activities. Prior to his day the Sun-Temple, Coricancha, had been the residence of the imperial family as well as the principal place of worship. This order of things had been inaugurated by the earliest Incas and had never been altered.[5] It did not accord, however, with

Roca's conception of the grandeur due to his family in the position to which it had now attained. He appears to have been the first of his dynasty to set about the systematic enlargement and embellishment of his capital city. In so doing he built for himself and his court a new and imposing palace called Cora-Cora, the Pastures, which was located in some open fields on the northern side of the Huaca-pata or Holy Terrace, the chief square of the city.[6] This palace was very large, over three hundred feet on a side. Part of it is still standing as though to display to us the architecture of the Incas at this period in their history. The masonry, particularly that shown in Figure 143, is very finely and solidly made, being in the style best designated by the term polygonal.

Behind the Cora-Cora palace was the Yachahuasi, Teachers' House or School, which was a foundation of this ruler's destined to the highly specialized training of the lads of the imperial caste. The instructors were certain professional sages who bore the title of *Amauta*, wise man, and their business was to fill the boys in their charge with all the lore of their class, in which we see a very clever and insidious method of creating a gulf between the rulers and the ruled.[7] The Incas had indeed been "getting on" since the days when they were but llama-herders led, in times of peril, by a temporary chieftain chosen from among them for the emergency.

The Coya of Inca Roca is, as usual, variously described by the divers Chroniclers. Garcilaso says that she was the Inca's sister, Mama Micay; Cieza states that she was the Inca's sister, Macay Cuca; Sarmiento goes into some detail, saying that Inca Roca took as his Queen "a great lady of the town of Pata-huayllacan, daughter of the Sinchi of that territory, named Soma Inca. Her name was Mama Micay." Cabello de Balboa avers that the Coya was chosen by the Inca's council and that she was a daughter of the valorous and rich Lordling of the Village of Guayllacan, her name being Mama Nicaz. Cobo affirms that "Inca-Roca married a lady named Mama-Michay, chieftainess of the village of Guayllacan," this being done by the special command of the Sun, transmitted through

Fig. 141. Ruins of the Sun-Temple, about one-fourth of a mile from the town of Pumatampu.

Fig. 142. The view from the summit of the Sun-Temple, looking toward the town of Pumatampu.

Photographs by courtesy of W. V. Alford, Esq.

FIG. 143.   Inca masonry in Cuzco. On the right is one wall of
Cora Cora, Palace of Inca Roca.

FIG. 144.   Last view of Cuzco. In the foreground is the great
north road of the Incas.

FIG. 145.   Agricultural terraces near Pisac, Urubamba Valley.
Terraces like these were built in all parts of the highlands.

Photographs by courtesy of W. V. Alford, Esq.

the priest of the Sun-Temple in Cuzco. Finally, Morúa completes the confusion by declaring that Inca Roca married Cusi Quicgsu, a lady otherwise unknown either to good or to bad fame. But subsequently he corrects himself by giving her name as Cusi Chimpu, otherwise known as Mama Micai.[8] In this connection, therefore, Garcilaso and Cieza stand together, both supporting the incestuous marriage version; the other Chroniclers cited agree to the extent of representing Mama Micay to be a native of the village of Huayllacan or Pata-Huayllacan, the location of which, by-the-bye, is not discoverable upon any map of which I know. It seems most probable that their version, rather than the incestuous version, is correct; and for reasons now to be set forth.

The sons and daughters of Inca Roca and Coya Mama Micay were numerous, including, among the sons, Titu Cusi Hualpa, Vica Quirao, Inca Paucar, Inca Huamán, and Inca Cazachicha.[9] Of these sons the second merits brief notice here, as he is generally neglected by modern historians. He was a youth of special nobility of spirit and affability of nature who early displayed great capacity as a leader in war, for he carried out some creditable campaigns in the region south and east of Cuzco where, apparently, the Inca's power was not fully consolidated, even thus late. It was in connection with the Inca's heir, however, Titu Cusi Hualpa, that the spirit of unrest made itself most painfully apparent at this time. The people of Huayllacan, the Coya's village, made so bold that they stole the young prince and carried him off to their country—probably south or southeast from Cuzco—and there held him captive. Hearing that the imperial child was there, the folk from all about came flocking to see him. Suddenly, while a great number of curious persons were staring at him, the child wept tears of blood, a circumstance which gave him the name by which he is best known, Yahuar Huaccac, He-who-weeps-blood. From this strange occurrence the child's captors took fright, and they hastily returned him whence they had wrongly taken him, humbly rendering homage, at the same time, to the child's father, Inca Roca.[10]

It seems fairly clear that Yahuar Huaccac, *circa* 1315–1347, was unique among the Incas because of his having been feckless, cowardly, and unenterprising. True, Garcilaso ascribes to him some of the conquests made in the east during Inca Roca's reign, but even he is obliged, apologist of the Incas though he be, to admit that this Inca "was not warlike, and that he was intimidated by the evil augury of his name. . . ."[11] Cobo portrays him as an arrant coward who did not dare to go to battle; and Father Cabello states that he "was so much given to venereal delights that he greatly shortened his life, as anyone will do who runs such a course with a slack rein."[12] His uninspiring character may have been the product of his early vicissitudes. At any rate, only a small amount of conquering was done in this reign, and that in the far south, in the regions of Llipi and of Atacama, where campaigns were conducted by the Inca's brother, Apu Mayta, or Vica Quirao, and, no doubt, by other close kinsmen of the ruler.[13]

Yahuar Huaccac's Coya was Mama Chiclla or Chiquia, of the Ayamarca tribe whose influence was so noticeable in the politics of this period. For a wonder all the major Chroniclers are in substantial agreement on this point.[14] This is of decided importance for anyone who is disposed to view the Inca dynasty from the eugenic angle for, even though incestuous marriages may have been entered into before this—by no means an established fact—fresh blood was certainly brought into the family by Yahuar Huaccac through his marriage to a woman from outside of his family.

The most celebrated of the sons of this marriage was the Prince Hatun Tupac,[15] better known as Viracocha Inca, which name he took for reasons soon to be made clear. When this prince had come to manhood the smouldering enmity of the Chancas suddenly burst into devouring flame. Fortunately for the Inca dynasty the son was a far better man than his father, and, disgusted by his parent's pusillanimity, he determined stoutly to resist the vast power of the foe from which the old Inca would have been glad enough to fly.

The Chancas were marching down from the west in a force

of thirty thousand fierce warriors under the leadership of three of their greatest chieftains. The subjects of Yahuar Huaccac were in a panic; Cuzco was not properly garrisoned; the Inca himself and his court were in retreat at Muyna, south of the city; Prince Hatun Tupac, who had always been at odds with his father, had lately been disgraced and sent into exile on the plain of Chita, lying high between Cuzco and the Urupampa Valley. It was a moment fraught with dire peril for the empire.

At this juncture the young Prince, while dozing one day at noon near the flock of llamas whose shepherd he was, received a visitation from an apparition in the form of a grave and imposing old man who announced himself to be Viracocha, the Creator-God and a forebear of the Inca line. He bade the Prince to hasten to Muyna and there to inform the Inca of the impetuous onrush of the Chancas towards Cuzco. The Prince was to command his parent, in the name of Viracocha, to bestir himself for the defence of the city and of the realm. The apparition concluded by saying that he would always protect and aid the Prince, and that great good fortune awaited the young man.

Immediately the Prince roused up and quickly went to his father. First of all he urged him to take strong measures for saving the empire, but, perceiving that the Inca would have none of him and would not follow the divine advice, he resolved to take matters into his own hands. Accordingly the Prince hastily assembled some four thousand young warriors and, with these as a nucleus, marched northwards along the road to Cuzco. At intervals new contingents of troops came flocking to him so that, by the time the city was reached, he had eight thousand men at his back. For a short while the Prince halted in Cuzco, strengthening the defences of the capital and preparing a garrison to defend it if need were.

After that Prince Hatun Tupac and his army of lusty young men marched out of Cuzco by the Huaca Puncu—Holy Gate —and took the road that led to the plain of Xaquixahuana, called Sacsahuana in early Spanish times and now known as the plain of Anta or of Zúrite. On arriving there the Prince quickly disposed his troops for battle, knowing well the while that the Chancas were coming swiftly and were now not far off. He could rely upon his men to fight to the death, for they were all of Inca blood; but vassal troops were now coming up in great numbers and were taking their station on the rounded slopes which hem in the broad plain.

The young Prince, we may suppose, set his jaws firmly, commended himself and his followers to his kinsman, the God Viracocha,—and waited. He knew well enough that those vassals of his father were biding their time until they should see whom victory would favor in the impending struggle.

Scouts brought in tidings that the enemy were at Rimac Tampu (modern Limatambo) hard by. The next day, at dawn, the Chancas poured into the plain from the western side and, with a savage brandishing of weapons and a wild chorus of fierce cries, they came rapidly across the flat valley-bottom. Battle was joined. It began with the Inca troops alone against the invaders. Both sides advanced to the stirring sound of clay trumpets, of tambours, of flutes, and of resonant clarion shells. Hand-to-hand fighting, with clubs and star-headed maces, began almost at once. From the rear, on both sides, slingers and archers and javelin-throwers hurled their missiles with deadly effect. Back and forth the swaying lines of fighters swung, fortune favoring now one side, now the other. The young Prince was everywhere, exhorting his soldiers to do their utmost, himself slaying many a foeman. For hours the strife rolled back and forth. At length the Chancas were forced back perceptibly. This induced the vassals, still hesitant upon the hills, to sweep in their squadrons down upon the plain to aid, belatedly, their liege. Their added numbers turned the balance permanently in the Incas' favor, and soon the Chancas were in full retreat. In the triumph of the pursuit the Inca warriors cried out to the flying enemy that the very stones and bushes of the hillsides were turning into men to fight for the Prince and his Father, the Sun. This completely disrupted the morale of the Chancas, and those of them who were not slain or captured fled precipitately towards their own homes. The victory of the Prince was unconditional. At length he could pause in the clear light of the Andean sundown and lean wearily, but happily, upon his death-dealing mace. The day was his. A glorious future was assured to his House.

After the victory of Xaquixahuana, Prince Hatun Tupac despatched three messengers southwards with the good news, one to the Sun-Temple and the priests there, one to the House of the Chosen Women, and one to the Inca, Yahuar Huaccac, still in shameful retirement at Muyna. The message borne by the last-mentioned envoy contained an imperious command to the old ruler that he remain where he was until his son should come.

The Prince then took command of a contingent of six thousand picked men whom he led in pursuit of the Chancas, in order to drive them to their homes and to complete the conquest of their territory. Perhaps the Chancas, lords of Antahuaylla, had not been too benign as masters for, according to Garcilaso,[16] "the women and children came forth to meet him [the Prince] with green boughs, rejoicing and saying, 'Sole Lord, child of the Sun, friend of the poor, have mercy upon us and pardon us.'" The Prince did exactly that, treating his new subjects with firmness, but with kindness. He made a thorough inspection of the country, setting up the machinery of government on Incaic lines, and stamping out the last embers of resentment by his justice tempered with mercy. It is entirely consonant with the character of the Incas, as we understand it to-day, that this policy should have been followed. Their benignity proceeded, not from an ethical appreciation of the worth of mercy, but rather from practicality. They were fully aware of the stupidity of vengefulness. The conquered peoples were not regarded so much as troublesome foes as they were as future subjects whose welfare must be fostered.

Having done so much, Prince Hatun Tupac journeyed back to Cuzco to enjoy the fruits of his victory. With him went those of the Chanca chieftains whom he had captured, for it was his intention to hold them, on honorable terms, as hostages. Descending from his litter he entered Cuzco on foot to show that he was a soldier as well as a Prince, and, at the head of his army, he passed through the Huaca Puncu and so to the Huaca Pata. His mother, the Coya Mama Chiclla, at the head of a throng of princesses and noblewomen, was waiting there to hail him and to acclaim him the victor. They embraced him, weeping with joy, cleansed the sweat from his face, and shook the dust of the highway from his raiment. Waving fair fronds of flowers, scattering sweet-smelling herbs upon his path, and singing songs of triumph, the Coya and her ladies led the Prince to the Sun-Temple, Coricancha, which he entered barefoot in order to give thanks for the epochal victory which had been won so opportunely by the aid of Viracocha.[17]

A description of the triumphal entry into Coricancha is given by Father Cabello de Balboa in language vivid enough to make it worthwhile to translate it fully here. It runs thus:

First of all the most valiant Captains entered into Curicancha making, with their arms and liveries, a sightly parade. After them entered many Soldiers of less renown who haled along numerous prisoners, bound. After these entered the wives and daughters of the captives, singing funeral songs in accordance with their custom, and bewailing their calamities and misfortunes, because it was commanded that they should do so. Afterwards entered in the common people, laden down with a hitherto unequalled quantity of spoils, and dragging the weapons of their foes after them upon the ground. Then came a squadron of lancers with their lances aloft and surmounted, each one, by the head of an enemy impaled upon the point, each head having its hair hanging loose and dishevelled. Then came another squadron, this one being composed of the nobility of the Empire, as well those who had gone to the war as those who had remained behind to govern the commonwealth. Amongst them they bore upon a litter of gold the Emperor, . . . with that austere countenance of his and those eyes of a cruel Tiger with which he killed and terrified the World. He wore, during this spectacle, the complete insignia of the Emperor. Afterwards came the Rearguard in which marched men of great importance, accompanied by groups of light-armed men who made a million movements with their bodies and legs, representing thereby the ardour and courage with which they had fought against their enemies. In that order they marched around the empty square. Then all the prisoners were ordered to lie down upon the earth, their faces on the ground. Then, [the Prince] leading the way, they walked over them, placing their feet upon the necks of the prostrate, without any prisoner's daring to raise or move his head; and, at the same time, they sang a verse which, in our language means "My enemies I tread upon." All this was carried out before the statue and image of the Sun, and at the same time he was besought to consider himself honoured by what was done and always to give them similar victories. With these prayers and ceremonies the triumphal festivals were concluded.[18]

Shortly thereafter the Prince again went southwards, this time to Muyna in order to see his father. Yahuar Huaccac received him with characteristic glumness at their public meeting, and in the private interview which speedily followed the Prince bluntly told his father that, since he had chosen to abandon Cuzco and all its sacred institutions to their fate, he must never see the capital again. He took the crimson fillet of sovereignty from the brow of Yahuar Huaccac and placed it upon his own. The deposed monarch spent the twilight of his inglorious day in deepest retirement, at Rumi Colca, not far from Muyna.[19]

Inca Viracocha, *circa* 1347–1400, was a great emperor. In honor of his kinsman, the apparition, he had given up the name of Hatun Tupac and had taken that of Viracocha. His reign is more notable for internal progress, due to the necessity of strengthening the empire within after the dire peril through which it had but lately passed under the inept rule of Yahuar Huaccac, than it is for conquests. Nevertheless, certain additions to the realm were made in his time, of which it is well to speak briefly now. Five provinces, named Huamanca, Pocra, Asancaru, Parcu, and Acos, occupying a considerable area in what is now the Department of Ayacucho, were added to the empire by the usual methods and were intensively developed along Incaic lines.[20] In this way did Viracocha underscore his conquest of the Chancas, pushing his power into country beyond that held by his vanquished enemies.

In this reign, also, a very important region—that of Tucma (modern Tucumán) in northwestern Argentina—came into the empire under singular circumstances. Garcilaso tells the story in these words:

While the Inca was in the province of Charcas, envoys arrived from a kingdom called Tucma, which the Spaniards called Tucuman. It is two hundred leagues to the south-east of Charcas. Having been brought before him they said, "Sapa Inca Viracocha, the fame of the deeds of the Incas your ancestors, of the impartiality and rectitude of their justice, of the excellence of their laws, of the care taken of their subjects, of their goodness, piety, and kindness, and of the great wonders that your father the Sun has lately worked through you, have reached to the utmost limits of our land, and have even passed beyond it. Understanding all these things, the Curacas of the whole kingdom of Tucma have sent us to pray that they may be received into your empire, and be permitted to be called your vassals, that they may enjoy your bounty, and may be held worthy to receive Incas of the blood royal to lead them from their barbarous customs, and to teach them the religion we ought to hold, and the laws we ought to obey. In the name, therefore, of all our people we worship you as a child of the Sun, and in testimony of our submission we offer our persons and the fruits of our land, as a sign that we belong to you." Saying this they presented much cotton cloth, good honey, maize, and other products of their country. They brought some of each product, that he might take possession of all. They did not bring gold or silver, because these Indians had none, nor is any found there now, in spite of careful search that has been made for it.

Having offered the presents, the envoys went down on their knees according to custom, and worshipped the Inca as their god and king. He received them with much kindness, and after receiving the presents in token of his possession of the whole of that kingdom, he ordered his relations to drink with the envoys, which was considered as an inestimable favour. After drinking he directed that they should be told that the Inca was highly pleased at their having submitted to his sway of their own accords, and that they would be treated with greater favour than others, because their love and good will merited more than the obedience of those who were forced to submit. He ordered that their chiefs should be given much woollen cloth of the fine quality made for the Inca, and other things made for his own use by the chosen virgins, which were looked upon as sacred. The envoys also received many gifts. He directed that Incas, his own relations, should instruct these Indians in their idolatry, and abolish former abuses, teaching the people the laws and ordinances of the Incas. He also appointed officials to make irrigation channels, and cultivate the lands, so as to increase the revenues of the Sun and of the king.

The envoys, after having been in attendance some days, and having understood the excellent laws and the customs of the court, compared them with their own, and said that these were laws of men who were children of the Sun, and that those were fit only for beasts without reason. Thus moved with zeal, they said to the Inca, when they departed, "Sole lord! there should be no one in the world who does not enjoy the religion, laws, and government which we have now been taught. But far away from our land, to the south and west, there is a great kingdom called Chili, which is well peopled, but with which we have no intercourse, on account of a great chain of snowy mountains that separates us. But we have heard of this people from our fathers and grandfathers, and we tell you of them because you may see fit to conquer that land and reduce it to submission, that its people may know your religion and worship the Sun, thus enjoying the benefits such knowledge confers." The Inca ordered this information to be recorded, and gave to the envoys permission to return to their own country.[21]

This matter of the entrance of Tucma into the empire of the Incas is of great interest and importance. Don Roberto Levillier has given careful attention to it,[22] showing that Garcilaso, in accordance with his somewhat snobbish tendency to portray the Incas as infinitely superior to all the peoples around them, has failed to credit the folk of Tucma—the Diaguitas—with any degree of civilization and culture. As a matter of fact—and to it the nature of the gifts sent to the Inca from Tucma amply testify—that remote southern region had long been the seat of advanced peoples whose civilization was akin in quality to that of the Incas and of the earlier high-cultured folk of Peru. The archæology of northwestern Argentina, moreover, makes it perfectly clear that, for centuries, the Diaguitas and their associates had long been the possessors of no mean skill in the arts. True, their social organization was perhaps looser and less efficient than that of the Inca empire; but in most other respects the folk of Tucma and adjacent regions were not inferior to the Peruvians, either of Incaic or of pre-Incaic times.

Because of the admirable common sense which informs it, I here translate in full Don Roberto Levillier's interpretation of the Tucma submission: "It is probable that, being in the province of Charcas, at no great distance from the Diaguitas' country, and being resolved to conquer them whether they wished it or not, the Inca sent emissaries to give them a hint that they would better submit forthwith, warning them that he would subjugate them if they should spurn the honor. The rights of the most civilized were already recognized, no doubt! Forced to choose between pacific domination and unequal strife, the people of Tucumán preferred to play a bit of comedy, and so assumed, as though spontaneously, an attitude imposed upon them by force. The very terms of Viracocha's reply support this deduction. The Incas 'treated better nations which submitted with good will than those which were rebels,' which is equivalent to considering that all nations owed them submission. Holding this belief, how could they fail to become vain? Nothing is more justifiable. From the very beginning of their advance towards the four cardinal points, what was the history of the Sons of the Sun but a succession of conquests? The opportune genuflexions of the ambassadors from Tucumán saved their people from graver harms, and turned the impetus of the imperialist monarchs towards Chile, whose annexation was accomplished by Tupac Yupanqui some hundred years later, not without great difficulties, and with but scanty results, for the coming of the Spaniards left them in the enjoyment of their triumph only a few years."[23] With this interpretation I find myself in complete agreement.

As I have already remarked, the Inca Viracocha was particularly interested in internal improvements and, especially so in works of irrigation. He was aware, apparently, that they served two purposes, namely, the obvious one of bringing much unused land under cultivation, and that of filling the people whose country they benefited with awe and respect which performed wonders in the way of pro-Incaic propaganda. One justly celebrated irrigation channel was twelve feet wide and twelve feet deep and was laid for one hundred and fifty miles through country lately conquered and through districts won from the Chancas and their associates. Beginning near the summit of the mountains near Parcu, at some beautiful springs that rise there, this great channel was carried along a semi-circular line that bent towards the west and, embracing in a wide southward curve a great area that had hitherto been very imperfectly utilized, it ended in the country of the Quechuas, near Cotapampa. Regarded as a piece of engineering it was a wonderful accomplishment, for it was so graded as to run at a very slight angle along the eastern slope of the Maritime Cordillera just above the head-waters of the streams that rise there. Although the Incas—as all other natives of America—were ignorant of the principle of the true keystone arch, they were adepts in the arts of grading, of causeway-building, of terrace-making, and of tunnelling. What they lacked in mechanical appliances was amply compensated for by their ability to bring unlimited numbers of human hands to any task that they might undertake, with the natural result that they were able to build public works which no modern society, always governed in its enterprises by the monetary factor, could hope to accomplish in those regions with financial profit. In Spanish times this amazing channel fell into disuse and ruin, but enough of it is left to justify Garcilaso's assertions concerning it.[24] Complementary to the main channel was an elaborate system of minor aqueducts of varying size and importance in which the flow of water could be controlled by sluices.[25] By means of these beneficial public works the Incas increased the yield of their realm tremendously and built up for themselves a renown which has never faded away.

The reign of the Inca Viracocha, and his victory over the Chancas, is also commemorated by an architectural achievement to which I shall revert in Chapter XII. It is the temple to the god Viracocha, his "kinsman," at Racche, south of Cuzco.

The Coya of the Inca Viracocha was Mama Runtu or Runtu Caya, so called because of the singular whiteness of her complexion, the word *runtu* signifying egg. Garcilaso claims that she was the Inca's sister; but Cobo and Sarmiento say that she was a daughter of the Lord of Anta, which is one of the towns adjacent to the plain of Xaquixaguana where Viracocha vanquished the Chancas. Cieza contents himself by calling her simply "one of the principal ladies."[26] The most important son of this pair is known to history as Pachacutec Inca Yupanqui.

In his youth, while his father was still reigning, he, like all the lads of the imperial caste, received a thorough education in the *yachahuasi,* the schools, founded by the Inca Roca. There he was scrupulously trained in the military science of his people and in such other lore and wisdom as was known to them. On attaining to the age of puberty—an event always celebrated by the formal donning of the breech-clout, the piercing of the ear-lobes, and the first arming of the youths[27]—he was given a prolonged and grilling instruction in the art of war and in that of administration.

Towards the end of Viracocha's reign a very picturesque event befell. Hanco-Huallu, chief of the subjugated Chancas, together with as many of his people as would or could follow him, fled away from the Inca's sway, proceeding at first northwardly with their women and children, then eastwardly, settling at last in the woodland country around Muyupampa (Moyobamba).[28] In this movement we see a retreat of more than usual significance, for the Chancas, originally a woodland people, after dwelling for some generations in the highlands until they met with defeat at the hands of a mountain people stronger than themselves, withdrew in discouragement but in undimmed pride to the sylvan wildernesses whence, long ago, they had come. Their going has an epic quality that is stirring.

The death of the Inca Viracocha marks the close of the

middle period of Incaic history. Up to this point we have had to rely on the often conflicting statements of Chroniclers who had widely divergent conceptions of the course of events. The Inca Garcilaso is the one whom we have chiefly followed, and we have done so because he presents the most completely authoritative and confidence-inspiring narrative of the early and middle reigns. It is true that, at times, one must offset his natural prejudices in favor of his kinsmen the Incas, either by consulting other and less biased authorities or by having recourse to pure reason; but nevertheless he is, on the whole, a reliable guide. From this time forward, however, all the major Chroniclers are in substantial agreement on the chief points.

The empire left by the Inca Viracocha contained about 155,000 square miles of territory and was therefore approximately equal to New England, New York, New Jersey, Delaware, Maryland, and the eastern half of Virginia added together or, in other words, to Italy with Switzerland and Bavaria. It was, moreover, a very thoroughly organized state rigidly subjected to the central authority in the person of the Inca, yet, so far as the mass of the people was concerned, strongly regionalistic in character, each tribe having its own organization and local activities and being bound to the imperial government only through the hierarchy of tribal and imperial officials. True, the Incas made it a practice to establish in each region conquered by them certain institutions of their own—particularly their religion, their language, and various economic measures—but their doing so did not break down the deeply rooted regionalistic tendency of the bulk of their subjects, nor was it their purpose to do so. The only people in the empire who experienced what may be called a feeling of imperial solidarity were the official classes—the élite. That, for the purposes of the Incas, was sufficient.

The Inca Pachacutec, *circa* 1400–1448, devoted the first three years of his reign to administrative measures, living the while in Cuzco, and the following three years to a painstaking tour of inspection through his wide dominions. Naturally he could not visit personally every valley and plain of his realm as his ancestors had been able to do; but he studied the state of affairs as thoroughly as he could, either in person or through trusted aides of his. Himself a very great man, perhaps the greatest ever sprung from the native race of America,[29] he had the inestimable advantage of being ably seconded by skilled generals and wise councillors, all close kinsmen of his own. Thus, one of his brothers was appointed to be governor and commandant of Cuzco and, at the same time, others were placed at the head of portions of the army, the most celebrated of these generals being the Inca's brother, Capac Yupanqui.[30] These arrangements made it possible for the Inca to divide his time between war and administration, in both of which he was supremely proficient.

The earliest conquests of Pachacutec lay in that part of the Urupampa (Urubamba) Valley which is downstream from Ollantaytampu. The region indicated bore—and still bears in popular parlance—the general name of Vilcapampa. Prior to Pachacutec's time the Incas' frontier in that direction had been at Ollantaytampu, but he, doubtless having in mind those incursions of savages from the forest-country that had given rise to the Chanca Confederacy and to the formidable struggle with it, determined to push his power farther down the stream. He did so by the usual Inca methods, combining guile and diplomacy with military aggression. In this campaign the province of Viticos or Vitcos and that of Vilcapampa, the key of which is the bridge of Chuqui-chaca (the Bridge of the Lance), were definitively added to the empire. The citadel of Machu Picchu rises in the heart of this region, and it is highly probable that the Inca Pachacutec gave orders for its construction, intending it to be thenceforward an eastern bulwark of his empire. At this same time the chiefs of the neighboring Pampaconas Valley and of the Amaypampa Valley voluntarily paid homage to the Inca.[31]

In considering these early conquests of Pachacutec we must remember that, though the empire inherited by this Inca was very large and, environmentally, highly diversified, Cuzco, the capital city, was still uncomfortably near to the frontier of the realm, Ollantaytampu being only some forty miles from Cuzco, on the upper margin of the zone often called the *ceja de la montaña*. It seems likely enough that the earlier Incas had been deterred from conquering in that direction by environmental conditions not propitious to highlanders. But by the time of Pachacutec, the Incas had perfected a military organization and a political system too efficient to be controlled altogether by such considerations as those, and it is quite logical that the great Inca may have deemed it politic to exercise at least some sort of power in the country between his "home counties" and the land of sylvan savages. Hence arose the construction of the magnificent border-citadel of Machu Picchu, not far from the lower margin of the *ceja de la montaña,* at a point where it commanded the narrow canyon of the Urupampa through which dangerous foes might attempt to come upwards towards the highlands.

After the Vilcapampa campaign the next task which confronted the Inca Pachacutec was the formidable one of carrying his power north-northwestwardly along the inter-cordilleran plateaux, beginning at his remotest province, on that side, Huamanca. With an army of 30,000 or 40,000 men at their backs, the Inca and his brother, General Capac Yupanqui, marched thence into the country of the Huancas, whose chief place was Sausa (Jauja). These people had small, well-fortified villages; they were extremely warlike and were wont to burn the captives whom they took in war, keeping bits of burnt skin as trophies and also making drum-heads out of the hides of their slain enemies. They had a strange cult for the dog, worshipping that worthy animal and, at the same time, paradoxically esteeming its flesh as a delicacy for dinner. They likewise had a somewhat ghastly custom of making trumpets out of dog-skulls and of using them to dance to, the music then being very sweet to their ears, or, in wartime, to terrify their foes. Far pleasanter is the Huancas' account of their origin: They believed that they were descended from a man and a woman who came forth from a

fountain called Huarivilca, where they built an imposing
temple to commemorate their progenitors.[32]

True to their bellicose traditions, the Huancas put up a
stiff fight, but they were eventually crushed. After master-
ing them, Pachacutec suppressed some of their more absurd
and nastier customs and, to do away with squabbles about
land, divided their country into three provinces, Sausa, Marcavilca (alias Huancavilca, the modern Huancavelica), and
Llacsapallanca. Their land was long and rather narrow, lying
between the Maritime and the Eastern Cordilleras in what
is to-day a part of the Departments of Junín and Huancavelica. They were dextrous slingers and brave fighters who,
after their submission to the Child of the Sun, served him
faithfully and well, for, as usual, their country was thoroughly Inca-ized by its new masters.

Supplementary to the conquest of the Huancas were two
other series of conquests, the one on the eastern slopes of the
Eastern Cordillera in the provinces of Tarma and Pumpu
(Bombón), the other on the western side of the Maritime
Cordillera in the provinces of Yauyu (Yauyos) and Huarochirí.
In the former of these regions the people "had a custom of
celebrating their marriages by the bridegroom giving the
bride a kiss, either on the forehead or the cheek. Widows
shaved their heads in sign of mourning, and were not allowed to marry within the year. Men, when they observed
fasts, neither ate meat, nor salt, nor pepper, nor did they
sleep with their wives."[33] At about the same time, also, the
General Capac Yupanqui made an incursion into the province
of Chucurpu, which lay in the ceja de la montaña, to the east
of Tarma and Pumpu. The people there were barbarous and
warlike, worshipping the puma as a god because of its ferocity.
After something of a struggle they submitted to the Inca's
authority and accepted the higher degree of culture which he
introduced among them.[34]

Thereafter, proceeding northwards along the inter-Cordilleran plateaux, the provinces of Ancara, Huayllas, Piscopampa,
and Cunchucu were successively added to the empire in the

customary manner. Their inhabitants were all on the neo-archaic plane of culture which, as explained on earlier pages, was general throughout the highlands prior to the Inca conquests. A little later, the upper portion of the Santa Valley, generally known to modern geography as the Callejón de Huaylas or Corridor of Huaylas, albeit the folk called Huaylas dwelt farther south than the Corridor, was conquered, being an important addition to the empire because of the richness of the soil and the comparative advancement of the people. Finally, the provinces of Huamachuco and Casamarca were invaded and subjugated after a considerable resistance on the part of their inhabitants.[35]

It goes without saying that these immense accessions of territory were not won in a brief time. The Chroniclers, and especially Garcilaso, make it clear that the various campaigns lasted months and years and that between them came long periods devoted to tours of inspection, to administrative measures, and to jovial relaxation at Cuzco. It was ever the custom of the Inca to make his control over newly acquired lands and peoples complete before going on to further conquests. Moreover, Pachacutec, like all great rulers, placed a proper value upon pleasure and repose, and therefore he saw to it that he had a fair portion of them between the strenuous periods of military expansion. In this way, then, steadily by jerks, as it were, a long and relatively narrow strip of mountain country, bounded on the west by the Maritime Cordillera and on the east by the *ceja de la montaña,* along which, at this latitude, the mighty Marañón River flows north-northeastwardly, was brought into the empire.

The pomps and splendors attendant upon the triumphal return of the Inca Pachacutec, of General Capac Yupanqui, and of the young heir to the *llautu,* Prince Tupac Yupanqui (who had taken a part in the more recent campaigns), to the imperial city of Cuzco are brilliantly described by Garcilaso. After them came a longer than usual interval of peace during which, we may be sure, Pachacutec not only saw to it that the highland territories which he had conquered were efficiently imperialized but also made his preparations for the conquest of the long strip of highly civilized coast-country lying west of them.

The overlordship of the seaboard states was the result of another long series of campaigns in which the Inca Pachacutec personally led his forces—60,000 troops, evenly divided into two divisions—with General Capac Yupanqui and Prince Tupac Yupanqui as his chief generals. With the Nazca Valley already a part of the empire, as a base, Pachacutec carefully prepared and successfully carried out the vanquishment by force of arms, of the Valleys of Ica, Pisco and Chincha. Of these the first, according to Garcilaso, submitted peacefully because, being neighbors to the already Inca-ized province of Nazca, they were well acquainted with the virtues of Incaic rule; but the powerful Lord of Chincha, who was the southernmost of the great kings of the coast, stoutly and haughtily resisted, and so had to be beaten into submission. In like manner, Chuquimancu, Lord of Runahuanac, Huarcu, Mala, and Chilca, and Cuismancu, Lord of Pachacamac, Rimac, Chancay, and Huamán, first opposed the invaders from the highlands and later were forcibly overwhelmed by them.[36]

In these campaigns the Incas showed that they had learnt a valuable lesson concerning the effect of coastal conditions on highland soldiery. They had found out that the large-lunged mountaineers could not be healthy for protracted periods in the hot, dense airs of the shore-country, and that, after a time, they were apt to sicken of one or more of the maladies prevalent there, being particularly prone to such diseases as tuberculosis, malaria, and bubonic plague. Perhaps all this danger to mountain folk transplanted to the lowlands is in part the result of definite physiological changes suffered by them in their new environment. These changes have to do with the volume and composition of the blood and with conditions set up in the respiratory organs. The corollary to the proposition now under consideration, namely, the effect of high altitudes on lowlanders, was studied in 1922 by a commission sent out to Peru by the Royal Society of London.[37]

There is no reason to suppose that the effects of coastal conditions upon highlanders would be any less deleterious than those of highland conditions upon lowlanders. Indeed, anyone who has had occasion to employ highland Indians for household purposes in Lima or elsewhere on the coast cannot have failed to notice their tendency towards poor health while in the lowlands.

No doubt the Incas were, in a vague way, aware of these truths. Therefore, before attempting any prolonged campaigns upon the coast, they worked out a very efficient system whereby the army was divided into relays, each of which was subjected to only a few months of active service on the coast, and was later sent home to recuperate.[38] As a result of these wise measures the Incas were able, in a series of campaigns, to conquer even the strongest of the great coastal states.

The prestige of these conquests arose not only from the great extent of territory which they brought into the empire but also from the antiquity and splendor of the cities therein. Pachacamac, for example, had been celebrated as a holy-place ever since Tiahuanaco II times, of which fact the Incas took characteristic advantage for, instead of obliterating the ancient cult observed in the majestic temple of the Creator-God, Pachacamac or Irma, they merely added to it their own worship of the Sun and Stars, building therefor a suitable sanctuary, and also a house of the Chosen Women. Like the Romans, the Incas were aware of the expediency of sometimes admitting new deities into their pantheon—provided their local prestige and intrinsic worth were great enough to win them that honor. In the present case, of course, the Incas had to do with a god closely akin to, if not identical with, their own Creator-God, Viracocha. Again, Rimac, near the site of the modern city of Lima, was the seat of a time-hallowed oracle widely revered up and down the coast, and the whole of the Rimac Valley was thickly sprinkled with pyramids, temples, palaces, and humbler habitations many of which dated from the earliest period of the coast culture, and many of which still exist, neglected but mournfully imposing.

The kingdoms of Chuquimancu and Cuismancu were conquered by arms but reconciled by kindness; for, having successfully concluded his campaigns against them, Pachacutec brought these monarchs and some of their chief vassals to his court at Cuzco, where he lavished upon them hospitality of the most regal description and, after a time, sent them home again, loaded with honors and filled with admiration for the Incaic idea. Thereafter, and with perfect safety, he allowed them to continue in office, but as mediatized princes subject to himself.[39]

The Inca's sway now extended to the southern frontier of the greatest of all the coast kingdoms, that of the Chimu. It was a frontier formidably defended by the grim fortress of Parmunca, the imposing proportions of which are clearly shown in the remarkable aerial photograph taken by Major Otto Holstein and reproduced by his kind permission in Figure 32. It rose—and still rises—terrace on terrace from the summit of an arid eminence in a green and fertile valley. Dead and abandoned though it now is, it fills the beholder with a realization of the defiant pride of its builders; bristling as it then was, with a well-armed garrison provided with spears and spear-throwers, with bows and arrows, with stones and slings, with maces, clubs, and knives of copper, bronze, silver, and gold, arrogant with banners, a-shout with battle-cries, it must indeed have presented itself as a redoubtable obstacle to further progress northwards on the part of the Inca's army.[40]

It is not surprising, therefore, that the Inca Pachacutec should have allowed six years to elapse before attacking a kingdom so formidably protected. The intervening time was devoted by the great Emperor to all manner of internal reforms and to strengthening the imperial power throughout its vast realm. There was, besides, the necessity of preparing huge armies for the impending campaign in the northern half of the coast-country.

In due course, however, the war against the Chimu was begun. The post of generalissimo was now entrusted to the

Prince Tupac Yupanqui, who had been thoroughly trained for the heavy task by his father and by his uncle, General Capac Yupanqui. Under the Prince were five other generals, all close kinsmen of his. There were some 40,000 highland troops in the newly assembled army, not to mention a large number of auxiliaries, who were vassals of Cuismancu and of Chuquimancu. These coast troops, bearing in mind the ancient enmities between their own people and those subject to the Chimu, fought with special violence to overwhelm their traditional foes. Nevertheless, it seems that, in the end, it was the pacificatory influence of the Chimu's own councillors rather than military force from without that terminated the struggle. The Chimu himself ardently wished to fight to the death; but his advisers were less hot-headed and more practical. Presently it was borne in upon the Chimu that, if he did not give in to his councillors' wishes, they would speedily incite the people to rise against his authority. For this the end of the Naymlap dynasty gave them a perfect precedent. Ultimately, after much procrastination, the Chimu submitted, and accepted the overlordship of the Inca.

Characteristically, Pachacutec made matters as pleasant as possible for his vanquished enemy, treating him as handsomely and as generously as he had treated Chuquimancu and Cuismancu. Sons of all these coastland kings were sent to Cuzco to enjoy the amenities of the imperial Court, to be instructed in the Incaic idea, and, incidentally, to be hostages for their fathers' continued good behavior—but this aspect of the matter, we may suppose, was politely disguised.[41]

I have made it clear, I hope, that the Inca Pachacutec was not merely a great soldier; he was more than that, for he was a soldier so great that he could recognize military ability in others and, without experiencing the ignoble emotion of jealousy, could employ their skill in order to accomplish his purposes. In his reign, therefore, partly as a result of his own warlike activities, but still more as a result of those of his brother, his son, and his other generals, he increased his empire from about 155,000 square miles to about 260,000, roughly equivalent to New England, New York, New Jersey, Delaware, Maryland, Virginia, and the two Carolinas, or, in European terms, to Italy, Switzerland, Luxembourg, Belgium, and Holland added together. In this vast area all kinds of environment known to western South America were present, and also native peoples ranging from the low-cultured folk of Chucurpu to the highly civilized subjects of the Chimu.

These facts are, however, far from constituting the sole claim of Pachacutec to be considered a genius of the highest order. In addition to everything else, he succeeded in attaining to intellectual distinction in various directions. For one thing he re-organized the *yachahuasi* or schools which had been founded by Inca Roca, his great-grandfather, providing them with fine new buildings and with an enlarged staff of instructors drawn from the profession of the *amautas*, or sages. Henceforward not only the youths of the Inca caste but also the sons of mediatized lords and kings were given a thorough training in Quechua, in the sciences and arts of the Incas, and in such political, military, economic, and cultural matters as it was deemed proper to teach them.

Some notion of the intellectual stature of the man can be gained by reading a selection of his sententious sayings, preserved for us by Father Blas Valera, S. J., and transmitted to us through the pages of the Inca Garcilaso de la Vega:

When subjects, captains and Curacas cordially obey the King, then the kingdom enjoys perfect peace and quiet.

Envy is a worm that gnaws and consumes the entrails of the envious.

He that envies another, injures himself.

He that kills another without authority or just cause condemns himself to death.

It is very just that he who is a thief should be put to death. (This is reminiscent of Early Chimu law; see p. 62.)

Adulterers, who destroy the peace and happiness of others, ought to be declared thieves, and condemned to death without mercy.

The noble and generous man is known by the patience he shows in adversity.

Judges who secretly receive gifts from suitors ought to be looked upon as thieves, and punished with death as such.

The physician herbalist who is ignorant of the virtues of herbs, or who, knowing the uses of some, has not attained to a knowledge of all, understands little or nothing. He ought to work until he knows all, as well the useful as the injurious plants, in order to deserve the name to which he pretends.

He who attempts to count the stars, not even knowing how to count the marks and knots of the *quipus*, ought to be held in derision.

Drunkenness, anger and madness go together; but the first two are voluntary and to be removed, whereas the last is perpetual.[42]

There was a great king indeed; a great king, a great social philosopher, and a great gentleman.

* * *

The most remarkable intellectual achievement of the Inca Pachacutec lay in the field of religion, but to that I shall return in a later chapter.

The Coya of the Inca Pachacutec was Mama Anahuarque or Añahuarqui. According to Garcilaso she was the monarch's sister; but Cobo, Cabello de Balboa, and Sarmiento de Gamboa all state that she came from the village of Choco, not far from Cuzco.[43] At all events he was fortunate in having by the Coya a number of sons, of whom the most famous was the heir, Prince Tupac Yupanqui, a man capable through natural ability and through training of carrying on his great task. Nevertheless, as in the case of that other puissant King, Louis XIV, an atmosphere of vague foreboding hovered around Pachacutec in his last days. The most stirring account of his death comes from the pen of Sarmiento, that arch-enemy of the Inca family. It runs thus:

He [Pachacutec] . . . sent for the Incas *orejones* [nobles] of Cuzco, his relations, and for Tupac Inca his son to whom he spoke, with a few words, in this manner: "Son! you now see how many great nations I leave to you, and you know what labour they have cost me. Mind that you be the man to keep and augment them. No one must raise his two eyes against you and live, even if he be your own brother. I leave you these our relations that they may be your councillors. Care for them and they shall serve you. When I am dead, take care of my body, and put it in my houses at Patallacta. Have my golden image [set up] in the House of the Sun, and make my subjects, in all the provinces, offer up solemn sacrifice, after which keep the feast of *purucaya,* that I may go to rest with my father the Sun."[44]

Thereupon, in a low, sad voice, he sang some verses the gist of which is this:

> I was born as a flower of the field;
> As a flower I was cherished in my youth.
> I came to my full age; I grew old.
> Now I am withered, and I die.

Although the empire was subsequently larger than it was when Pachacutec died, it was never more truly great with inward greatness. It was the perfect application of the monarch's character and capabilities to his tasks and opportunities that made it so.

The Inca Tupac Yupanqui, *circa* 1448–1482, was, as it were, a resounding echo of his father's voice. As his father had been, so was he uneasy about the eastern frontiers of his realm at the latitude of Cuzco. In provinces known by divers names and peopled by savage folk of the Musu (Moxos or Mojos), Anti, Chuncho and other wild tribes who inhabit the country beyond the already well Inca-ized portions of the Urupampa and Paucartampu Valleys, Inca Tupac Yupanqui made his first campaigns. These regions, veined by deep canyons sonorous with the onrush of hasting waters, choked by an all but impenetrable jungle, and stifled by dense, warm airs, were profoundly unsuited to the mountain folk; but, because the dwellers therein constantly menaced the peace and solidarity of the empire, the Inca determined to win at least a measure of authority over them. He did so in a series of campaigns, albeit one suspects that his overlordship was more a matter of theory than a political actuality. Nevertheless, he was able, after two years' preparations, to build a fleet of canoes sufficiently numerous to carry ten thousand troops down the

Amaru Mayu (literally Serpent River, *i. e.*, the Madre de Dios River) and even onwards down the upper part of the Beni River into which the Amaru Mayu flows. The fleet of canoes must have been rather impressive, consisting as it did of between two hundred and three hundred canoes each of which contained, amidships, a platform upon which were placed the supplies of the army. As the expedition went along the Chunchos and other savages through whose country it passed swam out into the stream to attack the invaders, so that it was only after much sharp fighting that the Incas finally forced their woodland foes to submit; to submit, that is, to the extent of sending annual tribute to Cuzco in the form of macaws, monkeys, honey, wax, and other products of their country, which tribute continued to be sent until after the Spanish conquest of Peru. As a matter of fact, however, these sylvan peoples, and notably the redoubtable Musus, became allies, rather than vassals, of the Inca, albeit they embraced the religion, laws, and customs of the Cuzco dynasty. Thus, though only in a limited sense, the upper portions of the Beni River drainage became a part of the empire. In like manner, but with even less success, Tupac Yupanqui sought to extend his power over the fierce Chiriguanos who dwelt—and still dwell—in the wide regions east of the province of Tucumán.[45]

After these preliminary campaigns the Inca Tupac Yupanqui devoted himself during some years to the internal administration of the enormous empire. When at length he was ready to do so, he, acting upon information that had been given to the Inca Viracocha by the envoys from Tucma, proceeded to Chile with two armies of 10,000 men each. He himself was general-in-chief, and he was aided in the command by various close relatives of his. In a long series of campaigns he conquered all of Chile down to the River Maule. His enemies in this war were the admirable and freedom-loving Araucanos whom, more than a century later, the great poet Don Alonso de Ercilla y Zúñiga so justly honored in his epic, *La Araucana*. In temperament they were like the best of our own Plains Indians, and they were in a similar stage of culture, midway between the savage folk of the eastern forests and the disciplined sedentary and agricultural peoples within the empire. The Araucanos had an orderly mode of government and a semi-nomadic way of living, with the result that they had such political strength and physical robustness that neither the Incas nor, later, the Spaniards ever succeeded in crushing their spirited resistance. The most that their invaders could do was to push them southwards and ever southwards. In the northern parts of the region in question the resistance to Incaic overlordship was slight; but as the Inca's armies went towards the south, from valley to valley, both in the mountains and on the coast, the difficulties became constantly greater, the strife fiercer and fiercer. At length it was decided that the River Maule should be the southernmost frontier of the empire, and no attempt was ever made by the Incas to pass beyond it.[46]

After another interval of internal consolidation and of courtly relaxation had supervened, the Inca Tupac Yupanqui turned his face to the north, as his father had done, and, marching with a very large army, went to Casamarca, his northernmost mountain province. There he established his base for military operations farther north. But before pushing onwards, so the Inca found, he must conquer and reorganize certain provinces to the south and east of Casamarca. Therefore he began a series of campaigns in the region of Huánucu (Huánuco), which lies in the uppermost part of the Huallaga River drainage. There the Inca found interesting vestiges of ancient occupation by a high-cultured people who, in all likelihood, were influenced by the builders of the Tiahuanaco II empire, and, delighted by the charms of the countryside, he there erected some noteworthy buildings, public works, and baths.[47] Thence he proceeded down the Marañón Valley, reaching in due course the province of Huacrachucu, whose people were warlike. They worshipped serpents and kept idols representing them in their temples and houses. Their distinguishing headdress was a black woollen fillet with white tassels on the sides, surmounted by the antler of a deer. Still farther down the Marañón River, and somewhat to the east of it, the Inca entered the province of Chachapuya (Chachapoyas) whose inhabitants likewise worshipped serpents but who had the Condor for their chief deity. In all these provinces the Inca met with stout but vain resistance; but the province of Muyupampa (Moyobamba), to the east of Chachapuya in a valley tributary to the Huallaga, submitted without difficulty to Inca domination. It was here that, long ago, the Chanca refugees under Hanco-Huallu had found an asylum. In like manner, the province of Cascayunca, in the Marañón Valley, north of Casamarca, yielded peacefully to the Inca's demand for their homage.[48]

Having thus broadened out the empire on the east by the addition of a strip of territory somewhat larger than New England and containing many peoples capable of being made into excellent subjects, the Inca Tupac Yupanqui, in succeeding campaigns, vanquished the folk of the mountain provinces of Huancapampa (Huancabamba) and Ayahuaca (Ayavaca), the former of which lies in a valley tributary to the Marañón and the latter in the uppermost part of the Chira Valley.[49]

The regions added to the empire as a result of these early campaigns were varied in their geographical aspects; for the eastern portion of the area in question was tropical—though not enough so to prevent intensive occupation by the Incas—and the western portion was mountainous, albeit less elevated than the highland regions to north and south.

In this manner the Inca Tupac Yupanqui extended his empire to the frontier of what is now Ecuador and of what was then the kingdom of Quitu. A general notion of the pre-Incaic history of that kingdom has been given in Chapter IV. At the time of the Inca Tupac Yupanqui "the noteworthy and very flourishing Province of Quito, rival in fertility and abundance and number of inhabitants of all the provinces of this New World,"[50] was ruled by a native dynasty whose realm was perceptibly larger than Massachusetts, Connecticut, and Rhode Island taken together. In each of the natural regions formed in this realm by transverse ranges of mountains between the Cordilleras there dwelt tribes of fairly high cultural attainments, each with its own chiefs and ruling class. In a word, it was a state similar to that of the Incas in the time of Inca Roca.

The southernmost tribe of the region in question, and consequently the first to be brought into contact with the Incas as they advanced from the south, was that of the Cañaris. Even among the generally warlike inhabitants of the north Andean highlands they were famous for their skill and ferocity in fighting. To overcome them was a difficult task, but once they were fairly conquered they became loyal vassals of the Incas and remained so until the Spanish conquest. To do the Cañaris special honor, and also to strengthen his hold upon their country and to cause his renown to spread throughout those regions, the Inca Tupac Yupanqui caused to be built remarkable roads provided with inns, storehouses, post-runners; and, for his own convenience, the Inca erected sumptuous palaces, as well as strong fortresses and imposing Sun-Temples. In the words of Garcilaso, "Tupac Inca Yupanqui, and afterwards his son Huayna Capac, greatly favoured these provinces of the Cañaris, and that called Tumipampa, erecting palaces and other edifices, the walls of which were adorned with herbs, plants, and animals, imitated from nature in gold and silver. They built a famous temple of the Sun, also covered with plates of gold and silver. For these Indians exerted themselves to beautify the dwellings of their kings, and so they expended all their treasure on the temples and palaces."[51] Cieza de León and Garcilaso are responsible for a belief that prevails in many quarters to the effect that the stones wherewith Tumipampa (Tomebamba) was constructed were dragged thither all the way from Cuzco. True, Cieza does not make a flat statement to this effect; he merely says, "Some of the Indians pretend that most of the stones" were brought from Cuzco. But Garcilaso, first citing Cieza, says that it was so, and that the Inca sought in this way specially to honor the city of Tumipampa and its region.[52] Furthermore, in order to display his trust in the Cañaris after their submission to him, the Inca Tupac Yupanqui created an imperial body-guard composed of the best Cañari warriors, whose privilege it was to be ever near the sovereign's person. The Cañari guards were important in the later campaigns of the Incas in what is now Ecuador.

After an interval of several years of peace, Inca Tupac Yupanqui assembled a very large army on the northern borders of Tumipampa, and from there he pushed his power northwards, passing through the country as far as the confines of the kingdom of Quitu proper. Some of the provinces added to the empire in this way were underpopulated and poor, as well as low-cultured, so that it was a good deal more trouble to Inca-ize them than to conquer them. Nevertheless, the fabric of Incaic civilization had, of necessity, to be spread over the whole land. But it was not deemed worth while to build, in these rude regions, Sun-Temples and Houses of the Chosen Women. So useless were some of these provinces that the Inca, in a humorous mood, exacted from them a tribute of lice. One instinctively wonders how this precious donation was delivered, and whether it was paid dead or alive.[53]

Still another interval of peace followed upon these campaigns. The Inca then collected 40,000 men at Tumipampa and sent thence the customary conciliatory messages to the king of Quitu, his next prospective adversary. Garcilaso's language is here so vivid that it merits quotation: "As the land was rough and wild, so was its king barbarous and warlike, feared by all his neighbours for his great power, and for the extent of his lordships. Confident in his strength, he proudly replied that he was lord, and that he would acknowledge no other, that he wanted no new laws, as he decreed those that pleased him to his vassals, nor would he abandon the gods of his ancestors, which were good enough for him, being deer and great trees, that furnished fuel and meat for the support of life. The Inca received the reply, but, while commencing the war, he continued his attempts at conciliation in accordance with the tradition of his ancestors. The people of Quitu, however, showed themselves to be as proud as the Inca was gentle.

Hence the war lasted for many months and years, with skirmishes, encounters, and indecisive battles, in which many were killed and wounded on both sides."[54]

This passage gives an insight into the political status of Quitu at that time. Clearly the chief of Quitu was locally powerful, quite enough so to make matters difficult for the Inca, because of the latter's would-be gentleness.

An important, indeed, a conclusive, part in the conquest of Quitu was taken by the twenty-year-old son of the Inca Tupac Yupanqui, the Prince Titu Cusi Hualpa, better known to history as Huayna Capac. In spite of his youthfulness, the heir was placed in charge of operations in Quitu—ably counselled, of course, by older kinsmen of his—so that the Inca himself might return to Cuzco to attend to the administration of the now enormous empire. The young Prince completed the work of bringing the kingdom of Quitu into the empire, and he also conquered the provinces north of there as far as the Ancas Mayu (Blue River, now called Patia River), the provinces of Carchi and Pastu being the two most northerly in the highlands of the empire.[55]

On the coast, likewise, the Inca Tupac Yupanqui waged war successfully against the Huancavilcas and other tribes living along the shore of the Gulf of Guayaquil; and he further strengthened his grasp upon the western part of the modern Department of Piura, in which region a number of local chiefs became his vassals.

While the Inca Tupac Yupanqui was on the coast something took place that gave rise to one of the most picturesque exploits of the Incas. We are told that certain merchants arrived at Tumbez, where the Inca then was, by sea and from the west, sailing upon great rafts with masts and sails. They came, so they said, from two islands far out in the ocean, called Avachumpi and Ninachumpi. According to the merchants, these islands were well peopled and also rich in gold. Made curious by these tales, the Inca Tupac Yupanqui determined to conquer these isles and to add them to his empire, thereby challenging his happy fortune to see whether it be as steadfast by sea as it had always been by land. But the Inca was a trifle doubtful about the veracity of his informants, and he took the precaution to consult his chief necromancer, named Antarqui, skilled in omens and in magic, as to the actuality of the islands. Antarqui, after a due amount of professional hocus-pocus, reported that the islands were real. Thereupon the Inca determined to seek them out.

A great flotilla of rafts was prepared by his command. Father Cabello describes them thus: ". . . they were made of certain particularly light logs strongly lashed one to another, with a platform of interwoven canes above, making a very safe and commodious sort of vessel of the kind called *Balsas*." Upon these craft a force of 20,000 men is said to have been placed, under the orders of the Inca himself and of his brother Tilca Yupanqui. Another army, commanded by Apu (General) Yupanqui, was left on the mainland.

The Inca, with his following, navigated until he reached two islands which, presumably, he made his own. At any rate, we are told that he brought thence some "Indian prisoners, black in colour, much gold and silver, a seat of brass, and the hides of animals like horses" (according to Father Cabello). Captain Sarmiento de Gamboa who, being himself a navigator, quite naturally took an interest in this naval expedition of the Inca, accepts the story unreservedly and adds that the trophies mentioned were preserved in the fortress of Cuzco, *i. e.*, Sacsahuamán, until long after the Spanish conquest. Moreover, he specifically identifies the islands of Ninachumpi (Fire Island) and Hahua-chumpi (Outer Island) with the Galápagos archipelago which he, Sarmiento, discovered in November, 1567.

The imperial expedition was absent nine months or a year, and the greatest anxiety was felt in the empire for the Inca's safety. In a somewhat ill-considered attempt to allay the popular misgivings, Apu Yupanqui caused it to be reported that the Inca had returned, and great rejoicings were held in his camp to give color to the report. They cost the General his life; for, when the Inca really did return, it was represented to him that Apu Yupanqui had in truth been celebrating his sovereign's untimely disappearance, and that he had been doing so with treasonable intent.[56]

It now becomes necessary to speak briefly of the private life and domestic arrangements of the Inca Tupac Yupanqui. All leading Chroniclers agree that he took for his Coya his own sister, Mama Ocllo.[57] He had by her six sons, of whom the most famous was Prince Titu Cusi Hualpa, better known in history as Huayna Capac. As I have indicated from time to time on earlier pages, former Incas may have made incestuous marriages; but this is the first of the kind that has never been called in question by any writer of note. In this indubitably incestuous marriage, therefore, we see the full florescence of Inca pride, pride which had been steadily growing in the dynasty throughout the period of its rise from humble beginnings to vast imperial power.

Another manifestation of that pride ought here to be mentioned at least briefly. That was the construction, by this Inca, of the southern walls of the fortress of Sacsahuamán. The Chroniclers, in speaking of the matter, usually say that the Inca erected "the fortress of Cuzco,"[58] but they fail to differentiate, as they should do, between the northern walls— which are megalithic in style, and far older than the Incas— and the southern walls, which overlook the city and are in the late Incaic style, having well-cut stones laid in regular courses. These walls probably do date from the reign of Pachacutec or from that of Tupac Yupanqui, for they are not dissimilar to the buildings erected by these rulers at Machu Picchu, at Pisac, and in various parts of Ecuador. To the architectural aspects of this matter I shall return in Chapter XII.

After causing the construction of the southern walls of the fortress, the Inca Tupac Yupanqui withdrew with the Coya and a few favored members of his court to Chinchero, on the plain of Chita, where, by his command, a palace was erected for his lodgement in the midst of gardens. A portion of it, perhaps the wall of one of the garden terraces, still stands, facing a charming vale with a flat and fertile bottom. There the Emperor passed his last years. His health was so poor that he wished neither to receive visitors nor to be harried by the care of rulership. It is a strange thing that, in their last years, both he and his successor were ill of grave infirmities, a point which is commended to the attention of medical readers as one worthy of study.[59] Gradually the Inca grew more and more ill until, feeling that death was nigh, he sent to Cuzco for his nearest kin and greatest nobles. When they were come into his presence, he addressed them, saying that his Father the Sun was calling him to rest and that he now solemnly appointed as his successor the Prince Titu Cusi Hualpa, his son by the Coya Mama Ocllo, his sister and wife. To this the nobles cordially agreed.[60] Soon thereafter the Inca expired.

In accordance with his father's wish, Prince Titu Cusi Hualpa assumed the *suntur paucar* and ruled as Inca Huayna Capac from 1482 to 1529. He did not do so without some difficulty, for a half-brother of his, Capac Huari, son of the Inca Tupac Yupanqui by his concubine, Curi Ocllo, pretended—on no just grounds whatsoever—to the imperial office, in which he was aided and abetted by his mother who, subsequently, was put to death as a witch and a traitress. Although the pretender had a considerable following, the majority of the nobles and of the people stood by the will of Tupac Yupanqui, acclaiming the chosen heir as their sovereign, in accordance with the old Emperor's command. The new ruler was very young at the time—hence the honorific name by which he is usually known, which means The Young Chief Rich in Virtues—but from the outset his was a personal rule, with the occasional, yet very influential, counsel of close kinsmen of the Inca who were often associated with him in the administration of the gigantic empire.[61]

The early years of his reign were spent by the Inca Huayna Capac in prolonged journeys of inspection all over his realm. In the quaint wording of Acosta, "Hee was very wise, planting good orders thorowout his whole realme, hee was a bold and resolute man, valiant and very happy in warre."[62] One day, when he was in the southern part of the empire, word was brought to him that there was grave unrest in several parts of the kingdom of Quitu. Therefore, after a brief pause at Cuzco in order to take the necessary administrative and military measures, he led a force of 200,000 men northwards into the most recently acquired part of the empire. The bare statement of this number is a trifle incredible, but Cieza's wording of the matter carries conviction. He puts it thus:

> The king called a general assembly of his forces throughout all the provinces of his government, and such numbers came from all parts that they covered the plains. After there had been festivities and drinking-bouts, and the affairs of Cuzco had been regulated, the Inca Huayna Capac set out with *yscay-pacha-huaranca-runa-cuna*, which means 200,000 men of war; besides the *yana-conas* (servitors) and women, of whose number no account was taken. The Inca took with him two thousand women, and left in Cuzco more than four thousand.[62]

The reign of Huayna Capac is sometimes regarded as the apogee of Inca greatness. But to me it represents the beginning of a decline whose trajectory we cannot trace because it was cut short by the advent of the Spaniards; or, rather, because it was led to instant catastrophe thereby. The fundamental evil in the case seems to me to have been this: Personal rule and supervision by the Inca—such as had been the chief source of imperial strength in the earlier reigns—was impossible in a realm so vast as the Inca empire was now become. Moreover, the distances were so great and the complexities of the country and of the people so various and intricate that, given the means of communication then in use, the Inca could not thoroughly know and control the problems active in all his provinces, could not do so even with the most rational governmental machine that man has ever built up. The situation with which the Inca was vainly contending presents a curious analogy to that in which, during the colonial period, the kings of Castile found themselves with regard to their vast and remote American possessions.

The reign of Huayna Capac was, therefore, full of gloom and evil portents. Unrest seems to have been general in various parts of the empire, particularly in the northern provinces. Expeditions against peoples along the borders of the realm were sometimes driven back with heavy losses. Nevertheless, various small additions to the empire were made, notably along what is now the Ecuadorian coast. In this Inca's time the empire reached its greatest geographical extent. It contained some 380,000 square miles, an area approximately equal to all of the Atlantic seaboard states added together and, consequently, somewhat larger than Italy, Switzerland, Luxembourg, Holland, Belgium and France added together. It was a majestic political edifice, but an edifice that was already giving alarming signs of cracking apart of its own weight.

The marriages and concubinages of the Inca Huayna Capac were the source of much confusion and strife in after days. His first legitimate wife was a somewhat elderly sister of his whose name is variously given by the Chroniclers. As she bore no children she was supplanted—or perhaps one should say supplemented—by a younger sister, Mama Rahua Ocllo, who bore the legitimate heir, Tupac (or Inti) Cusi Hualpa, better known as Huáscar.[63] Still another bedmate of the Inca Huayna Capac was the mother of the cherished bastard, Atahualpa, who was destined to lead such a stormy life and to meet such a lamentable end. The identity of this lady is rather a problem. Sarmiento says that she was Tocto Coca, of the lineage of Pachacutec and therefore a cousin of Huayna Capac.[64] Cieza affirms that she was "a woman of Quilaco, (in Chile) named Tupac Palla"[65] which means Princess Tupac. He adds that Atahualpa was older than Huáscar and that both were born in Cuzco. Much more authoritative, and certainly far more picturesque, is Garcilaso's version, which relates that the mother of Atahualpa was the eldest daughter of the deposed king of Quitu.[66] She was captured by Huayna Capac during one of his earliest northern campaigns and was taken by him to Cuzco where she was shut up in the convent of the Chosen Women—which, of course, was simply his harem—and there, in due course, she bore the Inca his belovéd bastard son, Atahualpa. This Princess is styled Paccha Duchicela by the eighteenth-century Jesuit historian Father Velasco. Except for the Incas' conquest of Quitu, she would have been Queen of that kingdom. In wedding her, or at any rate in mating with her, Huayna Capac provided himself with a wife who could give him a son who should be the logical heir to the Kingdom of Quitu. I am inclined to think that this story is true in the main, notwithstanding the fact that nowadays Father Velasco is largely discredited among historians, as explained on pages 146–155. It is certain that the affiliations of the Inca Huayna Capac, at any rate in his later years, were all with the northern third of his empire. Besides conquering the coast of Ecuador, he strengthened his power in the northernmost part of the Peruvian seaboard, that is the Pacasmayu and the Tumpiz (Tumbez) Valleys and all the valleys between them, including the Chira and Piura Valleys.[67] He never went back to Cuzco, apparently, after leading his vast army thither. Leaving the administration of affairs at the capital in the hands of trusted kinsmen, part of whose duty it was to prepare Huáscar for rulership, he himself went northwards, taking Atahualpa with him, whose mother was already dead.[68] During the remainder of his reign Huayna Capac resided chiefly at Tumipampa, where he caused sumptuous palaces to be built, and at Quitu. In his very last years, when sick in body and perhaps in mind, the Inca Huayna Capac sought to separate the Kingdom of Quitu from the rest of the empire and to erect it into a distinct state to be ruled by Atahualpa by right of his maternal ancestors. To this proposition Huayna Capac obtained the consent of the injured party, Huáscar, who made a special journey from Cuzco to Quitu in order to hear and accede to his father's request. Then, taking leave of the Inca, Huáscar returned to Cuzco, to continue his preparations for becoming emperor of the southern four-fifths of the empire.[69] After all, the sacrifice that was asked of him, and to which he gave his assent, was no great hardship; indeed, some rulers would have esteemed it a blessing.

These events took place in 1523 or 1524. A few years thereafter, while the Inca was at Tumipampa, and in very poor health with which, one suspects, that prodigious harem of his had something to do, the tidings were brought to him that a strange, white folk, travelling in outlandish craft of great size, had been seen off the coast. Three years later, after an interval of profound peace throughout the empire, the Inca Huayna Capac, filled now with forebodings of evil soon to befall his House, died at Quitu, leaving his empire divided, in accordance with his wish, between Huáscar and Atahualpa. The embalmed body of the dead emperor was taken to Cuzco for burial, but his heart was laid away with due pomp in that city of Quitu which he loved so well. It almost seems as though that far separation of his remnants were symbolical of the disintegration which was shortly to come upon his realm.

Before ending this chapter let me speak briefly of the history of art under the Incas. On pages 198 and 234 I referred to the art of the earliest times in the Incaic period and now, in a manner frankly "tabloid," I shall merely indicate what seems to me to have been the trend of art in the middle and the later reigns.

At its purest and best Incaic art is typified by the stately and graceful aryballus embellished with paintings in rich and usually somewhat sombre colors arranged with extraordinary balance and precision in geometric patterns. The only part of the decoration of the purest type of aryballus which has any reference to life-forms is a small nubbin with a roughly indicated animal-head (usually feline) at the base of the neck. This nubbin and the two handles at the widest part of the pot served to hold the carrying-rope in place when the aryballus was carried upon someone's back, the rope being passed through the handles and over the nubbin, after which the ends of the rope fell over the carrier's shoulder and were held by his hands on his chest. This arrangement brought it about that the side of the aryballus which would rest upon the carrier's back was left undecorated, all the ornamentation being concentrated on the other side, that which bore the nubbin. I have seen, however, aryballi with decoration on both sides which, we may suppose, were not used for carrying liquids in.

Two magnificent examples of the simon-pure type of aryballus appear in Figures 146 and 147. Let it not be supposed, however, that the aryballus was the sole form of pot made by the potters of the Incaic period. Dr. Bingham, in his recent work,[70] describes and pictures aryballi, pedestal cooking-pots, bowls, jars, kettles, ladles, plates, jugs, cups, and other sorts of Incaic vessels. Nevertheless, it remains true that the aryballus is the most typical of all Incaic ceramic forms and, in its purest type, it bears decorations identical with or similar to those already mentioned and pictured here. Moreover, as I said long ago,[71] the spread of Incaic power gave rise to a very wide distribution of typical Incaic pottery. From northern Ecuador down into northwestern Argentina (the Diaguite area) and central Chile, and, of course, throughout Peru proper especially, we find in archæological sites a stratum of characteristic Incaic pottery, and it is always at the top.

The point which I wish to make here is this: in the latest reigns, say from the death of Pachacutec to that of Huayna Capac, Incaic art fell away from the austere, but beautiful, geometric ornamentation already mentioned. This was caused in part, no doubt, by an increasing flamboyancy in matters of taste, and in part to the influence of the realistic or other tradition prevailing in the art of the numerous peoples who were brought into the empire. However charming some of these late designs on Incaic pottery may be—and some of them were very attractive as Figures 148, 149, and 150 show—it is well to bear in mind that, at any rate so far as pure Incaicism in art is concerned, designs containing elements derived from life-forms are decadent, exactly as was the empire whose contrasting peoples produced them.[72]

Into the welter of wars and tumults that began with the fratricidal strife between Huáscar, the legitimate heir, and Atahualpa, the bastard but favorite son of Huayna Capac, that continued with the Spanish invasion, and terminated only after many years of internecine struggles between various Spanish factions, I do not mean to enter here. It is enough to say that the Empire of the Incas collapsed in a cloud of golden dust through which flitted away the dismayed ghosts of Incaic aspirations, pursued remorselessly by the steel-clad myrmidons of an Emperor even mightier than Huayna Capac.

NOTES TO CHAPTER VII

[1] Garcilaso, Pt. I, Bk. IV, Ch. xv. Cieza, Pt. II, Chs. xliv and xlv. Cabello de Balboa, Pt. III, Chs. xiv and xv. Cobo, Bk. XII, Chs. ix and x. Sarmiento de Gamboa, Chs. xxv and xxvi. Betánzos, Chs. vi–x, inclusive.

[2] Lafone Quevedo, 1912, 1912b.

[3] Garcilaso, Pt. I, Bk. IV, Ch. xvi. Cobo, Bk. XII, Ch. ix.

[4] Garcilaso, Pt. I, Bk. IV, Ch. xviii.

[5] Cabello, Pt. III, Ch. x, p. 402. Cieza, Pt. II, Ch. viii. Morúa, Bk. I, Ch. iii. Sarmiento, Ch. xvi. Lehmann-Nitsche, 1928, pp. 21–29.

[6] Garcilaso, Pt. I, Bk. VII, Ch. x, translates the term Huacaypata as meaning "the terrace or square for enjoyment and delight," a loose translation, but accurate enough in this connection. Huacapata is a more accurate spelling and means Holy Terrace.

[7] Garcilaso, place cited above; also, Bk. IV, Chs. xviii and xix. See also Baudin, 1927, a very important study of the élite and its formation under the Incas.

[8] Garcilaso, Pt. I, Bk. IV, Ch. xviii. Cieza, Pt. II, Ch. xxxv. Sarmiento, Ch. xix. Cabello, Pt. III, Ch. xiii, pp. 445–446. Cobo, Bk. XII, Ch. ix. Morúa, Bk. I, Ch. ix, and Chs. xvi–xxvii, inclusive, where the lives of the Coyas are discussed.

[9] Cabello, Pt. III, Ch. xviii, pp. 446–447. Sarmiento, Ch. xix.

[10] Cabello, Pt. III, Ch. xviii. Sarmiento, Chs. xx–xxii, inclusive. Sir Clements Markham, in Ch. vi of *The Incas of Peru*, would have us believe that the Huayllacans stole the child at the behest of their powerful neighbors, the folk called Ayamarcas, whose chief, Tocay Capac, had been the betrothed of Mama Micay before she married Inca Roca. The jilted lover then terrorized the Huayllacans into capturing the first-born of Mama Micay, as a vengeance upon her and Tocay Capac's successful rival. This story, though quaint, seems to me to lack adequate documentary support.

[11] Garcilaso, Pt. I, Bk. IV, Ch. xvi, and Ch. xxii.

[12] Cobo, Bk. XII, Ch. x. Cabello, Pt. III, Ch. xiii, pp. 449–450.

[13] Garcilaso, Pt. II, Bk. IV, Ch. xx.

[14] Garcilaso, Pt. I, Bk. V, Ch. xx. Cieza, Pt. II, Ch. xxxv. Cobo, Bk. XII, Ch. x. Cabello, Pt. III, Ch. xiii, pp. 449–450. Oliva, Ch. vi of Ternaux-Compans's edition. Sarmiento, Ch. xxii, calls this Coya Mama Chiquia and makes her the daughter of Tocay Capac, curaca of Ayamarca, and adds that this potentate married Curi Ocllo, a daughter of Inca Roca.

[15] Sarmiento, Ch. xxiv.

[16] Garcilaso, Pt. I, Bk. VI, Ch. xx.

[17] The Chanca War and the Battle of Xaquixahuana are described by nearly all of the Chroniclers, but with appalling divergences as to details. The

account here given is woven, with due regard for verisimilitude and probability, from materials provided by: Garcilaso, Pt. I, Bk. IV, Chs. xxiii and xxiv; Bk. V, Chs. xvii–xxvi, inclusive. Betánzos, Chs. vi–x, inclusive. Sarmiento, Ch. xxiv. Cieza, Pt. II, Chs. xliv–l, inclusive. Cobo, Bk. XII, Ch. x. Cabello, Pt. III, Ch. xiv.

18 Cabello, Pt. III, Ch. xiv, pp. 467–468.

19 Garcilaso, Pt. I, Bk. V, Ch. xx. Cobo, Bk. XII, Ch. x.

20 Cieza, Pt. I, Ch. lxxxv, describes the buildings erected in this region in such a way as to give a good idea of the intensiveness with which the Incas occupied newly acquired districts. See also: Garcilaso, Pt. I, Bk. V, Ch. xxiv.

21 This quotation is taken from Garcilaso, Pt. I, Bk. V, Ch. xxv, Vol. II, pp. 79–81 of Markham's translation.

22 R. Levillier, 1927, Ch. i, discusses the whole matter of the Inca's acquisition of the kingdom of Tucma with great sagacity and brilliance, deriving valuable data from various little-known early documents and books. Among the sixteenth-century materials cited by him are: Góngora Marmolejo, 1862; Lovera, 1865; and Lizárraga, 1914. (These dates, of course, are those of publication, as will be seen on consulting the bibliography of this volume.)

23 R. Levillier, 1927, p. 17.

24 Garcilaso, Pt. I, Bk. V, Ch. xxiv.

25 Markham, in a note on pp. 236–237 of his translation of Cieza, Pt. I, gives some valuable data concerning Incaic irrigation works. See also Prescott, Bk. I, Ch. iv; Enock, 1912, pp. 20–25; Bingham, 1922, p. 56; and Joyce, 1912, pp. 119–120 and 220–221.

26 Garcilaso, Pt. I, Bk. V, Ch. xxviii. Cobo, Bk. XII, Ch. xi. Sarmiento, Ch. xxiv. Cieza, Pt. II, Ch. xxxviii.

27 Garcilaso, Pt. I, Bk. VI, Chs. xxiv and xxv. Cieza, Pt. II, Ch. xxxi. Acosta, Bk. V, Ch. xxviii. Sarmiento, Chs. xii, xiii, xv, and xxxi. Cobo, Bk. XIV, Ch. vi. Molina of Cuzco, pp. 34–35 of Markham's edition. Santa Cruz Pachacuti-yamqui Salcamayhua, p. 80 of Markham's edition.

28 Garcilaso, Pt. I, Bk. V, Ch. xxvi. Cieza, Pt. I, Ch. lxxviii; Pt. II, Ch. l. Sarmiento, Ch. xxxviii. Cabello, Pt. III, Ch. xvi.

29 This was the opinion of the late Sir Clements Markham who, in a letter to me, dated from London, June 8th, 1915, styles Pachacutec "the greatest man that the aboriginal race of America has produced." In this opinion I concur.

30 Garcilaso, Pt. I, Bk. VI, Ch. x. Cieza, Pt. II, Ch. xlix. Sarmiento, Ch. xxxviii. Cabello, Pt. III, Ch. xvi. Cobo, Bk. XII, Ch. xii.

31 Cobo (in Bk. XII, Ch. xii) is the Chronicler who gives the most complete account of these preliminary conquests of Pachacutec. Dr. Bingham (1914b, and 1922, Chs. xiii and xiv) vividly describes the country in question. His claim that Machu Picchu was Tampu Toco and so far earlier than the time of Pachacutec is eloquently set forth in Ch. ix of Bingham, 1930; but, I regret to say, his arguments do not carry conviction, as I shall explain in Chapter XII hereafter, which deals with architecture. See also my review of his book in The Times Book Review for May 4, 1930.

32 Garcilaso, Pt. I, Bk. VI, Ch. x. Cieza, Pt. I, Ch. lxxxiv; Pt. II, Ch. xlix.

33 Garcilaso, Pt. I, Bk. VI, Ch. xi, Vol. II, p. 130, of Markham's translation.

34 Garcilaso, Pt. I, Bk. VI, Ch. xi.

[35] Garcilaso, Pt. I, Bk. VI, Chs. xi-xv, inclusive. Sarmiento, Chs. xxxiv and xxxv, xxxviii and xxxix, xliv. Cobo, Bk. XII, Ch. xiii.

[36] Garcilaso, Pt. I, Bk. VI, Chs. xvii and xviii, xxix-xxxi, inclusive. Cobo, Bk. XII, Ch. xiii.

[37] Barcroft, J.; Binger, C. A.; Bock, A. V.; Doggart, J. H.; Forbes, H. S.; Harrop, G.; Meakins, J. C.; and Redfield, A. C.: *Observations upon the Effect of High Altitude on the Physiological Processes of the Human Body, carried out in the Peruvian Andes, chiefly at Cerro de Pasco.* In *Philosophical Transactions of the Royal Society of London*, Series B, Vol. 211, pp. 351–480. London, 1922.

[38] Garcilaso, Pt. I, Bk. VI, Ch. xvii.

[39] Garcilaso, Pt. I, Bk. VI, Ch. xxxi.

[40] Garcilaso, Pt. I, Bk. VI, Ch. xxxii. Cieza, Pt. I, Ch. lxx; Pt. II, Ch. lviii. Proctor, 1825, p. 175. Squier, 1877, pp. 101–102.

[41] Garcilaso, Pt. I, Bk. VI, Chs. x-xix and xxix-xxxv, inclusive. Cieza, Pt. II, Chs. xlvi-liii, inclusive. Cobo, Bk. XII, Chs. xii and xiii. Cabello, Pt. III, Chs. xv and xvi. Sarmiento, Chs. xxx-xlvii, inclusive.

[42] Garcilaso, Pt. I, Bk. VI, Ch. xxxvi.

[43] Garcilaso, Pt. I, Bk. VI, Ch. xxx. Cobo, Bk. XII, Ch. xii. Cabello, Pt. III, Ch. xv. Sarmiento, Chs. xxxiv and xlvii; but in Ch. xl he says that she was the Inca's sister.

[44] Sarmiento, Ch. xlvii.

[45] Garcilaso, Pt. I, Bk. VII, Chs. xiii-xvii, inclusive. Cieza, Pt. II, Chs. xxii and lv. Sarmiento, Ch. xlix. Cabello, Pt. III, Ch. xviii. Cobo, Bk. XII, Ch. xiv. Polo de Ondegardo, p. 168 of Markham's translation.

[46] Garcilaso, Pt. I, Bk. VII, Chs. xviii-xx, inclusive. Cieza, Pt. II, Ch. lx. Cobo, Bk. XII, Ch. xiv. Sarmiento, Ch. l.

[47] Data on the archæological remains at Huánuco Viejo—as it is now called—are to be found in: Markham's note on pp. 284-285 of his edition of Cieza, Pt. I; in Squier, 1877, pp. 216-218; in Enock, 1904, and 1907, Ch. xxii. The British Museum possesses in its Manuscript Room, under the signature 17671.n., an interesting plan made by Padre Sobreviela and a draughtsman named Sierra in 1786, which will repay study.

[48] Garcilaso, Pt. I, Bk. VIII, Chs. i-iii, inclusive. Cieza, Pt. II, Ch. lvi. Cobo, Bk. XII, Ch. xiv. Sarmiento, Ch. xliv, gives a detail that does not appear in other works. Of this Inca he says, "In Chachapoyas the fortress of Piajajalca fell before him, and he took prisoner a very rich chief named Chuqui Sota." Suta, or Sota, is a village of the Chachapuya folk, somewhat to the south of Chachapuya town. Interesting modern accounts of this region are to be found in: Maw, 1829; and in Dyott, 1922, Chs. iii and iv.

[49] Garcilaso, Pt. I, Bk. VIII, Chs. iii and iv. Cieza, Pt. II, Ch. lvi.

[50] Cabello, Pt. III, Ch. vii, p. 499, of N. Y. P. L. MS.

[51] Garcilaso, Pt. I, Bk. VIII, Ch. v. Cieza, Pt. II, Ch. lvi. Cobo, Bk. XII, Ch. xiv.

[52] Cieza, Pt. I, Ch. xliv. Garcilaso, Pt. I, Bk. VIII, Ch. v.

[53] Garcilaso, Pt. I, Bk. VIII, Ch. vi.

[54] Garcilaso, Pt. I, Bk. VIII, Ch. vii.

[55] Garcilaso, Pt. I, Bk. VIII, Ch. vii. Sarmiento, Chs. liv-lx, inclusive.

Cieza, Pt. I, Ch. xl; Pt. II, Chs. lvi and lvii. Cobo, Bk. XII, Chs. xiv–xvii, inclusive. Cabello, Pt. III, Chs. xvii and xx–xxiii, inclusive. Modern data for the Incaic period in Ecuador will be found in: Juan and Ulloa, 1748, Pt. I, Bk. VI, Ch. ix, Vol. II, pp. 616–640. Cevallos, 1870. González Suárez, 1878, 1892, 1890–1903, 1904, 1908, 1915, and 1922. Faliès, n.d. Jijón y Caamaño, 1920. Jijón and Larrea, 1918. Larrea, 1919, 1919b. Vega Toral, 1921. Dorsey, 1901. Uhle, 1923d.

56 Materials relative to this voyage occur in: Sarmiento, Ch. xlvi. Cabello, Pt. III, Ch. xvii, pp. 503–506 of N. Y. P. L. MS. It is generally assumed that the islands in question are the Galápagos Islands, more poetically known as The Enchanted Isles. As they are some 700 miles from Ecuador there is some doubt as to whether they were in reality the islands to which the Inca went. In 1871 Sir Clements Markham expressed this doubt (in a footnote on p. 342 of Vol. II of his translation of Garcilaso). Twenty years later Don Marcos Jiménez de la Espada mentioned the matter without committing himself either for or against the historicity of the voyage. (Jiménez de la Espada, 1891, pp. 19–26.) In 1907 (in a footnote on p. 136 of Sarmiento) and again in 1915 (in a private letter to me), Sir Clements supported the historicity of the voyage. Finally, Miss Ruth Rose (in Ch. xvi of Beebe, 1924), cites Sarmiento, but not Cabello, with reference to this voyage, at the same time pointing out that the Galápagos Islands "are one of the few places on earth where aboriginal man never existed." On the whole, however, she seems to think the voyage a possibility. Personally I am not sure whether the Inca's destination was the Galápagos Islands; I think it more likely to have been Gorgona or La Plata Island. If, however, even a tiny scrap of Incaic pottery or some other artifact of Incaic type is ever discovered on the Galápagos, the question will be settled affirmatively for all time. But this remark is not to be construed as a hint to some enterprising publicity-fiend to go thither in order to "plant" some evidence!

57 Garcilaso, Pt. I, Bk. VIII, Ch. viii. Cieza, Pt. II, Ch. lv. Cabello, Pt. III, Ch. xix. Cobo, Bk. XII, Ch. xiv. Sarmiento, Ch. xliii. Garcilaso tells us that the Inca Tupac Yupanqui and the Coya Mama Ocllo had in all six sons. Huayna Capac was the eldest. The fourth son, Hualpa Tupac Inca Yupanqui, was the maternal grandfather of the historian of the Incas.

58 Garcilaso, Pt. I, Bk. VII, Ch. xxvii–xxix, inclusive. Sarmiento, Ch. liii.

59 The suggested medical investigation will be facilitated by the following data: In 1559 the Licentiate Don Juan Polo de Ondegardo found in Cuzco the well-preserved bodies of the Inca Viracocha and his Coya, Mama Runtu; those of the Inca Tupac Yupanqui and the Coya Mama Ocllo; and that of the Inca Huayna Capac. The bodies were subsequently interred, by order of the Viceroy Marquis of Cañete, in the courtyard of the Hospital of San Andrés (Hospital for Indians), in Lima. This information is drawn from Markham's notes on p. 226 of Cieza, Pt. I, and p. 273 of Garcilaso, Pt. I, Vol. I. No doubt properly qualified investigators could obtain permission from the Peruvian government to exhume, study, and re-inter the five imperial cadavers.

60 Sarmiento, Ch. liv.

61 Cieza, Pt. II, Ch. lxi. Cobo, Bk. XII, Ch. xvi. Cabello, Pt. III, Ch. xx. Sarmiento, Ch. lv, tells the story substantially as it is related here. It is clear

that there was some political disturbance early in Huayna Capac's reign. Garcilaso, Pt. I, Bk. VIII, Ch. vii, simply says that Huayna Capac was put in command of affairs in Quito during his father's time, who also arranged his marriages for him.

[62] Acosta, Bk. VI, Ch. xxii, p. 433 of Markham's edition.

[63] Garcilaso, Pt. I, Bk. VIII, Ch. viii. Sarmiento, Ch. lx. Cieza, Pt. II, Ch. lxix. Cobo, Bk. XII, Ch. xviii.

[64] Sarmiento, Ch. lxiii. Santa Cruz Pachacuti-yamqui Salcamayhua, p. 107 of Markham's edition.

[65] Cieza, Pt. II, Ch. lxix.

[66] Garcilaso, Pt. I, Bk. IX, Chs. ii and xii.

[67] Garcilaso, Pt. I, Bk. IX, Ch. ii. Sarmiento, Ch. xlvi.

[68] Cabello, Pt. III, Ch. xxi.

[69] Garcilaso, Pt. I, Bk. IX, Ch. xii.

[70] Bingham, 1930, Ch. vi.

[71] Means, 1917c, pp. 379–381.

[72] In addition to the authors already cited on Incaic art, see: Lehmann and Doering, 1924, Pls. 89–98. Schmidt, 1929, Pls. 349–356.

CHAPTER VIII

THE ECONOMIC, GOVERNMENTAL, AND SOCIAL
ASPECTS OF INCAIC CIVILIZATION

In earlier chapters an account has been given of the pre-Spanish civilizations which ran their course in Peru and in adjacent territories. Incidentally references have been made to the social and governmental institutions which were in force during the several periods; but, in the present chapter, I aim to describe with more particularity the economic, governmental and social institutions prevalent in Incaic times. In so doing I shall dwell but briefly upon pre-Incaic institutions, believing that enough has already been said about them to reveal their salient characteristics.

The Chroniclers—from whom all of our information is derived—are in far more complete agreement regarding these aspects of the Incaic civilization than they are on the historical aspects thereof. They are even in substantial agreement regarding the conditions social and political prevailing in Peru in the period immediately prior to the rise of the Incas. In general terms, the situation which they portray is as follows:

There was a complete lack of centralized government on a large scale, the entire Andean area—both highlands and coastlands—being filled with innumerable states of more or less localized purview. There was, to be sure, a considerable divergency among these states, both as regards the extent of their territory and as regards the intricacy of their organization. The simplest and smallest of them consisted merely of a few households which combined to form an *ayllu* or tribe under the leadership, in times of war or danger, of a temporary *sinchi* or chief elected by the men of the tribe. Somewhat more advanced were those states in which there were several *ayllucuna* joined together under the rule of a permanent chief,

284

styled *curaca,* whose authority was transmitted by inheritance. The territory of the *sinchi*-ruled *ayllu* consisted of a hamlet of roughly built houses having near it a *pucará* or fortified hill-top, and round it fields for farming and herding. These fields were held in common and were periodically distributed among the heads of families. The *curaca*-ruled states were similar to those ruled by sinchis save that the office of ruler was permanent and hereditary, that the territory was larger and contained several villages, and that the civic strength was no doubt greater. States of both these classes were constantly in a condition of war, for, in spite of the communal possession of land, there was among them an intense desire to possess good fields for agriculture and for flock-raising. The weapons used by the mountain-folk in their wars—and most of the states in these two categories were in the mountains—were slings, clubs with star-shaped heads of stone or possibly of copper, and lances.

As it may be said that the curaca-ruled state was an outgrowth from the sinchi-ruled state, so may it be said that from the curaca-ruled state grew a third class of state, which may be called the compound state. It was a union of several curacadoms whose combined territories might well include a sizable area with several large and populous valleys, whose social system might closely resemble that of feudal Europe, or whose curacas might simply be allies of one another rather than vassals to the most powerful among them. Examples of compound states are the Colla confederacy, in the Titicaca basin; the Chanca confederacy, in Andahuayllas; and the Chincha confederacy on the coast. The two first-mentioned were of the allied character; the third of the feudal, the lord of Chincha being clearly the liege of his less powerful neighbors.

Finally, from the third category—the compound state—there grew the great feudal kingdoms of the coast, the imposing and intricately organized states ruled by Chuquimancu, Cuismancu, and the great Chimu. In the highlands a similar feudal state is seen in the kingdom of Quitu.

The general cultural status of these four classes of states

formed an exquisitely logical parallel with their social characteristics, the first two being in a neo-archaic stage of culture (having in most cases relapsed from a higher plane formerly occupied in Tiahuanaco II times); the third and fourth classes being decidedly more advanced in general attainments and in social intricacy.[1]

A word must be said concerning the chronological aspect of these four categories of states. Although examples of all of them were in existence in late pre-Incaic and early Incaic times, some of them were exceedingly old and were possessed of a civilization which has been studied in earlier chapters. In general it may be said that the break-down of the Tiahuanaco II empire called into being in the highlands numerous states of the first and second categories, out of which, in some cases, grew states of the third and fourth categories. The fourth-category states on the coast, on the other hand, were much more ancient, having been built up by similar processes, but at a much earlier period. It can scarcely be doubted that, during the period in which the coast was receiving its first settlers, there were states of the first, second, and third classes all along the seaboard, states which, at about the beginning of our Era, gave rise to states of the fourth category.[2]

All students of the subject recognize to-day that the *ayllu* or tribe is the fundamental social group common to all Andean societies, great and small, ancient and modern. Enough is known to-day to banish forever the old idea, fostered chiefly by the Inca Garcilaso de la Vega, that all order, well-being, and social stability in the Andean area was due to the Incas. We now know that the foundations of their polity were laid long before they rose to power; we also know that, at any rate for a few generations, they were only a highland ayllu ruled by a sinchi, exactly as were scores of other ayllus throughout the mountains. The very name of the earliest head of the Inca tribe to possess historicity is significant—Sinchi Roca, or Roca, temporary war-chief.

The march of the Incas on Cuzco from Tampu Toco is so much shrouded in myth and mystery as to be almost a fabulous event. It is at any rate certain that the Incas were intruders in the Valley of Cuzco and that they early imposed their rule upon the people whom they found there, doing so by force of arms aided by guile which overcame the resistance of the six ayllus already in residence in the Valley.[3] Their invasion of, and the establishment of their mastery over these tribes was their first step on the road from being a simple ayllu to being an imperial caste.

Enough has been said to show that the materials wherewith the Incas constructed their social polity were in existence long before their day. The ayllu was not only the fundamental social group, but also the oldest; in addition to it there were the inchoate institutions of the states belonging to the second and third categories mentioned above; and, finally, there were the full-fledged feudal states on the coast. All of these elements came to be woven into the fabric of the Inca empire as it grew; the elements themselves, therefore, were pre-Incaic; it was only the uses to which they were put and the final form that they were given which were purely Incaic.

It is my purpose to present here a brief account of the social and political aspects of the Incaic state as it was in the time of Pachacutec and afterwards, with occasional references to the growth of the institutions and practices which will be mentioned as the account proceeds.

For us of to-day, who are the heirs of and the participants in a civilization which, for some thousands of years, has had coinage and has, therefore, come to regard "value" and "money" almost as synonymous terms, it is extremely difficult to visualize a society in which the concept of "value" existed but in which the concept of "money" did not exist. To us a state in which gold and silver did not represent "value" because they could readily be converted into "money" is almost inconceivable; only by a violent prodding of the imagination can we make ourselves understand that gold and silver possessed "value" among the ancient Peruvians only because they were metals which could readily be made into beautiful objects fit for the use and adornment of the rulers of the land, but not at all fit to be used as a symbol of "value." Yet, to the student of ancient Andean institutions, it seems reasonable enough that the concept of "money" should be lacking even whilst the concept of "value" was present and very important. It is true that there have been claims, both ancient and modern, that the concept of "money" *was* known to the ancient Andeans and that their "coinage" consisted of such material substances as pepper, dried fish, copper, cotton, maize, frozen potato, feathers, salt, coca-leaves, and sea-shells.[4] The folly of looking upon such substances as "coinage" or even as a substitute therefor is obvious; they were used in trade, certainly, but merely as merchandize suitable for exchange against other merchandize. In no sense were they "money"; their "value" arose simply from their usefulness as foodstuffs or as raw materials from which useful objects could be manufactured. If a man had a superfluity of maize but a supply of cotton insufficient for the needs of his household, he merely exchanged a reasonable amount of maize for the required quantity of cotton.

The concept of "money" being quite lacking, where, then, did the concept of "value" find tangible representation? A study of all that has been said by ancient and by modern writers on this intricate subject convinces me that, in the last analysis, land was the sole material form that "value" possessed in early Peru. Land, whether for farming, for herd-raising, for hunting, as a haven for fisher-folk to return to from their labors, or for mining, was the fundamental form of "value," fundamental because it underlay all resultant and secondary forms that "value" might assume.

One will search in vain, however, for anything even faintly resembling the individual ownership of land as we understand the term. The ayllu, from the earliest times, was the cell of the social organism. If a state consisted of a single ayllu, it was simply a unicellular organism. But in every sort of state, whether small and simple or. large and complex, the ayllu owned the land collectively, distributing the usufruct of it among the heads of the households in the ayllu. Under the Incas the ayllu continued to own its land collectively, but with this difference: all the land was not in the hands of the ayllus. Land was divided into three portions: one for the Sun, i. e., the state religion; one for the Inca; and one for the ayllus. Whether or not these three divisions were equal in size and in quality is not perfectly clear. It is certain, however, that the portion reserved to the ayllus was always sufficient to maintain in comfort the people belonging to the district in question. Under the later Incas, at any rate, the theory was that all the land in the country belonged by right of eminent domain to the Inca who graciously distributed the usufruct of parts of it to the Sun and to the ayllus. In practice, however, the distribution of the soil was made as follows: Each married couple received a *tupu* of land of which they enjoyed, not the ownership, but the usufruct. A *tupu* was an area measuring about sixty paces by fifty, and it was the unit of measurement for land, being held to be sufficient for the maintenance of a married couple without children.[5] Garcilaso goes on to say:

As soon as he (the newly married Indian) had children another *tupu* was granted for each boy, and half a *tupu* for each girl. When a boy married, the father handed one *tupu* over to him, which had been granted for his sustenance, because when the son left his home the father could not retain what had been given for his son's use.

The daughters did not take their half *tupus* when they married, because they had not been granted as dowers but as the sources of their maintenance; and as land had to be granted to their husbands they could not take away these. For no account was taken of married women, only of women who were not provided with husbands to maintain them before marriage, or after they became widows. The fathers retained the lands granted for the sustenance of their daughters if they required them; and if not they reverted to the State, for no one was allowed to sell or buy land.[6]

Father Cobo gives a very clear account of the manner in which the heads of households were put in possession of the usufruct of land. The chiefs of the ayllu made an annual distribution of land among the heads of families, giving to each as much as the size of his family required. The land so given was tilled by the recipient with the aid of his neighbors and fellow-members in the ayllu, and proper care was also taken of the land held by men who were absent in the army or on other rightful business. There was no such thing as private property in land as we understand the term for, although the Inca, or some great vassal of his, might give some portion of his own land to an especially favored individual, it was a life-gift only; and, at the death of the original grantee, his sons shared the land equally, and on their deaths their sons did like-wise with each share, so that the original gift was broken up in the course of a few generations. At the same time, the land so passed from generation to generation was worked in com-munal fashion by the holders collectively, and the products of the soil were evenly distributed among them.[7]

A question that suggests itself is this: When it became need-ful that a household be given additional *tupus* of land, where was the land situate that was allotted to meet the need? An important modern German authority, Herr Trimborn, thinks that, as the population increased, the people were called upon to work harder and harder with the lands they already pos-sessed without receiving additional acreage; but there is not the slightest ground for such an opinion. It is altogether in-conceivable that a dynasty which spared no effort to main-tain the material well-being of its subjects should thus delib-erately overwork them. Far more reasonable, and far better supported by the Chroniclers, is the belief that additional *tupus* were taken, when needed, from the lands of the Inca.[8]

The order in which the fields were tilled is variously given by the divers Chroniclers. Garcilaso affirms that the order was as follows: First the fields of the Sun were cultivated. Second those of the poor, by which term were designated not persons lacking wealth—for such a thing was impossible to conceive of under the Incaic system—but the unfortunate, the widows, orphans, the aged, the sick, and the absent, all of whom had their lands worked for them by fellow ayllu-members under the direction of officials called *llacta-camayoc,* village-officers. Third the lands of the heads of households were tilled by them-selves, their families, and, if need were, their neighbors.

Fourth the lands of the curaca or chief of the district. Fifth the lands of the Inca.[9] This almost superhumanly benevolent dispensation is called in question, however, by Cobo and by Polo who lead us to suppose that the lands of the Sun and those of the Inca were cultivated before those of the ayllu-members.[10] Even if this was the case it was no great hardship upon the people, for a very large part of the produce of the Inca's lands eventually found its way back to them, via the imperial storehouses, of which more will be said presently.

Enough has now been said to support my contention that land was, among the subjects of the Incas, the fundamental tangible representative of the concept of "value." It was the basis not only of the social structure but also of the economic structure of the Incaic state.

We must now turn to a consideration of the administrative hierarchy whereby the Incaic state and its material wealth were governed. As I have already indicated, there were throughout the Andean highlands, and also on the coast, a great number of states of varying size and importance which, as the power of the Incas spread, were brought into the empire. Because each state thus added to the realm already possessed its own social structure, ranging in elaborateness from the simple single ayllu up to the great feudal kingdom, the Incas found ready to their hands excellent materials wherewith to strengthen the social fabric of a growing empire. Their genius in such matters was great, largely because of a strong tendency on their part towards numerical regularity. The pre-existent social groupings were irregular, inharmonious as to size, and divers as to functions. The Incas took them over and reduced them all to suitable places in a symmetrical administrative pyramid.

We may safely suppose that it was the ayllu which first felt the influence of the Incas' tendency towards numerical regularity. At the beginning of their career they themselves were no more than an ayllu, and the neighbors among whom they thrust themselves in the Cuzco Valley were also ayllu-members, the Incas' ayllu attaining supremacy over the rest. It is altogether likely that the first step taken by the Incas after achieving mastery over Cuzco and its district consisted in the regularizing of the ayllu which, previously, had been of no fixed size and of rather loose internal structure. Under the Incas' rule the old ayllu was arbitrarily converted into the *pachaca*, a social group composed of one hundred households with an official at the head of it.[11]

The Chroniclers differ somewhat as to the grades which made up the Incaic administrative pyramid; yet it is fairly clear, on the authority of the writers named below, that the ranks of the hierarchy were as follows:

1. *Chunca-camayu-cuna*—Officials (*camayu-cuna*) in charge of ten (*chunca*) households. (Garcilaso; *Horden*, MS.; Sarmiento; Cobo; Morúa; Falcón; Polo de Ondegardo.)
2. *Pichca-chunca-camayu-cuna*—Officials in charge of fifty (*pichca-chunca*) households. (*Horden*, MS.; Cobo; Morúa; Falcón.)
3. *Pachaca-camayu-cuna*—Officials in charge of one hundred (*pachaca*) households. Sometimes called also *Llacta-camayu-cuna*, village-officials. (Garcilaso; *Horden*, MS.; Sarmiento; Falcón; Cobo; Polo.)
4. *Pichca-pachaca-camayu-cuna*—Officials in charge of five hundred households. (Garcilaso; Sarmiento; Cobo; Falcón.)
5. *Huaranca-camayu-cuna*—Officials in charge of one thousand (*huaranca*) households. (Garcilaso; *Horden*, MS.; Sarmiento; Cobo; Polo; Falcón; Santillán.)
6. *Hunu-camayu-cuna*—Officials in charge of ten thousand (*hunu*) households. (*Horden*, MS.; Cobo; Polo; Falcón; Sarmiento; Santillán.)
7. *Tucuiricuc-cuna*—They-who-see-all, officials ruling jurisdictions containing forty thousand households and called *guamán*, equivalent to the term "province." (Garcilaso; Santillán; Montesinos; Sarmiento, Ch. lii; Cabello, Pt. III, Ch. xviii.)
8. *Apu-cuna* or *Hatun apu-cuna*—Officials, four in number, each of whom was in charge of one of the four quarters (*suyu-cuna*) of the empire. Spanish writers designate them as "viceroys" or "governors-general." They formed a sort of imperial council for the Inca, and resided at Court a good part of the time. (Cobo; Polo; Falcón; Sarmiento, Ch. lii.)
9. *H. I. M., the Sapa Inca*—The pinnacle of the pyramid.

Obviously, this hierarchy was logical and symmetrical; that it was also efficient becomes apparent when we study it. No small part of its strength arose from the fact that all three of the social classes in the State, *i. e.*, the Inca and the imperial caste, the nobility, and the people, participated in it. Officials of the two lowest ranks were of the people; officials of the rank of *pachaca-camayu* and upwards were styled *curaca,* which term has here the force of "gentleman" or "nobleman";[12] officials of the two highest ranks were very often, if not invariably, of the blood imperial and depended directly from the Inca himself. The *tucuiricuc-cuna* were appointed either by the Inca personally or by the *apu-cuna,* and in general each rank of officials was filled by the appointment of its immediate superior in the scale. The *chunca-camayu-cuna* and the *pichca-chunca-camayu-cuna* were appointed from among the heads of households in their respective groups of ten households or of five *chuncas,* and they were little more than overseers or leaders of manual labor.[13]

The manner in which conquered states were woven into the fabric of the empire's administrative system was logical and effective. The rank given to a conquered chief depended entirely upon the size of the state ruled by him. If he were of but moderate importance he was made a *pachaca-camayu* or perhaps a *huaranca-camayu,* and his vassals were given subaltern positions under him. If his state were more populous, the conquered chief was made a *hunu-camayu.* In the case of the great kings of the coast it is likely that they were made *tucuiricuc-cuna.*[14] In some cases, naturally, the Inca replaced the vanquished rulers by men of his own, although in general he tended to keep them in their places and to weave them into the Incaic system.

Taking the old ayllu as a point of departure, and transforming it, by what arbitrary methods one cannot exactly say, into a group of one hundred households, the *pachaca,* the Incas built up an extraordinary social structure in which each rank of officials was firmly rivetted to those above and below it, and in which the current of authority flowed ever downwards from the source of all earthly power—the Inca—with no contact at all between officials of equal rank.

Because they were themselves of the people, the *chunca-camayu-cuna* and the *pichca-chunca-camayau-cuna* came more closely into daily personal contact with the mass of the population than did the higher officials. Their duties were three-fold: they supervised the labor of the heads of households under them, at the same time seeing to it that they had a sufficiency of food, clothing, seeds, tools, etc.; they maintained discipline and administered punishments such as flogging or stoning for minor offences, reporting the graver infractions of good order to their superior officers; and they kept a record of the vital statistics in their groups, reporting them to the higher officials every month.[15]

As the fundamental principle of the Incaic system was this: Every man must serve the state in one way or another according to his age and capacity, the whole purpose of the hierarchy was that of extracting from the land its maximum yield of valuable merchandise. It has been seen in passing that the household, not the individual, was the unit of society. Nevertheless, as a means of producing the greatest amount possible, the state took a special sort of cognizance of the individual, drawing up a series of categories of persons based upon their capacity for work. The series was arranged thus:

1. *Mosoc-caparic*—Babe newly born and still in arms.
2. *Saya-huamrac*—Child able to stand, about one year old.
3. *Macta-puric*—Child between one and six years old.
4. *Ttanta-raquizic*—Bread-receiver, a child six to eight years old.
5. *Pucllac-huamrac*—Boy playing about, eight to sixteen years old.
6. *Cuca-pallac*—Coca-picker, doing light manual labor, sixteen to twenty years old.
7. *Ima-huayna*—Almost a youth, aiding his elders in their tasks, twenty to twenty-five years old.
8. *Puric*—The able-bodied man, head of a household and payer of tribute, from twenty-five to fifty years old.
9. *Chaupi-rucu*—Half old, doing light work, fifty to sixty.
10. *Puñuc-rucu*—Old man sleeping, sixty and upwards.[16]

As here described the official hierarchy implies the existence of an arithmetical rigidity in the grouping of the puric-households of which society was composed. Professor Baudin has called attention to this point, saying that, if at some given moment the grouping were mathematically accurate, it would not long remain so.[17] There are several possible ways of explaining how this situation was met; but, unfortunately, all of them are guess-work, because the Chroniclers are silent on the subject. German students of the matter, notably Cunow and Trimborn, have assumed that the original *pachaca* of one hundred households came in course of time to contain very many more households than that, the term *pachaca* becoming meaningless save as a label for a social group of this rank.[18] Another explanation—and one which, I think, is more valid —is that the proportions of the *pachaca* and of the other groups were maintained as closely as possible to their theoretical numbers, this being done sometimes by an arbitrary re-allocation of households, sometimes by a deliberate creation of new groups, sometimes by other artificial adjustments. Obviously, it would be far easier to keep the smaller groups, the *chunca*, the *pichca-chunca*, and the *pachaca* at their theoretical proportions than it would be to maintain the larger groups at the proper size.

Direct supervision of these matters was in the hands of certain extra-hierarchical officials, usually of the blood imperial, who periodically and incognito penetrated every corner of the land, being the direct personal representatives of the Inca and performing for him the duties of inspection—and at times of espionage—which the early Incas had been able to perform in person.[19] Father Cabello de Balboa calls these officials *michic*, which term he translates as "guardian," adding that they were spies and informers. But Garcilaso says that the term *michec* had the meaning of "shepherd,"[20] which is less baleful than the other. As a matter of fact, these inspectors constituted a very important check upon the hierarchy, their activities being in general benevolent, although, no doubt, they could on occasion be very terrible. The Inca himself would be so upon discovering any abuse of the powers reposing in the various grades of functionaries.

That such a check should be necessary becomes apparent

when we consider not only the immense extent of the empire, but the large population which it must have had. The *puric* household has been variously estimated to contain from five to ten individuals.[21] From this it follows that the *chunca* contained from 50 to 100 people, the *pachaca* or Incaized ayllu from 500 to 1,000, the *huaranca* from 5,000 to 10,000, the *hunu* from 50,000 to 100,000, and the *guamán* or province ruled by a *tucuiricuc* consisting of four *hunu-cuna* from 200,000 to 400,-000. In an attempt to arrive at some notion of the total population of the realm at the time of its greatest extension we are hampered by a lack of knowledge as to how many *guamán-cuna* were contained in each of the four *suyu-cuna* or quarters ruled by the four viceroys or *apu-cuna*. A careful study of the map of the empire published by Sir Clements R. Markham (Hakluyt Society) and of that issued by Dr. Horacio H. Urteaga under the auspices of Don Rafael Larco-Herrera (Lima, 1927) convinces me that each *suyu* must have contained at least twenty *guamán-cuna*. This figure gives to each *suyu* a population of between 4,000,000 and 8,000,000 and to the Empire of Ttahua-ntin-suyu a population of between 16,000,000 and 32,000,000. Assuming, for caution's sake, that it was much closer to the lower of these two figures than to the higher, we find that the population of the empire was approximately twice as great as that of the same territory to-day.

This brings me to a somewhat difficult question, namely that of the number and character of the social classes in the empire. Above, on page 293, I stated that there were three such classes: the Inca and the imperial caste, the nobility, and the people. I wish now to justify this assertion, doing so because Professor Baudin has classified the population in a somewhat different manner. He lists the classes thus: The Inca; the élite; the people; and the *yana-cuna*.[22] I now purpose to examine this matter in detail.

To begin with the most lowly grade of persons named, the *yana-cuna*, we find the following situation to have existed. The most detailed account of the origin of the *yana-cuna* is that given by Father Cabello de Balboa.[23] He tells us that a brother of the Inca Tupac Yupanqui dared to plot against the ruler and that he and his assistants in the plot were all captured. Having put to death his brother and the minor leaders, the Inca assembled in a village called Yanayacu six thousand Indian lance-makers who had also been implicated in the treason, doing so with the intent to slay them also. But the clement Coya, Mama Ocllo, interceded for the condemned and induced her brother-husband to spare their lives. He did so, however, with the proviso that thenceforward the pardoned men and their families constitute a special class whose duty it would be to serve the religious establishment and the Incas in the rôle of field-laborers, shepherds, and domestic servants. They were to be exempted in perpetuity from the ordinary duties and obligations of the people, and they were to form a special element in the state. As this measure was taken at the village of Yanayacu the members of the class thus created were called *Yanayacu-cuna,* which term was shortened to *yana-cuna* in common parlance.

Other Chroniclers, notably Cieza de León and Santillán, make very clear the status of the *yana-cuna.* The former speaks of the *"anaconas,* which is the name for perpetual servants who sufficed to till the royal fields, and do service in the palaces." Elsewhere he speaks of them as mere chattels and, in a description of certain military preparations made by the Inca Huayna Capac, mentions "the *yana-conas* and women, of whose number no account was taken."[24] Santillán speaks of them in like terms.[25]

It thus becomes apparent that the *yana-cuna* were an extra-social element, in some ways analogous to those persons who, while living within the Roman empire, formed no part of the Roman state. If they were not slaves or serfs—neither of which terms truly describe them—they were at all events hereditary servitors who were forever to be excluded from all connection with the polity of the Inca empire. Moreover, as Father Cabello makes clear, they developed only late in the history of the empire.

In strong contrast with them, therefore, were the heads of

households who were members of the ayllus, who were called *puric-cuna, aucapuric-cuna,* or *hatun-runa-cuna.* The second and third of these terms demand a word of explanation. *Auca* signifies "enemy" and its use in conjunction with the term *puric* probably indicates conquest, an enemy who has become a *puric* or head of a household. *Hatun-runa* means "a great man," probably in the sense of "a full-grown man." The functions of this class of men, though laborious, were distinctly honorable.

They were so because they served directly the two major activities of the Incaic state, namely, the collection of tribute and the carrying on of war for expansion and defence of the realm. Both of these general headings had a multiplicity of aspects and divers ramifications, some of the chief of which I shall now try to indicate.

Tribute was paid in a variety of ways of which the most important was manual labor in one or another of its many forms. In large sections of the empire tribute was paid by the heads of families in the form of agricultural toil. "The ancient tribute," says Polo de Ondegardo, "was to sow the crops for the Inca and for religion (*i. e.,* the state cult of the Sun), and to reap them and carry the harvests to the store-houses, where there was always a superfluity."[26] This work was done by turns or spells called *mita-cuna* in Quechua, so calculated as not to be oppressive.[27] Labor in the mines and elsewhere for the good of the state was arranged in like fashion, it being a fixed policy of the Incas that everyone should have an ample measure of repose.[28] The dignified position held by manual labor in the Incaic polity is made apparent by the fact that everyone, from the Inca downwards, participated in it. That this was more than a mere gesture such as the laying of a corner-stone with a golden trowel wielded by some bored potentate is made evident by Garcilaso, who tells us that, in the Spring (September), the terrace called Collcampata (shown in Figure 151), on the northern margin of Cuzco immediately below the fortress of Sacsahuamán, ceremonial cultivation of the soil for the benefit of the Sun was carried on. "This land,"

Fig. 146 (*left*). An aryballus of the purest Incaic type.

Fig. 147 (*centre*). A small aryballus of pure Incaic type.

Fig. 148 (*right*). A late Incaic ladle with a design of realistic frogs in the central panel and various not wholly Incaic motives in other panels.

Photographs by courtesy of the Museum of the University of Pennsylvania.

Fig. 149 (*left*). From Cuzco, an Incaic vessel, late in style, with plant-motive.

Fig. 150 (*right*). A late Incaic aryballus with design of condors and other birds. *After Lehmann and Doering.*

The originals are in the Ethnological Museum, Berlin.

FIG. 151. Part of the Colcampata Palace, just above the city of Cuzco. In the foreground is the "Field of the Sun."

Photograph by courtesy of W. V. Alford, Esq.

FIG. 152. A portion of a dwelling-house near the Temple of Viracocha, at Racche (or Urcos).

Photograph by L. D. Gismondi, La Paz.

says the Inca historian, "was cultivated by persons of the blood royal, and none but Incas and Pallas (Ladies) could work on it. The work was performed with great rejoicing, especially the ploughing, when the Incas came forth in their richest clothes. All the songs that were sung in praise of the Sun and of their Kings were composed with reference to the meaning of the word *Haylli,* which in the general language of Peru means 'triumph.' Thus they were said to triumph over the earth by ploughing it, and turning it up so that it might yield fruit. In these songs they inserted graceful references to discreet lovers and to valiant soldiers, all bearing on the triumph over the land that they were tilling. The refrain of each couplet was the word *Haylli.* . . ."[29] Somewhat more in the nature of a gesture was the manner of inaugurating the cultivation of the "lands of the religion" in other parts of the empire. Cobo describes it thus: "The people gathered to cultivate these lands in this fashion: That if by chance the Inca himself was present, or his governor or some other great Lord, he was the first to put a hand to the task, doing so with a *taclla,* or plough, of gold which they brought to him for the purpose, and, following his example, all the Lords and gentlemen who accompanied him did likewise. But the Inca desisted soon from the work, and the Lords and chief men did so as well, in due order, and they sat down with the King to hold their banquets and festivals, which on those days were very solemn." He goes on to say that the *curacas-pachacas* continued at work a while longer than the greater nobles and, after ceasing, supervised the toil of the men under them, who, in turn, were assisted by their children, wives, and members of their respective households.[30]

It is to Father Blas Valera that we owe the preservation of the general laws of the Incas governing labor and tribute, laws so inviolable that even the Inca himself might not contravene them. The chief of them were as follows:

1. No person exempted from tribute could ever be called upon for any contribution of merchandise or of work. The exempted classes were:

   A. All persons of the blood imperial, and all Curacas and their families.

   B. All officers of the army down to the rank of centurions, and their sons and grandsons.

   C. All subaltern officials, if sprung from the people; while in office.

   D. All soldiers while on active service.

   E. All males under 25 years of age.

   F. All men over fifty. (But Youths and Elderly Men were expected to help their kinsmen with their tasks.)

   G. All women.

   H. All sick persons.

   I. All incapable persons (blind, lame, or maimed). The deaf and dumb were given work suited to them.

   J. All priests of the Sun.

2. Tribute was to consist solely of labor, time, or skill as a workman or artisan, or as a soldier. All men were equal in this respect, he being held to be rich who had children to aid him in making up his appointed amount of tribute, and he who had none being considered to be poor.

3. Except for work as a husbandman or as a soldier, for which any *puric* might be called upon, no man was compelled to work at any craft save his own.

4. If tribute took the form of merchandise produced by the payer's labor only the produce of his own region could be demanded of him, it being held to be unjust to demand from him fruits that his own land did not yield.

5. Every craftsman who labored in the service of the Inca or of his Curaca must be provided with all the raw materials for his labor, so that his contribution consisted only of his time, work, and dexterity. His employment in this way was not to be more than two or three months in the year.

6. A craftsman was to be supplied with food, clothes, and medicine at need while he was working, and if his wife and children were aiding him, they were to be supplied with those things also. In this sort of work not time, but a special stint of accomplishment was required of the tribute-payer, so that if he had help from his family, he could finish his task sooner than by himself, and could not be called upon again that year.

7. This law was on the subject of collecting the tribute. At a certain time the collectors and accountants assembled in the chief village of each province, with the *quipu-camayoc-cuna* (knot-record keepers), and by means of the quipus and also of little pebbles the accounts and reckonings were cast up with perfect

accuracy in the presence of the official in charge, probably a *hunu-camayoc* or a *tucuiricuc*. Father Valera says as follows on this score: "They saw, by the knots, the amount of labour that the Indians had performed, the crafts they had worked at, the roads they had travelled over by order of their superiors, and other tasks on which they had been employed. All this was deducted from the tribute that was due. Then they showed the collectors and the governor each thing by itself that was stored in the royal depots, such as the provisions, pepper, clothes, shoes, arms, and all other things that the Indians gave as tribute, down to the gold, silver, precious stones, and copper belonging to the King and the Sun, each item being recorded separately. They also reported what was in store in the depots of each village. The law ordained that the Inca governor of the province should have a duplicate of the accounts in his own custody, to check any error on the part either of the collectors or of the payers of tribute."

8. The surplus of the tribute, after the royal wants had been satisfied, were placed on deposit and drawn upon for the good of the people as required. Certain specially prized goods, such as gold, silver, copper, precious stones, feathers, paints, and dyestuffs, were restricted to the use of the imperial caste and to such favored curacas as might be honored with permission to use them.

9. In special cases tribute was paid in the form of work upon the roads, upon the temples, palaces, aqueducts, bridges, storehouses, or other public works. In other cases the tribute-payers were called upon to serve as *chasqui-cuna* (post-runners) or as litter-bearers or as miners.

"Besides these things," says Father Valera, "the people were obliged to do other things for the common good, or for the service of the Curacas or the King. But as, in those times, there was such a multitude of Indians, each man had very light work, because their turns were regulated with great exactness, and one never had more to do than another."[31] I think my readers will agree with me that the world has never seen a code of laws more exquisitely logical nor more sublimely just.

The lot of the *hatun-runa-cuna* was not, we may be sure, a bad one while the power of the Incas lasted. It had, no doubt, its portions of sorrow and perplexity; but the major calamities were as infrequent as they can be where humankind is concerned. If to call the subjects of the empire "a menagerie of happy men" is to verge upon hyperbole—and who can surely say that it is?—at any rate they were men whose material wants were normally well protected. It has been charged that equality in poverty made all the Indians rich;[32] but, as we have seen, there was no concept of money, and being rich consisted merely in possessing a family of sufficient size to enable the householder to complete his tribute-stint in as short a time as possible, thereby leaving himself a maximum of time in which to attend to his own affairs. Moreover, as two important modern writers have pointed out, actual practice differed in ancient Peru from theoretical practice nearly as much as in our own society. As we are theoretically "dry" but practically "wetter" than ever before, so was the Incaic empire theoretically a state wherein no private property existed but practically one in which there was in fact quite considerable private property in a moral, if not in a legal, sense. Professor Baudin has shown that the crops raised by the *hatun-runa-cuna* on their *tupus* were their own property, as were also their houses, small domestic animals (dogs, guinea-pigs, etc.), their garments, and their household utensils, and their weapons. This concept is also expressed by Señor Latcham, in a somewhat broader interpretation.[33]

One final point, for the moment, concerning the *hatun-runa-cuna* is this: Their position was one of honor and of dignity, in the strongest possible contrast to that of the *yana-cuna*. The latter were obliged to toil constantly for their masters without sharing in or directly contributing to the life of the empire; the former toiled a certain proportion of their time for the state, serving as the firm base upon which it rested and participating fully in its benefits. The remainder of their time and strength was their own. The contrast was not unlike that between the helots and the citizens in ancient Athens.

We are now come to the question of the upper classes of the Incaic state, *i. e.*, the nobility, and the imperial caste.

Most writers, both ancient and modern, tend to lump them together into one class. But this, I venture to think, is a mistake; for even some of the Chroniclers, among them Cobo, Garcilaso, and Santillán, provide us with materials upon which to base a distinction. The first of these authorities says in so many words that the officials in the administrative hierarchy "enjoyed the immunities and privileges of noblemen" in an equal degree with the *orejones;* but he does *not* say that they were *orejones*.[34] Garcilaso repeatedly makes it clear that conquered chiefs who finally submitted with good grace, and chiefs of states who came into the empire without resisting the Inca, were continued in office and were fitted into the hierarchy of the Incaic administration, each one taking a rank therein to which his position prior to conquest entitled him. Only contumacious chiefs were cast down and replaced by others of the Inca's appointment or of his viceroy's appointment.[35] It was of the newly absorbed officials, and of their families, that the nobility, properly speaking, was constituted. It was, however, a nobility in which there was no such thing as primogeniture, nor were the places in it always filled by inheritance of any sort. When, for example, a *pachaca-camayu* died, so Santillán tells us, "there was chosen from the same *pachaca,* and not from some other, the one who was most manly and most virtuous, whom they were wont to style *ochamanchay,* which signifies 'fearful of sinning'; and this choice rested with the most important lord of the whole province or valley, who made it without reference to the sons and brothers of the dead curaca if there were someone else more fit for ruling than any of them. And when the lord of a huaranca died, the lordship of it came to that one of the lords of the other nine pachacas subject to him whom the most important lord of the whole valley considered to be most fit to rule. And when the lord of the whole valley died the Inca gave the post to whomever he judged most fit to rule and whom he believed had served him best, provided always the choice were made from among the lords of the same valley."[36] Thus, in spite of the vagueness of terms, we see that personal merit played a far greater part in the matter than did the accident of blood-relationship.

The imperial caste, on the other hand, was in large measure determined by blood. As Cobo says, "The title and privilege of nobles were enjoyed, in the first place, by all Incas of the blood royal, whom our Spaniards call *Orejones* (Big-Ears), because their ears were bored and enlarged to remarkable size; these and some other gentlemen of other lineages who, by grant of the King, also bored their ears, constituted the order of knighthood. . . ."[34] To this rather bare statement Garcilaso adds interesting details. He says, "Beginning with the name Inca, it must be understood that when applied to the royal person it meant king or emperor; but when given to those of his lineage it signified a person of the blood royal, and the name was applied to all who were descendants in the male, but not in the female line. They called their kings Sapa Inca, which means sole king or sole emperor or sole lord; for *Sapa* means sole."[37] Garcilaso then goes on to say that there were various other royal titles to which I shall return in a moment. Incas in general were sometimes styled *Intip-churi*, Son of the Sun. Unmarried princes of the blood royal were called *Auqui* and unmarried princesses were styled *Ñusta*. On marrying they became *Inca* or *Atauchi* and *Palla*, respectively. "These," adds Garcilaso, "were the royal titles which I heard the Incas use among each other and to the Pallas; for my chief intercourse, in my childhood, was with them. The Curacas, how great lords soever they might be, could not use these titles, nor their wives and children; for they appertained exclusively to the blood royal, in the male line."[38] This remark proves conclusively, I think, that there was a sharp distinction between the nobility and the imperial caste. Persons who were accorded the privilege of being Incas-by-grant, having been specially honored by the Sapa Inca with that rank, were for all practical purposes members of the imperial caste.[39]

The titles peculiar to the sovereign and his chief wife are interesting and eloquent of the aims of the dynasty. In addition to the formal designations, Sapa Inca and Coya, Emperor and Empress, there were certain laudatory vocatives, such as *Huaccha-cuyac,* Lover and Benefactor of the Unfortunate, applied to the monarch, and *Mamanchic,* Our Mother, given to the Empress.[37] These honorific appellatives indicate the general benignity of the imperial intentions, but they give but a slight indication of the absolute power wielded by the Inca. Europe and Asia have seen sovereigns whose power was enormous; but none among them exceeded in absoluteness the Incas from Pachacutec onward. It was not merely a question of tremendous earthly grandeur; it was also one of unlimited superiority to the rest of mankind, a superiority that was largely composed of sanctity, and a superiority which found tangible expression in a simple fact: No one, how great soever he might be, was permitted to enter the Inca's presence with shod feet, with shoulders not weighted with a symbolical burden, with eyes lifted to the countenance of the Intip Churi.[40]

This well-nigh immeasurable greatness was surrounded and supported by lesser degrees of greatness in the persons of the *orejones* and of the nobility. Their greatness arose not merely from place and from political power, but also from superior education. When the Inca Roca founded the *Yacha-huasi* or College at Cuzco, he enunciated a great social principle, namely, "that the children of the common people should not learn the sciences, which should be known only by the nobles, lest the lower classes should become proud and endanger the commonwealth."[41] In the time of the Inca Pachacutec the College was greatly enlarged and improved, remaining, however, true to the ideal of its founder. Garcilaso speaks interestingly on the subject, as follows: "In the Indian language they call the schools *Yacha-huasi,* which means 'the house of teaching.' Here lived the wise men and masters of that commonwealth, called Amautas or philosophers, and the Haravecs or poets. They were much esteemed by the Incas and by all the people. Many disciples lived with them, chiefly of the blood royal."[42]

The *Amauta-cuna* and the *Haravec-cuna* constituted together an extremely important section of the nobility, perhaps, in some cases, of the imperial caste; for, in their hands were concentrated all the wisdom and all the intellectual amenities of life under the Incaic régime. They had, therefore, an immense and irresistible influence over the formation of the collective mentality of the élite—to use Professor Baudin's term —of the empire.[43] It is not too much to say that the *Yachahuasi* was the brain of the state. The course of instruction, according to Morúa, was one of four years. In the first year those lads who had come from provinces where Quechua was not spoken were taught that language. The second year was taken up with a study of theology, ritual, and kindred matters. The third year the pupils began to learn how to understand the quipu or knot-record. The fourth and final year they went further into that study, learning history and many other things from the knot-records.[44] Thus we see that, as reformed by Pachacutec, the College received not only members of the imperial caste, but also youths of the provincial nobility. This formed an integral part of the Incas' policy of having the heirs of provincial chiefs reside in and be educated in Cuzco where, besides being hostages for the good behavior of their parents, they could be deeply imbued with the Incaic idea and so come to be important agents for the dissemination of pro-Incaic propaganda.[45]

Two more points must be referred to before my account of the structure of the Incaic state can be said to be complete. The first refers to the established religion of the state and the priests thereof. As these matters will be fully discussed in a later chapter, it is enough to say here that the hierarchy of the religious organization was roughly parallel to that of the social organization, the summit of both being the Inca.

More difficult, because more obscure, is the problem of the significance of the two *parcialidades* or moieties which were present in the city of Cuzco and in most other parts of the empire. It is said by Garcilaso, quoting directly from an Inca who was his maternal uncle, that Manco Capac "began to settle this our imperial city, dividing it into two parts, called *Hanan Cuzco,* which . . . means Upper Cuzco, and *Hurin*

Cuzco, which is Lower Cuzco. The people who followed the king wished to settle in Hanan Cuzco, and for that reason it received the name; and those who were gathered together by the queen settled in Hurin Cuzco, and it was therefore called the lower town."[46] He goes on to say that there was no greater contrast in honor between the two than there is between the right arm and the left, the people of the upper town merely being elder brothers to those of the lower, and the whole idea of the division being that of perpetuating the memory of the fact that both the king and the queen had worked to assemble the inhabitants of the city.

Garcilaso, therefore, implies that the division was early Incaic in date; but other writers, among them Castro and Ortega Morejón, in their report on Chincha, and Casas, give us to understand that the moieties were the creation of Pachacutec or of Tupac Yupanqui.[47] On the other hand, Father Montesinos and Sarmiento would have us believe that the moieties were a great deal more ancient than the Incas.[48] Most modern writers see in the moieties merely a distinct grouping of the original inhabitants of a district and of the invading and conquering folk who, forcing themselves among them, took the part of the land not yet occupied.[49] In a former study I departed somewhat from this explanation of the matter, saying that, when a valley was conquered, its original inhabitants were placed in the *hurin* or lower moiety where, perhaps, the land was less desirable, whilst the conquerors took the best lands and constituted themselves into the *hanan,* or upper, moiety.[50] This explanation is incomplete, however, for the Incas down to and including Inca Roca were Hurin-Cuzco folk, and from Yahuar-Huaccac onward they were of Hanan-Cuzco. In this change some students, notably Professor Baudin,[51] have seen the symptoms of a revolution. But Sarmiento gives a far more likely explanation of the matter. Speaking of the Inca Roca, he says: ". . . while his ancestors had always lived in the lower part of Cuzco, and were therefore called Hurincuzcos, he ordered that those who sprang from him should form another party, and be called Hanan-cuzcos, which means the Cuzcos of the upper part. So that from this Inca began the party of upper or Hanan-cuzcos, for presently he and his successors left their residence in the House of the Sun, and established themselves away from it, building palaces where they lived, in the upper part of the town."[52] It was, then, merely a question of a change of residence, brought about partly, no doubt, by plans for the enlargement and embellishment of Coricancha, the Sun-Temple, but chiefly, I strongly suspect, by a desire to live amid fresher airs than those of Lower Cuzco.

On the whole we may safely say that the Incas took over the moieties, as they did so many other social groupings, which had long existed in highland societies, and adapted them to their own purposes, intending thereby to make the collective will less uniform and to create two parties each of which would exercise surveillance over the other, intending also to facilitate the keeping of vital statistics and economic statistics.[53]

This brings me to the final phase of this chapter, namely, to the consideration of the methods by which an empire so divided, sub-divided, and sub-sub-divided again and again, was made into a compactly organized political fabric. The fact which must never be lost to sight is that the Inca was not only the source of all authority but was also the ultimate director of the lives of all his subjects. His being so was made possible by the structure of the official hierarchy which was so constructed that, although there was no direct contact between officials of the same rank, there was always the closest kind of contact between officials of a given rank with a number of officials of immediately inferior rank. At the top of the structure, the Inca had direct dealings with the four *hatun-apu-cuna* or viceroys and, through them, with the entire empire and with every aspect of its economic life.

It is now necessary for me to describe as briefly as may be the divers means whereby the official hierarchy was rendered efficient. As a convenient point of departure nothing can serve us better than a glance at the economic life of the empire.

Professor Baudin, in one pithy sentence, has summed up the

fundamental economic policy of the Incas. He says: "In Peru the needs of the populace were few, and the Incas had a genius for preventing them from growing."[54] In order to comprehend the full significance of this remark one must know exactly what were the requirements of the masses in the Incaic state. These may be summarized thus:

Diet. Normally the masses lived upon *charqui* or dried ("jerked") meat, mostly of the llama, supplemented by maize either roasted or boiled, and by roasted or boiled potatoes. There was also a preparation called *chuño* made from potatoes that had been alternately frozen and warmed until they became a sort of flour which, when used in conjunction with *charqui,* hot water, *uchu* (red pepper) and other herbs, was not a bad dish. Salt was seldom put into the food, but a chunk of rock-salt was kept handy at meals and was lapped from time to time by the eaters. There was a dish, however, called *chupe,* which was made of salt, pepper, water, and potato, a rather nasty thin potato gruel which, nevertheless, is nourishing, if not gastronomically pleasing. Moreover, there were soups made from *quinúa* leaves and from *oca* roots. Finally, there were three kinds of bread, all made from *sara,* maize, either hard, called *muruchu,* or soft, called *capia,* the three kinds of bread being *ttanta,* ordinary bread for daily use, *huminta,* a finer bread used only on special occasions, and *cancu* or *zancu,* used only for sacrifices. As a great treat the Indians were sometimes given fresh meat, llama, huanaco, or even venison.[55] Of such materials as these did the morning and the sundown repasts of the ordinary *puric* household consist. The diet was not a poor one, particularly if we assume that it was better cooked than is that of the highland peasants to-day—and it certainly could not have been worse cooked—but the economic point which must be made concerning it is this: that it could be entirely derived from each household's own garden-plot and therefore contributed little or nothing to the trade of the empire. The only foodstuffs which did so contribute were the delicacies enjoyed by the upper classes, to which matter I shall return presently.

Beverages. The national drink was maize-beer, nowadays called *chicha,* but anciently called *aca.* It was—and, alas, is—made from maize-grains which have been chewed by old women and men who spit it out into warm, brackish water—the more brackish the better—wherein fermentation takes place in about eight days. This brew was commonly imbibed to excess by all classes. More potent still was a drink called *viñapu* made by allowing maize to soak and to sprout in water, after which, in the same water, it was mashed and then left to ferment. This liquor, which drove the drinker quite mad, was prohibited by the Inca, and we may be sure that the prohibition was more effective than modern attempts of the sort usually are.[56] Milder than *aca,* and more in the nature of our tea or coffee, were certain infusions derived from the berries of the *mulli* tree and from the *chuchau* or maguey plant's leaves.[57]

Narcotics. Cuca was pre-eminently the narcotic of ancient Peru; it is the bane—or one of the banes—of modern Peru. That strange aberrant genius, the late Dr. W. Golden Mortimer, wrote a thick volume in eloquent praise of coca, hailing it as "the divine plant of the Incas."[58] So it is a wonderful plant, but one whose dried leaves are woefully easy to misuse to the hurt of mankind, a fact which the Incas themselves fully recognized; for, in addition to making it one of the government monopolies, they carefully restricted and regulated its consumption, allowing the masses to have it to chew, mixed with lime, only for special purposes, as on occasions when they would be subjected to unusual strains.[59] *Sayri,* tobacco, was known, but it was taken only in the form of snuff and with medicinal intent, to clear the nasal passages.[60] Thus we see that *cuca* and *sayri,* which might perhaps have been important articles of commerce, were used in a way so highly restricted that they probably did not bulk very large in the trade of the empire.

Housing. In ancient times, and likewise among the modern peasantry, the dwellings of the people were no more than rectangular, usually windowless structures with thatch roofs and containing usually one room, but sometimes two or even three. The floors were of trodden earth. Such windows as there were had no sort of closure-device. There were no chimneys. Crude niches sometimes were present to serve as cupboards. The lower-class dwellings of the coast were, no doubt, somewhat more commodious, being made of sun-dried bricks or of adobe, and having better ventilation in response to a more benignant climate. Squalor, enlivened by throngs of guinea-pigs, dogs, fleas, and miscellaneous vermin, was probably general, much as it is to-day in the houses of the Indians. Nevertheless, it is to be doubted whether, in the matter of lodgement, the *puric* household was less comfortable than the peasant household of any southern European country prior to the twentieth century. True, certain things which even the most humble European has always considered indispensable were lacking, such things as chairs, tables, dressers, objects of iron, glass, and brass or pewter, wheeled tools of every kind, and milk, butter, eggs, and fowls; but, there were either effective substitutes for these, or else conditions were such that they were not needed and were not much used even after the Spaniards introduced them. It is, therefore, apparent that the domiciles of the masses were so simple that they contributed little or nothing to the commerce of the empire.

Mode of living in general. The kingdom of women, under the Incas, was pre-eminently the home. The domestic offices were all performed there, including the manufacture of all the clothing of the family. This, in its simplest forms, consisted, for the men, of the *huara* or breech-cloth, of the *uncu* or shirt-like tunic, of the *yacolla* or mantle, of the *usuta* or sandals, and of various accessories such as a *chuspa* or pouch, a fillet for the head, and numerous ornaments; for the women, of the *anacu* or long tunic, of the *lliclla* or mantle, together with accessories, such as sandals, pins (*tupu*), headgear, and so on.[61] On their wedding-day a couple received, as a present from the state, two complete outfits each of clothing, one being finer than the other and destined to use of festival-days.[62] The materials, in general, were cotton and wool. In this respect, therefore, the masses did contribute rather heavily to the commerce of the empire, for wool, being a state monopoly for the most part, had to be distributed throughout the country, and cotton, grown only on the coast, had to be brought up into the mountain regions. The clothing of the well-established household, as contrasted with the newly founded, was all made at home, and great care was taken of it. The method of mending tears or burns was exactly the same as that used by French *stoppeurs* and was of the kind that we call invisible mending or re-weaving, paying therefor a great price.[63] Cooking was done on clay or stone stoves with several holes above the fire-chamber, on exactly the same principle as our kitchen-ranges. Finally, the household furnishings were almost entirely of home manufacture, consisting simply of a variety of vessels of pottery, stone, or wood, of wooden spoons, of gourds of divers shapes and sizes, and of sundry minor articles.

It would seem, therefore, that, in general, every *puric* household was practically self-sufficient because self-supporting. If this be true, it will naturally follow that almost the only contribution made by the masses to the commerce of the realm were in the matter of cotton and wool, in the matter of distributing tribute-merchandise to the imperial storehouses, and in supplying the elaborate material requirements of the upper classes.

The state of affairs here hinted at is so difficult to believe in that it becomes imperative for us to examine more deeply into the facts with a view to ascertaining their exact nature and meaning.

If we concede that the allotment of land to families in proportion to the number of individuals therein had as its first purpose that of supplying the needs of the family, and secondly of the production of a surplus for the use of the state, we may also concede that, theoretically, the amount of usable merchandise produced by the families of the empire would be more or less uniform throughout. Theoretically this is correct. Practically, however, various factors making for great inequalities in the amounts produced by families came into play, such factors as variations in the qualities of the soil, as the difference in the numbers of persons in the family—which would effect not only the amount of land available to the family but also the amount of hard work that could be accomplished on it—as the skill and application of the workers, all of which factors tended to bring about a general lack of uniformity in the amounts of merchandise produced by different households. Thus, a household consisting of a *puric* and his wife and three daughters would have two and one-half *tupu-cuna* of land whilst their neighbors, a family consisting of a *puric*, his wife, six unmarried daughters and four unmarried sons, would have eight *tupu-cuna*. Not only that, but the first family would have but one pair of masculine arms and four feminine ones whilst the second would have five masculine pairs and seven feminine pairs. Yet each family would stand on equality with regard to quotas of tribute to be paid, whether that tribute were in the form of labor upon the lands of the Inca or of the Sun or whether it were in the form of merchandise to be paid over to the state having been produced by the *puric* and his household. Hence arose the distinction mentioned above, on page 302, between "rich" and "poor," a family having many pairs of arms and an abundance of land being able to get through with its tribute-stint far more easily and quickly than a family of few arms and less land.

As families tended to be numerous, in spite of a high rate of infant mortality due to the rigors and neglect which surrounded young children, there was usually a considerable surplus of merchandise over and above the requirements of the family and of the tribute. It was this surplus that had to be taken to market and there disposed of to advantage. Naturally, if every family produced enough of every sort of merchandise to meet its own needs and to pay its share of the tribute, there would be no purchasers, and the surplus would be wasted. But, if we can judge by the methods prevailing to-day, this was not the case; for one family would raise potatoes, another *ocas*, another peppers, and so on. Therefore, trade was made possible by the fact that a family would send to market the surplus of material that it had raised in order to exchange it for those sorts of merchandise which it had not raised, but which it required.

Markets, consequently, were general and frequent under the Incaic régime. Various descriptions of markets ancient and modern are easily available to us. Father Blas Valera, quoted in full by Garcilaso, speaking of the Inca Pachacutec's economic measures, says: "In order that labour might not be so continuous as to become oppressive, the Inca ordained that there should be three holidays every month, in which the people should divert themselves with various games. He also commanded that there should be three fairs every month, when the labourers in the field should come to the market and hear anything that the Inca or his Council might have ordained. They call these assemblies *Catu,* and they took place on the holidays."[64] Again, Don Miguel de Estete, on entering Sausa (Jauja) in the train of Don Hernando Pizarro in March, 1533, found an immense commercial activity to be thriving vigorously.[65] Father Cobo makes some exceedingly important remarks on the subject of commerce, as follows: "Although they (the American natives) knew and esteemed gold, silver, and other metals, and made use of them in various ways, of none of them did they make money, nor was the use of money known in any part of America until the Spaniards introduced it. Instead of purchasing and selling, they bartered certain things against certain others. . . . It is true that certain things were most generally used in this way and served as money wherewith to buy all those other things that were needful for daily life. These were ordinarily the foodstuffs which were used as bread. . . . In this kingdom of Peru maize was most often made use of for this purpose, and to the present day the Indians use it in order to buy other kinds of viands; because of this there has been introduced the custom which we see today in the villages of the Spaniards where the Indian women (for they it is who commonly sell garden truck, fruits, and other things of that kind) are wont to exchange those things for bread, and thus they are wont to buy these trifling things with bread. *No value nor standard was fixed in these exchanges by any public authority, for this was left to the satisfaction of the parties,* just as we find it today in almost all the Indian villages of this kingdom; for on feast-days the women go out to make exchanges in the plazas, each one bringing the merchandise which she has. Some bring fruit, others maize, others cooked meat, others fish, others pieces of raw meat, salt, coca, red-pepper, and other things of this sort in which they deal. And they make their exchanges, one woman giving a plate of fruit for a plate of cooked meat, whilst another with red-pepper buys salt, and another with maize buys meat, and so on; with the result that all obtain what they need by giving in exchange of that which they had in superfluity. And in sooth no little entertainment can be derived by Spaniards who chance to be present if they set themselves to watch how these contracts and exchanges are arranged, for these people observe therein a custom of their own, which I have seen several times. It is as follows: The Indian women place all their merchandise, or a part of it, if it is fruit or something of that sort, in a row of little piles before them, each pile being worth half a *real* or a *real,** or, if it is meat, in rows of pieces of the same value, and in like manner with other kinds of goods. The Indian woman who comes to buy with maize instead of money sits herself down very slowly close to the seller and makes a little pile of maize wherewith she thinks to buy what she desires, neither woman speaking to the other the while. She who sells fixes her eyes upon the maize, and if it appears to her little, says naught, nor makes any sign other than to continue looking, and so long as she continues thus it is understood that she is not contented with the price offered. Meanwhile, she who buys has her eyes fixed on the seller, and all the while that she sees her remain thus unmoved, she keeps adding a few grains more to her pile of maize, and this goes on little by little until she who sells is content with the price and declares her approbation, not by

*He is speaking of post-Conquest markets; but the ancient ones were exactly similar in principle.

word—for from beginning to end they say nothing to one another even though the bargaining last for half an hour— but by the act of extending her hand and gathering the maize to herself."[66]

This long passage, and particularly that portion of it which I have italicized, proves conclusively that the concept of *money* was wanting among the pre-Spanish Peruvians, but that the concept of *value* was operative among them. The story, as told here by Father Cobo, is incomplete, however, for he fails to tell us how the buyer, if angered by the avarice of the seller, can rise in a silent dudgeon and take herself off to some less grasping vendor. One may see to this very day exactly the same procedure in any Andean market-place, as, for instance, in Figure 153. True, the range of merchandise offered is now more extensive than formerly—including even such things as patent-medicines, electric flash-lights, sewing-machines, and harmonicas—but the principle of barter is the same. Dr. Wrigley has given an admirable account of the Andean fairs or markets,[67] and I have studied them at Cuzco, La Paz, Huancayo, and Huancabamba in the highlands and at Querocotillo (Chira Valley) and at Catacaos (lower Piura Valley) on the coast, at all of which places I have seen exactly the same customs that Father Cobo describes.

A point of considerable importance must now be made: These markets were of local character only. They were attended by members of households within reasonable walking distance of the places at which they were held. At a guess, I would say that every village which was the seat of a *huaranca-camayoc* there was a periodical market or fair. But into this matter, no doubt, the hierarchical principle entered, in this way: The village of a *huaranca-camayoc* would have its market; that of a *hunu-camayoc* would have a more important market; and the capital of each *guamán* or province ruled by a *tucuiricuc* would have a very important market. I have failed to find any information on this head in the Chronicles of Peru; but I am inclined to think that the smaller the market, the more frequent its sessions, and that those of the

FIG. 153. A market being held in modern Cuzco, precisely as in the days of the Incas.

FIG. 154. Ruins of an Incaic bridge over the upper part of the Mantaro River.
Photographs by courtesy of W. V. Alford, Esq.

FIG. 155. The curving wall of the Temple of the Sun (now the Monastery of Saint Dominic) in Cuzco.

FIG. 156. A street scene in Cuzco showing, on the left, the exterior wall of the palace of Tupac Yupanqui.

Photographs by Max Vargas, Arequipa.

highest rank were probably semi-annual or annual affairs to which people of all classes, in their best attire and in festive mood, would repair from every hamlet throughout a large province. It is not to be supposed, however, that the *puric* households of the whole province attended *en masse;* rather, it is probable that each *pachaca* or *huaranca* sent representatives thither, charged with the duty of disposing of specially selected merchandise, of unusual value on account of its rarity or beauty, to advantage.

All this is admittedly conjecture, but it is conjecture which is supported in a measure by certain well-known facts regarding the Incaic administrative system, described above, and by the rather vague testimony—second-hand at that—of Father Román y Zamora, who leads us to believe that, in general, commerce was a purely local affair.[68] Such a hierarchy of fairs or markets as I have suggested, taken together with the system of *mitima-cuna* or transferred communities, of which more presently, would in a measure account for the wide distribution which certain classes of merchandise are known to have had in ancient times, and under the Incas.

It now becomes incumbent upon me to dwell briefly on those classes of merchandise. They were chiefly, but not entirely, of the type of articles of luxury, and they came from all three of the longitudinal zones into which the Andean area is divided by nature. The coast gave to the Incaic world cotton—not an article of luxury, since it was used by all classes—many vegetables, many fruits, many kinds of fish, sea-shells, algarroba wood and balsa wood; the highlands yielded all the metals then used, wool—of which only that derived from the vicuña was a luxury—various vegetables such as maize, potatoes and sundry tubers, meat both fresh and dried, and fine building-stone; the forests or *montaña* gave many sorts of timber, of which the *chonta* (a hardwood palm) was specially prized, *cuca*, medicinal plants, dyestuffs, and splendidly colored feathers. Of course this is not a complete enumeration of the products of the three zones, but it does indicate the major elements composing the sort of commerce under consideration.

The mode of living of the upper classes was closely connected with that commerce, was, indeed, only made possible because of it. Cuzco, navel of the empire, goal of all men's desires under the Incas—much as Paris is the goal of every Frenchman's—Cuzco, centre and summing-up of the Incaic idea, was the focus upon which converged all commerce, all thought, all adoration. (See Figures 144 and 157.) It is there, consequently, that we must study the pomps and elegances, the amenities and beauties with which, in the later reigns of the Inca dynasty, the imperial caste and the nobility surrounded their daily existence. It is not with the Cuzco of the earlier Incas, huddled upon a narrow strip of southwestwardly sloping land between the Huatanay and the Tullumayu whose rather noisome waters trickled or rushed—according to the season—from the heights of Sacsahuamán to the Cusimayu, that we have to deal; rather, it is with late Incaic Cuzco, whose splendors Inca Roca first envisioned, which Pachacutec created during twenty years, with the aid of tens of thousands of workmen, that we must concern ourselves. Nevertheless, some attention we must give to the older part of the city. At its northwestern end towers the hill of Sacsahuamán, crowned by the stately old fortress; at the southeastern end are the fields of Pumap Chupan (Puma-Tail). Between these points, and bounded on the other sides by the two streamlets, lies oldest and most venerated Cuzco. About midway its length, and on the western side, lay the Huacay Pata, the Holy Terrace or Square, some six hundred feet on a side, which was ever the very axis of the empire's being. To the northwest of it and of the Anti-suyu road running from it at right angles to the rivers was Upper Cuzco, Hanan Cuzco; to the southeast was Lower Cuzco, Hurin Cuzco, undoubtedly the older and the holier of the two. Beyond the two rivers, to the west and to the east respectively, there grew up in later Incaic times a series of suburban wards which contained no buildings of prime importance but which housed the general population of the capital. On the farther side of the Huatanay, and separated from the Huacay Pata only by the stream, was the

Cusi Pata (Joy Terrace or Square), twice as large as the other, but wholly given over to the people, just as was the adjacent square to the élite. The earlier Incas, down to and including Inca Roca, dwelt in Coricancha, the Temple of the Sun; but the palaces of the Incas from Roca to Huáscar, son of Huayna Capac, cluster in close proximity to the Huacay Pata, the remainder of the interfluvial strip—and particularly the street now called St. Augustine—contained the city mansions of the imperial caste and of the highest provincial nobles.

Although the strictly architectural features of the various chief buildings will be treated in a later chapter it will be in order to speak of them in general terms here. The ancient streets of Cuzco—and the more recent Spanish streets, too, for that matter—are narrow and, on the whole, tolerably straight. Because of the massive, dark-hued masonry unrelieved by windows and having only a few doorways, the streets have a grim aspect not a little heightened by their appalling filthiness. (See Figures 143 and 156.) Whether or not this last feature existed in Incaic times I cannot say; but I am inclined to think that ancient Cuzco was reasonably clean, fully as much so, at any rate, as were contemporary cities in Europe and perhaps conspicuously more so. In general the buildings were of but one story, but that in most cases was high, twenty feet or more. As a result of this fact and of the immense stretches of unbroken wall the streets must have been drafty and chilly as well as darksome, but impressive nevertheless.

The dimensions of the buildings, whether palaces or state edifices of various kinds, were very large. The Cora-Cora (Pastures) palace, built by Inca Roca, was the first of the individual imperial palaces. It was about three hundred feet square, an impressive structure in the polygonal style of architecture. (See Figure 143.) It stood on the northwestern side of the Huacay Pata, and behind it was the Yacha-huasi or College, measuring about four hundred feet by five hundred. The palace of the Inca Viracocha, part of whose site is now occupied by the cathedral, was somewhat larger than the Cora-Cora. Pachacutec's palace, known as Hatun Cancha (Great

Enclosure), stood at the eastern corner of the Huacay Pata and measured some five hundred feet by three hundred. Pachacutec also built a palace called Cassana (Freezing with wonder) which was an assembly place of some kind. The palace of the Inca Tupac Yupanqui, known as Puca Marca (the Red Ward), about four hundred and fifty feet by two hundred and fifty, stood approximately midway between the Huacay Pata and the Temple of the Sun. Finally, so far as the palaces are concerned, Amaru Cancha (Serpent Enclosure), the palace of the Inca Huayna Capac, measured nearly four hundred feet square and stood at the southern corner of the Huacay Pata. Of the state edifices the most important were the Yachahuasi, about four hundred feet by three hundred, standing behind the Cora-Cora and the Cassana palaces and fronting on the Huatanay; the Aclla-huasi (House of the Chosen Women), about two hundred feet by four hundred, standing next to the Puca Marca; and the Temple of the Sun, some five hundred feet square, with its garden, of the same length on its southeastern side. Consult Figure 157.

When in use these structures did not depend upon mere bulk for their impressiveness. They were profusely adorned with gold, that metal even being used, in some of them, for mortar. All sorts of animals, birds, and plants were delicately wrought in gold and silver, and sometimes human figures also. With these objects of art they adorned the walls of the apartments in the palaces. To quote Garcilaso:

The Inca usually sat on a stool of solid gold called *tiana* . . . without arms or back, and with a concave surface for the seat. It was placed on a great square slab of gold. All the cups for the whole service of the house, as well for the table as for the kitchen, were, large and small, of gold and silver; and some were placed in each depot for the use of the king when travelling. This was done to avoid the necessity of carrying them about with him, and thus every royal lodging, whether on the roads or in the provinces, was fully supplied with all he required when he marched with his armies, or visited his people. . . .

There was also great store of new clothing, both for wearing and for the bed, for the Inca never put on the same dress twice, but gave

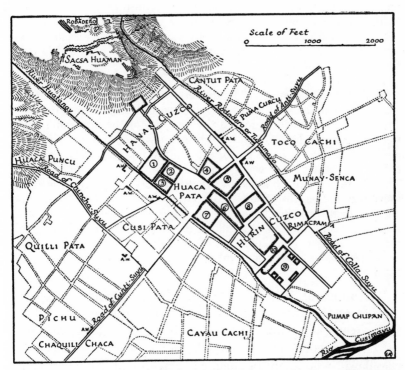

Fig. 157. A plan of ancient Cuzco based on Markham's plan, in Vol. II of his edition of Garcilaso.

1. Yachahuasi, or Teachers' House, *i. e.*, Schools, founded by Inca Roca.
2. Cora-Cora (the Pastures), palace of Inca Roca.
3. Cassana, said by Garcilaso to have been the palace of the Inca Pachacutec, but more probably this structure was an exercise-hall or gymnasium for the youths of the Inca caste.
4. Palace of the Inca Viracocha. A part of this site was occupied by a temple called Quishuar-Cancha, dedicated to the Creator-God, Viracocha.
5. Probable site of the palace of the Inca Pachacutec.
6. Aclla-huasi or House of the Chosen Women.
7. Amaru Cancha, palace of the Inca Huayna Capac.
8. Puca Marca, the palace of the Inca Tupac Yupanqui.
9. Coricancha, the Temple of the Sun. The Golden Garden of the Sun lay between the rounded apse and the River Huatanay.
10. Intip Pampa, or Square of the Sun.

it to one of his relations. All his bed clothes were woollen, woven from the wool of the vicuñas, which is so fine that, among other things belonging to that land, it has been brought over for the bed of the king, Don Philip II. These blankets were placed both under and over. They did not use mattresses, because they did not want them, for when they saw those used by the Spaniards they would not have them in their houses. They seemed to be too great a luxury, and too artificial to be in conformity with the natural life that they profess to lead.

They did not have tapestry for the walls, because they were covered with gold and silver. The dinners were very plentiful, as they were prepared for all the Inca's relations who might come to dine with the king, as well as for all the servants of the household, who were numerous. The hour for the principal meal, both for the Inca and for the people, was eight or nine in the morning. They supped before the light of day was gone, and these were their only meals. They were generally bad eaters; that is to say, they ate little. But they were not so abstemious in drinking. They did not drink during the meal, but they made up for it afterwards, and their potations were continued until night. This was the custom of the rich, for the poor had only sufficient of all things, though no scarcity. They went to bed early, and got up very early to do the business of the day.[69]

It is apparent, therefore, that in spite of its golden splendor the life of the Inca—and, by implication, that of the ruling classes generally—was fundamentally simple, almost austere. As for the splendor, it undoubtedly existed, for not only Garcilaso—who might be inclined to overpaint the scene—but all the other Chroniclers tell of it in much the same sort of language.[70] It was, however, a splendor that concerned only the Inca and the ruling classes; moreover, it was a splendor that did not separate those who enjoyed it from close contact with nature. We may, I think, visualize imperial Cuzco as a large city—perhaps having as many as 200,000 people in it— with a central, river-bordered strip of sombre magnificence. Herein were crowded the vast palaces of the rulers—many of them, as time went on, uninhabited, because of the custom of each successive Inca to abandon his father's house and build one for himself—enclosed within high and massive walls within which were a great number of courts, gardens, halls, apartments, and chambers. Imposing and shiningly adorned though these mansions were, they differed not at all in principle from the dwellings of the nobility, for in all alike were to be seen the same magnificent masonry, the same thatched roof— made with care and nicety, no doubt, but thatch all the same, and the same paucity of what we call furniture.[71] Indeed, the contrast between the abode of a *puric* and that of a great *curaca* or that of the Sapa Inca himself was more a matter of size than anything else. The breezes of heaven could play on the spines of all of them as they ate their suppers. Consonant with that contrast were others: the imperial caste and the élite ate and drank from silver and gold vessels closely similar in shape to the pottery, wooden, and calabash vessels of the people; the *puñuna-cuna,* beds, of the highly placed were of fine vicuña wool, light and yet warm, or, on the coast, of exquisitely wrought hammocks made from cotton or from bast fibre, but here again they differed only in quality from the coarse, llama-wool *chusi-cuna,* blankets, in which the people slept; the women of the people used mirrors of bronze, but the Ñustas and Pallas had dainty affairs of obsidian, pyrite, or silver in which to admire themselves; the diet of the rulers differed from that of the ruled only through the addition of such delicacies as fresh fish and as the delicate and delicious tubers called *ynchic* and *cuchuchu,* of which the commonalty rarely if ever tasted.

Where, then, in all this, do we discover evidences of great commercial activity? Frankly, I can discern no traces of anything of the sort. It is true that at Cuzco, in the dwellings of the mighty, there were various articles of use and adornment that had been derived from all parts of the empire. The Inca, if minded to partake of fresh fish from the sea or from Lake Titicaca, undoubtedly was able thus to cosset his fancy;[72] if feathers of dazzling hue were desired for the embellishment of favored persons' apparel they were available in abundance; if the wondrously wrought gold beads called *chaquira* of the coast, or if the mother-of-pearl and the fine shell of that region, if the *umiña-cuna,* emeralds, of the Ecuadorian coast were needed for the embellishment of the dress or possessions of persons permited to use them, they were to be had;[73] if the ladies of Cuzco desired their looms to be of fitting elegance, they caused them to be of the hard, lustrous wood of the *chonta* palm.

None of these things, however, was derived through channels that can properly be called commercial. They were made available through the activity of the Inca's servants—*chasquicuna* and tribute collectors. Only a small part of society was allowed to use them, and it was natural enough that the Inca or his representatives should have charge of obtaining and distributing them. The empire was thickly sprinkled with storehouses, each one serving a not very extensive district, serving both as a point for the reception of tribute and as a point for the dispensing of material benefits. If it became necessary to bring one class or another of luxury merchandise to any given point from a long distance away, the Inca's messengers or servants looked after its transportation. Garcilaso makes it clear enough that even the victualling and supplying of the Inca's household needs was, on the whole, a local affair. He writes thus:

The attendants for the service of the palace, such as sweepers, water-carriers, and wood-cutters, as well as cooks for the table of the courtiers (for that of the Inca himself was served by his concubines), porters, keepers of the wardrobe, warders of the treasure, gardeners, domestics, and all other servants holding similar positions to those in the houses of the kings and emperors, were not persons chosen by chance. But each office was filled by natives of particular villages, whose duty it was to supply faithful and efficient men in sufficient number. They were changed at certain intervals, and this was the form that the tribute took in those villages. Any negligence or inefficiency on the part of these servants was looked upon as an offense committed by their village, and for one man's fault all the inhabitants were chastised more or less severely according to the offense. If the offense was committed against the royal majesty, the village was levelled with the ground. It must not be understood that the wood-cutters went to the forest for fuel, but that they found it provided in the palace, being brought there by the vassals, as well as all other things for the royal service. And these employments were much prized among the Indians, as they enabled them to be nearer to the royal person, which was an honour they most esteemed.

The villages which furnished these servants were those within six or seven leagues (eighteen to twenty-one miles) of the city of Cuzco, and were the first which the Inca Manco Capac ordered to be formed by the savages whom he reduced to subjection. The inhabitants of them, by his special grace and bounty, he called Incas, and they received the insignia and dress of the royal person. . . .[74]

This quotation shows several things quite clearly, viz., that the service of the imperial palace was a local matter; that none of the supplies for the Court were provided through commercial channels, but rather were brought in by the Inca's own vassals as a part of their tribute; and that the service of the royal person was held to be a great honor in spite of its ardors and risks of punishment.

If, therefore, there *were* far-journeying merchants in Incaic Peru—which I doubt—I am at a loss to know what kinds of goods they carried, or what it profited them to do so. The commerce of the nation, as I see it in the light of the evidence adduced, was chiefly a local matter conducted under governmental supervision at the various grades of fairs or markets, supplemented by long-distance traffic which was wholly in the hands of the imperial authorities.

This being so, it naturally follows that the Incas must have been in the closest possible touch with every corner of their vast empire, not only in order that they might keep themselves informed concerning the resources and the productions of each district, but also that they might hold the enormous fabric which they had created firmly to their own selves, thereby ensuring its continued solidity.

They did all of that. The means whereby they accomplished a purpose so many-sided were various; study of them is profoundly illuminating. The first of them to demand our attention is the system of statistics which provided the ruler with exact information concerning the material wealth, the value, existent in each district, and also concerning the man-power

therein. Writing being unknown—and Dr. Bingham is the
sole important scholar of our day who accepts Montesinos's
statement that there *was* writing in early Peru[75]—the Incas
had to depend upon the *quipu* for the preservation of their
records. Although various Chroniclers lead us to suppose that
the *quipu* or knot-record had a narrative character, at any rate
in some instances,[76] it has been demonstrated fairly conclusively by modern writers that the majority of *quipu-cuna* now
extant have only a mnemonic and mathematical character.[77]
By means of the *quipu* the *quipu-camayoc*, knot-record keeper,
could enumerate and calculate in the decimal system.[78] In this
respect the Incas were far ahead of the Romans, with their
clumsy system of figures, and even of the modern British, with
their absurd £. s. d. A good idea of the value and importance
of the *quipu* is given by a passage in Cieza which, in spite of
one inaccuracy, is worth quoting: "The system (of accounting)
of the Peruvians was by *quipus*. These were long ropes made
of knotted cords, and those who were accountants and understood the arrangement of these knots, could, by their means,
give an account of the expenditure, and of other things during
a long course of years. On these knots they counted from one
to ten, and from ten to a hundred, and from a hundred to a
thousand. On one of the ropes are the units, on another the
tens, and so on." (This is the inaccuracy. Modern writers already cited have shown that units, tens, etc., were all recorded
on one string.) Cieza continues: "Each ruler of a province was
provided with accountants who were called *quipucamayos*, and
by these knots they kept account of what tribute was to be
paid in the district, with respect to silver, gold, cloth, flocks,
down to fire-wood and other minute details. By these same
quipus they could report to those who were commissioned to
take the account at the end of a year, or of ten or of twenty
years, with such accuracy that so much as a pair of sandals
would not be missing."[79] Captain Pedro de Cieza de León, one
of the most honorable and Christian, as well as one of the
most intelligent, Spaniards who ever went to Peru then proceeds to tell us how, with his own eyes, he saw the *quipu*

utilized for his instruction by an Indian lord who was a friend of his, Guacarapora, lord of Marcavilca in the province of Xauxa, and he concludes his chapter with eloquent praise of the *quipus* which, to no slight extent, enabled the Indians to maintain good order in their affairs notwithstanding the cruelties and oppression to which they were subjected by the Spanish *conquistadores.*

We may be sure, therefore, that, in spite of its humble and primitive appearance, the *quipu* was a really efficient mathematical and statistical instrument, fully on a par with the abacus and, in well-trained hands, almost equal to the modern slide-ruler. To the possible narrative functions of the *quipu* I shall refer later.

Moreover, it may not have been the sole instrument of the sort. There exists, in various archæological collections, a curious class of artifacts that has always puzzled the student. I refer to the terraced and compartmented objects now generally called "counters" of which characteristic examples appear in Figure 158. The first of these objects to be found was discovered at Patecte, near Chordeleg in the province of Cuenca, Ecuador, in 1869. It formed a part of the very rich furnishings of a grave in which the body lay *at length* amid an amazing array of beautiful and curious things.[80] This counter is made of wood, perhaps *chonta,* and is beautifully executed and finished. It is small, measuring 33 centimetres by 27. On its sides are designs which are certainly not in the Incaic style, resembling Late Chimu art far more closely. The rectangular bottom of the artifact bears a simple but tasteful design of rosettes. Oddly enough, its dainty carvings notwithstanding, the object was originally covered with a thin sheet of silver affixed to it with pin-like nails.[81]

Other objects of analogous kind are available for study. One, from Caraz in the Corridor of Huaylas, is very similar to the Patecte specimen save that it is made of stone; another specimen, also from Caraz, is likewise of stone, but is broken. The corner "towers" of this specimen had but one story, not two.[82] Wiener found two stone rectangular specimens in the moun-

tainous parts of the department of Ancachs,[83] both of them
being of the same type, with minor differences in proportions
and arrangement. A third, also from that region, is more nearly
oval and is less perfectly symmetrical. It is some ten inches
long.[84] Finally, we have two specimens from the coast of Peru.
One, a very crude piece of work in yellowish-gray porphyritic
serpentine, is only some six inches square. It comes from the
Chicama Valley.[85] The other, from Pachacamac, is circular
and is made of light, thin wood, having a diameter of only 80
millimetres.[86]

What, in verity, were these artifacts originally intended to
be? The first suggestion made concerning them was that they
were models or maps of structures, this being put forth first by
Bastian, with some measure of caution, and, with none, by
González Suárez, both cited in note 81. Almost at once thereafter, and more sagaciously, Charles Wiener hailed them as
"counters."[83] This theory receives some slight support from
Gutiérrez de Santa Clara and from Acosta, the first of whom
tells us that the natives of Peru cast up accounts with small
stones, the second of whom says vaguely: "Besides these Quip-
pos of thred, they have an other, as it were a kinde of writing
with small stones, by means whereof they learne punctually
the words they desire to know by heart. . . . It is a pleasant
thing to see them correct themselves when they doe erre; for
all their correction consisteth onely in beholding of their small
stones."[87] My personal opinion is, however, that these objects
were parts of the game of *chuncara* which is described by
Cobo thus: "*Chuncara* was another game of five small hollows
scooped out in some flat stone or in a board. They played it
with beans of various colours, throwing the die, and, according
to how it fell they moved their beans through their houses until the end was reached. The first house counted ten, the rest
mounted up by tens until the fifth was reached, which was
worth fifty."[88] I concede that this description does not fit perfectly with the arrangement of the objects under consideration; but they may have been unusually elaborate *chuncara*-
boards. As a matter of fact, the "counter" theory may be correct, in which case these objects may well have been extremely

Fɪɢ. 158. "Contadores" or counters of various materials from several sites, as follows:

1. From Laurel, Chicama Valley, made of Serpentine. (*Original in the Ethnological Museum, Berlin.*)
2. From Caraz, corridor of Huaylas, made of stone. (*Original in the Greuter Collection, Berlin.*)
3. From Patecte, near Chordeleg, southern Ecuador, made of wood.
4. From Cabana or Urcon in the Province of Pallasca, Department of Ancachs, Peru, made of stone. (*Original in the Musée du Trocadéro, Paris.*)
5 and 6. Other views of No. 3.

After Verneau and Rivet, 1912, Plate XV.

FIG. 159. A sealskin balsa, of the type used in the southerly part of the coast. *After Frézier.*

FIG. 160. The most elaborate type of early Peruvian ship. *After Humboldt.*

useful for calculations, much as the abacus was to the people possessing it.

If the *quipu* and the possible "counter" were the instruments for the acquisition of accurate information, the roads and their adjuncts were the instruments whereby central authority made itself felt throughout the empire.

The roads, or rather, the footways of the Incas! These extraordinary arteries of an astonishing empire, these strong bonds which held to a central peg an immense cluster of varied societies, are, in reality, replete with the simplicity of true greatness; yet they have had the misfortune to inspire a greater number of silly remarks than almost anything else in the whole range of ancient Andean history—with the possible exception of the ruins of Tiahuanaco. The truth lies midway between the belittling statement of the Abbé Raynal to the effect that they were merely lines of posts intended to guide travellers and the fantastic statement of a modern imaginist to the effect that the roads leaped gaily from peak to peak and across lakes.[89] As a matter of fact, the truth was so amazing as to render flights of the imagination pale and ridiculous, and so admirable as to give the lie direct to would-be detractors.

Two main highways, both of them passing through Cuzco, bound the entire coast and the entire highland zone to the capital. Under Huayna Capac, in whose time the network of footways attained to its fullest development, the highland road followed this route: Pastu—Quitu—Latacunga—Tumipampa—Ayavaca—Huancapampa—Casamarca—Huamachucu—Huaraz—Pumpu—Sausa—Picoy—Huamanca—Urumarca—Vilcas—Amancay—CUZCO—Vilcañota Pass—Hatun Colla—Huaqui—Desaguadero Valley—Chuquisaca—Kingdom of Tucma.

The shore-country road had Tumbez as its northern terminal and ran thence along the coast to Nazca, serving all the great states of that region. It went inland from Nazca to Apucara, Vilcas, Amancay, and CUZCO, thence through Chumpivilca to Arequipa, Moquehua, Tacna, Arica, and so down the length of Chile as far as the Maule River.

Vilcas, it will be observed, was the junction-point of the two routes, not Cuzco. This seems rather surprising at first, but Cieza explains it by informing us that Vilcas, or Vilcas-Huamán, was anciently regarded as the geographical centre of the empire. He also informs us that he saw in the vicinity of Vilcas three roads successively built by Pachacutec, Tupac Yupanqui, and Huayna Capac as memorials to their campaigns and conquests, the last and most impressive of the three being an integral part of the highway system here considered.[90]

Supplementary to these two major highways was an intricate network of secondary roads almost equal in usefulness. Father Cobo mentions several of them: one went from Tumbez up into the mountains; another went from Chan-Chan up to Casamarca and Chachapuya; another from Parmunca mounted to Sausa; another went from Rimac up to Sausa; and still another went from the coast up to the province of Chuqui-apu (La Paz) and thence down into the Chuncho country in the *Montaña*.[91] These secondary roads were, therefore, transversal routes in the main. In addition to them, we may be very sure, there were infinitely numerous lesser roads reaching into every part of the empire. Of such the road by which the citadel of Machu Picchu was connected with Cuzco, as described by Dr. Bingham, is a good example.[92]

Characteristically—for the Incas tended to go straight to their objective—the roads ran, whenever possible, in straight lines. Those in the mountains were paved and stepped wherever necessary; those on the coast were surfaced with foot-beaten earth and were lined with walls of adobe or with large wooden posts set at intervals to mark the way. The greatest care was taken to preserve the roads in neatness and in perfect repair. On the mountain roads there were numerous turn-outs where litter-bearers might pause for breath whilst their imperial or noble passenger might enjoy the view spread before him. The coast roads had long stretches that were shaded by trees whose fruit-laden branches arched over the way, while many birds frolicked about in the foliage. In short, the claim made by Gutiérrez de Santa Clara—who, be it remembered, saw them soon after the Conquest—that the roads of the Incas surpassed those of the Romans is probably justified by the facts.

Causeways and suspension bridges were cleverly constructed in order to carry the roads over swampy ground or over rivers. An excellent example of causeway is that in the Xaquixahuana Valley (now called Anta or Zúrite), near Cuzco. Cieza describes it,[93] and I have ridden over it. The suspension bridges were sufficiently terrifying contraptions at best—and more so than ever if one happens to remember Mr. Thornton Wilder's classic work while in the middle of one of them. Three aloe-fibre ropes about a foot thick were thrown across the chasm to be crossed and were securely fastened to massive masonry piers on the banks. Figure 154 shows characteristic piers of this kind. On these ropes was laid the flooring consisting of sticks firmly lashed together and covered with strong, coarse matting which made a footway from six to eight feet wide and as much as one hundred and fifty yards long. Two other aloe-fibre ropes of the same size ran along the sides of the footway, to which they were solidly lashed in such a way as to make a sort of balustrade. So far all sounds reasonably comfortable. The terror of the thing came from the necessarily steep pitch from the bank to the centre of the hanging bridge and from there up to the other bank. Still worse was the circumstance that the whole fabric would swing alarmingly in the slightest wind. Nevertheless, at least under the Incas, the bridges were safe and serviceable, as was also a less common type of structure which consisted of a single aloe-fibre rope upon which was slung a large basket in which the unfortunate traveller was ensconced—perhaps in a swooning condition—while, by means of smaller ropes, the basket was drawn across the abyss. With respect to bridges, then, we must in fairness concede that the Romans were ahead of the Incas, except that a very special bridge, floating on reed-pontoons, that crossed the Desaguadero River near Lake Titicaca, would have compelled even Cæsar's admiration, redoubtable builder of bridges though he was, because of its ingenuity.[94]

Above I spoke of adjuncts to the roads. These included the *chasqui-cuna,* couriers or post-runners, the *tampu-cuna,* inns or supply-stations and rest-houses, and the litters of the very great. I shall speak of them in that order.

The youths of Ttahua-ntin-suyu (the land of the Four Parts) were always adepts at the art and science of running steadily and swiftly; they were called upon to do so in the *huarachicui* ceremonies which marked their arrival at the age of puberty. Acosta, speaking of this matter running in general, says: "For this cause there were men of great agilitie, which served as curriers, to goe and come, whom they did nourish in this exercise of running from their youth, labouring to have them well breathed, that they might runne to the toppe of a high hill without wearines. . . . And in Cusco when they made their solemne feast of Capacrayme (Capac Raymi), the novices did runne who could fastest vp the rocke of Yanacauri. And the exercise of running is generally much used among the Indians."[95] Their aptitude for running, be it noted in passing, comes not so much from the power of their legs, which are somewhat short and not particularly strong, as from their extraordinary pulmonary development. It was of these circumstances that the Inca Pachacutec availed himself when he established the service of *chasqui-cuna* or post-runners throughout his empire.[96]

At the time of its perfection—and so excellent was it that it even survived the Spanish conquest, as we shall see—the *chasqui*-system was worked in this way: All along the footways of the empire there were set up post-houses called *chuclla-cuna*[97] in which the couriers on duty were stationed. There is considerable confusion regarding the distance between them, for Garcilaso and Santillán state that the post-houses were a quarter of a league (less than a mile) apart; Sarmiento, Cieza, and Morúa say half a league; Montesinos says one league; and Acosta and Gutiérrez de Santa Clara say a league and a half. As Professor Baudin has said, the distance probably varied in accordance with the nature of the country. It is quite conceivable that a specially trained man, reared in greatest simplicity, could run at full speed for a league and a half (about four and a half miles) in flat country.[98]

Each post-house or, according to Garcilaso, pair of post-houses, had in attendance two, four, six or more couriers who took turns in watching the road so that there should be no loss of time if a message should come in either direction. On seeing a *chasqui* approaching from the next station on either side, the runner whose duty it would be to relieve him would go out to meet him and would run along with him long enough to learn the message, which was usually of telegraphic brevity, or to receive the *quipu* with any words that might accompany it, or to grasp the burden, as the case might be, all this being accomplished without any diminution of pace at the post-houses. "So well was the running performed," observes Cieza de León, who probably saw the system in operation, "that in a short time they knew, at a distance of 300 leagues, 500, and even 800, what had passed, or what was needed or required. With such secrecy did the runners keep the messages that were entrusted to them, that neither entreaty nor menace could ever extort a relation of what they had thus heard, although the news had already passed onwards. The roads pass over rugged mountains, over snow-covered ridges, over stony wildernesses, and forests full of thorny thickets, in such sort that it may be taken as quite certain that the news could not have been conveyed with greater speed on swift horses or mules, than by these foot posts. For the men on foot have no impediments, and one of them can do more in a day than a mounted messenger could do in three. I do not mean one single Indian, but one running for one-half league, and another for the next, according to the established order. And it must be understood that neither storms nor anything else prevent the due service of the posts in the wildest parts, and as soon as one started another arrived to wait in his place."[99]

The last sentence of this quotation is very similar in spirit to the admirable inscription which adorns the outside of the U. S. Post-Office in New York City. It is of interest, for the sake of seeing how well the *chasqui*-system lived up to this high ideal, to note some of the records made by it. A few pertinent data are as follows:

Quito to Tiahuanaco, one way, 8 days (Morúa, Bk. III, Ch. xv).
Quito to Cuzco, one way, 5 days (Gutiérrez, Bk. III, Ch. lxiii).
Quito to Cuzco, go and return, 20 days (Polo, 1873, p. 169).
Quito to Cuzco, go and return, 12 days (Cobo, Bk. XII, Ch. xxxii).
Cuzco to Lima, one way, 3 days (Cobo, as cited; Polo, as cited)
Coast to Cuzco, with fresh fish, 2 days (Cobo, as cited).

Nor was this all. Garcilaso says: "They had another way of sending messages, which was by raising smoke at each station by day, or a flame by night. For this purpose the *Chasquis* always had the fire ready, and it was constantly watched, so that it might be ready the moment an occasion arose. This method of sending news by fires was only adopted when there was a rebellion in some great province, so that the Inca might know it within two or three hours at the most (even if the outbreak was at a distance of 500 or 600 leagues from the Court) and give the necessary orders the moment that the insurrection was reported."[100]

At the present time a telegraph message sent from Cuzco to Quito, or *vice versa,* would, in all likelihood, take a week. A traveller between those points, by rail, steamer, and rail again, would be on his way fully a fortnight. It happens that, in October, 1914, being minded to go from Cuzco to Lima and wishful to reserve a room in the hotel at Lima, I telegraphed for one. The next day I began my journey. It occupied me at least a week, perhaps more, and my telegram reached the Lima hotel *after* I did! So much for "modern improvements" as contrasted with the Incaic idea. As for the authenticity of the records given above, only the second and the fourth, implying an average speed of 11 to 13 miles per hour, are hard to believe, and the fifth was made *after* the Conquest, according to Polo. The third record, allowing 20 days for a distance of about 2,500 miles, implies an average speed of between 4 and 5 miles per hour, which is not, in the postulated circumstances, incredible.

The *tampu-cuna,* commonly called *tambos,* or inns, now demand consideration. Father Cobo's description of them is the most illuminating. He tells us that, in addition to the towns and villages which lay along the roads, there were, at intervals of four or six leagues (twelve or eighteen miles), *tambos* or *aposentos reales* (literally, royal apartments) which were built, served, and provisioned by the provinces in which they stood. It was incumbent upon the local authorities to see that they were kept in perfect repair and cleanliness. In these establishments were lodged, wholly at the expense of the Inca, the various classes of official travellers—and there were none but officially sanctioned travellers—who had occasion to journey along the highways. All their wants were met from the storehouses attached to every *tampu,* the provisioning of which was a local tribute-duty.[101]

Although Father Cobo, in the place cited, says that the tambos consisted only of a single room, from 100 to 300 feet in length and from 30 to 50 feet in width, there is ample evidence, afforded by the remains of ancient tambos at various localities in the Andean area, that, in addition to the large room, there was also a congeries of smaller chambers destined to various uses, such as private apartments, kitchens, guardrooms, and store-rooms. These were all conveniently arranged around one or more courtyards. At Piñasñiyoc, just below the Pass of Panticalla, which leads from the Urupampa Valley near Ollantaytampu over into the Lucumayu Valley, there are some very interesting ruins consisting of a long range of well-made *pirca* masonry storehouses, lined with plaster and having ventilator-holes, and, hard by, the vestiges of a sizable tambo of several chambers.[102] Again, at the Pass of Vilcañota (*alias* La Raya), where the Incas' mountain highway passes into the Colla country, Squier found a tambo "which may be taken as a type of this kind of structures in general, although no two are precisely alike. It is a building with a front of 180 feet in length, with wings extending inwards at either extremity, forming three sides of a court. This court is extended down to the waters of the little lake by rough stone walls, and the ground falls off by low terraces. [It is shown in Figure 161.] The main front has but three rooms, each about sixty feet long; the central one alone having entrances from the outside. The corner rooms open into the court, and each has a smaller inner room that can only be reached through it. . . .

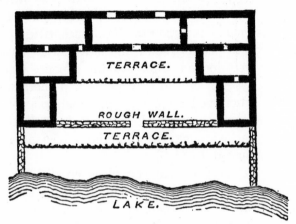

Fig. 161.   Plan of Inca Tambo, La Raya.
After Squier.

The rooms have small niches on their sides, sunk in the walls, which are from two to three feet thick, composed of rough stones laid in clay."[103] It seems to me that the building referred to here by Squier was probably destined to the use of the great who might be journeying that way; no doubt there were less important and less well-built edifices round about it that have since vanished. Dr. Bingham refers to various ruined houses in the immediate vicinity of the Pass, as well as to the ancient wall by which, according to Father Lizárraga, it was formerly defended.[104] In Father Cobo's experience, the two most elaborate and best preserved tambos were those at Vilcas and at Moho, the latter place being in the region of Chuqui-apu (La Paz).[101] We are given a vivid picture of the thoroughness with which the Incaic roads were provided with tambos at the end of each day's march, namely, at distances ranging from four to eight leagues, in a letter written in 1566 by the Licentiate Matienzo to the King of Castile. The road of which he speaks in detail is the great highway of the Incas through the Diaguite country in what is now northwestern Argentina.[105]

It is well to bear in mind that there was a fundamental difference between the purposes of the Incas' roads and those of Europe (bad though they were at that period). The *ñan-cuna* or *purina-cuna*, footways, of the empire were destined entirely to official uses and to officially approved journeyings. They were travelled over by armies, couriers, colonists, officials, and burden-bearers employed by the state. The people could use them only to attend the established fairs and to return thence home. Even the individual courier saw but little of any given road, for he spent his term of service in passing back and forth, shuttle-wise, between his own post and those next to it on either side. In this we see a manifestation of the limited geographical orbit within which the mass of the people spent their lives.[106]

In the greatest contrast thereto were the immense distances covered by the Emperor and others privileged to travel by litter. Cieza speaks thus of the subject: "When the Incas visited the provinces of their empire in time of peace, they travelled in great majesty, seated in rich litters fitted with loose poles of excellent wood, long and enriched with gold and silver work. Over the litter there were two high arches of gold set with precious stones, and long mantles fell round all sides of the litter so as to cover it completely. If the inmate did not wish to be seen, the mantles remained down, but they were raised when he got in or came out. In order that he might see the road, and have fresh air, holes were made in the curtains. Over all parts of these mantles or curtains there was rich ornamentation. On some were embroidered the sun and the moon, on others great curving serpents, and what appeared to be sticks passing across them. These were borne as insignia or arms. The litters were raised on the shoulders of the greatest and most important lords of the kingdom, and he who was employed most frequently on this duty, was held to be most honoured and in highest favour." Around the imperial litter marched the Cañari guard, who always surrounded the monarch's person to the number of two thousand. In front of the litter marched five thousand slingers, and after it came two thousand warriors of the Inca caste. All this multitude passed slowly onward in religious silence broken only by the rhythmic shuffle of innumerable sandals. Every little while a halt was made, in order to rest the litter-bearers and to afford the sovereign a chance to admire the view or to hear the plaints of his subjects, who, in vast throngs, lined the roadway to see their divine liege pass on his journey. *They* were not silent, for, as the litter passed along they shouted, "Most high Lord, Child of the Sun, Thou art the sole and belovéd Lord. The whole earth truly obeys Thee."[106]

In the quaint, unpublished manuscript work of Don Felipe Huamán Poma de Ayala, written about 1613, and lavishly illustrated with pen-and-ink drawings somewhat like those in Thackeray's earlier manner, there are several pictures of litters. One, reproduced herewith, in Figure 163, shows the Inca Tupac Yupanqui and his Coya in a handsome, plume-canopied travelling litter. It is of interest to note that the Inca is sufficiently courteous *to ride backwards!* In which he differs from modern European monarchs who, on state occasions, seat their wives on their left in the royal carriage. Huamán also shows us a very light war-litter used by the Inca Huayna Capac, as well as two funeral-litters, one of them large enough to contain two mummy-bundles, a priest, and a number of sacred vessels. This litter, also, belonged to Huayna Capac.[107]

Pleasantries aside, the litter of the Inca must have been a vehicle fully as comfortable as the coaches used in Europe down to the seventeenth century. The use of litters was, however, very closely restricted to the greatest and holiest of the realm, for, although I do not find it specifically mentioned, it may have been one of the many privileges conceded by the Inca to favored vassals. Certainly we cannot, in reason, suppose that members of the imperial caste walked about like ordinary mortals nor that a great mediatized king like the Chimu would be expected to do so, his ancestors having, from time immemorial, travelled in litters. Garcilaso and Cobo tell us that the men of Hatun Rucana and Rucana were specially trained to carry litters with a maximum of smoothness, there being some 15,000 *vecinos, i. e.,* tribute-payers, in those provinces, which implies that there must have been a considerable

FIG. 162. The Coya Mama Huaca and her handmaidens.

FIG. 163. The Inca Tupac Yupanqui and his Coya being borne in a litter.

From the drawings by Felipe Huamán Poma de Ayala, after Montell, 1929.

number of litter-bearers in the realm and, consequently, a goodly number of people privileged to use litters.[106]

The roads of the empire, therefore, together with the adjuncts thereto—the *chasqui-cuna,* the *tampu-cuna,* and the *huantu-runa-cuna* (litters)—assured to the Incaic state far more efficient and commodious communications than any that existed in Europe between the downfall of Rome and the Industrial Revolution. On the whole, then, the dictum of von Tschudi is justified; he says: "There is not in Peru at the present time (1842) any modern road in the most remote degree comparable to the Incas' highway."[108] I am told, however, that there is now (1930) a good motor-road that leads from Cuzco out into the country for twenty-odd miles. The only trouble with it is that it leads nowhere in particular. There are also, of course, a moderate number of fairly passable roads in the various coastal valleys, and around Lima.

If the land-communications of the Incas were admirable, their communications by water were equally remarkable, but, in this case, for their amazing inadequacy. The natives of South America were singularly inexpert in the matter of navigation. It is worth while, however, to examine the point briefly.

Reference was made in Chapter VII to the incursions of the Incas into the *montaña* and to the canoes employed in connection therewith. They were dug-outs made from the abundant hardwood timber of those parts, and were, on the whole, an adequate craft for use on the rivers, particularly as there was no lack of men to paddle them. Dug-outs were likewise made by the people of the Peruvian coast, the material used there being the strong, light wood of the *ceyba* tree which attains to great size in that region. Dug-outs of this description were very swift and easily handled, whether with paddles or with sails, but they were very easily capsized. Anciently these craft ranged in dimensions from little boats for two or three people up to vessels fifty or sixty feet in length capable of holding thirty persons. To this day bathers at Payta are wont to use tiny dug-outs called *chingos* in which they paddle about in their bathing-suits, the idea being, apparently, that a shark will not swallow a bather if he has to swallow a *chingo* as well.

Pontoon-rafts of two types were in use, the one being common on the southern part of the coast and consisting of two seal-skins, inflated, held together, catamaran-fashion, by a wooden platform, as shown in Figure 159; the other being a wooden platform supported by a number of seal-skins, this crude contraption serving principally as a rustic ferry on rivers.

Then there were the totora-reed boats on Lake Titicaca, which, with their pointed ends and matting sails on rickety

A-shaped masts, form a picturesque element in the scenery. Some of these boats, all of which are made of three parallel bundles of totora-reed so lashed together as to form a bow and a stern, have no sails, and it is possible that, anciently, none of them had. One of the exciting features of these boats is that, when they reach the saturation-point, they suddenly sink with all hands on board. Until that unhappy moment arrives, however, they are practically unsinkable, yet they are never quite dry.[109] A wretched and forlorn craft indeed! See Figure 67.

Finally the great raft of the northern part of the Peruvian coast and of the shore of what is now Ecuador must be considered; for it was the *chef-d'œuvre* of native Andean naval architecture. It consisted of seven, nine, eleven, and perhaps more logs of the light *balsa*-wood so arranged that the central log was longest and the others were shorter and shorter as the outer edge of the raft was approached. A wooden platform, perhaps with a crude roof, stood in the middle, and near the bow was the mast for the cotton-cloth sail. Sometimes there was a second mast at the stern. It was necessary to use paddles in order to steer the clumsy thing, which is shown in Figure 160.[110] As this was the best the ancient Peruvians could do in the way of ship-building, it is not wonderful that they were dumbfounded when the ships of the Spaniards dawned on their horizon. Yet it was on a fleet of rafts like these that the Inca Tupac Yupanqui made his mysterious maritime excursion, mentioned on pages 270–272. Likewise, it was a vessel of this description, richly laden with gold, silver, fine woollen cloths, and carrying a number of well-dressed men and women, that the Pilot Bartolomé Ruiz encountered in 1527. A great deal has been said about that *balsa* out of Tumbez which so astonished Pilot Ruiz. Professor Baudin, for example, holds that it is an evidence that the subjects of the Inca were wont to engage in foreign commerce. It seems to me far more likely, however, that the party on board the *balsa* was some chieftain and his court in quest of a new home, or perhaps some emissary of the *curaca* of Tumbez sent forth to found a colony somewhere along the shore. It is possible that such enterprises were fairly common, because, at the time of the Conquest, there was a fairly definite knowledge, among the people of Panamá, of the existence of a great empire in the south.[110]

It is evident, therefore, that the science of navigation was in a stage so rudimentary under the Incas that it cannot have contributed appreciably to the task of holding the empire together. Yet, poor, clumsy things though they were, the Tumbez-type *balsas* sufficed to fill Huayna Capac with a naïve pleasure so great that he caused a number of them to be brought from Tumbez up to the Lake of Pumpu (Junín), for his amusement.[111]

The development to which land transportation had attained under the Incas implies that those rulers were possessed of an extensive and profound geographical knowledge. Consonant therewith is what Sarmiento has to say concerning an administrative measure taken by the Inca Pachacutec, who, so he tells us, "ordered visitors to go through all the subdued provinces, with orders to measure and survey them, and to bring him models of the natural features in clay. This was done. The models and reports were brought before the Inca. He examined them and considered the mountainous fastnesses and the plains. He ordered the visitors to look well to what he would do. He then began to demolish the fastnesses and to have their inhabitants moved to plain country, and those of the plains were moved to mountainous regions, so far from each other, and each so far from their native country, that they could not return to it. Next the Inca ordered the visitors to go and do with the people what they had seen him do with the models. They went and did so."[112]

In this passage we have the most definite sort of evidence —and from a deadly foe of the Inca dynasty—that the Sons of the Sun possessed the science of making maps in relief. Nor is corroborative evidence lacking. Garcilaso speaks of plans, models and designs of provinces and of towns, particularly of a plan of Cuzco which he saw in his youth. Betánzos likewise mentions a plan of Cuzco worked in clay. Finally, there is mention, in the verse of Don Juan de Castellanos (about 1575), of a map of the kingdom of Quitu that was made upon cloth by order of a chief named Chaparra for the information of the conqueror Don Sebastián de Benalcázar at the time of his entry into that region.[113] It is easy enough to understand, therefore, why certain writers, on seeing the "counters" mentioned above on page 327, should have jumped at the conclusion that they were plans or models.

At the time of the map-making mentioned above, the Inca Pachacutec despatched various lesser officials in company with the *tucuiricuc-cuna*, to whom he had shown the map, into all the districts of the empire, with instructions to select in each of them from thirty to one hundred young men with their wives and to bring them to Cuzco. The young couples thus selected were first presented to the Inca—an overwhelming honor—who then sent those from Chinchay-suyu (the northern quarter of the empire) to dwell in Anti-suyu (the eastern quarter), and those of Cunti-suyu (the western quarter) to dwell in Colla-suyu (the southern quarter). They were bidden to settle down in their new homes, for which purpose they were well provided with all things needful; and they were commanded to learn the native languages there without, however, forgetting Quechua; and finally, they were instructed to spy upon their new neighbors, whose houses they were licensed to enter at any hour, and to report their misdoings to the authorities.

Thus does Sarmiento describe the foundation, by Pachacutec, of the system of *mitmac-cuna* or colonists. Cieza also ascribes it to Pachacutec, but Oliva, incredibly enough, states that Yahuar-Huaccac, whom we know to have been a poor thing, founded it.[114] Into his account of the *mitimaes*—for we might as well fall in with general custom and use the Spanish corruption of the original term—Sarmiento de Gamboa characteristically injects a note of tyranny. Garcilaso, however, in speaking of the mitimaes established by the Inca Pachacutec, writes as follows: "The Inca took Indians of Nanasca

(Nazca) and transported them to the banks of the river
Apurimac, near the highroad from Cuzco to Rimac (Lima).
For that river flows through a region which is so hot that the
Indians of the cold and temperate climate of the Sierra soon
sicken and die in it. . . . The order of the Incas was that,
when Indians were thus transported from one province to another, . . . they should always be sent to a climate similar
to that of their native land, that the change might do them no
injury. It was therefore forbidden to send Indians of the
Sierra to the *Llanos,* because they would certainly die in a few
days.* The Inca, mindful of this danger, took Indians from
one hot climate to inhabit another. It was only necessary to
send a few to the banks of the river Apurimac, because it flows
between very lofty and precipitous mountains, and has very
little available land on either side of its current. The Inca desired that this small strip of land should not be lost, but should
be turned into a garden for raising the numerous and excellent
fruits which ripen on the banks of that famous river."[115]

Dr. Bowman provides us with data that reveal fully the significance of the Inca historian's remarks and of his great ancestor's economic strategy; for he shows that the valley-floor
of the Apurimac is at about 4,000 feet elevation whilst mountains of some 18,000 feet rise in close proximity thereto, there
being between these extremes every environmental gradation
known to the Andean highlands. Intensive cultivation is possible only on very small areas in the valley-bottom and on the
alluvial fans adjacent thereto.[116]

Garcilaso's version of the motive for the mitimaes is, therefore, very different in tenor, and probably more just, than is
that of Sarmiento. Later on, Garcilaso says with commend-
able candor as follows: "The Incas transplanted Indians from
one province to another for special reasons, some for the good
of their vassals, and others for their own purposes and to secure their dominions from insurrections. In the course of their
conquests the Incas found some provinces to be naturally fertile, but thinly populated. To these districts they sent Indians

*This, of course, is a great exaggeration.—P. A. M.

who were natives of other provinces with a similar climate. This precaution was taken that no injury might befall the settlers. On other occasions, when the inhabitants of a locality multiplied rapidly, so that their province was not large enough to hold them, they removed a certain proportion of the people to some other district. They also removed Indians from barren and sterile tracts to such as were fertile and prolific, with a view to the benefit both of those that remained and of those that went; because, being relations, they would help each other with their harvests. . . . Colonists were also sent to other provinces for a reason of state. When some warlike kingdom was conquered, of which it might be feared that, owing to its distance from Cuzco and the fierce disposition of the natives, it would not remain loyal or tranquil, then some, and not infrequently all, the inhabitants were removed to a loyal district, where they would be surrounded on all sides by faithful vassals of the Inca, and thus would themselves become loyal and bow their necks to the yoke. . . ."[116]

An integral part of the *mitmac* system was the practice of causing the heirs of lords of vassals to dwell at the Court in Cuzco, not only that they and their servants might absorb the Incaic idea, but also that they might be hostages for the good behavior of their fathers. Thus it came about that most parts of Cuzco—except, we may suppose, the central strip mentioned on pages 317–319—contained many mitimaes from all parts of the realm.[117]

The geographical aspect of the system of colonization is emphasized by Cieza and by Cobo, who make it quite clear that all colonists were moved into regions that would be congenial and wholesome for them.[118] An apparent exception to this rule is a special type of colony mentioned by Cieza, who tells us that, because the Collao was incapable of producing a sufficiency of food for its people, and because the fertile, warmer valleys of Anti-suyu were not far off, the Incas caused a certain number of households to be taken from each Collao village and established in the eastern valleys so that they might there raise enough food for their kinsmen at home as well as for themselves.[119] But this contradiction is, I think, only apparent; for the valleys in question were probably those of the *ceja de la montaña,* not those of the *montaña* proper, and, therefore, the contrast in environment was not drastic. It is to be noted, in this connection, that when the Inca Tupac Yupanqui settled the representatives of no less than forty-two peoples in the vicinity of Copacavana and on the adjacent islands of Titicaca and Coati—the district indicated being one of the greatest holy-places of the realm—he chose principally mountain folk for the purpose, drawing them from all parts of the highland zone or else from the relatively cool land of Chile.[120]

Mitimaes were particularly useful to the Inca Tupac Yupanqui in the pacification of the turbulent northern provinces —in the Palta country, and at Huancapampa, Ayavaca, and Caxas—and he also sent a colony of 15,000 Cañaris with their wives to dwell in Cuzco. With them he formed the redoubtable Cañari Guard, to which reference was made above on page 269. At Caxas, according to Cieza, there were mitimaes who, with their governor, occupied certain splendid buildings and busied themselves with the collection of tribute from the surrounding country.[121]

The only class of mitimaes not yet touched upon was that composed of garrisons established all along the inland frontiers of the empire, often under the command of members of the imperial caste. The prime duty of these garrisons was that of protecting the Ttahua-ntin-suyu from incursions by woodland savages such as the Chunchos—against whom the citadel of Machu Picchu was probably intended as a defence—such also as the Musus, the Chiriguanos and many other sylvan or formidable folk east and northeast of the empire, as well as in southern Chile and in parts of what is now Argentina. Garrisons of this kind had their headquarters in forts called *pucara-cuna,* which were manned by troops drawn from the provinces that they were designed to defend. Cieza makes it clear that these frontier troops received special rewards. He says: "The recompense for their service consisted in orders that were given, on certain occasions, to bestow upon them woollen clothing, feathers, or bracelets of gold and silver, after they had shown themselves to be valiant. They were also presented with women from among the great number that were kept, in each province, for the service of the Inca, and as most of them were beautiful they were highly valued."[122]

In short, the system of mitimaes was an admirable and efficacious contrivance designed to serve three purposes: First, to distribute the population of the empire evenly so that no district should be either over-worked or under-utilized; second, to reduce to a minimum the risks of insurrection and invasion; third, to disseminate the Incas' peculiar brand of civilization, and especially their language, throughout a huge territory filled with divers peoples in various stages of culture.[123]

Yet there is a tinge of remorselessness in its practicality. So is there also in other parts of the Incaic polity, notably in the dispensing of justice. This important activity of the state was in the hands of the divers grades of officials, the arrangement being that each man's immediate superior in the scale had jurisdiction over him. If the crime were very serious—treason, lèse-majesté, or if it involved more than one province ruled by a *tucuiricuc*—the Inca personally, or at any rate his Council of the four *apu-cuna*, took cognizance of it; and this was also done in cases where the person charged was of the rank of *hunu-camayoc* or higher, or a member of the imperial caste.[124]

Such was the machinery whereby justice was administered. The punishments meted out, albeit they differed in accordance with the rank of the criminal, were severe, nay, ferocious. Thieves were publicly flogged or stoned for the first offence, subjected to sundry ingenious and spirit-corroding torments for the second, and lingeringly slain for the third. Vagabonds, gossip-spreaders, and all persons who had failed in their appointed duties were either lashed with a sling or, if the crime were heinous, hanged by the feet until they were dead.[125] A decided humanitarian note is sounded, however, in the Law's differentiation between a robbery from malice aforethought, for which the doer was chastized, and a robbery committed in need of food or of other necessary thing, for which punishment was inflicted upon the official who ought to have forestalled the need.[126] Certain crimes of passion—such as the rape of a Chosen Virgin, sodomy, etc.—were punished not only by the violent death of the guilty parties but also by the obliteration of their villages and the slaughter of all living things therein.[127]

Such was the general tenor of the Incaic penal code to whose penalties the masses were liable.[128] For the upper classes there were other punishments whose terrors were as much psychological as physical. It was held—perhaps with reason—that to a member of the imperial caste a public reprimand was more dreadful than was a public stoning or a public shaving of the head to an ordinary man. For graver offences there were such penalties as demotion from office, loss of privileges, etc.

Treason and disobedience were specially dreaded by the Incas. To repress them Inca Tupac Yupanqui built at Sanca Cancha, hard by Cuzco, a subterranean dungeon with so many blind doors and tortuous passages that it resembled the dwelling of the Minotaur in Crete, all of which were strewn with sharp flint points. There he placed a great number of wild beasts, pumas, jaguars, bears, and, among the flints upon the pavement, toads, vipers, and vermin. Into this loathsome menagerie were thrust to die all traitors and disobedient persons. At Pimpilla, half a league from Cuzco, was an equally horrible prison into which were thrown, to die, malevolent wizards, poisoners, spell-casters, and false prophets. Finally, at Tancar, also close to Cuzco, the Incas maintained a kind of Bastille in which erring aristocrats were incarcerated for life.[129]

As Garcilaso has sententiously remarked, ". . . the Incas never made laws to frighten their vassals, but always with the intention of enforcing them on those who ventured to transgress them."[130] It is easy to imagine the blistering contempt that the Incas would feel could they behold the state of affairs in our country in this year of Grace, 1930. And yet there would have been an element of amusement in it for them, too, when they saw our mild and sweetly padded prisons, crammed with resentful inmates, and contrasted them with their own frightful dungeons whose sole inhabitants were of the brute creation.

Stern though the Laws of the Incas undoubtedly were as regards the punishments which they provided, nevertheless they clearly had for their fundamental purpose the good of society as a whole. For example, there was the law against the killing of female llamas, alpacas, and vicuñas, which carried very painful penalties for disobedience; nevertheless, this law had a merciful motive, namely, the wish that the species in question should multiply exceedingly, to the end that there should be ample provision of wool for clothing wherewith all classes might dress themselves warmly.[131] Akin thereto was the law that no game-birds, nor larger game, should be taken save under special conditions and with special permission. The object of this law was to prevent the people from falling into idle habits.[132] Yet, here again, the note of benevolence is present for, at stated intervals, there were imperial hunts called *chacu-cuna* in which vast numbers of the people participated and in whose catch they shared.

It is worth while to animadvert upon the art of the chase as practiced under the Incas. A great throng of men was assembled in the chosen locality to act as beaters, there being usually from ten to sixty thousand men in the throng. The tents from which the Inca was to watch the spectacle were set up in some place whence a wide view was to be enjoyed over the stretch of country, some twenty or thirty leagues in circuit. A vast circle was formed by the beaters who, at the beginning, stood at some distance from one another; but, as they advanced shouting and making a fearful din by every known method, they gradually drew closer and closer together, driving all the animals within the circle before them. At length the yelling beaters were close enough together to take hands, each with his neighbors, and so they proceeded under the observant eye of the Inca, the circle drawing ever closer and closer until it became necessary to form two or more concentric rings of beaters. As the walls of human beings closed in upon the frightened, struggling animals of many kinds, the racket and confusion grew ever greater and greater until at length the signal was given for the slaughter to begin. Thereupon certain

specially trained slayers, armed with *ayllu-cuna* (here meaning *bolas*), clubs, and sticks, plunged in among the prey and
set about seizing and slaying the poor, terrified beasts. Females were always spared.

Such hunts as these occupied several days and they were
held in any given stretch of country only once in three years.
The animals sought were: the wild vicuña, whose exquisitely
fine wool was reserved to the Inca; the wild huanaco, whose
coarser wool was distributed among the people who had helped
in the hunt; and several sorts of deer. Between twenty and
forty thousand head were taken in these hunts, not to mention vast quantities of pumas, bears, foxes, wild-cats and other
creatures which were slaughtered without mercy because of
their harmfulness to animals useful to man. Every province
was divided into four hunt-areas, one of which was hunted in
turn every year, either under the auspices of the Inca, or under
those of the *tucuiricuc*.

A great feature of these hunts was the fact that they were
not designed solely for the selfish pleasure of the great. They
were, in fact, serious business rather than mere pastimes, and
it was an integral part of the hunt-policy that the people
should have a generous share of all that was taken, either
directly receiving portions of venison or of dried meat, or of
wool, or else deriving indirect benefit through the various
things which were sent from the hunt—skins, feathers, wool,
hides—to the store-houses.[133]

To conclude this chapter I will submit to the reader that,
however stern the Incaic rule may have been, it was never unjust; however much the greatness and splendor of the highly
placed may have been served and enhanced, the well-being of
the humble was never lost to sight; however much may have
been demanded of the people in the way of personal labor and
of tribute, society as a whole was well compensated by the
measure of peace and security, of plenty and of leisure, that
was assured to it by the Incaic rule. Captain Pedro de Cieza
de León, who saw Peru in the early days of its being Spanish,
describes thus the sway of the Incas:

Having established a governor, with garrisons of soldiers, the army then advanced, and if the new province were large, it was presently ordered that a temple of the Sun should be built, and women collected for its service, and that a palace should be erected for the lord. Tribute was collected, care being taken that too much was not exacted, and that no injustice was done in anything; but that the new subjects were made acquainted with the imperial policy, and with the art of building, of clothing themselves, and of living together in towns. And if they needed anything, care was taken to supply it, and to teach them how to sow and cultivate their lands. So thoroughly was this policy carried into effect, that we know of many places where there were no flocks originally, but where there has been abundance since they were subjugated by the Incas; and others where formerly there was no maize, but where now they have large crops. In many provinces they went about like savages, badly clothed, and barefooted, until they came under the sway of the Incas; and from that time they have worn shirts and mantles, both men and women, so that they always hold the change in their memories.[134]

NOTES TO CHAPTER VIII

[1] A more detailed study of the social institutions of pre-Incaic Peru will be found in Means, 1925, pp. 409–425, where full references to the source materials are given. Extremely important is the admirable monograph of Prof. Louis Baudin, of Dijon University, especially, in the present connection, Baudin, 1928, Chs. iii–v, inclusive.

[2] A general bibliography of the subject treated in this chapter should include the following works:

Works, ancient and modern, bearing on the subject of this chapter include the following: Argüedas, 1919. Baudin, 1927; 1927b; 1927c; 1928; 1929. Belaúnde, 1908. Bustamante Cisneros, 1918; 1919. Cosio, 1916. Cúneo Vidal, 1914; 1919. Cunow, 1896; 1898. Deberle, 1876. Diaz, 1898. Eguiguren, 1914. Hanstein, 1923; 1925. Latcham, 1909; 1923; 1927. Lissón, 1887. McBride, 1921. Means, 1921c; 1921d; 1925. Minnaert, 1928. Miró Quesada, 1907; 1916. Osores, 1918. Riva-Agüero y Osma, 1910. Saavedra, 1913. Trimborn, 1923–1924; 1925; 1927. Tudela y Varela, 1905. Ugarte, 1918. Uhle, 1911. Valdez de la Torre, 1921. Valcárcel, 1914. Villarán, 1907. Wiesse, 1913. Zurkalowski, 1919.

[3] Sarmiento, Chs. ix and xi. Garcilaso, Pt. I, Bk. I, Chs. xvi–xviii, inclusive. Cieza, Bk. II, Chs. vi–viii, inclusive. Cabello, Pt. III, Chs. ix and x. Cobo, Bk. XIII, Ch. iii. Santillán, 1879, paragraph 2.

[4] See Baudin, 1928, pp. 174–175, for a fully documented account of this matter.

[5] As Baudin points out, 1928, pp. 90–91, modern estimates of the size of the *tupu* vary considerably. Inasmuch as the *tupu* was a quantity of land called upon to support a married couple without children, it is natural that its

extent should depend upon the quality of the soil in it. Where land of aver-
agely good quality was in question the *tupu* did possess the dimensions given
by Markham. At the present time one may see in many parts of highland
Peru fields of a *tupu* each which have approximately those dimensions. Early
references to the *tupu* include: Garcilaso, Pt. I, Bk. V, Ch. iii. Cieza, Pt. II,
Ch. xv. Sarmiento, Ch. lii. (Unfortunately the word *tupu* or *topu* was used
also to designate distance markers on the highways and also the large pins
used to hold garments together. Much confusion has arisen from this.)

[6] Garcilaso, Pt. I, Bk. V, Ch. iii, Vol. I, p. 10 of Markham's translation.

[7] Cobo, Bk. XII, Ch. xxviii.

[8] Compare Trimborn, 1923-1924, p. 586, with Baudin, 1928, p. 93. Garcilaso,
Pt. I, Bk. V, Ch. i, is very specific in saying that the lands of the Inca were
drawn upon in this way.

[9] Garcilaso, Pt. I, Bk. V, Ch. ii.

[10] Cobo, Bk. XII, Ch. xxviii. Polo, pp. 155-158 of Markham's translation.

[11] My account of the Incaic hierarchy is based upon: Garcilaso, Pt. I,
Bk. II, Chs. xi-xiv, inclusive. Morúa, Bk. III, Ch. v. Cobo, Bk. XII, Ch. xxv.
Santillán, 1879, pp. 17-19. Polo de Ondegardo, 1872, 1916b, 1917b. Montesinos,
Ch. vi. Sarmiento, Ch. 1. *Horden que el Ynga tubo en la governaçion del Piru.*
MS. In British Museum, Add. MSS. 13,992, folios 411-415. Falcón, 1918. See
also Baudin, 1928, pp. 118-124, and Means, 1925, pp. 448-452.

[12] Cobo, Bk. XII, Chs. xxv and xxvii. Father Blas Valera, quoted by Garcilaso in Pt. I, Bk. V, Ch. xiii.

[13] Garcilaso, Pt. I, Bk. II, Ch. xi. Baudin, 1928, pp. 118-120.

[14] Cobo, Bk. XII, Ch. xxv. Garcilaso, Pt. I, Bk. VI, Ch. xxxiii.

[15] Garcilaso, Pt. I, Bk. II, Chs. xii and xiv. *Horden,* MS. Baudin, 1928,
p. 120.

[16] Santillán, 1879, pp. 19-20.

[17] Baudin, 1928, pp. 121-122.

[18] Cunow, 1896, p. 107. Trimborn, 1923-1924, p. 993.

[19] Falcón, 1918, p. 147. Santillán, p. 22. Garcilaso, Pt. I, Bk. II, Ch. xiv.
Cieza, Pt. II, Ch. xviii. Cabello, Pt. III, Ch. xviii, p. 537 of the N. Y. P. L. MS.
Sarmiento, Ch. lii.

[20] Garcilaso, Pt. I, Bk. VIII, Ch. xvi.

[21] Means, 1925, p. 456. Castaing, 1884, p. 20. Tello and Miranda, 1923,
p. 508.

[22] Baudin, 1928, Ch. v, pp. 59-79.

[23] Cabello, Pt. III, Ch. xix, pp. 547-551 of N. Y. P. L. MS. Sarmiento,
Ch. li.

[24] Cieza, Pt. II, Chs. xviii, xxviii, and lxiii.

[25] Santillán, 1879, p. 21.

[26] Polo de Ondegardo, 1873, p. 162.

[27] Father Blas Valera, quoted *in extenso* by Garcilaso, Pt. I, Bk. V, Chs.
xi, xv, and xvi.

[28] Cobo, Bk. XII, Ch. xxxiii. Cieza, Pt. II, Ch. xviii.

[29] Garcilaso, Pt. I, Bk. V, Ch. ii. Vol. II, pp. 7-8 of Markham's translation.

[30] Cobo, Bk. XII, Ch. xxviii, Vol. III, pp. 247-248.

[31] The tabulation of these laws here presented is an arrangement of the

material preserved from the writings of Father Blas Valera and quoted *in extenso* by Garcilaso in Pt. I, Bk. V, Chs. xv and xvi.

[32] Morúa, 1922, p. 114.

[33] Baudin, 1928, pp. 99–100. Latcham, 1927, pp. 225–227.

[34] Cobo, Bk. XII, Ch. xxviii, Vol. III, p. 234.

[35] Garcilaso's statements to this effect are so numerous that it is idle to cite them. See also Acosta, Bk. VI, Ch. xiii.

[36] Santillán, 1879, p. 25. See also pp. 53–55.

[37] Garcilaso, Pt. I, Bk. I, Ch. xxvi. Vol. I, p. 95 of Markham's translation.

[38] Garcilaso, Vol. I, p. 97 of Markham's edition. On his own showing the great historian had no right to the title of Inca, which he used, for his imperial blood came to him through his mother. Yet, let us accord it to him, in recognition of his services in perpetuating the memory of the Imperial dynasty of Ttahua-ntin-suyu.

[39] Garcilaso, Pt. I, Bk. V, Ch. xxiii.

[40] Zárate, Ch. xi. Casas, 1892, Ch. xxi. Cieza, Pt. II, Ch. xiii.

[41] Father Blas Valera, cited by Garcilaso, Pt. I, Bk. IV, Ch. xix.

[42] Garcilaso, Pt. I, Bk. VII, Ch. x. Vol. II, pp. 247–248 of Markham's translation.

[43] Baudin, 1928, pp. 68–70.

[44] Morúa, Bk. III, Ch. iv.

[45] See Garcilaso, Pt. I, Bk. VII, Chs. ii–iv, inclusive.

[46] Garcilaso, Pt. I, Bk. I, Ch. xvi. Vol. I, p. 67 of Markham's translation.

[47] Castro and Ortega Morejón, p. 208. Casas, 1892, Ch. xvii.

[48] Montesinos, Ch. vi. Sarmiento, Chs. vi and viii.

[49] Uhle, 1911; 1912b, p. 302. Zurkalowski, 1919, p. 493. Cúneo Vidal, 1919, p. 311.

[50] Means, 1925, pp. 437–438.

[51] Baudin, 1928, p. 124.

[52] Sarmiento, Ch. xix. P. 72 of Markham's translation.

[53] Cobo, Bk. XII, Ch. xxiv.

[54] Baudin, 1928, p. 137: "Précisément, au Pérou, les besoins de la population étaient très réduits, et les Inka se sont ingéniés à les empêcher de croître."

[55] A vast amount of material on the diet of the early Andeans is provided by the Chroniclers. Important citations include the following: Acosta, Bk. IV, Chs. xvi, xvii, xix, and xx. Cieza, Pt. II, Ch. xviii. Cobo, Bk. IV, Chs. ii–v, inclusive, vii, viii, xiii, xiv, xxi, xxv, xxvi–xxviii, inclusive, Bk. XII, Ch. v. Garcilaso, Pt. I, Bk. IV, Ch. xiv, wherein methods of cooking are described; Bk. VI, Ch. xi, wherein the royal hunts are described; Bk. VIII, Chs. ix–xi, inclusive, in which an account of the foodstuffs is given. Cabello, Pt. III, Ch. v. See also, Baudin, 1928, pp. 137–138, and Eaton, 1925.

[56] Garcilaso, Pt. I, Bk. VIII, Ch. ix.

[57] Garcilaso, Pt. I, Bk. VIII, Chs. xii and xiii.

[58] Mortimer, 1901.

[59] Acosta, Bk. IV, Ch. xxii. Cobo, Bk. V, Ch. xxix. Garcilaso, Pt. I, Bk. VIII, Ch. xv.

[60] Garcilaso, Pt. I, Bk. II, Ch. xxv. Acosta, Bk. IV, Ch. xxix.

[61] The best general account of the dress of all classes under the Incas is

that given by Father Atienza in his Ch. v. See also: Benzoni, Smyth's translation, 1857, p. 249. Cieza, Pt. I, Ch. xli. Cobo, Bk. XII, Ch. ii. Garcilaso, Pt. I, Bk. IV, Ch. ii. Molina, of Cuzco, Markham's translation, pp. 39–41. Morúa, Bk. III, Chs. iv and xi. Montell, 1929, pp. 189–233, is the best modern account of the matter of dress.

62 Betánzos, Ch. xiii.

63 Garcilaso, Pt. I, Bk. IV, Ch. xiv.

64 Garcilaso, Pt. I, Bk. VI, Ch. xxxv. Vol. II, p. 206 of Markham's translation.

65 Estete, in Xerez, 1534. P. 90 of Markham's translation, 1872.

66 Cobo, Bk. XI, Ch. viii, Vol. III, pp. 43–44.

67 Wrigley, 1919.

68 Román y Zamora, 1595, Bk. II, Chs. xii–xvi, inclusive.

69 Garcilaso, Pt. I, Bk. VI, Ch. i. Vol. II, pp. 100–101 of Markham's translation.

70 Cieza, Pt. I, Chs. xxi, xli, xliv, lxxx, xciii, *inter alia.* Zárate, Bk. I, Ch. xiv. Cobo, Bk. XIV, Chs. ii–v, inclusive. Morúa, Bk. III, Chs. i–v, inclusive. Cabello, Pt. III, Ch. xxi, pp. 582–583 of N. Y. P. L. MS.

71 My descriptive passages referring to Cuzco are based upon my personal recollections of the place and upon various writings ancient and modern, among them: Garcilaso, Pt. I, Bk. VI, Chs. i–iv, inclusive, Bk. VII, Chs. viii–xi, inclusive. Betánzos, Ch. xvi. Cobo, in addition to chapters already cited, Bk. XIV, Ch. xii. Cieza, Pt. I, Chs. xcii–xciv, inclusive. Contreras y Valverde, 1885, pp. 179–183. Román, Pt. III, Ch. v. Lizárraga, Pt. I, Ch. lxxx. Carli, Pte. I, Letter VI. Baudin, 1928, pp. 160–161. Valcárcel, 1924.

72 Polo de Ondegardo, p. 169 of Markham's translation. Montesinos, Ch. vii.

73 Garcilaso, Pt. I, Bk. VIII, Ch. v. Cieza, Pt. I, Chs. xlvi and l. Cobo, Bk. III, Ch. xxxi. Acosta, Bk. IV, Ch. xiv.

74 Garcilaso, Pt. I, Bk. VI, Ch. iii. Vol. II, pp. 107–108 of Markham's translation.

75 Montesinos, Chs. vii, xiv, and xv. Bingham, 1922, Ch. xvi; 1929, Ch. ix.

76 Acosta, Bk. VI, Chs. viii and xix. Cabello, Pt. III, Ch. x. Calancha, Bk. I, Ch. xiv. All these ascribe a narrative character to the ancient *quipu.* Cieza, Pt. I, Ch. lxxxii, where he says that the *quipu* was used for accounts; Pt. II, Ch. xii, where he emphasizes arithmetical uses of the *quipu;* Chs. xviii and xix, where he says that the *quipu* was used to record vital statistics; Ch. lii, where he implies that the *quipu* had a narrative value. Cobo, Bk. XII, Chs. ii and xxxvii, in latter of which he ascribes both an arithmetical and a narrative character to the *quipu.* Garcilaso, Pt. I, Bk. II, Chs. xiii and xxvi; Bk. VI, Ch. vi, in all these chapters the Inca historian emphasizes the arithmetical and statistical character the *quipu;* in Bk. VI, Chs. viii and ix, he does so again, but implies that they also served as *an aid to the memory* in preserving narratives. Molina, of Cuzco, pp. 10–11 of Markham's translation, ascribes both an arithmetical and a narrative character to the *quipu.* Montesinos, Ch. xv, *quipu* used in place of letters. Morúa, Bk. III, Ch. xxv, ascribes statistical and narrative functions to the *quipu.* Oliva, Bk. I, Ch. ii, strongly supports the narrative character. Polo

de Ondegardo, p. 169 of Markham's translation, does likewise. Sarmiento, Ch. ix, ascribes arithmetical and mnemonic functions to the *quipu*. Zárate, Bk. I, Ch. v, speaks of arithmetical character. Gutiérrez de Santa Clara, Bk. III, Ch. lxiii, seeks to give *quipu* almost the same value as a book.

[77] Among the modern writers who hold that the principal function of the *quipu* was mathematical or statistical are: Larrabure y Unánue, 1893, pp. 187–189. Markham, 1910, pp. 139–141, also concedes the mnemonic function. Guimaraes, 1907. Locke, 1912; 1923, p. 31, concludes that, while the *quipu* was mainly mathematical, it probably had a mnemonic function also. Nordenskiöld, 1925 and 1925b does likewise, but draws attention to the calendrical functions of the *quipu*.

[78] Baudin, 1928, pp. 124–136.

[79] Cieza, Pt. II, Ch. xii. Pp. 33–35 of Markham's translation.

[80] Heuzey, 1870.

[81] Descriptions of this artifact appear in: Bastian, 1877, p. 149. González Suárez, 1878, pp. 25–26, and Pl. V; 1890–1903, Atlas, pp. 67–75, and Pls. III and IV. Verneau and Rivet, 1912, pp. 244–250, and Pl. XV. Baudin, 1928, pp. 125–126. Unfortunately the original specimen is lost, but reproductions of it exist in the Ethnological Museum, Berlin, and in the Museum at Santiago de Chile.

[82] Verneau and Rivet, 1912, pp. 245–246, and Pl. XV, Fig. 2.

[83] Wiener, 1880, pp. 776–778.

[84] Verneau and Rivet, 1912, p. 245, and Pl. XV, Fig. 4. The original is in the Trocadéro.

[85] Verneau and Rivet, 1912, p. 245, and Pl. XV, Fig. 1. The original is in the Ethnological Museum, Berlin.

[86] Baessler, 1902–1903, Fig. 417. Verneau and Rivet, 1912, p. 246.

[87] Gutiérrez de Santa Clara, Bk. III, Ch. lxiii. Acosta, Bk. VI, Ch. viii.

[88] Cobo, Bk. XIV, Ch. xvii, Vol. IV, p. 228. Garcilaso, Pt. I, Bk. II, Ch. xiv.

[89] Raynal, 1770, II, p. 147. Deberle, 1876, p. 29.

[90] Cieza, Pt. I, Ch. lxxxix; Pt. II, Ch. xv.

[91] Cobo, Bk. XII, Ch. xxxi.

[92] Bingham, 1930, Ch. ii.

[93] Cieza, Pt. I, Ch. xci.

[94] Source material on roads and bridges includes the following: Cieza, Pt. I, Chs. lx and xci; Pt. II, Ch. xv. Cobo, Bk. XII, Ch. xxxi; Bk. XIV, Ch. xiii. Garcilaso, Pt. I, Bk. III, Chs. vii, viii, xv, and xvi; Bk. IX, Ch. xiii. Gutiérrez de Santa Clara, Bk. III, Chs. lxii and lxiii. Morúa, Bk. III, Chs. xxvii and xxix. Sarmiento, Ch. xlv. Xerez, p. 29 of Markham's translation. More modern writers who have discussed the matter include: Baudin, 1928, Ch. xi. Beuchat, 1912, pp. 649–651. Bingham, 1922, pp. 84–86.

[95] Acosta, Bk. VI, Ch. x. P. 409 of Markham's edition.

[96] Garcilaso, Pt. I, Bk. VI, Ch. vii, tells us that the Quechua word for messenger or envoy was *chaca*, but that the word for courier was *chasqui*, meaning exchange, because they exchanged messages and burdens from one man to the next. The establishment of the *chasqui* service is credited to Pachacutec by: Sarmiento, Ch. xxxviii. Cieza, Pt. II, Ch. xxi. But Morúa,

Bk. III, Ch. xxiv, credits it to Tupac Yupanqui. And Montesinos, Ch. vii, makes the *chasqui* system greatly ante-date the Incas, ascribing it by implication to the Tiahuanaco II period, about 700 A. D.

[97] Cobo, Bk. XII, Ch. xxxi, Vol. III, p. 268.

[98] Garcilaso, Pt. I, Bk. VI, Ch. vi. Bk. IX, Ch. xiii. Santillán, 1879, p. 40. Sarmiento, Ch. xxxviii. Cieza, Pt. II, Ch. xxi. Morúa, Bk. III, Ch. xxiv. Montesinos, Ch. vii. Acosta, Bk. VI, Ch. xvii. Gutiérrez de Santa Clara, Bk. III, Ch. lxiii. Baudin, 1928, p. 196.

[99] Cieza, Pt. II, Ch. xxi. Pp. 65–66 of Markham's translation.

[100] Garcilaso, Pt. I, Bk. VI, Ch. vi. Vol. II, pp. 120–121 of Markham's translation.

[101] Cobo, Bk. XII, Ch. xxxii.

[102] Bingham, 1922, p. 207.

[103] Squier, 1877, pp. 400–401.

[104] Bingham, 1922, pp. 117–118. Lizárraga, Pt. I, Ch. lxv.

[105] See Boman, 1908, pp. 698–706.

[106] Cieza, Pt. II, Ch. xx. Pp. 61–63 of Markham's translation. See also: Morúa, Bk. III, Chs. i and iii. Garcilaso, Pt. I, Bk. VI, Ch. iii. Cobo, Bk. XII, Ch. xxxiii.

[107] Huamán Poma de Ayala, MS., in Royal Library, Copenhagen, pp. 289, 331, 333, and 377. Means, 1923.

[108] Tschudi, 1847, p. 323; 1847b, p. 226.

[109] Bandelier, 1910, pp. 12–15. Bingham, 1922, pp. 97–98. Ogilvie, 1922, p. 165.

[110] References to native navigation in the Andean area and on the coasts thereof will be found in: Benzoni, Bk. III, pp. 242–243 of Smyth's translation. Cobo, Bk. XIV, Ch. xiv. P. Pizarro, 1921, I, 138–139. Gutiérrez de Santa Clara, Bk. III, Ch. lxi. Cieza, Pt. I, Ch. lxxxv; Pt. II, Ch. xxxix. Zárate, Bk. I, Ch. vi. Frézier, 1717, pp. 120–121. Juan and Ulloa, 1748, Bk. IV, Ch. ix, paragraphs 465–473. Prescott, 1847, I, pp. 244–247. Baudin, 1928, pp. 170–171 and 200–202. Means, 1925, pp. 456–460. Urteaga, 1919.

[111] Xerez, p. 87 of Markham's translation.

[112] Sarmiento, Ch. xxxix. P. 120 of Markham's translation. It is to be noted that Sir Clements translated the Spanish word *visitadores* a trifle too literally; it really means inspectors.

[113] Garcilaso, Pt. I, Bk. II, Ch. xxvi. Betánzos, 1880, p. 108. Verneau and Rivet, 1912, pp. 244–250, give various references, including a quotation from Castellanos in which a map on cloth is definitely ascribed to the chief Chaparra.

[114] Sarmiento, Ch. xxxix. Cieza, Pt. II, Ch. xxii. Oliva, 1857, p. 51.

[115] Bowman, 1916, pp. 58–60.

[116] Garcilaso, Pt. I, Bk. VII, Ch. i. Vol. II, pp. 213 and 215 of Markham's translation.

[117] Garcilaso, Pt. I, Bk. VII, Ch. ii. Cieza, Pt. I, Ch. xcii.

[118] Cieza, Pt. I, Ch. xli; Pt. II, Chs. xiii and xxii. Cobo, Bk. XII, Ch. xxiii.

[119] Cieza, Pt. I, Ch. xcix.

[120] Ramos Gavilán, Bk. I, Ch. xii. Cobo, Bk. XIII, Ch. xviii.

[121] Cieza, Pt. I, Ch. lviii; Pt. II, Ch. lvi.

[122] Cieza, Pt. II, Ch. xxii, pp. 69–70 of Markham's translation.

[123] Cobo, Bk. XII, Ch. xxiii.

[124] Morúa, Bk. III, Ch. xxi.

[125] Morúa, Bk. III, Ch. xx.

[126] Valera, 1879, p. 204, Law xxiii.

[127] Garcilaso, Pt. I, Bk. III, Ch. xiii; Bk. IV, Ch. iii; Bk. VI, Ch. xi.

[128] Useful references concerning the penal code are as follows: Cabello de Balboa, Pt. III, Ch. xx, pp. 560–562 of N. Y. P. L. MS. Cobo, Bk. XII, Ch. xxvi. Cieza, Pt. II, Ch. xxvi. Garcilaso, Pt. I, Bk. II, Ch. xiii. *Horden*, MS., folio 413. Morúa, Bk. III, Chs. xx, xxi, and xxiii. Román y Zamora, Bk. II, Ch. xiv. Baudin, 1928, pp. 182–186.

[129] Cabello, pp. 561–562 of N. Y. P. L. MS.

[130] Garcilaso, Pt. I, Bk. IV, Ch. iii. Vol. I, p. 299 of Markham's translation.

[131] Cieza, Pt. II, Ch. xvi.

[132] Garcilaso, Pt. I, Bk. VI, Ch. vi.

[133] Acosta, Bk. IV, Chs. xxxiv and xl. Cieza, Pt. II, Ch. xvi. Cobo, Bk. XIV, Ch. xvi.

[134] Cieza, Pt. II, Ch. xvii, pp. 49–50 of Markham's translation.

CHAPTER IX

THE CEREMONIAL LIFE AND OFFICIAL RELIGION OF THE INCAIC STATE

MODERN states—particularly those of them which have the good fortune to be ruled by dictators—tend to instil into the minds of their people a perhaps exaggerated notion of the blessings to be derived from being married; they tend to make it slightly uncomfortable for persons who are selfish enough— or should I say canny enough?—to stick fast to bachelorhood or to spinsterhood. Among the Incas these tendencies existed in a marked degree, for bachelorhood and spinsterhood in persons past the age for marrying was almost non-existent. Practically everyone was married, in one way or another, at least once in their lives; and many were married often. Matrimonial matters were, to describe them briefly, arranged and conducted as follows.

Polygamy existed; indeed, among the upper classes, it was general, being regarded as a delectable state fitting only to the highly placed and to those favored by the Sapa Inca who, either in his own person or else through the agency of some official acting for him, conferred concubines upon men whom he sought to reward for valor in the field. The first woman whom a man received, either as a reward for valor or in the ordinary course of things, was his wife-in-chief, remaining so until death parted the pair. She was the only one whom the man married with any degree of pomp, the manner of doing so being this:

Having received his wife at the hands of the Inca, or of the Inca's representative official, the bridegroom led her to the house of her father, a throng of his own kinsfolk accompanying the young couple on the way. At her father's house the bride's relatives were in waiting, and her father, in the presence of the two groups of kinsmen, handed her over to the

358

bridegroom. Thereupon the young man knelt down and shod his bride's right foot with a sandal of wool (if she were a maiden) or with one of *ichu* grass if she were a widow. After that ceremony, performed as a sign that the bridegroom accepted the bride as his wife-in-chief, he led her to their destined home, which had been made ready beforehand, the relatives of both of them following after. On arriving there the bride took from her *chumpi* (girdle) a shirt of fine wool, a *llautu* (fillet), and a breast ornament, all of which she gave to her husband, who donned them forthwith. From that moment until night was well advanced the two young people were kept apart, each of them being in company with elder persons of the same sex who were supposed to instruct them in the meaning and obligations of marriage. During this interval many gifts were presented to both the man and the girl and, after the contracting parties had come together again, a festival began which, as the hours flew by, became an orgy.

Points of interest concerning this mode of marrying are these: in the first place, the priesthood had nothing whatever to do with it; in the second place, a woman so wedded could never be repudiated nor abandoned, and, even though her husband later received from the Inca, or from his representative, a woman of nobler blood, she remained all her life his chief wife; finally, only the chief wife was so wedded, the secondary wives being no more than authorized concubines were merely taken and enjoyed without any formalities, and, at the same time, they always remained wholly subservient to the chief wife.

If, however, the first wife died, the husband might marry again after a year or more of mourning, taking as his new wife-in-chief some woman not already a member of his household, and going through the same ceremonies as before. Widowerhood was a chill and cheerless condition among the Incas' subjects, especially for the monogamous plebeians, to whom, sometimes, a new wife was not allotted for as many as two or three years so that, during a long interval, the bereaved husband had to pass through the early Peruvian equivalent

for the sink-full-of-unwashed-dishes state of affairs. The man
who, blissfully polygamous, lost his chief wife by death was,
at any rate in a material way, better off than the monogamous
man; for there remained to him his concubines to serve and
to solace him. The priority of the first wife was again emphasized at her death; for there were held, in the house of her
husband, mourning ceremonies of an exceedingly lachrymose
description in which the widower, the deceased wife's kinsfolk,
and all the secondary wives wept noisily and lengthily. The
concubines could do so with at least some degree of sincerity,
and quite without secret plans for capturing the empty place,
because by custom, if not by law, none of them could ever become wife-in-chief. If the widower ever did remarry, it was
always with some lady not previously of his household. This
custom, as Father Cobo wisely observes, prevented the secondary wives from slaying one another in a grand squabble for
the first place. Deceased secondary wives were mourned only
by their own kinsfolk, and that not in the house of the
husband.[1]

There were several ways of acquiring secondary wives,
among them the following: Highly born parents were wont
to place their sons in the care of nurse-maids while they were
still young lads, and these women remained with their charges
until they had attained to manhood, tending and washing
them in childhood and, later, teaching them the carnal delights, sleeping with them, and so on, all this being done with
the approval of the parents. Subsequently, when the lads took
chief wives—I am speaking here of the upper classes—the old
nurses remained in the new households as concubines. Although good Father Cobo seems rather shocked by all this, it
really was not a bad system. Again, if an orphan boy was
given over to the care of a childless widow who devoted herself to bringing him up, she eventually became his concubine
and remained so even after the authorities had given him a
chief wife; and the relationship between the old widow and
the young man continued until it was agreed between them
that he had fully repaid her for the trouble of rearing him;

or, if they failed to agree, the proper official determined when the obligation had been discharged. Still another mode of acquiring secondary wives was by war, the officers of a conquering army being wont to distribute among themselves any women who might be captured. More decent was the custom of the Inca to confer secondary wives upon the valiant fighters, taking them from the imperial supplies of women. Finally, secondary wives came to a man by inheritance, a son succeeding to the secondary wives of his deceased father or even of his deceased brother, always with the proviso, however, that he have no carnal relations with his own mother.

Incestuous marriages, according to Father Cobo,[2] were prohibited to all until Inca Tupac Yupanqui married his own sister, at the same time ordaining that only the monarch or the heir-apparent should do so, albeit he permitted men of high rank to marry their paternal half-sisters. But all that was a very modern development. Of great age, however, was the custom of marrying a first cousin, who was granted to a young man by the Inca, or by the proper officials, on the demand of the bridegroom's parents or of the bridegroom himself. This was done in order to further and intensify the adoration of the mummies of the couple's mutual ancestors.

Thus far I have been treating chiefly of the matrimonial arrangements of the upper classes, particularly those of Cuzco, in whose marriages the Sapa Inca could, and very often did, take a personal interest in bringing the young couple together in the first place. In the provinces, the official in charge of each village periodically assembled the youths and maidens of marriageable age into two groups and then paired them off in couples. Modern writers have generally assumed that this was a rather arbitrary and cold-blooded proceeding, but it is quite probable that there were artful dodges whereby a lad and a lass who felt drawn to one another could manage to be paired together. Having thus been joined by civil authority, the couple went through the marriage solemnities described above, with incidental entertainments of whatever degree of lavishness their station in life made suitable.

Among humble folk, in certain provinces, the marriage-ceremony was more simple. In the Collao, for example, it consisted merely of the young man's going to the mother of the girl appointed by the proper official to be his wife and of making a present to her in the form of a pouch full of coca; if the old lady accepted it, the marriage was considered to be an accomplished fact. In other regions it was the custom for the young man to serve the parents of the appointed bride by doing household chores for them, such as carrying wood and water, during several days, in which period the kinsfolk of both parties came together and observed suitable urbanities towards one another.

This account of the marriage-customs is based upon the work of Father Bernabé Cobo;[3] only a little additional light is thrown upon the matter by other Chroniclers. Garcilaso tells us that the girls to be married were from eighteen to twenty years of age, and the men twenty-four and upwards.[4] In this respect the Jesuit and the Inca historians contradict one another, for the former makes the ages of both sexes at marriage much less than does the latter. The Inca Garcilaso is right, however, as a study of the age-categories into which the populace was divided—related on page 294 of the preceding chapter—will amply prove. Garcilaso also implies that the couples, at any rate those of the imperial caste, paired themselves off according to their personal predilections and merely had their hands officially joined by the Inca.[4] Santillán, on the other hand, leads us to believe that the pairing was done among the provincial lower classes by an official whom he calls *visitador,* by which term he may mean the *tucuiricuc,* and that it was entirely arbitrary, the wishes of the contracting parties not being consulted at all.[5] The pretty ceremony of the *usuta* or sandal always followed upon the official joining of hands, as Father Acosta, in complete corroboration of Father Cobo, makes clear.[6] Captain Pedro de Cieza de León speaks only of the Incas' marriages, giving us an idea of the size of the imperial seraglio when he says that none of the sovereigns "had less than 700 women for the service of their house and for their pleasure." They were guarded by persons especially appointed therefor; but, as in the case of the less lofty ranks of society, the wife-in-chief, the Coya or Empress, was emphatically pre-eminent over all the rest.[7]

Strange to relate, there is, in the Chroniclers' accounts of marriages under the Incas, singularly little evidence of that lusty carnality which is usually an integral part of marriages among both primitive and civilized peoples. We search in vain for signs, in early Peru, of any great degree of fleshliness and for specific injunctions of the increase-and-multiply sort. Presumably all that was taken for granted, for it is certain that the Incas and their subjects were exceedingly prolific. Moreover, only one Chronicler, Santa Cruz Pachacuti-yamqui Salcamayhua, gives us a definite insight into the presence of romantic love, as we of to-day understand the term, among the Incas' subjects. He tells us that, in the days of Sinchi Roca Inca, youths and maidens loved one another so dearly that they could not live apart, their passion having some obscure connection with certain small, round stones which the lovers cherished. Likewise, he tells us of a poor, ragged *llama-michec* (llama-herder), whose charms were so great that he was able to woo away a maiden from Sinchi Roca himself, doing so with the aid of a *huacanqui* or lovephiltre given to him by a demon with whom he had made a pact in a certain cave.[8]

On the whole, however, the marriage arrangements of the Incas and their subjects were of a practical and economic aspect rather than a romantic. They were, as we have seen, directly under the supervision of the State; and the State saw to it that each new household received an abode, domestic equipment, and fields adequate to its requirements and to its status in society.

Childhood, in early Peru, was a difficult time to survive, for it was filled with all manner of hardships and vicissitudes. The Inca Viracocha, who had evidently pondered the matter deeply, pronounced upon it as follows: "Fathers are often the cause that their sons are lost or corrupted by evil habits which they are allowed to learn in their childhood. For some bring up their sons with too much indulgence and good nature, and, being overjoyed by the beauty and tenderness of their children, they leave them to do as they please, without caring for the future when they shall become men, or thinking of what will then happen. Others there are who treat their children with too much severity and harshness, which also ruins them. For too much indulgence weakens the powers both of body and mind, and too much severity enfeebles and weakens the spirit, making the child lose the hope of learning and hate instruction. Those who are made to fear everything cannot have the courage to perform deeds worthy of men. The proper way is to bring children up by a middle course, so that they may turn out strong and courageous in war, wise and judicious in peace."[9]

All this, excellent though it is, seems to have been entirely theoretical, if not merely rhetorical. In actual fact the rigors of infancy and of childhood were formidable. When a wife felt herself to be on the point of giving birth, she, and also her husband, fasted, that is, they abstained from certain foods, and she confessed herself and made propitiatory prayers to the *huacas* or minor deities to whom she was devout. When the moment of giving birth came, the woman drew apart for a brief while from her people and, without even such aid as a mid-wife might have given, brought her child into the world, presently going with it to the nearest stream in whose waters she washed both herself and the babe, no matter how cold the atmosphere and the water might be. This procedure, exactly, is common to this day.

Soon after that the infant was tightly swaddled and placed in a *quirau* or cradle which had four legs, one of them shorter than the rest in order to facilitate rocking. The wrappings were loosened from around the baby's body every morning so that it might be washed, often with water de-chilled by being held for a space in the mother's mouth, a process which was believed to be beneficial to the child. The arms of the little creature were not unwrapped, however, for three months or more, as it was thought that doing so would weaken the arms. Moreover, the infant spent practically all its time in the *quirau,* never being taken up into its mother's arms because it was held that to do so would make it howl to be there always. The mother gave her bairnie to suck only thrice daily— early in the morn, at noon, and at sundown—for the Incas and their subjects had noted that the animals suckled their young at fixed times, and they held that to do so more often would tend to make the baby vomit when young and to be gluttonous when grown. No matter how high her rank every mother in the realm, provided her health were good, fed her children, wet-nursing being resorted to only when the mother's health made it necessary. The child was kept entirely on a mother's milk diet until, after two years or so, it was weaned. During this period the mother had no sexual intercourse, as it was considered to have a bad effect on her milk, which would render the child *ayusca* (incapable, anæmic). A baby able to crawl on all fours took its meals kneeling whilst the mother bent over it, and, as it was never allowed on her lap, it had to go around the mother on its hands and knees if it wished to feed from the other teat, for it knelt beside her, not in front of her.

All this seems cosey and natural enough, but both Garcilaso and Cobo, from whom the best data on Incaic infancy are derived, say with unpleasant clearness that the young of Ttahua-ntin-suyu were much neglected, untidy, and more or less abandoned to their own devices. The custom of always carrying the child on the back, cradle and all being swathed in a shawl, a custom, by-the-bye, still general in the Andean highlands, may have been convenient for the mother as she went about her tasks, but it cannot have been very pleasant for the infant. Worse was in store, however, for children too old for cradles were wrapped up in any cloths that came handy and placed in holes dug in the ground which came up to their arm-pits. There they were left to jump and kick, and to amuse themselves as best they could with whatever trifling toys the mother saw fit to set down in front of them upon the ground.[10]

Certain ceremonies marked the passage of the infant years. The first of them took place at the time of weaning and was a rite that corresponded to our baptism, save that, as in the case of the marriage ceremony, the priesthood had nothing to do with it. All the relatives and friends of the child's parents came together to dance and to drink with much joviality, and the most venerable uncle of the child, with due solemnity, cut its hair and nails for the first time, using the sharpened stone implements which, uncomfortably enough one would think, they employed for such purposes. Thereafter all the company made presents to the child suitable to its station in life, the favorite gifts being clothes, arms or spinning-implements, *queros* or drinking-cups, and so on. The fineness and beauty of the gifts varied, naturally, according to the class of society of those interested, but they all had an emphatically useful aspect. In the case of the heir to the imperial fillet, only, did the priesthood have the remotest connection with the matter, and then it merely consisted in the *Villac Umu* or High Priest of the Sun acting as sponsor to the child who, more often than not, was in any case his nephew, the greatest *curaca-cuna* of the realm attending in order to make superb gifts to their destined liege.[10] This was the *rutuchicui* or haircutting ceremony.

The name given to the child at this time was of a temporary nature only, destined to be replaced by a permanent name when he or she reached the age of puberty. At that time an even more important ceremony was held, that of the boys being called *huarachicui* or breeching-ceremony, and that of the girls *quicuchicui* or combing-ceremony.[11] Although more extended mention of the puberty ceremony for boys will be made further on, it is well to note here that both sexes, on attaining to recognized adult age at their respective festivals, received presents from their parents, kinsfolk, and friends, as well as the names which they were to bear through life, Puma, Cuntur, Amaru, Huamán (Lion, Condor, Serpent, Falcon) and the like for boys, and names of gentler import for the girls.

The ceremonies and festivals held for the benefit and the enjoyment of adults, not to mention the delectation of the gods, were, naturally enough, more numerous and more elaborate than those centring upon the infant population. The *huata* or year of the Incas and their subjects was, indeed, plentifully sprinkled with festivals and ceremonial observances. Father Cobo sapiently divides these into two categories: those which occurred in celebration of special events, such as the commencement of a new reign, the beginning of an important war, or an attempt to break a drought by propitiating the gods; and those which fell at stated times through the year. The latter class of ceremonies brings us to the subject of Incaic calendrical lore. Although the astronomical knowledge of the Incas was vastly inferior to that of the Mayas of Yucatan and to that of the Aztecs of Mexico, it was quite sufficient to enable them to form an accurate idea of the duration and division of the solar year. Not only were they fully aware of the times when the solstices and the equinoxes occurred, but also they were able to adjust the lunar year, with its twelve complete cycles of phases, to the solar year by means of intercalating eleven supernumerary days which according to Sir Clements Markham, were called *allcancanquis,* a term meaning "you are missing."[12] Candor compels me to state, however, that I have been unable to find this word in any of the Chronicles of Peru.

As might be expected, the Chroniclers differ considerably from one another concerning the composition of the *huata,* with its *quilla-cuna,* months or moons, and its *punchau-cuna,* days; but by a careful study of the data which they provide it is possible to arrive at a fairly accurate notion of the Incaic year and its divers festivals. They seem to have been arranged as follows:

I. *Intip Raimi,* or *Yntip Raymi,* was the month beginning with the June solstice and continuing for about thirty days. At this time was held the Solemn Feast of the Sun, which

Garcilaso describes as follows: ". . . They celebrated this festival of the Sun in acknowledgement that they held and adored Him as the sole universal God who, by His light and power, creates and sustains all things upon earth; and that He was the natural father of the first Inca Manco Capac and of his wife Mama Ocllo Huaco, and all their descendants, who were sent to this earth for the benefit of all people. For these reasons, as they themselves say, this was their most solemn feast."[13]

All who were noblest and most influential in the empire were participants in the great feast of the Sun. At Cuzco, where the ceremonies were naturally most solemn and splendid, the rites were conducted in part by the Sapa Inca, as first-born of the Sun, and in part by the Villac Umu, High Priest of the Sun, his uncle or his brother. Curacas from all parts of the empire, each one attended by a numerous and an impressive retinue, assembled in order to pay homage to the chief god of their liege. Those from certain mountain districts came in robes fashioned from puma-skin; from the east and north came others whose raiment was gorgeous with the brilliant plumage of birds; and from the long-civilized coastal states came powerful lords resplendent in beautiful apparel of finely woven cotton cloth glowing with many colors. Perhaps the most imposing of all were those chiefs who came in wonderful condor-costumes provided with outstretched wings. In short, it must have been a wildly picturesque congregation that poured into the capital city at this time, whence all strangers of low degree were temporarily banished. The din of barbaric music proceeding from syrinxes, trumpets, shell-clarions, and all manner of drums and rattles no doubt increased the nervous tension of those present.

A three-day fast preceded the festival proper. During the night before the feast the *aclla-cuna* or Chosen Women (of whom more, further on) were industriously preparing *canca*, the maize-bread or maize-pudding used ceremonially in the rites, and at the same time priests were making ready the living things destined to be immolated in the sacrifices.

At dawn of the great day the Sapa Inca and a vast following of great men in magnificent raiment came forth from his palace in a stately procession and made their way to the *Huaca Pata*, Holy Terrace, or Great Square. On arriving there they all prostrated themselves in such a way as to rest upon their elbows, the hands apart and the face upwards towards the Sun. In this posture they kissed the sunbeams, solemnly, fervently, thus adoring their God. Only the Sapa Inca and the men of the blood imperial were privileged to go to the *Huaca Pata*, the curacas and all other honored guests being assembled in like manner in the *Cusi Pata*, Joy Terrace, hard by, across the little Huatanay River, whence all that was done could be seen without difficulty.

The ritual must have been impressive. Garcilaso describes it thus:

. . . Presently the King rose to his feet, the rest being still prostrate, and took two cups of gold, called *aquilla*, full of the beverage that they drink. He performed this ceremony as the first-born, in the name of his father, the Sun, and, with the cup in his right hand, invited all his relations to drink. This custom of inviting each other to drink was the usual mode by which superiors showed favour and complacency to inferiors, and by which one friend saluted another.

Having given the invitation to drink, the Inca emptied the vase in his right hand, which was dedicated to the Sun, into a jar of gold, whence the liquor flowed down a stone conduit of very beautiful masonry from the great square to the temple of the Sun, thus being looked upon as drunk by the Deity. From the vase in his left hand the Inca himself drank, that being his share, and then divided what remained among the other Incas, pouring it into other cups of gold and silver. Gradually the principal vase, which the Inca held, was emptied; and the partakers thus received such virtue from it as was imparted by its having been sanctified by the Sun or the Inca, or rather by both together. Each member of the blood royal drank of this liquor. The curacas in the other square received drinks of the beverage made by the chosen virgins, but not that which had also been sanctified by the Inca.

This ceremony having been performed, which was but a foretaste of what would have to be drunk afterwards, all went in a procession to the temple of the Sun. All took off their shoes, except the King, at two hundred paces before reaching the doors; but the King remained with his shoes on, until he came to the doors. The Inca and his relations then entered the temple as legitimate children of the deity, and there worshipped the image of the Sun. But the Curacas, being unworthy of so great an honour, remained outside in a large square before the temple doors.

The Inca offered to the Sun the golden vases with which he had performed the ceremony, and the other members of his family gave up their cups to the Inca priests, who were set apart for that office; for persons who were not priests, even if they were of the royal blood, were not allowed to perform the priestly office. Having offered up the cups of the Incas, the priests came to the doors to receive those of the Curacas, who took their places according to their seniority as vassals, and presented the gold and silver articles which they had brought from their provinces as offerings to the Sun. These gifts were in the form of sheep, lambs, lizards, toads, serpents, foxes, tigers, lions, and many sorts of birds, in short, of all the animals in the provinces, each imitated from nature in gold and silver, though the size of each article was not great.[14]

In this passage the hierarchical principle with which the Incaic idea was so deeply imbued stands out most clearly. Here, as so often, there was a fine gradation of privileges, eloquent of the gradations of society itself. Another point worthy of special remark is the method whereby the curacas arranged themselves, according to their seniority as vassals. In this we have a very definite bit of evidence that the Incas' subjects had a developed historical sense, for, without it, they could not have known anything about the relative antiquity of the various conquests made by the ruling Inca and by his predecessors.

Garcilaso goes on to relate that a black llama from the herds of the Sun was formally sacrificed. A black llama was chosen for special honors because a white or a colored llama, how perfect so ever it might be otherwise, always had a black nose, which, so they held, constituted a blemish, whereas a black llama was of the same hue all over and was consequently a more perfect thing than a white or a piebald beast could be. This black paschal llama was placed with its head to the east and, whilst four Incas sat upon it to keep it still, its left side was slashed open by the officiating priest who then plunged his hands into the wound in order to drag forth the still living heart, lungs, and gullet, all of which had to be removed entire and without cutting. The viscous matter thus surgically acquired was regarded as having great prognostic value, for, if the lungs were still palpitating when separated from the victim's carcass, the omen was declared to be highly favorable, so much so that, even though other and minor omens were unfavorable at the same time, they were disregarded, the potency of the pulmonary omen being considered great enough to annul the evil effect of the lesser portents. If the first sacrifice of this kind furnished unpropitious signs, such as the cessation of movement on the part of the lungs or such as the escape of the llama from its recumbent position, they made a second and even a third attempt. If all three were unfavorable, the festival continued nevertheless, albeit the participants were sad, dreading cruel wars, epidemics, failure of crops, and all manner of calamities. When the omens were propitious, their joy was correspondingly great.

The sacrificing of the black llama having been completed, a great holocaust of many other animals, also from the herds of the Sun, was offered up. These victims were all beheaded first, and their blood and hearts were made a special offering to the Sun; but their carcasses were piled up and consumed by fire. Garcilaso tells us how this was done, as follows: ". . . It was necessary that the fire for the sacrifice should be new, and given by the hand of the Sun, as they expressed it. For this purpose they took a large bracelet, called *chipana* (like those they usually wear on the left wrist). This was held by the high priest, and had on it a highly polished concave plate, about the diameter of an orange. They put this towards the Sun, at an angle, so that the reflected rays might concentrate on one point, where they had placed a little cotton wool well pulled out, for they did not know how to make tinder; but the cotton was soon lighted in the natural way."[15]

If, unfortunately, the countenance of the Sun were veiled from his children by clouds, recourse was had to two sticks which were rubbed together until a spark was obtained. These sticks, *uyaca,* were the usual fire-making implements of the Incas' subjects. It was considered very unlucky, however, if they had to be used in order to obtain new fire for the sacrifice; for it was said that the Sun was angry with his people and so refused to give the new fire himself.

The flesh of the sacrificed animals was well roasted, and afterwards it was distributed among all the people in both the squares, all those present partaking of it in a ceremonial mood. The sacred festal bread, *canca,* was likewise distributed, as well as many other foods, all of which were partaken of with due solemnity. Finally, when all the victuals had been eaten, the serious business of the day began; for the people of Ttahua-ntin-suyu, wise in the science of gastronomy, never ate and drank at the same time. Instead, they prepared within themselves a solid basis for the floods of liquor which would presently be poured down. At the beginning of the drinking there was a great measure of pomp and etiquette, as was proper enough where libations of ritualistic character were concerned; but, as the celebrants warmed to their work, the proceedings rapidly assumed an exceedingly jovial, and finally, a frankly orgiastic aspect. This sort of thing went on for nine days, at the end of which time all the assembled curacas returned to their own homes well content, carefully preserving the golden cups out of which they had pledged the Inca's health and from which, during the course of the drinking-bout, he had drunk a great or a small amount, according to the degree in which he esteemed the chief who proffered him his cup.

When it chanced that the Intip Raimi came around whilst the Sapa Inca was elsewhere than in his capital, he celebrated the feast wherever he might be, albeit with diminished splendor. The High Priest of the Sun and other Incas of the blood imperial celebrated it fittingly in Cuzco without, however, the presence of the provincial lords who, in these circumstances, went to the seat of their respective *tucuiricuc-cuna* in order to observe the rites of the season. From this we may deduce that the festival of Intip Raimi at Cuzco was most brilliant during those periods of rest which recurred between the campaigns of the Incas.[16]

II. *Chahuar Huarquiz,* about July 22nd to about August 22nd, was the second month in the list officially approved by the Church Council held at Lima in 1582–1583. Oddly enough Father Molina of Cuzco, who was present at the Council, lists the months in a very confused—and confusing—way; whereas Father Calancha, who was not born until two years after the Council, gives the list in the form approved by that congregation after prolonged and careful research into the matter; and finally, Father Acosta, who was the official historian of the Council's proceedings, does not trouble himself even to name all of the months of the Incaic *huata.*[17] It is bibliographical situations such as this that cause writers on early Peru to go prematurely white-haired!

It is clear enough, however, that this month of *Chahuar Huarquiz* was devoted mainly to ploughing and to making the irrigation ditches clean, as well as repairing them wherever necessary. Father Cobo relates a pleasing legend in this connection, telling us that, in the time of Inca Roca, a certain spring called Tocori was giving very little water. The Inca made sacrifices to it, and ended by plunging his arm into the spring. From that time onward its yield was far greater than before, being more than sufficient to irrigate the district. Naturally enough, the spring was ever afterwards regarded as a *huaca,* or holy-thing.[18]

III. *Yapaquiz,* about August 22nd to about September 22nd, was the month of sowing and during it, in order to bring about good crops, a festival was held called *huayara.* On that occasion fifteen brown llamas were sacrificed to each of the *huaca-cuna* in the vicinity of Cuzco, the animals being selected from the flocks of the Sun and from those of the Inca. In this month, also, the farms of the Sun were ploughed with special rites by priests and priestesses of the state cult. A white llama having golden ornaments in its ears accompanied them as they worked, apparently as a guardian or mascot, and a great quantity of maize-beer was sprinkled over the fields to do him honor. When the sowing was completed there was a great sacrifice consisting of the aforesaid white llama, of hundreds of guinea-pigs, much maize, coca, richly colored plumage and many sea-shells, *mullu,* the object being, of course, to propitiate the Air, Water, Ice, and Thunder, in order that they might favor the crops. To make good fortune doubly sure, the priests refrained, during the period between the planting and the sprouting of the maize, from eating anything save herbs without salt and toasted maize-kernels; and they also abstained from chewing coca and from drinking anything save an inferior sort of beer called *cunchu.*[19]

IV. *Coya Raimi,* about September 22nd to about October 22nd, contained an important festival called *Situa* which was closely interwoven with the Moon-cult and was intended, among other things, to ward off sickness and other evils attendant, unless checked, upon the beginning of the annual rains. Previous to. the commencement of the *Situa* was the formality of causing all provincial persons, all individuals suffering from physical defects, and all dogs, to leave the city of Cuzco; the first were sent out because they were not descendants of the Moon; the second because they bore upon them the marks of faults which made them unworthy to observe the festival; and the third because they were apt to bark and howl at awkward moments. Then, at the proper moment, the Sapa Inca, the nobility, and most of the persons left in the city repaired to Coricancha, the Temple of the Sun. At this time the Sapa Inca, the Villac Umu (High Priest of the Sun) and other great ones arranged between them exactly what form the ceremonies should have that year, for they were different in detail from year to year, and at the same time the figure of the Creator, Viracocha, was brought forth from its own temple called Quishuarcancha, and that of Thunder, Chuqui-illapa, was brought from its temple named Puca-marca, both being stationed in the square before Coricancha. During this same period of preparation, a great urn of gold was set up in the centre of the temple square so that, in the sight of all, libations of maize-beer might be solemnly poured into it. Around this urn were stationed four hundred warriors, armed as if for war, a group of one hundred facing toward each one of the cardinal points.

All these preparations having been carried out, the concourse of people waited in silence until the new Moon should make her appearance in the heavens. Thereupon, at a concerted signal, all present burst out into loud cries, shouting: "O sickness, disasters, misfortunes, and perils, go forth from the land." Immediately the cry was taken up in all parts of the city and, at the same moment, each one of the four groups of one hundred warriors began running rapidly in the direction towards which its faces were set, crying the while: "Go forth all evils, go forth all evils." Thus vociferating they sped beyond the bournes of the city and out into the country where the provincial folk were camped; these in turn took up the supplicatory and menacing shout, so that, in a very brief space of time, the chant against the evil foes of mankind spread far from Cuzco in ever-widening circles of clamor under the calm argentine rays of the Andean moon. Meanwhile, the great ones of the realm, gathered in the square before Coricancha, solemnly prayed to the god Viracocha, chanting: "Let evil go forth! Ah, how greatly belovéd of us is this festival! Oh, Creator, permit it to befall that this feast shall take place again next year!"

A little later, in certain rivers which were known to flow into distant regions beyond the sway of the Sapa Inca, the four groups of warriors, each having run its appointed course, could be seen bathing under the moonbeams, laving themselves ceremonially in waters which would carry evils and misfortunes out of the country; and at the same time the whole populace was bathing with proper rites in order to purify themselves for the coming year.

Thereafter a sort of maize-gruel, called *sancu,* was made and, while it was still hot, all householders used it to anoint their faces, their thresholds, and the niches where food was kept. All the fountains of the city were likewise anointed with *sancu,* as were also the mummies of the dead, each one of which was carried to its favorite bathing-place and there washed before being smeared with *sancu*. When these rites had been observed everyone sat down to a mighty feast consisting of all the most delicious food that they knew how to make, followed by a colossal drinking of the best maize-beer; nor, in these restorative pleasures, were the mummies and the innumerable minor idols forgotten. In front of each of them was burnt a generous portion of the richest viands, the idea being, apparently, that in this way the idols and the dead could be bribed into a year's benevolence towards the living.

Dawn was by now approaching, and all the people in Cuzco, carrying with them their idols and their ancestral mummies, both living and dead arrayed in their richest attire, assembled in kindred groups in the great square of the city. A *taqui* or dance, special to this occasion, was performed by dancers wearing long red tunics and, also, diadems of brilliant feathers. They trod the appointed measure to the sound of *antara-cuna*, pan-pipes or syrinxes, whose music was of the kind called *tica-tica*, flowery. In this fashion thanks were given to all the gods from the Creator downwards to the humblest *huaca* or minor deity, and their favor was besought that the coming year might be filled with good fortune. The feasting, followed by drinking that went on all day, was marked by the pouring of libations to the gods into the great golden urn, which had a duct leading to Coricancha, and as the drinking-ceremonies proceeded the Inca pledged the gods, the priests pledged one another, and, in general, everyone drank to the health of everyone else. A charmingly genial jollification it must, indeed, have been.

Towards the close of the festival of *Situa* the provincial folk who had been sent out of the city were invited to come into it again. Assembling, in kindred groups, in the *Cusi-pata*, Joy Terrace, they observed the closing ceremonies of the season. Thirty spotless white llamas, of the type called *cuyllu*, brought thither from every part of the empire, were now sacrificed by means of a fire ritualistically composed of thirty bundles of saffron-scented *quishuar*-wood. The fleece of the animals—which had never been shorn—and their flesh were used in sundry ceremonial manners, all of a propitiatory nature. For one, the blood of the animals was mixed with maize to make *yahuar-sancu,* blood-pudding, which was made up into a vast number of little loaves. These, after being heaped upon huge golden platters, were carried through the throng by Chosen Women of the Sun, every person taking a loaf for himself and for any sick relatives that he or she might have at home. This was done in order that all, high and low, Cuzco folk (both Hanan and Hurin) and provincials, might be bound to the Sun and to the Inca; for it was held that he who, after partaking of *yahuar-sancu,* spoke disrespectfully of the Sun or of the Inca would surely be found out. Loaves of *yahuar-sancu* were likewise sent to every *huaca* great and small throughout the empire, and in order that each of these might receive promptly his portion there were Indians present from each of the shrines who received a portion of the blood-pudding and went with it swiftly to his respective *huaca.*

This sort of thing continued for several days, one day being consecrated to the Creator and to the Sun, another to the Moon and the Earth, and another to visits paid by many *huaca-cuna,* borne in litters by their priests, to the Creator, and to the Sun, to whom they made ritualistic obeisances. In short, it was an intricate, but well-planned, sequence of ceremonies intended to placate the wrath of the gods in general and to ensure their good-will towards men. The *Situa,* naturally enough, was most splendid and elaborate at Cuzco, where the Sapa Inca was, and also the Villac Umu, but it was likewise celebrated, albeit with less magnificence, in every provincial capital, the *tucuiricuc* acting as presiding officer. It is interesting to note, incidentally, that Pachacutec is said to have given this festival its final development.[20]

V. *Uma Raymi,* about October 22nd to about November 22nd, was a relatively quiet month given up to brewing maize-beer, to ensuring a good rainfall by means of tying a black llama of the Sun in the fields of the Sun and not feeding it until, in pity, the god sent rain, and to boring holes in the ears of boys who were soon to be breeched, on which occasion they were also to don the fine raiment that their mothers now began to make for them.

VI. *Ayamarca Raimi,* about November 22nd to about December 22nd, was likewise a quiet month chiefly devoted to preparations for the puberty ceremonials. The youths who were to undergo those ceremonials went to the hill of Huanacauri in order to ask the *huaca* of that name for permission to become fully armed warriors. The youths passed a day and a night on the hill of Huanacauri, during which time each one of them sacrificed a llama to the *huaca* and, afterwards, daubed his face with the blood of the dead animal. This period was spent in fasting, and on the morrow, when the lads returned to the city, every one of them bore a load of straw wherewith to make a seat from which his relatives would be able to watch the impending puberty ceremonies. Having reached their homes again, the lads aided in the making of maize-beer, their strong young jaws bruising and crushing the kernels with eager violence, whilst their elders brought jars for them to expectorate the mass into. Water was fetched, also by the elders, from the spring called Calispuquiu and it was added to the masticated maize in order to make a beer of peculiar potency and ripeness.[21]

VII. *Capac Raimi,* about December 22nd to about January 22nd, was perhaps the most important month in the year; certainly it was so for the youth of the imperial caste, of both sexes. In this month were held the ceremonies which marked the entrance of boys into years of discretion.

The *huarachicu* or breeching-ceremony is frequently called by both ancient and modern writers a "knighthood" ceremony. As a matter of fact, it was merely a celebration of the arrival at puberty of the lads belonging to the imperial caste; nevertheless, if one bears in mind that the rite of arming a youth as a knight, in mediæval Europe, was also, in a sense, a puberty ceremony, the term is not, after all, a misnomer, for it ushered the young males of the ruling caste into manhood and into the privileges and the responsibilities appertaining thereto.

Quite frankly the rites of the *huarachicu* were in the nature of an ordeal which had for its purpose the testing of the virility, the endurance, the strength, and the discipline of the youths whom it concerned. Introductory to the ceremony proper was a course of instruction in the arts of war, particularly in the making and management of weapons and in the manufacture of *usuta-cuna*, sandals, and other equipment. This course, given by certain elderly Incas of wide martial experience, had for its lecture-room the charming terrace in front of the Collcampata palace, whence an inspiring view of the city of Cuzco is to be enjoyed and where there is ample space for drills and exercises of all kinds. Just overhead rise the southern walls, of Incaic construction, of the Sacsahuamán fortress, the Bastile of the Incas. It is a place redolent of martial tradition and, in our day, it is wrapt in a wistfulness shot through with grievous memories of that tradition's tragic vanquishment.

The instruction and the examination of the candidates having been concluded, the lads fasted for six days, during which period they partook of no nourishment save raw maize and water. The fast ended, however, they were generously fed, and we may safely suppose that they pounced upon their dinners with a right good will. Thereafter—but, let us hope, with an interval for digestion—a race was run from the hill of Huanacauri to the plain on the northern side of Sacsahuamán. Huanacauri, it will be remembered, was closely associated with the march of the first Incas into the Cuzco Valley; the hill is one of the peaks on the southern rim of the valley, and, in Incaic times, it was one of the most sacred of the *huaca-cuna* worshipped by the imperial caste. Because Huanacauri was the place where one of Manco Capac's brothers—some say Ayar Uchu and others Ayar Cache—was turned into stone, on which occasion he specially bade his surviving brethren to remember him at the time when the *huarachicu* was held, this hill, some four to five miles from Sacsahuamán, became peculiarly linked with the puberty ceremonies. Upon it were placed various animals—a falcon, a vicuña, a fox, a humming-

bird, a vulture, an ostrich,[22] a serpent, a toad—which seem to
have been regarded as in some way aiding or protecting the
contestants in the race; or, they may have been merely totemic or heraldic emblems.

Starting from Huanacauri and running swiftly through the
sharp, cold air of the highlands, the eager youths sped across
the Valley in a northerly direction, finally reaching the above-
mentioned plain below the northern walls of the fortress. As
they approached, their popping eyes were cheered by the sight
of the Inca and his court sitting upon the seats carved in the
living rock to their right as they ran, sitting there in readiness
to distribute praise and dispraise among the contestants. The
boy who won the race was made captain over all the rest, and
the second, third, and fourth, down to the tenth, were greatly
commended for their strength and swiftness, and all others
who were deemed to have done creditably were given propor-
tionate praise. But the lot of the sluggards who came in
tardily, and still more that of those weaklings who did not
come in at all, was scorn and derision, and the unpleasant
obligation of wearing a shameful breech-clout of black cloth
instead of the triumphant white breech-clout trimmed with
camantira, gay feathers, which those who had done well were
now allowed to don.

The next phase of the ordeal seems to have been made up of
sham battles. The successful candidates were divided into
two "armies," one of which held and the other attacked the fortress of Sacsahuamán. The next day the rôles were exchanged.
All this was a part of the military training which was an important element in the puberty ceremonies, and it was all in
the nature of a preliminary to the *huarachicu* proper, such
further tests of endurance as exercises, floggings, and dances
also being included in the programme.

Finally, the day of the ceremony itself arrived. The Sapa
Inca emphasized its political and military importance by taking a leading part in the rites of the day. The culminating
moment was that in which the lads' ear-lobes were ceremonially pierced (the actual piercing having been done two

months before, as stated above), by the Inca in person, using certain golden pins which were left in the holes to keep them open. Into these holes ear-studs were presently fitted which were frequently exchanged for larger ones until, by the time the boys were adult men, their ear-lobes had become greatly enlarged because of the weight of the studs in them. From this situation arose the term *orejón,* big-ear, by which the Spaniards were wont, after the Conquest, to designate members of the imperial caste. When the rite of piercing was concluded, each novice passed on to other Incas who dressed him in breech-clout, sandals, and gave him weapons. The general austerity of the rites was pleasantly broken by the graceful act of garlanding the youths with *cantut* flowers, which are shaped like lilies and are colored yellow, purple and red, and with *chihuayhua* blooms, similar to yellow carnations, both of these flowers being reserved to the use of the imperial caste; and, upon their brows, the lads wore wreaths of a plant called *uñay huayna,* which means ever young.

All the ceremonies having been felicitously concluded, and, on this occasion, with no relapse into that orgiastic bibulosity to which the Incas were so prone, the young "knights" went to bathe in the spring called Calispuquiu, which is the source of the Huatanay River, behind Sacsahuamán. After that, they repaired to the Huaca Pata, where each lad was greeted by his nearest kinsman and from him received a shield, a club, a javelin, and a sling. From that moment the lad was a man at the service of his sovereign lord.[23]

It is eloquent of the rigor of Incaic discipline and of the starkness of that unparalleled dynasty's morale that, when the heir to the sovereignty was among the novices, he, far from receiving the snobbishly softened treatment with which a European prince in like case would have been flattered, was subjected to much greater severity than were his companions. The idea was that, as his responsibilities would be far greater than theirs, so must his strength be, and the trials were calculated so as to reveal whether or not his strength was great enough to meet the demands upon it. In this concept, and also in the years of practical military experience on campaign through which the heir always passed during his father's lifetime, we see the underlying cause of the almost unvarying excellence of the Inca rulers.

VIII. *Camay,* about January 22nd to about February 22nd, was a month during which there were held in the Huaca Pata various military exhibitions and exercises participated in by the newly armed warriors, both those of Hanan Cuzco and those of Hurin Cuzco, as a means of finding out which ones among the young men had the greatest bodily strength. These exercises included sham fights with slings, the missiles being fruit, and also hand-to-hand combat, probably in the nature of wrestling, the purpose of which was to test the power of the contestants' arm muscles. During these proceedings the costumes worn consisted of black tunics under tawny-colored mantles and of head-gear made from the fair white plumes of the *ttucu,* a kind of owl. The new "knights" passed through this phase of their experience fasting, which, perhaps, made them all the more active in the ritualistic sports of the season. After a suitable period had been devoted to these things, the Sapa Inca, always an interested spectator, rose from his *tiana* (throne) and made a gesture that stilled the tumult. Immediately thereafter the hungry young warriors were cheered by a copious meal.

Certain of the other rites with which this month was filled demand at any rate brief mention here because of their quaintness and significance. On the day of the new moon a great number of old llamas from all of the four *suyu-cuna* or quarters of the realm were assembled in the Huaca Pata and, with much solemnity, their ears were pierced by persons appointed thereto; thereafter, the animals were known by the title of *apu-rucu,* meaning "chief who is old." The significance of this curious rite is a point that demands close study.

Again, on the day of the full moon, being the fifteenth of the month, there came into the great square a vast multitude of people before whom ten llamas of all colors were sacrificed in order to ensure the health of the Inca, after which everyone joined in a dance called *yahuayra* that was performed in all of the streets of the city throughout the night and terminated, at dawn, in the square, where a sacrificial burning took place of ten costumes of the finest red-and-white cloth, two being offered up to each of the major gods: Viracocha, the Sun, the Moon, Thunder, and Earth. At once thereafter two white baby-llamas were sacrificed for the health of the public in general.

As the morning of this, the sixteenth day of the month of Camay, advanced, the priests brought forth the images of the major and minor gods, and likewise were brought forth the mummies of the illustrious dead, all of which were duly arranged in their appointed places in the square. At the same time a very long, thick cable, braided from wool colored black, white, red, and yellow, was likewise taken to the square from its abiding-place near Coricancha. This cable was a ceremonial object of most unusual character. In Quechua it was called variously *huascar,* meaning simply cable or rope, and *muru-urcu,* which means spotted male. It was used in the following fashion: Men lined up along one side of the *huascar* and women on the other, both sexes grasping it all along its great length in such a way that a long, serpentine group of people was formed with the brightly colored rope running down the middle, its forward end being a large ball of red wool like a head. In this quaint formation the group solemnly marched around the edges of the square, partly, no doubt, to get the *muru-urcu* stretched out at full length. As they passed in front of the idols and of the Inca, the dancers made low obeisances, which must have imparted an interesting undulation to the group as it moved along. Then, having surrounded the square, the dancers gradually began to form a coil, slowly drawing in the convolutions as closely as possible. When this process was completed, they dropped the *huascar* upon the ground and went away from it, leaving it all curled up on the pavement like a monstrous serpent. Of all the rites of the Incas this dance of the cable must surely have been one of the most charming. The famous "golden chain" which was

made, toward the end of the Incaic period, to celebrate the
birth of the ruler known as Huascar, was merely a rope such
as that here described but one adorned most lavishly with
strands and ornaments of gold.[24]

IX. *Hatun-Pucuy,* about February 22nd to about March
22nd, was a quiet month during which the rains were at their
height and the crops were ripening. There were very few rites
in this month.

X. *Pacha-Pucuy,* or *Paucar-Huara,* about March 22nd to
about April 22nd, contained the *mosoc-nina,* new fire, festival,
the meaning of which, and its relation to the new fire of the
Intip Raimi, are obscure.

XI. *Ayrihua,* about April 22nd to about May 22nd, was a
month devoted to harvesting and, fittingly enough, it contained more of hard work than it did of festivity. Nevertheless, there was held in this month the *quicuchicu,* the puberty-
ceremony for girls, with rites and instruction no less suitable
to them than were those of the *huarachicu* for boys.[25]

XII. *Hatun Cuzqui,* about May 22nd to about June 22nd,
closed the year with the festival of *Aymoray* in celebration
of the bringing in of the harvest. In this month five *apu-rucu*
llamas were among the animals sacrificed, their flesh being
eaten raw in small quantities, but for what purpose is not
clear.

Less obscure is the rite of harvesting the maize at Sauasera,
near the modern San Sebastián, south of Cuzco. At that place
was the *chácara* or farm of the Sun. On the first day of the
ritualistic—as well as actual—harvesting at Sauasera, the
warriors who had been armed that year, arrayed in their best
apparel, brought into Cuzco a part of the crop, using large
bags for the purpose, and as they came along the road they
sang joyfully many a *yaraví* or lyric. On the following days
all the great folk of Cuzco went out to Sauasera in order to
bring in the rest of the Sun's crop and, when it had been
wholly garnered, the ground was immediately ploughed anew
by the highest dignitaries of the empire.

Finally, and also in this month, the people observed a

quaint rite in honor of *Mama-Sara,* Mother Maize, of whom all families were devotees. Every householder took a small amount of maize and, wrapping it up in the richest cloth he had, placed it in a little hole called *pirua* in the soil of his *chácara* or farm. That hole then became the maize-mother for the farm, and it continued to be venerated until the wizards, who were consulted annually, announced that its efficacy was worn out. After that a new *Mama-Sara* had to be prepared in the same way.[26]

Such was the *huata* or Incaic year, described succinctly on a basis of very confused evidence and, necessarily, with many details omitted for the sake of avoiding what the Chroniclers called "prolixity." Enough has been said, I hope, to give a general idea of the *huata,* and to show that, when its multitude of rites, each one of them surrounded by an esoteric etiquette of extreme intricacy, is considered as a whole, it stands forth to the mind of one looking back upon it as an epic of old will do, if sympathetically regarded. Indeed, it *was* an epic, an epic of worship in which homage, propitiation, and praise were nicely blended. Not one of those elements that made for the greatness and increase of the empire failed to be duly honored at some time or other in the course of the year. Truth to tell, one receives the impression that there was something important, exciting, or amusing going on at least half of the time, and he wonders how, amid such a maze of ritualistic observances, the average *puric* household ever did any serious and sustained manual labor. The answer is, of course, that a considerable proportion of the rites were participated in only by the upper classes. Moreover, certain times of the year—solstices and equinoxes—were more crowded with ceremonial events than were the periods between them; and this, too, gave some relief to the nervous tension of all concerned.

The astronomical knowledge of the Incas, and of still earlier Peruvians, now demands our attention because on it was based not only the *huata* and its divisions, but also, in large part, the state religion. It is impossible to claim for the Incas or for their predecessors anything even remotely approaching in intellectual dignity the hieroglyphic and calendar systems formerly existing in Yucatan and in Mexico. Nevertheless, they did possess mathematical, astronomical and calendrical knowledge of a rudimentary sort that is not without interest.

At Cuzco, according to Garcilaso, the positions of the sun and of the moon were studied with solicitous attention, and in order to measure the movements of the sun there were erected two sets of eight towers, one set being on the hills west of Cuzco, the other on the eastern rim of the Cuzco basin. In each set the eight towers were so arranged that they formed a quadrangular group with the four tall towers at the corners and the short ones between them, thus:

$$O \quad o \quad o \quad O$$

$$O \quad o \quad o \quad O$$

The high towers, probably thirty feet or more in height (for Garcilaso remarks that they were much higher than the watch-towers so common in Spain), appear to have been used as observatories, but in just what manner is somewhat obscure. At any rate we know that, whether the towers were pierced by holes near the top through which the sun shone, or whether the sun was sighted between the towers in some way, or whether the shadows cast by the sun upon the pavement surrounding the towers were the determining factors, these observatories enabled the Incas to fix with accuracy the time at which the solstices came around. The equinoxes, however, were determined by means of another device, consisting of a single pillar or gnomon erected in the centre of a circle across which a diametrical line was drawn or carved in such a way that, at the equinoxes, the shadow of the pillar lay along that line all day.

The tower-observatories were called *sucanca*, meaning "that which is about to be furrowed," a fanciful reference, as

Markham pointed out, to the alternating play of light and shadow upon the ground as the sun shone between the towers. The gnomon device was called *inti-huatana*, "place where the sun is tied." The most important of the *inti-huatana-cuna* was, no doubt, that in front of Coricancha; but there are excellent examples of the contrivance at Pisac, at Amancay (modern Abancay), at Ollantaytampu, and at Machu Picchu.[27] See Figures 166 and 167.

By means of these two devices, the one for observing the solstices and the other for the equinoxes, the Incas were able to achieve an accuracy of knowledge concerning the formation of the solar year. That accuracy was heightened, and an adjustment with the lunar year was arrived at, by means of inserting six extra days now and then through the year, and of having a group of five such days—called *allcancanqui*, "you are missing"—at the end of the year.

It is probable that the Incas had no other aids to calendrical calculation than these; but there is some reason for thinking that the Tiahuanaco II people had a device which, although crude as compared with the Aztec calendar-stone, was more nearly a true calendar than anything else of which we know in early Peru. I refer to a certain gold plaque which was seen and closely studied by Markham, in Lima, in 1853, and afterwards discussed by Bollaert at a meeting of the Society of Antiquaries, in London, in 1860. This plaque—generally known as the Echenique plaque, its original owner having been General J. R. Echenique—was lost to the sight of scientists in England and America for many years. It was reposing safely, however, in the possession of Dr. Gaffron, the celebrated German collector of Peruvian antiquities, and from him, in 1912, Mr. George Heye bought it for the Museum of the American Indian, in New York City.

Various beliefs have been held concerning the significance of the Echenique plaque. Markham and Bollaert both considered it to be a calendar. Mr. Saville is non-committal as to the purpose of the artifact and studies it objectively, concluding that it is Tiahuanaco in style, not Incaic. Dr. Tello ascribes to it a mystical and cosmogonic significance.[28] In spite of the differences in their views, the theories of Saville and of Tello with regard to the plaque are worth examining with some care. See Figure 164.

Mr. Saville distinguished upon the rim of the plaque twenty small decorated areas whose designs, however, were not all different from one another. As an aid to identification he, after careful study, supplied each individual design with a letter. It then became clear that:

A appears twice;
B appears four times;
C appears twice;
D appears twice;
E appears four times;
F appears twice;
G appears twice;
H appears twice.

Adhering, for the moment, to Mr. Saville's lettering, I would point out that both the central face and the designs around it are exquisitely symmetrical in design. The two figures marked A come opposite to one another. Reading clockwise from the upper A we find that the figures follow in a certain sequence which is precisely repeated if one reads clockwise from the lower A. The nicety of this symmetry becomes still more apparent when we examine Tello's lettering which differs from that of Saville. Dr. Tello sees but four signs, each of which occurs twice, always at opposite sides of the disc, and always in rhythmical and symmetrical succession. Thus it works out that:

Tello's A is made up of the G and H figures of Saville;
Tello's B is made up of the C and D figures of Saville;
Tello's C is made up of the E, A, and B figures of Saville;
Tello's D is made up of the E, F, and B figures of Saville.

A fact, possibly of great hidden importance, leaps into sight when the Saville and Tello arrangements are compared; for it is clear that Tello's figures C and D both contain the designs which Saville labels E and B, and it is precisely these designs

FIG. 164.   The Echenique plaque.
After Saville.

which occur *four* times instead of *twice* as all the other designs do.

These objective facts are to us incomprehensible as yet. Nevertheless, I shall not be surprised if, at some future time, it is conclusively proven that the plaque refers to solstices and equinoxes rather than to months. At a guess, I would say that Tello's A and B figures refer to those recurrent phenomena, and that his C and D figures have some lunar significance. But this is frankly a guess.

As for the age of the relic, it is agreed by all who have discussed it that it is of the Tiahuanaco period, not the Incaic. Obviously there is a resemblance between the central face of the disc and that of the Weeping God on the monolithic gateway at Tiahuanaco. Dr. Tello, with less than his usual perspicacity, describes the face as feline. Why, I do not know, unless its dentition has recalled to his mind Tenniel's portrait of the Cheshire Cat.

Seriously, however, the belief that the Echenique plaque is a Tiahuanaco-period calendar receives support of a sort from Montesinos, who avers that various early highland kings made reforms in the calendar, among them Capac Raymi Amauta, with whom, but rather obscurely, Montesinos connects the use of the *sucanca* type of shadow-clock. According to my calculations the calendar reforms of Capac Raymi Amauta and those of his predecessor of two generations earlier fell in the sixth century of our era, or, in other words, just prior to the full florescence of the Tiahuanaco II period. Montesinos adds that the month, Capac Raymi, took its name from the reformer-king.[29]

Such were the instruments whereby the Incas and the Tiahuanaco folk gained knowledge of the heavenly bodies. Nor, as we shall see as this chapter progresses, was their knowledge confined to the sun and the moon. It is but natural that these luminaries should appear like gods to a relatively simpleminded people and that, around their supposed personalities, an intricate and by no means despicable cult should have been built up.

It is this aspect of the population of the sky that we must now examine. The state religion of the Inca empire, linked with the destinies and the administration of that empire in the most invariable intimacy, was worship of the Sun, greatest and brightest Being visible to man. The name given to the Sun, as a god, was, in Incaic times, *Inti* or *Ynti*, a term whose history, although it is obscure, merits consideration. According to Captain Sarmiento de Gamboa, Manco Capac and all the Incas down to Inca Pachacutec Yupanqui had a *huauqui,* brother or familiar spirit, in the form of a bird called *Indi* or *Inti* who was a falcon.[30] Flying high into the firmament, after the manner of his kind, Inti the falcon-brother of the Incas managed to confuse his identity with that of the Sun whose realm he seemed to invade, with the result that his name became transferred to the Sun which, regarded merely as a giver of light, was called *Punchau*, a term that also signifies day. The sister-spouse of *Inti*, the Sun, *Mama Quilla*, Mother Moon, also styled *Pacsa Mama*, Resplendent Mother, was much revered in her capacity of wife to Inti, but the degree of divinity ascribed to her is variously—and very confusingly—reported by the Chroniclers. Dr. Lehmann-Nitsche, in his extremely important recent work, *Coricancha*, defines three distinct views of the matter: 1. The Sun is regarded as a man and the Moon as a woman, without any kinship existing between them. The Sun is the god peculiar to men; the women, in like fashion, adore the Moon. 2. The Sun is held to be the husband of the Moon, and the stars were thought to be the children of both of them. 3. The Sun and the Moon, children of the Creator, are regarded as being incestuously married. The Moon, in addition to being Queen of the Sky, was goddess of the sea and of the winds, of queens and princesses, and of childbirth.[32]

Opposed to these views is that of Garcilaso, who states that, although her shrine was adjacent to that of the Sun, and although she was considered to be "the sister and wife of the Sun, and mother of the Incas," the Moon, *Mama Quilla*, received no sacrifices, albeit the custom of entering her shrine in order to commend themselves to her was observed by all visitors to Coricancha.[31] Father Cobo has still another version of the matter, for he avers that, although the Moon was the wife of the Sun, she was less divine than Thunder, who occupied second place in the Incaic pantheon.[33]

The confusion regarding these points can best be mitigated by studying the plan, content, and significance of *Coricancha*, the Golden Enclosure, otherwise the Temple of the Sun. It so happened that, when the Spaniards took possession of

Cuzco, in November, 1533, joyously dividing up among themselves the property of the imperial family, the Temple of the Sun fell to the lot of Don Juan Pizarro, brother of the Conqueror. He, presumably in return for spiritual favors, gave it to the Dominicans, and it has been the Monastery of Santo Domingo ever since. Between 1534, when the donation was made, and 1541, the friars made many modifications in the structure, doing so largely under the direction of Bishop Don Vicente de Valverde, the ecclesiastical ruffian who was so largely responsible for the death of Atahualpa and who, in 1541, was so condignly punished, while journeying towards Spain, by being murdered by the Indians near the Island of Puná, in the Gulf of Guayaquil. As time went on, further changes were made in order that the house of pagan idols might better serve as a house of Christian idols. The result is that, although certain very interesting vestiges of the Temple remain to delight the beholder, the great building as a whole has forever lost its original plan and character, as Figure 155 makes all too evident. Nevertheless, three modern writers, von Tschudi, Squier, and, most recent and most thorough of all, Dr. Lehmann-Nitsche, have, on the basis of the existing remains and of the basis afforded by Chroniclers who saw the Temple while it was still relatively intact, been able to give us a fairly complete picture of Coricancha as it must have been in the days of its grandeur.[34] Upon their accounts, and upon those of the Chroniclers whom they cite, are based my own remarks concerning this amazing structure.

Temples of the Sun were important foundations in all parts of the empire, for an invariable policy prevailed of introducing Sun-worship wherever Inca power penetrated. Naturally enough, the Temple of the Sun at Cuzco was the greatest of the fanes of the official cult. That Temple was, in effect, the holiest spot in a city altogether holy. The idea of the sacredness of Cuzco was carried to such a length that if two Indians of equal rank met on the road, one coming from Cuzco and the other going towards it, the first was regarded as the more sanctified and so took precedence. As Garcilaso puts it,

"Whatever came from Cuzco, although not in reality superior, was preferred solely for that reason. Being thus held in such veneration, these kings ennobled the capital to the utmost of

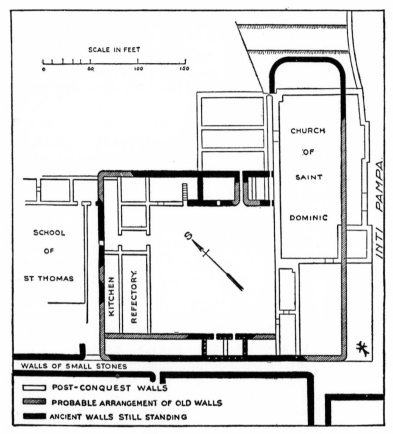

SCALE IN FEET

SCHOOL
OF
ST. THOMAS

KITCHEN

REFECTORY.

CHURCH
OF
SAINT
DOMINIC

INTI PAMPA.

WALLS OF SMALL STONES

☐ POST-CONQUEST WALLS
▨ PROBABLE ARRANGEMENT OF OLD WALLS
■ ANCIENT WALLS STILL STANDING

FIG. 165. Plan of Coricancha and of the monastery of St. Dominic.
After Squier and Lehmann-Nitsche.

their power, with sumptuous edifices and royal palaces. . . ."[35]
This being so, it was logical that Coricancha should be, as it emphatically was, the finest and most splendid of the buildings erected by the Incas. It had existed from the earliest reigns, being in those days, no doubt, a relatively rude and cramped adoratory attached to the residence of the sovereigns,

but the great emperor Pachacutec Yupanqui brought it to
that high state of magnificence in which the Spaniards found
it.[35] Traces of different styles of masonry—to which reference will be made in Chapter XII—are to be found in the
existing ancient walls, and it is a reasonable assumption that
they represent as many different periods in the history of the
edifice. A study of Figures 155, 165 and 168 will here be of
help to the reader.

According to Captain Cieza de León, who probably knew it
well, the Temple was more than 400 paces—say 1,200 feet—
in circuit, which figure accords well with Squier's measurements made while he lived in the Monastery of Santo Domingo.[36] From the outside world there was but one entrance,
and that led from the *Intip-Pampa,* Square of the Sun, directly into the main sanctuary. This last was an immense
room, some 296 feet long by 52 feet wide, and, like the rest
of the edifice, it was built of the finest masonry, having at its
westerly end a beautifully made elliptical apse which, happily,
still exists in part. The gabled roof, constructed of carefully
woven thatch always maintained in good condition, had an
inner shell of wood, finely wrought and embellished with very
thin sheets of beaten gold. Similar sheets were attached to a
large part of the masonry walls, also, being kept in place by
wooden pegs or by stout thorns, sockets for which appear in
the stones of several parts of the edifice.[37]

At the eastern end was the high altar, with its adjuncts, of
which the Indian Chronicler, Santa Cruz Pachacuti-yamqui
Salcamayhua, has left us a deeply interesting graphic representation. His picture, or rather diagram, has had a quaint
history which it is well to mention here. Made in the first
twenty years of the seventeenth century, probably with the collaboration of the missionary, Father Francisco de Ávila, among
whose papers the manuscript was found, the diagram remained unknown until, in 1873, it was published by Markham,
and, in 1879, by Jiménez de la Espada in their respective publications of Santa Cruz's work. From that time onwards the diagram has been assumed to be of an esoteric and astrological na-

Fig. 166. A general view of the upper ward of Pisac.
Photograph by courtesy of W. V. Alford, Esq.

Fig. 167. The Intihuatana, Pisac.
Photograph by Max Vargas, Arequipa.

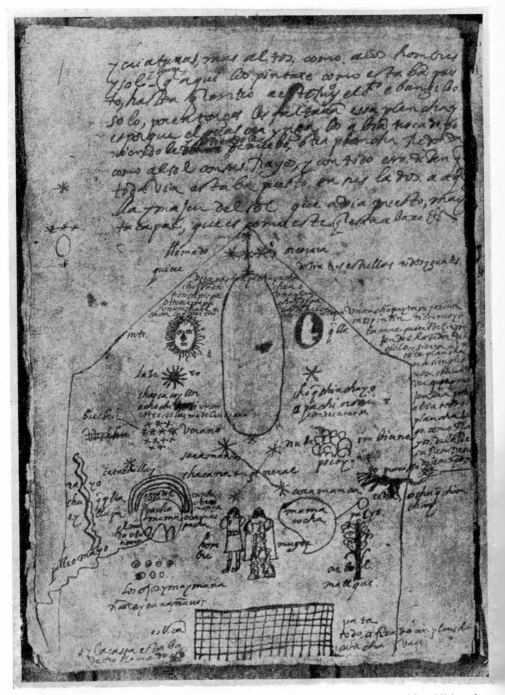

FIG. 168. Diagram of the High Altar in Coricancha, drawn by Santa Cruz, with additions by Father Ávila. *After Lehmann-Nitsche.*

ture, with the result that an amazing amount of balderdash has been written about it by ignorant and impetuous persons and even by well-informed persons who ought to have known better. It remained for Dr. Lehmann-Nitsche to put us forever in his debt by revealing the simple but hitherto unsuspected fact that the drawing is merely a rough representation of the altar and the objects around it as they stood in the sanctuary of the Sun.

It is a difficult matter to deal clearly and briefly with this group of objects graphically represented for us by the Indian Chronicler, Santa Cruz, and accompanied by legend in the writing of Father de Ávila, difficult not only because of the historical points involved, but also because of the intricacy of the ideas anciently attaching to the objects themselves. See Figure 168.

The oval figure in the middle of the wall and near its apex will serve the discussion as a point of departure. In the Santa Cruz *cum* Ávila diagram it is labelled Viracocha, but that is a fact that requires explanation. There were three distinct gold plates in this place at different times: the first, nearly circular, is said to have been set up by Manco Capac at the time when Coricancha was founded; the second, oval in shape, was set up by Inca Mayta Capac—this being the one which appears in the diagram; the third, circular, set up by Huáscar at the beginning of his ill-fated reign.[38] The latest of the three plates had a curious history, for, at the time when Huáscar was at war with his half-brother, Atahualpa, a few years after the death of their father, Inca Huayna Capac, he, Huáscar, sent the great circular image northwards, in the care of his general, Atoc. Father Cabello de Balboa relates the matter thus: "When Atoc (Captain General of Guascar) set forth from Cuzco, he took with him the statue of the Sun, thinking to persuade Atahuallpa, by means of its presence, promptly to surrender himself as a prisoner."[39] Later, after the Spaniards had entered the country, the image fell into the hands of the rebel, Inca Manco, who carried it off with him to his refuge-capital in Vilcapampa. In this way it came into the hands of the Inca Tupac Amaru I, who, unfortunately, was captured in 1572 by a near kinsman of Saint Ignatius of Lóyola. Although the great Viceroy, Don Francisco de Toledo, with that sub-acid humor that sometimes characterized him, suggested that the image, source and inspiration of all the pagan idolatry, be presented to His Holiness, the Spaniards contented themselves with merely melting it up for its bullion worth, which was undoubtedly very great.

Returning now to the image shown in the Santa Cruz diagram, that is, to the second image in the series of three, to the image which was in Coricancha during all the best days of the Inca empire, we may note that Dr. Lehmann-Nitsche makes it very clear that the oval disc, although labelled Viracocha, represented a confusion of the Creator-god's personality with that of the Sun-god, Inti, rather than the more philosophic aspect of Viracocha's personality. To Viracocha, the Creator, there had been erected in the Huaca-Pata, on land now partly occupied by the Cathedral, a great temple known as Quishuarcancha,[40] to which I shall refer more at length further on. Between the cult of the material god, the Sun, and that of the abstract Creator-god, Viracocha, there was a prolonged struggle represented by various religious ideas which surged to the surface at one time or another, and which sometimes came close to the concept, prevalent in the classical world of ancient times, of the cosmic egg, source of all things.[41]

To summarize the significance of the oval disc shown by Santa Cruz, we may say, then, that it represented the solar aspect of Viracocha. Quite logically, therefore, it had on its right and on its left (in the heraldic sense of the words) representations of Inti the Sun and of Mama Quilla the Moon.

Here another historical digression becomes necessary. One of the most picturesque anecdotes of early Spanish days is the tale which relates how a conqueror, Don Mancio Sierra de Leguízamo, who, in the sack of Coricancha, had possessed himself of "a figure (i. e., face) of the Sun, made of gold, which the Ingas had placed in the house of the Sun, in Cuzko" staked the image in a card-game and lost it in a wild night of play.[42] It has always been assumed that Sierra's image was the great figure of the Sun, but, as related above, Dr. Lehmann-Nitsche has made it plain that that image was not in Cuzco when the Spaniards took the city. He goes on to show that Sierra's image was not even the smaller disc of the Sun, but was merely the golden cover of a large stone vessel which, standing in the cloister of the temple, was used as a receptacle for libations of maize-beer wherewith the Sun was honored.[43]

Having said all that seems necessary regarding the great central disc in the Santa Cruz diagram, I shall now briefly comment upon the other images of the altar, following closely in the footsteps of Dr. Lehmann-Nitsche, whose arrangement does not admit of any improvement in the presentation of the material. See Figure 168.

Above the central disc, then, is seen a cruciform group of five stars labelled *orcorara,* a corruption of the Colla (or Aimará) word *urcorara,* also used in Quechua, meaning band of men or of male animals. Three of the stars are linked vertically by lines, and these stars are identified by Dr. Lehmann-Nitsche as being the baldric of Orion. The Spaniards call them *Las Tres Marías.* To the right of them (in heraldic sense) is shown the star Rigel, and on the left is Betelgeuze, the five stars representing a train of three male llamas with a herder on either side, in which we see that the ancients of the Andes had a far more active and accurate imagery in such matters than did the ancients of Greece.[44]

Immediately below the great central disc we see a group of five stars which is labelled *chacana en general.* Although, as Dr. Lehmann-Nitsche points out, dictionaries ancient and modern translate this term, *chacana,* as meaning ladder, and also as meaning a litter in which to carry the dead, it also means a cross. The upper right-hand star (in heraldic sense) and the lower left-hand star are labelled, respectively, *sara-manca* and *coca-manca.* There two compound words offer no difficulties, *sara* meaning maize, *coca—cuca* would be more correct—being self-evident, and *manca* meaning pot. Dr. Lehmann-Nitsche presents convincing evidence that the cross in this group is the Southern Cross and that, to the Indian mind, it represented a hearth, with a pot full of maize and a pot full of *coca* beside it.[45]

Below the Southern Cross and just above the altar proper are drawn a man and a woman, clearly labelled *hombre* and *muger*. Their costumes, although very crudely represented, are in accordance with what we know of Incaic costume. Dr. Lehmann-Nitsche thinks that these figures represent finely wrought statues of gold and that they stand for Manco Capac and Mama Ocllo.[46]

The remaining figures on the diagram go in pairs, which Dr. Lehmann-Nitsche studies in order, beginning at the top. On either side of the great central disc we see two minor discs, the one having a human face engraved upon it and rays issuing from it, the other showing, rather crudely, a human profile. These are clearly labelled *inti* and *quilla*, sun and moon, respectively. Below them come a second pair of figures, the one a stout star with many rays, the other a thin star with few rays. Of these the first is labelled *luzero*, a Spanish word meaning morning star, and also *chasca coyllur*, a Quechua phrase meaning the long-haired star. A third label attaching to this figure is *achachi ururi*, a Colla phrase meaning the grandfather who rises early, and to it is appended, probably in Father de Ávila's writing, *este es el luzero de la mañana,* this is the morning star. In like manner, the star on the other side is labelled in Quechua, Colla, and Spanish, as follows, respectively, *choquechinchay* meaning that which makes gold stand forth, *apachi ocori* meaning the old woman who eats with a full mouth, *este de la tarde* meaning this [star] of the evening. In this pair of figures, therefore, we do not have, as in the preceding pair, *two* heavenly bodies, but two aspects of *one,* namely, Venus as the morning star and Venus as the evening star.[47]

In similar fashion are rendered two aspects of the constellation which we of European tradition call the Pleiades, the first being the summer aspect, represented by thirteen small stars (the correct number would be seven), which Santa Cruz labelled *Vvchhu,* a word that Father de Ávila scratched out, placing *Sucsu* instead. *Vvchhu,* or, more correctly, *uuchhu* or *ussu,* is a Colla word meaning sickness in general, while *sucsu,* from the verb *sucsuni,* is the Quechua term for the same idea. The summer aspect of the Pleiades, therefore, was associated with sickness, both in Colla and in Quechua. The winter aspect of the same thirteen stars is cleverly represented for each of them is neatly wrapped up in a cloud, Santa Cruz having labelled it *nube,* cloud, to which Ávila added *niebla,* mist. In Santa Cruz's hand also is the Quechua word *pocoy,* meaning autumn, or time of ripening.[48]

The next pair of figures in order is represented by only one of its members, Santa Cruz and Ávila having forgotten, apparently, to complete the pair. That which does appear is a star called *catachillay* meaning wild female llama. According to Father Cobo she should be accompanied by a baby llama, *uñachillay* and by *urcuchillay,* the wild male llama; but only the mother appears in the Santa Cruz *cum* Avila diagram.[49] Of these groups of stars, and of the Pleiades, it may be said that they were honored by being represented at the altar because it was held that they could aid mankind to preserve good health, to have good crops, and to possess prosperous herds.

At the outer edges of the end wall, and about half-way up to the roof, were two figures of great interest. One, shown by two zig-zag, or rather, wavy lines, is labelled *rayo,* Spanish for thunderbolt, *chuqueylla,* Quechua for splendor of gold, and *yllapa,* Quechua for that which shines repeatedly. Dr. Lehmann-Nitsche presents excellent evidence for believing that, by representing the thunderbolt by zig-zag lines, Santa Cruz was following European rather than South American ideation. It would have been much more in accordance with native notions if he had shown the constellation *Haucha,* the furious man, who, armed with a club and a sling, was the god of storms, and master of the thunderbolt, which he hurled with his sling, the lightning being caused by the flash of his glittering apparel as he turned. Thunder and lightning were closely associated with rain and hail, which were held to proceed from a heavenly river which is what we call the Milky Way.[50] Balancing this indication of thunder is a very curious figure in the form of a feline animal, a puma or an ounce, which had something to do with hail, *granisso* on the diagram, the animal itself being marked *cosu,* a Colla term meaning the flashing, and *chuque chinchay,* Quechua for an idea of the same sort and also for an animal of the ounce kind. This animal was thought to have charge of the hail and also to be in the habit of trying to devour the sun and the moon, thereby causing eclipses of those bodies.[51]

Inwards from the pair of figures just treated of is another pair, also of great interest. The first member of it is a sort of panorama of the earth, shown as a circle with three mountain-peaks in it from between two of which a river flows far away, whilst over the whole arches the rainbow, shown as four parallel lines. This rather intricate figure is labelled in Quechua and in Spanish, the earth being called *el mundo o la tierra,* the world or the earth, and *pacha mama* or *camac pacha,* which mean, respectively, earth-mother and creator-earth; the rainbow is called *arco del cielo* and, in Quechua, *cuyichi* (properly *cuychi*) and *turo manya* (properly *turumaya*), both of which mean rainbow. Finally, the river is called *pillcomayo* (properly *pillcumayu*), which means red river.

Dr. Lehmann-Nitsche finds some difficulty in believing that the Pillcomayu referred to on the Santa Cruz *cum* Ávila diagram is the mighty river of that name which, rising in central Bolivia, merges its waters with those of the Paraguay. Nor does he accept the idea that it is the Río Bermejo (Vermilion River) somewhat to the south of the other and running parallel with it. On the other hand he does believe that it may be the Río Colorado (Red River) which flows into the Lagoon of Uinamarca (the southern lobe of Lake Titicaca). He adds, however, a reference to another Pillcomayu, which, rising in the Lake of Pumpu (modern Bombón or Junín), flows into the Huallaga,[52] but I can find no account of that river other than the very brief one cited by Dr. Lehmann-Nitsche. It seems to me that, instead of being three special peaks in the vicinity of Lake Titicaca, as the great Argentinian authority suggests, they are merely the Andean mountains in general. As Dr. Lehmann-Nitsche shows, many of the streams flowing out of the highlands on the westerly side are reddish in color because of the mineral substances in them. This, taken in conjunction with the fact that westward-flowing streams were used for ceremonial bathing—as noted on page 375 above— because they would bear uncleanlinesses and sicknesses alto- gether out of the empire, and with the further fact that this same idea is carried out by the drawing of the river in the dia- gram, leads me to believe that the stream there represented is simply a symbol for any one of the great westwardly flowing rivers.

The figure that balances the one just described is likewise of geographical import. It consists of a roughly heart-shaped area labelled *mama cocha,* mother-lake, which term, in Dr. Lehmann-Nitsche's judgment, designates Lake Titicaca, not the Pacific. He supports his contention by pointing out the fact that the figure bears a faint resemblance to the actual shape of Lake Titicaca, a resemblance, I may say, quite as great as that between the form of the Lake as it appears on certain early Spanish maps and the form which Viracocha really gave to it. Attached to *mama cocha* by a straight line is a much smaller circular area marked *pucyo* (correctly *puquiu*), Quechua for spring or fountain. Concerning this spring there is also some doubt, for it has been suggested that it represents Lake Poopó, the line being the Desaguadero River. The simpler interpretation would be, of course, that it signifies simply springs in general which pour their waters into the Lake. Personally, I am not entirely satisfied that *mama cocha* does indicate Lake Titicaca. As Cobo has shown, the Ocean Sea, *i. e.,* the Pacific, was adored by the ancient Peruvians, and in particular by the dwellers on the coast. It seems to me not unlikely, therefore, that *mama cocha* here indicates the ocean, for the habit of the Incas to incorporate the deities of conquered peoples into their own pantheon is well known. Obviously, however, all these interpretations are mere conjectures none of which is susceptible to absolute proof; it is certain, on the other hand, that the linked areas, *mama cocha* and *pucyo* are indications that the Incas were well versed in the rudiments of geography.[53]

The final pair of figures, slightly above the ends of the altar, consists of a group of seven circles and of a tree-like design. The first is labelled in Spanish *los ojos,* the eyes, and in Quechua, *ymaymana ñaoray cunap ñauin,* the last letters of the two final words being added in Ávila's writing to Santa Cruz's original legend. As they stand they mean "The eyes of all kinds of things." The concept contained in the word *ymaymana,* "everything," is associated with Viracocha who, according to Molina of Cuzco, had two sons, one of them named Ymaymana Viracocha,[54] but whether the late Dr. Lafone Quevedo was correct in identifying the figure on the diagram with the son of Viracocha[55] is a point discussed by Dr. Lehmann-Nitsche, who comes to the conclusion that the "eyes" and the Peruvian constellation, *collca*—which word appears below the eyes—or "the granary," combine to form a concept whose sense is "The granary watched over by the eyes of Viracocha creator of all things of all kinds," the said concept being connected with the constellations which we call the Hyades and the Pleiades,[56] and being regarded by the ancient Peruvians as beneficial to agriculture.

The tree-design, which completes this final pair of figures, is labelled *arbol* in Spanish and *mallqui* in Quechua, both of which terms mean tree.[57]

At the very bottom of the Santa Cruz *cum* Ávila diagram is a large rectangular block containing seven horizontal and eighteen vertical lines. It is labelled *pata,* Quechua for "terrace" or "platform." I am not able to agree with Dr. Lehmann-Nitsche, who thinks that the word *pata* and the mode of drawing the rectangle are meant to indicate a design of "steps or a staircase shown in primitive perspective."[58] My reasons for disagreement are two: 1. If more than one terrace or platform had been intended, Santa Cruz would have written either *pata-pata* or *pata-cuna;* 2. It is clear to me that the *pata*, terrace or platform, refers quite straightforwardly to some massive block, probably of stone encased in sheets of gold, which served as an altar, just as did the magnificent block of granite in the Main Temple at Machu Picchu.[59]

Finally, an inscription which straddles the altar reads, in Spanish and in Quechua, as follows: *y lacassa estaba todo a fixado con planchas de oro llamado cori cancha vaçi*, which means "and the house was all affixed with plates of gold called golden enclosure house."

Such, stated with the greatest succinctness possible in treating of so intricate a subject, was the high altar with its accompaniments in the Temple of the Sun, Coricancha. We must not forget that although the Santa Cruz *cum* Ávila diagram is æsthetically crude, it is, after all, merely a diagram, not in any sense a picture. Every indication that we have leads us to suppose that the altar, its fittings, and the whole Temple were stunningly gorgeous, glittering, and splendid. Whether or not modern taste would pronounce them beautiful we can only guess.

The sanctuary of the Sun, in addition to containing the high altar and its appurtenances, held the mummies of the dead emperors of the Inca line. They were seated upon chairs of gold, according to Garcilaso, or on benches of wood beautifully carved and painted and adorned with feather-work, according to Betánzos.[60] There is some doubt in my mind whether the Incas down to and including Yahuar-Huaccac were there, so to speak, in person; for Betánzos, in speaking of how Pachacutec arranged the dead in the presence of the Sun, says: *"Hizo hacer muy muchos bultos, y tantos, cuantos Señores habían sucedido desde Manco Capac hasta su padre Viracocha Inca . . ."* which I translate thus: "He caused to be made many bundles, as many as there had been Lords who had succeeded, from Manco Capac down to his father, Inca Viracocha. . . ." This, as I see it, can mean but one thing, namely, that Pachacutec, not having the actual mummies of the earlier Incas, caused mummy-like bundles to be made in order that they might be represented in the series. His father's actual body, embalmed and mummified, he had, naturally enough.[61] At any rate, we know that the mummies—false or real—were arranged close to the altar, most of them facing towards the people in the sanctuary; but Huayna Capac—who alone of the Incas was deified in his life-time—was specially honored by being placed so as to face the image of the Sun.

Probably the sanctuary also contained certain objects which Father Cobo describes as ". . . three other statues of the Sun which were made of some very thick and closely woven mantles so fashioned that they could stand up without artificial aid. Each one had on its head a *llautu* made of very thick braids of wool so as to form a mitre, save that it was all closed over, and each one had very large ear-studs like those which the Incas wore."[62] These oddly contrived images are also mentioned by Father Acosta who was a good deal scandalized by them on account of what he held to be a diabolical imitation of "the mysterie of the holy Trinitie," the names of the statues being *Apu-Inti,* Chief Sun, *Churi-Inti,* Son-Sun, and *Inti-Huauque,* Son-Brother. Father Cobo, however, takes a saner view of the matter, giving three not very interesting interpretations of these statues. They were probably minor phases of the Sun's personality.[63]

Behind the sanctuary there was a quadrangle or cloister of which one side was formed by the southerly wall of the fane, in exactly the same manner that the southerly wall of the church of Saint Dominic forms one side of the monastery cloister at the present time. The quadrangle of Coricancha was formed by a massive wall against which were set five spacious chambers, each with a pyramidal roof wrought of fine thatch, four of them being shrines and the fifth a special chamber. Of the shrines that nearest to the sanctuary of the Sun was dedicated to Mama Quilla, Mother Moon, who was venerated as being the wife of the Sun and Mother of the Incas. Fittingly enough the mummies—or bundles representing mummies—of the *Coya-cuna* were ranged beside her, that of Coya Mama Ocllo, mother of the Inca Huayna Capac, alone having the honor of facing the image of the Moon. This arrangement exactly expresses the status of the empresses in the social fabric of the Incaic state.

Adjacent to the shrine of the Moon was that dedicated to Chasca, the "star with long, curly hair," *i. e.*, Venus, and to the Pleiades, all of which stars were regarded, according to Garcilaso, as handmaidens of the Moon, not of the Sun, since they appeared always in her company, never in his.

On the opposite side of the quadrangle were two other shrines, viz., those of *Illapa*, Thunder-Lightning-Thunderbolts, of whom we have spoken above, and of *Chuychu*, the Rainbow. True, there is no documentary authority for my statement that these shrines were opposite the other two; but a careful study of Squier's plan leads me to think that the four shrines, measuring about forty feet long by about thirty feet from front to back in the case of the Moon's and Chasca's shrines and about forty feet by about twenty feet in the case of the others, *were* arranged in pairs, facing one another. At all events, both Illapa and Chuychu were held to be servants of the Sun, if we are to trust Garcilaso, who tells us that the Incas were aware that the rainbow "proceeded from the Sun" and that, because of this, the Incas, after the Conquest, took the rainbow as a crest for their coat-of-arms.

Opposite to the sanctuary of the Sun, if my reasoning is correct—and Squier partly confirms my guess as to the location (but not as to the dimensions) of the shrines and of the "sacristy"[64]—was the last-mentioned chamber, given over to the use of the Villac Umu, High Priest of the Sun. According to Squier's plan there are no traces of ancient walls on that side of the quadrangle save the long back-wall and the side-walls of the quadrangle itself. This leads me to think that the "sacristy" occupied the space now taken by the refectory, the kitchen and the four smaller apartments beyond them, in which case the sacristy must have measured about one hundred and seventy feet by about fifty-five, and the quadrangle about one hundred and twenty-five feet square.[65]

In addition to the buildings mentioned the temple contained many other apartments and structures—quarters for the numerous servitors such as guards, water-carriers, porters, cooks, and so on—as well as the sleeping-chambers of the priests on duty. The temple received its supply of water through deeply laid pipes (of gold, according to Garcilaso) which served five fountains having golden spouts. Of these five fountains one is still in place—but lacking the spout—in the middle of the monastery courtyard. It is seven feet long, four wide, and three deep, all of one great stone magnificently wrought. It was the golden cover of this imposing tub that fell to the lot of the gamester conqueror, Don Mancio Sierra, as related above on page 396.[66]

Lying immediately south of the temple-structure proper, but of course within the high and massive wall which surrounded the whole establishment, were certain terraces sloping towards the River Huatanay, terraces of which many vestiges remain. Their total area is about three hundred feet in width by six hundred in length. From them one may enjoy a superb view over the Valley of Cuzco towards the mountains on its southern rim. On this choice terrein there existed, in Incaic days, the celebrated Garden of the Sun where, so Garcilaso and others assure us, the herbs, flowers, shrubs, trees, animals, birds, reptiles and human beings were all wrought of finest gold.[67] This glittering garden was not a mere pompous and vainglorious gesture on the part of the Incas as it would have been for a people to whom gold had a monetary value; rather, it was a thank-offering to their god, wrought in the sightliest and most resplendent material of which they knew. Furthermore, I suspect, it had a significance that does not meet the eye, a subtle connection between the golden sheen of the metal and the golden quality of the sunlight. Only thus can one explain so violent a departure from that practicality which was a chief trait of the Incas' temperament. Another point in this connection is as follows: Incaic art, in its pure state, was not realistic; it was geometrical. Therefore, it is probable that the artisans who wrought the multitude of golden objects in the Garden of the Sun were imported to Cuzco from the coast for that very purpose. A like importation is implicit in some of the pottery from Machu Picchu, notably the great arybal and the two butterfly dishes shown by Dr. Bingham.[68] In all of this there is a chronological element, for such importations of coastland artisans, skilled in realistic art in metals and in pottery could have been arranged only after the conquest of the coast or, in other words, in the time of the Inca Pachacutec and his successors.

The personnel of the Sun-cult was in keeping with the importance of the solar church in the Incaic state. The High Priest or Pontiff of that religion was known by the title of *Villac Umu,* Soothsayer-who-speaks, *umu* signifying soothsayer, and *villac,* one who speaks. According to most Chroniclers the holder of this lofty office was always an uncle or a brother of the Sapa Inca. He stood at the pinnacle of the established church as did the monarch at the pinnacle of the empire. The same authorities tell us that the priests of Coricancha were arranged in two categories, those who performed the most solemn rites being always Incas-by-blood and those who officiated in the less important ceremonies being always Incas-by-privilege, that is, members of the families of powerful provincial curacas whom the Inca honored by elevation into the Incaic caste. The clergy of the temples elsewhere than in Cuzco—and there was a Sun-Temple in every important town—were selected from the families of local chiefs whom the Inca thus sapiently welded to his régime by spiritual bonds.[69]

Although the usual account of the solar clergy is that just given, we must note in passing that there are other versions of the matter. Father Cobo tells us that there were several ranks of priests, some of whom were appointed to office by the Inca, others of whom inherited the priestly function. He goes on to say that the priests of the Sun were always of the *ayllu* or tribe of Tarpuntay. According to Sarmiento this was the name of one of the ayllus whom the first Inca led down from the barren heights into the fertile Valley of Cuzco. Furthermore, both Cobo and Cieza say that the Villac Umu lived always in Coricancha. Cieza adds that he held office for life, that he was married, that he vied in power and prestige with the Inca himself, but he does *not* say that the High Priest of the Sun was a brother of the Inca.[70]

In short, Cobo and Cieza would have us believe that there was a priestly family or tribe which passed the headship of the church from father to son, and which, unconnected by blood with the imperial family, threatened its supremacy in the state. In other words, if they speak truly, the Incas were menaced by a potential ecclesiastical shogunate. It seems to me, however, that the discrepancy between the two accounts is not so great as it might at first appear to be. The crux of the matter is this: the Tarpuntay ayllu did go to the Cuzco Valley with the primitive Inca ayllu. What could be more natural—nay, inevitable—than that the two should early blend? It may well be that, in the earliest reign or two, the High Priest was a Tarpuntay and that the name of the family was soon transferred to the office. If this is so, we may easily imagine that the Inca family would not long delay in making the office of *tarpuntay*, or sacrificing priest, one of its numerous appanages.

Forming a part of the clergy was a very large number of women whose lives were consecrated to the service of the Sun. These were the celebrated *Intip chinan*, handmaidens of Inti, the Sun. In romantic language they are styled the Virgins of the Sun, but it is far more accurate simply to call them by the most usual Quechua term, *aclla-cuna*, or *acllas*, meaning Chosen Women. They dwelt in vast conventual establishments close to, but distinct from, the Temple of the Sun. These convents, the *aclla-huasi-cuna*, houses of the Chosen Women, were numerous throughout the provinces, for it was deemed a great honor if the Inca deigned to establish one in a newly conquered district. The greatest *aclla-huasi* was, of course, that in Cuzco. It stood some five hundred feet from Coricancha, between the *Huaca Pata*, Holy Terrace or Square, and the Temple. This separation, which Garcilaso emphasizes because of his annoyance at the innuendoes which certain writers had indulged in at the *acllas'* expense, was made, so he says, because ". . . it was the intention of the Kings Incas that no man should enter the house of the virgins, and that no woman should enter the temple of the Sun."[71]

The inmates were chosen early in life, between eight and fifteen years of age. All had to be virgins, of course, and those *acllas* who were sheltered in the Cuzco convent all had to be of the blood imperial. Their number was great, fifteen hundred, according to Garcilaso, which seems excessive. They were divided into groups, each of which was supervised by an older woman who had herself been an *aclla,* and who, in her matronly capacity, became one of the *mamacuna,* or mothers, of the secluded and hallowed girls. The cloistered women, both matrons and damsels, were well supported by the produce of the estates of the Sun, their comfort being further enhanced by five hundred virgin girls who served them as handmaidens and belonged to the class of Incas-by-privilege, they having *mamacuna* of like station to watch over them.

The *aclla-huasi* in Cuzco, of which a considerable part is still standing, was a huge building of fine masonry. It was much longer than broad, and had but one portal, that being at one of the narrow ends. A passage ran the length of the building, beginning at a vestibule just inside the doorway. There a group of porters waited whose duty it was to keep out intruders and to receive the provender of the establishment, which they were permitted to carry only to the inner door of the vestibule. Along the passage were many apartments used as work-rooms, storehouses, dormitories and so on. At the inner end was a great room where the *acllas* spent the chief of their time performing the sacred duties which were theirs. These included the weaving of all the clothing worn by the Inca and the Coya and the preparation of certain foods and beverages for use in the public ceremonials in honor of the Sun. The handiwork of the *acllas* was so greatly venerated that only the Inca and the Coya might, ordinarily, use it.[72]

Garcilaso would have us believe that the *aclla-cuna* "lived in perpetual seclusion to the end of their lives, and preserved their virginity." He avers that even the Inca did not see them and converse with them, and that he sent the Coya and her daughters to make them visits of courteous enquiry on his behalf. Nevertheless, there was a stringent law designed to meet the case of the *aclla* who transgressed the rule of her order. Such a one was to be buried alive, and her partner in sin was to be strangled; but in addition to this, all his kinsfolk were to be obliterated as persons utterly accursed. But, so Garcilaso says, this law was never called into activity, because it was never violated.[73]

Other accounts of the *aclla-cuna* differ from that of the Inca historian. The Augustinian friar, Alonso Ramos Gavilán, for example, says that the chosen damsels were kept in the convents from the age of eight to that of sixteen years. After that, they were either immolated in honor of the Sun or else they were brought before the Inca in order that he might give them as wives to men whom he wished to favor. Others, the most beautiful and highly born, he himself took as concubines. Friar Alonso goes on to say, in connection with his account of the *aclla-huasi* on the Island of Titicaca, that there were three classes of girls, based upon their degree of beauty. These classes were: the *Guayruro,* the most lovely ones; the *Yurac-aclla,* not quite so fair; and the *Paco-aclla,* still less fair. I can find no meaning for *Guayruro,* but *yurac* or *yurak* means white, and *paco* or *pacco* is one of the terms for red or ruddy. Ramos also tells us that, in addition to spinning and weaving, the *acllas* also kept the temples in order and, on certain occasions, served as sacrificial victims at the festivals.[74]

Father Ramón y Zamora tells us that the Inca Pachacutec instituted the order of the *acllas* so that they might sweep and garnish the temples, but he adds that every three years the Inca or his *tucuiricuc,* chief of a province, assembled all the Chosen Women in his jurisdiction, and from the number of those who were of marriageable age, selected four or five as brides for the Sun. The girls thus designated preserved their virginity through life. The other maidens of like age were taken either by the Inca or by the *tucuiricuc,* the rest being distributed among the great vassals or other favored personages. That having been done, the roster of the virgins was filled up again with girls of noble blood who were over ten years old.[75]

According to Polo de Ondegardo the supervision of the *aclla-cuna* was in the hands of the *apu-panacas,* rulers over the *hunus* (ten thousand households). By them girls were chosen at the age of eight or nine and were placed under the authority of matrons who looked to their education in womanly matters. When they came to a suitable age, they either became wives of the Inca or of favorites of his, or joined the ranks of the *mamacuna,* or met death by being sacrificed in the rites. Polo leads us to believe that the girls thus taken over by the state were looked upon merely as so much tribute.[76]

Much the same notion is expressed by Father Cobo, according to whom the Inca chose girls ten or twelve years old as part of the tribute to be paid to him by each province, selecting always the most beautiful and most nobly born. In the provinces, the *apu-panacas* had general supervision over the *acllas.* Although this author says much the same as does Garcilaso about the dire punishment inflicted upon the unchaste *aclla* and her partner, he also avers that the Inca himself would occasionally steal into the convent and enjoy one of the consecrated women. In such a case, the porter who was on duty at the outer door at the time would go to the great square when next the Inca was sacrificing to the Sun. Going up close behind the Inca, the porter would pluck the imperial mantle and, in a low voice, would say, "Inca, last night thou didst enter the Sun's mansion and didst have carnal relations with one of his wives." Then the Inca, also in a low voice, would reply, "I sinned," and the porter would know that he was absolved from all neglect of his duty. Cobo also tells us that there was in each house one *aclla* who was regarded as *the* wife of the Sun, and that she ruled the rest and managed all the business affairs of the convent much as the chief wife in any ordinary household would do. The head *aclla* of the convent in Cuzco was usually a sister of the Inca.[77]

Finally we come to the account of the matter given by Father Morúa, who informs us that there were six kinds of houses full of women. The differences between them were merely questions of rank on the part of the inmates and also of their beauty. The girls made marvellous *cumbi*, correctly *cumpi*, fine cloth of wool, for the use of the Inca, spending sometimes as much as one year on a single piece. The guardians of the houses were eunuchs whose noses and lips were slit as a badge of their office.[78]

It is apparent, therefore, that the perpetual virginity theory, advocated by Garcilaso, breaks down. Indeed, the Inca historian himself admits that there were many convents throughout the empire patterned after that in Cuzco and that from these provincial houses girls were taken systematically for wifehood. In the provincial *aclla-huasi-cuna* there were maidens of the blood imperial and also members of the families of curacas, as well as some uncommonly pretty daughters of the people. From among their number some were chosen for the Inca's embrace, and when he was aweary of them, if they were not legitimately of the imperial blood, they were given in marriage by the Inca to some one whom he wished to flatter. Legitimate daughters of the imperial house were, however, always inviolate save to the Inca himself, and discarded concubines of his, instead of returning to the convent, became handmaidens of the Coya until such a time as they were allowed to return to their homes. When they did so they received houses and lands for their support, and they were much venerated by their neighbors. The inmates of the provincial convents lived in much the same fashion as those in Cuzco, but with this difference, that they were supported by produce of the Inca's land, not by that of the estates of the Sun.[79]

As has been said, the ceremonial life of the people was based on the *huata* or year; that was based in the movements of the sun; and of the Sun the Incas made a god, benevolent and yet sufficiently awesome to command respect. It is true that the worship of the Sun and of the other heavenly bodies who were adored was materialistic rather than spiritual, but there was mingled with it no small amount of imagery and symbolism, involving such elements as propitiation, supplication, and thanksgiving, which enabled a person well endowed with imaginative powers to find ample exercise for them. The simpler-minded folk, on the other hand, probably worshipped more irreflectively and more materialistically, with the result that there must have been as great a contrast between Sun-worship as practiced by a lowly peasant and Sun-worship as practiced by a member of the imperial caste, as there is between the Catholicism of a Spanish sheep-herder and that of a highly educated man of the same nation.

Nor was Sun-worship all. As I shall now endeavor to show, in the next chapter, it stood, among the religions of pre-Spanish Peru, midway between the ancient idol- and fetich-cults of the people on the one hand and the likewise ancient cult for the Creator-god of the enlightened on the other hand.

NOTES TO CHAPTER IX

1 Cobo, Vol. IV, pp. 183–184. Garcilaso, Pt. I, Bk. I, Ch. xiv.
2 Cobo, Vol. IV, pp. 185–186.
3 Cobo, Bk. XIV, Ch. vii.
4 Garcilaso, Pt. I, Bk. IV, Ch. viii.
5 Santillán, 1879, p. 24.
6 Acosta, Bk. VI, Ch. xviii.
7 Cieza, Pt. II, Ch. x.
8 Santa Cruz Pachacuti-yamqui Salcamayhua, 1873, p. 81; 1879, pp. 251–252. See also, for general data on marriage, Morúa, Bk. III, Chs. xxx–xxxiv, inclusive.
9 Quoted from Father Blas Valera by Garcilaso, Pt. I, Bk. V, Ch. xxix, Vol. II, pp. 94–95 of Markham's translation.
10 Garcilaso, Pt. I, Bk. IV, Chs. xi and xii. Cobo, Bk. XIV, Ch. vi.
11 Molina of Cuzco, 1873, p. 53. Santa Cruz, 1873, p. 80.
12 Markham, 1910, pp. 117–120.
13 Garcilaso, Pt. I, Bk. VI, Ch. xx. Vol. II, pp. 155–156, of Markham's translation.
14 Garcilaso, Pt. I, Bk. VI, Ch. xxi. Vol. II, pp. 159–160, of Markham's translation.
15 Garcilaso, Pt. I, Bk. VI, Ch. xxii. Vol. II, pp. 162–163, of Markham's

translation. Molina of Cuzco, 1873, pp. 16–18. Cobo, Bk. XIII, Ch. xviii. Acosta, Bk. V, Ch. xviii.

[16] Garcilaso, Pt. I, Bk. VI, Chs. xxii and xxiii. Sarmiento, Ch. xxxi. Molina of Cuzco, 1873, pp. 16–19.

[17] Means, 1928, pp. 287–295, 326–334, and 395–399. Molina of Cuzco, place cited. Acosta, Bk. V, Ch. xxviii.

[18] Cobo, Bk. XIII, Ch. xxviii. Molina of Cuzco, 1873, p. 19.

[19] Cobo, place cited. Molina of Cuzco, 1873, pp. 19–20.

[20] Cobo, Bk. XIII, Ch. xxix. Molina of Cuzco, 1873, pp. 20–34.

[21] Cobo, Bk. XIII, Ch. xxx. Molina of Cuzco, 1873, pp. 34–36.

[22] The "ostrich" here mentioned is, of course, the rhea-bird, or American ostrich, called *suri* in Quechua and *nandú* in Guaraní. Its habitat was in the country around Tucumán and in the territories now called Paraguay and Brazil, but living rheas were brought to Cuzco under the Incas. Its plumage is less beautiful than that of the African ostrich, but its feathers have commercial value, nevertheless, and they were prized by the Incas and their subjects. See: Garcilaso, Pt. I, Bk. V, Ch. x. Santa Cruz, 1873, p. 80. Cobo, Bk. VIII, Ch. lix.

[23] Cabello de Balboa, Bk. III, Chs. ix and x of N. Y. P. L. MS. Sarmiento, Chs. xii–xiv, inclusive, xxxi and xxxii. Cobo, Bk. XIII, Ch. xxv. Cieza, Pt. II, Chs. vii, viii, xxviii, and xxxii. Garcilaso, Pt. I, Bk. VI, Chs. xxiv and xxvi. Molina of Cuzco, 1873, pp. 36–47. Santa Cruz, 1873, p. 80.

[24] Cobo, Bk. XIII, Ch. xxvi. Molina of Cuzco, 1873, pp. 47–51. Markham, 1910, p. 241.

[25] Cobo, Bk. XIII, Ch. xxvii. Molina of Cuzco, 1873, pp. 51–54.

[26] Cobo, Bk. XIII, Ch. xxvi.

[27] Garcilaso, Pt. I, Bk. II, Ch. xxii. Cieza, Pt. I, Ch. xcii. Acosta, Bk. VI, Ch. iii. Sarmiento, Ch. xxx. Rivero and von Tschudi, 1851, Ch. vi. Squier, 1877, pp. 524–529. Markham, 1910, Ch. ix. Bingham, 1930, Ch. iii.

[28] The literature of the golden Echenique plaque consists of: Markham, 1910, pp. 119–130. Bollaert, 1860. Saville, 1921. Tello, in *Inca*, I, pp. 224–230, Lima, 1923.

[29] Montesinos, Chs. xi and xii; Table III of the Hakluyt Society's edition, 1920.

[30] Sarmiento, Ch. xii. Cobo, Bk. XIII, Ch. ix. Alexander, 1920, p. 249.

[31] Garcilaso, Pt. I, Bk. III, Ch. xxi.

[32] Lehmann-Nitsche, 1928, pp. 112–113. Santillán, 1879, pp. 30–31. López de Gómara, Ch. cxxi. Cobo, Bk. XIII, Chs. v and vi. Morúa, Bk. III, Ch. i. Garcilaso, place cited. Valera, 1879, pp. 138–139.

[33] Cobo, Bk. XIII, Chs. v and vi.

[34] Tschudi, 1891. Squier, 1877, pp. 438–444. Lehmann-Nitsche, 1928, pp. 21–56.

[35] Garcilaso, Bk. III, Ch. xx.

[36] Cieza, Pt. II, Ch. xxvii.

[37] Lehmann-Nitsche, 1928, Figure 2. Jijón y Caamaño, 1929, Plate III. It seems to me that these illustrations show the same area of wall, that of Dr. Lehmann-Nitsche being, however, set horizontally, which is incorrect, as a glance at Señor Jijón's illustration will show.

[38] Lehmann-Nitsche, 1928, pp. 24–25. Santa Cruz, 1879, pp. 244 and 256–257.

[39] Cabello de Balboa, Pt. III, Ch. xxviii, pp. 695–696 of N. Y. P. L. MS.

[40] Lehmann-Nitsche, 1928, pp. 27–28, and 64. Valera, 1879, p. 148. Cobo, Bk. XIII, Ch. iv. Betánzos, Ch. xi.

[41] Lehmann-Nitsche, 1928, pp. 64–76.

[42] Lehmann-Nitsche, 1928, pp. 41–42.

[43] Lehmann-Nitsche, 1928, pp. 41–43. Calancha, Bk. I, Ch. xiv.

[44] Lehmann-Nitsche, 1928, pp. 77–80.

[45] Lehmann-Nitsche, 1928, pp. 106–109.

[46] Lehmann-Nitsche, 1928, pp. 110–111.

[47] Lehmann-Nitsche, 1928, pp. 111–124.

[48] Lehmann-Nitsche, 1928, pp. 124–133.

[49] Lehmann-Nitsche, 1928, pp. 133–142. Cobo, Bk. XIII, Ch. vi, Vol. III, pp. 329–331.

[50] Lehmann-Nitsche, 1928, pp. 142–155. Cobo, place cited.

[51] Lehmann-Nitsche, 1928, pp. 157–180.

[52] Lehmann-Nitsche, 1928, pp. 181–184.

[53] Lehmann-Nitsche, 1928, pp. 184–186.

[54] Molina of Cuzco, 1873, pp. 6–7.

[55] Lafone Quevedo, 1900.

[56] Lehmann-Nitsche, 1928, pp. 186–209.

[57] Lehmann-Nitsche, 1928, p. 209.

[58] Lehmann-Nitsche, 1928, pp. 210–211.

[59] See the numerous illustrations of this granite block published in the various works of Dr. Bingham, and especially Bingham, 1930, Figs. 37, 38 and 39.

[60] Garcilaso, Pt. I, Bk. III, Ch. xx. Betánzos, 1924, p. 127. Lehmann-Nitsche, 1928, pp. 32–34.

[61] See Note 59 to Chapter VII, above. Also pp. 272–273 of this volume.

[62] Cobo, Vol. III, pp. 325–326.

[63] Acosta, Bk. V, Ch. xxviii. Cobo, Bk. XIII, Ch. v.

[64] Squier, 1877, p. 442.

[65] Lehmann-Nitsche, 1928, pp. 43–47. Garcilaso, Pt. I, Bk. III, Ch. xxi.

[66] Lehmann-Nitsche, 1928, pp. 49–51.

[67] Garcilaso, Pt. I, Bk. III, Ch. xxiv. Gutiérrez de Santa Clara, Bk. III, Ch. i. Cieza, Pt. II, Ch. xxvii. Cobo, Bk. XIII, Ch. xii. Santa Cruz, 1873, pp. 76 and 84–85. Pedro Pizarro, 1921, pp. 254–255. Tschudi, 1891, pp. 84–85. Lehmann-Nitsche, 1928, pp. 53–56.

[68] Bingham, 1930, Figs. 78, 79 and 122.

[69] Garcilaso, Pt. I, Bk. III, Ch. xxii. Acosta, Bk. V, Chs. ii–vii, inclusive. Arriaga, Ch. iii. Román y Zamora, Pt. III, Bk. I, Ch. vii.

[70] Cobo, Bk. XIII, Ch. xxxiii. Sarmiento, Ch. xi. Cieza, Pt. II, Chs. xxvii and xxx.

[71] Garcilaso, Pt. I, Bk. IV, Ch. i.

[72] Garcilaso, Pt. I, Bk. IV, Chs. i–iii, inclusive.

[73] Garcilaso, Pt. I, Bk. IV, Ch. ii.

[74] Ramos Gavilán, Bk. I, Ch. xviii.

[75] Román y Zamora, Pt. III, Bk. I, Ch. viii.

[76] Polo de Ondegardo, 1873, pp. 165–167.

[77] Cobo, Bk. XIII, Ch. xxxvii.

[78] Morúa, Bk. III, Chs. xxxvi–xliii, inclusive, particularly Ch. xl, for the question of eunuchs, who are also mentioned by López de Gómara, Ch. cxxi. *Corasca* is the Quechua word for eunuch.

[79] Garcilaso, Pt. I, Bk. IV, Chs. iv and vi.

CHAPTER X

SOME OTHER RELIGIONS OF THE ANCIENT ANDEANS, AND THEIR INTELLECTUAL LIFE IN GENERAL

THE state religion and ceremonial life of the Incas as they existed during the later reigns of the solar dynasty of Cuzco were studied in the previous chapter; in the present chapter we shall examine other cults and rites which, although possessing very great importance, did not wear an official aspect. The fact that they were all much older than the official Sun-worship is the one thing that they have in common; for some among them were extremely humble from an intellectual point of view whilst others were very advanced, the state religion lying, if intellectually considered, midway between the extremes represented in the range of religions.

Archaic man, in the Andean area as elsewhere, lives in a mysterious universe which is constantly showing him new phenomena that he cannot comprehend immediately, if at all. At the same time, he is impelled through his days by certain fundamental requirements compounded of instincts with but a small proportion of reason in them, requirements that touch poignantly upon such needs as those for food, for shelter, for bodily covering, and—most powerful of all—for reproduction of the race. Under the imperious necessity of satisfying these needs, archaic man passes blunderingly through his period of mundane existence, in the course of which he frequently finds himself in the presence of natural forces some of which fill him with awe or even with terror because of their irresistible opposition to his will, others of which awaken his gratitude by favoring his plans. Archaic man, therefore, spends a large part of his time in being afraid of this or that natural force or object; yet another large part of his time is spent in thanking those other things of nature which he finds to be his friends. From all this the earliest forms of religion take their rise, motivated by two emotions: fear, coupled with a wish to propitiate; gratitude, coupled with a wish to reward.

The oldest and humblest grade of religions discernible in the Andean area is that series of cults wherein lifeless, or at any rate sub-human, objects are conceived to have a soul and a personality capable of working good and evil upon men. The soul and the personality are reverenced and, frequently, worshipped, by the folk who believe in them, the attention accorded to them being the product of dread or of thankfulness blended with incomprehension. Objects which receive this kind of religious observance are, in the Andean area, designated by the convenient generic term *huaca*, a Quechua word meaning a holy thing, whether animate or inanimate.[1]

In brief, then, it may be said that veneration and even adoration were accorded to springs, rivers, mountains, cliffs, any strange rock formation, gnarled trees, ferocious or curious animals, and animals esteemed for their usefulness to man. Of these things, all of them the creations of nature, not of man, all of them mundane, not celestial, was the lowliest and simplest class of *huacas* composed. The outstanding trait of these cults was irreflective wonderment, either of a pleased or of an apprehensive kind. The things reverenced or adored were regarded objectively and venerated incuriously, uncontemplatively, exactly as they were in other parts of America and in other continents of the world. Don Jacinto Jijón y Caamaño makes it very clear that cults of this general type are very widely distributed.[2]

The devotion accorded to the *huacas* was of a simplicity consistent with the objective character of the things venerated, being carried on sometimes without the intervention of any sort of priesthood, sometimes—if a simple shrine or prayer-place were in question—under the guidance of self-appointed priests who acted as servitors and guardians of the *huaca*. Father Arriaga, the most informative of the Chroniclers in this connection, tells us that the act of worship in honor of any given *huaca* was not an everyday matter, but one obligatory only at stated times. Furthermore, he shows clearly the simplicity of the ritual involved: women engaged in planting the new seeds would talk to their Mother, the Earth, praying her to make the crop a success, and making a propitiatory sacrifice by scattering maize-beer and milled maize upon the soil; travellers wishful to cross a river, would drink a little of its water and thereafter beseech the stream to let them cross in safety. Finally, in speaking of mountaineers who, in Colonial times, were brought down to the coast to serve as forced laborers, Father Arriaga tells us that they were wont to make a prayer to the sea, entreating it to send them health and prosperity and to let them return to their homes soon and sound.[3] In this practice of post-Conquest times we see, no doubt, a survival of the usages prevalent in the days when the Incas were wont to send relays of mountain soldiers down to the coast-country in order to fight.

All of these little observances are rather charming in their simplicity and imagery. Others there were, naturally, which were either bloody or nasty, albeit artless and spontaneous. Pedro Pizarro, for example, gives a vivid account of the river-oracle, Apurimac, the lord-who-speaks, who, in late Incaic times, was represented by a set of idols smeared with blood but richly dressed who were in charge of a lady styled Asarpay who belonged to the imperial caste.[4] In this we see, no doubt, one of a multitude of cases in which the Incas took over an ancient *huaca* and incorporated it into the official pantheon. The blood-offerings were, we may suppose, in the nature of propitiatory sacrifices whose purpose was that of securing the benevolence of the river-god.

Comparable with the *huacas* were the *conopas,* the chief difference between them being that the former were objects of worship to a tribe or even to a whole province, whereas the *conopas* were household or personal gods analogous, as Father Arriaga points out, to the *Lares* and *Penates* of the Romans. They probably included many sorts of objects, ranging from small, unworked pebbles or shells of unusual forms to beautifully wrought artifacts of pottery, metal, stone, wood, shell, and other materials. Worn on or carried about the person they were of a peculiarly intimate nature to their possessors, partaking of the character of amulets, charms, and fetishes. Sometimes the *conopas* verged upon the realm of medicine, as in the case of bezoar-stones, which were prized in accordance with their place of origin, those derived from the bellies of vicuñas being the most highly regarded, those from deer next in value, and those from llamas or huanacos least.[5] In general, however, the purpose and character of the *conopas* are indicated by the generic term applied to them in Quechua, *huasi-camayoc,* literally, house-guardian.

Lack of space forbids that I say more here regarding the very interesting and intricate subject of the *huacas* and the *conopas.* Although, as I have said, they represent at once the lowest and the oldest of the classes of cults anciently existent in the Andean area, I do not wish to imply that they died out when higher types of religion came into being. They did not; far from it. Even to-day the lives of the purely Indian element in Andean society turn very largely upon surviving forms of *huaca*-worship and *conopa*-worship. In some cases it will be found that the cults to which I refer are unmodified by contact with Europeans and are now exactly what they were at any time during these past two thousand years; but, in other cases, it will be found that *huaca*-cults have been modified by Catholicism either through the arbitrary suppression of some artless indecency or else through adaptation to the requirements of Catholic dogma.

In short, although *huaca*-worship is undoubtedly the oldest and lowliest manifestation of religiosity in the Andean area— just as worship of the same type is so in most other countries —it is also the most long-lived. As other forms of religion arose, however, requiring a greater degree of intellectuality both from their originators and from their adherents, *huaca*-worship was more and more definitely relegated to the lower orders of society, becoming at last their peculiar property and an outward sign of their inferiority in the state.

Here I would make a point significant for the study of ancient Andean cultural history. Accounts of very old local cults abound in the writings of Father Arriaga and other missionary churchmen who, filled with indignation by the low moral value—from their point of view—of those cults, wrote of them in tones of horrified contempt and so, paradoxically enough, immortalized them. At the same time many of the Chroniclers were preserving for us data concerning the ancient local idioms which existed in early times throughout the Andean area. It seems to me that these hoary cults and tongues should, at any rate in this connection, be considered together; for, most likely, they are in truth manifestations of a partial survival into later times of the underlying archaic culture. I use the words "underlying archaic culture" in a double sense, meaning not only that the archaic culture in Peru, as in so many lands, underlies all more advanced culture, but also that the lower classes of society remained partly archaic in culture even after the élite had passed beyond the bournes of the archaic stage. It is this contrast between the cultural attainments of the masses and those of the élite that best indicates the great intellectual gulf that came into existence between them. When, however, the power of the élite was blasted—as at the end of the Tiahuanaco II period—the masses and their brand of culture were all that was left. As a natural result of this there came into being, at any rate until a new élite could be formed, the condition of neo-archaicism to which I referred in Chapter V.

Inevitably, the transitions in the evolution of the mentality of the élite as manifested by religious beliefs was slow, at times almost imperceptible. No doubt they advanced simultaneously with the progress made in other departments of culture, each step forward denoting a definite enlargement of the intellectual life of the people by whom such a step was made. The trend was away from an objective and superstitious regard for lowly objects and for animals and towards an examination into the causes of natural phenomena. Animism remained a feature of even the most deeply searching of the new faiths, but it was an animism whose horizon was always broadening so that, at last, it came to include extra-mundane objects and powers. The men who first ceased to regard only that part of the universe which lay upon the terrestrial plane and directed a questioning gaze to the winds, the rain, the clouds, the thunder and lightning, and, at length, to the visible but inscrutable denizens of the skies were men whose minds and whose psyches were expanding. Looked at from this angle, Sun-worship itself is but an outgrowth of animistic *huaca*-worship, the chief departure from the old beliefs being the new habit of contemplating things beyond the bournes of this planet. It is far from clear whether the credit for beginning this novel variety of animism belongs to the Incas of Cuzco. It may be that some relatively simple form of Sun-worship existed in the highlands before they rose to power and that they merely systematized and embellished it. We only know that they did so shape its tenets and so regulate its ritual that it became a wholly adequate state religion with which they incorporated, as their empire spread, many of the more respect-worthy *huaca* cults which commanded reverence among their conquered subjects.

In the course of that same process of conquest the Incas must inevitably have encountered local cults of many kinds, ranging from the weird and rather terrible worship accorded to the gods whom we see portrayed on the pottery of the coast to the concept of a Creator-god, sometimes thought of as material, sometimes held to be immaterial, which under various guises, existed in many parts of the sierra.

The Creator-god most celebrated in the Chronicles of Peru is one known under various names who is definitely associated with the Tiahuanaco II cultural period. He has generally been referred to on earlier pages as Viracocha or as Pachacamac, the former designation being usual in the highlands, the latter on the coast. Both of them, however, are Quechua and, consequently, more or less late in date. It seems clear enough that pre-Incaic names for the Creator-god were Con, Con-Tici, Illa Tici, and sundry approximations thereto, sometimes prefixed to the name Viracocha in later times, these names being general in the pre-Incaic highlands, albeit the Inca Garcilaso avers that they were all post-Conquest. On the coast in days prior to the advent there of the lords of Cuzco the Creator-god was generally known as Irma.

Associated with Con or Viracocha in the myths of the highlands are two servitors, the one variously styled Tarapaca, Taguapaca, or Tuapaca, the other being Tonapa whom Santa Cruz Pachacuti Salcamayhua blandly identifies with "the glorious Apostle Saint Thomas." Sarmiento, however, tells us that Taguapaca was one of three men who were spared by Viracocha at the time of the universal flood by means of which he destroyed the first human race upon the earth. Ungratefully enough Taguapaca disobeyed his master who was obliged to tie up the rebel and to place him upon a balsa on Lake Titicaca. Blaspheming against Viracocha, and swearing to return and avenge himself, Taguapaca was carried on his frail craft down the Desaguadero River and never heard of more. The question of whether or not there is any historical and ethnic connection between this personage and the desert region now known as Tarapacá is one that I recommend to the attention of students. Cieza de León tells us that Tuapaca— a variation of the name under consideration—was merely the designation of Viracocha general in the Collao. As for Tonapa, the second associate of Viracocha, it suffices to say that he was the object of an extensive cult widespread in territory now known as northwestern Argentina. Still another pre-Incaic name for the Creator-god was Iraya, or Coniraya, the ancient designation for Pachacamac in the province of Huarochirí which lies in the mountains to the east of the Rimac and Pachacamac Valleys.[6]

These very brief remarks will serve to show the intricacy of the subject of Creator-gods in ancient times among the Andean folk. For our present purposes it is enough to say that the most widely accepted designations of the Creator-god were Viracocha and Pachacamac, with the occasional addition of some descriptive epithet. That the cult of this God greatly antedates the Incas and that it was definitely linked with the Tiahuanaco II culture is made abundantly clear by a long list of the most important Chroniclers.[7] Having thus established this fundamental fact, I shall now show that Viracocha-worship, and by implication Pachacamac-worship, was of the greatest importance in pre-Incaic times, both in the highlands and on the coast. Father Blas Valera, whose ideas in this connection are preserved by Father Montesinos, makes it clear that the earliest mountain chiefs recognized Viracocha as an all-powerful God. To this we may add the evidence of the quaint full-blooded Indian Chronicler, Don Felipe Huamán Poma de Ayala, who tells us that the first race of men in Peru bore the generic name of Viracocha which fact we may interpret as an indication that they were worshippers of that God. These facts, taken in conjunction with the definite link between Viracocha-worship and the Tiahuanaco II culture, bring us to the question of whether or not the Weeping God figure on the monolithic gateway at Tiahuanaco and on many other objects representing Tiahuanaco II art is the same personage as that designated by the name Viracocha. To my mind there is no doubt but that the Weeping God is Viracocha; for, in the myths of that period Viracocha is the chief personage, a sort of culture-hero as well as a Creator-god, and in the art of that culture the Weeping God, or derivatives from him, is the leading figure. Therefore they must be the same.

Turning now to the objective aspect of the Weeping God, or of Viracocha, as he appears on the monolithic gateway, we perceive certain traits which make it obvious that he was a sky-deity of some sort. No one can be more chary than I am as a general rule of subjective interpretations of ancient decorative designs; but here the indications are so clear that they admit of no doubt. The Weeping God's head is certainly of a solar character, his headdress with its erect fringe-like embellishment representing the rays of the sun, his conventionalized human face representing the human character ascribed to the sun, and his tears typifying the rain which falls from the sky and causes life to prosper here on earth. These points have been most interestingly set forth by Mr. Joyce, of the British Museum, in an article published some seventeen years ago.[8] As for the lesser figures on the monolithic gateway, it is safe enough to say that the weeping birds are messengers of the God who employed them to scatter rain over the earth. and that the weeping men were other messengers of his.

This brings us to the subject of Irma-worship or Pachacamac-worship on the coast. Most of the important Chroniclers give some account of the great pilgrimage-city, seat of the oracular Creator-god Irma or Pachacamac, some twelve miles down the coast from Lima.[9] Garcilaso avers that, when the Inca Pachacutec conquered the place, he had the great temple cleared of its ancient idols, which had the forms of fishes and of a fox. Again, at the time of the Spanish conquest, there was, according to Don Miguel de Estete, who saw the shrine in 1533, "a piece of wood fixed in the ground with the figure of a man badly carved and shaped upon the upper end of it, and at its foot many trifling things of gold and silver . . ." which were offerings that had been made to the God.[10] In the anonymous *Conquista del Peru* which, if not written by Estete himself, was at any rate written by a fellow eye-witness of the first visit to the shrine by Spaniards in 1533, we read concerning Pachacamac as follows: "This town is larger than Rome. In the temple was a Devil who used to speak to the Indians in a very dark room which was as dirty as himself. . . ."[11]

Such, then, was the nature of the worship carried on at Pachacamac at the time of the Inca conquest and at the time of the Spanish conquest. At both periods it was a low type of image-worship, maintained in a maculate and fetid holy of holies that stood atop the otherwise superbly magnificent temple. It was on an infinitely lower plane, both æsthetically and intellectually, as well as morally, than the worship of the sky-god Viracocha at Tiahuanaco; for, however strange to us his figure upon the monolithic gateway may be, it is clear enough that it represents a rich and a beautiful nature-worship well provided with sound philosophy.

How can we explain this discrepancy between the Creator-god cult of the highlands and that of the coast? Dr. Max Uhle, in his great monograph on Pachacamac, shows clearly enough that the earliest culture at that site was of the Tiahuanaco II type, that it was followed by an intermediate period and by an Incaic period. Furthermore, he shows that Irma was emphatically a more ancient name for the god and for the place than was Pachacamac.[12] Therefore was may conclude that the cult of Irma, equivalent to that of Con or Viracocha in the mountains, was introduced into the coast-country in Tiahuanaco II times, probably as a part of the conquest of the littoral by the people whose cultural centre was at Tiahuanaco. It is likely that, in its original form, the cult was observed by different classes of society in different ways, the ruling class conceiving of a Creator who united in His person every possible kind of godly attribute and power, the lower classes concerning themselves only with such simpler manifestations of His complex personality as were made visible to them by the images and symbols present in the artistic productions of the time. Precisely the same sort of contrast may be seen to-day if one compares the abject hyperdulia of an Andalusian or a Calabrian peasant with the exalted spirituality of an upper-class Belgian, English, French, or Spanish Catholic.

The gross and sordid character of the worship of Pachacamac as it was when the Incas arrived on the coast, and, still more so, as it was when the Spaniards came into Peru is to be explained, I think, by the habits of the coastal mentality. We have but to study certain unpublishable classes of Early Chimu pottery to realize the abnormal, nay, pathological, animality towards which the thoughts of its makers were wont to stray; we need only to see the grotesque and unnatural figures upon Early Nazca pots to understand how easy it would be for people with such minds as they must have had to distort into coarse earthiness even a religion filled with philosophic imagery.

The position held by Viracocha-worship in Incaic times must now be considered. In the next preceding chapter some reference was made in an incidental way to this matter; but it is well to deal with it now more specifically. Cieza and Sarmiento aver that even the earliest Incas revered Viracocha fully as much as they did the Sun; Father Cobo and Santa Cruz tell us that He was represented by an image in Coricancha, and of these two Chroniclers the former also speaks of a special temple to Viracocha in Cuzco, on the site now partly occupied by the Cathedral, called Quishuarcancha.[13]

It is probable, however, that only in the time of the Inca Viracocha, namesake of the God who saved the Inca dynasty from the Chancas, did the cult of the Creator-god begin to assume special significance to the ruling caste, and the final touches seem to have been put to His worship by Pachacutec. The manner in which this took place is told by Father Cabello, as follows:

The Inca Pachacutec entirely rebuilt Coricancha, in Cuzco, and, after the work was completed, he convoked there all the priests from every part of his realms so that sacerdotal and religious matters might be duly set in good order. This council allotted the highest place in the pantheon to the Sun, and gave to each of the other heavenly bodies suitable rank in the divine hierarchy. The rites and ceremonies of the official religion were systematized, the priesthood was regulated, and every other aspect of the state cult was carefully considered and ordered, all this being done under the personal supervision of the Inca. When all these things had been carried out to his liking, the Emperor, in reflective mood, asked the assembled priests whether, after all, they could not conceive of some god even higher and mightier than the Sun. He pointed out to them that that luminary, though excellent and useful to man, went always on the same path, performing the same tasks, appearing to possess no will and freedom of his own. His power was not limitless; he could not appear by night; his radiance was obscured by every passing cloud. But the priests were unable to imagine any greater god. There-

fore the Inca addressed them at some length, chiding them
because they were themselves beguiled by the very dogmas
which had been contrived to beguile the commonalty of the
empire. The Inca then presented to them his concept of a
great, omnipotent Creator-god, Viracocha or Pachacamac, The
Foundation of all that is Excellent, Maker of the World.
Filled with wonderment, the priests accepted the teachings of
their master and accorded to this God the supremacy of sky
and earth. But His cult was only to be for the ruling caste,
being deemed too subtle for the masses. Thereafter, the Inca
when addressing the Sun spoke as to a friend and kinsman;
but when he prayed to Viracocha he supplicated Him with
greatest humility.[14]

In some such way came into being the final phase of Viracocha-worship among the imperial caste of the Incas during
the later reigns. The God was held to be maker and ruler of
all things in heaven, on earth, everywhere. So great was He
that the Inca did not allot to Him estates and tribute, as he
did to the Sun, for Viracocha was already master of the entire
universe.[15] Nor, as a general rule, were temples erected in
His honor, the only two on record being that of Quishuarcancha, in Cuzco, wherein He was symbolized by a massive
golden image about the size of a ten-year-old boy, and that at
Racche which the Inca Viracocha built after the conquest of
the Chancas. See Figure 170. The fewness of the temples to
Viracocha is, I think, a fact of deeper significance than has
been generally suspected. The reign of the Inca Viracocha,
formerly known as Prince Hatun Tupac, may fairly be regarded as the one in which the empire entered in upon its
greatness, its destiny having then been revealed by the decisive victory which the Inca, acting on the commands and
under the patronage of the god Viracocha, won against a
formidable foe. The reality underlying this legend is not
difficult to guess at; probably the worship of Viracocha had
been gaining adherents among the Inca caste for some time,
and Prince Hatun Tupac may have deemed it wise, in this
crucial moment of his family's career, to put the power of the

Creator-god to the test once and for all. The outcome forever confirmed the Inca caste in the belief that the god Viracocha was their special deity and protector. As He had naught to do with the masses, it was unnecessary to popularize His worship by building temples everywhere. Therefore He was represented only in Coricancha, in his special fane, Quishuar-cancha, and at Racche. Apparently no effort was made by the Incas to lift His cult from the degraded state into which it had fallen at Pachacamac, and in this fact we may see still another manifestation of the Incas' belief that Viracocha was a god peculiar to themselves.

In short there are plentiful indications that the élite, in both pre-Incaic and Incaic times, were capable of not inconsiderable philosophic flights. This statement, however, does not tell the whole story; for, from quite another part of the Andean area than any hitherto mentioned, we derive important evidence that it is incorrect to suppose that merely because a deity was a Creator-god he was the object of a highly philosophic cult. This material is provided by two Augustinian missionaries who, in 1551, arrived at Huamachuco, in the mountains northeast of Chan-Chan, in order to convert the people to Christianity. They found there a curious cult which we must now briefly consider.

The Indians of Huamachuco worshipped a god named Ataguju, who was said to be "Creator of all things." He created two servants or subjects, variously known as Sagradzabra and Vaungrabad, as Sugadcabra and Uciozgrabad, and as Uvigaicho and Vustiqui. It is clear enough that these servants or subjects were regarded by the people as powerful intercessors, for frequent prayers were addressed to them by folk who sought all manner of benefits. When the maize was in flower the people would say to them, "Beseech Ataguju to let no hail fall upon the maize, and beg him to give us much maize, and many sons and llamas, and an abundance of all other things that we need."

Sacrifices were made to Ataguju under the direction of the high priest of his cult, called Xulumango. They took the form of offerings of guinea-pigs, of maize-beer, or maize-meal, and of coca. The ceremonies of the cult were held in certain enclosures built of stone wherein ritualistic dances were held.

At the same time that Ataguju created his two servants he also made a personage named Guamansiri who came to earth at Huamachuco where he discovered two brothers named Guachemin. They had a sister called Cautaguan whom they kept in hiding. But Guamansiri, who was wandering about in the guise of a poor old man, contrived to rape her, and in due course she bore two eggs, dying in egg-birth. The two brothers, disgusted with their sister and with her strange offspring, threw the eggs upon a rubbish-heap. Presently two lads came forth shouting from the eggs, and they were adopted by a woman who chanced to be passing by. Their names were Cepocatequil or Catequil and Piguerao. They went to the place where their mother had died and Catequil managed to recall her to life. Thereupon she gave them two slings which Guamansiri had left behind for his egg-children and, with these weapons, they slew or drove away their uncles who had abandoned their mother and themselves. After that Catequil went up to the sky where he besought Ataguju to create Indians to populate the earth.

A cult grew up around the personality of Catequil, a curious outgrowth of the cult for Ataguju, it would seem. It had its chief shrine at Porcón, four leagues from Huamachuco. There are three peaks at that place which, so the Indians believed, were Cautaguan with her sons Catequil and Piguerao. On the peak that represented Catequil a stone statue of a man, as skilfully wrought as the artistry of the Indians permitted, was set up. This was the idol or image of Catequil to which the people of Huamachuco paid special homage. Below the shrine where the image was, a large village housed the priests, stewards, and numerous servants of the idol. Worshippers came thither from far and wide, bringing offerings of gold, silver, and other prized things, with the result that the idol gathered a large and varied treasure, just as that of Pachacamac did.[16]

In this cult of Ataguju and the personages associated with or derived from him we have, in all probability, a Creator-god cult which was peculiar to the provinces of Huamachuco and Casamarca, in which region it was extremely ancient. In the course of time the personality of Ataguju was to a large extent superseded by that of Catequil. For us the chief interest in all this lies in the fact that the Ataguju-Catequil cult, though partaking of the nature of a Creator-god religion, was apparently bereft of philosophical traits, being hardly superior, intellectually, to *huaca*-worship.

Brief though my account of the various religions heretofore mentioned necessarily is, it will suffice, I hope, to show that the religions of ancient times in the Andean area were exceedingly various, both as to their outward aspects and their inward meanings. At the lower end of the scale we have the rather sordid and materialistic *huaca*-cults; at the upper end we find the subtle and philosophic Viracocha-worship of the Inca caste, a worship derived in large part, we may be very sure, from scattered remnants of the religion which had flourished in Tiahuanaco II times. Almost exactly in the middle of the scale was the official Sun-cult which, as it was in the later reigns, incorporated many local cults surrounding a variety of *huacas* and so converged, for political reasons, upon the lower order of faiths, but which also included, at any rate by implication, veneration of the Creator-god, thereby impingeing upon the highest order of religious concepts. In the form which it had from the time of the Inca Viracocha onward, the Sun-cult was very largely a thing of compromises and of adaptations, a state-engendered organization whose tenets were sufficiently elastic to permit its adherents to be either objectively minded worshippers of things visible and tangible or else to be highly philosophic adorers of abstract forces, laws and principles. In this quality of elasticity, as well as in the fact of its being a state-supported and state-controlled establishment, the Sun-worship of the Incas bears a startling, and in some ways a comic, resemblance to the Church of England.

It will have been noticed that, in this chapter and in the preceding one, I have made only the slightest allusion to the religions of the coast-people in pre-Tiahuanaco II times. True, in earlier chapters I have referred to them, albeit warily and briefly; but, when it comes to attempting a description of their forms of religious observance and their tenets of faith, I feel obliged to remain silent for the reason that no definite and concrete knowledge on those points is available. Therefore I can say concerning them only this much: They seem, from the visual evidence presented to us by Early Chimu and Early Nazca pottery designs, to have been in the nature of *huaca*-worship, turning upon deities partly animal and partly human in shape, deities who, because of the advanced abilities of the artists of the day, were portrayed in innumerable esoteric guises of great intricacy. That the deities in question were terrible rather than benign is also made clear enough by the manner in which they are presented to our gaze in the designs and by the prevalence therein of decapitated heads of sacrificial victims.

This brings me to the vexed question of human sacrifice in the Andean area in ancient times. Garcilaso, speaking on his own authority and also citing Father Blas Valera, says that human sacrifice was absolutely alien to the spirit of Incaic Sun-worship, but that it had been common prior to the rise to power of that dynasty. On the other hand, other authoritative Chroniclers would have us believe that human beings, chiefly women and children, were offered up to the Sun, but only on the very greatest occasions and then under the direct control either of the Inca himself or of some high-born official representing him.[17] There is a trace, too, of another type of human sacrifice said to have been practiced in Incaic days. Speaking of the death of the Inca Pachacutec, Santa Cruz tells us that there was general and sincere mourning throughout the realm and that food, wool, and clothing were distributed among the people. At the same time many of his old captains were buried with him, and also all his pages, the idea being that the dead emperor would have need of their services in the other life. Additional light is thrown on this matter by Father Molina, of Cuzco, who informs us that the Incas and their subjects believed that the soul did not die with the body. The spirits of good people went to rest with the Creator and those of bad folk went to a realm of perpetual torment ruled by a demon named Supay. In the hope that the departed were in the land of bliss the best of everything was offered up to their spirits by those of their kinsmen who remained alive. The immolation of captains and of pages was but an extension of this practice. The realm of Supay, we may note in passing, was a place where the wicked suffered hunger and thirst, their food being charcoal, snakes, toads, and other unpleasant things. His name was always greeted by violent expectoration upon the ground.[18]

One thing that is sometimes cited in support of the claim that human sacrifices on a large scale were practiced in Incaic times is the so-called cemetery of the sacrificed women in the precinct of the Sun Temple at Pachacamac. Dr. Uhle found there the remains of very many women whose deaths had been violent. As the great archæologist says, one's first guess would be that these were the bodies of *Aclla-cuna* who had broken their vows and had been condignly punished by strangulation. But he goes on to show that this conjecture is made untenable by the fact that the bodies in question had been buried very honorably, their graves being furnished with various objects which the sacrificed women had used and cherished during their lives. The validity of this argument is borne out by a passage in Betánzos wherein that author first gives a long list of the animals offered up at the more ordinary sort of ceremonies, after which he goes on to say that children were also sacrificed by being buried alive in couples, and that with them were placed all the utensils that a married couple would usually have, everything being of the finest quality.[19] In view of this evidence it is clear that the ornate burials at Pachacamac were, as Dr. Uhle has said, the burials of women ceremonially sacrificed in honor of the Sun. But the said cemetery does not prove that such sacrifices were practiced on a large scale, for there is nothing to prove that the burials there were all made at one period; they are just as likely to have been made a few at a time during a long stretch of years. Finally, in the important relation written in 1586 by Don Juan de Ulloa Mogollón, Corregidor of the Province of Collaguas, near Arequipa, we read that, in addition to the ordinary animal sacrifices, there were special human sacrifices designed to propitiate angry *huacas,* such sacrifices being made only by express command of the Inca.[20]

It seems probable, on the whole, that human sacrifices did form a recognized part of the Incaic polity, both for religious and for personal motives. But it was employed sparingly, no such chronic and systematic misuse of human life as that which prevailed in Mexico and Yucatan ever having been countenanced by the Incas. The right to authorize human sacrifices was a prerogative of the sovereign, and they were made only on his specific order, not only to the Sun and to such *huacas* as continued to be officially recognized, but to the more-than-usually illustrious dead.

Manifestations of the intellectual life of the early Andeans other than those appertaining to religion abound. There is that which, for want of a more accurate term, we must call their literature, albeit we candidly admit that, strictly speaking, it is incorrect to speak of literature where no letters are in question. Yet, in Incaic times, there were poetical compositions and other compositions verbally perpetuated by professional bards called *haravecs* which, in all save a technical sense, were literature. Of lyrical verse, unrhymed, but at any rate either rhythmical or cadenced, there was probably a goodly amount at the Incas' court. It is inconceivable that a people who had evolved for the honor of their rulers so elaborate a ritualistic etiquette as we know that they had should not also have produced some form or other of lyrical poetry, presumably in large part of the complimentary variety usual in palaces the world over.

Garcilaso copies from Father Blas Valera one of the most charming and most celebrated of these court poems. It is

based on a pretty fable which the Inca historian tells thus:
"They say that the Creator placed a maiden, the daughter of a
king, in the sky, who holds a vase full of water, to pour out
when the earth requires it. Occasionally her brother is supposed to break it, and the blow causes thunder, lightning, and
thunderbolts. They say that these are caused by a man, because they are the deeds of a ferocious man, and not of a
tender woman. But the maiden causes the snow, hail and rain
to fall, because they are more kind and gentle acts and produce great benefits."[21] Garcilaso then goes on to tell us that
the poem was preserved in knot-records which were interpreted to Father Valera by the official who had charge of
them. He adds that he had heard this myth in his youth. I
offer a translation of the poem, the original Quechua version
of which is quoted by Garcilaso from Father Valera, in the
place cited above. The sense of the lyric is as follows:

> Beautiful princess,
> thy dear brother
> thy cup
> is now breaking.
> So for this
> there is thunder,
> lightning,
> thunderbolts falling.
> But, princess,
> thy water,
> dropping, rains
> where sometimes also
> there will be hail,
> there will be snow.
> The maker of the earth,
> Pachacamac
> Viracocha
> for this duty
> has placed thee,
> has created thee.

It is clear enough that the matter of this lyric is purely Indian. The imagery in it is simple, but delicate. Nevertheless,

a well trained and careful student of literature, Dr. E. C. Hills, would have us believe that the lyric is a Spanish composition of the sort which, in Garcilaso's day, was called *redondilla*.[22] In this opinion I cannot concur because the *matter* of the poem is obviously purely Andean and because its *form*—so far as it can be said to have poetic form—is so simple that it might occur anywhere.

Equally Andean are two compositions which have been preserved by Don Felipe Huamán Poma de Ayala. The first is a lament by a woman who had been caught in adultery and bound by her hair to a lofty crag where she was left to perish. Its sense is as follows:

Father Condor, carry me hence, brother Falcon guide me hence.
Intercede for me with my dear mother.
Now for five days I have had neither food nor drink.
Father messenger, bearer of tidings, swift runner, take away my
    tongue and my bowels.
Make intercession for me with my dear father and my dear mother.[23]

The second poem sounds a note more fierce, virile, and warlike:

From his skull we shall drink;
we shall adorn ourselves with his teeth;
his bones shall serve us as flutes;
with his skin for a drum, we shall dance.[24]

Still another note is sounded by a very simple but very touching love-song which runs:

To this my song
Thou shalt sleep.
In the dead of night
I shall come.[25]

In the four compositions thus far examined we find four distinct notes, namely, the mystical, the pathetic, the martial, and the amatory. Yet, despite the differences between them, these four specimens of Incaic literature—if that term be per-

missible—have one element in common: they are all typically
Andean in tone and in spirit.

Altogether different from the foregoing compositions, save
for the Andean quality that pervades them all, are the hymns
or prayers said to have been addressed to one god or another
by this Inca or by that. A few of them may be given here
for the purpose of showing their general characteristics. The
sense of one of the most celebrated of these supplications is as
follows:

> Viracocha, Lord of the Universe!
> Whether male or female,
> at any rate commander of heat and reproduction,
> being one who,
> even with His spittle. can work sorcery.
> Where art Thou?
> Would that Thou wert not hidden from this son of Thine!
> He may be above;
> He may be below;
> or, perchance, abroad in space.
> Where is His mighty judgement-seat?
> Hear me!
> He may be spread abroad among the upper waters;
> or, among the lower waters and their sands
> He may be dwelling.
> Creator of the world,
> Creator of man,
> great among my ancestors,
> before Thee
> my eyes fail me,
> though I long to see Thee;
> for, seeing Thee,
> knowing Thee,
> learning from Thee,
> understanding Thee,
> I shall be seen by Thee,
> and Thou wilt know me.
> The Sun—the Moon;
> the Day—the Night;
> Summer—Winter;
> not in vain,
> in orderly succession,

do they march
to their destined place,
to their goal.
They arrive
wherever
Thy royal staff
Thou bearest.
Oh! Harken to me,
listen to me,
let it not befall
that I grow weary
and die.[26]

This beautiful, groping supplication has almost the quality of some of the Psalms of David. In it we see bewilderment coupled with a passionate longing to know the truth of the Creator's personality and with a definite attempt to reason out the nature of His being. It fairly represents, I think, the state of mind and of spirit that must have possessed the great Inca Pachacutec in the days before he made his momentous address to the assembled priesthood of the empire concerning the supremacy of Viracocha.

A note of much greater sureness, indeed, of complete conviction concerning the nature of the Creator, is sounded in an orison preserved by Father Molina, of Cuzco, and by Father Morúa which may be rendered into English thus:

O conquering Viracocha!
Ever-present Viracocha!
Thou who art without equal upon the earth!
Thou who art from the beginnings of the world until its end!
Thou gavest life and valour to men, saying,
"Let this be a man."
And to woman, saying,
"Let this be a woman."
Thou madest them and gavest them being.
Watch over them, that they may live in health and in peace.
Thou who art in the highest heavens,
and among the clouds of the tempest,
grant them long life,
and accept this our sacrifice,
O Creator.[27]

On a closely similar plane is a prayer addressed to Pachacamac, which has been preserved by Bishop Oré, the sense of
which is this:

> O Pachacamac!
> Thou who hast existed from the beginning,
> Thou who shalt exist until the end,
> powerful but merciful,
> Who didst create man by saying,
> "Let man be,"
> Who defendest us from evil,
> and preservest our life and our health,
> art Thou in the sky or upon the earth?
> in the clouds or in the deeps?
> Hear the voice of him who implores Thee,
> and grant him his petitions.
> Give us life everlasting,
> preserve us, and accept this our sacrifice.[28]

These selections will suffice to show to what philosophic
heights the minds of the élite in Incaic times were capable of
attaining. It is but right to mention, in passing, that writers
of the "discouragistic" school, those dour souls who refuse to
concede that the early Andeans were anything more than
savages wallowing in the darkness of complete ignorance and
superstition, would try to convince us that these poems were
Catholic or Biblical in source and in content. It is true, as I
have hinted above, that they do have something of the fresh-
ness and fervor which pervade the most moving parts of the
Old Testament. A study of the writings of the many Catholic
missionaries who flocked to Peru after the Conquest will convince any reasonable person, however, that those missionaries
found evidences of exalted spirituality already existing in the
people, duly honoring it and utilizing it in their own labors
for the conversion of the people to Christianity. The similarity in quality between the lore embodied in the Old Testament and that represented by these selections is to be explained on the ground of an approximate likeness in mental
culture between the folk of ancient Palestine and the folk of

ancient Peru, rather than on the ground of a supposititious priestly influence after the Conquest.

We are now come to the hotly contested question of whether or not the Incas possessed anything resembling dramatic art. There is a play in Quechua called variously *Ollanta, Ollantay,* or *Apu Ollanta* which has attained to a certain degree of renown, not so much on account of its rather modest literary merits as on account of the prolonged debate among writers as to its age. There have been a number of respect-worthy critics, among them Johann Jakob von Tschudi and Sir Clements Markham, who have held the opinion that the drama in question is, in theme and in wording, altogether pre-Spanish. This is the extreme of opinion on the one side; the other, to the effect that *Ollanta* was composed in the last quarter of the eighteenth century, has been held by Middendorf, Dr. Hills, and other competent judges.[29]

It seems to me that the plot of *Ollanta* and the incidents of the drama suffice to make manifest its spuriousness as an antique dramatic composition. The plot is both trivial and preposterous, dealing as it does with the love-passages between Ollanta, a warrior not of the Incaic caste, and a daughter of the Inca Pachacutec. It is unthinkable that any man in the empire, save perhaps some very high and powerful chief, should have had the temerity to entertain a wish to woo the Inca's daughter. Furthermore, had an insignificant upstart such as Ollanta done so, in spite of every obstacle, and done so successfully, his very boldness and his very prowess as a lover would have aureoled his name with a celebrity even greater than that of his flouted sovereign. He would have been so very famous, this audacious and highly treasonable lover, that this story would have been one of the first tales to be related to the Spaniards upon their arrival in the country. But not a word of any such story is to be found in the writings of any Chronicler. The nearest approach to anything of the sort is the tale told by Father Cabello de Balboa concerning the loves of a youth named Quilaco Yupanqui, of the imperial caste, and an *aclla* named Cori-Coyllur (Golden Star), this affair having befallen in the time of Huáscar, just prior to the Conquest.[30] The resemblance is, therefore, very slight.

Moreover, in the course of the play, various incidents—such as disrespectful speeches by persons of low degree to Incas of high rank and even to the sovereign himself, such also as a tendency on the part of various ladies and gentlemen to stroll about in the *acllahuasi*—are represented as taking place in a manner wholly lacking in verisimilitude. It is, therefore, clear that, at any rate in its present form, *Ollanta* is not a true Incaic drama;[31] but it does seem to contain a number of ancient indigenous lyrics which are woven into the thread of the action.

Although *Ollanta* cannot be regarded as an example of Incaic dramatic art, it is certain that the court at Cuzco, and probably also the provincial courts, witnessed frequently a variety of dramatic or pseudo-dramatic performances. These included, no doubt, the antics of mimes, the posturings of dancers, the lyrics of the *haravec-cuna* (bards), and the lengthier recitations of the *amauta-cuna* (sages, historians, wisemen). In connection with these things Father Acosta writes as follows: "At Peru I have seene plaies in maner of combats, where the men of both sides were sometimes so chafed that often their *Puclla* (which was the name of this exercise) fell out to be dangerous. I have also seene divers sortes of dances, wherein they did counterfait and represent certaine trades and offices, as sheepheards, laborers, fishers, and hunters, and commonly they made all those dances with a very grave sound and pase: there were other dances and maskes, which they called cuacones, whose actions were pure representations of the divell. There were also men that dance on the shoulders one of another, as they do in Portugall, the which they call Paellas. The greatest part of these dances were superstitions and kindes of idolatries: for they honoured their idolls and Guacas in that maner. . . . In these dances they vse sundry sortes of instruments, whereof some are like flutes or little Canons, others like drummes, and others like shells: but commonly they sing all with the voyce, and first

one or two sing the song, then all the rest answer them. Some
of these songs were very wittily composed, contayning histories, others were full of superstitions, and some were meere
follies."[32]

Garcilaso also tells us that the *amautas* or sages attached to
the court were wont to compose tragedies on such subjects as
war and the heroic deeds of former kings, and comedies about
homely life and husbandry. Both sorts of plays were, he says,
acted by Incas and others of high rank for the delectation of
the court. In all of this Cieza de León agrees.[33]

There is ample reason for believing, therefore, that in
ancient times the imaginative powers of the Andean élite
were considerable, and that they found expression in verbal
compositions of one sort or another. In a volume which is a
curiously touching and little-known memorial to the aboriginal Andean mentality there are several tales, obviously native in plot and in language, that display the characteristics
of the Indian mind as it existed in ancient Peru. I refer to a
pathetic and moving bi-lingual volume entitled *Tarmapap
Pacha-Huaraynin. Azucenas Quechuas. Por unos Parías,*
which was brought out at Tarma (Peru), in 1905. Although
it is now many years since I saw a copy of this book—it is
extremely rare in spite of being only a quarter of a century
old—the impression which it made upon my sympathies has
never faded. The "Pariahs" who issued it evidently sought,
and with success, to gather a series of stories illustrative of the
quality of their race's sentiments and aspirations. Of all the
tales which it contains that entitled *La Mariposa Blanca,* The
White Butterfly, is, I think, the most beautiful and the most
typical. It runs somewhat as follows:

A young Indian warrior was living happily with his wife in their
rough stone hut. Time went by, and the wife bore a man-child,
greatly to her husband's delight and her own. When the boy was a
year or two old, the father had to go away from home in order to
serve in the army. So he went off, leaving his wife and child well
provided for in the hut. In his absence the woman worked all day
at her duties, and in the evenings, sitting in the doorway of the hut,

busied herself by sewing or by playing with the little boy. On several such evenings a pretty white butterfly came fluttering into the hut and, flying around the fire in the centre of it, made strange shadows on the roof and on the walls. The woman liked to have the butterfly come, and sometimes she would speak to it at some length. One night, while she was doing so, the little boy asked her who the butterfly was, that she spoke to him so much. She, filled with tender thoughts of her absent husband, answered softly, "He is my lover."

In due course the husband returned safely from the wars and was tenderly greeted by his wife and child. Presently he sent the woman away upon an errand, and then asked the lad how she had employed herself during his absence. The child replied, "She talked much with her lover in the evenings." The husband, in a fury of jealousy, went forth and found his wife. Knocking her down, he disembowelled her. Afterwards, repentant of his violent passion and of his crime, he went sadly back to his hut.

One night, not long after, while the father was mournfully sitting beside his little son in the doorway, the white butterfly came again, and the lad cried out, "Look, father, there is the lover of my mother who used to come to her." Then the poor father knew the whole of his crime. In his despair and remorse he went forth and ended his life.

The various materials here presented make it clear enough that melancholy was a salient characteristic of the Andean mentality in olden days. Almost equally prominent and frequent are such traits as martial fierceness, amative tenderness, and philosophical reflectiveness. Humor is much less often met with in the vestiges of the verbal literature that have come down to us. Wit, or perhaps sententiousness would be a more accurate term, is chiefly represented in the aphorisms of Pachacutec, preserved by Garcilaso and mentioned on page 262 above.

The musical heritage of modern inhabitants of Ecuador, Peru, and Bolivia, derived in large part from the music of the Incas, has been carefully studied during the past twenty years by various competent musicians of those countries and, with special success, by M. and Mme. d'Harcourt, of Paris, with the collaboration of Mme. Paul Rivet, who is by birth an Ecuadorian, and of others. Some two hundred songs have been collected by them from all parts of the Andean area. Although a large proportion of these show quite plainly the influence of Spanish culture, certain others are purely native in quality and content. In ancient times the musical instruments all fell within one or the other of two technical categories: percussion instruments and wind instruments. Both of these, however, contained many types of contrivances, the most elaborate of which was the pan-pipe or syrinx, called *quena* in Quechua, sometimes made of reeds, sometimes of pottery, examples of the latter type being often of great beauty. Trumpets fashioned from shell, from wood, from clay, and from metal have been found, some of them elaborate in design and finish, but none of them provided with a reed. Flutes of many sorts likewise abound in collections, as well as a great variety of bells, whistles, and so on. Nor were these instruments by any means all of the Incaic period; for there is plentiful evidence that all the previous cultures of the Andean area possessed a wide range of musical instruments of the classes here referred to. With reason, therefore, do M. and Mme. d'Harcourt remark that, as regards musical advancement, ancient Peru stands at the forefront of the pre-Spanish peoples of America.[33]

Before bringing this chapter to an end I wish to mention, if only very briefly, a matter of great intricacy and fascination, namely, the medical lore and practice of the ancient Andeans. Rich materials for an extended study of the subject exist in the pages of Acosta, Cobo, Garcilaso and other Chroniclers, as well as in those of specially medical authors such as Dr. Francisco Hernandez and Dr. Nicolás Monardes.[34]

According to González Holguín the general word in Quechua for doctor was *hampi-camayoc*, literally remedy-keeper. The best medical practice known to the Incas included a knowledge of purging and bleeding. One of the commonest and best of their many purgative herbs was the root called *huachancana*. This the patient took in the form of an infusion and after imbibing it he would sit in the warm sunlight until overcome by sickness and vertigo, coupled with a tickling sensation all over his body. Very soon after that violent evacuation by both ways began during which worms or any poisons that the patient might be suffering from were gotten rid of. After a time the sickness wore off, and the patient felt himself to be bursting with rude health and also to be extremely hungry. Bleeding was effected by means of punctures in the epidermis with a sharp flint or crystal lancet fixed in a wooden handle, the point of the incision being the nearest possible to the apparent seat of the pain. Practitioners in good standing, who in general ministered only to the imperial caste and to the aristocracy, included both men and women well advanced in years for the most part. Although such persons as these knew that a white-coated tongue was a sign of stomach trouble, they were ignorant of such simple diagnostic methods as taking the pulse and as examining the urine and the fæces, nor did they know aught of clysters. All their medicaments were simple herbs, not compounds. A few of them may well be described briefly here.

The resin of the *mulli* tree, very common in the region of Cuzco and elsewhere in the high Andes, was used with remarkable results on wounds, which it caused to heal rapidly. Leaves of the low bush called *chilca* were heated, presumably in water, in a clay pot and then applied as a sort of poultice to joints or sprains into which the cold had made its way. *Ractania*, a sort of geranium, was a plant whose roots were charred and, while still very hot, packed around the teeth and left there until cool. This was painful, but it was a treatment often resorted to by people suffering from bad gums, for it burned away the diseased flesh and allowed new, healthy flesh to come in its stead. Leaves of *sayri*, which we call tobacco, were reduced to a fine powder which was snuffed up the nose in order to clear the nasal passages. It was not used for smoking. Juice of the leaf of the water-plant called *matecllu* was employed with great success in order to clear the eyes, and a poultice made from the bruised leaves of this plant was very efficacious in correcting some forms of blindness and in relieving pains of the eye.[35]

These examples will suffice to indicate the general character of the materia medica of the Incas. Nor should the *cuca,* the most highly prized by them of all the plants which they knew, be passed over in silence. To them it was the greatest blessing derived from the vegetable kingdom, for it relieved them of much anguish. In cocaine, a derivative of the plant, the world has one of its most potent and, under proper control, most beneficial drugs. Its use, in ancient times, was most strictly controlled by the state, but there was a widespread appreciation of the various medicinal uses of the *cuca* plant. It seems, on the whole, to have been a benefit to mankind, but one full of danger because of the ease with which it can be abused.[36]

Another great medicine which was given to the world by Peru, namely, Chinchona or quinine, now universally employed as a febrifuge, was probably known to the ancient Andeans only in a limited way and in a restricted region. This, however, is a point which has not been definitely settled.[37]

Finally I must mention that the great and difficult surgical operation known as trephining, *i. e.,* cutting away a part of the osseous substance of the head of a living person, was brought to a high state of perfection in Incaic times, and was practiced with great frequency, as the somatological collections in our museums clearly show. That the art was not originated by the Incas, but was practiced on the coast in earlier times has recently been made evident by Dr. Julio Tello, of Lima.[38]

NOTES TO CHAPTER X

[1] The word *huaca* has, however, many shades of meaning. The one here employed is the most important of them. Consult: González Holguín, 1607–1608, I, pp. 158–159. Torres Rubio, 1603, article, *huaca.* Tschudi, 1853. Markham, 1864. Jijón y Caamaño, 1919, pp. 72–97.

[2] Jijón, 1919, Ch. i.

[3] Arriaga, 1621, p. 11.

[4] Pedro Pizarro, 1921, pp. 241–244.

[5] Arriaga, 1621, pp. 11–16. Cobo, Bk. III, Ch. xxix. Jijón, 1919, pp. 99–102. The Quechua words for bezoar-stones are *quicu* and *illa.*

[6] Ávila, 1873, Ch. ii. Betánzos, Chs. i and ii. Cieza, Pt. II, Ch. v. Cobo,

Bk. XIII, Ch. iv. Garcilaso, Pt. I, Bk. II, Ch. ii. Molina, of Cuzco, 1873, pp. 26–34. Santa Cruz Pachacuti-yamqui Salcamayhua, 1873, pp. 70–72. Santillán, 1879, p. 32. Sarmiento, Ch. vii. Alexander, 1920, pp. 232–242. Jiménez de la Espada, 1879; and 1887, p. 118. Lafone Quevedo, 1892b. Uhle, 1903, pp. 47–52.

7 Acosta, Bk. I, Ch. xxv. Calancha, Bk. I, Ch. xiv. Casas, 1892, Ch. xvi. Cieza, Pt. I, Ch. xxxviii; Pt. II, Chs. iv and v. Huamán Poma de Ayala, 1613. Lizárraga, Pt. I, Ch. xviii. Montesinos, Ch. i. Oré, 1598, Ch. ix.

8 Joyce, 1913c.

9 Cieza, Pt. I, Ch. lxxii; Pt. II, Chs. lviii and lxv. Cobo, Bk. XIII, Ch. xvii. Garcilaso, Pt. I, Bk. VI, Chs. xxx and xxxi. Pizarro, 1921, pp. 209–210. Sancho, 1917, pp. 97–98.

10 Estete, 1918, pp. 27–28.

11 Anonymous conquest, 1929, pp. 37–38.

12 Uhle, 1903, Chs. x–xv, inclusive. Bandelier, 1910, p. 277.

13 Cieza, Pt. II, Ch. viii. Cobo, Bk. XIII, Ch. iv. Santa Cruz, 1873, p. 76. Sarmiento, Ch. xxxi.

14 Cabello, Pt. III, Ch. xv, pp. 472–480 of N. Y. P. L. MS. Cobo, Bk. XII, Ch. xii. Sarmiento, Ch. xxxi.

15 Cieza, Pt. I, Ch. xliii and xcviii and ci; Pt. II, Ch. v. Cobo, Bk. XIII, Ch. iv. Garcilaso, Pt. I, Bk. II, Chs. ii and xxvii. Román y Zamora, Pt. III, Bk. I, Ch. iii.

16 San Pedro and Canto, 1865. Arriaga, 1621, Ch. ii. Sarmiento, Ch. lxi.

17 Cieza, Pt. II, Chs. xxv and xxviii. Cobo, Bk. XIII, Ch. xxi. Garcilaso, Pt. I, Bk. II, Ch. viii. Santillán, 1879, p. 32.

18 Cieza, Pt. I, Ch. lxii; Pt. II, Ch. v. Garcilaso, Pt. I, Bk. II, Ch. ii; Bk. VIII, Ch. xxi. Molina, of Cuzco, 1873, p. 48. Santa Cruz, 1873, p. 100.

19 Betánzos, Ch. xvii. Garcilaso, Pt. I, Bk. IV, Ch. ii. Uhle, 1903, pp. 86–88.

20 Ulloa Mogollón, 1885, pp. 44–45.

21 Garcilaso, Pt. I, Bk. II, Ch. xxvii.

22 Hills, 1914, pp. 153–154.

23 Hills, 1914, p. 156, gives the Quechua text and another translation of this lament.

24 Hills, 1914, pp. 156–157.

25 Garcilaso, Pt. I, Bk. II, Ch. xxvii.

26 The Quechua text of this supplication, derived from Santa Cruz, appears with the emendations of the great Quechua-scholar, Dr. Miguel Mossi, in Lafone Quevedo, 1892b, p. 339. At that place will be found also Dr. Lafone Quevedo's translation of the emended text into Spanish. Another English version of it than that given by me will be found in Markham, 1910, pp. 100–101 and in Alexander, 1920, pp. 237–238. The original and unemended text in Quechua, as given by Santa Cruz, varies considerably between the editions of Jiménez de la Espada and of Markham. Compare Santa Cruz, 1879, p. 248 and Santa Cruz, 1873, p. 79. The English version which I give is based upon materials provided in Lafone Quevedo's article, cited above.

27 Molina, of Cuzco, 1873, p. 33. Somewhat, but very little, different is the version of this orison given by Morúa, Bk. I Ch. vii.

28 Oré, 1598, Ch. ix. Todd, 1914, pp. 177–178.

[29] Against the antiquity of *Ollanta* are ranged: Hills, 1914; Middendorf, 1890; 1890b; 1890c; and 1891b; Mitré, 1881. The strongest possible argument in favor of the antiquity of the drama is that given by Markham in a carefully documented but rather peppery essay which precedes his translation of Cieza, Pt. II. For the best version in English of the play see Markham, 1910, pp. 321–407.

[30] Cabello, Pt. III, Chs. xxx–xxxiii, inclusive, pp. 729–799 of the N. Y. P. L. MS., provides the source material for this tale. Markham gives a good résumé of it in pp. lv–lx of the volume containing his translation of Cieza, Pt. II.

[31] Hills, 1914, p. 176.

[32] Acosta, Bk. VI, Ch. xxviii. Cieza, Pt. II, Ch. xii. Garcilaso, Pt. I, Bk. II, Ch. xxvii.

[33] Harcourt, R. and M. d', 1925, p. 87.

[34] General data on the *materia medica,* diagnostics, etc., of the Indians in Peru before the Spanish Conquest will be found in Acosta, Bk. IV; Cobo, Bk. XIII, Ch. xxxv; Bk. XIV, Ch. x; Garcilaso, Pt. I, Bk. II, Chs. xxiv and xxv. Concerning the two Spanish medical writers mentioned here I can speak only briefly. Dr. Francisco Hernández was commissioned by King Philip II to go to Mexico (then called New Spain) in order to make an exhaustive study of the native medicinal plants and other curative substances. He did so, and, according to Acosta, caused over 1,200 paintings of plants to be made wherewith to illustrate his text. The first edition of his book, entitled *Quatro libros de la Naturaleza y Virtudes de las plantas y animales que estan recevidos en el uso de Medicina en la Nueva España,* was printed in Mexico City by the widow of Diego López Dávalos, in 1615. As many of the plants and animals described by Dr. Hernández existed also in Peru, his book is valuable for students of native Andean medical lore.

The work of Dr. Nicolás Monardes was first, but only in part, printed in Seville in 1565. The most important early edition in Spanish was entitled *Primera y segunda y tercera partes de la Historia medicinal de las cosas que se traén de nuestras Indias Occidentales que sirven de Medicina.* It was brought out in Seville by Alonso Escrivano, in 1574, and again in Seville, by Fernando Diaz, in 1580. The book was early translated into Latin, Italian, French, and English, the first edition in English being entitled *Ioyfull Newes out of the Newfound Worlde.* The translator was John Frampton, the publisher was E. Allde, and the date was London, 1596. (These notes of mine are frankly superficial, but are based upon excellent materials, namely, the Catalogue of the John Carter Brown Library, the fully documented catalogues of Messrs. Maggs Bros., of London, and Palau's *Manual del Librero Hispano-Americano.*)

[35] These examples of remedies used in Incaic times are mentioned by Garcilaso, Pt. I, Bk. II, Chs. xxiv and xxv; Cobo, Bk. XIII, Ch. xxxv, and Bk. XIV, Ch. x. For more ample treatment of some of the medicines mentioned see: Cobo, Bk. VI, Ch. lxxvii (*mulli*); Bk. V, Ch. xliv (*chilca*); Bk. IV, Ch. lvi (*sayri*).

[36] Cobo, Bk. V, Ch. xxix. Garcilaso, Pt. I, Bk. VIII, Ch. xv. Acosta, Bk. IV, Ch. xxii. Mortimer, 1901.

[37] Markham, 1880, p. 5. Mr. Markham (as he then was) took the leading part in introducing Chinchona into British India and in thus making it commercially important.

[38] Tello, 1912; 1929, pp. 145–150. Muñiz and McGee, 1895.

CHAPTER XI

THE ART OF THE LOOM IN ANCIENT PERU

Weaving, or at any rate some form of industrial art very closely related to it, appears at the time when a given people is beginning to pass from the hunter-and-fisher stage of culture into the pastoral and agricultural stage. At that point in their advancement along cultural lines a progressing people becomes aware that the skins of animals and the feathers of birds are not very convenient or very satisfactory coverings for the human body. They therefore look about them to see what better materials can be found. The commencement of weaving, and also the commencement of pottery-making, is symptomatic of a people's becoming sedentary, that is, of their abandoning the primitive phase of culture and of their entering the archaic phase.

Andean archæology provides us with at least one example of a people so low in the cultural scale that they were barely within the archaic horizon. I refer to the earliest known folk of the Arica district. They had no knowledge of ceramic art, nor of the use of any metals. Their textile art was of the most rudimentary description, consisting merely of knitting and braiding with totora-fibre from which they fashioned crude garments wherewith they supplemented those made from skins of animals.[1]

The situation here briefly referred to represents the lowest of the textile arts in the Andean area of ancient times; in this chapter we shall chiefly study the higher manifestations of the art of the loom as it was known to the pre-Spanish Andean folk.

1. The Raw Materials

Of the four principal textile fibres known to the world as a whole—i. e., linen, silk, cotton, and wool—only the two last

450

named were known in ancient Peru. They were not, however, the only substances used for the fashioning of fabrics; other materials were employed likewise, as will be noted presently, their importance being secondary, for in general most of the textiles made by the ancient Andeans were either of cotton or of wool, or else of a combination of the two.

This being so, it is well to give a little space to each of these materials.

Cotton belongs to the genus *Gossypium* of the natural order of the *Malvaceæ*. The leading South American tongues possess words for cotton, those interesting to us being: *Utcu*, the Quechua word; *qhuea*, the Colla (Aymará); *jam*, pronounced *hahm*, the Mochica; *amandiyú*, the Guaraní; and *amariy'ú*, the Tupi.[2] There are many varieties of cotton now in commercial use throughout the world, a goodly proportion of which are grown with profit in modern Peru. In the botanical writings of Linnæus, Lamarck, Cavanilles, and other justly celebrated specialists[3] one can find a wealth of descriptive material regarding the varieties of cotton known to mankind. For us, however, only a few varieties of the plant are important, those being:

Gossypium hirsutum, Linnæus, is an American cotton, probably of Mexican origin. This was the plant which supplied the Mayas and other advanced peoples of Middle America with the raw material for their well developed textile arts.[4] It may have been known in early Peru, also, but of this we cannot be certain.

Gossypium religiosum, Linnæus, is a rather large perennial plant which grows wild in the *montaña* zone of Peru and in western Brazil. It has leaves with three sharp lobes. Hitherto it has not attained to commercial importance because its seeds stick together in a kidney-shaped mass which can be separated from the fibre only with difficulty. Jean Lérius, a Frenchman who was in Brazil from 1557 to 1558, shows that the natives of that country did use the fibre of this plant for textile purposes, among others the weaving of hammocks.[5]

Gossypium vitifolium, Lamarck, grows in the Department

of Piura, northern Peru, where it was seen and studied by an able, but now almost forgotten, botanist, Richard Spruce. It appears to be an older and a wilder kind of cotton than most others, and it may be an ancestral form of better known and more widely spread varieties.[6]

Gossypium peruvianum, Cavanilles, known to modern commerce as Peruvian Full Rough or Peruvian Moderate Rough, is undoubtedly the most important kind of cotton for our consideration in the present connection.

The plant grows to a height of fifteen feet or more. At present it is peculiar, in Peru, to the Department of Piura in the northernmost part of the coast and to that of Ica in the southern part. It has been introduced into other countries, but the process of acclimitization has usually been accompanied by a loss of those prized traits which distinguish the plant in Peru. It does grow in the Ecuadorian province of Imbabura, being common there up to an altitude of 8,000 feet above the sea.[7]

The above-mentioned prized traits of *Gossypium peruvianum* are: the length of its fibres, ranging from an inch to very close on two inches in ancient specimens; and, the presence of tiny, hook-shaped projections along the fibres which give this cotton that "rough" quality that has made it so valuable in ancient as well as in modern times. It is a fibre which lent itself especially well to the modes of spinning and weaving anciently employed by the Andean peoples. Still another point in favor of *Gossypium peruvianum* is the fact that it is perennial, not annual. It can live and bear as long as twenty years, albeit as a rule modern planters cut it down after the eighth year.

Strangely enough Father Acosta is the only one of the Chroniclers of Peru who gives any extended notice to the cotton of that country; Father Cobo, so informative on most points relative to the plant-life and animal-life of pre-Spanish America, does not even mention it. Father Acosta, who wrote between 1587 and 1590, speaks of *Gossypium peruvianum* as follows:

Cotton likewise growes vpon small shrubs and great trees like to little apples, which doe open and yeelde forth this webbe; which being gathered, they spinne to make stuffes. It is one of the things at the Indies of greatest profite, and most in vse, for it serves them both insteed of flaxe and wooll to make their garments. It groweth in hote soyle, and there is a great store in the vallies and sea coast of Peru, in New Spaine, the Philippines and China. But the greatest store of any place that I know is in the province of Tucuman, in that of Santa Cruz de la Sierra, and at Paraguay, whereas Cotton is their chiefe revenue. They carry cotton into Spaine from the Iland of Santo Domingo; and the yeare that I spake of there came 64,000 *arrobas*. At the Indies whereas this cotton growes, they make cloth, which both the men and women vse commonly, making table napkins thereof, yea and sailes for their shippes. There is some coarse, and other that is fine and delicate; they dye it into diverse colours, as wee doe our woollen cloth in Europe.[8]

This quaint passage is of interest to us chiefly because it indicates that two regions within the borders of the Inca empire, namely, the Peruvian coast and Tucumán, were cotton-producing, and that one, Santa Cruz de la Sierra, on its margin, was so as well. It will be remembered that among the products of Tucma or Tucumán brought to the Inca Viracocha by the ambassadors from the chiefs of that kingdom cotton cloth was mentioned. In view of this fact and in view, also, of the passage just copied from Father Acosta, it is strange that the late M. Boman should have hesitated to believe that cotton was cultivated in Tucumán.[9] It is quite clear, from his mention of "small shrubs and great trees," that Father Acosta had in mind at least two sorts of cotton. This is a point to which I shall revert very soon.

It is well to mention, in passing, that the noted French voyager, Amédée François Frézier, who was in Peru between 1712 and 1714, made rather interesting but very inaccurate observations upon *Gossypium peruvianum* in the course of which he emphasized the perennial character of the plant.[10]

I have no intention of attempting to unravel the knotty problem of the botanical origins of cotton in America. It will suffice to point out that possibly *Gossypium religiosum* and *Gossypium vitifolium* represent species of cotton which, at some time or other, were hybridized by the agency of man and so gave rise to the cultivated cottons of ancient America, in especial to *Gossypium peruvianum*. Still more striking is the suggestion made by Sir George Watt, who points out that *Gossypium Darwinii*, Watt, was found growing wild in the Galápagos Islands in 1835, at which time no cotton was cultivated there. Sir George Watt shows that it is very probable that this wild cotton of the Galápagos is an ancestral type of *Gossypium peruvianum*.[11] If so, we may suppose that it formerly grew on the mainland also.

Returning now to the industrial aspect of cotton in ancient Peru, it may be safely said that *Gossypium peruvianum* was cultivated on the coast of Peru as early as the opening centuries of the Christian Era and that it then served as one of the raw materials for a highly developed textile art.[12] Although some students have thought that two kinds of cotton were anciently used in Peru, the one being *Gossypium peruvianum* and the other perhaps *Gossypium hirsutum*, the specimens of ancient cotton examined by me in many collections during many years have all been without doubt *Gossypium peruvianum*. Not only does the length of the staple indicate this, but also the appearance of the fibres under the microscope. The difference in color between specimens is, nevertheless, somewhat confusing. Cotton of snowy whiteness is frequently found in the work-baskets which occur in women's burials; but cotton of various shades of brown occur almost as often. It has been thought that the brown cottons are of a species distinct from the white.[13] Likewise one finds now and then cotton of a bluish or bluish-gray or of a yellowish tint. On several occasions, particularly with reference to a series of such tinted cottons which I arranged in the National Museum of Archæology in Lima in 1920, I have sought information on this matter of tinting from specialists, but they failed to establish the presence of any cotton other than *Gossypium peruvianum* and they also failed to show positively whether the colors were natural, or caused by the action of pests, or the result of dyes. Let me point out, in this connection, that rather definite information is afforded by Don Pedro Gutiérrez de Santa Clara, who wrote about 1550, in the interesting passage where he says: ". . . there is in this country much cotton which of itself is blue, brown, tawny, yellow, and the colour is so fine that it is something to be noted, as though it had been in dye for a long time, for the painter of the world gave to it those vivid colours."[14] It is well that we should bear in mind, pending future research, the possibility that other kinds of cotton, grown, as Acosta says, on "small shrubs" were anciently used for textiles in Tucumán and in other regions. At the present itme, however, I am inclined to believe that *Gossypium peruvianum* was the only cotton used in Peruvian weaving in pre-Spanish days, and that both pests and dyes worked upon its naturally white color, bringing about the variations of tint mentioned above.

The wool employed by the early Andean weavers all came from certain indigenous animals belonging to the natural order of the *Camelidæ*. The four animals in question are the *guanaco* or *huanacu*, the *llama*, the *alpaca*, and the *vicuña*. Competent zoologists think that the guanaco is the oldest form. It is of relatively slight importance as a wool-bearer, but is much valued as game, its flesh being esteemed as an article of diet. The llama is used as a carrier of burdens up to 100 pounds in weight, as a food, and as a bearer of coarse, tough wool. The wool of the alpaca is finer in quality and is noteworthy for the wide range of its natural colors which include white, bluish-gray, tawny, orange, light brown, and dark brown.[15] In ancient times the natural shades of the wool of both the llama and the alpaca were skilfully utilized in creating the designs of woollen cloths. The vicuña, whose wool is the finest and most highly prized of all, was never domesticated. These four animals, then, are kindred, and all descend from primitive *Camelidæ* whose habitat was North America. One branch moved southwards and eventually gave rise to the four animals here mentioned; the other moved into Asia and gave rise to the much larger beasts from which the comforting Dr. Jaeger derived his well-earned millions.

It may be said, in general terms, that the environment in the highlands was inimical to the raising of cotton and that on the coast it was hostile to the health of wool-bearing animals. During the archaic stage of culture each of these zones adhered, we may suppose, to that raw material for textiles which was natural to it. In the subsequent periods of greater cultural advancement an interchange of commodities came into being, as a result of which we find fabrics containing both these materials in all parts of Peru, and in many cases representing periods long before the Incas.

The secondary raw materials of ancient textile art in Peru require no more than brief mention.

The nearest approach to linen was a bast fibre derived from the maguey plant. In Quechua it was called *chuchau,* and in Colla *tauca.* Although there was no attempt to use it for fine fabrics, maguey-fibre was employed in making ropes, cords, and coarse threads; it was sometimes used in sandals, in network, and in a burlap-like cloth in which mummies were encased.

More puzzling, and at the same time more interesting, is the question of whether or not the filaments produced by the *ceyba* tree were ever used for textile purposes by the ancient Andeans. The tree in question is very common in northern Peru and in the adjacent portions of Ecuador. It grows to an immense height, and at certain seasons puts forth masses of silky white cotton or tree-wool of exceeding fineness and smoothness. This substance is the kapok of modern commerce. Manufacturers of to-day do not consider this fibre to be suitable for use in the loom; but I am inclined to believe that it was used in ancient times for the making of very delicate and subtle fabrics of great luxury. The glutinous saliva of the Indians—of which more anon—freely used during the process of spinning would obviate all difficulty in the fashioning of thread from a fibre so smooth. Moreover, the evidence given us by Francis Petty, who accompanied the famous buccaneer Thomas Cavendish on his circumnavigation of the globe in 1586–1588, leaves us in no doubt that the people of Puná were wont to gather ceyba cotton,[17] presumably for textile purposes. Against this possibility, however, must be set down two facts: first, that Father Cobo, in his chapter on the ceyba, makes no mention of any such thing;[18] second, that no fabric made of ceyba "cotton" has ever been seen by me in the collections which I have studied during the past eighteen years.

Finally, one occasionally runs across references to various strange animal substances as being used in textiles. Garcilaso states that the *viscacha,* a large, long-tailed rodent which inhabits the high Andes, was used by the Incas' subjects "in weaving, to vary the colours of their fine cloths. Its colour is a clear yellow, and a cloth mixed with it was much valued amongst the Indians, and was only used for the dresses of the nobles."[19] Human hair was likewise used, often for the purpose of giving special lustre and beauty to vicuña or alpaca wool cloth. In the wonderful archæological collection which belonged to the late Dr. Don Javier Prado y Ugarteche, of Lima, there were several pieces of fine cloth made of vicuña wool which were embellished by narrow weft stripes of fine blue-black substance that can only have been human hair. The use of this same material for the comparatively humble business of holding leather sandals to the wearer's feet is also recorded, as is also a slipper-like sandal partly woven from human hair.[20]

2. The Processes of Spinning and Weaving

The methods used by the ancient Andeans in spinning thread and in weaving fabrics have often been discussed with quite unnecessary elaboration. Simplicity was the outstanding characteristic of early Peruvian textile technology, and it is just as well that this fact be not lost sight of. Paradoxically enough, however, the simplicity of the methods employed entirely failed to restrict the rich diversity of the masterpieces produced upon a myriad of simple old Andean looms; indeed, if anything, the utter simplicity of the processes and implements employed augmented the intricacy of the webs then manufactured, doing so because of the scope that they gave to the hands of the weavers. Even in the pride of this mechanized twentieth century of ours it is wholesome for us to remember that no tool was ever invented that had greater perfection than the human hand; and *that* was not an invention of Man.

The threads, whether of cotton or of wool, used in early Peruvian stuffs of the highest quality were in every respect perfect, each in its kind.[21] Yet they were the product of rudimentary methods, the processes of thread-making varying somewhat according as the material involved was cotton or wool.[22]

Cotton, after being picked from the bursting bolls, was rid of seeds by hand, precisely as cotton was so treated everywhere in days before Whitney's cotton-gin. The seeded cotton was then bundled together into convenient lots which were then carded in order to straighten the fibres and to lay them approximately parallel with one another. It is not certain just how this was done in early days; some think that it was a process performed by a raking motion with the fingers; others, with perhaps greater reason, believe that the combs of various degrees of fineness which occur by the thousand in Peruvian burial-grounds and in ancient work-baskets were carding-combs rather than hair-combs. It seems to me that they may well have served both purposes, at the will of their owners.

After the cotton had been seeded and carded it was ready to be placed upon the distaff. This tool was a slender stick, less thick than a finger and about a foot in length, having at one end a small ring not quite closed at the upper end. Into this was fitted a convenient amount of cotton, the two ends of the mass being fluffed out somewhat in order to make it easier to finger. The lower end of the distaff was held by the spinner's left armpit or else in her left hand. Sometimes the mass of carded cotton was merely held in the left hand without the aid of a wooden distaff.

The cotton was now ready to be transferred in the form of

one-ply thread to the spindle. It is not surprising that a people so well developed æsthetically as the early Andeans should have adorned their spindles and the always present spindle-whorls with rich and delicate designs. The shafts of the spindles are usually finely carved or painted, and the whorls or weights which surround the shafts in order to give them momentum and steadiness of motion are equally rich in ornamentation, their material being either pottery, stone, bone, or wood. In most Peruvian spindles the whorls are either smallish rings located midway the length of the shaft, or else on the lower half of it. In the National Museum of Archæology, in Lima, there were a number of spindles which had cylindrical wooden whorls fixed over the middle third of the shaft's length, the shaft being tightly settled in a hole drilled through the axis of the whorl. This type of spindle was unusual, however, the more common type being the *chonta*-wood shaft with a pottery or a stone whorl. The dimensions of the spindle are usually these, approximately: the shaft is about ten or twelve inches long, sometimes as little as six inches; its thickness is between one quarter and one half an inch. The diameter of the usual ring-whorl ranges from an inch to two inches; that of the cylindrical wooden whorl is, if I remember correctly, a trifle over an inch.

At the present time one of the most characteristic and picturesque customs of the Indian women of Ecuador, Peru, and Bolivia is that of spinning as they walk about and even as they carry burdens or children on their backs. The distaff is commonly held by the left armpit and the cotton (or wool) is drawn from it by the thumb and index finger of the left hand, constantly and copiously moistened in the mouth of the spinner. The spindle hangs at the waist or even at the knees of its manipulator, and it whirls steadily giving a tight, even twist, well wetted with saliva, to the thread. Mr. Crawford would have us believe that the custom of ambulatory spinning was unknown in ancient times, his sole argument in favor of the contention being an exceedingly poor, would-be realistic pot in the American Museum of Natural History which shows a person of indeterminate sex spinning with a wretchedly represented spindle whose type is by no means clear. Mr. Crawford naïvely describes this sorry pottle as "a famous picture vase"![23]

Even though it were not inherently improbable that a habit now so general should be of recent growth, we have proof that Mr. Crawford's contention is incorrect. Both Garcilaso and Father Cobo affirm that peripatetic spinning and thread-twisting were customary in ancient times.[24] Furthermore, Mr. Crawford makes a distinction where there is no real difference between spinning and twisting the thread. When, as was very often the case, a newly made single-ply thread was doubled and tightly twisted into a two-ply thread, the same implements and the same application of saliva entered into the process which was, in effect, merely an extension of the process of spinning.

That spinning and twisting were anciently practiced sitting down as well as walking or standing is made evident not only by the two Chroniclers just cited but also by the presence in very numerous work-baskets of small, shallow bowls of pottery, stone, shell, or gourd. When the spinner was seated she, or he,—for both sexes spun and wove—would rest the lower point of the spindle in the bow in order to impart to it a greater smoothness and steadiness of motion, tension on the thread being maintained by the weight of the tilted spindle. I am inclined to believe that the spindles, which occur frequently, with two whorls were used chiefly in seated or bowl-spinning, the upper whorl giving added weight to the spindle and so keeping the tension what it should be. Father Cobo specifically mentions bowl-spinning in the chapter cited above.

Saliva was an important element in Andean spinning in the early days; indeed, it is so still, but apparently with less efficacy than formerly, for no thread now spun in the Andean area can equal for fineness and evenness the best of the ancient cotton threads. Whether the saliva of modern Andeans is less adhesive and glutinous than that of their ancestors, and whether, if it be so, this is caused by modifications in the diet, are points which I leave to some competent specialist in medical matters to settle.

The preparation of woollen thread was very like that of cotton. After being removed from the animal the wool was washed in water, but not so thoroughly as to free it entirely from its natural oils. These, in combination with the saliva supplied by the spinner, helped to give to the woollen thread, and especially that derived from the vicuña, a noteworthy pliability and smoothness.

So far as cotton threads are concerned, those of ancient Peru have been excelled in fineness only by the Dacca cotton of India and by a small amount of modern cotton spun at Manchester (England) as an exhibition piece. Early Peruvian cotton threads range from a rating of 300 down to 130 for single-ply threads, and from 150 to 110 for threads of more than one ply. The finest thread now made from Peruvian Full Rough ranges only as high as 70.[25]

Woollen threads, naturally, are in general less fine than cotton. Single-ply vicuña wool thread fine enough to give a weft-count of 240 to the inch has been seen by me, in the specimen of Tiahuanaco II style weaving shown in Figure 177. More usually the best woollen threads of ancient Peru ranged from 200 to 180 weft threads to the inch for one-ply threads, and from 190 to 130 for two-ply. The finest modern woollen threads made from vicuña wool give a weft-count of between 90 and 70.[25]

This brings us to the subject of the ancient Andean loom. Here, again, we meet with a situation of the uttermost simplicity which, nevertheless, most writers have persisted in treating as though it were very complicated.

The early looms of Peru—and those of the same type still used in that country—were literally hand looms; for only the hands and fingers of the weaver took part in their operation. They were chiefly of the type known as vertical, albeit in actual use they often assumed a position almost horizontal. But this did not signify much, for in all cases the warps were maintained at the proper tension by the pull of the heavy lower loom-bar. Sometimes this was attached by a belt to the weaver's body so as to enable him or her to increase the tension merely by leaning backward. All this is brought out very clearly by Figures 2, 169, and 172, the first of which represents

Fig. 169. A pen-and-ink drawing by Don Felipe Huamán Poma de Ayala, about 1610, showing the type of hand-loom used by the Incas' subjects and other early peoples of Peru.

After Montell.

an Early Chimu weave-shop, the second and third the loom of Incaic times, surviving into our own day. In making large pieces of cloth a somewhat different type of hand-loom was used: two bars about as thick as a person's forearm were fixed to stakes driven into the ground, the bars being parallel and at a distance of four and a half or five feet. The warp was stretched in a horizontal position from one to the other, and as the weaving progressed the finished cloth was wound up on the bar nearer to the weaver. Another variant of the hand-loom was that in which the upper bar was held in horizontal position by two stout crotched sticks set up in the ground close to a wall, the lower bar hanging free supported by the warp threads and close to the ground. The worker at a loom of this kind sat, knelt, and finally stood as his finished work's upper margin gradually rose towards the upper bar.[26] See Figure 172.

Notwithstanding these minor variations all Peruvian looms are of the same general character, albeit they varied considerably in point of size according to the purposes for which they were intended. Some looms were over four feet in width, though these were uncommon; usually they were about two feet wide. Smaller looms were likewise used, specimens of only half an inch in width being known. In such looms as these very narrow fabrics—girdles, fillets, slings, binding-bands—were woven.

Looms intended for the production of ordinary cloth had but few parts. The simplest of them consisted merely of two strong rods or bars each of which had a stout cord lashed along its length. From one of these cords to the other the warp threads were stretched in a close spiral that began, usually, at the left and was continued towards the right until the series of closely set warps had attained to the desired width. In the simplest weaving the weft was worked in and out between the warps by the fingers alone or, perhaps, by the fingers assisted by a weave-dagger which was used to make a short shed into which weft could be inserted.

The next step in loom planning was the introduction among the warp threads of a pair of smaller rods set parallel between the two mentioned above. The uneven numbered warps were passed over the lower of these two rods and under the upper; the even numbered warps were passed under the lower rod and over the upper. In this way a primitive shedding device was arrived at which, though clumsy, inflexible, and awkward, did at least give two sheds through each of which in turn weft could be delivered. The main drawback to this contrivance was the difficulty of working each delivery of weft down into its place in the fell (finished fabric). Wefts passed through the lower of the two sheds could be so worked down with comparative ease; but, in the case of wefts passed through the upper shed, it was necessary to remove the lower rod each time, work the weft into place, and re-set the rod—obviously a slow and cumbrous procedure.

A far more efficient type of loom consisted of the same bars at top and bottom and of a rudimentary heddle, clearly shown in Figure 172, wherein the woman's hands are seen resting upon it. This device consisted of a light rod to which the even numbered warps were attached by loops that passed between the odd numbered warps. To supply the necessary weight for keeping the even numbered warps below the odd numbered save when they were pulled upwards by the action of the heddle and its loops a special bar or rod was laid between the two sets of warps in the manner shown very well in Figure 169 and in Figure 173. When shed A was being used the even numbered warps, weighted down by the bar, hung below the odd numbered and the weft was delivered through the shed thus formed, after which it was beaten up with a somewhat heavy weave-sword whose length was greater than the width of the fabric. After that the weaver removed the weave-sword from the warps and, by pulling up the even numbered warps with the aid of the heddle and its loops, formed shed B, through which weft was again delivered, and so on.[27]

A point made by Mr. Crawford[28] requires enlargement here: He points out that, in ancient Peruvian weaving, shedding devices were decidedly less important than the weavers' skill with the wefting-implement. There is some vagueness as to the distinction, in early Andean weaving, between the spindle and the bobbin. In many cases the spindle, when filled with thread as a result of the process of spinning or of twisting two plies together, was used as a bobbin. But sometimes, usually in work that required only one or two colors which would be passed through long sheds, a true bobbin was used that consisted of a slender and smooth piece of *chonta*-wood or other

FIG. 170. The median wall of the Temple of Viracocha at Racche (or Urcos).
Photograph by Max Vargas, Arequipa.

FIG. 171. A doorway at Ollantaytambo showing the irregular courses of the masonry
and the use of niches.
Photograph by courtesy of W. V. Alford, Esq.

FIG. 172. A native woman in northern Peru weaving upon a loom of the ancient type (with very slight modifications).

Photograph by courtesy of W. V. Alford, Esq.

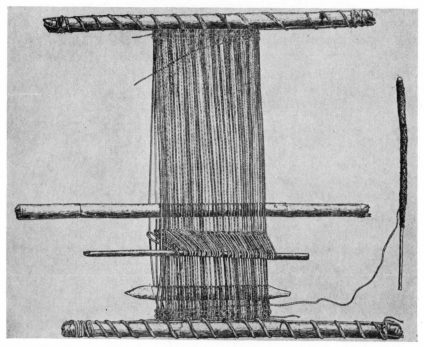

FIG. 173. The most elaborate type of loom known in ancient Peru. *After Schmidt.*

hard wood having one end thicker or more blunt than the other, and it was from this end of the bobbin that the weft was paid off as the bobbin passed through each successive shed. Neither the true bobbin nor the spindle-used-as-a-bobbin was ever *thrown* through the shed as in a foot-loom or in a power-loom; it was *pushed* through slowly and painstakingly by the hand of the weaver. For this purpose the right hand was usually employed, the fingers of the left, and sometimes the whole left hand, being busied in forming the shed, this being especially true of tapestry looms which were without anything resembling a heddle.

Considering the extremely important place which weaving occupied in the daily life of the people during all periods of advanced culture in the Andean area, it is very strange that the more realistic examples of early ceramic art should have preserved almost no representations of weaving. Indeed, I know of but one such scene, namely, that in Figure 2, a design which has already been studied in these pages and also by Mr. T. A. Joyce.[29]

Although, if we regard it as an example of Early Chimu art, this design lacks conspicuous merit, its documentary value is great, for it displays before us with a remarkable wealth of detail an Early Chimu cloth-factory. For the sake of convenience in describing the design, it may be divided into four scenes or sections. In the first we see a richly dressed person who presides over the cooking of some venison or other meat. In the background are two shallow vessels, one containing fruit, the other fish. Another person, in the background, may be a servitor. In the foreground are two small vessels for holding liquid refreshment, that on the left having herbs protruding from it in a manner suggestive of mint-julep. In scene two we are shown three weavers of indeterminate sex each with a loom upon which tapestry is being woven. The two end weavers in the scene have each a model which is being faithfully copied; the middle weaver has no model and appears to be composing a variant of the design. Scene three contains four figures. That on the left is a richly arrayed personage of the warrior caste, as is shown by the axe-head in his turban. He receives from a well-clad attendant, who wears a long tunic with sleeves, a bowl of food or of drink. The two remaining figures appear to be singing or declaiming to the warrior as he feasts. Finally, in scene four, there are five weavers of whom the first and second have models which they are carefully reproducing whilst the third is composing a new design that has not gone very far and the fourth and fifth are following their models with very little fidelity. In all the scenes various water or liquor vases appear, all of them being of typical Early Chimu forms. All of the eight looms shown are tapestry looms without heddles, exactly as described above. That the designs being worked by the eight weavers are elaborate can be deduced from the fact that they have from four to nine bobbins each. The whole factory, including the warrior who seems to own or manage it, including also his attendants, his entertainers, the cook, the cook's aide, and the eight weavers, is housed in an airy shelter with a rustic roof held up by algarroba poles, very similar to that shown in Figure 172.

It is noteworthy that the looms shown in this design from an Early Chimu vase dating from the period between 200 and 500 A. D. are exactly the same as those which occur in graves representing various other periods of Andean pre-Spanish history. Moreover, looms like them are still in use in the remoter parts of Peru, Ecuador and Bolivia to this day, for the ancient textile arts survive strongly among the peasants of many parts of the Andean area.

3. Dyes and Dyeing

Although rich coloring is an outstanding trait of early Andean textiles, very little study has been given as yet to the subject of the ancient dye-stuffs. There is a general but erroneous belief that all the coloring matters used in that day were of a vegetable kind. Many of them, indeed, most of them, were so. But the early Peruvian weavers fully understood that to give depth and fastness to their chromatic designs, and in especial to certain shades therein, a mordant was required. The function of the mordant was to corrode the fibres to a slight extent and so to render them somewhat rough and porous with the result that they would become highly receptive to dye and retentive of it after its application.

Mordants always belong to the mineral kingdom. Tin has been used as a mordant by such notable weavers as the Copts of Egypt—whose woven stuffs are all too frequently mixed in with the Peruvian fabrics in our museums, to the utter bewilderment of the popular mind—as the Persians, and as the Gobelin family. Aluminium and oxide of iron were mordants used by the Chinese, the Hindoos, and the ancient Egyptians.

The late Paul Berthon carried to France a number of textile specimens found by him in Peru. Of these five were analyzed by M. Valette for the purpose of learning something about their dyes. It was discovered that silicate of chalk, aluminium, silicate of aluminium, and oxide of iron were all used in ancient Peru as mordants. It was also shown that cochineal, an animal substance, provided the red shades and that some of the blues were derived from indigo.[30]

It is possible that the ancient Andean weavers availed themselves of the natural colors of their cotton and wool to a greater extent than has hitherto been recognized. It was pointed out above that cotton naturally shaded brown and even shaded blue was known, as well as white, and that wools of several natural hues occurred in abundance. It seems very likely that these natural and therefore permanent tints were made use of to a great extent.

Finally, as a study of the series of specimens described hereafter will make clear, nearly all dyeing was done in the thread and not in the piece. We have ample evidence of this, provided both by ancient work-baskets and by looms which have survived from the distant past with unfinished fabrics in them. Moreover, the nature of the majority of the cloths themselves precludes the possibility of piece-dyeing. Only in the small class of tie-dyed and resist-dyed fabrics, to be described in due course, is there any approximation to piece-dyeing.

4. General Data Regarding Andean Textiles and Clothing

Dr. Gösta Montell, of Gothenburg, Sweden, has recently published a most valuable volume entitled "Dress and Ornaments in Ancient Peru."[31] It is an important additon to the long list of contributions made by Swedish scientists to the study of ancient American culture. The technique of his treatment of this intricate subject is chronological, the material being grouped in three major historical divisions, viz., the pre-Incan Age, the Incan Age, and the post-Columbian Age. The first of these begins with the rudimentary skin and totora-fibre clothes worn by the very ancient archaic-cultured fisher-folk of the Peruvian coast and proceeds with a detailed study of the richly and beautifully ornamented raiment used during the Early Chimu and Early Nazca periods in the first 600 years of our Era, concluding with a thorough discussion of the wearing-apparel of the Tiahuanaco II period on the coast between 600 and 900 A. D. Each part of the costume—breech-clout, shirt or tunic, mantle, foot-gear, headdress, and also such accessories as trinkets, face-painting, and hair-dressing—is fully set forth, the material being based not only on actual specimens of the various objects mentioned but also on vase-designs of great documentary value. It is noteworthy, by the bye, that only a few of the realistically adorned vessels referred to and pictured by Dr. Montell represent women. This is consistent with the general rarity of feminine figures in early Peruvian art.

In considering the dress worn in the Incaic period, Dr. Montell draws upon the rich—if sometimes contradictory—material given to us by the Chroniclers. Particularly instructive, and also amusing, are the quaint pen-and-ink sketches by Don Felipe Huamán Poma de Ayala, whose as yet unpublished manuscript belongs to The Royal Library, Copenhagen. One of his drawings is reproduced by Dr. Montell and is repeated here in Figure 169.

It is very clear that the fundamental parts of the costume, viz., the breech-clout, shirt or tunic, mantle, foot-gear, and headdress, are present in every period of pre-Spanish Andean civilization, albeit with considerable variations from age to age and from region to region. The clothing used in the time of the Incas and other woven goods then in daily use are treated not only by Dr. Montell but also by a Peruvian writer, Señor Torres-Luna, whose work is valuable for the latest period that concerns us here.[32]

We have very ample evidence that the textile art of the Early Chimu people had reached a high stage of development. Not only does the weave-shop scene, already mentioned, prove this, but also, if less directly, it is proved by a study of the costumes worn by the personages shown in the portrait-vases, and in the many scenes painted or modelled or in relief upon the vessels of this period. Oddly enough, however, our museum collections do not contain specimens of cloth which indubitably represent the Early Chimu culture. True, they do contain innumerable specimens which *may* date from that period but, as it happens, they might with equal probability be assigned to the Late Chimu period. This situation is due to the fact that Early Chimu art, in pottery, is essentially realistic, and therefore it cannot be compared with any known textile designs, these latter being wrought in a medium hostile to realistic forms. The raiment and other stuffs shown in the scenes and portraits which embellish Early Chimu pots are of a formal and geometrical type so far as the designs worked upon them are concerned and, therefore, they resemble the stuffs of the Late Chimu period so closely that it is impossible to tell which of the two produced any given specimen of the kind ascribable to either of them. Some day, let us hope, really satisfactory stratigraphical excavations on a large scale will be made all up and down the Peruvian coast, for, when that is done, we shall know at last exactly what kind of textiles is representative of the Early Chimu period.

Concerning the fabrics of the Early Nazca culture, on the other hand, there is no doubt whatever, for we have a great number of stuffs that bear exactly the same decorative motifs as those which occur so plentifully on Early Nazca pottery.

It is true that the general loss of realism on the part of Early
Nazca art as compared with Early Chimu deprives the former
of a large measure of that "documentary" value of which I
have spoken, with the result that we are less perfectly informed as to how the Early Nazca folk dressed; but this is
compensated for by the large number of actual garments
which have come down to us from that culture. The art of
the Tiahuanaco II period, being still more remote from realism, gives us still less information about the dress of its
people; but here again we have ample material wherewith to
form an opinion, our archæological treasuries being rich in
specimens of Tiahuanaco II raiment. Finally, for the Incaic
period, we have reliable information from the Chroniclers—
and particularly from Huamán Poma de Ayala's drawings—
supplemented by examples of the objects whereof those writers tell us.

5. Costume During the Several Pre-Incaic Periods

The embellishments of Early Chimu pots show us costumes
that range from stark nakedness to the most elaborate kind of
apparel. In certain of the battle scenes, such as Figure 13, we
see a marked contrast between the dress of the warriors on the
losing side and that of those on the winning side. The former
are either not clad at all or else wear hardly more than a
breech-clout. Their victorious opponents, on the other hand,
are fully and richly dressed. As I have said elsewhere, this
contrast may represent a real divergence in point of culture
between the two contending parties; or, as seems equally
probable, it may indicate that the victors were in the habit of
stripping their foes before slaying them.

At any rate we may say that the breech-clout was one of
the earliest articles of dress to be developed, and one of the
most constantly employed thereafter. It consisted of a strip
of cloth that was secured around the waist by strings or tapes,
and it was passed between the legs and then passed over the
strings behind in such a way that it hung below them to some

extent. It was an utterly simple garment, but one whose convenience made it inevitable that it should be very generally employed.[33]

The shirt or tunic was worn over the breech-clout and next to the torso. Its length varied quite considerably, sometimes barely reaching to the waist, sometimes falling to the knees. It varied also with regard to sleeves, both sleeveless and sleeved examples being shown on the pottery, of which the latter seem to be somewhat more numerous in this period. Although one cannot make a hard and fast rule about this point it does seem that the garments of this sort that are long enough to be called tunics rather than shirts almost always have sleeves, whereas the shorter garments are almost always sleeveless. Long tunics with sleeves appear in Figures 2, 4, 5, 6, 7, 9, 20 and 21. A short shirt without sleeves appears in Figure 3. A question that now arises is this: Was not a sort of kilt worn in some cases that hung from the waist to the mid-thigh, leaving the torso bare? Such a garment is very clearly shown in Figure 5, where it is worn by one of the hunters. This is a point that demands special study. I can only say, at the present time, that I have never seen a garment of this kind in any museum collection.[34]

The Early Chimu mantle was in principle a rectangular piece of cloth considerably longer than wide. It was worn over the shoulders and was knotted or otherwise fastened on the wearer's chest, falling down behind to the level of the knees and sometimes even to the ground. Good examples of the mantle are seen in Figures 22 and 26. Simple though the structure of the mantle was, it allowed a good deal of scope to the decorative abilities of the modistes of that day; indeed, there are many pots which lead us to suppose that mantles were often richly wrought. In the little-known work of Lope de Atienza (about 1582) there is mention of cotton mantles measuring two and one-half *varas* (about seven feet) by two *varas*.[35] True, Atienza is here speaking of the Incaic days, but there are Early Chimu pots which show mantles as capacious as this which, being white, may well have been of cotton. Because of their great length they could be pulled up over the head, after the manner of a monk's cowl.[36]

This brings us to the subject of Early Chimu headdresses. A glance at Figures 2, 3, 4, 5, 6, 7, 12, 13, 21, 22, 23, 24, 25, 26, 27 and 28 will inform the reader as to the general characteristic headdresses of this period. It may be said that in principle the headdress consisted of three chief parts, i. e., the cap covering the top of the head, the curtain-like flap falling down behind, and the chin- and cheek-band. Of these three the last was quite often omitted. Built up on this underlying plan, the headdress of the Early Chimu nobles assumed an endless variety of forms, some of them obviously intended for use in peace-times, others for use in war. The aspect of the peace-time headdresses is one of extremely neat elegance coupled with practicality, for it is clear that the basic material is cotton and it is probable that the designs were worked in wool, a combination making for coolness and lightness with the addition of richness. The curtain behind, besides protecting the neck from the hot sun, gave a peculiar dignity to the whole. It is interesting to note that the designs upon such headdresses as those in Figures 26, 27, and 28 are strongly reminiscent of the fabrics being wrought in the weave-shop scene in Figure 2. Although similar in principle to the peace-time headdresses, the helmets are almost invariably distinguished by having somewhere about them an adornment that resembles an axe-head. This appears very prominently in Figures 4, 5, 6, 12, 13, 21, etc. Whether or not an actual axe-head was in some way affixed to the helmet—which must have made it rather top-heavy—we cannot tell; it may be that an imitation of an axe-head was contrived out of cloth on some sort of a frame. In certain cases, such as that in Figure 16, the axe-head was clearly of ornamental character only; indeed, it is there almost more a fan-shaped affair than an axe-head, and in other cases, such as Figure 7, left-hand man, it is without any resemblance to a true axe-head, being frankly a fan-shaped ornament, made of feathers.[37]

There are a number of attractive but puzzling ceremonial

scenes in the corpus of Early Chimu pottery. Figure 6, for instance, shows us what appears to be a man masked as a fox who presides over a conference of five semi-personified foxes; Figure 12 displays a charming dance full of rushing movement participated in by six men wearing bird-masks and feathered wings and tails. In their headdresses are various animal-symbols—bats and indeterminate animals—and the dancers appear in association with various natural objects such as a cactus, a bird, and sea-water washing up on a beach (this last being a guess on my part). Naturally, the inner meaning of a scene like this is lost to us, probably forever, yet its charm of line and arrangement is left to be enjoyed. Quite often headdresses were made, apparently, of animal-skins and animal-heads; that the animal-headdresses were of totemic or heraldic significance is as good a guess as any.

It is almost impossible to judge of the Early Chimu footgear from the type of pots which we have been consulting. When the feet are shown at all clearly they are either naked or else are painted in such a way as to suggest stockings or socks. There is no evidence, however, that stockings were known in any pre-Spanish Peruvian period, no specimen of such things being found in any collection of archæological objects. That the feet, calves, and knee-caps were painted in various fashions is the only other possible explanation. It is safe to assume, however, that sandals similar to those associated with later periods were in use in Early Chimu times.[38]

Into the subject of Early Chimu finery—ear-studs, nose-ornaments, breast-ornaments, collars, face-painting, and so on—I cannot enter here.

Early Nazca art, being on the whole decidedly less realistic than Early Chimu art, affords us less documentary evidence in the form of pottery than does its northern contemporary. Nevertheless, there are a few portrait-vases of the Early Nazca culture which are fully as informative as Early Chimu portrait-vases. In Figures 37 and 38 we see two outstandingly important Early Nazca portrait-vessels. In some respects the costumes of the two personages shown closely resemble those of Early Chimu personages, particularly as regards the mantle and the mode of knotting it upon the chest. In Figure 38 we see very clearly the breech-clout with a simple but neat edging which matches that of the wearer's short shirt whereon, at the bottom hem and at the ends of the sleeves, the same edging is to be seen, thus following out the *ensemble* idea so cherished by dressmakers in our own time. The most striking difference between Early Nazca dress and Early Chimu, if we use these two pots as representatives of the former, is that the Early Nazca headdress is much more simple and rather less attractive than Early Chimu. It takes the form of a peaked bonnet that covers only the rearward portions of the head, and it is affixed to the wearer's person by means of long, bandage-like swathings. Both men, be it noted, are chewing coca-quids.

Examples of Early Nazca hunting-costumes appear in Figure 39. They consist of breech-clouts, long, streaming girdles, short shirts with short sleeves, and simple headdresses of more or less the sort that we have seen before. Indeed, the only new element here is the girdle.

The chief glory of Early Nazca costume was, beyond doubt, the shawl or mantle. The personages in Figures 37 and 38 both wear it, but the specimens of Early Nazca mantles that have survived into our own day are more informative than any ceramic representation of them can be. Therefore I shall speak of the mantle in greater detail further on, when discussing actual garments or other specimens.

Tiahuanaco II costume, if we try to judge of it from the pottery, is somewhat hard to know about. As I have said on earlier pages there is a steady decline in the degree of realism as one proceeds from Early Chimu art to that of Early Nazca and thence to the Tiahuanaco II art. Nevertheless, the portrait-pot persists throughout these three phases of art, existing in the later phases in spite of the ever-growing tendency towards formalism and conventionalization. This paradoxical situation is to be explained, I think, on the ground that realism itself was a very definite and a very vigorous tradition which had many adherents who were consciously or unconsciously its defenders and preservers against hostile formalistic traditions. If this be so it is quite natural that realism should have survived most vigorously on the coast, as, clearly enough, it did. Figure 175, for instance, shows us a full-length portrait pot from Pachacamac. Although its general style and the place where it was found prove beyond question that it represents the Tiahuanaco II period of the coast, the intention, if not the execution, of the artist who made it was of the purest realism. It shows us a man dressed in a severely simple knee-length tunic with sleeves. Again, Figure 176, although less realistic and, at the same time, more elaborate, shows us a man dressed in a knee-length sleeved tunic. As the rendering of his lower extremities is vague we can only guess at the nature of the garment which clothes his legs; but it seems to be a kilt affair held up by broad and richly decorated bands which cross the tunic and pass over his shoulders. These bands are strongly reminiscent of those which appear on the Early Nazca portrait-pot shown in Figure 37. Yet this Figure 175 undoubtedly represents the Tiahuanaco II period, for the animal-heads upon his braces, the rendering of his headdress, and his four-digit hands clearly prove this.

At Tiahuanaco itself, as we might expect, the art of this period is still less realistic. Nevertheless, it is quite obvious that the figure of Viracocha on the Monolithic Gateway, shown in Figures 70 and 71, wears a belted kilt held up by bands almost exactly like those on the personage shown in Figure 176. His square face with its slit-like mouth is framed in a nearly rectangular headdress, and in this fact as well as in his four-digit hands, we see further resemblance between the personage in Figure 175 and the Viracocha of the Monolithic Gateway. As to the nature of the garment—if any—under Viracocha's braces we can only guess; but it is not unlikely that it was a long, sleeved tunic such as that worn by the man in Figure 176.

For the present discussion it is important that the lateral figures on the Monolithic Gateway are clad in wing-like fringed mantles strongly reminiscent of the winged and masked dancers shown in the Early Chimu design displayed in Figure 12. This goes to prove that, in dress as in artistic tradition generally, there was a strong vein of continuity that connected Early Chimu and Early Nazca art with that of Tiahuanaco II. Certain minor novelties did come in, it is true, with Early Nazca art, notably the girdle and the braces, both of which have already been mentioned, and both of which are prominent in the Viracocha figure of the Monolithic Gateway.

Turning now to an attempt to define the dress of the central personage on the Raimondi monolith, shown in Figure 80, we find that realism has been so submerged by the rising tide of conventionalization as to render impossible any statement more conclusive than that the creature wears a belt decorated laterally with serpent-heads. The other specimens of Chavín art are so incoherent that they throw no light whatever on the subject of dress.

In Late Chimu art, which is really no more than a recrudescence—with diminished vigor—of the Early Chimu tradition, we find, both in the pottery and in specimens of actual garments, no great difference from the garb already described in connection with the Early Chimu costume. So true is this that it is needless to cite more than a few specific examples, as, for instance, the group as clearly shown in Figure 174. It is a magnificent example of Late Chimu black-ware pottery from the Chicama Valley. Upon it we see portrayed a llama led by a man in very simple garb, whose bonnet is secured by a band that passes under the chin, and whose body is covered by an undecorated sleeveless knee-length tunic. It is to be supposed, from the man's occupation, that we see here a representative of the people, and, if this be so, the specimen in question is of peculiar value, for, generally speaking, only the proud and the great are shown on the pottery, whether of the Early Chimu or of the Late Chimu periods.[89]

To sum up the matter of pre-Incaic costume I will say this: In all the pre-Incaic periods studied here the dress is of more

Fig. 174. A Late Chimu black-ware pot showing a man leading a llama. From the Chicama Valley. *After Lehmann and Doering.*

*The original is in the Gaffron Collection,
Schlachtensee.*

Fig. 175. A portrait pot from Pachacamac, in the Tiahuanaco II style. *After
Schmidt, 1929.*

*The original is in the Gretzer Collection,
Ethnological Museum, Berlin.*

Fig. 176. Painted design from a vase found at Pachacamac showing the costume used in
the Tiahuanaco period of the coast. About 600–900 A. D. *After Montell.*

Fig. 177. Textile Specimen No. 1. A fragment of Tiahuanaco II tapestry. (I, B.)
In the National Museum of Archæology, Lima.

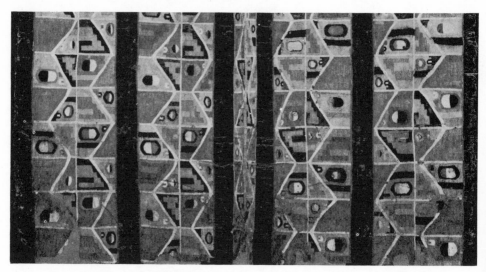

Fig. 178. Textile Specimen No. 2. A tunic of wool-on-cotton tapestry. (I, B.)
Courtesy of H. A. Elsberg, Esq.

or less the same type, such variations as there are being only of a minor kind. It is clear, moreover, that the garb of high and low was based on the same principles, the difference being only in the richness of the ornamentation seen in the apparel of the ruling class as compared with the plainness of that of the lowly folk.

One observation, however, remains to be made. Although it is safe to guess that some three-fourths of the cloth woven in these early periods went into articles of attire, we must not forget that fine fabrics were also used for curtains, hangings, and other household requirements. In a private collection at Pacasmayo I saw, many years ago, a pot which showed a sanctuary atop a terraced pyramid. In the doorway was a rich curtain supported by a stout bar. Unfortunately there were human figures before it engaged in a rite which made reproduction of the specimen impossible in decent pages such as these. Nor are other evidences of the use of curtains and hangings wanting in the range of pre-Incaic pottery. It is but natural that skilled weavers should use their handiwork as embellishments for their houses and public buildings.

6. The Textile Arts and the Dress of the Incaic Period

As might be expected, the Quechua language is very rich in terms that designate one or another object or process connected with the art of the loom. A few of the leading terms may well be mentioned here: The loom itself was called *ahuana; alluyni* was a convenient verb meaning "to set up the warp in the loom"; the warp itself was called *mini* and the weft was *ahuay;* the weave-sword was styled *comana;* the word for spindle was *calla* and another word for it was *puchca;* in fact, the list could be continued almost indefinitely.[40]

All this indicates very clearly that the subjects of the Incas were no less adepts in weaving than their various predecessors had been. The Chroniclers tell us, indeed, that they made several kinds of cloth which may be defined as follows: A cloth called *abasca* or *avasca* was made from the lowest grade of llama-wool and was used by the humble classes for their garments and other requirements. A thick and heavy stuff called *chusi*, probably like a thick baize or perhaps like a thick felt, was not used for clothing but was much employed as a floor-covering and for bedding. The great folk of the empire wore *cumpi*, which was made out of the fine wool of vicuñas, specially fine *cumpi* being made from the wool of lambkin vicuñas. It is probable that most of the fine woollen tapestry cloth that exists in museum collections is to be regarded as *cumpi*. The looms in which *cumpi* was made were frames of considerable size, the function of the lateral beams being to give rigidity and a proper tautness to the warp. There were no heddles in these frames, all the work being done by the weaver's fingers and by spindles or bobbins carrying the colored weft-threads which were beaten up, after insertion, by the use of the weave-dagger. Father Cobo tells us that the weavers were usually men who were styled *cumpi-camayoc-cuna*, but that *aclla-cuna* or Chosen Women made the finest *cumpi* of all, mixing with the vicuña wool the soft hair of the vizcacha and of the bat. Even more highly prized than *cumpi* was the cloth, usually cotton, but sometimes, at any rate according to Father Cobo, wool, which was so densely covered over with innumerable tiny feathers of many colors that the fabric of the cloth was hidden. As Father Cobo says: "The luster, splendour, and sheen of these fabrics of feather-work were of such rare beauty that it is impossible to make them understood, unless by showing them." He goes on to say that the Spaniards, when they entered the country, found the imperial storehouses to contain great quantities of precious feathers for use in this way.[41] Even more sumptuous, if that were possible, was the material called *chaquira*, which was fine cloth richly adorned with gold, silver, and burnished copper in the form either of tiny bells or else of spangles. It was, no doubt, with a metal-spangled garment of this kind that the Shining Mantle episode, related above on page 209, was enacted. Unfortunately, specimens of *chaquira* are rare in most museum collections, but I remember several very beautiful *chaquira* garments in the collection of the late Dr. Don Javier Prado y Ugarteche, of Lima, one of which was a sleeved shirt densely spangled with small discs of gold, silver, and copper, arranged in regular sequence in such a way as to form a charmingly lustrous pattern of three metallic hues. Finally, in the list of kinds of cloth made in Incaic times, I must mention a sort of fabric called *tocapu* which, according to Sarmiento, was invented by the Inca Viracocha and so was called *Viracocha-tocapu*. It seems to have been in the nature of embroidered stuff or else of brocaded cloth, the difference between the two being, at times, lamentably vague, as will be seen when we come to actually existent specimens.[42]

A point which I must make here is this: The Incas, in their textile arts as in so many other things, were not really originators but rather were merely the heirs of more ancient cultures and adapters of long-existing techniques. All of the varieties of fabrics known to and used by them had been manufactured and employed in days long prior to their own time. All that they did to modify the art of the loom in ancient Peru was to impress upon it their own type of æsthetic design, and even in doing that much they received no small amount of suggestion from their predecessors. All this will be made clear as we study the specimens to be presented in later pages.

The garb of men in Incaic times was, in its fundamentals, not greatly different from the costumes of earlier times. The breech-clout or *huara* was first put on and over it went a shirt-like tunic without sleeves called *uncu* or *cusma* which was shaped in the loom, not tailored. To tell the truth, these shirts were far from subtle in form, for they were merely bag-like affairs with a hole for the head in the middle of the top margin and two holes for the arms in the corners, the lower margin being open. Over the shirt a mantle, called *yacolla*, was worn, being drawn over the shoulders and knotted on the chest. When a man wished to engage in active exercise or in labor, he laid his mantle aside. To judge by the drawings of Huamán Poma de Ayala there was a good deal of latitude in the manner of donning the *yacolla* which, being merely a large oblong of cloth, perhaps with a seam down its middle, could be knotted and draped in a variety of ways, sometimes on one shoulder or the other, sometimes on the stomach—this being the habit, apparently, of men who had attained to a pleasant plumpness—and sometimes tightly tied around the waist. Men usually wore a pouch called *chuspa* which had long tapes or strings that rested on the right shoulder over the *uncu,* allowing the pouch to lie upon the left hip. A smaller bag, called *pira,* was sometimes carried in the hand or over the forearm.

These were the essentials of the men's costumes. In the garb of the Inca and of the nobles the desirable elegance was achieved by means of various accessories, such as arm-bands of gold or of silver, pectoral patens of the same metals, head-dresses of finely braided or woven fillets supplemented by fringes, feather-work, and gold or silver, knee-ornaments of feathers, and so on. It goes without saying, of course, that the clothes of humble men were of course *abasca* and that those of the highly placed were of *cumpi,* feather-work, or *chaquira.* It was the headdress, however, that constituted the chief peculiarity of the Incaic costume. Known variously as *llautu* and as *masca-paicha,* it was the distinctive headgear of the Inca and of the imperial and noble classes. It consisted of a braid that was narrow and thick which was bound around the head several times in such a way that it formed a band four or five inches wide. At its lower edge there was a fringe which hung down to the eyebrows and ran from temple to temple. The variations in the color and arrangement of the *llautu* were innumerable, each class and each tribe having its distinguishing form of it. Montesinos, who calls it *huincha,* not *llautu,* says that the Sapa Inca's fillet was crimson and blue, and Garcilaso says that it was of several colors but that the fringe was crimson. Noblemen's fillets were either of stiff, upright feathers forming a sort of tiara known as *pilcucara,* or else were *llautu-cuna* of yellow and crimson, for members of the blood imperial, or of black for Incas-by-privilege. On special occasions ornaments of flowers and of feathers were added to the *llautu*. The *masca-paicha* appears to have been a tassel which was either on the forehead or else over the left temple. Dr. Uhle has suggested that *paicha* refers to the object itself, and that the word *masca* is a memorial to the Masca tribe which was one of those who inhabited the Cuzco Valley before the Incas came there and which originally wore the ornament called *paicha*.[43]

The woman's tunic, called *anacu*, was a large rectangular piece of cloth which was bound around the body just under the arms, much in the same fashion as a Javanese *sarong*. It was held in place by pins with fan-shaped heads called *tupu* and by a broad, richly woven sash or girdle called *chumpi*. The *anacu* fell to the middle of the calf or even to the feet, but when the wearer walked it would open at the side to some extent, displaying the greater part of the leg. This shocked the Spaniards of that day to such an extent that soon after the Conquest they made skirts obligatory for women. Sometimes the broad girdle was supplemented by a long, narrow and bright-colored band that was wound around the torso outside the *chumpi*, in which case the broad sash was called *mama-chumpi* and the narrow *chumpi*.[44] The woman's mantle was called *lliclla*, which was much like the *yacolla* of a man save that it was secured by *tupu-cuna* instead of being knotted in front. Upper-class women wore on their heads a piece of *cumpi* which was folded lengthwise three or four times and then fastened to the hair in such a way that one end hung over the forehead and the other covered the top and back of the head and almost reached to the waist. This graceful head-covering was variously called *ñañaca, iñaca,* and *pampacuna*.[45]

Both sexes wore sandals, the general word for which was *usuta*, but another term, *llanquisi*, was also used, albeit less often. Father Cobo tells us that the soles of the sandals were shorter than the length of the wearers' feet in order to allow the projecting toes to aid locomotion over rough surfaces by gripping the ground. The soles were of leather, and sometimes the straps were likewise, but Cobo informs us that the cords which held the sandals in place were usually of soft, finely wrought wool and had delicate patterns worked in them.[46]

In short, the costume worn in Incaic times, by both sexes, lacked neither variety nor dignity. Although it was simple enough in its essential parts, it was susceptible to great embellishment, and whenever desirable it could be given a decided elegance of material and of decoration without losing the practicality which was one of its fundamental characteristics. The numerous accessories of the costume aided, also, in giving to it that richness which was a natural attribute of the upper-class apparel in the empire of the Incas, as it has been in all other empires, with the result that we may be sure that the sartorial aspect of the Inca and the Coya and of their Court was as diversified and as splendid as that of any similar group of people elsewhere.

Ancient Andean weaving, whether of the pre-Incaic or of the Incaic period, chiefly had to do with dress, as I have said above, but a certain portion of it supplied other needs, such as hangings and curtains. Taken as a whole it was one of the greatest textile arts the world has ever known, and this notwithstanding the lack of such fibres as silk and linen. The looms upon which the divers cloths of ancient Peru were wrought never attained to mechanical intricacy and yet their productions were sometimes in the highest degree elaborate and original. This seemingly paradoxical situation is due, I think, to the double fact that the human fingers—which, after all, are the greatest and most subtle of all tools—had a maximum part to play in the processes of cloth-making, and that time was an element of no importance whatever. When one considers the matter from this angle, he understands how such astonishing fabrics could have been produced by people who almost entirely lacked mechanical contrivances.

For the last ten years or so the world in general has gradually been learning to appreciate early Peruvian textiles at their true worth, and likewise to appreciate other artistic productions of the ancient Andean peoples. Gone is the day when such things were regarded as mere ethnology rather than as art. In European museums and private collections they are accorded the same respectful admiration as are the vestiges of Chinese, Egyptian or Classical antiquity; in our own country The Boston Museum of Fine Arts, thanks in large measure to the intelligent appreciation of Dr. Denman Ross, led the way for museums of that kind by installing in its halls superb examples of Peruvian tapestry and embroidery, and to-day The Metropolitan Museum of Art in New York and many first-rank museums of art throughout the country are doing likewise. This is all a part of the larger process of becoming fashionable, as a witty archæologist once put it, through which American archæology has been passing these fifteen or twenty years past.

7. Technological Classification of Ancient Andean Textiles

In that same period the art of the loom in ancient Peru has been studied by textile experts in a way that had never been attempted before. Nevertheless, no generally recognized classification of early Peruvian weaves has yet been drawn up; one wonders sometimes if it ever will be drawn up. The baffling element is the fact that the inventiveness and resource of the early Andean weavers were so great that they frequently created stuffs which combine harmoniously two or more techniques in a tissue that cannot be fitted into any one standard category. It is, therefore, with a feeling of diffidence, and quite without any claim to finality, that I offer here a classification which I have found to be fairly satisfactory in working with series of ancient Andean textiles.

I. TAPESTRY.
  A. Plain, or monochrome.
  B. Multi-colored, but with interlocking wefts.
  C. Multi-colored, but with vertical slits or *jours* between the color areas in the weft.
  D. Brocaded.
  E. Embroidered.

II. PLAIN WEBS, OR ORDINARY WEAVING.
  A. Undecorated.

      B. Striped in the warp.
      C. Striped in the weft.
      D. Check-patterns and ginghams.
      E. Embroidered.
      F. Brocaded.
      G. Painted, or perhaps printed.

III. DOUBLE-FACED CLOTHS.

IV. FEATHER-WORK.

V. CHAQUIRA.

VI. GAUZE AND VOILE.
      A. Undecorated.
      B. With tapestry borders.
      C. Brocaded.
      D. Embroidered.
      E. Tie-dyed.

VII. NETWORK, OR RETICULATED MESHES.
      A. Plain.
      B. Figured.

VIII. MISCELLANEOUS AND COMBINED TECHNIQUES.
      A. Sundry combinations of techniques.
      B. Braided, crocheted, and knitted fabrics.
      C. Tassels and fringes.
      D. Rare or indeterminate weaves.

Each of these classes and sub-classes of ancient Peruvian weaving must now be discussed with some care in order fully to reveal their characteristics.

Class I, *A:* Tapestry, plain or monochrome.
    The salient characteristic of tapestry is that the warp threads are wholly concealed from view by the weft threads which are beaten up over them so closely, after each insertion of weft, that no interval remains between them through which the warp threads could show. In Peruvian tapestries the warp is of cotton far more often than it is of wool. In all the pre-Spanish Peruvian tapestries known to me the weft is of wool; but there is a magnificent piece of all-cotton tapestry (seventeenth century) in my possession which suggests that all-cotton tapestries may have been made in pre-Spanish times also.

A tapestry all in one color is very infrequently met with in collections. In tapestry of this rare kind there is but one weft thread and that invariably passes from side to side of the fabric. In a cloth of this kind only the invisibility of the warp, due to the painstaking and close beating-up during weaving, identifies the cloth as a tapestry rather than as a plain web.

It is but fair to the reader and to specialists to point out that this definition of tapestry does not agree with the skilful and now generally accepted definitions given by Miss Reath, of The Pennsylvania Museum, Philadelphia. According to her Table of Hand-Loom Weaves, tapestry may be either a simple cloth or a simple twill. But in each one of these two kinds of fabric, as defined by Miss Reath, both the warp and the weft are visible, and both aid in forming the pattern. Tapestry, as I define it for present purposes, is, therefore, quite outside the categories of "plain cloth" and "twill" as defined by Miss Reath.[47] Fundamental facts regarding all early Peruvian tapestries are these: 1. The shedding has been done only by the weaver's fingers or by use of the weave dagger with no help from any kind of heddle. 2. The process of beating-up has been so perfectly carried out that the warp threads are completely covered.

Class I, *B:* Tapestry, multi-colored, but with interlocking wefts

In tapestry of this sort there are many weft-threads, each of a different color from the others. Any given weft-thread covers only that portion of the warp where its particular color is required by the designer. The color areas, in this sort of tapestry, are locked together by any one of several processes, all of which obviate anything in the nature of a vertical slit between the patches of color.

Class I, *C:* Tapestry, multi-colored, but with vertical slits or *jours* between the color areas in the weft.

Tapestry of this sort is often called *kelim* tapestry or tapestry à *jours.* It is very characteristic of early Peruvian weaving. The chief feature of it is that a slit or *jour* is purposely left between the color areas, sharply dividing them vertically, each one from its horizontal neighbors. This slit was made by systematically not linking with weft two warps which lay at the borders of adjacent color areas, with the result that great emphasis was laid upon certain lines of the design. Naturally, the slits or *jours* considerably weakened the strength of the fabric, but tapestries in which they are found were clearly not intended to receive rough usage. Most European tapestries were made with these slits, but they were sewn up from the back when the *jour* was long enough to make doing so desirable. Peruvian slit tapestry, on the other hand, made the *jours* æsthetically important as integral parts of the pattern of the tapestry.

Class I, *D* and *E:* Tapestry, brocaded or embroidered.

Tapestries of these sub-classes are relatively rare. The most important facts concerning them are these: 1. Brocaded tapestry differs from other tapestry in that it has, here and there, an extra weft inserted during weaving for the purpose of making a design. 2. Embroidered tapestry is decorated by means of a needle after the tapestry itself has been finished and taken from the loom.

Class II, *A:* Plain Webs, undecorated.

Most of the undecorated plain webs which have come down to us from the Andean past are trimmed with tapestry borders, with borders wrought in other techniques, with fringes, or with tassels, none of which is, technologically, a part of the undecorated plain web itself. Webs of this kind are of cotton far more often than of wool; but both materials do occur in the form of plain webs.

Class II, *B, C,* and *D:* Plain Webs, striped in the warp, striped in the weft, check-patterned, and ginghams.

The designations of these sub-classes of fabrics are self-explanatory. Examples of webs of these kinds occur made both of wool and of cotton. In the case of the woollens, it will be found, in many specimens, that clever use was made of two or more natural shades of the fibre; the same is true, though to a less extent, of the cottons. They were the plebeian stuffs of ancient Andean weaving.

Class II, *E:* Plain Webs, embroidered.

There is a large class of Peruvian fabrics which consists of cotton cloth embroidered in wools of many colors. Less usual are cotton cloths embroidered with cotton, and still more uncommon are woollen cloths embroidered with wool. I have never seen a woollen cloth embroidered with cotton.

In the case of the cotton cloths embroidered in wools it is always apparent that the base fabric was finished as a thing complete in itself before its embellishment through embroidery with a needle carrying decorative woollen yarn was begun. If the stitches show on both sides of the base fabric equally well, we may be sure that we have before us a specimen of embroidery. The usual stitches were crewel-stitch, chain-stitch, and a modified feather-stitch.[48]

Class II, *F:* Plain Webs, brocaded.

Brocaded cloth—whether tapestry or plain webs—differs from embroidered cloth, which it superficially resembles, in that the decorative threads are really a supernumerary weft which is woven into the warps in such a way as to conceal the true weft at systematically determined points. Very often the brocade-weft was thicker than the true weft-thread. The decorative threads thus woven into the fabric show very slightly on the reverse side. The commonest kind of brocade in ancient Peru had an all-cotton base and brocading of wool. Cottons brocaded with cotton and woollens with wool are more rare, but both do occur in collections.

Class II, *G:* Plain Webs, painted, or perhaps printed.

All the cloths of this sub-class that I have ever seen are of cotton. Some of them are obviously painted free-hand, much as an artist paints a picture upon his canvas. In other specimens, however, the design, usually geometric or highly conventionalized, suggests that perhaps it was applied by means of a cylindrical roller stamp or by means of a press stamp. Examples of both kinds of stamps occur in burials, sometimes made of pottery, sometimes of wood. In a work-basket from Ancón, in the National Museum of Archæology in Lima, there was a cylindrical pottery stamp with a hole through its axis in which there still remained a slender rod that probably served as an axle or handle. Traces of red dye were still visible on the stamp, which bore a conventionalized fish-design set in diamond-shaped medallions, and it was clear enough that the cylinder had been rolled over the surface to be decorated by the aid of the rod in the longitudinal hole. In this, we may note in passing, there was a remarkably close approximation to the wheel. This stamp convinces me that at least some of the cloths which have been regarded as painted cloths were in reality printed. Fabrics bearing designs that regularly repeat themselves upon their surface should be carefully measured point by point and if every part of the design has precisely the same dimensions and conformation in each repetition, we may be sure that it was printed, not painted.

Class III: Double-faced Cloth.

Cloth of this kind is made by employing two sets of warps and two sets of wefts, all of which are worked from both sides of the loom during manufacture. Inasmuch as both warps and both wefts appear in turn on both surfaces of the fabric, the cloth becomes a strong and coherent whole as weaving progresses. The design is the same on both surfaces except that areas colored *A* on the front are colored *B* on the back, and vice versa. The possibilities of the double-face technique were numerous, but in early Peru the uses to which it was put were relatively few and trifling, being mostly pouches, belts, fillets, and so on. But larger and more important pieces of double-faced cloth do sometimes occur in collections; notably in that of the Boston Museum of Fine Arts.

Class IV: Feather-work.

Only a few regions of the world have produced really beautiful feather-work. Of these regions two, namely Mexico and Peru, are in America.

The feather-work of ancient Peru was a special glory of the textile art of that country. Father Cobo tells us that the cloth basis to which the feathers were applied was *cumpi*, or fine woollen cloth, the feathers being laid on so thickly that the surface of the fabric quite disappeared beneath them. Birds whose plumage was brilliantly colored abound in all parts of Peru, but the feathers most used by the Incas were those of the *quenti* or humming-bird upon the tiny chest of which was a greenish golden spot whence could be plucked very small but very beautiful feathers much prized for feather-work. Other birds important in this connection were numerous, including the *camantira*, an exquisite creature the size of a swallow whose head is green, whose wings are blue with touches of bright red near the shoulders, whose throat is bluish-purple, and the rest of whose feathers are black; the *chayna*, beautifully colored black and yellow; the *tanagra*, blue and black; and the *tandia*, a valiant bird the size of a parrot, colored black, white, yellow, green, and red. There were many others besides, including various birds from both the coast and the forest-country. Father Cobo tells us that at the time of the Spanish Conquest the warehouses of the Inca were found to contain immense quantities of many sorts of precious feathers destined for use in sundry ways.[49]

As noted above, Father Cobo leads us to suppose that fine woollen cloth was the basis for feather-work; but all the specimens of feather-work known to me have cotton cloth for a base fabric. We must, therefore, either suppose that woollen cloth was formerly used in that way or else that the term *cumpi* was sometimes applied also to cotton cloth of good quality.

In the manufacture of feather-work the following processes were carried out: The base fabric was made first, and shaped to its destined use as a garment, headdress, hanging, or whatever else it might be. Then the feathers were laid on, each feather's quill being hooked over a thread and secured by a knot in a second thread which ran parallel to the first and secured each feather in turn.

Sometimes, for the sake of greater firmness, two tie-threads were used, the object being to hold the feathers in a vertical position.[50] When, in this manner, one row of closely set feathers had been completed, it was sewn to the cloth at the bottom edge thereof. The next row of feathers was then completed in like manner and was sewn upon the cloth in such a way as to conceal the quills of the first row of feathers, leaving only the colored portion visible. Thus, row by row the whole cloth was densely covered with feathers, with the result that a fabric of lustrous richness, fully as beautiful as silk or satin could be, was created. When plumes of various colors were used to make a design, the arrangement of the feathers of each tint had to be planned out carefully beforehand in order that every feather might come in its appointed place in the scheme. Upon the skill of this planning depended the sharpness of the lines of the design in the finished fabric.

Class V: Chaquira.

Enough has been said concerning this sort of fabric to show what its character was. Because of the monetary value of the metals used in chaquira very little of it has survived into our time. Mr. Mead mentions a fabric in which eight discs of silver 5⅝ inches in diameter occur, each surrounded by three rows of feathers, colored blue, red, and blue, respectively.[51] This is important as showing that these two techniques—which have points in common—were sometimes combined.

Class VI, A: Gauze and Voile, undecorated.

The peculiarity of gauze is that the warp-threads are paired and twisted loosely around each other, spirally, throughout their length in such a way that one or more wefts can be passed through the loose bends which they combine in forming. The fabric resulting from this technique is a delicate transparent web of no great textile strength but of considerable sightliness, because of its crinkled surface and its lightness. In general it may be said that undecorated gauze was rare in early Peru, for garments made from it were usually provided with a tapestry border or with some other edging technologically distinct from the gauze itself. All the specimens of gauze which I have ever seen have been made of cotton, although woollen gauzes may have been made also.

Voiles, in contrast with gauze, are merely loosely woven fabrics without the element of twisting. In some voiles the warps are paired, in some the wefts are paired, and in some both are paired, but there is no twisting.

Class VI, *B:* Gauze and Voile, with Tapestry borders.

The borders of tapestry are technologically separate and are sewn on the margins of the gauze after both tapestry and gauze have been independently made.

Class VI, *C:* Gauze and Voile, brocaded.

This sub-class of fabrics consists merely of gauzes or voiles treated with the brocading technique already referred to under the headings of Class I, *D,* and Class II, *F.*

Class VI, *D:* Gauze and Voile, embroidered.

Finished gauze or voiles was embellished with needlework after being taken out of the loom, as were the stuffs mentioned under the headings of Class I, *E,* and Class II, *E.*

Class VI, *E:* Gauze and Voile, tie-dyed.

Tie-dyeing is a form of resist-dyeing, a process which has been much used in Asia but which was unknown to all parts of America except Peru, and which existed there only in its simplest forms. As practiced by the early Andeans, tie-dyeing consisted of two types of procedure. In the more common the finished fabric, usually a gauze, was systematically puckered up into a number of sac-like bulges so arranged as to form rows or groups. Each pucker probably contained a small pebble or a pellet of clay beneath which there was formed a sort of shank made of the gauze, a shank which was tightly bound with waxed thread or with some other material impervious to dye. In each case the area covered by the thread was a circular or a nearly rectangular one, according as the gauze was adjusted during the process of binding. By careful manipulation of the size and distribution of the puckers, the clever operator could work out a rather intricate design composed of thread-clad areas surrounding so many puckers. When all was in readiness the whole fabric was placed in the dye-pot where all of it, save the areas covered by the waxed thread, received the chosen color.

The other method of tie-dyeing is known to me only through Mr. Crawford's description of it.[52] According to him the fabric was rolled into a tight cylinder which was then tightly bound with dye-resistant thread at intervals suitable to the operator's purpose. The prepared cylinder of gauze was then placed in the dye. The result of this method was a striped gauze.

Class VII, *A:* Network, or Reticulated Meshes, plain.

Network, or reticulated meshes, differs from other fabrics in that it has neither a true warp nor a true weft, for any given thread will now run vertically, now horizontally, through the fabric. Network may be wrought by knitting, by crocheting, or merely by looping, twining, and knotting the threads with the fingers, all of these processes being carried out "in air" rather than in a frame or on a loom.

Class VII, *B:* Network, or Reticulated Meshes, figured.

This group of fabrics is similar to the foregoing save that, during manufacture, some or all of the threads have been diverted from their normal lines of march and twisted or knotted around one another in pairs or groups in such a manner as to form designs, some of them intricate, which superficially resemble certain European laces.

Class VIII: Miscellaneous and Combined Techniques.

The fabrics belonging to this class are so strongly individual that it will be best to speak only of specific examples.

8. Description of a Series of Ancient Andean Textiles

The remainder of this chapter will be taken up with a brief study of characteristic examples of ancient Andean textile art. All the specimens studied are in accessible collections, both public and private, the resting-place of each specimen being clearly indicated in each case. Obviously, in a work of this sort one has to select with great care from a very wide range of possible examples, but, I believe, the specimens here presented to the reader will indicate in the broad the general character of ancient textile art in Peru.

The classification of fabrics given above is adhered to throughout the discussion. Each class and sub-class will—so far as possible—be studied in turn, the specimens belonging to it being arranged, whenever it is feasible to do so, in chronological order. The purpose underlying this scheme is to bring out the fact that ancient Andean weaving was a constant and vital element in all periods of pre-Hispanic history in the Andean area.

Finally, I must crave the indulgence of my readers for incompletenesses and inconsistencies which they may find in these brief descriptive notes. In spite of my best efforts to whip my data into shape, the fact that these notes have been gathered in many widely separated places and under varying circumstances during the past eleven years will, I fear, peep out occasionally from between the lines.

9. Specimens of Tapestry

No. 1.—Figure 177. A Fragment of Tiahuanaco II Tapestry (I, *B*). Width about 47 inches.

The warp threads of this specimen are either of cotton or else of llama-wool; they are of fine two-ply thread, tightly twisted. The weft threads are of very fine vicuña-wood, particularly rich and glossy in appearance. The fabric feels like a closely woven, heavy, silken stuff of great flexibility. There are between 51 and 54 warp threads to the inch and between 190 and 240 weft threads. Notwithstanding this variation the weave is a marvel of evenness and fineness. The colors are noteworthy, being: golden yellow, greenish yellow, yellowish brown, deep crimson, light crimson, white, and black.

Although Dr. Uhle, in his never-finished catalogue of The National Museum of Archæology, asserts that this specimen came from Ica or from Nazca, I incline, on historical and æsthetic grounds, to think that it may have come from the highlands, perhaps from Tiahuanaco or its vicinity. The design obviously represents Tiahuanaco II art in its last stages, but those last stages were different in the highlands from what they were on the coast. In the former region they were typified by a general loss of coherence in design, by an æsthetic chaos, and this is what the specimen shows us. On the coast Tiahuanaco II art lost in skill as it grew older, but not in coherence, and the ancient naturalistic tendency of coastal art reasserted itself, particularly in pottery. The specimen is of decided beauty because of the richness of its coloring and the excellence of its weave. I date it as being of the middle of the ninth century.[53]

No. 2.—Figure 178. A Tunic of Wool-on-Cotton Tapestry, Tiahuanaco II Style (I, *B*). Length 42 inches, width 40 inches. (Only part shown.)

The warp, running horizontally, is of cotton. The weft is of wool, probably vicuña wool. There are about 27 warp threads per inch and from about 80 to about 160 weft threads. The colors are: dark brown, in the plain vertical stripes, medium brown, light reddish brown, crimson, pinkish lavender, deep pink, greenish blue, and white.

The design is a chaos of miscellaneous Tiahuanaco II motives arranged harmoniously but without any attempt to build them into a picture. The great beauty of the specimen arises from its magnificent coloring and from the daring with which seemingly inimical shades are placed side by side. Study of the design reveals the fact that the strong, dark vertical lines of brown and the slender vertical or vertically zig-zag lines of white provide enough neutral coloring to relieve the eye and to prevent all unpleasant clashes between color areas.

Probable date, middle of the ninth century or a trifle earlier.

No. 3.—Figure 179. A Tapestry Border, with Fringe, Late Chimu Style (I, *B*). Length about 14½ inches, width about 6½ inches. The fringe is about 6 inches deep.

The warp threads are of fine cotton. The white weft threads are also of cotton, the remainder of the weft being of vicuña wool. The colors are: pink, yellow, black, and white.

In this specimen the design consists of several horizontal bands of plain color which serve to emphasize the bands of step-sided frets near the top and the bottom, respectively, and the broader central band of interlocking fish-head motives arranged in bold slanting stripes between step-sided borders. Most of the color areas are edged or limned with black, which prevents all confusion in the design, only those color areas which contrast without clashing not being limned.

The fringe is sewn on and is technologically a separate piece of weaving.

The specimen represents the Late Chimu period not long after its beginning. The survival of Tiahuanaco II influence is apparent in the step-sided frets and in the use of stepped lines elsewhere. Probable date, between 900 and 1100.

No. 4.—Figure 180.   A Tunic or Shirt of Vicuña Wool, Incaic
Style (I, *B*). Length about 36 inches, width about 30 inches.

The warp threads and the weft threads of this specimen are
all of wool, the former being of llama-wool, the latter of the
finest vicuña-wool. There are about 30 warp threads to the
inch and from 120–160 weft threads. The colors are: brown,
yellow, olive green, and crimson.

The austerely beautiful design wrought with matchless skill
in this specimen represents the æsthetic ideas of the Incaic
period in their utmost purity. As I said on page 277, when
discussing Incaic pottery, geometric patterns such as this
were typical of Incaic art whenever it was uninfluenced by
the artistic tradition of other cultures. Most of the textiles of
the Incaic period which exist in collections display at least a
slight connection with life-forms—human- or animal-figures,
perhaps no more than a feather-motive—but now and again
one finds a piece of weaving which, like this specimen, is
purely geometrical in its design.[54]

As an example of fine weaving this specimen commands
hearty admiration. Not only are the many slanting lines of
the pattern executed with unusual nicety by use of eccentric
wefting very skilfully executed, but also the horizontal wefting is wrought with exceptional skill which implies a careful beating-up of each weft as it was inserted in the fabric.
Because of the fineness of the warp and the still greater fineness of the weft the several color areas, although in reality
they interlock, are clear-cut to a noteworthy degree. A final
elegance and finish is given to this superb *uncu* or shirt by
the excellent buttonhole stitching around the openings for the
neck and arms and around the bottom. At the bottom there
is also an attractive zig-zag stitch.

Unfortunately there is no record of the place where this
specimen was found. Incaic tunics more or less like it have
been recovered both in the vicinity of Lake Titicaca and in
the neighborhood of Ica, on the coast. I am, therefore, inclined to date it as of the early part of the fifteenth century,

FIG. 179. Textile Specimen No. 3. A tapestry border with fringe, Late Chimu style. (I, *B*.)
In the Museum of Fine Arts, Boston.

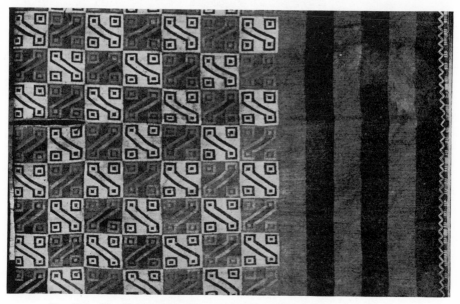

FIG. 180. Textile Specimen No. 4. A tunic or shirt of vicuña wool. (I, *B*.)
In the National Museum of Archæology, Lima.

Fig. 181. Textile Specimen No. 5. A fragment of tapestry with slits. (I, C.)

Fig. 182. Textile Specimen No. 7. A panel of tapestry with slits. (I, C.)

Courtesy of H. A. Elsberg, Esq.

at which time Incaic art was highly developed and Incaic conquests in the shore-country had begun. In addition to these considerations is the fact that the tendency to separate the pattern into small areas grouped in panels or bands of decoration was almost certainly derived by the Incas from the suggestion given to them by what they saw of Tiahuanaco II art when they conquered the Titicaca basin.

This brings us to the technical group I, C. It consists of tapestries with vertical slits between the color areas in the weft, sometimes called tapestries à jours, sometimes also called kelim-technique tapestries. It is a very important group of fabrics, both æsthetically and numerically.

I do not wish to imply that every color area is separated from every one of its horizontal neighbors by a slit; I merely wish to imply that vertical slits do occur and that, very often, they constitute an integral part of the pattern. The great question now is: when did the practice of making slits come into general use? In a recent publication I presented evidence of the probability that the tapestry technique originated, so far as ancient Peru is concerned, early in the Tiahuanaco II period.[55] Its immediate ancestor was Early Nazca embroidery, of which I shall speak further on in this chapter.

The problem of how best to give the full chromatic value to each color area in a design seems to have engaged the attention of weavers almost from the very moment when tapestry came into use. Some of the Tiahuanaco period designers either begged the question altogether by simply allowing each color to speak for itself, as it were, through its inherent contrast with its neighbors, as in Specimen No. 1; others, dimly groping for some mode of color emphasis, worked out a technique such as that mentioned in connection with Specimen No. 2; none of them seem to have hit upon either one of two possible methods of achieving color emphasis. The two methods in question are: 1, Limning, that is, outlining insufficiently contrasted color areas with a thin line of neutral shade—usually black or white—which could separate them enough to permit each to attain to its fullest value; and, 2, the making of slits. Both of these methods will now be seen in operation. Tentatively—while awaiting opportunities to study specimens still unknown to me—I am of the opinion that both limning and the making of slits are post-Tiahuanaco II and also that both are also pre-Incaic. Limning, to be sure, frequently occurs in the Early Nazca designs upon pottery, but I know of no specimen of Tiahuanaco II textile which shows its presence as a deliberately introduced element in the pattern. Nor, at the moment, do I recall a definitely Tiahuanaco II textile which contains a true system of slits, albeit there are one or two Tiahuanaco II textiles which show inept and unsystematic attempts at using slits.

No. 5.—Figure 181.   A Fragment of Tapestry with Slits (I, C). Length 20½ inches, width 6 inches.

The warp is of cotton and the weft of wool. The colors are: red, pink, dark brown, medium brown, light brownish yellow, greenish blue, black, and white (cotton).

The pattern, arranged within a border of step-sided frets, consists of two types of panels. One type contains bird-figures which, although they are reminiscent of Tiahuanaco II art, are surprisingly vital, much as are the bird-men figures on the Monolithic Gateway at Tiahuanaco. The other type of panel contains highly conventionalized llama-heads together with various decorative elements not assignable to any special life-form. If one were to consider these panels alone he would be justified in declaring this specimen to represent Tiahuanaco II art as it was when in the final stages of æsthetic evolution. But the bird-panels seem to contradict this interpretation for, although they display a marked influence from Tiahuanaco II art, they resemble even more closely the bird-figures so often seen in the earlier phases of Late Chimu art.[56]

We have, therefore, in this specimen, two æsthetic elements of chronological significance, namely, the very late Tiahuanaco II llama-head panels, and the bird-panels representing the opening phases of the Late Chimu period. In addition to these points one should also mention the fact that the *jours* or slits are too long and too ineptly placed to aid effectively in the design and that, moreover such limning as is to be found here is curiously imprecise and ineffectual, all of which seems to suggest that this piece was something of an experiment with both jouring and limning, the jouring here being decidedly overworked.

All things considered I think that it is fairly clear that this piece is of the first half of the tenth century.

No. 6.—Figure 183. Tapestry Border of a Garment (I, *C*).
Length 21½ inches, greatest width 13 inches.

The warp threads are of cotton and the weft threads are all of wool. The count is not particularly high. The colors, however, are rich and varied, being: pale yellow (ground), dark blue, crimson, deep pink, dark purple, dark green, black, and white.

We have here a pattern which displays a strong influence from Tiahuanaco II art. There are two sets of zoomorphic figures in the pattern, namely, a densely packed triangular area containing what may be highly conventionalized sharks and a band of indeterminate creatures. There is an interesting combination here of rather skilful limning with equally effective jouring with the result that all of the figures in the design stand forth most sharply.

A striking feature of this piece of weaving is the fringe of tabs along the lower margin. The fringe, to which I shall refer again later on when speaking of fringes in general, is an integral part of the fabric, each tab being, in fact, a tiny bit of plain or monochrome tapestry of Class I, *A*, in the classification here used.

Because of the combination here of marked Tiahuanaco II influence with typical Late Chimu figures I date this specimen as of the opening of the Late Chimu period, in the tenth century.

No. 7.—Figure 182. A Panel of Tapestry with Slits (I, *C*).
Length 20½ inches, width 5½ inches.

The warp is of cotton and the weft principally of wool. The
weft count is fairly high, ranging from about 75 to about 120
picks to the inch. The colors are: deep pink (ground), dark
brown, medium brown, and white (cotton).

The design consists of highly conventionalized human
figures displaying strong influence from Tiahuanaco II art.
The headdress of the lower figure is, however, typical of Late
Chimu art. There is no limning in this specimen, but the
system of slits is very interesting. It is clear that the designer would have liked to make a number of slanting slits;
but that, of course, was not possible. Therefore he came as
near to doing so as he could by making a great number of
short slits separated from one another, in each series, by only
one warp, the effect being very effective, particularly along
the sides of the headdress. Very wisely the designer did not
weaken his fabric by making long *jours* along the vertical sides
of the personages' bodies, as he could have done; instead, he
bridges the gap with a pick or two of weft at irregular
intervals.

This specimen seems to me to represent the opening of
the Late Chimu period, tenth century.

No. 8.—Figure 185. Fragment of Tapestry with Slits (I, *C*).
Length 8¼ inches, width 5½ inches.

The warp is of cotton and the weft is of both cotton and
wool, in almost equal proportions, which is most unusual.
The count is not especially high. The colors are: white
(ground, of cotton), olive-green, crimson, yellow, and buff (all
these of wool).

The warrior depicted here with his entire aspect speaks in
loud tones of the influence of Tiahuanaco II art. In four-digit
hands he holds ceremonial staffs which rest upon the heads of
small human figures who may be captives, servitors, or
adorers. This warrior, in spite of the high degree of formalism

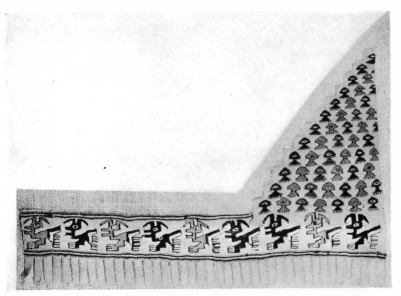

Fig. 183. Textile Specimen No. 6. Tapestry border of a garment. (I, *C*.)

Fig. 184. Textile Specimen No. 9. Fragment of tapestry with slits. (I, *C*.)
Courtesy of H. A. Elsberg, Esq.

FIG. 185.   Textile Specimen No. 8.   A fragment of tapestry with slits.   (I, C.)
Courtesy of H. A. Elsberg, Esq.

FIG. 186.   Textile Specimen No. 10.   A tapestry border with slits.   (I, C.)
Courtesy of the Museum of Fine Arts, Boston.

which inspired the design, displays here and there quaint touches of realism as, for example, at his elbows and in the attempt to represent the natural configuration of the nose. A touch of humor, probably unconscious, is present also, in the drawing of his odd little bandy legs.

Were one to judge this panel only by the lower two-thirds of it, he would be inclined to date it as of the Tiahuanaco II period. The headdress, however, precludes one's doing so; for it is typical of the Late Chimu period.[57] This specimen, therefore, may be said to be a combination of the formalistic tendency of Tiahuanaco II influence with the realistic tendency inherent in coastal art. That the specimen is Late Chimu is made abundantly clear not only by the aforementioned headdress but also by the very carefully planned and executed system of slits. Almost every vertical line in the piece that separates different colors is emphasized by a *jour*, some of them very short, others quite long. A good many of the slits are, however, not strictly necessary for clarity because of the contrast inherent in the adjacent colors concerned. This is particularly true at the ends of the headdress. This point has chronological significance because it suggests that the specimen was made prior to the time when the Late Chimu folk had mastered the science of jouring and the reasons for having a system of slits.

On the whole, I think, this piece may be safely dated as Late Chimu of the tenth century.

No. 9.—Figure 184.   A Fragment of Tapestry with Slits (I, *C*). Length 10 inches, width 9 inches.

The warp is of cotton, and the weft of wool. The count of the weft varies considerably, ranging from about 70 to about 130 threads to the inch. The colors are: four shades of brown from light to medium, crimson, pink, violet, and black.

The design consists of a series of square panels each of which bears an animal- or bird-figure, highly conventionalized. Between the panels are bands of tapestry with spirals worked in them by means of a painstaking use of eccentric wefting. These spirals are, in fact, a valiant attempt to get away from the rectangularity which usually pervades textile designs, and the attempt is, on the whole, successful. A feature of this piece is the exaggerated use of jours coupled with the use of limning. Not only are some of the slits very long, but some of them are double or triple, their parts being separated vertically by one or two warp threads closely bound with tightly packed weft. The long jours at the sides of the square panels are occasionally interrupted at irregular intervals by one or two weft threads which jump across them, this measure having been taken, we may suppose, for the sake of greater solidity.

As there is no particular Tiahuanaco II influence visible in this specimen we may date it, I think, as Late Chimu of about 1100 A. D.

> No. 10.—Figure 186.   A Tapestry Border with Slits (I, C). Length about 17½ inches, width about 6¾ inches, depth of fringe about 7 inches.

The warp is of cotton, and the white areas in the weft are also of cotton, the remainder of the weft being of fine vicuña wool. The count is high, from about 75 to about 105 weft threads to the inch. The colors are: crimson, deep pink, yellow, black and white.

The design consists of two bands of decoration at top and bottom respectively each of which bears an arrangement of step-sided frets enclosed between narrow stripes of plain color. Between these two bands is another and broader band upon which are displayed six highly conventionalized creatures beautifully executed, in part with very subtle and skilful use of eccentric wefting. Both jouring and limning appear in this specimen, being used in the most efficacious way imaginable to bring out the full value of each color area. As a result, this fabric is, from the æsthetic point of view, a masterpiece of rhythm, symmetry, and color harmony.

The general character of the design leads me to date it as of the latter part of the Late Chimu period, somewhere between about 1000 and 1400 A. D.

No. 11.—Figure 187. Part of a Tunic of Brocaded Tapestry (I, D). Width 15½ inches, length 10½ inches.

The warp is of cotton and the weft of fine vicuña wool. In the part of the fabric that is of ordinary tapestry the count is high. The colors are: crimson, dark brown, yellow-brown, yellow, and black.

A large part of this fabric is of ordinary tapestry, beautifully executed and very sightly. Near the left-hand side there is a curious irregularity arising from an inexplicable pairing of the warps, each pair of threads being covered with weft in the usual fashion. The distinctive features of the piece, however, are the vertical bands and the chevron-shaped areas of brocading which give a more than usually great richness to the fabric. Mr. Crawford calls this sort of work "bobbin-weave,"[58] and he may be correct in so describing it. Personally, however, I can only consider it to be brocading. Both sides, be it noted, are equally sightly. In any case, whether this specimen be regarded as being "bobbin-weave" or as brocaded tapestry, it is of singular richness and beauty. The slits which occur here have nothing to do with the chromatic values of the design and some of them have been sewn up.

The conventionalized design with bird- and fish-motives very distinct from those of Tiahuanaco II art are typical of the art of the later part of the Late Chimu period. Therefore I date this specimen between 1100 and 1400.

No. 12.—Figure 188. A Border of Brocaded Tapestry (I, D). Length 14 inches, width 12 inches.

The base-fabric of this specimen is a tapestry with a cotton warp and a woollen weft. The count is not high. The colors of the base-fabric are: medium brown, light yellow, blue, and two shades of olive-green. The brocading, which, in the illustration, looks as though it had been inserted after manufacture with a needle (in which case it would be, not brocading, but embroidery), really is brocading, having been inserted during manufacture, as a close study of the piece makes clear, the reverse of the fabric displaying a great number of floats.[59] The colors in the brocading are: crimson, olive-green, pinkish lavender, and white (this being of cotton).

The unbrocaded part of the tapestry bears a simple arrangement of plain-colored stripes. The brocaded portion of the fabric bears innumerable hollow squares all of them formed by extra weft threads inserted during weaving. The squares are so grouped as to build up an intricate pattern of interlocking step-sided frets, this pattern being less clear in some colors than in others, and being clearest in the case of the crimson and the white. The effect is one of unusual richness and attractiveness.

It is impossible to date this specimen with any degree of preciseness, but it is certainly Late Chimu, that is, of date somewhere between 900 and 1400.

Two sorts of tapestry have not been pictured here. These are plain or monochrome tapestry (I, A) and embroidered tapestry (I, E). They are both, to a certain extent, theoretical groups rather than actual. It so happens that I have never seen a large piece of perfectly plain tapestry; yet there may have been such. Indeed, if some of the monochrome areas of specimens which we have examined were to be torn or cut loose from their places, or if, as I hinted above on page 497, any one of the tiny tabs of the tab-fringe shown in Figure 183 were to be exhibited alone, we would then have a monochrome tapestry.

The case of embroidered tapestry (I, E) is a little different. It is clear that there is no inherent reason why tapestry should *not* have been embroidered with a needle after manufacture; yet, at the moment, I do not recall having seen any specimen of pre-Hispanic Peruvian tapestry that had

FIG. 187. Textile Specimen No. 11. Part of a tunic of brocaded tapestry. (I, *D.*)
Courtesy of the Museum of Fine Arts, Boston.

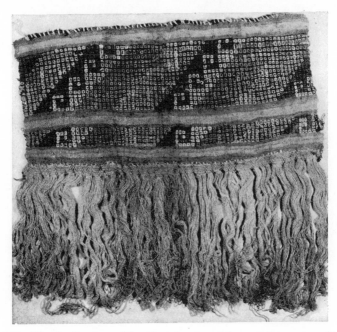

FIG. 188. Textile Specimen No. 12. A border of brocaded tapestry. (I, *D.*)
Courtesy of H. A. Elsberg, Esq.

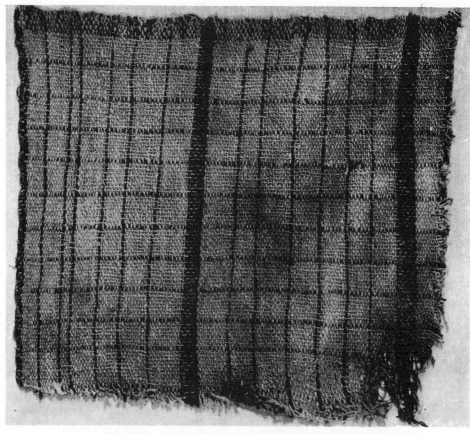

Fig. 189. Textile Specimen No. 13. A fragment of gingham. (II, *D*.)

Fig. 190. Textile Specimen No. 14. A shawl-like garment, embroidered. Early Nazca.
(II, *E*.)

Photographs by courtesy of the Museum of Fine Arts, Boston.

been so embellished. There does exist, however, a magnificent tapestry in cotton, of very high weft-count, which was to have been embroidered. None of the embroidery was ever executed, but the elaborate pattern for it is all laid out in sepia drawing. The piece to which I refer is seventeenth century.[60] Because of the fact that pre-Hispanic embroidered tapestry may at any time come to some well-known collection, I have thought it wise to provide a place for it in the classification.

10. Specimens of Plain Webs, or Ordinary Weaving

Fabrics of Class II, *A* to *D*, inclusive, are almost always of cotton; Class II, *E* and *F*, always have a cotton base fabric with embroidery or brocading in wool; Class II, *G*, is always of cotton.

Groups *A* to *D* of this class are so simple that it is hardly worth while to illustrate them profusely. Group *B* (Plain Webs Striped in Warp) have warp threads of two or more shades which form stripes vertically. Group *C* (Plain Webs Striped in Weft) have weft threads of two or more shades which form stripes horizontally, in like manner. Group *D* (check-patterns and ginghams) have two or more shades in both warp and weft with the result that they sum up the characteristics of the preceding two, as is made clear in Figure 189, Specimen No. 13.

It is Class II, *E* to *G*, inclusive, which demand our more detailed inspection here. I will now briefly discuss a few specimens representing these groups.

No. 14.—Figure 190. A Shawl-Like Garment, Embroidered (II, *E*). Length about 7 feet.

The base fabric is a rather coarse plain web of cotton dyed black. The figures embroidered upon it are worked in wool of rich and varied colors. At each corner is an oblong panel of stitching in light yellow each of which contains two figures like the others but arranged vice-versa fashion and worked in colored wool. Each of the figures in the central part of the shawl is about six inches in height, and those on the corner panels are about the same size. The greater part of the embroidery is in the outline stitch. Light is thrown on the methods of the maker of this shawl—and of others like it— by the two unfinished and somewhat smaller figures at the left-hand end of the garment. One of the two is completely outlined and is ready for filling in; the other is only partly outlined. The stitching of the outlines is of the outline sort.

The embroidered figures represent men either winged or with outstretched fringed shawls. Their headdresses, ornaments, and general aspect are all typical of Early Nazca art, and for that reason I date this specimen as being of the Early Nazca period, between about 100 and about 600.

No. 15.—Figure 191. A Fragment of Plain Web, Embroidered (II, *E*). About 6½ inches square.

The base fabric of this embroidery is a rather coarse cotton cloth of somewhat irregular weave. The embroidery on this specimen is of the crewel sort, a larger example of which was recently acquired by The Metropolitan Museum of Art and described by me in an article concerning the origins of tapestry in Peru.[61] As I there pointed out, embroidery of this particular kind was probably the immediate forerunner of tapestry. Certainly the embroidered surfaces bear a close superficial resemblance to tapestry. All that had to be done was to omit the horizontal threads of the base fabric. The technique here in question likewise superficially resembles brocading, but the absence of floats at the back, and the equal sightliness of the two sides of the fabric, clearly indicate that it is not brocading, but is embroidery.

The rather rich design is wrought in wool, the colors being: dark red, two shades of yellow, dark green, and black. The design represents the Tiahuanaco II period and, as it is a pre-tapestry Tiahuanaco II piece, I incline to date it early in that period, or very soon after 600, perhaps even a trifle before that date.

Fig. 191.   Textile Specimen No. 15. A fragment of plain web, embroidered.   (II, *E*.)
By courtesy of the Museum of Fine Arts, Boston.

Fig. 192.   Textile Specimen No. 16. Part of a plain web, embroidered.   (II, *E*.)   *After
Harcourt.*
By courtesy of M. Albert Morancé.
Original in the Musée du Trocadéro, Paris.

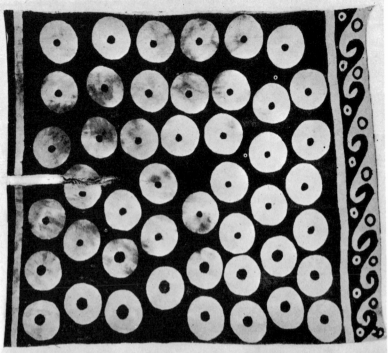

Fig. 193. Textile Specimen No. 17. Part of a plain web, brocaded. (II, F.)

By courtesy of the Art Association of Montreal.

Fig. 194. Textile Specimen No. 18. A shirt or tunic of plain web, painted. (II, G.)

By courtesy of H. A. Elsberg, Esq.

No. 16.—Figure 192.   Part of a Plain Web, Embroidered (II, *E*).
Length of the portion shown about 8 inches.

The base-fabric of this specimen is of unusual interest. It is of cotton, loosely but evenly woven. At the right-hand margin of the fabric there is a broad vertical stripe of handsome light blue color, also of cotton. My study of the piece itself convinces me that we have here an example of that naturally tinted blue cotton to which reference was made on page 454. A part of the embroidery, namely, the central band of conventional motives, is of the same blue cotton. Above it there are slanting bands of conventionalized bird-figures wrought in dark brown wool, and below it there are two indeterminate zoomorphic figures, that on the left being worked in the blue cotton and that on the right having a brown woollen head and a crimson woollen body.

The character of the design stamps the specimen as being of the Late Chimu period, probably of the latter part thereof, between 1100 and 1400.

No. 17.—Figure 193.   Part of a Plain Web, Brocaded (II, *F*).
Size of the rectangles 6 by 6¾ inches.

The base-fabric is a cotton cloth of beautiful and even weave. The brocade-weft is of fine, glossy vicuña wool of a very sightly light golden-yellow color.

This specimen, which I have already described elsewhere,[62] is one of the most attractive and dainty pieces of early Peruvian weaving that I know. It was wrought in the manner which Mr. Crawford has explained in the diagram herewith. The pattern was the result of a systematic shedding of warps in such a manner that the base fabric made its appearance at predetermined intervals among the threads of the decorative brocade-weft. In this piece the brocaded weft is predominant on one side of the cloth and is correspondingly in the minority on the other side. Each surface, however, is entirely sightly, the design being much clearer on the side not shown here than on this side. The surface here illustrated is, however, the richer of the two from the standpoint of color.

The style of this specimen marks it as of the more recent part of the Late Chimu period, between 1100 and 1400.

No. 18.—Figure 194. A Shirt or Tunic of Plain Web, Painted (II, *G*). Width as here shown 36 inches.

The material of this tunic is a rather heavy and closely woven cotton cloth which has been painted with a thickish dark brown pigment in such a way as to form a pattern consisting of a number of irregularly distributed and irregularly shaped figures strongly resembling the traditional doughnut of New England. Along the lower margin is a more formal design of interlocking curvilinear frets in which the "doughnut" motive is repeated on a smaller scale. Were it not for this design and the neat stripes at the top of the tunic, the decoration of this garment would possess a naïveté bordering on the puerile. As it is, the tunic represents almost the simplest possible kind of painted cloth.

It is difficult to date a specimen so indeterminate in design as this, but, at a guess, I would say that this cloth is of the most recent part of the Late Chimu period, perhaps the fourteenth century.

No. 19.—Figure 195. A Shirt of Plain Web, Painted or Printed (II, *G*). Width 3 feet 6 inches, length about 12 inches.

This broad, short shirt, with short sleeves, is made of finely woven cotton cloth. It bears a design in pigment laid on after the cloth was manufactured. The colors of the design are four shades of brown.

It is a question whether this design is painted or printed. It is quite likely that both methods were used, for it is well known that pottery stamps, wooden stamps, and perhaps even metal stamps were used as a means of applying pigment to the surface of woven stuffs.[63] The subject of stamped, or printed, fabrics in Peru is one which I venture to recommend to the special attention of my fellow-workers, and more especially to Baron Erland Nordenskiöld and his associates, in

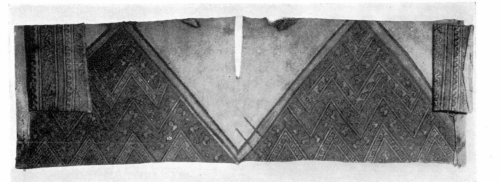

FIG. 195. Textile Specimen No. 19. A shirt of plain web, painted or printed. (II, *G*.)
Courtesy of the Museum of Fine Arts, Boston.

FIG. 196. Textile Specimen No. 20. Part of a tunic of plain web, painted. (II, *G*.)
Courtesy of the Peabody Museum, Harvard University.

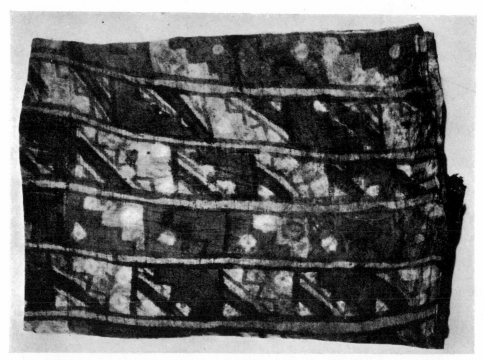

FIG. 197. Textile Specimen No. 21. Part of a mantle of plain web, painted (II, *G*.)
Courtesy of the Peabody Museum, Harvard University.

FIG. 198. Textile Specimen No. 22. Fragment of double-faced cloth. (III.)
Courtesy of the Art Association of Montreal.

Sweden. In the present case it seems not unlikely that the zig-zag stripes bearing conventional motives may have been applied by means of roller-stamps of the sort mentioned above, on page 487; it is likewise possible that the bird- and animal-figures may have been made with press-stamps. As I said, on the page just cited, a sure proof of the employment of stamps of one type or another would be the exact uniformity of the repeated figures; but even slight variations in the respective dimensions thereof would not necessarily disprove the use of stamps, for there might easily be minor fluctuations in the degree of capillarity in the cloth itself which would account for them.

No. 20.—Figure 196. Part of a Tunic of Plain Web, Painted (II, *G*). Portion shown about 2 feet square. Found in the vicinity of Huancabamba, Department of Piura, by Dr. Julio Tello.

The material of this specimen is brownish white cotton, rather loosely woven and then boldly but crudely painted in designs strongly suggestive of Tiahuanaco II art in its later and in its more provincial forms. There is nothing peculiar about this tunic save, perhaps, the looseness with which its two longitudinal parts are laced together by a cord instead of being neatly sewn as is usually the case.

No. 21.—Figure 197. Part of a Mantle of Plain Web, Painted (II, *G*). Portion shown about 2 feet wide. Found in the vicinity of Huancabamba.

This specimen, likewise of cotton, is somewhat better woven than the specimen mentioned immediately above. The design, painted in sombre browns and black relieved with touches of lighter shade, is even more clearly related to the Tiahuanaco II style than is the preceding specimen.

Specimens 20 and 21 are particularly interesting for the reason that their place of origin and other circumstances relating to them are better known than are those of most of the specimens in museums. These two painted fabrics and four others of the same general sort, as well as a small fragment of plain network (possibly a fish-net or a carrying-net), were found with a flexed mummy in some burial caves about 25 miles northwest from Huancabamba.

These examples of Group II, *G,* will suffice to give a general idea of the characteristics of this type of early Peruvian textiles. At this point, however, one collides with what may be called a philosophical difficulty. There is a large and most illuminating class of cotton cloths bearing elaborate painted embellishment of considerable documentary value. Most of them represent the Late Chimu period. Superb examples of them are shown by Schmidt.[64] The difficulty is that such cloths as those referred to belong properly to the graphic arts rather than to the textile arts. The painted scene, not the fabric that bears it, is the important thing. One would hardly look upon Velazquez's *Las Meninas* as a bit of well-made canvas adorned with a painted design!

11. Specimens of Double-Faced Cloths

Double-faced Cloth is, perhaps, the least commented upon of Peruvian weaves; yet it is one of the most characteristic, most commonsense, and most charming products of the ancient Andean loom.

In general—and to this rule there are very few exceptions— the material of double-faced cloths is cotton; and, as a rule, there are only two colors in any given piece. This last feature is a natural outcome of the structure of the cloth—described above, on pages 487–488; for, if each of the two sets of warp-and-weft were to have more than two colors, they would have to have additional *pairs* of colors in order to permit of the chromatic interchange from side to side of the fabric, which interchange is the salient trait of double-faced cloth. It so happens that I do not now recall having seen any specimen of this sort of weaving that had more than two colors, but it is quite possible that some exist. We may be sure that their rarity was not due to any lack of daring in design or of skill in workmanship on the part of the Peruvian loom-masters; rather, it may be explained by the completeness with which they achieved the most felicitous effects with only two shades.

No. 22.—Figure 198. Fragment of Double-Faced Cloth (III). Length about 6 inches.

The colors of this specimen are medium brown and white, the weave being ordinary basket-weave. The weave is singularly neat and even, and the weight of the fabric is, of course, twice what that of the ordinary cotton basket-weave cloth would be.

The design, geometrical in character, is arranged in rectangular panels, and is strongly reminiscent of the influence of Tiahuanaco II art. Therefore I date this specimen as Late Chimu, but probably of the earlier part of that period, between 900 and 1100, in which I differ somewhat from the date (before 1450) which I have ascribed to this specimen elsewhere.[65]

No. 23.—Figure 199. A Fragment of Double-Faced Cloth (III). Length about 4¼ inches as shown.

In this very striking specimen the colors are brownish black and white. The weave is somewhat uneven due to the fact that both warp threads and weft threads are occasionally paired, but without any discernible rule and system in the pairing. This does not detract, however, from the sightliness of the cloth.

The design consists of rows of highly conventionalized pelicans which, notwithstanding the conventionalization, possess no small degree of liveliness. Interspersed with them are many smaller bird-figures, also conventionalized. Only by taking such a fabric as this into one's hands can one appreciate the nicety with which the color areas interchange with each other from side to side of the fabric.

The design here is typical of the later phases of the Late Chimu period, between about 1100 and about 1400.

Let it not be thought, merely because the two examples of double-faced cloth here shown are simple, that this kind of weaving was never elaborate. It was often highly intricate, both in the matter of design and in that of execution. The Museum für Völkerkunde, in Berlin, has some very ornate and exquisitely made double-faced cloths of which one admirable piece has been illustrated by Drs. Lehmann and Doering in their admirable volume.[66] Far and away the most impressive collection of fabrics of this category known to me, however, is that recently acquired by The Museum of Fine Arts, Boston, which includes a number of large garments fashioned from very richly wrought double-faced cloths.[67]

Feather-work, which is our next category of ancient Peruvian stuffs, would require a volume to itself were one to treat of it adequately. Above, on pages 488–489, the salient characteristics of this kind of fabric have been expressed briefly, and to the remarks there made I can add nothing here beyond giving a short description of one supreme example of Peruvian feather-work.

No. 24.   See Frontispiece of this volume. Half of a Feather-Work Tunic. As shown 18 inches by 35 inches.

Without question this is the finest specimen of early Peruvian feather-work known to me in any public or private collection. In North American collections—so far as I know them—it has no rivals, and even the magnificent specimens of feather-work in some of the German museums do not imperil its supremacy.[68] Good though the color-plate which serves (through Mr. Elsberg's kindly generosity) as a frontispiece for this volume is, it does not convey to the eye the whole sum of vital brilliance and subtlety of the original fabric. An enumeration of the almost unnamable hues which glow upon its surface may be of some help; they are: pale yellow (ground), orange (tooth-motive, at the bottom), dark bluish purple, electric blue, light brown, dark green, and light green.

Throughout the design the color areas are limned with black which here—as so often elsewhere—obviates all infelicitous combinations of tones, giving to each of them the full value of its splendor. An exception to the general rule of limning occurs, however, in the case of the ground-colors of the four panels which make the central band of the composition. They are not separated from one another by lines of black, nor do they need to be, for their hues are nicely calculated to harmonize with each other without confusion and without clashing.

The chronological aspect of this specimen is important because, although the personage represented in four different color-schemes on the four panels is predominantly Early Nazca in style, he here has certain attributes strongly indicative of Tiahuanaco II influence. For instance, the headdress —seen best in the two panels to the right—is very like the square or conical caps which may sometimes be seen in collections of Tiahuanaco II art; again, the conventionalized animal-heads shown upside down on the torsos of the personage in the first, third, and fourth panels are typical of Tiahuanaco II art, that in the first panel being particularly clear.

On account of this juxtaposition of Early Nazca art with elements plainly derived from the highland art, I date this specimen about 600, at which time the two arts were meeting and blending.

Chaquira, Class V in our classification, is briefly described above on page 489. Unhappily there are very few pieces of it extant for the simple reason that the avarice of the conquistadores and, more recently, of grave-plunderers, the *huaqueros* who, buzzards of the archæological field as they are, exploit thousands of graves for gain rather than for science, has compassed the destruction of nearly every piece of chaquira ever found, the gold, silver, or copper bangles and bells and beads being ruthlessly torn from the cloth for their bullion worth. In all my experience both in the field and in museums I have never seen specimens of chaquira except in the magnificent private collection of the late Dr. Don Javier

Prado y Ugarteche, in Lima. He did possess one—and perhaps more, but of this I am not sure—very fine example of chaquira, a short-sleeved tunic, hip-length, with ornamental feather-work around the bottom of the sleeves and of the tunic itself. The cloth of which the tunic was fashioned was finely spun and woven cotton of a rich dark brown shade, natural, not dyed, and upon it were thickly sewn innumerable thin bangles in the form of fishes cunningly wrought in silver and varying in length from about half an inch to about three inches. All my efforts to obtain a photograph of this specimen have been in vain, due to the lamented death of my old friend, the owner. Where this and Dr. Prado's other treasures may now abide I do not know; I fear that they may have been lost amid the turmoil and destruction wherewith the present dictator of Peru celebrated his triumphant snatch at power, in the dark days of July and August, 1919.*

Chaquira must have been—and the specimen of which I speak was—scintillantly splendid, a proud and arrogant sort of fabric suitable for raiment of special brilliance. It played its part, too, in the coming of the Incas to kingship, as was duly told in Chapter VII. Yet, as I say, its very magnificence was the cause of the loss of most of it. No doubt many a sun-scorched rag lying neglected beside a plundered grave once glowed and flashed with bangles, beads, and bells of gold, of silver, and of ruddy copper or bronze.

12. Specimens of Voiles and Gauzes

Class VI, Voiles and Gauzes, is one of the least studied classes of Peruvian textiles because, no doubt, it presents no ostentatious magnificence to the eye. Nevertheless, on the technical side, the class is very well worth studying, as the specimens now to be described will show. The primary material was cotton, wool, when it occurs at all, being usually of auxiliary importance only.

---

*The Dictator, Leguía, was driven from power late in August, 1930, while this volume was in press.

<table>
<tr><td>

FIG. 199. Textile Specimen No. 23. A fragment of double-faced cloth. (III.)

Courtesy of the Museum of Fine Arts, Boston.

</td><td>

FIG. 200. Textile Specimen No. 25. Part of a voile shawl. (VI, *A*.)

Courtesy of the Art Association of Montreal.

</td></tr>
</table>

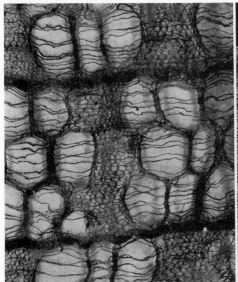

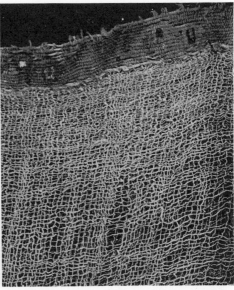

FIG. 201. Textile Specimen No. 26. Part of a gauze shawl. (VI, *A*.)

FIG. 202. Textile Specimen No. 27. Part of a voile shawl with tapestry border. (VI, *B*.)

Courtesy of the Art Association of Montreal.

FIG. 203.   Textile Specimen No. 28.   Part of a gauze fabric, embroidered.   (VI, *D*.)
Courtesy of the Museum of Fine Arts, Boston.

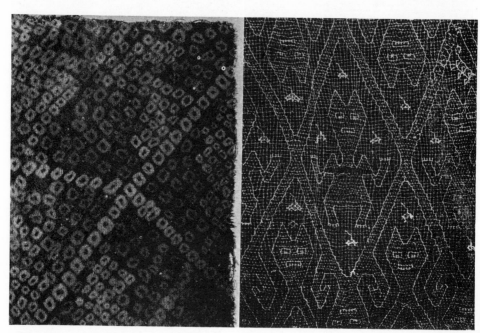

FIG. 204.   Textile Specimen No. 29.   A
fragment of voile, tie-dyed.   (VI, *E*.)

*Courtesy of the Museum of Fine Arts,
Boston.*

FIG. 205.   Textile Specimen No. 30.   A figured
network.   (VII, *B*.)   *After Harcourt.*

By courtesy of M. Albert Morancé.

No. 25.—Figure 200. Part of a Voile Shawl (VI, *A*). Portion shown about 2 inches square.

The material of this specimen is rather crinkly cotton thread which varies considerably in diameter. As a result of these irregularities the fabric has something of the character of a primitive chiffon or a primitive crêpe. Such stuff as this was probably used for shawls, head-coverings for women, or perhaps for hangings in houses, but it is of no strength and durability which would enable it to stand rough usage.

No. 26.—Figure 201. Part of a Gauze Shawl (VI, *A*). Portion shown about 4 inches high.

Strictly speaking this specimen does not fit accurately into the category in which I have placed it, for only a part of this fabric is plain undecorated gauze. There seems, however, to be no better place for it in the scheme of things here used. The material is cotton, of two shades of brown. Between the areas of undecorated gauze there are open spaces, probably originally six-sided, which are bordered by bunched-together threads and are crossed irregularly by errant threads that display the crinkliness of the material used.

A sort of pattern is, therefore, formed by the bunching-together of threads to form lines of greater or less thickness, and by the openings already mentioned. Aside from these features this specimen is an excellent example of gauze.

No. 27.—Figure 202. Part of a Voile Shawl with Tapestry Border (VI, *B*). Average height of portion shown about 3½ inches.

This specimen consists of two loosely woven cotton voiles laid parallel and held together at the edges where the narrow tapestry border is sewn on. This gives double strength and double warmth to the shawl which was perhaps used as a head-covering as well as for a shoulder-garment.

No. 28.—Figure 203. Part of a Gauze Fabric, Embroidered (VI, *D*). Length of portion shown 11 inches.

The gauze here shown is medium brown in color and is of cotton. Upon it is worked a design in wool, colored: crimson, dark brown, light brown, olive-green and bluish black. The design is a very attractive geometric pattern based on the triangle. The handiwork in this specimen bears a close technological resemblance to the *buratto* work which was made in Italy from the seventeenth century onwards.

No. 29.—Figure 204.   A Fragment of Voile, Tie-Dyed (VI, *E*). Height about 6½ inches.

On page 490 the methods of tie-dyeing practiced in pre-Incaic Peru were succinctly described. The present specimen represents the more common of the two methods. A large number of small puckers were made in the cloth, in the manner already described, no particular plan or design—save for certain long and straight lines of puckers which clearly show—having been followed. The cloth was then submersed in a dye of olive-green hue. Circular areas covered with waxed thread did not receive the dye, but the rest of the fabric did. The variation in the coloring of the rings is to be explained, I think, by after-painting with a dilution of the dye, so that some of the rings are left in the natural white shade of the cotton fabric whereas others have been made pale olive greenish in hue.

It is impossible to date a specimen such as this. I suspect that it was an experimental piece.

Unfortunately I have been able to find no good example of the roll- or cylinder-method of tie-dyeing described by Mr. Crawford and by Dr. Dixon[52] and mentioned above, on page 490. There is no great mystery concerning it, however, and it may fairly be assumed that it was used only for rather ordinary fabrics.

13. A Specimen of Figured Network

Figured network or reticulated meshes were used for many purposes varying from fish-nets to hair-nets, from small bags to be attached to beam-scales to veils. Specimens of this Class VII of our classification are rather rare. Although cotton was the most usual material, maguey-fibre and other bast fibres were often employed for the rougher sorts of network. Dr. Uhle has given us grounds for thinking that network is perhaps the oldest technological form of textile in Peru.[69] The subject would well repay exhaustive study.

No. 30.—Figure 205.   A Figured Network (VII, *B*).   Height about 5 inches.

Upon a basis of network which, if it had no decoration, would serve to illustrate Class VII, *A*, a charming pattern is worked, partly with extra threads and partly by means of a skilful manipulation of the threads of the basic network. The material, needless to say, is cotton.

The main lines of the design are emphasized by what appears to be a thicker thread than that used elsewhere in the fabric, but which is, in reality, merely a doubling, tripling or even quadrupling of the ordinary thread so as to make a twisted cord of thickness sufficient for the purpose of the designer.

As the pattern here, consisting of lozenge-shaped areas terminating in conventionalized cats' heads and enclosing conventionalized cat-headed figures, is typical of the Late Chimu period, and as there is no particular Tiahuanaco II influence, I date this specimen at between 1100 and 1400.

14. Specimens of Miscellaneous and Combined Techniques

Naturally this Class VIII of our classification does not possess much unity or cohesion, being as it is the category in which all specimens are placed that do not fit in easily elsewhere. Nevertheless, it contains many of the most spectacular and most beautiful of the products of ancient Peruvian looms. Of these a few, but only a very few, examples will be shown here.

No. 31.—Figures 206 and 207. Part of a Fabric of Plain Web
with Superimposed Embellishment of Tapestry (VIII, *A*).
Width of portion shown about 5½ inches. The original was
found near Lima.

The base-fabric of this specimen is a closely woven cotton
cloth whose warps run in pairs and whose wefts are somewhat
irregularly spaced. There are systematically arranged areas
of Plain Web on the under side of the fabric which combine
to form a geometric pattern which is repeated by the bare
areas of Plain Web on the upper side of the cloth.

The embellishment is of wool, the general color being a
rich dark reddish brown relieved and varied by small patches
of other hues: light brown, medium brown, medium greenish
blue, dark greenish blue, and bluish black. There is, consequently, a sharp and striking contrast between the cream-
white of the cotton base-fabric and the generally sombre
tonality of the woollen embellishment, a contrast which
greatly enhances the sightliness of the piece.

Although this specimen seems, at first glance, to be a Plain
Web, embroidered, and to have a soft, velvety gloss which is
brought out fairly well by the general photograph of it reproduced in Figure 206, it is in reality a strange two-storied sort
of cloth, as the detailed photograph in Figure 207 shows. The
base fabric, already described, is, as it were, the lower story;
the upper story is a tapestry which has for its warps one or
more pairs of the general warp of the cloth, the weft of the
tapestry being, in miniature, exactly like that of an ordinary
tapestry save that, in some parts, the weft threads do not lie
exactly horizontal. In other parts, however, they are entirely
smooth and regular. The tapestry-covered areas are so
arranged as to form a geometrical pattern relieved by conventionalized animal-heads, this pattern being echoed, as I
have said, on the lower surface of the fabric.

This specimen represents, I think, the latter part of the
Late Chimu period, between about 1100 and about 1400. As
it comes from near Lima we may take it as a production of

Fig. 206. Textile Specimen No. 31. Part of a fabric of plain web with superimposed embellishment of tapestry. (VIII, A.)

Fig. 207. Detail of Textile Specimen No. 31.

Courtesy of the Museum of Fine Arts, Boston.

Fig. 208. Textile Specimen No. 32. A brocade with occasional tapestry stripes. (VIII, *A*.)

Fig. 209. Textile Specimen No. 33. Embroidery on a concealed base-fabric. (VIII, *A*.)
Courtesy of H. A. Elsberg, Esq.

the subjects of Cuismancu, Lord of Rimac, Pachacamac and other valleys.

No. 32.—Figure 208. A Brocade with Occasional Tapestry Stripes (VIII, *A*). Length 14¾ inches, width 12 inches.

The peculiarity of this specimen is that it consists of two quite different kinds of fabrics which utilize the same warp. The base-fabric is a voile of brown cotton. Brocaded upon it, in the form of an extra weft of wool, are three horizontal bands of rich decoration in crimson, light brown, medium brown, dark brown, and pinkish lavender wool, and in white cotton. Near the top and the bottom of the piece there are narrow bands of brocading showing little men in a row, all very much conventionalized. The broad central band of brocading has a superb crimson ground relieved by rectangular panels of light brown upon each of which is wrought a conventionalized human figure similar to those already mentioned, but much larger. The base-fabric shows through the brocading comparatively little, but where it does appear it serves to emphasize the rich softness and depth of the large expanses of crimson and brown. Conversely, the back of the fabric is distinguished by the large number of rather long floats which it carries, the floats crossing all areas where their color is not needed on the face of the fabric.

Between the bands of brocading there are stripes of tapestry which have for their warps pairs of the same warp threads that serve the brocaded areas. The weft of the base-fabric is absent in those parts which have tapestry weft, either because it was not inserted when the base-fabric was made or else because it was removed to make way for the tapestry weft.

There is a strong Tiahuanaco II influence in the mode of showing the eyes, hands, and feet of the human figures yet the style of the decoration is undoubtedly Late Chimu. Therefore I date the specimen as of the first part of that period, between 900 and 1100.

No. 33.—Figure 209.   Embroidery on a Concealed Base-Fabric
(VIII, *A*).   Measurement 7 inches by 12 inches.

The base-fabric of this elaborate piece of embroidery is of
dark brown cotton, but it does not appear except in one or
two spots where the embroidery has worn through with the
passage of time.

The colors of the embroidery are: crimson, light red, yellow,
green, dark blue, olive-green, dark brown, brownish purple,
reddish buff, black, and white, all of them, with the possible
exception of the white, being of fine vicuña wool. Most of the
stitching is figure-stitch, but outline-stitch also covers a part
of the surface, and chain-stitch appears along the upper and
the lower margins of the fabric proper. In the design, which is
divided into two principal bands of decoration each of which
is subdivided into panels bearing single figures no two of
which are alike, there is an admirable use of limning. Here,
as in the polychrome pottery of the Early Nazca period, limning, chiefly in black but occasionally in other colors, prevents
not only unfelicitous juxtaposition of tints, but also preserves
the coherence of the various figures.

An interesting feature of this specimen is the manner in
which its two long edges are finished. The lower one has
a thick and handsome fringe which is an integral part of the
fabric. It consists of innumerable delicate woollen threads
twisted together in pairs so as to form small cords. The upper
edge of the fabric carries a number of hollow-square tabs
which, superficially, resemble tapestry. In truth, however, as
the better preserved of them make clear, they are herring-
bone stitch embroidery from which the base-fabric has been
removed.

Unquestionably this specimen represents Early Nazca art
at its height, probably between 400 and 600.

No. 34.—Figure 210.   A Fine Cotton Web of Unusual Weave
(VIII, *D*).   Portion shown about 5¾ inches by 4¾ inches.

The solid portion of this fabric is a fine cotton cloth in
basket or linen weave. The decorated portion consists of

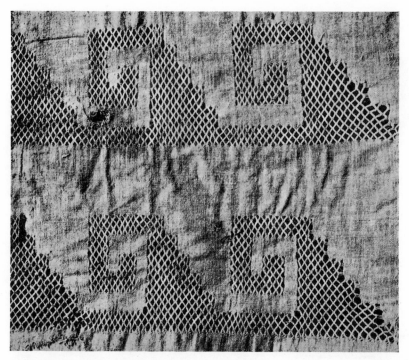

FIG. 210. Textile Specimen No. 34. A fine cotton web of unusual weave.
(VIII, D.) *After Harcourt.*
By courtesy of M. Albert Morancé.

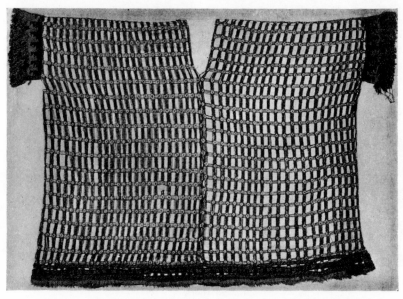

FIG. 211. Textile Specimen No. 35. A shirt of unusual type. (VIII, D.)
Courtesy of the Museum of Fine Arts, Boston.

FIG. 212. The pyramid of Maranga, in the Rimac Valley, below Lima.

FIG. 213. A detail of the construction of Maranga. Note the traces of finish-plaster, which have now disappeared. (This picture was taken in 1918.)

FIG. 214. A view in the Rimac Valley showing the vast mound-like structures which abound there.

Photographs by the Author.

groups of warp threads taken by threes and fours and braided. The braids thus formed are arranged diamond-wise by means of being attached each one to its neighbors on either side at regular intervals, the attachment being effected by a delicate interlacing of one or two of the threads in each braid with one or two of the threads in the braid with which junction is to be made. The braided cords vary in length according to the exigencies of the design. The general appearance of the fabric is not dissimilar to that of the bobbin-made laces of Europe.[70]

It is difficult to say whether a design so very simple as this is—from an æsthetic point of view, not a technological—belongs to the Tiahuanaco II period or to the Late Chimu period; my own judgment inclines towards the latter.

No. 35.—Figure 211. A Shirt of Unusual Type (VIII, *D*). Length about 30 inches.

The technique of this garment is in the highest degree unusual. The greater part of it is of light brownish cotton treated in such a way as to resemble drawn-work. There is, however, a carefully executed system of small areas left undrawn. These, examined with a powerful glass, are seen to be ordinary basket-weave; moreover, by means of tie-dyeing, they have been enabled to retain their natural white color while the rest of the fabric was being tinted light brown, including a small dot in the middle of each undrawn area.

The short sleeves and the border of the shirt are of tapestry of several types, including slit-tapestry and brocaded tapestry. The appearance of the garment as a whole is attractive and out of the ordinary. Presumably it was worn with some other garment under it.

Owing to the indeterminate quality of the specimen from the chronological point of view it is impossible to date it with accuracy. The chances are that it is Late Chimu.

15. Conclusion

It goes without saying that the series of early Peruvian fabrics here examined gives only a bird's eye view of the whole vast subject of the art of the loom in ancient Peru. I have sought, however, at any rate to indicate the scope of the matter and to describe a few salient and yet characteristic examples of that art. In my treatment of it there are many *lacunæ,* of which I am fully aware, but which I cannot avoid or remedy in the present volume, partly from lack of illustrative material, partly from lack of complete knowledge of various processes used by the loom-masters of long ago in Peru. I would have liked, for instance, to give a detailed description of the justly celebrated Paracas textile, already referred to in these pages, which has been ably discussed by Mme. Levillier.[71] But circumstances have made it impossible for me to obtain the detail-photographs of the figures in its border which I would require. Inasmuch as, with the available materials for study before them, well-trained experts in textile matters have given me their opinions as to the technique of those figures, no two of the said opinions exactly agreeing, I have decided not to embark now on an attempt of my own. I hope that, in the future, an opportunity will arise to settle, once and for all, the question of how the border of the Paracas textile was made.

With this implication that much future work is needed before ancient Peruvian fabrics can be said to be fully understood I close this lengthy chapter.

NOTES TO CHAPTER XI

[1] Montell, 1929, pp. 6–7. Uhle, 1919, 1919b.

[2] González Holguín, 1608. Bertonio, 1879. Middendorf, 1892. Carrera, 1880. Ruiz de Montoya, 1876. Platzmann, 1901.

[3] Miller, 1731. Linnæus, 1753, II, p. 693; 1766–1768, II, p. 462. Lamarck, 1783–1808, II, p. 135. Cavanilles, 1785–1790, II, p. 313. Parlatore, 1866, pp. 54–56. Watt, 1907; 1908, pp. 575–576.

[4] Watt, 1908, pp. 575–576. Linnæus, 1766–1768, II, p. 462. Morley, 1920, p. 3.

[5] Lérius's account appears in Purchas, 1905–1907, XVI, pp. 539–540.

[6] Lamarck, 1783–1808, II, p. 135. Spruce, 1864, pp. 67–73.

[7] Cieza, Pt. I, Ch. xl, implies that cotton was grown in the warm valleys near Quito. Spruce, 1864. Wolf, 1892, pp. 432 and 548. Watt, 1907, pp. 217–219.

[8] Acosta, Bk. IV, Ch. xxiii, I, p. 249, of Markham's edition.

[9] Boman, 1908, pp. 140 and 202.

[10] Frézier, 1717.

[11] Watt, 1907, pp. 68–69 and 166–167, also, Pls. 4, 38 and 45.

[12] Rochebrune, 1879.

[13] Crawford, 1916c.

[14] Gutiérrez de Santa Clara, Bk. III, Ch. lix.

[15] Thomas, 1891. Scott, 1913, pp. 215 and 386–391. Means, 1918c. Hollister, 1918. Barker and Garnett, 1920. Acosta, Bk. IV, Ch. xl. Cobo, Bk. IX, Ch. lviii.

[16] Cobo, Bk. V, Chs. xx, xxi, and xxii. Garcilaso, Pt. I, Bk. VIII, Ch. xiii.

[17] Petty's narrative will be found in Hakluyt, 1903–1905, XI, p. 316.

[18] Cobo, Bk. VI, Ch. cxxvi.

[19] Acosta, Bk. IV, Ch. xxxix. Garcilaso, Pt. I, Bk. VIII, Ch. xiii. Cobo, Bk. IX, Ch. xlviii.

[20] Montell, 1929, pp. 131–132 and Figs. 65 and 66.

[21] Murphy, 1912, III, p. 83.

[22] Crawford, 1915, 1916, 1916d, 1924, pp. 50–60. Frödin and Nordenskiöld, 1918. Hooper, 1915. Schmidt, 1910, 1910b.

[23] Crawford, 1915, p. 74, calls this sorry pottle "a famous picture vase."

[24] Garcilaso, Pt. I, Bk. IV, Ch. xiii. Cobo, Bk. XIV, Ch. xi.

[25] These figures are taken from my note-books of researches made in Lima, in various European collections, and in sundry American collections during the past twelve years. See also Crawford, 1915, pp. 80–81.

[26] Montell, 1929, pp. 181–182. Garcilaso, Pt. I, Bk. V, Ch. vi. Bowman, 1916, Fig. 42.

[27] My description of these looms is based upon the material in Schmidt, 1910, and Crawford, 1915 and 1916. I have also drawn upon my own observations in the collections which I have examined.

[28] Crawford, 1915, p. 86.

[29] Joyce, 1921, 1922.

[30] Valette, 1913.

[31] Montell, 1929.

[32] Torres-Luna, 1923.

[33] Montell, 1929, pp. 31–32.

[34] Montell, 1929, pp. 32–37, 40–41. Uhle, 1889, Pls. 27 and 28.

[35] Atienza, Ch. v.

[36] Montell, 1929, pp. 37–40.

[37] Montell, 1929, pp. 44–61, especially p. 53.

[38] Montell, 1929, p. 44.

[39] Montell, 1929, pp. 15–23.

[40] González Holguín, 1607–1608. Cobo, Bk. XIV, Chs. ii and ix. Torres-Luna, 1923.

[41] Cobo, Bk. XIV, Ch. xi.

[42] General references for Incaic textile art are as follows: Cobo, Bk. XIV, Chs. ii, ix, and xi. Atienza, Ch. v. Garcilaso, Pt. I, Bk. IV, Ch. ii; Bk. VI, Chs. xvi, xxii, and xxiv; Bk. VIII, Ch. v. Cieza, Pt. I, Chs. xli and xlvi. Santa Cruz Pachacuti-yamqui Salcamayhua, 1873, pp. 88, 97–99, 105, and 118. Molina, of Cuzco, 1873, pp. 20 and 38. Torres-Luna, 1923. Montell, 1929, pp. 173–236.

[43] Uhle, 1907.

[44] See *Relaciones Geográficas de Indias*, I, p. 189, where the dress of the folk of Hatun Rucana, near Huamanga (the modern Ayacucho), is described in a report dated 1586. See also: Uhle, 1903, Pl. 19, Figs. 1–5. Montell, 1929, p. 231.

[45] Cobo, Bk. XIV, Ch. xi. González Holguín, 1607–1608. Valera, 1879, p. 184. Montell, 1929, p. 232.

[46] Cieza, Pt. I, Ch. xli. Garcilaso, Pt. I, Bk. I, Ch. xxi; Bk. VI, Ch. xxv. Molina, of Cuzco, 1873, pp. 36 and 40. Santa Cruz, 1873, pp. 80 and 106. Sarmiento, Ch. 1. González Holguín, 1607, p. 360. Torres-Luna, 1923. Montell, 1929, pp. 208–211 and 233.

[47] Reath, 1927, pp. 4, 8–11, 19–20, 27–29.

[48] Day and Buckle, 1901, pp. 28–37, and 40–46.

[49] Cobo, Bk. VIII, Chs. xxvii, xxix, xxxiv-xxxvi, inclusive; Bk. XIV, Ch. ii. Garcilaso, Pt. I, Bk. VIII, Chs. xx and xxi.

[50] For methods of attaching feathers see Mead, 1907.

[51] Mead, 1907, p. 12.

[52] Crawford, 1916, pp. 153–156. Dixon, 1928, pp. 197–198.

[53] Means, 1925b, pp. 9–13.

[54] Uhle, 1913b. Means, 1917c, pp. 381–382. Harcourt, R. and M., 1924b, Pl. 40. Jiménez de la Espada, 1923. Schmidt, 1929, p. 485, Fig. 1.

[55] Means, 1930.

[56] Harcourt, 1924b, Pl. 26, a, and 27, a and c.

[57] Schmidt, 1929, Pls. XII, XIII, and XIV. Harcourt, 1924b, Pl. 22. Lehmann and Doering, Pls. 118 and 119.

[58] Crawford, 1916, pp. 147–153.

[59] A float is a thread that runs free for a space without being interwoven with other threads. Reath, 1927, p. 7.

[60] The piece in question formerly belonged to me.

[61] Means, 1930, p. 21, and Pl. I, 1930c,

[62] Means, 1925b, pp. 18–20.

[63] References on the subject of stamps include: Wissler, 1922, p. 282; Schmidt, 1929, p. 536.

[64] Schmidt, 1910; 1929, pp. 507, and 512–514, inclusive.

[65] Means, 1925b, pp. 22–23.

[66] Lehmann and Doering, 1924, Pl. 117.

[67] None of the specimens to which I here refer has yet been published. They came from the collection of Don Mauro Pando, of Lima, and were bought through the sagacious generosity of Mr. Edward J. Holmes, Director of The Museum of Fine Arts, Boston, in consultation with Miss Gertrude Townsend, Curator of the Textiles Department. It is a most important acquisition.

[68] Lehmann and Doering, 1924, Pl. XII. Schmidt, 1929, Pl. XVII.

[69] Uhle, 1919b.

[70] Barnett, 1909.

[71] Mme. Levillier, 1928.

Note: I wish here to make one more acknowledgment to Miss Marian Hague, Miss Gertrude Townsend, Miss Germaine Merlange, Miss Nancy Andrews Reath, and Mr. H. A. Elsberg for all the counsel and encouragement which I have had from them during years past in connection with work upon this chapter. To Mr. Joseph Breck, of The Metropolitan Museum of Art, and to his associates there, I am grateful for opportunities to study and to describe Peruvian fabrics of great importance, some of which are treated of in an earlier writing of mine (1930).

CHAPTER XII

FINAL POINTS, AND CONCLUSION

Obviously enough a book so brief as this one cannot well claim to treat exhaustively a subject so vast and so complex as the ancient civilizations of Peru and adjacent regions. At the most it can only indicate the salient facts under each heading, as it were. Therefore, in this chapter, I shall deal briefly with various points which require further notice even in a book of admittedly preliminary character such as the present volume.

1. Architecture

The subject of this section, if exhaustively treated, would fill a volume by itself. Here, however, I shall attempt to do no more than to point out various important characteristics of the architecture of sundry regions and periods.

The coast of Peru is pre-eminently the home of the pyramidal style of architecture. True, artificial, or partly artificial, elevations occur elsewhere in the Andean area than on the coast; for we have the burial mounds, or *tolas,* of Ecuador which are said to have been the peculiar property of the Caran folk; we have also stepped pyramids built, or rather faced, with stone at Chavín, Huánuco, Vilcashuamán, Pumatampu, and Tiahuanaco. But it is on the coast that this type of structure attains to the most imposing proportions. In Chapter III this matter has been referred to before, but here I mention it again, and more concretely. It is apparent that a structure like the five-terraced pyramid of Maranga, near Lima, now partially ruined, as Figure 212 shows, and built, as the wall shown in Figure 213 displays, of a type of adobe closely similar in appearance and texture to concrete, forms a class of pyramid distinct from the rounded hills of immense size that are scattered over the flat part of the Rimac Valley as is shown in Figure 214. The outlines of Maranga are clear-cut and decidedly elegant, but the forms of the elevations in the third picture are vague and they are hardly more to the eye than so many tremendous accumulations of earth. Only when such a mound is cut through is its true character revealed, as it is in Figure 215, showing that the material is billions and billions of rectangular sun-dried adobe bricks laid in regular courses.

To structures of both the sorts here referred to the modern Peruvian applies the term *huaca*, failing, it would seem, to distinguish the one style of building from the other. The question is now which of these two styles of architecture is the older. Or are they, perchance, contemporaries? Certain facts are clear. In the first place, the "concrete" sort of adobe construction is found in the vicinity of Chan-Chan; Paramunca (now called Paramonga) is largely, if not wholly, composed of it; at Pachacamac it is very common; and in other sites (such as the Chincha Valley), it occurs plentifully. So far as dating is concerned, it can be shown to have been in use in the Early Chimu period—the Early Chimu frescoes shown in Figure 34 demonstrate this fact—and to have continued in use throughout the coast country until after the Incaic conquest of that region. Walls such as those shown in Figures 124 and 125 are of the "concrete" type of adobe construction and they represent the Late Chimu period, the arabesque patterns wrought on the surface of the wall being highly characteristic of the art of that period. On the other hand, the brick type of construction is equally well distributed, both as regards place and as regards period. Moreover, it is quite obvious that such an edifice as that shown in Figure 215 could not have been created in less than a thousand years, for the height of the mass of adobes is not much less than two hundred feet and its length is more than two thousand feet, the brick type of construction being used throughout. We may safely assume therefore that the oldest part of the mass dates from the Early Chimu period. From all this I conclude that both types of architecture were in use on the coast from the earliest civilized times down to the Spanish conquest.

But only very rarely, if ever, were the two styles combined in one building.

In earlier chapters reference has been made to the military architecture of the coast, and Figures 32 and 130 show characteristic examples of it. It is safe to say that no pre-firearm fortress in the world is better adapted to purposes of defense than that of Paramunca, an admirable air photograph of which, by Major Holstein, is reproduced in Figure 32. But here I wish to call attention to a smaller but equally admirable military construction. It is shown in Figure 216 which displays a narrow entrance in one of the innumerable defensive walls near Maranga in the Rimac Valley. Flanking the entrance, and several feet above it, are two L-shaped niches on the inner side of the wall. In them, in times of war, guards were stationed, one on each side of the entrance, who could without difficulty hold the opening against a large number of attackers. In this simply planned but efficacious defensive work we observe the use of the "concrete" type of construction.

Although general comment on the domiciliary architecture of the coast people has been made above, on pages 80–83, I wish here to speak briefly of a certain very interesting ruined palace to which I have given some attention. It stands about a mile north of the pyramid of Maranga and it bears the suggestive name of House of the Chief. As shown in Figure 217, it consists of an adobe platform raised some three feet above the ground and surrounded on three sides by massive adobe "concrete" walls about eleven feet high, the fourth side or front of the platform being left open and facing upon what appears to have been a large patio or a small public square. A wide doorway at the middle of the back wall gives upon a now much ruined corridor leading to a number of secondary chambers disposed behind and beside the main apartment. The noteworthy point about the House of the Chief is the arabesque ornamentation upon the walls of the platform chamber and upon the front of the platform itself. The patterns which appear there are typical of Late Chimu art and were probably derived from the textile art of the

Fig. 215. A cutting through a huge mound in the Rimac Valley, near Lima. Note the construction, consisting of rectangular adobe bricks.

Photograph by courtesy of The Foundation Company.

Fig. 216. A defended gateway in a defensive wall near the pyramid of Maranga, Rimac Valley.

Photograph by the Author.

FIG. 217.   A detail of the house of the Chief, near Maranga, Rimac Valley.

FIG. 218.   Details of Tiahuanaco II stone-cutting, at Pumapuncu, close to Tiahuanaco, Bolivia.

FIG. 219.   Two Tiahuanaco II stones joined by a copper cramp, at Pumapuncu
Photographs by the Author.

period. Originally the entire wall-surface was covered with tinted plaster, the raised part of the design being blue and the depressed part light buff. Of this coloring there were distinct traces at the time of my first visit in 1917; but when I was there last, in May, 1921, they had almost disappeared. Other stucco ornamentations appear in Figures 124 and 125.

There is but little doubt in my mind concerning the purpose of this structure. It formerly had a roof of some sort held up by columns and beams of wood whose sockets—albeit much corroded by time and the elements—still may be seen in Figure 217. In short, I think that it must have been a pavilion not unlike those mentioned in Chapter III. No doubt the chief of Maranga in Late Chimu times, or perhaps even the great Cuismancu himself, held here his court and issued his commands to his lesser vassals gathered in the square before the platform.[1]

Turning now to the highlands I shall make a few brief comments on the architecture of that region at various periods. In the structures of the Tiahuanaco II period there were several sorts of joinings employed for holding stones firmly to their neighbors. Figures 218 and 219 show the three most important. In Figure 218 the stone to the left is beautifully wrought and the tenon-like lower margin was no doubt intended to fit into a corresponding groove in some other stone. To the right we see a T-shaped slot typical of those which were often made by the Tiahuanaco masons for the reception of copper clamps or cramps. A similar slot, not visible in the photograph, is near the right-hand corner of the same block, and we may assume that a corresponding pair of slots existed in the stone to which it was intended to join this one, the cramps, of which Baron Nordenskiöld studies several examples,[2] being probably of pure copper in the form of two Ts set end to end and so effectually linking the adjoining stones. In Figure 219 we see a distinct and more rare type of cramp, also of copper, which has two downward projecting pegs that fit nicely into holes cut for their reception in the two stones concerned. An examination of this cramp and of the traces of copper adjacent to it led me to wonder whether or not the copper had been poured into its destined place while in a molten condition. The appearance of the stones and of the clamp and the traces of copper dribbled along the line of junction would seem to indicate that this had been done.

Because of meticulous care in regard to details of construction Tiahuanaco II architecture at its best must have had an aspect of austere majesty difficult to equal. That is to say, it must have had such an aspect if the city were ever, in truth, erected in accordance with its designers' plans. As to that there is some doubt. At any rate the stone-cutting and finishing there in the period to which I refer was wholly admirable, as a study of Figure 65 will reveal. In that picture we see a group of scattered blocks of many shapes but all beautifully wrought, their color being lighter than that of the stones behind them because they have been lately excavated. These stones form a part of the so-called Palace of Sarcophagi which lies just to the west of the southwestern corner of Calasasaya. In Figure 64 we see some further admirable stone-cutting. The structure here shown is the so-called monolithic stairway which lies in the middle of the eastern side of Calasasaya. Obviously, it is not really a monolith at all; rather it is composed of a series of great stones most of which are large enough to be styled monoliths. Although much weathered, this stairway, flanked as it is by great monolithic uprights, makes a dignified appearance in which the fondness of the Tiahuanaco II people for long, straight. regular lines in their masonry is noticeable.

Elsewhere in the highlands are various constructions which may safely be assumed to be more or less contemporary with the edifices of the two periods of Tiahuanaco. Close to Cuzco we see the famous northern walls of Sacsahuamán, three roughly parallel lines of superbly solid masonry rising in tiers above a long plain. Figures 59 and 60 show them well about midway of their east-west length. Although the construction here is no less firm than any at Tiahuanaco or elsewhere it is so because of the immense weight of the stones and the great care with which each one was cut so as to fit into a special space among its neighbors.

Some of the Chroniclers[3] would have us believe that the northern walls of Sacsahuamán were built by the Inca Tupac Yupanqui as an exhibition of strength and power, in which case they would date only from late Incaic times. But everything about those walls indicates for them a much greater age than that. At least such is the opinion of most modern authorities on this subject. It is conceivable, of course, that future research will adduce evidence to the contrary, in which case our ideas concerning Incaic architecture will have to be revised.

Certain walls in Ollantaytambo, shown in Figure 61 now demand comment. We have here three terraces of which the two uppermost resemble in some ways the masonry of the Tiahuanaco II style. The enormous upright pilons in the highest terrace-wall are set much more closely together than the pilons of any wall at Tiahuanaco itself are, being separated, indeed, only by series of thin slabs nicely set edgewise between them. It is probable that this arrangement is merely the result of some ancient architect's whim. The second terrace, and particularly the largest stone in it, is typical of the best Tiahuanaco II masonry. There is some doubt whether the lowermost terrace-wall is contemporaneous with the other two or whether it was built later by the Incas in order to supplement them. If so, it was carefully made in imitation of the simpler parts of the masonry in the middle terrace.

This brings us to the question of architectural development during the Incaic period. Told as briefly as possible, its history was as follows:

At the time when the earliest Incas were emerging from obscurity a type of masonry called *pirca*—already mentioned in this volume—was in general use throughout the highlands of the Andean area. Figures 137 and 138 give excellent views of *pirca* buildings. They consist merely of rough stones laid in mud, moss, clay, or any primitive binding material. Later, perhaps acting under the inspiration afforded by the northern walls of Sacsahuamán, the Incas worked out a style of masonry which may be called "modified polygonal" to distinguish it from the real megalithic masonry of Sacsahuamán. In Cuzco itself there are a number of buildings, including the palace of the Inca Roca, shown in Figure 143, and a part of the Yacha-Huasi (Schools) founded by him, which are in this style of construction. So likewise is a good proportion of the Colcampata palace, on the southern slope of Sacsahuamán, just above Cuzco. Figure 151 shows admirably the "modified megalithic" masonry at Colcampata and makes it evident that, when pains were taken with it, this kind of construction was not unsightly. Another excellent example appears in Figure 152.

The next step, made under the palpable influence of the Tiahuanaco II masonry, was a type of masonry represented in Figures 170 and 171. It consists of stones carefully wrought, and fitted each one to its neighbors such a way that distinct courses of stone are formed. Their lines waver, however, and occasionally break, as in Figures 62, 152, 170, and 171. In spite of these irregularities, however, there is an evident effort to achieve coursed ashlar masonry. A feature often, but by no means always, present in masonry of this category is the use of adobe in juxtaposition with the stonework. As seen in Figures 152 and 170, adobe, when present, is the material whereof the upper parts of the walls are composed. The fact that, during many centuries, the adobe has withstood the annual rains and the other inclemencies of the highland climate proves that it was a material of no mean worth.

The temple of Viracocha at Racche (otherwise known as Urcos), south of Cuzco and north of the Pass of Vilcañota, is the most celebrated of the edifices built in the combination of materials mentioned, as Figure 170 shows. The chief feature of this fane, built by the Inca Viracocha as a thank-offering to the god Viracocha who aided him in the war against the Chancas, is a median wall over 300 feet in length and, originally, over 50 feet in height. This wall, consisting of ten massive piers joined at the top, carried the ridge-pole of the building and divided it into two broad aisles. The masonry part of each pier is between five and six feet thick and about eight feet high, serving as a sure foundation for the 40-odd feet of adobe above. In the masonry there are niches where, according to Garcilaso, porters or guardians were wont to sit. It was in this type of construction that niches, so characteristic of the later Incaic architecture, made their first appearance. Still another point of note in connection with the temple of Viracocha is the fact that it contained two and perhaps three stories, which was very rare in Incaic buildings. In short, this great fane is unique, not only in Peru but in ancient America as a whole for its height, its size, and its plan. It is a *tour de force* of the Inca's architects, built at a time when that dynasty stood on the threshold of its imperial greatness, and never duplicated.[4]

This brings us to final florescence of Incaic masonry, to the style which is their peculiar property, their special monument in stone: the regular, austere, and beautiful course-ashlar masonry of the latest reigns, in use from the time of the Inca Pachacutec onwards.

At Pisac, in the upper Urubamba Valley some fifteen miles northeast of Cuzco, there are the impressively situated and very beautiful ruins of an Incaic citadel a part of which, crowning a ridge that commands panoramas unsurpassed, even in the Andes, for majesty and for charm, is built in the finest architectural style of the Incas. Figures 145, 166 and 167 give characteristic glimpses of the place and of the ruined buildings, made of fine pinkish-white granite, which adorn it. Nowhere in Inca-Land is the masonry here seen excelled for solidity, regularity, and for austere dignity. In Figure 166 we see a general view of the upper ward of Pisac with its walls of meticulously cut stones laid in mathematically accurate courses. We see the interior of houses whose thatched roofs have long since mouldered away exposing to the sunlight the rows of gracefully tapering niches with their solid lintels and, in the room nearest to us, the stumps of cylindrical stone roof-pegs used not merely for ornament but also for the practical business of affording a necessary projection to which the beams of the now vanished roof could be lashed. As Dr. Bingham has made clear in his recent book,[5] the roof of Incaic dwellings was, in spite of the comparatively humble material wherewith it was fashioned, no less elaborately contrived than was the rest of the building, and these projecting pegs, which some writers have held to be nothing but reminiscences, in stone, of earlier wooden constructions, were in reality a vital part of Incaic house-erection.

In the distance of this same picture one sees the *Intihuatana* or sun-dial of Pisac with its beautiful doorway and its exquisitely wrought curving wall. A nearer view of this edifice is given in Figure 167. Only at Cuzco, at Machu Picchu, and, far to the north, in the Ecuadorian province of Asuay,[6] does one find curving walls equal in construction to this one. In fact, the celebrated curving wall in Cuzco is less beautiful than the others because of the sombre-hued material in which it is built. Figure 155 shows it well and displays also the fact that the marvellously wrought and fitted stones, in perfect courses, are but a veneer over the coarser masonry of an earlier period. This wall, a part of Coricancha, the Temple of the Sun, now the Monastery of Saint Dominic, is eloquent proof of the improvement introduced into the Temple by the Incas Viracocha and Pachacutec. The upper parts of the building as it now stands are, needless to say, Spanish handiwork, composed for the most part of stones pillaged from the ancient temple, and laid with very little skill.

This brings us to the subject of domestic architecture in Incaic times. In the beginning of the Incaic period, when *pirca* masonry was the only kind in use, the dwellings of all classes, including the greatest people in the land, must have been emphatically squalid. The uncut stones laid in mud were continually working loose from their proper places; windows and doorways were few, small, and crudely made; and the thatched roofs teemed with vermin whilst *cuy-cuna* (guinea-pigs) ran about on the earthen floor. Luckily for the comfort of the inhabitants the cooking was done out of doors whenever possible but when, in bad weather, it had to be done indoors the smoke and smells added themselves to the normal discomfort of the cold, damp, ill-ventilated hovel in which only an occasional roof-peg of wood or a still more rare wooden beam or strut afforded a poor hanging place for odd clothing and utensils. At night—and one who has been in the highlands of Peru will know how cold the nocturnal hours are there—the family and most of its domestic animals huddled together in a malodorous heap to which, no doubt, a large number of fleas, mice, rats and other little guests added themselves. In short, conditions very like those to be found in the huts of modern peasants in the remoter districts of Peru and neighboring countries were then common to all.

As time went on, however, domestic comfort increased, at any rate for the great. Niches in which utensils could be kept, more adequate windows and doorways, better-made roofs and floors, and other ameliorations came into use, such as those seen in Figure 221. In the time of the Inca Pachacutec and his successors course-ashlar masonry was usually employed in all better-class houses. It was at this point in their history that the Incas worked out the final form of the gabled domicile of which there were two quite distinct types, namely, the one-family dwelling—in which the gable-ends supporting the ridge-pole were at the middle of the end walls—and the two-family dwelling—in which there was a median wall, usually with niches in it, immediately under the ridge-pole. Figure 220 shows the interior of such a house and the plan of it. While, to our pampered gaze, such an interior, with its neat niches and its simple pegs for hanging things upon and its floor of well-tamped and carefully finished earth, looks decidedly bleak, it was in reality no more so than the interiors of European castles of the period between the fall of Roman civilization and the beginning of the Renaissance. When occupied the Incaic houses were not, we may safely assume, entirely without mitigations: curtains hung in the doorways; llama-pelts and vicuña-pelts were doubtless scattered about, as our rugs are, upon the floor, and perhaps even the pelts of pumas and other large animals were used in this way; plaster, usually tinted, lined the rooms and detracted from the grimness and grayness which naked masonry would inevitably have. Besides skins, the people had of course, hangings, beds made of coarsely woven stuff laid down in piles and finished at the top with finer materials to which reference has been made on earlier pages.

The arrangement of the houses, whether single-family or two-family, varied greatly. In some towns, like that of Racche where the temple of Viracocha stands, they were disposed in regular lines; elsewhere, as in Cuzco itself and at Machu Picchu, there was almost no definite plan, owing in part to the configuration of the land and in part to the gradual growth of the city. We may picture the Inca's own palace as a vast series of gabled chambers grouped around courts filled with flowers and shrubs, adorned, too, by an ever-shifting throng of gaily clad vassals and courtiers, and, finally, brilliantly embellished by beautiful pottery and by works of art in gold, silver, carved wood, and other prized materials. Such buildings, on the street side, were no more than dreary expanses of blank wall, as Figure 156 makes clear.

In short, to be perfectly candid, although some progress was made beyond the absolute squalor which had been the lot of everyone under the earliest Incas and before their time, even in the latest reigns only the great lived in conditions that modern folk would regard as distantly approaching to tolerable comfort. As each successive style of masonry was perfected in the order described above it became the exclusive property of the ruling class; the earlier styles, while being retained in use, were relegated to the purposes and occupation of the humble. It is on this account that Machu Picchu, a citadel that certainly does not ante-date the Inca Pachacutec, contains examples of all the kinds of architecture here mentioned. They are there used, however, in the closest juxtaposition with one another, a fact which is eloquent of their contemporaneity and also, perhaps, of haste in the building of that citadel.

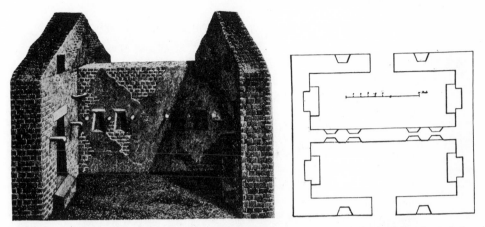

FIG. 220. Ground-plan and interior of a house of the best type of the late Incaic period. The exterior length of the building is about 20 feet. *After Humboldt.*

FIG. 221. Houses on the hillside above Ollantaytambo. Note that, although the masonry is only "modified polygonal" in style, they already have the carefully made doors and windows characteristic of the best Incaic architecture.

Photograph by courtesy of W. V. Alford, Esq.

FIG. 222. Modern Indians near Huánuco ploughing with the traditional *taclla* or footplough.

FIG. 223. A short respite from toil whilst a new quid of coca is made ready.
Photographs by courtesy of W. V. Alford, Esq.

To sum up, then, the subject of ancient Andean architecture, here very shortly dealt with because of lack of space, it may be said that, at all periods of high culture there was a tendency towards grandeur rather than towards what we of to-day regard as comfort or convenience. Such considerations, in all probability, would have awakened the scorn and derision of the Incas who in such matters were austere and fearful of becoming effeminate through a loss of that hardiness which is the product of close contact with Nature. As for the squalor in which—beyond doubt—the populace of the empire dwelt one can only say that it was probably no worse than that in which the populace of Europe dwelt until the Industrial Revolution, no worse than that which prevails throughout the East and throughout Africa to-day, no worse in fact than that which may be found in any great city of the modern world—our own proud towns among them. Moreover, under the Incas, the lowly were exempt from the embittering experience of seeing some of their fellow beings living in immeasurably greater comfort than themselves; for, a careful reading of the most reliable chronicles will bring home to one the significant fact that the grandeur of the ruling caste did not cater to a loftier grade of bodily luxury and comfort so much as it served to create a background of superlative æsthetic glory for the greatest in the land.

2. Material Lacks in Incaic Culture

The Incas, in common with all others of the native American peoples, were without certain material elements which we, of European extraction (both as regards blood and as regards culture) have, during many centuries, regarded as indispensable to civilized life. The basic constitutive elements of Old World culture include: cereals such as wheat, rye, barley, oats, and rice; draught- and burden-bearing animals such as reindeer, yaks, camels, dromedaries, elephants, horses, asses, mules, and dogs, food-yielding animals such as cattle, sheep, pigs, and poultry; foods derived from animals, such as milk, cheese, and eggs; metallic substances such as iron and its daughter, steel; mechanical devices involving one or more applications of the principle of the wheel, whether for the fashioning of vehicles or for the confection of tools varying greatly in kind and in elaboration; forms of building based upon the principle of the keystone arch, whether for simple arches or for domes, or for vaultings. These things, taken together, not only characterize Old World civilization, but define it.

Let us now take each one of these elements and categories in turn and seek for the American equivalents or parallels therefor. To begin with, if the natives of the New World lacked the useful Old World plants named above, had not they full compensation in such plants as maize, the potato, the oca, squashes, and all the rest of the forty plants listed by the great botanist, Candolle,[7] as being native to and characteristic of native American culture? In the article of draught- and burden-bearing animals, on the other hand, the peoples of this hemisphere had no effective substitute; for the feeble, lethargic, and saliva-erupting llama is not to be mentioned in the same breath with the noble and laborious beasts cited above, and even he was confined to the Andean area. Dogs, to be sure, the early Peruvians did have, and likewise other folk of America, but they were kept merely as pets and as an aid in the chase. Again, the llama, the vicuña, and their kin were the sole animals which yielded, in America, anything even faintly resembling butcher's meat; and eggs, milk, butter, and cheese were totally unknown in pre-Spanish times. As regards iron it may be said that, although the Incas had a word for it, *quillay*, its use and value were totally unknown to them and to all natives of America.[8] But in the use of such metals as they did know—copper, bronze, silver, and gold—the pre-Spanish folk of this hemisphere were as skilful as any in the Old World prior to the Renaissance. Of steel, naturally, they were totally ignorant. Moreover, wheeled contrivances of every kind were universally unknown in ancient America, the nearest approaches to them, such as firedrills and spindles, being purely fortuitous and quite without any application of the wheel-principle. Finally, the lack of knowledge concerning the arch inevitably limited the scope of architects' imaginations to such edifices as the stepped-in vault could compass and, in ancient Peru, that was used but rarely, the roofs of early Andean structures being, as already said, their least admirable feature.

We find, therefore, that there was a certain amount of equivalency in ancient America for the fundamental constitutive elements of Old World civilization. True, certain things, such as glass, were wholly wanting in the New World, but for this a fairly effective substitute was found in burnished metal or in the lustrous surface of iron-pyrites, obsidian, quartz-crystal and such things. A far-reaching lack of complex causation, not mentioned elsewhere that I know of, is this: no people of native stock in America ever thought of harnessing the energy latent in natural power—in water-power and in wind-power. This is the direct outcome of ignorance of the wheel and its potentialities. The only approach to a use of natural energy was in the sailing-craft—sufficiently crude though even the best of them were—employed by some of the American peoples.

If we set off against these apparent deficiencies in American culture generally and Andean culture in particular their undeniable accomplishments in the fields of government, agriculture, pottery, textiles, metal-work, sculpture, and architecture —all of which, so far as the early Andean civilizations are concerned, have been treated in this volume—we shall find, I think, that the native peoples of this continent, or rather the most highly developed among them, are well worthy to stand among the advanced nations who, prior to the Renaissance in Europe, shared the Earth among them. We shall find, moreover, that the very contrasts between the constitutive elements under consideration are an eloquent argument, indeed, a proof, of the wholly American origin of all the New World cultures and, more especially, of the New World civilizations.[9] Bone, flesh, and blood, and these alone, did the native folk of this hemisphere derive from the Old World.

3. The Soul of the Subject. Conclusion

Archæology in the Andean countries is a living science which has to do not only with the past, but also with the present and with the future. In Egypt, in Turkestan, in Cambodia, in the classic fields of Greece and Italy, in divers other lands, archæology is a matter of purely intellectual interest, being so either because the materials with which it deals are the products of peoples who have quite vanished from this world, or because those peoples' descendants are to-day so modified, whether for the better or for the worst, that practical lessons derived from those products and applicable to the capacities and mental habits of their modern successors can be only very rare.

But note the difference that we find when we turn to an examination of Andean archæology! Here is a vital thing at once full of the purest sort of intellectual appeal and of potentialities of application to intensely practical purposes. This is true because of one fundamental fact, namely, that the race which created even the oldest, the choicest, the rarest, and, for us, the most exotic artifacts from the ancient periods of the Andean area, is still living and, relatively speaking, is almost unchanged in custom, character, and genius. Years of observant wandering and diligent study have convinced me that of all the ancient and still-surviving peoples none is more tenacious of its past, and none more likely—under favorable circumstances—to surprise the world some day with a splendid renascence of its former genius than is the venerable native stock which to-day comprises more than half of the Andean population. In spite of all the evils that have weighed upon them for four centuries their spirits are not crushed, as a glance at Figures 172, 222 and 223 will make clear.

He who has dwelt among these people, amid all the smoke, and grime and stink of their hovels, and has known the whole story of their muted, tortuous lives can never fail, so be it his soul contain one glimmer of sensibility and altruism, to understand at last that the hidden fires of artistic and political fervor still burn within the breasts of this oppressed, this miserable, this despised race. Mocked at for dullards, gulled for varlets fit only for the ox's toil, defended—when defended at all—only by the plausible, soap-tongued politician of demagogic proclivities and, usually, of Negro or of Oriental, rather than of Indian blood, the indigenes of the Andean region are indeed in a tragic plight. Not until a true understanding of their genius, of their requirements, and of their practical worth is won, will they come into their own, and in the ingredients of that understanding the materials provided by archæology will constitute the major part.

NOTES TO CHAPTER XII

[1] I owe my acquaintance with Maranga and its vicinity to my friend, Don José de la Riva Agüero y Osma, who is—or at any rate was—owner of much of the land in that neighborhood. He was kind enough to arrange several archæological excursions for my benefit to several of the less known sites in the country around Lima.

[2] Nordenskiöld, 1921, pp. 88–91.

[3] Garcilaso, Pt. I, Bk. VII, Ch. xxvii. Cieza de León, Pt. II, Ch. li. Sarmiento, Ch. liii.

[4] Authorities, both ancient and modern, vary greatly in their descriptions and measurements of the temple of Viracocha. I do not vouch, therefore, for the accuracy of the dimensions here given; I have, however, sought to come as near to the correct figures as the material within my reach permits. For accounts of the temple, see: Garcilaso, Pt. I, Bk. V, Ch. xxii. Cieza, Pt. II, Ch. iii.

[5] Bingham, 1930, Ch. iv. See especially Mr. Bumstead's reconstruction of an Incaic roof, on p. 77.

[6] Humboldt, 1910, Pl. 62. Jijón y Caamaño, 1929.

[7] Candolle, 1902. Wissler, 1922, p. 392.

[8] Cobo, Bk. III, Ch. xliii. González Holguín, 1608, p. 176. Wissler, 1922, p. 392. Beuchat, 1912, pp. 152–159.

[9] Wissler, 1922, Chs. xx and xxi.

Sketch map of the
ÁNDEAN ÁREA
showing the chief
ARCHÆOLOGICALLY IMPORTANT PLACES
compiled by
PHILIP AINSWORTH MEANS
from the best available sources
Drawn by Erwin J. Raisz

Scale 0 _____ 500 Miles

BIBLIOGRAPHY

BIBLIOGRAPHY

OF WORKS CONSULTED, CITED AND QUOTED IN THE COURSE
OF THE PRESENT BOOK

ABBREVIATIONS

AA *American Anthropologist.*
AASP *American Antiquarian Society, Proceedings.* (Worcester, Mass.)
AGSB *American Geographical Society, Bulletin.* (New York.)
AJS *American Journal of Science.* (New Haven.)
AMJ *American Museum of Natural History, Journal.* (New York.)
APAMNH *Anthropological Papers of the American Museum of Natural History.* (New York.)
ARBAE *Annual Report, Bureau of American Ethnology.* (Washington.)
ASAF *Archives de la Société Américaine de France.* (Paris.)
AUC *Anales de la Universidad Central.* (Quito.)
BAE *Bureau of American Ethnology.* (Washington.)
BANH *Boletín de la Academia Nacional de Historia.* (Quito.)
BIGA *Boletín del Instituto Geográfico Argentino.* (Buenos Aires.)
BIGBA *Boletín del Instituto Geográfico de Buenos Aires.*
BNBC *Bulletin of the Needle and Bobbin Club.* (New York.)
PSEEHA *Boletín de la Sociedad Ecuatoriana de Estudios Históricos Americanos.* (Quito.)
BSGL *Boletín de la Sociedad Geográfica de Lima.*
CLDHP *Colección de libros y documentos referentes a la historia del Perú.* (Lima.)
FFLA *Facultad de Filosofía y Letras. Publicaciones de la Sección Antropológica.* (Buenos Aires.)
GJ *Journal of the Royal Geographical Society.* (London.)
GR *Geographical Review, American Geographical Society.* (New York.)
HAHR *Hispanic American Historical Review.* (Durham, N. C.)
ICA *International Congress of Americanists.*
IN *Indian Notes, Museum of the American Indian, Heye Foundation.* (New York.)
JAP *Journal de la Société des Américanistes de Paris.*
MCAAS *Memoirs of the Connecticut Academy of Arts and Sciences.* (New Haven.)
MJ *Museum Journal, Museum of the University of Pennsylvania.* (Philadelphia.)
MP *Mercurio Peruano.* (Lima.)
NGM *National Geographic Magazine.* (Washington.)
NH *Natural History, American Museum of Natural History.* (New York.)
PMP *Peabody Museum Papers.* (Cambridge, Mass.)
RCHG *Revista Chilena de Historia y Geografía.* (Santiago de Chile.)
RGI *Relaciones Geográficas de Indias.* (Madrid.)

RH   *Revista Histórica.* (Lima.)
RMLP   *Revista del Museo de La Plata.* (La Plata, Argentina.)
RUBA   *Revista de la Universidad de Buenos Aires.*
TCAAS   *Transactions of the Connecticut Academy of Arts and Sciences.*
            (New Haven.)
UCPAAE   *University of California Publications in American Archæology
            and Ethnology.* (Berkeley, Calif.)
ZE   *Zeitschrift für Ethnologie.* (Berlin.)

LIST OF WORKS

ACOSTA, Father José de: (1540–1600; in Peru 1569–1583. Jesuit.)
1588   *De Natura Novi Orbis Libri duo* . . . Salamanca. (Guillermo
            Foquel.)
1590   *Historia Natural y Moral de las Indias* . . . Seville. (Juan de
            Leon.)
1604   *The Naturall and Morall Historie of the East and West Indies*
            . . . Translated by E. G. (Edward Grimston). London. (Ed-
            ward Blount and William Aspley.)
1880   *The Natural & Moral History of the Indies.* Edited by Clements
            R. Markham. London. (Hakluyt Society.) 2 vols.
AGUSTINOS, Los Primeros Religiosos:
            See San Pedro and Canta.
ALCEDO, Antonio de:
1786–1789   *Diccionario geográfico-histórico de las Indias Occidentales, ó
            América.* Madrid. 5 vols.
1812–1815   *The Geographical and Historical Dictionary of America and the
            West Indies.* With additions by G. A. Thompson. London.
            5 vols.
ALEXANDER, Hartley Burr:
1920   *The Mythology of All Races—Latin American.* Boston.
ALGAROTTI, Count:
1764   *Saggio sopra l'imperio degl'Incas.* Leghorn.
ALMANAQUE DE "LA CRÓNICA":
1918   Lima.
AMBROSETTI, Juan B.:
1897   *La antigua ciudad de Quilmés.* BIGBA, XVIII, Nos. 2 and 3.
            Buenos Aires.
1897b   *La industria vinícola.* Buenos Aires.
1897c   *Los monumentos megalíticos del valle de Tafi (Tucumán).*
            Buenos Aires.
1899   *Notas de arqueología calchaquí.* Buenos Aires.
1901   *Noticias sobre la alfarería prehistórica de Santiago del Estero.*
            Buenos Aires.
1902   *Antigüedades calchaquíes, datos arqueológicos sobre la provincia
            de Jujuy.* Buenos Aires.
1902b   *Arqueología Argentina. Algunos vasos ceremoniales de la región
            calchaquí.* Buenos Aires.
1902c   *Arqueología Argentina. El sepulcro de "La Paya" últimamente
            descubierto en los valles calchaquíes.* Buenos Aires.
1903   *La antigüedad del Nuevo Mundo.* Buenos Aires.
1904   *El bronce en la región calchaquí.* Buenos Aires.

1904b   *Viaje en la puna de Atacama de Salta a Caurchari.* Buenos Aires.

1904c   *Apuntes sobre la arqueología de la puna de Atacama.* La Plata.

1905   *Arqueología Argentina; el bronce en la región calchaquí.* Buenos Aires.

1905b   *Arqueología Argentina; insignia lítica de mando de tipo chileno.* Buenos Aires.

1906   *Exploraciones arqueológicas en la Pampa Grande.* Buenos Aires.

1907   *Exploraciones arqueológicas en la ciudad prehistórica de "La Paya."* Buenos Aires.

1908   *La question calchaquí.* ICA, XVI. Vienna.

1910   *Resultados de las exploraciones arqueológicas en el Pukara de Tilcara.* ICA, XVII. Buenos Aires.

ANGRAND, Léonce:

1866   *Lettre sur les antiquités de Tiaguanaco et l'origine présumable de la plus ancienne civilisation du Haut-Pérou.* Paris.

ANONYMOUS CONQUEST: (Perhaps by Xerez, *q. v.*)

1534   *La conquista del Perú.* Seville. (Bartholomé Perez.) Excessively rare. A copy in the New York Public Library.

1929   *The Conquest of Peru.* Reproduced in facsimile from 1534 edition and translated by Joseph H. Sinclair. New York. (New York Public Library.)

ANONYMOUS PERUVIAN:

1791   *Idea general de los monumentos del antiguo Perú, é introducción a su estudio.* MP, I, pp. 201–208. Lima.

ANONYMOUS RELATION:

     See Valera.

ANTIGUALLA PERUANA, Una:

     See Quipucamayocs.

APARICIO, Francisco de:

1928   *Investigaciones arqueológicas en la región serrana de la provincia de San Luís (Rep. Argentina).* ICA, XXII, Pt. I, pp. 453–466. Rome.

ARCA PARRÓ, A.:

1923   *¿Dónde vivían los Chankas?* Inca, I, pp. 971–974.

ARCTOWSKI, H.:

1910–1913   *Studies in Climate and Crops.* AGSB, XLIII, pp. 270–282, 481–495; XLIV, pp. 598–606, 754–760; XLV, pp. 117–131.

ARGÜEDAS, Alcides:

1919   *Pueblo enfermo.* Barcelona.

ARRIAGA, Father Jesús:

1922   *Apuntes de arqueología Cañar.* Cuenca (Ecuador).

ARRIAGA, Father Pablo José de: (In Peru 1582–1622.)

1621   *Extirpación de la idolatría del Piru.* Lima. (Geronymo de Contreras.)

1920   *Extirpación,* etc. Edited by Drs. Carlos A. Romero and Horacio H. Urteaga. CLDHP, 2d ser., I. Lima.

ARSANDAUX, H.; and, RIVET, Paul:

1923   *L'orfévrerie du Chiriquí et de Colombie.* JAP, n. s., XV, pp. 169–181.

ATIENZA, Father Lope de: (Flourished between 1580 and 1585.)

1585 (?)   *Compendio historial de los Yndios del Piru* . . . Unpublished

MS., of which the original is lost. Two copies of it exist in the New York Public Library.

ÁVILA, Father Francisco de: (Born in Cuzco in 1565. Died 1647.)
1873   *A Narrative of the Errors, False Gods, and other Superstitions and Diabolical Rites in which the Indians of Huarochiri lived in Ancient Times.* Translated and edited by Clements R. Markham in *Rites and Laws of the Yncas,* pp. 122–147. London. (Hakluyt Society.)
     NOTE: This translation is based upon the original MS., dated 1608, which is in the National Library, Madrid.

BAESSLER, Arthur:
1902–1903   *Ancient Peruvian Art.* Berlin and New York. 4 vols.
1906   *Altperuanische Metallgeräte.* Berlin.

BALLIVIÁN, Manuel Vicente:
1910   *Monumentos prehistóricos de Tiahuanaco.* La Paz.

BALLIVIÁN, Manuel Vicente; and, CEVALLOS TOVAR, Walter:
1914   *Noticia histórica y clasificación de la papa de Bolivia.* La Paz.

BAMPS, Anatole:
1879   *Les antiquités équatoriennes du Musée Royal d'Antiquités de Bruxelles.* ICA, III, vol. II, pp. 47–143, and Atlas. Brussels.
1887   *Tomebamba.* Louvain.

BANDELIER, Adolf Francis:
1905   *The aboriginal Ruins of Sillustani, Peru.* AA, n. s., VII, pp. 49–68.
1907   *The Indians and aboriginal Ruins near Chachapoyas, Northern Peru.* New York.
1910   *The Islands of Titicaca and Koati.* New York.
1911   *The Ruins at Tiahuanaco.* AASP, XXI, pp. 218–265.

BARKER, Alfred F.; and, GARNETT, Francis W.:
1920   *Alpaca and Llama Research.* Yorkshire Observer, August 12, 1920. Reprinted in the West Coast Leader (Lima), October 2, 1920.

BARNETT, Anna:
1909   *Étude technologique d'un tissu péruvien* . . . JAP, VI, pp. 265–268.
1910   *Étude sur le mode de fabrication des frondes péruviennes antiques.* JAP, VII, pp. 117–120.

BARRERA, Isaac J.:
1918   *El Padre D. Juan de Velasco.* BSEEHA, I, pp. 136–144.

BARRETT, S. A.:
1925   *The Cayapa Indians of Ecuador.* Museum of the American Indian. New York. 2 vols., paged *seriatim.*

BASLER, Adolphe; and, BRUMMER, Ernest:
1928   *L'Art Précolombien.* Paris.

BASTIAN, Adolf:
1877   *Aus der ethnologischen Sammlung des königlichen Museums zu Berlin.* ZE, IX, pp. 143–150.
1878–1889   *Die Culturländer des alten America.* Berlin. 3 vols. usually bound as 4, the 3d in two parts.

BAUDIN, Louis:
1927   *La formation de l'élite et l'enseignment de l'histoire dans l'Empire des Inka.* Rev. des Études Historiques, 93d year, pp. 107–114. Paris.

1927b　　La statistique au temps des Inka. Rev. politique et parlemen-
taire, CXXXII, pp. 460–465. Paris.

1927c　　Une expérience socialiste: le Pérou des Inka. Journal des Écono-
mistes, LXXXVII, pp. 506–519. Paris.

1928　　L'Empire socialiste des Inka. Institut d'Ethnologie, Traveaux et
Mémoires, V. Paris.

1929　　L'organisation économique de l'Empire des Incas. Rev. de l'Amérique Latine, XVII, pp. 385–393. Paris.

BEEBE, William:
1924　　Galápagos World's End. New York.

BELAÚNDE, Victor Andrés:
1908　　El Perú antiguo y los modernos sociólogos. Lima.

BENNERS, Ethel Ellis:
1920　　Ancient Peruvian Textiles. MJ, September, 1920, pp. 140–147.

BERTHON, Paul:
1911　　Étude sur le précolombien du Bas-Pérou. Nouvelles archives des
missions scientifiques, fascicule 4. Paris.

BERTONIO, Ludovico: (Flourished 1600–1612.)
1879　　Vocabulario de la lengua aymará. Edited by Julius Platzmann.
Leipzig. 2 vols.

BETÁNZOS, Juan de: (Born in Spain in 1510; in Cuzco 1540–1576.)
1551　　Suma y narración de los yngas que los yndios llamaron Capaccuna
que fueron señores en la ciudad del cuzco y de todo lo a ella
subjeto . . . Original MS. is lost; an early copy of it exists in
the library of the Escorial under the signature L. I. 5.

1880　　Suma y narración de los Incas . . . Edited by Don Marcos
Jiménez de la Espada. Biblioteca Hispano-Ultramarina, II.
Madrid.

1924　　Suma y narración de los Incas . . . Edited by Drs. Horacio H.
Urteaga and Carlos A. Romero, with a biographical note by
Friar Domingo Angulo. CLDHP, 2d ser., VIII. Lima.

BEUCHAT, Henri:
1912　　Manuel d'archéologie américaine. Paris.

BINGHAM, Hiram:
1911　　The Ruins of Choqquequirau. AA, n. s., XII, pp. 505–525.

1912　　Vitcos, the last Inca Capital. AASP, XXII, pp. 135–196.

1912b　　The Discovery of pre-historic human Remains near Cuzco, Peru.
AJS, XXXIII, pp. 297–305.

1913　　In the Wonderland of Peru. NGM, April, 1913.

1914　　The Ruins of Espiritu Pampa, Peru. AA, n. s., XVI, pp. 185–199.

1914b　　The Pampaconas River. GJ, XLIV, pp. 211–214.

1915　　The Story of Machu Picchu. NGM, February, 1915.

1915b　　Types of Machu Picchu Pottery. AA, n. s., XVII, pp. 251–271.

1916　　Further Explorations in the Land of the Incas. NGM, May, 1916.

1917　　The Inca Peoples and their Culture. ICA, XIX, pp. 253–260.
Washington.

1922　　Inca Land. Boston.

1930　　Machu Picchu, a Citadel of the Incas. New Haven.

BINGHAM, Millicent Todd:
1929　　Article on Peru. Encyclopædia Britannica, XIVth Edition.

BOLLAERT, William:
1853　　The pre-Incarial Ruins of Tiahuanaco . . . Intellectual Observer,
III, pp. 229–237. London.

1860   *Antiquarian, ethnological and other Researches in New Granada, Peru, and Chile* . . . London.

BOMAN, Eric:

1903   *Enterratorio prehistórico* . . . *en Jujuy.* Buenos Aires.

1904   *Groupes de tumulus préhispaniques dans la vallée de Lerma.* L'Homme Préhistorique, II, pp. 310–323. Paris.

1905   *Migrations précolombiens dans le Nord-Ouest de l'Argentine.* JAP, n. s., II, pp. 91–108.

1908   *Antiquités de la région andine de la république Argentine et du désert d'Atacama.* Paris. 2 vols., paged *seriatim.*

1921   *Los vestigios de industria humana en Miramar (República Argentina) y atribuidos a la época terciana.* RCHG, XXXIX, pp. 330–352.

1923   *Los ensayos de establecer una cronología prehispánica en la región diaguita.* BANH, VI, pp. 1–31.

1923b   *Alfarería del estilo draconiano de la región diaguita.* Buenos Aires.

BOWMAN, Isaiah:

1912   *The Cañon of the Urubamba.* GR, XLIV, pp. 881–896.

1912b   *The geologic Relations of the Cuzco Remains.* AJS, XXXIII, pp. 306–325.

1912c   *A buried Wall at Cuzco and its Relation to the Question of a Pre-Inca Race.* AJS, XXXIV, pp. 497–509.

1916   *The Andes of Southern Peru.* New York.

1924   *Desert Trails of Atacama.* New York.

BRASSEUR DE BOURBOURG, Charles-Étienne:

1857–1859   *Histoire des Nations civilisées du Mexique et de l'Amérique Centrale durant les siècles antérieurs à Christophe Colomb.* Paris. 4 vols.

BRINTON, Daniel Garrison:

1882   *The Maya Chronicles.* Philadelphia.

BROOKS, C. F.:

1916   *World-wide Changes of Temperature.* GR, II, pp. 249–255.

BRUCH, Carlos:

1910   *Las edificaciones antiguas del valle Calchaquí.* ICA, XVII, pp. 499–501. Buenos Aires.

1913   *Exploraciones arqueológicas en* . . . *Tucumán y Catamarca.* RMLP, XIX, pp. 1–196.

BUCHWALD, Otto von:

1908   *Die Kara.* Globus, XCIV, pp. 123–125. Brunswick, Germany.

1908b   *Altes und Neues vom Guayas.* Globus, XCIV, pp. 181–183.

1909   *Das Reich der Chimus.* Globus, XCV, pp. 149–151.

1909b   *Zur Wandersage der Kara.* Globus, XCV, pp. 316–319.

1909c   *Ecuatorianische Grabhügel.* Globus, XCVI, pp. 154–157.

1909–1910   *Zur Völkerkunde Südamerikas.* Globus, XCVI, pp. 317–320; XCVIII, pp. 74–76.

1918   *Tiahuanaco y Cuzco.* BSEEHA, I, pp. 105–108.

1918b   *Migraciones Sud-Americanas.* BSEEHA, I, pp. 227–236.

1918c   *Notas acerca de la arqueología del Guayas.* BSEEHA, I, pp. 237–275.

1919   *Los primeros Incas.* BSEEHA, VII, pp. 115–121.

1920   *Notas etnológicas del Ecuador Occidental.* BANH, IV, pp. 285–293.
1921   *Un sello cilíndrico.* BANH, III, pp. 155–156.
BUSTAMANTE CISNEROS, Ricardo:
1918   *Condición jurídica de las comunidades de indígenas en el Perú.* Lima.
1919   *Introducción al estudio de la sociología nacional.* Lima.
CABELLO DE BALBOA, Father Miguel: (In Peru 1566 to after 1602.)
1576–1586   *Miscelánea Antártica.* The original MS. is lost to sight, but a good copy, probably made between 1700 and 1725, exists in the New York Public Library, and it is to this that all references are made in the present volume.
CABRAL, Jorge:
1913   *Los cronistas é historiadores de Indias y el problema de las dinastías de la monarquía peruana.* Buenos Aires.
CALANCHA, Father Antonio de la: (Born in Chuquisaca, 1584, died in Lima, 1654.)
1638   *Coronica moralizada del orden de San Agustín en el Peru, con sucesos egenplares en esta monarquia.* Barcelona. (Pedro Lacavallería.) Save for a reissue, in 1639, by the same printer, this is the only edition of this work.
CANDOLLE, Alphonse de:
1902   *Origin of cultivated Plants.* New York.
CAPDEVILLE, Augusto:
1921   *Notas acerca de la arqueología de Taltal. I. Introducción.* BANH, II, pp. 1–16.
1921b   *Notas, etc. II. Civilización dolménica.* BANH, II, pp. 256–261.
1921c   *Notas, etc. III. Civilización de las gentes de los vasos pintados.* BANH, III, pp. 229–233.
1922   *Apuntes para la arqueología de Taltal. IV. Civilización de las gentes de los vasos figurados.* BANH, IV, pp. 115–118.
1923   *Un cementerio chincha-atacameño de Punta Grande, Taltal.* BANH, VII, pp. 34–49.
CARLI, Count Gianrinaldo:
1780   *Delle Lettere Americane.* Florence, 2 vols.
1788   *Lettres américaines.* Translated by Jean Baptiste Lefebvre de Villebrune. Boston and Paris. 2 vols.
1821   *Cartas americanas dirigidas . . . a su sobrino el Marqués de Pietra-Pelosa, desde el año de 1777 al de 1779.* Translated by D. Fernando Pimentel Ixtliulxuchilt (i. e., Don Augustín Pomposo Fernández de San Salvador). Mexico.
CARRERA, Father Fernando de la:
1644   *Arte de la lengua yunga de los valles del obispado de Truxillo del Peru . . .* Lima. (José de Contreras.)
1880   *Arte de la lengua yunga . . .* Edited by Dr. Manuel González de la Rosa. Lima.
CARRILLO Y ANCONA, Bishop Crescencio:
1883   *Historia antigua de Yucatán.* Mérida. (Yucatan.)
CARRIÓN CACHOT, Rebeca:
1923   *La mujer y el niño en el antiguo Perú.* Inca, I, pp. 329–354.
CASAS, Bishop Friar Bartolomé de las: (1474–1566.)

552 BIBLIOGRAPHY

1892   *De las antiguas gentes del Perú.* Edited by Don Marcos Jiménez de la Espada. Madrid.
NOTE: This volume is a series of consecutively arranged excerpts from Casas's *Apologética historia de las Indias*, written about 1550.

CASTAING, Alphonse:
1884   *Le communisme au Pérou.* Paris.
1888   *Le mythe de Manco Capac.* ASAF, n. s., VI, Pt. I, pp. 7–27.

CASTRO, Cristóbal de; and, ORTEGA MOREJÓN, Diego de: (1558.)
1867   *Relación y declaración del modo que este valle de Chincha y sus comarcanos se gobernaban antes que hobiese ingas y después que los hobo hasta que los cristianos entraron en esta tierra.* In Colección de documentos inéditos para la historia de España, L, pp. 206–220. Madrid.

CAVANILLES, Antoine Joseph de:
1785–1790   *Monadelphiae classis dissertationes decem.* Paris.

CEVALLOS, Pedro Fermín:
1870   *Resúmen de la historia del Ecuador.* Lima. 5 vols.
1886–1889   *Resúmen de la historia del Ecuador.* Guayaquil. 6 vols.

CHEESMAN SALINAS, Francisco:
1909   *El distrito de Lunahuaná.* BSGL, XXV, pp. 240–243. Lima.

CIEZA DE LEON, Pedro de: (Born 1519; in Peru 1532–1550.)
1553   *Parte primera de la Chronica del Peru.* Seville. (Martín de Montesdoca.)
1864   *The Travels of Pedro de Cieza de León, A. D. 1532–50, contained in the First Part of his Chronicle of Peru.* Translated and edited by Clements R. Markham. London. (Hakluyt Society.)
1880   *Segunda Parte de la Crónica del Perú.* Edited by Don Marcos Jiménez de la Espada. Biblioteca Hispano-Ultramarina, II. Madrid.
1883   *The Second Part of the Chronicle of Peru.* Translated and edited by Clements R. Markham. London. (Hakluyt Society.)

CIPRIANI, Lidio:
1928   *Su due "quipus" del Museo Nazionale di Antropología e Etnología di Firenze.* ICA, XXII, Pt. I, pp. 471–480. Rome.

CISNEROS, Carlos B.:
n. d.   *Atlás del Perú.* Lima.

CLAVIGERO, Francesco Saverio:
1780–1781   *Storia antica del Messico.* Cesena. (G. Biasini.) 4 vols.
1787   *The History of Mexico.* Translated by Charles Cullen. London. 2 vols.

COBO, Father Bernabé: (Born in 1582; in America, 1599–1657.)
1890–1893   *Historia del Nuevo Mundo.* Edited by Don Marcos Jiménez de la Espada. Seville. (Sociedad de Bibliófilos Andaluces.) 4 vols.

CONTRERAS Y VALVERDE, Vasco de: (Flourished about 1649.)
1885   *Relación de la ciudad del Cuzco* . . . RGI, II, pp. 174–198. Madrid.

COOK, O. F.:
1909   *Vegetation affected by Agriculture in Central America.* U. S. Bureau of Plant Industry, Bulletin 145. Washington.
1916   *Staircase Farms of the Ancients.* NGM, May, 1916.

CORDOBA Y SALINAS, Friar Diego de:
1650   *Teatro de la Santa Iglesia Metropolitana de la muy noble Ciudad de los Reyes, llamada comunmente Lima* . . . Original MS. in the New York Public Library. This still unpublished book contains, in Chapter XIV, valuable data on the archæology of the region of Lima.

COSIO, Felix:
1916   *La propiedad colectiva del ayllu.* Cuzco.

COURTY, Georges:
1909   *Les nouveaux aspects de la préhistoire américaine.* L'Homme Préhistorique, VII, pp. 65–72. Paris.

CRAWFORD, Morris De Camp:
1915   *Peruvian Textiles.* APAMNH, XII, Pt. 3. New York.
1916   *Peruvian Fabrics.* APAMNH, XII, Pt. 4. New York.
1916b   *The Cotton of Ancient Peru.* Boston.
1916c   *The Loom in the New World.* AMJ, XVI, pp. 381–386.
1924   *The Heritage of Cotton.* New York.

CRÉQUI-MONTFORT, Count G. de:
1906   *Fouilles de la mission scientifique française à Tiahuanaco* . . . ICA, XIV, Pt. 2, pp. 531–551. Stuttgart.
1906b   *Fouilles dans la nécropole préhispanique de Calama.* ICA, XIV, Pt. 2, pp. 551–567. Stuttgart.

CRÉQUI-MONTFORT, Count G. de; and, RIVET, Paul:
1914   *L'origine des aborigènes du Pérou et de la Bolivie.* Comptes-rendus des séances de l'Académie des Inscriptions et Belles Lettres, 1914, pp. 196–202. Paris.
1914b   *L'origine des aborigènes des hauts plateaux boliviens et péruviens.* Institut français d'anthropologie, II, p. 39.
1925–1927   *La lengua Uru ou Pukina.* JAP, XVII, pp. 211–244; XVIII, pp. 111–139; XIX, pp. 57–116.

CUMMINGS, Byron:
1923   *Cuicuilco, the oldest temple discovered in North America.* Art & Archæology, XVI, pp. 51–58. Washington.
1923b   *Cuicuilco and the archaic culture of Mexico.* Scientific Monthly, XXIII, pp. 289–304.

CÚNEO VIDAL, Rómulo:
1914   *Del Concepto del "Ayllu."* BSGL, XXX, pp. 4–9.
1919   *El cacicazgo de Tacna.* RH, VI, pp. 309–324. Lima.
1924   *La tumba del Inca historiador Garcilaso de la Vega en la catedral de Córdoba.* RH, VII, pp. 217–228.

CUNOW, Heinrich:
1896   *Die soziale Verfassung des Inkareichs.* Stuttgart.
1898   *Die soziale Verfassung des Inkareichs.* Brunswick.
1930   *El sistema de parentesco peruano y las comunidades gentilicias de los Incas.* Translated by María Woitscheck. Paris.

DAY, Lewis F.; and, BUCKLE, Mary:
1901   *Art in Needlework.* London.

DEBENEDETTI, Salvador:
1908   *Excursión arqueológica a las ruinas de Kipón.* FFLA, No. 4. Buenos Aires.
1910   *Exploración arqueológica en los cementerios prehistóricos de la Isla de Tilcara (Quebrada de Humahuaca, Provincia de Jujuy).* FFLA, No. 6. Buenos Aires.

1911   *Noticia de un cementerio indígena de Baradero.* RUBA, XIII, pp. 401–414.

1912   *Influencias de la cultura de Tiahuanaco en la región del Noroeste Argentino.* RUBA, XVII, pp. 326–352.

1912b   Abstract of the foregoing. ICA, XVIII, Pt. I, pp. 298–300. London.

1928   *Los yacimientos arqueológicos de las márgenes meridionales de las langunas Guanacache.* (*Rep. Argentina.*) ICA, XXII, Pt. I, pp. 505–508. Buenos Aires.

DEBERLE, A.:
1876   *Histoire de l'Amérique du Sud.* Paris.

DENIS, Pierre:
1927   *Amérique du Sud.* Paris. 2 vols., paged *seriatim.*

DIAZ, Eulogio:
1898   *Descripción del distrito de San Carlos de Bambamarca.* Cajamarca.

DIXON, Roland Burrage:
1928   *The Building of Cultures.* New York.

DORSEY, George A.:
1901   *Archæological Investigations on the Island of La Plata, Ecuador.* Field Columbian Museum, Publication No. 56. Chicago.

DYOTT, G. M.:
1922   *Silent Highways of the Jungle.* London.
1926   *On the Trail of the Unknown.* London.

EATON, George F.:
1912   *Report on the Remains of Man and of Lower Animals from the Vicinity of Cuzco, Peru.* AJS, XXXIII, pp. 325–333.
1913   *Vertebrate Remains in the Cuzco Gravels.* AJS, XXXVI, pp. 3–14.
1914   *Vertebrate Fossils from Ayusbamba, Peru.* AJS, XXXVII, pp. 141–154.
1916   *The Collection of Osteological Material from Machu Picchu.* MCAAS, V. New Haven.
1925   *Food Animals of the Peruvian Highlands.* ICA, XXI, Pt. II, pp. 61–66. Gothenburg.

EGUIGUREN, Luís A.:
1914   *El ayllu peruano y su condición legal.* Lima.

ENOCK, C. Reginald:
1904   *Las ruinas de Huánuco Viejo.* BSGL, XV, pp. 317–324.
1905   *The Ruins of "Huánuco Viejo" or Old Huanuco* . . . GJ, XXVI, pp. 153–179.
1907   *The Andes and the Amazon.* London.
1910   *Peru.* London.
1912   *Peru.* London. (3d edition, improved.)

ESTETE, Miguel de: (Born in Spain about 1510; in Peru 1532–1557.)
1534   *La relación del viage que hizo el señor Hernando Pizarro* . . . *desde el pueblo de Caxamalca a Parcama y de allí a Xauxa.* Seville. (Bartolomé Perez.)
       NOTE: This work is inserted into the text of Xerez, *q. v.,* below.
1535   *Noticia del Perú.* MS. preserved in the Archives of the Indies, at Seville.
1872   *The Narrative of the Journey made by* . . . *Hernando Pizarro* . . . *from the city of Caxamalca to Parcama, and thence to*

Xauxa. Translated and edited by Clements R. Markham, and inserted in pages 74–94 of his edition of Xerez, *q. v.* London. (Hakluyt Society.)

1919   *El descubrimiento y conquista del Perú.* Edited and reproduced in facsimile of the 1535 MS. by Carlos M. Larrea. Quito.

FALCÓN, Francisco: (Was in Peru about 1580–1585.)
1918   *Relación sobre el gobierno de los Incas.* Edited by Drs. Horacio H. Urteaga and Carlos A. Romero. CLDHP, 1st ser., XI, pp. 135–176. Lima.

FALIÈS, Louis:
n. d.   *Études historiques et philosophiques sur les civilisations.* Paris. 2 vols.

FARABEE, William Curtis:
1920   *Ancient American Gold.* MJ, XI, pp. 93–129.
1921   *The Use of Metals in Prehistoric America.* MJ, XII, pp. 35–42.
1921b   *A Golden Hoard from Ecuador.* MJ, XII, pp. 43–52.
1922   *Indian Tribes of Eastern Peru.* PMP, X.

FEYJOO DE SOSA, Miguel:
1763   *Relación descriptiva de la ciudad . . . de Truxillo . . .* Madrid.

FRÉZIER, Amédée François:
1717   *A Voyage to the South Sea, and along the Coasts of Chili and Peru.* London. (John Bowyer.)

FRÖDIN, Otto; and, NORDENSKIÖLD, Erland:
1918   *Über Zwirnen und Spinnen bei den Indianern Südamerikas.* Gothenburg.

GARCÍA Y MERINO, Manuel:
1894   *Proyectiles primitivos de los peruanos.* BSGL, IV, pp. 210–217.

GARCÍA ROSSELL, Ricardo:
1900 (?)   *Atlás geográfico del Perú.* Barcelona.
1903   *El departamento de Piura.* BSGL, XIII, pp. 193–242.

GARCILASO DE LA VEGA, El Inca: (Born in Cuzco, 1539; died in Spain, 1616.)
1609   *Primera Parte de los Commentarios Reales . . .* Lisbon. (Pedro Crasbeeck.)
1869–1871   *The First Part of the Royal Commentaries of the Yncas.* Translated and edited by Clements R. Markham. London. (Hakluyt Society.) 2 vols.

GAYTON, A. H.:
1927   *The Uhle Pottery Collections from Nievería.* UCPAAE, XXI, pp. 91–97.

GAYTON, A. H.; and, KROEBER, A. L.:
1927   *The Uhle Pottery Collections from Nazca.* UCPAAE, XXIV, pp. 1–46.

GENET, Jean:
1927   *Esquisse d'une civilisation oubliée.* Paris.

GENET, Jean; and, CHELBATZ, Pierre:
1927   *Histoire des Peuples Mayas-Quichés.* Paris.

GÓNGORA MARMOLEJO, Alonso de: (Flourished about 1575.)
1862   *Historia de Chile.* Edited by Don Diego Barros Arana. Santiago.

GONZÁLEZ HOLGUÍN, Father Diego:
1607–1608   *Vocabulario de la lengua general de todo el Perú llamada lengua*

Qquichua, o del Inca. Lima. (Francisco del Canto.) 2 vols., usually bound as one.

GONZÁLEZ DE LA ROSA, Manuel:
1907   *El Padre Valera primer historiador peruano.* RH, II, pp. 180–199.
1908   *Estudio de las antigüedades halladas bajo el huano.* RH, III, pp. 39–45.
1908b   *Los Comentarios Reales son la réplica de Valera a Sarmiento de Gamboa.* RH, III, pp. 296–306.
1908c   *Les Caras de l'Equateur et les premiers résultats de l'expédition G. Heye sous la direction de M. Saville.* JAP, n. s., V, pp. 85–93.
1910   *Les deux Tiahuanaco, leurs problèmes et leur solution.* ICA, XVI, pp. 405–428. Vienna.
1912   *Carácter legendario de Manco Capac.* ICA, XVII, pp. 269–272. Buenos Aires.

GONZÁLEZ SUÁREZ, Archbishop Federico:
1878   *Estudio histórico sobre los Cañaris, antiguos habitantes de la provincia del Azuay, en la República del Ecuador.* Quito.
1890–1903 *Historia general de la República del Ecuador.* Quito. 7 vols.
1892   *Atlás arqueológico.* Quito. 2 vols.
1904   *Prehistoria Ecuatoriana.* Quito.
1908   *Los aborígenes de Imbabura y del Carchi.* Quito.
1915   *Notas arqueológicas.* Quito.
1922   *Estudio histórico sobre los Cañaris, pobladores de la antigua provincia del Azuay.* Cuenca. (Ecuador.)

GRASSERIE, Raoul de la:
1894   *Langue Puquina.* Leipzig.

GREGORY, Herbert E.:
1914   *Geologic Reconnaissance of the Ayusbamba Fossil Beds.* AJS, XXXVII, pp. 125–140.
1916   *A Geologic Reconnaissance of the Cuzco Valley.* AJS, XLI, pp. 1–100.

GROUSSAC, Pablo (alias Paul):
1882   *El Tucumán antecolonial.* Buenos Aires.

GUEVARA, Tomás:
1898–1922 *Historia de la civilización araucana.* Santiago de Chile.
1928–1930 *Sobre el orígen de los Araucanos.* RCHG, LIX, pp. 128–168; LXIV, pp. 322–331.

GUIMARAES, Enrique de:
1907   *Algo sobre el quipus.* With a Note, by Max Uhle. RH, II, pp. 55–65.

GUTIÉRREZ DE SANTA CLARA, Pedro: (About 1525 to 1603.)
1904–1910 *Historia de las guerras civiles del Perú.* Edited by Don Manuel Serrano y Sanz. In Colección de libros y documentos referentes a la historia de América, II, III, IV, and IX. Madrid. 4 vols.

HAKLUYT, Richard:
1903–1905 *The Principal Navigations, voyages, traffiques, and discoveries of the English Nation.* Edinburgh and Glasgow. 12 vols.

HANSTEIN, Otfrid von:
1923   *Die Welt des Inka.* Dresden.
1925   *The World of the Incas.* Translated by Anna Barwell. London and New York.

HARCOURT, Raoul d':
1922   La céramique de Cajamarquilla-Nievería. JAP, n. s., XIV, pp.
            107–118.
1928   La fabrication de certains grelots métalliques chez les Yunka.
            ICA, XXII, Pt. I, pp. 541–543. Rome.
1928b   Les vêtements et les armes d'un guerrier Yunka d'après le décor
            d'un lécythe de la région de Trujillo. ICA, XXII, Pt. I, pp.
            545–548. Rome.
HARCOURT, Raoul and Marie d':
1924   La céramique ancienne du Pérou. Paris.
1924b   Les tissus indiens du Vieux Pérou. Paris.
1925   La musique des Incas et ses survivances. Paris. 2 vols.
HARTH-TERRÉ, Emilio:
1923   La fortaleza de Chuquimancu. Revista arqueológica del Museo
            Larco-Herrera, No. 2. Lima.
HEUZEY, L.:
1870   Le trésor de Cuenca. Gazette des Beaux-Arts, 2d period, IV, pp.
            113–127. Paris.
HILLS, Elijah Clarence:
1914   The Quechua Drama, "Ollanta." Romanic Review, V, pp. 126–
            176. New York.
HOLLISTER, N.:
1918   The Domestication of the Llama. Science, n. s., XLVII, p. 461.
HOLMES, William H.:
1885   A Study of the Textile Art. ARBAE, 1885, pp. 189–252.
1887   The Use of Gold and other Metals among the Ancient Inhabi-
            tants of Chiriquí, Isthmus of Darien. BAE, Bulletin 3.
1888   Ancient Art of the Province of Chiriquí, Colombia. ARBAE, VI,
            pp. 13–187.
1889   Textile Fabrics of Ancient Peru. BAE, Bulletin 7.
1907   On a Nephrite Statuette from San Andrés Tuxtla, Vera Cruz,
            Mexico. AA, n. s., IX, pp. 691–701.
1916   The Oldest Dated American Monument, a Nephrite Figurine
            from Mexico. Art & Archæology, IV, pp. 275–278. Washington.
HOLSTEIN, Otto:
1927   Chan-Chan: Capital of the Great Chimu. GR, XVII, pp. 36–61.
HOOPER, Luther:
1915   The Loom and Spindle, past, present and future. Smithsonian
            Report for 1914, pp. 629–678.
HORDEN QUE EL YNGA TUBO EN LA GOVERNACION DEL PIRU:
MS.   The unpublished anonymous document thus entitled is of the
            sixteenth century. It is in the British Museum under the signa-
            ture: Add.Mss., 13,992, folios 411–415.
HRDLIČKA, Aleš:
1907   Skeletal Remains suggesting . . . Early Man in North America.
            BAE, Bulletin 33.
1911   Some Results of recent Anthropological Exploration in Peru.
            Smithsonian Miscellaneous Publications, vol. 56, No. 16.
1912   Early Man in South America. BAE, Bulletin 52. (W. H.
            Holmes, Bailey Willis, F. E. Wright, and C. N. Fenner are co-
            authors.)

1912b   *Restes, dans l'Asie orientale, de la race qui a peuplé l'Amérique.* Congrès International d'Anthropologie et d'Archéologie préhistoriques, XIV, pp. 409–414. Geneva.

1912c   *Early Man in America.* AJS, XXXIV, pp. 543–554.

1912d   *Derivation and probable Place of Origin of the North American Indian.* ICA, XVIII, pp. 58–62. London.

1914   *Anthropological Work in Peru in 1913.* Smithsonian Miscellaneous Publications, vol. 61, No. 18.

1916   *The most Ancient Skeletal Remains of Man.* Smithsonian Institution, Washington. (2d edition.)

1916c   Review of Eaton, 1916. AJS, September, 1916, p. 281.

1917   *Transpacific Migrations.* Man, XVII, pp. 29–30.

1917b   *The Genesis of the American Indian.* ICA, XIX, pp. 559–568.

HUMBOLDT, Baron Alexander von:

1810   *Vues des cordillères et monumens des peuples indigènes de l'Amérique.* Paris.

HUNTINGTON, Ellsworth:

1914   *The Climatic Factor.* Washington. (Carnegie Institution.)

1914b   *The Solar Hypothesis of Climatic Changes.* Geological Society of America, Bulletin, XXV, pp. 477–490.

1915   *Civilization and Climate.* New Haven.

1917   *Maya Civilization and Climatic Changes.* ICA, XIX, pp. 150–164.

IZCUE, Elena:

1927   *El arte peruano en la escuela.* Paris. 2 vols.

JIJÓN Y CAAMAÑO, Jacinto:

1912   *El Tesoro del Itschimbia (Quito-Ecuador).* London.

1914   *Contribución al conocimiento de las aborígenes de la provincia de Imbabura en la República del Ecuador.* Madrid.

1918   *Examen crítico de la veracidad de la Historia del Reino de Quito del P. Juan de Velasco, de la Compañía de Jesús.* BSEEHA, I, pp. 33–63.

1918b   *Artefactos prehistóricos del Guayas.* BSEEHA, I, 253–275.

1919   *La religión del Imperio de los Incas.* Quito.

1919b   *Artefactos prehistóricos del Guayas.* Quito. (A reprint of 1918b.)

1920   *Nueva contribución al conocimiento de los aborígenes de la provincia de Imbabura.* Quito.

1920b   *Los Tincullpas y Notas acerca de la metalurgía de los aborígenes del Ecuador.* BANH, I, pp. 4–43.

1922   *La edad del bronce en la América del Sur.* BANH, IV, pp. 119–126.

1927   *Puruhá: contribución al conocimiento de los aborígenes de la provincia del Chimborazo, en la república del Ecuador.* Quito. 2 vols.

1929   *Notas de arqueología Cuzqueña.* Riobamba.

JIJÓN Y CAAMAÑO, Jacinto; and, LARREA, Carlos M.:

1918   *Un cementerio incásico y notas acerca de los Incas en el Ecuador.* Quito.

JIMÉNEZ DE LA ESPADA, Marcos:

1879   *Del hombre blanco y signo de la Cruz pre-colombianos en el Perú.* ICA, III, Pt. I, pp. 526–651. Brussels.

1879b   *Tres relaciones de antigüedades peruanas.* Madrid.

1887   *Del hombre blanco, etc.* Brussels. (Improved and separate edition.)

1891   *Las islas de los Galápagos y otras más á poniente.* Boletín de la
Sociedad Geográfica de Madrid, XXXI, pp. 351–402.

1923   *El cumpi-uncu hallado en Pachacámac.* Inca, I, pp. 904–928.
Lima.

JOYCE, Thomas Athol:

1912   *South American Archæology.* London and New York.

1913   *Note on a Gold Beaker from Lambayeque.* Man, XIII, pp. 65–
66. London.

1913b   *The Clan-ancestor in Animal Form as depicted on the Ancient
Pottery of the Peruvian Coast.* Man, XIII, pp. 113–117.

1913c   *The Weeping God.* In "Essays and Studies presented to William
Ridgeway . . . on his sixtieth birthday," pp. 365–375. Cambridge, England.

1921   *The Peruvian Loom in the Proto-Chimu Period.* Man, XXI, pp.
177–180.

1922   *Note on a Peruvian Loom of the Chimu Period.* Man, XXII,
pp. 1–2.

JUAN Y SANTACILIA, Jorge; and, ULLOA, Antonio de:

1748   *Relación histórica del viage a la América meridional hecho de
orden de S. Mag. para medir algunos grados de meridiano ter-
restre.* Madrid. 4 vols.

KEANE, A. H.:

1909–1911   *Central and South America.* Edited by Sir Clements R. Markham. London. 2 vols.

KELLY, Isabel T.:

1930   *Peruvian Cumbrous Bowls.* UCPAAE, XXIV, pp. 325–341.

KRICKEBERG, Walter:

1925   *Die Totonaken.* Baessler-Archiv, IX. Berlin.

KROEBER, A. L.:

1925   *The Uhle Pottery Collections from Moche.* UCPAAE, XXI, pp.
191–234.

1925b   *The Uhle Pottery Collections from Supe.* UCPAAE, XXI, pp.
235–264.

1926   *Archæological Explorations in Peru. Part I, Ancient Pottery from
Trujillo.* Chicago. (Field Museum.)

1926b   *The Uhle Pottery Collections from Chancay.* UCPAAE, XXI,
pp. 80–90.

1926c   *Culture Stratifications in Peru.* AA, n. s., XXVIII, pp. 331–351.

1927   *Coast and Highland in Prehistoric Peru.* AA, n. s., XXIX, pp.
625–653.

KROEBER, A. L.; and, STRONG, W. D.:

1924   *The Uhle Collections from Chincha.* UCPAAE, XXI, pp. 1–54.

1924b   *The Uhle Pottery Collections from Ica.* UCPAAE, XXI, pp.
95–133.

LAFONE QUEVEDO, Samuel A.:

1892   *Las Huacas de Chañar-Yaco.* RMLP, III, pp. 35–62.

1892b   *El culto de Tonapa.* RMLP, III, pp. 323–379.

1900   *Los ojos de Imaimana* . . . BIGA, XX, pp. 446–474.

1904   *Viaje a los menhires é intihuatana de Tafí y Santa María.*
RMLP, XI, pp. 123–128.

1905   *Viaje arqueológico en la región de Andalgalá.* RMLP, XII, pp.
73–108.

1908   Tipos de alfarería en la región Diaguito-Calchaquí. RMLP, XV,
        pp. 295–396.
1912   Pronomial classification of certain South American linguistic
        stocks. ICA, XVIII, pp. 111–115. London.
1912b   The great Chanca Confederacy . . . ICA, XVIII, pp. 115–125.
        London.
LAMARCK, J. B. P. A. de M. de:
1783–1808 Encyclopédie méthodique botanique. Paris. 8 vols.
LARCO HERRERA, Rafael:
1928   La civiltà Yunga. ICA, XXII, Pt. I, pp. 565–581. Rome.
LARRABURE Y UNÁNUE, Eugenio:
1874   Cañete, Apuntes geográficos y arqueológicos. Lima.
1893   Monografías histórico-americanas. Lima.
LARREA, Carlos M.:
1919   Nota acerca de dos objetos arqueológicos de oro hallados en Im-
        babura. BSEEHA, II, pp. 208–216.
LARREA, Carlos M.; and, JIJÓN Y CAAMAÑO, Jacinto:
1919   Notas acerca de la arqueología de la provincia de Esmeraldas.
        BSEEHA, III, pp. 85–109.
LATCHAM, R. E.:
1903   Notes on Chilean Anthropology. Journal of the Anthropological
        Institute, XXXIII, pp. 167–175. London.
1909   El comercio precolombiano en Chile i ostros países de América.
        Santiago de Chile.
1910   El comercio precolombiano en Chile. Santiago de Chile.
1914   Review of Posnansky, 1914. RCHG, XII, pp. 207–248.
1915   Costumbres mortuorias de los Indios de Chile y otras partes de
        América. Valparaiso.
1923   La existencia de la propiedad en el antiguo imperio de los Incas.
        Santiago.
1924   La organización social y las creencias religiosas de los antiguos
        Araucanos. Santiago.
1927   El dominio de la tierra y el sistema tributario en el antiguo im-
        perio de los Incas. RCGH, LII, pp. 201–257.
1927b   The Totemism of the Ancient Andean Peoples. Journal of the
        Royal Anthropological Institute, LVII, pp. 55–87.
1927–1928 Los Incas, sus orígenes y sus ayllus. Revista de la Universidad
        de Chile, n. s., V, pp. 1017–1154; VI, pp. 159–233.
1928   La alfarería indígena chilena. Santiago.
1928b   Chile prehispano. RCHG, LVII, pp. 44–91.
LEHMANN, Walter; and, DOERING, Heinrich:
1924   The Art of Old Peru. London.
LEHMANN-NITSCHE, Robert:
1904   Catálogo de las antigüedades de la provincia de Jujuy, con-
        servadas en el Museo de La Plata. RMLP, XI.
1928   Coricancha, el Templo del Sol en el Cuzco y las imágenes de su
        altar mayor. RMLP, XXXI, pp. 1–260.
LEVILLIER, Jean (Mme. Robert Levillier):
1928   Paracas, a contribution to the study of pre-Incaic textiles in an-
        cient Peru. Paris.
LEVILLIER, Robert:
1927   Nueva Crónica de la conquista de Tucumán. Buenos Aires.
LINNAEUS, Carolus (alias Carl von Linné):

1753   *Species plantarum.* Stockholm. 2 vols.
1766–1768 *Systema naturae.* Stockholm. 3 vols.
LINNÉ, Sigvald:
1929   *Darien in the Past.* Gothenburg.
LISSÓN, Carlos:
1887   *Breves apuntes sobre la sociología del Perú.* Lima.
LIZÁRRAGA, Friar Reginaldo de: (1540–1611.)
1909   *La descripción y población de las Indias.* Edited by Don Manuel Serrano y Sanz. Nueva Biblioteca de Autores Españoles, XV, pp. 485–660. Madrid. (Based on original MS. in the Library of the University of Saragossa, Spain.)
LOCKE, L. Leland:
1912   *The ancient Quipu, a Peruvian Knot-Record.* AA, XIV, pp. 325–332.
1923   *The ancient Quipu or Peruvian Knot-Record.* New York.
LÓPEZ, Felicísimo:
1907   *Atlás geográfico del Ecuador.* New York.
LÓPEZ DE COGOLLUDO, Diego:
1688   *Historia de Yucathan.* Madrid.
LÓPEZ DE GÓMARA, Francisco: (Lived from 1511 until after 1557.)
1553   *Primera y segunda parte de la historia general de las Indias.* Saragossa. (Agustín Millan.)
1849   *Historia general de las Indias.* Edited by B. C. Aribau. In Biblioteca de Autores Españoles, XII. Madrid.
LOTHROP, Samuel Kirkland:
1926   *Stone Sculptures from the Finca Arevalo, Guatemala.* IN, III, pp. 147–171. New York.
1926b   *Pottery of Costa Rica and Nicaragua.* New York. (Museum of the American Indian.) 2 vols.
1926c   *La Centinela, an Inca Ruin on the Coast of Peru.* The Independent, CXVI, pp. 13–16. Boston.
LOVERA, Mariño de: (Flourished about 1543.)
1865   *Crónica del Reino de Chile.* Edited by Don Diego Barros Arana. Colección de historiadores de Chile, VI. Santiago.
MacCURDY, George Grant:
1911   *A Study of Chiriquian Antiquities.* MCAAS, III. New Haven.
1924   *Human Origins.* New York and London. 2 vols.
MAGALLANES, Manuel M.:
1912   *El camino del Inca.* RCHG, III, pp. 44–75.
MARKHAM, Sir Clements Robert:
1864   *Contributions towards a Grammar and Dictionary of Quichua, the Language of the Yncas of Peru.* London.
1871   *On the Geographical Positions of the Tribes which formed the Empire of the Yncas* . . . GJ, XLI, pp. 281–338.
1892   *A History of Peru.* Chicago.
1910   *The Incas of Peru.* London and New York.
1910b   *A Comparison of the Ancient Peruvian Carvings and the Stones of Tiahuanacu and Chavín.* ICA, XVI, pp. 389–395. Vienna.
          NOTE: These are, of course, but a few of Markham's many writings. I here cite only those of his works which are specifically mentioned in these pages.
MASON, J. Alden:
1927   *Mirrors of Ancient America.* MJ, XVIII, pp. 201–209.

1928　　　　　　*Some Unusual Spearthrowers of Ancient America.* MJ, XIX,
　　　　　　　　pp. 290–324.

MAW, Henry Lister:

1829　　　　　　*Journal of a Passage from the Pacific to the Atlantic, crossing
　　　　　　　　the Andes in the northern Provinces of Peru.* London.

McBRIDE, George McCutchen:

1921　　　　　　*The Agrarian Indian Communities of Highland Bolivia.* New
　　　　　　　　York. (American Geographical Society.)

MEAD, Charles W.:

1903　　　　　　*The Musical Instruments of the Incas.* Guide Leaflet No. 11,
　　　　　　　　American Museum of Natural History. New York.

1907　　　　　　*Technique of some South American Feather-work.* APAMNH,
　　　　　　　　I, Pt. 1.

1915　　　　　　*Prehistoric Bronze in South America.* APAMNH, XII, Pt. 2.

1916　　　　　　*Ancient Peruvian Cloths.* AMJ, XVI, pp. 389–393.

1917　　　　　　*Peruvian Art.* Guide Leaflet No. 46, American Museum of Natu-
　　　　　　　　ral History. New York.

1921　　　　　　*Prehistoric Mining in Western South America.* NH, XXI, pp.
　　　　　　　　453–456.

MEANS, Philip Ainsworth:

1917　　　　　　*Culture Sequence in the Andean Area.* ICA, XIX, pp. 236–252.
　　　　　　　　Washington.

1917b　　　　　*History of the Spanish Conquest of Yucatan and of the Itzas.*
　　　　　　　　PMP, VII.

1917c　　　　　*A Survey of Ancient Peruvian Art.* TCAAS, XXI, pp. 315–442.

1918　　　　　　*Realism in the Art of Ancient Peru.* Art & Archæology, VI, pp.
　　　　　　　　235–246. Washington.

1918b　　　　　*A Note on the Guarani Invasions of the Inca Empire.* GR, IV,
　　　　　　　　pp. 482–484.

1918c　　　　　*The Domestication of the Llama.* Science, XLVII, pp. 268–269.

1918d　　　　　*Las relaciones entre Centro-América y Sud-América en la época
　　　　　　　　prehistórica.* BSGL, XXXIII, pp. 151–170.

1918e　　　　　*Racial Factors in Democracy.* Boston.

1918j　　　　　*Precolumbian Peruvian Chronology and Cultures.* Man, XVIII,
　　　　　　　　pp. 168–169.
　　　　　　　　Note: The break in the series of letters plus dates is here ex-
　　　　　　　　plained by the omission of various writings dealing with modern
　　　　　　　　Peru, not cited in this book.

1918k　　　　　*A Note on two Stone Objects from Southern Bolivia.* AA, XX,
　　　　　　　　pp. 245–246.

1919　　　　　　*La civilización precolombina de los Andes.* BSEEHA, III, pp.
　　　　　　　　213–242.

1919b　　　　　*Una nota sobre la prehistoria peruana.* Lima.

1919d　　　　　*Distribution and Use of Slings in Pre-Columbian America, with
　　　　　　　　Descriptive Catalogue of Ancient Peruvian Slings in the United
　　　　　　　　States National Museum.* Proceedings of the U. S. National
　　　　　　　　Museum, vol. 55, pp. 317–349. Washington.

1921　　　　　　*Aspectos estético-cronológicos de las civilizaciones andinas.* BANH,
　　　　　　　　I, pp. 195–226.

1921b　　　　　*Ciertos aspectos estéticos del arte antiguo del Perú.* MP, VI,
　　　　　　　　215–223.

1921c　　　　　*Indian Legislation in Peru.* HAHR, III, pp. 509–534.

1921d　　　　　*Breves apuntes sobre la sociología campestre del Perú.* Lima.

1923   *Some Comments on the Inedited Manuscript of Poma de Ayala.* AA, n. s., XXV, pp. 397–405.

1925   *A Study of Ancient Andean Social Institutions.* TCAAS, XVII, pp. 407–469.

1925b   *A Series of Ancient Andean Textiles.* BNBC, IX, pp. 3–27. New York.

1927   *A Group of Ancient Peruvian Fabrics.* BNBC, XI, pp. 10–25.

1928   *Biblioteca Andina, Part One.* TCAAS, XXIX, pp. 271–525.

1930   *Peruvian Textiles. Examples of the Pre-Incaic Period.* With an Introduction by Joseph Breck. New York. (Metropolitan Museum of Art.)

1930b   Review of Bingham, 1930. New York Times Book Review, May 4, 1930.

1930c   *The Origin of Tapestry Technique in Pre-Spanish Peru.* Metropolitan Museum Studies, III, Pt. 1, pp. 22–37.

MEDINA, José Toribio:

1882   *Los aborígenes de Chile.* Santiago de Chile.

MERCADO DE PEÑALOSA, Pedro de: (Flourished about 1580–1590.)

1885   *Relación de la provincia de los Pacajes.* RGI, II, pp. 51–64. Madrid.

MIDDENDORF, E. W.:

1890   *Ollanta.* Leipzig.

1890b   *Das Runa-Simi oder die Keshua-Sprache.* Leipzig.

1890c   *Wörterbuch des Runa-Simi.* Leipzig.

1891   *Die Aimará-Sprache.* Leipzig.

1891b   *Dramatische und Lyrische Dichtungen der Keshua-Sprache.* Leipzig.

1890–1892 *Die einheimischen Sprachen Perus.* Leipzig. 6 vols.

1892   *Das Muchik oder die Chimu-Sprache* . . . Leipzig.

1893–1895 *Peru.* Berlin. 3 vols.

MILLER, Philip:

1731   *The Gardener's Dictionary.* London.

MINNAERT, Paul:

1925   *Les institutions et le droit de l'Empire des Incas.* Ostende.

MIRÓ-QUESADA, Oscar:

1907   *Problemas ético-sociológicos.* Lima.

1916   *Bosquejo de una sociología integral.* Lima.

MITRÉ, Bartolomé:

1881   *Ollantay: Estudio sobre el drama Quichua.* Buenos Aires.

MOLINA, of Cuzco, Father Cristóbal de: (About 1535 to after 1590.)

1873   *The Fables and Rites of the Yncas.* Translated and edited by Clements R. Markham, in *Rites and Laws of the Yncas,* pp. 1–64. London. (Hakluyt Society.)

MONTELL, Gösta:

1925   *Le vrai poncho, son origine postcolombienne.* JAP, XVII, pp. 173–183.

1929   *Dress and Ornaments in Ancient Peru.* Gothenburg and London.

MONTENEGRO Y UBALDI, Juan Antonio:

1906   *Noticia de la ciudad de Moquegua.* RH, I, pp. 70–109.

MONTESINOS, Father Fernando: (From about 1600 until after 1640.)

1920   *Memorias antiguas historiales del Perú.* Translated and edited by P. A. Means, with an Introduction by the late Sir Clements R. Markham. London. (Hakluyt Society.)

MORLEY, Sylvanus Griswold:
1920   The Inscriptions at Copan. Washington. (Carnegie Institution.)
MORTIMER, W. Golden:
1901   Coca, the divine plant of the Incas. New York.
MORÚA, Friar Martín de: (From about 1560 until after 1590.)
1922   Historia de los Incas, reyes del Perú. Edited by Drs. Horacio H.
        Urteaga and Carlos A. Romero. CLDHP, 2d ser., IV. Lima.
MUÑIZ, Manuel Antonio; and, McGEE, W. J.:
1895   Primitive Trephining in Peru. ARBAE, XVI, pp. 1–72.
MURPHY, Robert Cushman:
1921   Bird Life in the Urubamba Valley. NH, XXI, pp. 507–512.
1923   The Oceanography of the Peruvian Littoral with Reference to the
        Abundance and Distribution of Marine Life. GR, XIII, pp.
        64–85.
1923b   Fisheries Resources in Peru. Scientific Monthly, XVI, pp. 594–
        607.
1925   Bird Islands of Peru. New York.
1926   Oceanic and Climatic Phenomena along the West Coast of South
        America during 1925. GR, XVI, pp. 26–54.
NESTLER, Julius:
1910   Die Bedeutung der Ruinenstätte von Tiahuanaco nach den Publi-
        kationen von Dr. Max Uhle und Sir Clements Markham. ICA,
        XVI, pp. 395–407.
1913   Beitrage zur Kenntnis der Ruinenstätte von Tiahuanaco. Vienna.
NEVEU-LEMAIRE, Maurice:
1907   Les lacs des hauts plateaux de l'Amérique du Sud. Paris.
1909   Los lagos de los altiplanos de la América del Sud. Translated by
        B. Diaz Romero. La Paz.
NOBLE, G. Kingsley:
1921   A Search for the Marsupial Frog. NH, XXI, pp. 474–485.
1921b   Pages from the Photographic Journal of the Harvard Peruvian
        Expedition. NH, XXI, pp. 486–493.
NORDENSKIÖLD, Baron Erland:
1906   Ethnologischen und archaeologischen Forschungen im Grenzgebiet
        zwischen Peru und Bolivia. ZE, XXXVIII, pp. 80–99. Berlin.
1906b   Arkeologiska Undersökningar i Peru och Bolivias gränstrakter
        1904–1905. Stockholm.
1917   The Guarani Invasion of the Inca Empire in the Sixteenth Cen-
        tury. GR, IV, pp. 103–121.
1921   The Copper and Bronze Ages in South America. Gothenburg.
1925   The Secret of the Peruvian Quipus. Gothenburg.
1925b   Calculations with Years and Months in the Peruvian Quipus.
        Gothenburg.
NUTTALL, Zelia:
1886   The Terra Cotta Heads of Teotihuacan. American Journal of
        Archæology, II, pp. 157–178; 318–330.
1901   Fundamental Principles of Old and New World Civilizations.
        PMP, II.
1906   The Astronomical Methods of the Ancient Mexicans. Boas Me-
        morial Volume. New York.
1928   Nouvelles lumières sur les civilisations américaines et le système
        du calendrier. ICA, XXII, Pt. I, pp. 119–148. Rome.

OGILVIE, Alan G.:
1922   Geography of the Central Andes. New York. (American Geographical Society.)

OLIVA, Father Juan Anello: (1572–1642.)
1857   Histoire du Pérou. Translated and edited by H. Ternaux-Compans. Paris.
1895   Historia del reino y provincias del Perú . . . Edited by Don Juan Pazos Varela and Don Luís Varela y Orbegoso. Lima.

O'NEALE, Lila M.; and, KROEBER, A. L.:
1930   Textile Periods in Ancient Peru. UCPAAE, XXVIII, pp. 23–56.

ORCHARD, William C.:
1930   Peruvian Gold and Gold Plating. IN, VII, pp. 466–474.

ORÉ, Bishop Luís Gerónimo de: (About 1547 to 1627.)
1598   Symbolo Catholico Indiano . . . Lima. (Antonio Ricardo.)

ORTON, James:
1870   The Andes and the Amazon. New York.

OSBORN, Henry Fairfield:
1915   Men of the Old Stone Age. New York.

OSORES, José Manuel:
1918   El medio y la legislación. Lima.

OYAGUE Y CALDERÓN, Carlos:
1904   Arquitectura incáica y construcción general. BSGL, XV, pp. 410–417.

PARLATORE, Filippo:
1866   Le specie dei cotoni. Florence.

PATRÓN, Pablo; and, ROMERO, Carlos A.:
1923   La Tribu Tampu y la lengua especial de los Inkas. Inca, I, pp. 432–439.

PAUW, Cornélius de:
1774   Recherches philosophiques sur les Américains. Berlin. 3 vols.

PAZ-SOLDÁN, Mariano Felipe:
1865   Atlás geográfico del Perú. Paris.
1877   Diccionario geográfico estadístico del Perú. Lima.

PAZ-SOLDÁN, Mateo; and, PAZ-SOLDÁN, Mariano Felipe:
1862–1863 Geografía del Perú. Paris. 2 vols.

PENCK, A.:
1914   The Shifting of the Climatic Belts. Scottish Geographical Magazine, XXX, pp. 281–293.

PERRONE DI SAN MARTINO, Count Giuseppe:
1922   Il Perù. Rome.

PI Y MARGALL, Francisco:
1888   Historia general de América. Barcelona.
1892   América en la época del descubrimiento. Madrid.
1892b   Historia de la América antecolombiana. Barcelona.

PIZARRO, Pedro: (From about 1515 until after 1572.)
1921   Relation of the Discovery and Conquest of the Kingdoms of Peru. Translated and edited by P. A. Means. New York. (Cortes Society.) 2 vols.

PLATZMANN, Julius (alias Julio):
1901   Das anonyme Wörterbuch Tupi-Deutsch und Deutsch-Tupi. Leipzig.

POLO, José Toribio:
1899   *La Piedra de Chavín.* BSGL, IX, pp. 192–231; 262–290.
1901   *Indios Uros del Perú y Bolivia.* BSGL, X, pp. 445–482.
POLO DE ONDEGARDO, Juan: (About 1510 to 1575.)
1872   *Relación de los fundamentos acerca del notable daño que resulta de no guardar a los Indios sus fueros.* Colección de documentos inéditos del archivo de Indias, XVII, pp. 1–177. Madrid.
1873   *Of the Lineage of the Yncas, and how they extended their Conquests.* Translated and edited by Clements R. Markham in *Rites and Laws of the Yncas,* pp. 151–170. London. (Hakluyt Society.)
1916   *Los errores y supersticiones de los indios.* Edited by Drs. Horacio H. Urteaga and Carlos A. Romero. CLDHP, III, pp. 3–43.
1916b   *Relación de los fundamentos,* etc. Edited by Drs. Urteaga and Romero. CLDHP, III, pp. 45–188.
1917   *Relación de los adoratorios de los indios en los cuatro caminos (zeques) que salían del Cuzco.* Edited by Drs. Urteaga and Romero. CLDHP, IV, pp. 3–44.
1917b   *Relación del linaje de los Incas y como extendieron éllos sus conquistas.* Edited by Drs. Urteaga and Romero. CLDHP, IV, pp. 45–94.
POSNANSKY, Arthur:
1911   *Tihuanacu y la civilización prehistórica en el Altiplano Andino.* La Paz.
1911b   *Razas y monumentos prehistóricos del Altiplano Andino.* Trabajos del IV Congreso Científico, XI, pp. 2–142.
1913   *El signo escalonado . . . con especial referencia a Tihuanacu.* Berlin.
1914   *Una metropolí en la América del Sud.* Berlin.
PRESCOTT, William Hickling:
1847   *History of the Conquest of Peru.* New York. 2 vols.
PROCTER, Robert:
1825   *Narrative of a Journey across the Cordillera of the Andes, and of a Residence in Lima and other Parts of Peru, in the Years 1823 and 1824.* London.
PURCHAS, Samuel: (1575–1626.)
1905–1907   *Hakluytus Posthumus, or Purchas his Pilgrimes.* Glasgow. 20 vols.
PUTNAM, E. K.:
1914   *The Davenport Collection of Nazca and other Peruvian pottery.* Proceedings of the Davenport Academy of Sciences, XIII, pp. 17–40. Davenport, Iowa.
QUESNAY, François: (Late eighteenth century.)
1888   *Œuvres économiques et philosophiques.* Edited by A. Oncken. Frankfort and Paris.
QUIPUCAMAYOCS: (Ca. 1541–1544.)
1920   *Discurso sobre la descendencia y gobierno de los Incas.* Edited by Drs. Horacio H. Urteaga and Carlos A. Romero. CLDHP. NOTE: This document was addressed to Governor C. Vaca de Castro, who ruled Peru from 1541 to 1544. It was first published in 1892, by Don Marcos Jiménez de la Espada, under the title of *Una antigualla peruana.*

RAIMONDI, Antonio:
1867 *On the Rivers San Gavan and Ayapata* . . . GJ, XXXVII, pp. 116–151.
1873 *El departamento de Ancachs* . . . Lima.
1874–1913 *El Perú.* Lima. 6 vols.
1901 *Ruinas de Huánuco Viejo.* BSGL, XI, pp. 397–400.
1903 *Enumeración de los vestigios de la antigua civilización entre Pacasmayo y la Cordillera.* BSGL, XIII, pp. 159–171.

RAMOS GAVILÁN, Friar Alonso: (From about 1580 until after 1621.)
1621 *Historia del celebre santuario de Nuestra Señora de Copacabana* . . . Lima. (Gerónymo de Contreras.)

RAYNAL, Abbé Guillaume Thomas François:
1770 *Histoire philosophique et politique des établissements et du commerce des Européens dans les deux Indes.* Paris. 2 vols.
1776 *A Philosophical and Political History of the Settlements and Trade of the Europeans in the East and West Indies.* London. 4 vols.

RÉAL, Daniel:
1925 (?) *La décoration primitive de l'Amérique Précolombienne.* Paris.

REATH, Nancy Andrews:
1927 *The Weaves of Hand-Loom Fabrics.* Philadelphia. (Pennsylvania Museum.)

REISS, Wilhelm; and, STÜBEL, Alphons:
1873 *Alturas tomadas en la República del Ecuador.* Quito.
1880–1887 *The Necropolis of Ancon in Peru.* Berlin. 3 vols.

RIVA AGÜERO, José de la:
1910 *La historia en el Perú.* Lima.
1921 *El Perú histórico y artístico.* Santander.

RIVERO, Mariano Eduardo de; and, TSCHUDI, Juan Diego de:
1851 *Antigüedades peruanas.* Vienna. 2 vols.

RIVET, Paul:
1913 *Influences des civilisations amazoniennes sur le haut plateau Andin.* JAP, X, pp. 684–685.

ROCHEBRUNE, A.-T. de:
1879 *Recherches d'ethnographie botanique sur la flore des sépultures péruviennes d'Ancon.* Actes de la Société Linéenne, XXXIII, pp. 343–358. Bordeaux.

ROMÁN Y ZAMORA, Friar Jerónimo de: (1536–1597.)
1575 *Repúblicas del mundo* . . . Medina del Campo. (Francisco del Canto.) 2 vols.
1595 *Repúblicas del mundo* . . . Salamanca. (Juan Fernández.) 3 vols.
1897 *Repúblicas de Indias* . . . Edited by D. L. d'Orvenipe. Colección de libros raros o curiosos que tratan de América, XIV and XV. Madrid.

ROSEN, Count Eric von:
1924 *Popular Account of Archœological Research during the Swedish Chaco-Cordillera Expedition, 1901–1902.*
1924b *Ethnographical Research Work during the Swedish Chaco-Cordillera Expedition, 1901–1902.* Stockholm. 2 vols. issued together.

RUIZ FOWLER, Luís:
1924   *Monografía histórico-geográfica del departamento de Ayacucho.* Lima.

RUIZ DE MONTOYA, Antonio: (Flourished about 1639.)
1876   *Arte de la lengua Guarani.* Edited by Julio (alias Julius) Platzmann. Leipzig.

SAAVEDRA, Bautista:
1913   *El ayllu.* La Paz.

SALINAS Y CORDOBA, Father Buenaventura de: (Flourished 1625–1655.)
1631   *Memorial de las historias del Nuevo Mundo . . .* Lima. (Gerónimo de Contreras.)

SANCHO DE LA HOZ, Pedro: (In Peru 1533 to about 1548.)
1917   *An Account of the Conquest of Peru.* Translated and edited by P. A. Means. New York. (Cortes Society.)

SAN PEDRO, Friar Juan de; and, CANTO, Friar Juan del: (About 1551.)
1865   *Relación de la religión y ritos del Perú, hecha por los primeros religiosos agustinos que allí pasaron para la conversión de los naturales.* Colección de documentos inéditos . . . del real archivo de Indias, III, pp. 5–58. Madrid.

SANTA CRUZ PACHACUTI-YAMQUI SALCAMAYHUA, Juan de: (Flourished about 1610.)
1873   *An Account of the Antiquities of Peru.* Translated and edited by Clements R. Markham in *Rites and Laws of the Yncas,* pp. 67–120. London. (Hakluyt Society.)
1879   *Relación de antigüedades deste reyno del Pirú.* Edited by Don Marcos Jiménez de la Espada in *Tres relaciones de antigüedades Peruanas,* pp. 231–328. Madrid.
    NOTE: Both these editions are based upon the original MS. which, together with the papers of Father de Ávila, is in the National Library, Madrid.

SANTILLÁN, Judge Fernando de: (Flourished 1550–1575.)
1879   *Relación del orígen, descendencia, política y gobierno de los Incas.* Edited by Don Marcos Jiménez de la Espada in *Tres relaciones,* etc., pp. 3–133. Madrid.
    NOTE: This, the sole edition of this work, is based upon the original MS. which is in the Library of the Escorial under the signature L. j. 5, folios 307–345.

SARMIENTO DE GAMBOA, Pedro: (From 1532 until after 1589.)
1906   *Geschichte des Inkareiches.* Original text and annotated translation by Richard Pietschmann. Berlin.
    NOTE: This edition is based upon the original MS. in the Library of the University of Göttingen, Germany.
1907   *History of the Incas.* Translated and edited by Sir Clements R. Markham. London. (Hakluyt Society.)

SAVILLE, Marshall H.:
1907–1910 *Antiquities of Manabí, Ecuador.* New York. (Museum of the American Indian.)
1921   *A Golden Breastplate from Cuzco, Peru.* New York. (Museum of the American Indian.)
1924   *The Gold Treasure of Sigsig, Ecuador.* New York. (Museum of the American Indian.)
1925   *Balance-beam Scales in Ancient Peru.* IN, II, pp. 266–285.
1926   *The Pottery Arybal of the Incas.* IN, III, pp. 111–119.

SCHMIDT, Max:
1909   Über Altperuanische Ornamentik. Archiv für Anthropologie, VII,
        pp. 22–38. Brunswick.
1910   Szenenhafte Darstellungen auf altperuanischen Gewebe. ZE,
        XLII, pp. 154–164.
1911   Über altperuanische Gewebe mit szenenhaften Darstellungen.
        Baessler-Archiv, I, pp. 1–61. Leipzig and Berlin.
1929   Kunst und Kultur von Peru. Berlin.
SCOTT, William Berryman:
1913   A History of Land-Mammals in the Western Hemisphere. New
        York.
SELER, Eduard:
1893   Peruanische Alterthumer. Berlin.
1912   Archäologische Reise in Süd- und Mittel-Amerika. ZE, pp. 201–
        242.
1923   Viaje arqueológico en el Perú . . . Inca, I, pp. 355–382. Lima.
1923b   Die buntbemalten Gefässe von Nasca im südlichen Peru und die
        Hauptelemente ihrer Verzierung. Edited by Caecilie Seler-
        Sachs, in Gesammelte Abhandlungen zur Amerikanischen
        Sprach- und Alterthumskunde, IV, pp. 171–138. Berlin.
SERRANO, Antonio:
1930   Los primitivos habitantes del territorio Argentino. Buenos Aires.
SEVER, Jacques:
1922   Chullpas des environs de Pucará (Bolivie). JAP, n. s., XIII, pp.
        55–58.
SINCLAIR, Joseph H.:
1929   Article on Ecuador in the Encyclopædia Britannica, 14th edition.
SPINDEN, Herbert J.:
1913   A Study of Maya Art. Memoirs of the Peabody Museum, VI.
        Cambridge, Mass.
1917   The Invention and Spread of Agriculture in America. AMJ,
        XVII, pp. 181–189.
1917b   The Archaic Type. On pp. 390–393 of Means, 1917c, which see.
1917c   The Origin and Distribution of Agriculture in America. ICA,
        XIX, pp. 269–276.
1924   The Reduction of Maya Dates. PMP, VI, No. 4. Cambridge,
        Mass.
SPRUCE, Richard:
1864   The Cultivation of Cotton in the Piura and Chira Valleys of
        northern Peru. London.
SQUIER, E. George:
1877   Peru, Incidents of Travel and Exploration in the Land of the
        Incas. New York.
STRONG, William Duncan:
1925   The Uhle Pottery Collections from Ancon. UCPAAE, XXI, pp.
        135–190.
STÜBEL, A.; and, UHLE, M.:
1892   Die Ruinenstaette von Tiahuanaco. Leipzig.
        NOTE: This monumental work was also issued, apparently, at
        Breslau, in the same year.
SYMONDS, Mary (Mrs. Guy Antrobus); and, PREECE, Louisa:
1928   Needlework through the Ages. London.

570 BIBLIOGRAPHY

TELLO, Julio C.:
1912   Prehistoric Trephining among the Yauyos of Peru. ICA, XVIII,
          pp. 75–83. London.
1917   Los antiguos cementerios del Valle de Nasca. Washington.
1918   El uso de las cabezas artificialmente momificadas en el antiguo
          arte peruano. Lima.
1921   Introducción a la historia antigua del Perú. Lima.
1923   Wira Kocha. Inca, I, pp. 93–320; 583–606.
1928   Los descubrimientos del Museo de Arqueología Peruana en la
          península de Paracas. ICA, XXII, Pt. 1, pp. 679–690. Rome.
1929   Antiguo Perú. Lima.
TELLO, Julio C.; and, MIRANDA, Próspero:
1923   Wallallo. Inca, I, pp. 475–549.
THOMAS, Oldfield:
1891   Notes on some ungulate Mammals. Proceedings of the Zoolog-
          ical Society of London, for 1891, pp. 384–389.
TORRES-LUNA, A.:
1923   El vestuario en la época incaica. Revista de Arqueología, I, pp.
          50–64. Lima.
TORRES RUBIO, Father Diego de:
1603   Grammatica y vocabulario en la lengua general del Peru, llamada
          Quichua. Seville.
TOTTEN, George Oakley:
1926   Maya Architecture. Washington.
TRIMBORN, Hermann:
1923–1924 Der Kollektivismus der Inkas in Peru. Anthropos, XVIII, pp.
          978–1001. Vienna.
1925   Straftat und Sühne in Alt-Peru. ZE, LVII, pp. 194–240.
1927   Die Gliederung der Staende im Inka-Reich. JAP, n. s., XIX,
          pp. 303–344.
TSCHUDI, Johann Jakob von:
1847   Travels in Peru, during the Years 1838–1842. Translated by
          Thomasina Ross. London.
1847b   Same work, by same translator, in different format. New York.
1853   Die Kechua-Sprache. Vienna. 3 vols.
1868   Reisen durch Sudamerika. Leipzig. 5 vols.
1891   Culturhistorische und sprachliche Beiträge zur Kenntniss des
          Alten Peru. Vienna.
TUDELA Y VARELA, Francisco:
1905   Socialismo peruano. Lima.
UGARTE, César Antonio:
1918   Los antecedentes históricos del régimen agrario peruano. Lima.
UHLE, Max:
1889–1890 Kultur und Industrie Südamerikanischer Völker. Berlin.
1903   Pachacamac. Philadelphia. (Museum of the University of Penn-
          sylvania.)
1906   Los Kjoekkenmoedings del Perú. RH, I, pp. 3–23.
1906b   Las llamitas de piedra del Cuzco. RH, I, pp. 388–392.
1906c   Bericht über die Ergebnisse meiner südamerikanischen Reisen.
          ICA, XIV, Pt. 2, pp. 567–579. Stuttgart.
1906d   Aus meinem Bericht über die Ergebnisse meiner Reise nach Süd-
          amerika 1889–1901. ICA, XIV, Pt. 2, pp. 581–592. Stuttgart.
1907   La masca paicha del Inca. RH, II, pp. 227–232.

1907b	*La estólica en el Perú.* RH, II, pp. 118–128.
1907c	See Guimaraes, 1907.
1908	*Über die Frühkulturen in der Umgebung von Lima.* ICA, XVI, pp. 347–370. Vienna.
1908b	*Zur Deutung der Intihuatana.* ICA, XVI, pp. 371–389. Vienna.
1909	*Peruvian Throwing-Sticks.* AA, n. s., XI, pp. 624–627.
1910	*Tipos de civilización en el Perú.* BSGL, XXV, pp. 289–294.
1910b	*Las relaciones pre-históricas entre el Perú y la Argentina.* ICA, XVII, pp. 509–540. Buenos Aires.
1911	*El aillu peruano.* BSGL, XXI, pp. 81–94.
1912	*Die Muschelhügel von Ancon.* ICA, XVIII, pp. 22–45. London.
1912b	*Los orígenes de los Incas.* ICA, XVII, pp. 302–353. Buenos Aires.
1913	*Die Ruinen von Moche.* JAP, n. s., X, pp. 95–117.
1913b	*Zur Chronologie der alten Culturen von Ica.* JAP, n. s., X, pp. 341–367.
1917	*Fortalezas incaicas . . .* RCHG, XXI, 154–170.
1917b	*Los aborígenes de Arica.* Santiago de Chile.
1919	*Fundamentos étnicos de la región de Arica y Tacna.* BSEEHA, II, pp. 1–37.
1919b	*La arqueología de Arica y Tacna.* BSEEHA, III, pp. 1–48.
1920	*Apuntes sobre la prehistoria de la región de Piura.* BSEEHA, IV, pp. 165–167.
1920b	*Los principios de las antiguas civilizaciones peruanas.* BSEEHA, IV, pp. 448–458.
1920c	*Los principios de la civilización en la sierra peruana.* BANH, I, pp. 44–56.
1922	*Orígenes centroamericanos.* BANH, IV, pp. 1–6.
1922b	*Sepulturas ricas de oro en la provincia del Azuay.* BANH, IV, pp. 108–114.
1922c	*Influencias Mayas en el alto Ecuador.* BANH, IV, pp. 205–240.
1923	*Civilizaciones mayoides de la Costa Pacífica de Sudamérica.* BANH, VI, pp. 87–92.
1923b	*Toltecas, Mayas y civilizaciones sudamericanas.* BANH, VII, pp. 1–33.
1923c	*Cronología y orígen de las antiguas civilizaciones argentinas.* BANH, VII, pp. 123–130.
1923d	*Las ruinas de Tomebamba.* Quito. 2 vols.
1924	*Explorations at Chincha.* UCPAAE, XXI, pp. 58–94.
1924b	*Notes on Ica Valley.* UCPAAE, XXI, pp. 121–123.
1924c	*Notes on sites and graves excavated.* UCPAAE, XXI, pp. 123–127.
1924d	*Ancient civilizations of Ica Valley.* UCPAAE, XXI, pp. 128–132.
1926	*Excavaciones arqueológicas en la región de Cumbayá.* AUC, XXXVII, pp. 1–33.
1928	*Las ruinas de Cuasmal.* AUC, XL, pp. 183–234.
1930	*El reino de Quito.* BANH, X, pp. 1–17.

ULLOA MOGOLLÓN, Juan de: (Flourished about 1586.)
| 1885 | *Relación de la provincia de los Collaguas.* RGI, II, pp. 38–50. |

URTEAGA, Horacio H.:
| 1909 | *El antiguo Perú a la luz de la arqueología y de la crítica.* RH, IV, pp. 200–223. |
| 1917 | *El fetichismo de los Yungas.* BSGL, XXXII, pp. 165–183. |

1919   El Perú. Bocetos históricos. Lima.
1921   La organización judicial en el imperio de los Incas. RH, IX, pp.
            1–50.

VALCÁRCEL, Luís:
1914   La cuestión agraria en el Cuzco. Cuzco.
1923   Tampu. Inca, I, pp. 79–82.
1924   El Cuzco precolombiano. Revista Universitaria del Cuzco, No.44.

VALDEZ DE LA TORRE, Carlos:
1920   El ayllu. MP, V, pp. 187–209.
1920b   Régimen de la propiedad durante los Incas. MP, V, pp. 399–413.
1921   Evolución de las comunidades de indígenas. Lima.

VALERA, Father Blas: (Born in Peru about 1540; died in Spain in 1597.)
1879   De las costumbres antiguas de los naturales del Perú. Edited by
            Don Marcos Jiménez de la Espada in Tres relaciones de an-
            tigüedades peruanas, pp. 137–227. Madrid.
            NOTE: The credit for identifying this work—which was pub-
            lished by Jiménez as anonymous—as the product of Father
            Valera's pen belongs to Dr. Manuel González de la Rosa, 1907,
            see above. Most of Father Valera's surviving passages are pre-
            served for us by Garcilaso, who frequently quotes them, always
            with credit to Valera. Montesinos, whom see, is also largely if
            not wholly based on Valera's writings, as explained on pages 68
            and 69 of the present volume.

VALETTE, M.:
1913   Note sur la teinture de tissus précolombiens du Bas-Pérou. JAP,
            X, pp. 43–46.

VEATCH, A. C.:
1917   Quito to Bogotá. New York.

VEGA TORAL, Tomás:
1921   La Tomebamba de los Incas. Cuenca.

VELASCO, Father Juan de:
1789   La historia del Reino de Quito en la América Meridional. MS. in
            the Library of the Jesuit monastery at Chamartín de la Rosa,
            near Madrid. Cf. Jijón, 1918, p. 35.
1789b   La historia del Reino de Quito, etc. Another MS., now preserved
            in the Royal Academy of History, Madrid.
1837–1839   La historia del Reino de Quito. Edited by Don Abel Victor
            Brandin and published under the auspices of Don José Modesto
            Larrea y Carrión. This edition is incomplete, going only to
            Book III of Part I, 60 pages having been printed in Paris and
            40 in Quito.
1840   Histoire du Royaume de Quito. Edited by Henri Ternaux-Com-
            pans. Paris. 2 vols.
1841–1844   Historia del Reino de Quito. Edited by Don Agustín Yerovi.
            Quito. 3 vols.
            NOTE: This is the most complete edition of this work.

VERNEAU, R.; and, RIVET, Paul:
1912–1922   Ethnographie ancienne de l'Équateur. Paris. 2 vols.

VILLAR CORDOVA, Pedro E.:
1923   Las ruinas de la provincia de Canta. Inca, I, pp. 1–24.

VILLARÁN, Manuel Vicente:
1907   Condición legal de las comunidades de indígenas. Lima.

VILLAVICENCIO, Manuel:
1858   *Geografía de la República del Ecuador.* New York.
VITERI LAFRONTE, Homero:
1917   *La Historia del Reino de Quito.* Revista de la Sociedad Jurídico-
            Literaria, XIX, pp. 162–181. Quito.
VOCABULARIO POLÍGLOTA INCAICO. Lima. 1905.
WATT, Sir George:
1907   *The Wild and Cultivated Cotton Plants of the World.* London
            and New York.
1908   *The Commercial Products of India.* London.
WHIFFEN, Thomas:
1915   *The North-West Amazons.* New York.
WHYMPER, Edward:
1892   *Travels amongst the Great Andes of the Equator.* New York.
            2 vols.
WIENER, Charles:
1880   *Pérou et Bolivie.* Paris.
WIESSE, Carlos:
1913   *Las civilizaciones primitivas del Perú.* Lima.
WISSLER, Clark:
1922   *The American Indian.* New York.
WOLF, Teodoro:
1879   *Viajes científicos por la República del Ecuador.* Guayaquil.
1892   *Geografía y geología del Ecuador.* Leipzig.
WRIGLEY, Gladys M.:
1919   *Fairs of the Central Andes.* GR, VII, pp. 65–80.
XEREZ, Francisco de: (From 1504 until after 1534.)
1872   *Narrative of the Conquest of Peru.* Translated and edited by
            Clements R. Markham in *Reports on the Discovery of Peru,*
            pp. 3–73. London. (Hakluyt Society.)
            NOTE: See also Anonymous Conquest and Estete.
ZÁRATE, Agustín de: (In Peru from 1544 to about 1551.)
1555   *Historia del descubrimiento y conquista del Perú* . . . Antwerp.
            (Martín Nucio.)
1577   *Historia,* etc. Seville. (Alonso Escrivano.)
ZURKALOWSKI, Erich:
1919   *Observaciones sobre la organización social del Perú antiguo.* MP,
            II, pp. 337–352; 480–495.

INDEX

Acapana, ruins of, at Tiahuanaco, 119; 124–125

Aclla-cuna, Chosen Women of the Sun, 408–412

Aclla-huasi, House of the Chosen Women of the Sun, 408–413

Agriculture, on the Coast, 12; in the Highlands, 20–21; of the Mayas, 36–37; see also Diet and *Huata*

Alaska, man entered America from Siberia by way of, 29

Alcaviquiza, a tribe of the Cuzco Valley in pre-Incaic times, 206

Altar, the High, in Coricancha, description of, 394–404

Amauta-cuna (or *Amautas*), sages, and instructors of youth, 240; 262; 305–306; 441–442

Amazon River, 17

Anacu, tunic for women, 431

Ancas Mayu (Blue River), northern limit of Inca Empire, 270

Ancón, archæology of, 187–189

Andean area, definition of, 1; natural divisions of, Ch. I

Anta, see Xaquixahuana

Antasaya, a native tribe of the Cuzco Valley, 206

Apurimac River, 16; shrine of the god of the, 419

Araucanos, of Chile, difficult conquest of by Tupac Yupanqui, 265–266

Architecture in Early Chimu times, 80–83; in Tiahuanaco I times, 108–113; in Tiahuanaco II times, 124–126; in *ceja de la costa* in Late Chimu times, 192–193; in Late Nazca times, 195–197; *pirca* and *chulpa* types of, 200–202; of Incas influenced by seeing Tiahuanaco, 228–229; polygonal, 240; character of Incaic, 251; general discussion of, 524–535

Argentina, archæology of, 169–170; history of, 249–250

Army, Incaic, see under the various Incas

Asángaro, antiquities of, 133

Asia, see Yellow-Brown Race of

Atacama, desert and *puna* of, 19

Ataguju, low type of Creator-God cult at Huamachuco, 429–432

Atahualpa, elder but bastard son of Huayna Capac, 275–276

Atau, son of Guayanay and Ciguar, 212; father of Manco Capac, 212–213

Atauillo or Atavillo, a Colla tribe in Canta Province, 202

Avachumpi and Ninachumpi, two islands, possibly of the Galápagos group, visited by Tupac Yupanqui, 269–272

Aviation, as an aid to geography, 9; as an aid to archæology, 129

Ayacucho, see Huamanga

Ayahuaca, Tupac Yupanqui's conquest of, 267

Ayar Auca, one of Manco Capac's brothers, 206; slain by Manco Capac, 218

Ayar Cachi, one of Manco Capac's brothers, 206; killed by a wizard, 218

Ayar Uchu, one of Manco Capac's brothers, 206; dies without children, 218

Ayllu, tribe, nature of, 223; 283; as nucleus of social organization, 286–287

Aymará, a Quechua-speaking folk in the Titicaca Basin, 134–136

Balsa, raft, 11; at the Desaguadero River, 228; of Tumbez and the Gulf of Guayaquil, 341–342; see also Navigation

Balsa tree and its uses, 10–11

Battle-scenes, on Early Chimu pottery, 78

Beacon fires, used for quick messages, 334

Beverages, under the Incas, 310; 369; see also Diet and Drink

Bird-Demon, a personage of Early Nazca art, 98

Black-on-white pottery at Chancay, 186–188

Blue River (Ancas Mayu), northern limit of Inca Empire, 270

Bridge, built across the Apurimac by Capac Yupanqui, 231

Bridges and causeways, 331

Burials, on the Coast, 52; 106–107; **in**